STATUTORY INSTRUMENTS 1973

PART III
(in four Sections)

SECTION 3

Published by Authority

LONDON
HER MAJESTY'S STATIONERY OFFICE
1974

PRINTED AND PUBLISHED BY HER MAJESTY'S STATIONERY OFFICE

To be purchased from
49 High Holborn, LONDON, WC1V 6HB
13a Castle Street, EDINBURGH, EH2 3AR
41 The Hayes, CARDIFF, CF1 1JW
Brazennose Street, MANCHESTER, M60 8AS
Southey House, Wine Street, BRISTOL, BS1 2BQ
258 Broad Street, BIRMINGHAM, B1 2HE
80 Chichester Street, BELFAST, BT1 4JY

or through booksellers

1974

Price for the four Sections: £21 net

PRINTED IN ENGLAND

ISBN 0 11 840127 0*

Contents of the Volume

PART I, Section 1

PART I, Section 2

PART II, Section 1

PART II, Section 2

PART III, Section 1

PART III, Section 2

PART III, Section 3

PART III, Section 4

Note: S.I. No. 1853 *is local: particulars of it will be found in Part III of the volume.*

STATUTORY INSTRUMENTS

1973 No. 1854

PENSIONS

The Occupational Pension Schemes (Recognition of Schemes) (No. 2) Regulations 1973

Made - - - -	*7th November* 1973
Laid before Parliament	*15th November* 1973
Coming into Operation	*6th April* 1975

The Secretary of State for Social Services, in exercise of his powers under sections 51(4)(*a*)(ii), (*b*) and (*e*), 52(1), 53(8), 54(4) and 58(3), (4) and (5) of, and paragraphs 3, 4, 5, 10 and 12 of Schedule 15 to, the Social Security Act 1973**(a)**, and of all other powers enabling him in that behalf, hereby makes the following regulations:—

Citation, interpretation and commencement

1. These regulations, which may be cited as the Occupational Pension Schemes (Recognition of Schemes) (No. 2) Regulations 1973, shall be read as one with the Occupational Pension Schemes (Recognition of Schemes) Regulations 1973**(b)** (hereinafter called "the principal regulations") and shall come into operation on 6th April 1975.

Transfer of benefit between schemes

2.—(1) For the purposes of section 58(4) of the Act (where the rules of a scheme provide for the allowance of transfer credits, then for the scheme to be recognised in relation to any employment it must provide for them, if and so far as they consist of recognition credits, to be in such form as may be prescribed) the prescribed forms shall be—

(*a*) in cases where the recognition credits are allowed in respect of rights accrued under another scheme which include—

(i) minimum personal pension, or

(ii) transfer credits previously allowed under any scheme, so far as representing or replacing, or otherwise allowed in respect of, benefits accrued under another scheme which included minimum personal pension,

the form of a right to benefit which includes some personal pension; and

(*b*) in cases where the recognition credits are allowed in respect of rights accrued under another scheme which include—

(i) minimum death benefit, or

(ii) transfer credits previously allowed under any scheme, so far as representing or replacing, or otherwise allowed in respect of, benefits

(a) 1973 c. 38.

(b) S.I. 1973/1470 (1973 II, p. 4481).

accrued under another scheme which included minimum death benefit,

the form of a right to benefit which includes some death benefit.

(2) For the purposes of section 58(3) of the Act (where, in relation to any employment, scheme rules allow for transfer of accrued rights to another scheme, then for the first scheme to be recognised in relation to that employment it must so provide that any transfer of minimum benefits or benefits including them or of recognition credits can be made only to recognised schemes or schemes which fall within a prescribed category), the prescribed category of schemes shall be one consisting of schemes—

(*a*) which are administered primarily or wholly outside the United Kingdom;

(*b*) whose rules allow the transfer of recognition credits only to other schemes in the category, or to other schemes which are recognised in relation to any employment; and

(*c*) which are approved (whether or not subject to conditions) for the purpose of this regulation by the Board.

(3) For the purposes of section 58(5) of the Act (provision for accrued rights to be transferred without the earner's consent to be inadmissible in relation to minimum benefits except in prescribed cases), the prescribed case shall be where—

(*a*) the transfer of accrued rights is to another scheme which relates to employment with the same employer or with another employer who is one of a group of companies consisting of a holding company and one or more subsidiaries within the meaning of section 154 of the Companies Act 1948**(a)**, being a group which includes the first-mentioned employer; and

(*b*) the rights allowed to the earner in the scheme to which the transfer is made are in the opinion of the trustees or managers of that scheme at least equal in value to the rights transferred.

Modification of section 54 *of the Act in relation to certain annuity contracts*

3.—(1) The provisions of section 54 of the Act (rate of minimum personal pension) shall, in the case of a scheme whose benefits are provided under an annuity contract for the time being approved by the Inland Revenue under section 226 or 226A of the Income and Corporation Taxes Act 1970**(b)** or which is a trust scheme approved by the Inland Revenue under either of those sections (such annuity contract or trust scheme being hereinafter referred to as an "approved annuity"), be subject to the modifications set out in the following paragraph of this regulation.

(2) Subsections (2), (4)(*b*) and (5) shall not apply, and subsection (1) shall have effect as if the section required that—

(*a*) the rate of minimum personal pension must be calculated in accordance with subsection (4)(*a*);

(*b*) the annual rates of minimum personal pension must be as mentioned in regulation 6(2)(*a*) and (3) of the principal regulations;

(*c*) the earner must be under a legal obligation to the employer to pay in respect of the approved annuity, by means of contributions or premiums, an amount equivalent to at least 5 per cent of his reckonable earnings;

(*d*) the terms of the approved annuity must specify the manner in which

(a) 1948 c. 38.   **(b)** 1970 c. 10.

the minimum personal pension and minimum death benefit are to be related to those contributions or premiums; and

(*e*) the earner's employer must be under a legal obligation to the earner to pay the earner, in relation to the approved annuity, an amount equivalent to at least 2·5 per cent of the earner's reckonable earnings, being an amount that is additional to the earner's earnings from the relevant employment to which the earner would have been entitled but for the employer's said obligation to him.

Derivation of resources of schemes

4. For the purposes of section 51(4)(*a*)(ii) of the Act (scheme can be recognised scheme only if the derivation of its resources satisfies certain requirements) the following are the prescribed payments:—

(*a*) in the case of a scheme whose members include persons employed by Her Majesty in Her private capacity, payments made by Her Majesty out of Her private resources;

(*b*) in the case of a scheme relating to persons employed by the Duke of Lancaster or by the Duke of Cornwall, payments made out of the revenues of the Duchy of Lancaster or the Duchy of Cornwall; and

(*c*) in the case of a scheme whose benefits are provided under an approved annuity, where either—

(i) the employment to which the approved annuity (being an annuity contract) relates is such that the earnings from it fall to be included in a computation of profits assessable to tax under Schedule D (as defined in section 108 of the Income and Corporation Taxes Act 1970) and the earner is also liable to pay Class 1 contributions in respect of them, or

(ii) the earner had paid before, or was paying at, 5th April 1974 contributions or premiums under an approved annuity in respect of earnings received in any employment with the same employer or his predecessor in that business, or

(iii) the earner had at any time paid contributions or premiums, under the same approved annuity as that which provides the benefits of the scheme in question, in respect of earnings received in any recognised pensionable employment,

payments made by the earner such as are mentioned in regulation 3(2)(*c*) above.

Determination of date from which earner has been in recognised pensionable employment

5. In a case where the trustees or managers of a scheme decide that past service of an earner in an employment to which the scheme relates shall qualify him (if his service continues for the appropriate period) for the minimum benefits of the scheme, the Board may determine that the earner has been in recognised pensionable employment from a date not earlier than the beginning of that past service, or the issue of a recognition certificate in respect of it, whichever is the later.

Modification of sections 53(1) *and* 55(6) *of the Act*

6.—(1) Section 53(1) of the Act (provision of minimum personal pension) and section 55(6) of the Act, as modified**(a)**, (persons to whom minimum death benefit is payable) shall be modified, in accordance with the provisions of paragraph (2) below, in their application to cases in which the person to whom minimum benefit is payable ("the beneficiary") is unable to act by reason of his minority, mental disorder or otherwise.

(2) The modification is that in relation to such cases the scheme may, with the approval of the Board, confer on the trustees or managers discretion to direct that, instead of being paid to the beneficiary, the benefit may be paid or applied for the maintenance of any one or more of the following persons, namely the beneficiary and his dependants.

Centralised schemes

7.—(1) In this and the following regulation "centralised scheme" means a scheme for whose benefits earners in employments under different employers qualify by virtue of their respective service in those employments, and "5 years' qualifying service" has the same meaning as in section 53(2)(*c*) and (3) of the Act.

(2) In its application to a case where an earner is in employment to which a centralised scheme applies, section 53(4)(*a*) of the Act (form of minimum personal pension) shall be modified so as to have effect as if it referred to a pension payable as from whichever is the latest of the following:—

(*a*) termination of the relevant employment;

(*b*) termination of the last of a series of employments of the earner—

(i) of which the relevant employment was one,

(ii) to all of which one centralised scheme applied, and

(iii) which occurred at such times that any interval between one employment in the series and the next, in a case where the earner had not completed 5 years' qualifying service in relation to that scheme, was not longer than 6 months or such longer period as the Board may allow; and

(*c*) attainment by the earner of pensionable age.

Termination and linking of periods of recognised pensionable employment

8.—(1) Subject to paragraph (2) below, an earner's employment shall be treated as having ceased to be recognised pensionable employment when any of the following circumstances applies:—

(*a*) the earner's contract of service has expired or been terminated;

(*b*) in the absence of a contract of service, the service itself has ended;

(*c*) he is no longer of requisite age (as defined in section 51(2) of the Act);

(*d*) cancellation or withdrawal of the recognition certificate by virtue of which his employment was recognised pensionable employment has taken effect;

(*e*) a variation of the recognition certificate by virtue of which his employment was recognised pensionable employment has taken effect such that the certificate no longer applies to his employment;

(*f*) the earner has ceased to be within the description of earners in relation to which the recognition certificate applies.

(a) *See* Regulation 23 of S.I. 1973/1470 (1973 II, p. 4481).

(2) In such cases as are specified in paragraph (3) below, an earner's employment shall not be treated as having ceased to be recognised pensionable employment by reason only of the circumstances mentioned in paragraph (1)(*a*) and (*b*) above where the service in question was in an employment which is one (other than the last) of a series of employments to all of which the same scheme applies.

(3) The cases mentioned in paragraph (2) above are—

(*a*) where all the employments are with the same employer or the same centralised scheme applies to them all, cases where—

(i) no reserve scheme premium has been paid in respect of the employment first mentioned in paragraph (2) above or any that has been paid has been refunded, and

(ii) (except in a case where a centralised scheme applies to all the employments and the earner has completed 5 years' qualifying service in relation to that scheme) any interval between one employment in the series and the next is not longer than 6 months or such longer period as the Board may allow in a particular case; and

(*b*) where all the employments are with one employer and his successors, such cases as the Board (whether or not subject to conditions) consider suitable.

(4) The total period of recognised pensionable employment which consists of a series of employments to which paragraph (2) above applies shall include any intervals between employments in the series, so however that the intervals shall not count towards calculation of minimum benefits.

(5) Where an earner dies during the interval between the end of a period of service in recognised pensionable employment and what would, apart from this paragraph, have been the end of the period allowed for payment of any reserve scheme premium which relates to that period of service, and at the time of his death no reserve scheme premium has been paid in respect of that employment, or any that has been paid has been refunded, that employment shall be treated as having come to an end on, and not before, the date of his death, so however that the period between the end of the service and the death shall not count towards calculation of minimum benefits.

Miscellaneous amendments to the principal regulations

9.—(1) The principal regulations shall be amended in accordance with the following provisions of this regulation.

(2) In regulation 2 (schemes administered outside Great Britain), after paragraph (3) there shall be inserted the following paragraph—

"(4) In the case of a scheme which is administered primarily or wholly outside the United Kingdom, the preceding paragraphs of this regulation shall not apply, but, for the purposes of section 51(4)(*e*) of the Act (means by which minimum benefits are secured), the minimum benefits of the scheme shall be secured in such manner as the Board may (whether or not subject to conditions) consider suitable."

(3) In regulation 5(2) (circumstances in which minimum benefit may be suspended), after sub-paragraph (*c*) there shall be inserted the following sub-paragraph—

"(*cc*) in any case where minimum personal pension is payable under a centralised scheme (namely a scheme for whose benefits earners in employments under different employers qualify by virtue of their respective service in those employments) and the earner has attained pensionable age, during any period when the earner is in employment to which that centralised scheme applies or would apply if the earner were of requisite age (as defined in section 51(2) of the Act);"

and in condition (ii), after the words "sub-paragraph (*c*)" there shall be inserted the words "or (*cc*)".

(4) In regulation 7(1) (calculation of minimum benefit based on earnings and length of service), for the words "paragraph (4)" there shall be substituted the words "paragraph (5)".

(5) In regulation 19 (surrender of deferred pension on re-employment by the same employer), after the words "the same" (in both places where they occur), there shall be inserted the words "or another".

(6) In regulation 21(2) (service which does not count for minimum benefits), after the words "that employment" (in both places where they occur), there shall be inserted the words "(or any other employment, being employment by reference to which he qualifies for the benefits of the scheme)".

Transitory provision

10.—(1) This regulation applies to—

(*a*) any scheme which existed on 5th April 1947 and in which no alterations have been made since that date other than alterations (if any) which have been approved by the Inland Revenue for the purposes of section 224(2) of the Income and Corporation Taxes Act 1970(**a**); and

(*b*) any other scheme which is associated with a scheme to which sub-paragraph (*a*) above applies, in such manner that in the opinion of the Board it should be treated as a scheme to which this regulation applies.

(2) The requirements of regulation 2 of the principal regulations (means of securing minimum benefits) shall have effect, in their application to the case of a scheme to which this regulation applies, so as to require that the minimum benefits of the scheme shall be secured either—

(*a*) by such irrevocable trust, policy of insurance or annuity contract as is mentioned in the said regulation 2, or

(*b*) by such trust, policy or contract in conjunction with an undertaking which is given by the trustees or managers of the scheme, and which the Board consider satisfactory, to provide the earner with minimum personal pension and minimum death benefit so as to satisfy the requirements of sections 53 to 60 of the Act.

(3) This regulation shall cease to have effect on 6th April 1980 and any recognition certificate issued by the Board in a case where an undertaking such as is mentioned in paragraph (2) of this regulation is given shall have effect for a period expiring not later than 5th April 1980.

Keith Joseph,
Secretary of State for Social Services.

7th November 1973.

(**a**) 1970 c. 10.

EXPLANATORY NOTE

(*This Note is not part of the Regulations.*)

These Regulations supplement and amend the provisions of the Occupational Pension Schemes (Recognition of Schemes) Regulations 1973, which relate to the recognition of occupational pension schemes, in relation to an earner's employment, under Part II of the Social Security Act 1973.

The principal matters dealt with are the transfer of benefit between schemes (Regulation 2), the use of certain annuity contracts for recognition purposes (Regulation 3), certain types of payment from which a scheme's resources may derive (Regulation 4), the commencement, termination and linking of periods of recognised pensionable employment (Regulations 5 and 8), and the payment of benefit for maintenance of beneficiaries unable to act(Regulation 6). There are also special provisions for centralised and overseas schemes, and a transitory provision affecting schemes which existed on 5th April 1947 and have undergone no alterations, or only limited alterations, since then, and other schemes associated with them.

1973 No. 1860 (S.149)

SHERIFF COURT, SCOTLAND

Act of Sederunt (Appeals against Poinding) 1973

Made - - - *7th November* 1973

Coming into Operation *1st January* 1974

The Lords of Council and Session, under and by virtue of the powers conferred on them by section 32 of the Sheriff Courts (Scotland) Act 1971(**a**), and of all other powers enabling them in that behalf, and after consultation with the Sheriff Court Rules Council, do hereby enact and declare as follows:—

1. This Act of Sederunt may be cited as the Act of Sederunt (Appeals against Poinding) 1973 and shall come into operation on 1st January 1974.

2.—(1) In this Act of Sederunt, unless the context otherwise requires— "the Act" means the Law Reform (Diligence) (Scotland) Act 1973(**b**); "appeal" means an appeal under section 1(4) of the Act; "Sheriff Clerk" includes Sheriff Clerk Depute.

(2) The Interpretation Act 1889(**c**) shall apply to the interpretation of this Act of Sederunt as it applies to the interpretation of an Act of Parliament.

3. On the execution of a poinding in a dwellinghouse the poinding Sheriff Officer or Messenger-at-Arms shall deliver to the possessor of the poinded effects a notice in the Form A in the Schedule hereto.

4. Appeals shall be made by lodging with the Sheriff Clerk a form in, or as nearly as it practicable in, the Form B in the Schedule hereto.

5. On the lodging of an appeal the Sheriff shall grant warrant for intimation and shall fix a date for hearing the appeal not sooner than the seventh day after such intimation, which warrant may be in the Form C in the Schedule hereto.

6. On the granting of a warrant for intimation the Sheriff Clerk shall forthwith intimate the appeal to the respondent and to the poinding Sheriff Officer or Messenger-at-Arms by transmitting a copy of the appeal and warrant, duly certified by him, by registered post or by recorded delivery first class service to each of the said respondent and Sheriff Officer or Messenger-at-Arms at the address or addresses stated in the Appeal. A certificate of execution of intimation may be in the Form D in the Schedule hereto.

(**a**) 1971 c. 58. (**b**) 1973 c. 22.
(**c**) 1889 c. 63.

7. All appeals shall be entered in a book to be kept for the purpose and such entries shall set forth the names and designations of the appellant, respondent, and poinding officer, the date of the poinding, the articles in respect of which the appeal is taken and the several deliverances and the dates thereof, which book shall be signed by the Sheriff. The determinations and deliverances of the Sheriff may be written on the principal appeal or separately, shall be signed by the Sheriff Clerk and shall have the force and effect of extract.

SCHEDULE

Form A.

Notice to the possessor of poinded effects.

The Law Reform (Diligence) (Scotland) Act, 1973 provides that an article shall not be liable to be poinded at the instance of a creditor in respect of a debt due to him by a debtor if it is an article to which the Act applies and, being at the time of the poinding in a dwellinghouse in which the debtor is residing, it is reasonably necessary to enable him and any other person living in family with him in that dwellinghouse to continue to reside there without undue hardship. The Act at present applies to beds or bedding material, chairs, tables, furniture or plenishings providing facilities for cooking, eating or storing food, and furniture or plenishings providing facilities for heating.

Where any article is poinded in respect of a debt, then, without prejudice to any other remedy available to him, a debtor may within seven days from the date of the poinding appeal to the Sheriff on the ground that, by virtue of the provisions of the Act, the said article is not liable to be poinded.

Any enquiry relating to the making of such an appeal may be directed to the Sheriff Clerk's Office at

Form B.

In the Sheriff Court at Appeal under section 1(4) of the Law Reform (Diligence) (Scotland) Act 1973.

Appeal by

Applicant

in the poinding at the instance of

Respondent

1. The Appellant is the defender in an action at the instance of the respondent in (Court) in which decree was granted on (date) against the Appellant for payment of (or as the case may be)

2. (name), Sheriff Officer, (Address), on the instructions of the respondent executed a poinding of the appellant's effects on (date) at the dwellinghouse at (address)

   Included amongst the effects poinded were the following articles:—

   (a)

   (b)

3. These articles are reasonably necessary to enable the appellant and the persons living in family with him in that dwellinghouse to continue to reside there without undue hardship.

4. This appeal is made under section 1(4) of the Law Reform (Diligence) (Scotland) Act 1973.

THEREFORE the Appellant craves the Court—

(a) To find that the articles referred to are articles to which section 1 of the Law Reform (Diligence) (Scotland) Act 1973 applies and are not liable to be poinded.

(b) To order that said articles be released from the poinding.

(c) To deal with the expenses of this Appeal as the Court may think fit.

(d) To sist meantime all further execution in respect of said articles.

Appellant
or
Appellant's Solicitors.

Form C.

Grants Warrant to intimate the foregoing Appeal and this warrant to the respondent and the therein designed Sheriff Officer/Messenger-at-Arms and Appoints them, if they intend to oppose the Appeal, to answer within the Sheriff Court at on the day of at o/clock noon. Further Appoints the said Sheriff Officer/Messenger-at-Arms to lodge a copy of the schedule of poinded effects in the hands of the clerk of court. Meantime, Grants interim sist of execution as craved.

Form D.

I, , Sheriff Clerk (Depute), did lawfully intimate the foregoing Appeal to the respondent and to the poinding Sheriff Officer/Messenger-at-Arms by posting a certified copy of the Appeal and warrant in a registered letter (or through the recorded delivery service) to each of them. The Post Office receipt for the said registered (or recorded delivery) letters are attached hereto.

Signed Sheriff Clerk or Sheriff Clerk Depute.

And the Lords appoint this Act of Sederunt to be inserted in the Books of Sederunt.

G. C. Emslie,
I.P.D.

Edinburgh,

7th November, 1973.

EXPLANATORY NOTE

(*This Note is not part of the Act of Sederunt.*)

This Act of Sederunt makes provision for the notice to be delivered by the poinding Sheriff Officer, and for the procedure to be followed for appeals to the Sheriff, under the Law Reform (Diligence) (Scotland) Act 1973.

STATUTORY INSTRUMENTS

1973 No. 1861

LOCAL GOVERNMENT, ENGLAND AND WALES

The Local Authorities (England) (Property etc.) Order 1973

Made - - - -	8*th November* 1973
Laid before Parliament	9*th November* 1973
Coming into Operation—	
For the purposes specified in article 1(2)(*a*)	21*st December* 1973
For all other purposes	1*st April* 1974

ARRANGEMENT OF ARTICLES

SCHEDULES

The Secretary of State for the Environment, in exercise of the powers conferred upon him by section 254(1) and (2)(*a*), (*b*) and (*d*) of the Local Government Act 1972(**a**) and by those provisions as extended by section 34(1) of, and paragraph 5(2)(*b*) of Schedule 6 to, the Water Act 1973(**b**) and of all other powers enabling him in that behalf, hereby makes the following order:—

Title and commencement

1.—(1) This order may be cited as the Local Authorities (England) (Property etc.) Order 1973.

(2) This order shall come into operation—

(*a*) for the purposes of the following provisions, namely:—

paragraphs (2) to (6) of article 10
article 11 in so far as it provides for agreements
article 12
paragraphs (1) to (3) and (5) of article 19
paragraph (3) of article 20
paragraphs (5) and (6) of article 23
paragraph (1) of article 25
articles 21, 22, 26, 27, 37 and 39
paragraph 3(*b*) and (*c*) of Schedule 2,

on 21st December 1973; and

(**a**) 1972 c. 70. (**b**) 1973 c. 37.

(*b*) for all other purposes, on 1st April 1974.

Territorial extent

2.—(1) Save as expressly provided in this order or in any other order made under section 254 of the Act—

(*a*) this order does not extend to the transfer of any matter from an authority whose area is wholly or partly in Wales;

(*b*) article 7(3) and (4) extend only to councils of counties and county boroughs in England;

(*c*) articles 29 and 32, in so far as they refer to property described in (*a*), (*b*) or (*e*) of article 9(1), articles 34(2) and 35 in so far as they deal with matters transferred by the Act, and article 38, extend only to England;

(*d*) article 36(1), (3) and (4) do not extend to any such authority as is described in (*a*);

(*e*) article 36(2) extends only to committees established in England;

(*f*) article 37 extends only to authorities whose areas are wholly in England.

(2) This order extends to the transfer of matters from the following authorities, namely—

The Severn River Authority
The Lancashire and Western Sea Fisheries Committee.

(3) Article 36(1) extends to the authorities named in paragraph (2) and to the Chester Port Health Authority.

(4) Article 36(3) and (4) extend to the authorities named in paragraph (2).

(5) Article 37 extends to the Severn-Trent Water Authority.

Exclusion of certain matters

3. Nothing in this order other than the express exceptions in the table in Schedule 2 and the definition in that Schedule of "police matters" applies to—

(*a*) property held by the council of any county or county borough for police purposes, including the purposes of section 81 of the Road Traffic Regulation Act 1967**(a)**;

(*b*) property held by the council of any county or any borough having a separate commission of the peace for the purposes of section 25 of the Justices of the Peace Act 1949**(b)**; or

(*c*) the land, buildings and works in Wales of any water undertaking,

or to any liabilities incurred, contracts, deeds, bonds, agreements and other instruments subsisting, notices given, actions and proceedings pending or causes of action or proceeding existing in relation to such matters.

Interpretation

4.—(1) The Interpretation Act 1889**(c)** shall apply for the interpretation of this order as it applies for the interpretation of an Act of Parliament.

(2) In this order—

"the Act" means the Local Government Act 1972;

"buildings", except in article 22, means buildings not within the meaning of the term "land";

(a) 1967 c. 76. **(b)** 1949 c. 101. **(c)** 1889 c. 63.

"corporate land" means corporate land within the meaning of the Local Government Act 1933**(a)**;

"divided parish" means the parish of Abbots Langley, Altcar, Alwalton, Aston, Birtley, Blagdon, Bold, Brafield-on-the-Green, Burnham, Burrington, Charlwood, Christchurch East, Collingtree, Compton Martin, Corton, Courteenhall, Datchworth, East Harptree, Ecton, Great Houghton, Harraton, Harworth, Heighington, Herringfleet, Horley, Kislingbury, Little Houghton, Loxton, Lydiate, Milton Malsor, Newton Longville, Orton Longueville, Orton Waterville, Overstone, Redbourn, Reedham, Rothersthorpe, St Michael Rural, Shenley Brook End, Shifnal, Slaugham, Sopley, South Biddick, Tattenhoe, Thorpe St Andrew, Ubley, Upton, West Harptree, Wexham, Whaddon, Wootton or Worth;

"historic and ceremonial property" does not include any property held (or under article 19, 20, 22 or 39 deemed to be held) for the purposes of any statutory functions;

"land" includes land covered by water and any interest or right in, to or over land;

"parish authority" means in the case of a parish having a separate parish council that council, and in any other case the parish meeting, or the representative body or the parish trustees, as may be appropriate;

the relevant class of authorities, in relation to any authority described in column (1) of the following table, means the class specified in respect thereof in column (2).

TABLE

(1)	(2)
A county council	In the case of areas included in metropolitan counties, metropolitan county councils
	In the case of other areas, non-metropolitan county councils
The corporation or council of a borough, or the council of an urban or rural district	In the case of areas included in metropolitan districts, metropolitan district councils
	In the case of other areas, non-metropolitan district councils;

"Wales" means the area consisting of the counties established by section 20 of the Act (new local government areas in Wales), and "England" does not include any area included in any of those counties; and

"water authority" means an authority established in accordance with section 2 of the Water Act 1973; and any reference to the area of a water authority, without more, means the area of that authority as defined in section 2(2)(*b*) of or Schedule 1 to that Act.

(3) In this order, unless the context otherwise requires, references to any enactment shall be construed as references to that enactment as amended, extended or applied by or under any other enactment.

(4) Any reference in this order to a numbered article or schedule shall, unless the reference is to an article or schedule of a specified order, be construed as a reference to the article or schedule bearing that number in this order.

(a) 1933 c. 51.

(5) Any reference in any article of this order to a numbered paragraph shall, unless the reference is to a paragraph of a specified article, be construed as a reference to the paragraph bearing that number in the first-mentioned article.

Other express provision

5. This order shall have effect subject to the express provision of—

(*a*) any other order made (whether before or after this order) under section 254 of the Act;

(*b*) any regulations made under section 7 or 8 of the Superannuation Act 1972**(a)**, or,

(*c*) section 16, 25 or 54(2) of the National Health Service Reorganisation Act 1973**(b)** or any order made under those sections.

Ancillary provision in relation to highways

6. There shall be transferred to and vest in or attach to a county council as the highway authority for any highway—

(*a*) the interest of the former highway authority, as such, in the highway, in so far as such interest is not vested in the county council by virtue of section 226 of the Highways Act 1959**(c)**;

(*b*) any land held by the former highway authority, as such, for the purposes of their functions in relation to the highway or which has been acquired by them as highway authority for the highway and not appropriated for any other purpose;

(*c*) any equipment on or near the highway belonging to the former highway authority as such, including any road lighting system within the meaning of Part III of the Local Government Act 1966**(d)** and any other lighting system belonging to the former highway authority as highway authority for the highway; and

(*d*) any traffic sign, on or near the highway, belonging to a county, county borough or county district council and not comprised in (*c*).

In this article "traffic sign" has the meaning attached to that expression in section 54(1) of the Road Traffic Regulation Act 1967**(e)**.

Particular matters

7.—(1) Any property described in column (2) of Schedule 1 (or of any extension thereof effected by any further order under section 254 of the Act made before 1st April 1974) of an authority named in column (1) shall by virtue of this order be transferred to and vest in the authority specified in respect of such property in column (3).

(2) The Teesside passenger transport undertaking shall be held by the District Council of Middlesbrough for the joint use and benefit of themselves and the District Councils of Langbaurgh and Stockton-on-Tees.

(3) Any liability of the council of any county or county borough to repay money borrowed for the provision of financial assistance in respect of works for water supply or sewerage or sewage disposal shall be transferred to and attach to the water authority for the area in which the works are situated.

Any other liability of the council of a county, county borough or county district to repay money borrowed under any statutory provision for the pro-

(a) 1972 c. 11. **(b)** 1973 c. 32. **(c)** 1959 c. 25.
(d) 1966 c. 42. **(e)** 1967 c. 76.

vision of financial assistance in respect of any works shall be transferred to and attach to the authority who would on and after 1st April 1974 be empowered by that statutory provision to provide such financial assistance in respect of such works.

Paragraphs (3) and (4) of article 18 shall apply to the liabilities transferred by this paragraph as they apply to the liabilities transferred by paragraph (2) of that article.

(4) This paragraph applies to the liability of the council of any county or county borough to make contributions to any authority in respect of any scheme under section 2 of the Rural Water Supplies and Sewerage Act 1944**(a)**.

Any such liability shall cease in respect of any payment falling to be made on or after 1st April 1974.

Where any payment falling to be made before 1st April 1974 is in fact made on or after that date it shall be made to the authority specified in column (2) of Part I or II of Schedule 4 in respect of the authority first referred to in this paragraph.

Sewers and sewage disposal works

8.—(1) Nothing in this article applies to any matter provided for in article 7 or in article 11(2) or (3) or 18 in their application to any property or liability transferred by article 7.

(2) Any public sewer (within the meaning of section 20(2) of the Public Health Act 1936**(b)** as that provision has effect at the date of the making of this order) which crosses the boundaries of the areas for sewerage and sewage disposal purposes of two or more water authorities, and any other public sewer discharging thereto, shall be transferred to and vest in the water authority within whose area for such purposes is situated the sewage disposal works, or where the sewer does not discharge to sewage disposal works the outfall, to which the first-mentioned sewer discharges.

(3) Any other public sewer or any sewage disposal works vested in a local authority by virtue of the Public Health Act 1936 shall be transferred to and vest in the water authority within whose area for sewerage and sewage disposal purposes the sewer is or the sewage disposal works are situated.

(4) In this article "sewer" includes manholes, ventilating shafts, pumping stations, pumps, pumping mains, storm overflows and associated overflow pipes and outfalls, storm flow balancing installations and any other accessories belonging to the sewer.

Transfer of specified classes of property, etc.

9.—(1) Nothing in this article applies to—

(*a*) any property held as sole trustee, exclusively for charitable purposes, by an existing local authority for an area outside Greater London, other than the parish council, parish meeting or representative body of a parish (but including the corporation of a borough included in a rural district) transferred by section 210 of the Act;

(*b*) any property so held by the parish council, parish meeting or representative body of an existing parish mentioned in paragraph 1 of Part IV of Schedule 1 to the Act or in paragraph (2) of article 3 of the New Parishes Order 1973**(c)** transferred by article 9(1) of that order;

(a) 1944 c. 26. **(b)** 1936 c. 49. **(c)** S.I. 1973/688.

(*c*) any other property held for the purposes of any charitable trust;

(*d*) any property vested in an authority described in column (1) of Part I or II of Schedule 4 transferred to the Secretary of State by section 16, 25 or 54(2) of the National Health Service Reorganisation Act 1973 or any liabilities incurred, contracts, deeds, bonds, agreements and other instruments subsisting, notices given, actions and proceedings pending or causes of action or proceeding existing in relation to such property;

(*e*) any property vested in a county council by virtue of section 226 of the Highways Act 1959;

(*f*) any matter provided for in article 6, 7 or 8;

(*g*) any matter provided for in article 11(1) in so far as it applies to rights ensured by article 23 in its application to any property transferred by article 6, 7 or 8;

(*h*) any matter provided for in article 11(2) or (3) in their application to any matter provided for in articles 7 and 8;

(*i*) any matter provided for in article 18 in its application to any matter described in the preceding items of this paragraph.

(2) Nothing in paragraphs (4) to (6) of this article applies to matters provided for in paragraphs (2) to (4) of article 18 in their application to any matters provided for in paragraph (3) of this article, and nothing in paragraphs (5) and (6) of this article applies to any matters provided for in paragraphs (3) and (4) of article 18 in their application to any liabilities provided for in paragraph (4) of this article.

(3) All property vested in an authority described in column (2) of the table in Schedule 2 (or of any extension thereof effected by any further order under section 254 of the Act made before 1st April 1974) and within any description of matters specified in respect of such authority in column (3) shall by virtue of this order be transferred to and vest in the authority specified in respect of such description of matters in column (4).

(4) All liabilities attaching to an authority described in the said column (2) and within any description of matters specified in respect of such authority in column (3) shall by virtue of this order be transferred to and attach to the authority specified in respect of such description of matters in column (4).

(5) All contracts, deeds, bonds, agreements and other instruments subsisting in favour of, or against, and all notices in force which were given (or have effect as if they had been given) by, or to, an authority described in the said column (2) and within any description of matters specified in respect of such authority in column (3) shall be of full force and effect in favour of, or against, the authority specified in respect of such description of matters in column (4).

(6) Any action or proceeding or any cause of action or proceeding, pending or existing at 1st April 1974, by, or against, an authority described in the said column (2) and within any description of matters specified in respect of such authority in column (3) shall not be prejudicially affected by reason of the Act or the Water Act 1973, and may be continued, prosecuted and enforced by, or against, the authority specified in respect of such description of matters in column (4).

(7) Save in so far as express provision is made in item No. 13 of the table in Schedule 2, this article does not extend to the historic and ceremonial property other than land and buildings, and in particular to the charters, insignia and plate, of any area.

Provision supplementary to article 9

10.—(1) The provision made in this article applies in the application of article 9.

(2) Any question as to the functions for the purposes of which any property is held, any liabilities have been incurred, any contract, deed, bond, agreement or other instrument subsists, any notice has been given or any action or proceeding or cause of action or proceeding relates shall, subject to the provision of paragraph (6), be determined by the transferor authority.

(3) Any question whether any property is historic or ceremonial property shall, subject to the provision of paragraph (6), be determined by the transferor authority.

(4)(*a*) Where any land or any part of any land vested immediately before 1st April 1974 in an authority described in column (2) of the table in Schedule 2 is situated in two or more areas specified in respect of that authority in the said table, the land or the part shall be deemed to be situated in the area so specified in which the greater proportion of it is situated.

(*b*) Where part of any land vested as aforesaid is situated (or is under (*a*) deemed to be situated) in an area specified in respect of an authority described in column (2) of the said table, any part of the land situated outside the area of that authority shall be deemed to be situated within the area so specified.

(*c*) Any question as to the area in which the greater proportion of the land or the part is situated shall, subject to the provision of paragraph (6), be determined by the transferor authority.

(5) Where in relation to any land held (or under article 19, 20 or 39 deemed to be held) for the purposes of the deposit of refuse—

(*a*) deposit has been completed; and

(*b*) it has been resolved that the land shall be used (otherwise than temporarily) for the purposes of a particular function,

the land shall be deemed to be held for those purposes and shall be held by the authority to whom it is transferred for those purposes.

Any question whether the deposit of refuse has been completed, or whether it has been resolved as described in (*b*), or whether any use is temporary, shall, subject to the provision of paragraph (6), be determined by the transferor authority.

(6) If notice is given by any authority that they are dissatisfied with any determination under paragraph (2), (3), (4) or (5), the question shall be determined by agreement between the authorities concerned or failing such agreement by the decision of a person agreed on by such authorities or in default of agreement appointed by the Secretary of State.

(7) The provisions of section 187(2) and (3) of the Act shall be disregarded.

(8) The provision of off-street parking places for vehicles shall be treated as a function exercisable on and after 1st April 1974 by both county and district councils.

Fittings, furniture, equipment and stores

11.—(1) Where by paragraph (1) of article 23 any right to the use of any accommodation is ensured for any authority other than the authority in whom the accommodation is vested on and after 1st April 1974, the fittings, furniture, equipment and stores in such accommodation which have been provided exclusively for the purposes of the functions described in (i) or (ii) of the said paragraph shall, except in so far as the first-mentioned authority shall otherwise agree, by virtue of this order be transferred to and vest in such authority.

(2) Subject to paragraph (1), where by article 7, 8 or 9 any building is transferred to and vested in any authority, the fittings, furniture and equipment of such building, and the stores therein which have been provided for the discharge of functions therein, shall, except in so far as such authority shall otherwise agree, by virtue of this order be transferred to and vest in such authority.

If the value of any stores transferred by this paragraph is included in any revenue balance, the necessary adjustment shall be made in such balance.

(3) Subject to paragraph (1), where by article 7, 8 or 9 any land to which paragraph (2) does not apply is transferred to and vested in any authority, the equipment of such land shall, except in so far as such authority shall otherwise agree, by virtue of this order be transferred to and vest in such authority.

(4) For the purposes of this article—

(*a*) "equipment" includes records; and

(*b*) any vehicles or other mobile equipment used wholly or mainly in the performance of the functions carried out in any accommodation or building or on any land shall be deemed to be equipment thereof.

Agreements as to the transfer of property other than land not transferred by the preceding articles

12.—(1) Paragraph (1) of article 9 applies to this article as it applies to article 9.

(2) Nothing in this article applies to any matter provided for in article 9 or in articles 11(2) and (3) and 18 in their application to any matter provided for in article 9.

(3) Any property other than land vested in an authority named in column (1) of Part I of Schedule 3 (or of any extension thereof effected by any further order under section 254 of the Act made before 1st April 1974) for the purposes of functions—

(*a*) which are not exercisable on and after 1st April 1974 by an authority of the specified class in relation to such authority; but

(*b*) which are so exercisable by the authorities specified in respect of such authority in column (2),

shall by virtue of this order be transferred to and vest in such one or more of the authorities specified in column (2) as may be agreed between them.

In this paragraph, the specified class of authorities, in relation to any authority described in column (1) of the following table, means the class specified in respect thereof in column (2).

TABLE

(1)	(2)
The council of a county	Non-metropolitan county councils
The corporation or council of a borough, or the council of an urban or rural district, wholly or partly comprised in metropolitan districts	Metropolitan district councils
The corporation or council of any other borough, or the council of any other urban or rural district	Non-metropolitan district councils

(4) Any property other than land vested in the council of any administrative county, county borough or county district for the purposes of functions which on 1st April 1974 become exercisable in any area partly by the county council and partly by the district council shall by virtue of this order be transferred to and vest in such one of those councils as may be agreed between them.

(5) Subject to the provisions of paragraphs (3) and (4), any property other than land vested in an authority named in column (1) of Part II of Schedule 3 (or of any extension thereof effected by any further order under section 254 of the Act made before 1st April 1974) shall by virtue of this order be transferred to and vest in such one or more of the authorities specified in respect of such authority in column (2) as may be agreed between them.

(6) Any agreement under paragraph (3), (4) or (5) may—

(*a*) provide for payment in respect of any property within such paragraph;

(*b*) extend to any matter arising under article 18 in its application to property within such paragraph; and

(*c*) provide that any authority concerned shall be entitled to the use of the property for such period and on such terms as may be agreed, whether for the purposes of the functions for which the property is used immediately before 1st April 1974 or for the purposes of any other functions exercisable by them.

(7) In default of agreement as to any matter arising under paragraph (3), (4), (5) or (6) or article 18 in its application to property within any such paragraph the matter shall be determined by the decision of a person agreed on by the authorities concerned or in default of agreement appointed by the Secretary of State.

(8) In this article—

"exercisable" means exercisable otherwise than by virtue of section 101, 110 or 187(2) or (3) of the Act; and

"property" does not include the balance on any fund or account.

Balances on accounts of undertakings

13.—(1) Subject to paragraph (2), nothing in articles 7 to 12, or in article 18 in its application to any undertaking transferred by any such article, shall be effective to transfer any amount standing as a balance (whether credit or debit) in respect of any undertaking in the revenue accounts of the transferor authority immediately before 1st April 1974.

(2) The provisions of this paragraph shall apply where a local authority maintain separate accounts in respect of any water undertaking transferred by article 7.

Where in such accounts for the period ending on 31st March 1974 as finally closed a credit balance is shown the transfer effected by article 7 shall include the amount shown as such balance.

Where in such accounts for such period as so closed a deficiency is shown the water authority to whom the undertaking (or the undertaking other than any land, buildings or works in Wales) is transferred shall as soon as practicable pay to the authority specified in respect of the local authority in column (2) of Part II of Schedule 4 the amount shown as such deficiency.

Certain county council funds

14.—(1) This article applies to the county councils of Berkshire, Buckingham, Chester, Durham, East Suffolk, East Sussex, Gloucestershire, Hampshire, Lancaster, Lincoln, Parts of Lindsey, Northumberland, Nottinghamshire, Somerset, Staffordshire, Surrey, Warwickshire, Worcestershire, Yorkshire, East Riding, Yorkshire, North Riding and Yorkshire, West Riding.

(2) The balances on the following funds, namely—

the county fund
any capital fund
any renewal and repairs fund
any fund of substantially similar nature to a capital fund or a renewal and repairs fund

of a county council to whom this article applies shall be apportioned between the new counties in which any parts of the area of such council are comprised in the proportions which the aggregate rateable value of all the hereditaments in the several parts, as shown in the valuation lists immediately before 1st April 1974, bear to the aggregate rateable value of all the hereditaments in all such parts, and the amounts so apportioned shall be payable to the councils of such counties.

Certain county borough and county district council funds

15.—(1) This article applies to the councils of the boroughs of Teesside and Whitley Bay, the urban districts of Ashton-in-Makerfield, Billinge-and-Winstanley, Golborne, Lakes, Queensbury and Shelf, Ramsbottom, Seaton Valley, Thurrock and Turton and the rural districts of Axbridge, Basford, Blackburn, Blofield and Flegg, Bridlington, Brixworth, Bucklow, Burnley, Castle Ward, Chelmsford, Chesterfield, Chester-le-Street, Chichester, Clutton, Croft, Cuckfield, Darlington, Dartford, Dorking and Horley, Droitwich, Easington, East Retford, Eastry, Epping and Ongar, Eton, Gloucester, Hemsworth, Hertford, Kettering, Lichfield, Lothingland, Market Bosworth, Meriden, Norman Cross, Northampton, Osgoldcross, Pershore, Preston, Ringwood and Fordingbridge, Runcorn, St. Albans, St. Thomas, Shifnal, Skipton, Sodbury, South East Derbyshire, Stockton, Stokesley, Stratford-on-Avon, Strood, Tadcaster, Thirsk, Thornbury, Tonbridge, Wantage, Watford, Wellingborough, West Lancashire, Wetherby, Wharfedale, Whiston, Wigan, Winchester, Winslow, Worksop, Worthing and Wortley.

(2) The balances on the following funds, namely—

the general rate fund, other than the housing revenue account;

any capital fund, renewal and repairs fund or fund of a similar nature to either such fund other than one maintained in connection with any undertaking transferred by article 7,

of a council to whom this article applies shall be apportioned between the districts in which any parts of the area of such council are comprised in the proportions which the aggregate rateable value of all the hereditaments in the several parts, as shown in the valuation lists immediately before 1st April 1974, bear to the aggregate rateable value of all the hereditaments in all such parts, and the amounts so apportioned shall be payable to the councils of such districts.

(3) This paragraph has effect in relation to the housing revenue account of a council to whom this article applies.

The working balance on such account shall be apportioned between the districts in which dwellings of the council are situated in the proportions which the numbers of such dwellings in the several districts bear to the total number of such dwellings, and the amounts so apportioned shall be payable to the councils of such districts and shall attach to the housing revenue accounts of the councils.

In this paragraph "dwellings" means Housing Revenue Account dwellings within the meaning of the Housing Finance Act 1972**(a)**.

Residual transfer of property, etc.

16.—(1) Save as provided in paragraph (2) of this article, paragraph (1) of article 9 applies to this article as it applies to article 9.

(2) The following entry in Schedule 4, namely—

"The representative body of any parish not included in the preceding items"

shall extend to property held by any such representative body for the purposes of charitable trusts.

(3) Subject to the provisions of articles 9 to 15 or of articles 11(2) and (3) and 18 in their application to any matters provided for in articles 9 to 15—

(*a*) all property and liabilities vested in or attaching to an authority described in column (1) of Part I or II of Schedule 4 (or of any extension thereof effected by any further order under section 254 of the Act made before 1st April 1974) shall by virtue of this order be transferred to and vest in or attach to the authority specified in respect of such authority in column (2);

(*b*) all contracts, deeds, bonds, agreements and other instruments subsisting in favour of, or against, and all notices in force which were given (or have effect as if they had been given) by, or to, an authority described in column (1) of Part I or II of Schedule 4 (or of any extension thereof as aforesaid) shall be of full force and effect in favour of, or against, the authority specified in respect of such authority in column (2);

(*c*) any action or proceeding or any cause of action or proceeding, pending or existing at 1st April 1974, by, or against, an authority described in column (1) of Part I or II of Schedule 4 (or of any extension thereof as aforesaid) shall not be prejudicially affected by reason of the Act or the Water Act 1973, and may be continued, prosecuted and enforced by, or against, the authority specified in respect of such authority in column (2); and

(*d*) any power to appoint any person to any body belonging to an authority described in column (1) of Part I or II of Schedule 4 (or of any extension thereof as aforesaid) in respect of any matter provided for in (*a*) or (*b*) shall be transferred to the authority specified in respect of such authority in column (2).

General saving for agreements

17.—(1) The authority to whom any account or fund is transferred, or any amount of any fund is payable, by virtue of any provision of this order, may agree that any particular amount in the account or fund shall be payable to any other authority.

(2) The authority to whom any other property other than land is transferred

(a) 1972 c. 47.

by the preceding articles of this order other than article 7 may by resolution agree that the property shall be transferred to any other authority specified in the resolution, and paragraphs (2) to (5) of article 18 shall apply accordingly.

(3) The transferee authority in respect of any matter other than property, provided for in paragraph (4), (5) or (6) of article 9 or in (*a*), (*b*) or (*c*) of paragraph (3) of article 16, and any other authority, may agree that that other authority shall be substituted for the transferee authority in the application of any such provision.

(4) The provision made by the preceding articles of this order, other than articles 12, 14 and 15, for the transfer of any matter is without prejudice to any agreement which may be made for payment in respect of such matter.

Liabilities, contracts etc., notices and proceedings in respect of transferred property, etc.

18.—(1) This article applies to the following matters, namely—

(*a*) any property described in (*a*), (*b*) or (*e*) of article 9(1); and

(*b*) any property transferred by this order.

(2) Subject to paragraph (6), all liabilities attaching to any authority in respect of any property to which this article applies shall by virtue of this order be transferred to and attach to the authority to whom such property is transferred.

(3) All contracts, deeds, bonds, agreements and other instruments subsisting in favour of, or against, and all notices in force which were given (or have effect as if they had been given) by, or to, the authority first mentioned in paragraph (2) in respect of any property to which this article applies, or in respect of liabilities transferred by paragraph (2), shall be of full force and effect in favour of, or against, the authority to whom such property and liabilities are transferred.

(4) Any action or proceeding or any cause of action or proceeding, pending or existing at 1st April 1974, by, or against, the authority first mentioned in paragraph (2) in respect of any property to which this article applies, or in respect of liabilities transferred by paragraph (2), shall not be prejudicially affected by reason of the Act or the Water Act 1973, and may be continued, prosecuted and enforced by, or against, the authority to whom such property and liabilities are transferred.

(5) Any power to appoint any person to any body belonging to the authority first mentioned in paragraph (2) in respect of any property (other than that described in (*a*) and (*b*) of article 9(1)) to which this article applies or any matter provided for in paragraphs (2) and (3) shall be transferred to the authority to whom such property or matter is transferred.

(6) Paragraph (2) shall not apply to the rights and liabilities described in entry (*a*) in item No. 19 in the table in Schedule 2, but paragraphs (3) to (5) shall apply in respect of such rights and liabilities.

Land held for several purposes

19.—(1) Where any land, not being a property described otherwise than as an undertaking in column (2) of Schedule 1 or of any extension thereof described in article 7, is held by an authority for the purposes of functions exercisable on and after 1st April 1974 by two or more authorities, or for the purposes of a function which will then be so exercisable, the land shall, subject to the provision of paragraphs (2) to (6), for the purposes of this order be deemed to be held for the purposes of the function exercisable by such one of those authorities as shall be determined by the first-mentioned authority to be the function for which the land is, immediately before that date, used to the greatest extent.

In such determination the first-mentioned authority shall disregard any use of the land which is temporary.

(2) In the application of paragraph (1), where any function is exercisable on and after 1st April 1974 by an authority of the relevant class in relation to the authority first mentioned in that paragraph and by any other authority, the function shall be deemed to be exercisable only by the authority of the relevant class.

(3) Subject to paragraph (2), two (but not more) functions exercisable on and after 1st April 1974 by an authority shall be treated as a single function in the application of paragraph (1).

(4) Any land to which paragraph (1) applies shall be held by the authority to whom it is transferred for the purposes of the function determined under that paragraph, or where two functions have been treated as a single function under paragraph (3) for the purposes of such one of those functions as is determined by the authority to whom the land is transferred.

(5) If notice is given by any authority that they are dissatisfied with the determination in paragraph (1) the purposes therein described shall be determined by agreement between the two or more authorities so described or failing such agreement by the decision of a person agreed on by such authorities or in default of agreement appointed by the Secretary of State, and paragraphs (1) and (4) shall have effect accordingly. Paragraphs (2) and (3) shall apply in the application of this paragraph.

(6) In this article, "exercisable" means exercisable otherwise than by virtue of section 101, 110 or 187(2) or (3) of the Act.

(7) In the application of this article, any reference to the purposes of functions includes a reference to the purposes of an undertaking transferred by article 7.

Property to be deemed to be held for the purposes of statutory functions

20.—(1) This article applies to—

(*a*) any property held under section 125 of the Local Government Act 1933;

(*b*) any land acquired under section 112, 114 or 119(1)(*a*) of the Town and Country Planning Act 1971**(a)** or any earlier provision corresponding to any such enactment;

(*c*) any corporate land;

(*d*) any land acquired under any provision empowering the acquisition of land for the benefit, improvement or development of any area and not allocated or appropriated for any statutory purpose; and

(*e*) any property acquired by a local authority as a gift otherwise than for charitable purposes.

(2) (*a*) Where any property to which this article applies is, immediately before 1st April 1974—

(i) in the case of property referred to in paragraph (1)(*a*), used wholly or substantially so for the purposes of a particular function being purposes authorised by enactments other than the said section 125,

(ii) in the case of property referred to in paragraph (1)(*b*), used wholly or

(a) 1971 c. 78.

mainly for the purposes of statutory functions other than those exercised under the Town and Country Planning Acts 1971 and 1972; or

(iii) in the case of property referred to in paragraph (1)(*c*), (*d*) and (*e*), used wholly or mainly for the purposes of any statutory function,

it shall for the purposes of this order be deemed to be held for the purposes of the function for which it is so used.

In the application of this sub-paragraph any temporary use of the property shall be disregarded.

(*b*) Two (but not more) functions shall be treated as a single function in the application of this paragraph.

(*c*) Any property to which this paragraph applies shall be held by the authority to whom it is transferred for the purposes of the function described in (i), (ii) or (iii) of sub-paragraph (*a*) or where two functions have been treated as a single function for the purposes of such one of those functions as is determined by the authority to whom the property is transferred.

(3) Any question whether any property to which this article applies is, immediately before 1st April 1974, used as described in (i), (ii) or (iii) of paragraph (2)(*a*) shall, subject to the following provision of this paragraph, be determined by the authority in whom the property is, before 1st April 1974, vested.

If notice is given by any authority that they are dissatisfied with any such determination the question shall be determined by agreement between the authorities concerned or failing such agreement by the decision of a person agreed on by such authorities or in default of agreement appointed by the Secretary of State, and sub-paragraph (*c*) of paragraph (2) shall apply accordingly. Sub-paragraph (*b*) of paragraph (2) shall apply in the application of this paragraph.

(4) In the application of this article, any reference to the purposes of functions includes a reference to the purposes of an undertaking transferred by article 7.

Questions as to appropriations

21. The provisions of this article shall have effect in relation to any land appropriated between 9th November 1973 and 1st April 1974 and to any financial adjustment made on the appropriation.

Any such land shall for the purposes of this order be treated as held for the purpose for which it has been appropriated, and any financial adjustment made on the appropriation shall be of full effect, unless a local authority, Passenger Transport Executive or water authority give notice that the land falls to be treated for the purposes of this order as being held for the purpose for which it was held before the appropriation, or that the financial adjustment falls to be varied. If such notice is given the question of the purpose for which the land is held or, as the case may be the adjustment to be made, shall be determined by agreement between the authorities concerned or failing such agreement by the decision of a person agreed on by such authorities or in default of agreement appointed by the Secretary of State.

Buildings to be replaced

22.—(1) The provisions of this article shall apply where—

(*a*) at 1st April 1974 any building or part of a building is to be wholly or substantially so replaced by another building which is completed or in course of erection or for the erection of which a contract has been entered into or by part of such building;

(*b*) it has been resolved by the transferor authority before the date of the making of this order that the first-mentioned building or part of a building or the site thereof is to be used for the purposes of some function other than the one for which it is held;

(*c*) the nature of the building or the location of its site is such as to make it peculiarly suited for use for the purposes of such function rather than other local government purposes,

and apart from the provisions of this article the two buildings or parts of buildings would be transferred to the same authority.

(2) The transferor authority may determine that for the purposes of this order the land on which the building or part of a building first mentioned in paragraph (1) is erected shall be deemed to be held for the purposes for which by the resolution described in item (*b*) of that paragraph it is to be used.

(3) If notice is given by any authority concerned that they question whether (*a*), (*b*) or (*c*) in paragraph (1) is satisfied, the determination shall be of no effect and the question of the purpose for which the land is to be deemed to be held shall be determined by agreement between the authorities concerned or failing such agreement by the decision of a person agreed on by such authorities or in default of agreement appointed by the Secretary of State.

User rights

23.—(1) This paragraph applies to—

(*a*) accommodation in any property transferred to and vested in any authority by virtue of this order (hereinafter referred to as "case (*a*)");

(*b*) accommodation in any property held by a parish authority and not transferred by virtue of this order (hereinafter referred to as "case (*b*)");

immediately before 1st April 1974 used (or in the case of accommodation not yet in occupation proposed to be used) otherwise than temporarily—

(i) in case (*a*) for the purposes of any functions which on and after 1st April 1974 are not exercisable (or not exercisable as regards any part of the area served from the accommodation) by the authority to whom the property is transferred;

(ii) in case (*b*) for the purposes of any functions which on and after 1st April 1974 are not exercisable (or not exercisable as regards any part of the area served from the accommodation) by a parish authority.

In the case of any accommodation to which this paragraph applies the authority exercising the functions described in (i) or (ii) in the area served by the accommodation or, as the case may be, the part thereof shall be entitled to the use of such accommodation, whether for the purposes of such functions or for the purposes of any other functions exercisable by them.

(2) Where—

(*a*) any property is immediately before 1st April 1974 used (or in the case of property not yet in use proposed to be used) otherwise than temporarily for the purposes of functions exercisable by one authority in relation to any area;

(*b*) the functions become exercisable on and after that day by two or more authorities; and (*c*) the property is by virtue of this order transferred to and vested in one of the authorities described in (*b*);

(hereinafter referred to as "case (*c*)") any other of the authorities described in (*b*) shall be entitled to the use of such property, whether for the purposes of such functions or for the purposes of any other functions exercisable by them.

(3) Where—

(*a*) any property to which paragraph (2) does not apply is immediately before 1st April 1974 held by the council of a county, county borough or county district under section 125 of the Local Government Act 1933; and

(*b*) the property is by virtue of this order transferred to and vested in the council of any relevant area,

(hereinafter referred to as "case (*d*)") the council of any other relevant area shall be entitled to the use of the property.

In this paragraph, "relevant areas" means—

in relation to a county, new counties and metropolitan districts;

in relation to a county borough or county district, new counties and districts,

being areas in which the area of the county, county borough or county district is comprised.

(4) Where—

(*a*) any property is immediately before 1st April 1974 used (or in the case of property not yet in use proposed to be used) otherwise than temporarily for the purposes of functions exercisable by two or more authorities;

(*b*) the property is by virtue of this order transferred to and vested in one authority;

(hereinafter referred to as "case (*e*)") any other authority exercising any of the functions described in (*a*) shall be entitled to the use of such property whether for the purposes of such functions or for the purposes of other functions exercisable by them.

(5) Any question—

(*a*) whether any accommodation in any property to which paragraph (1) applies is used (or proposed to be used) for the purposes described in (i) or (ii) of that paragraph;

(*b*) whether any property to which paragraph (2) applies is used (or proposed to be used) as described in (*a*) thereof;

(*c*) whether any property to which paragraph (4) applies is used (or proposed to be used) as described in (*a*) thereof; or

(*d*) without prejudice to (*c*) whether any use (or proposed use) is temporary,

shall, subject to the following provision of this paragraph, be determined by the authority in whom the property is, before 1st April 1974, vested.

If, before 1st April 1975, notice is given by any authority that they are dissatisfied with any such determination (or, no determination having been made, that a question exists) the question shall be determined by agreement between the authorities concerned or failing such agreement by the decision of a person agreed on by such authorities or in default of agreement appointed by the Secretary of State.

(6) The use of any accommodation or property by virtue of this article shall

be for such period and on such terms as may be determined by agreement between the authority entitled under this article to use the accommodation or property and, in case (*a*), (*c*), (*d*) or (*e*) the authority to whom the property is transferred and in case (*b*) the parish authority, or failing such agreement by the decision of a person agreed on by such authorities or in default of agreement appointed by the Secretary of State.

(7) In this article "exercisable" means exercisable otherwise than by virtue of section 101, 110 or 187(2) or (3) of the Act.

Charter trustees

24.—(1) It shall be the duty of the council of a district in which a city or town for which there are charter trustees is situated to provide accommodation for the proper discharge of the functions of the charter trustees.

(2) The accommodation to be provided and the terms on which it is provided shall be determined by agreement between the district council and the charter trustees, or failing such agreement by the decision of a person agreed on by them or in default of agreement appointed by the Secretary of State.

Corporate land

25.—(1) Any question whether any land vested in the corporation of a borough is corporate land shall, subject to the following provision of this paragraph, be determined by the council of the borough.

If notice is given by any authority that they are dissatisfied with any such determination the question shall be determined by agreement between the authorities concerned or failing such agreement by the decision of a person agreed on by such authorities or in default of agreement appointed by the Secretary of State.

(2) Any corporate land to which article 20(2) does not apply and which is transferred by this order to any authority shall be held by that authority as if it had been acquired by that authority under section 120(1)(*b*) or 124(1)(*b*), as the case may be, of the Act.

Inventories of road passenger transport undertakings

26. The council of any county borough from whom any road passenger transport undertaking will be transferred to a Passenger Transport Executive by article 7 shall, not later than 31st January 1974, supply to such Executive—

(*a*) an inventory of the land, buildings and vehicles comprised in the undertaking;

(*b*) a statement of the financial position of the undertaking;

(*c*) a statement of any appropriations subsequent to 9th November 1973 of land held for the purposes of the undertaking.

Inventories of property transferred to water authorities

27.—(1) Any authority from whom any water undertaking, or any water undertaking other than any land, buildings or works in Wales, will be transferred to a water authority by article 7 shall, not later than 31st January 1974, supply to such water authority—

(*a*) an inventory of the land, buildings, water mains, plant and other vehicles (other than any land, buildings or works in Wales) comprised in the undertaking;

(*b*) a statement of the financial position of the undertaking;

(*c*) a statement of any appropriations subsequent to 9th November 1973 of land held for the purposes of water supply.

(2) Any authority from whom any public sewer or any sewage disposal works will be transferred to a water authority by article 8 shall, not later than 31st January 1974, supply to such water authority an inventory of the sewers and sewage disposal works which will be transferred to such water authority.

Property and liabilities to attach to whole areas

28.—(1) Subject to paragraph (2), any interest in any property or any liability transferred by the preceding articles of this order to the authority for any county, district or parish shall be held or discharged by them in respect of the whole of such area.

(2) Paragraph (1)—

(*a*) shall not apply to any property or liability transferred by article 16 as extended by paragraph (2) thereof;

(*b*) shall not apply in respect of any interest in any property or any liability which by reason of agreements made by authorities abolished by the Act falls to be held or discharged in respect of any specific area; and

(*c*) shall have effect subject to the provision of subsections (4) and (5) of section 248 of the Act (freemen and inhabitants of existing boroughs).

Byelaws, etc.

29.—(1) Any byelaws in force for the regulation of any property described in (*a*) or (*b*) of article 9(1) or transferred by the preceding articles of this order shall have effect as if they had been made by the authority to whom such property is transferred.

(2) Any provision of any local Act or of any order made under or confirmed by any Act which applies to any property described in (*a*) or (*b*) of article 9(1) or transferred by the preceding articles of this order shall have effect with the substitution for any references to (or having effect as references to) the authority from whom such property is transferred of references to the authority to whom the property is transferred.

Vehicle licences

30. Any excise licence, operators' licence, public service vehicle licence, road service licence, plating certificate or other document issued in respect of any vehicle transferred by the preceding articles of this order shall have effect as if it had been issued to the authority to whom such vehicle is transferred, and any reference to the authority from whom the vehicle is transferred in any such licence or certificate or in any registration book or other document issued in respect of such vehicle shall have effect as a reference to the authority to whom the vehicle is transferred.

Markets

31. The expression "market authority" in Part III of the Food and Drugs Act 1955**(a)** shall include any district council to whom such a market as is described in section 49(2) of that Act is transferred by this order.

(a) 4 Eliz. 2 c. 16.

Loan sanctions

32. Any authorisation of the borrowing of money in force in respect of any property or liability described in (*a*), (*b*) or (*e*) of article 9(1) or transferred by the preceding articles of this order to the authority for any county, district or parish may, subject to the terms applicable thereto, be acted on by such authority.

Security for loans

33. Where under this order any liability or part of a liability charged indifferently on all the revenues of a public body or on any particular revenues or fund of such body is transferred to another public body, the liability or part of the liability shall be charged indifferently on all the revenues of the public body to whom it is transferred and shall cease to be a charge on any revenues or fund of the public body from whom it is transferred.

Capital and renewal and repairs funds

34.—(1) A local authority may transfer the balance on any capital fund or renewal and repairs fund transferred to them under article 16 or the amount of any such fund received by them under article 14 or 15 to the credit of a capital fund or a renewal and repairs fund, as the case may be, established by them under Schedule 13 to the Act.

(2) Where any matter in respect of which a repayable advance which has not been fully repaid has been made from a capital fund or a renewal and repairs fund is transferred by the Act or this order to any authority, that authority may treat the outstanding amount of the advance as an advance from a capital fund or a renewal and repairs fund established by them under Schedule 13 to the Act and make such payments to such fund as the authority consider appropriate, but otherwise any liability to make repayments in respect of the advance shall cease.

Loans pools and consolidated loans funds

35.—(1) This article applies where, if the Act had not been passed and this order had not been made, advances from a loans pool or consolidated loans fund would have fallen to be repaid in respect of any matter, and the matter is by virtue of the Act or this order transferred to an authority other than the authority to whom the pool or fund is transferred by article 7 or 16.

(2) Sums which would have become due and owing to the pool or fund in respect of such advances shall be paid by the authority first mentioned in paragraph (1) to the authority last mentioned therein:

Provided that the said authorities and the lender may agree for the transfer to the first-mentioned authority of the liability with respect to any outstanding loan.

(3) The outstanding amount in respect of any such advances shall be shown in the accounts of the authority first mentioned in paragraph (1) as loans from other local authorities and as advances to the appropriate borrowing account.

(4) The outstanding amount in respect of any such advances shall be shown in the accounts of the authority last mentioned in paragraph (1) as loans to other authorities.

Audit of accounts

36.—(1) The repeal effected by section 272 of, and Schedule 30 to, the Act of Part X of the Local Government Act 1933 shall not affect (*a*) any audit of accounts for any period preceding 1st April 1974; or

(*b*) any disallowance, surcharge, appeal, application or disqualification arising from any audit of such accounts by a district auditor (whether an audit completed before the said date or an audit falling within (*a*)),

but nothing in sections 154 to 167, 196(3) and 197(4) of or in section 251(1) in so far as it extends to paragraph 7(1) of Schedule 29 to, the Act shall apply to any accounts which are subject to district audit under the said Part X.

(2) The said Part X shall apply to the accounts of any committee established under section 264 of the Act, and of the sub-committees and officers thereof, as if the committee had been established under Part III of the Local Government Act 1933.

(3) In relation to the accounts of any authority described in column (1) of Part I or II of Schedule 4 (or of any extension thereof described in article 16) to whom Part X of the said Act of 1933 applied or of the committees or officers thereof, any action which had the Act not been passed would have fallen to be taken by such authority shall be taken by the authority specified in respect of such authority in column (2).

(4) If at any audit of the accounts of an authority described in column (1) of Part I or II of Schedule 4 (or of any extension thereof described in article 16) to whom Part X of the said Act of 1933 applied or of the committees and officers thereof any sum is certified by a district auditor as due from any person, that sum shall be paid to the authority specified in respect of that authority in column (2).

Inspection of documents

37. Any officer of the council of any county or district, of a Passenger Transport Executive or of a water authority, duly authorised in that behalf, shall, for the purposes of the functions of the authority by whom he is employed, be entitled during ordinary office hours to inspect and take extracts from any books or documents of any council dissolved by section 1(10) or 20(6) of the Act not in the custody of such authority.

Legal proceedings

38. All legal proceedings pending at 1st April 1974 may be amended in such manner as may be necessary or proper in consequence of the Act or the Water Act 1973 or the preceding articles of this order.

General provision as to disputes

39.—(1) Any question as to the interpretation of this order may be determined by the decision of a person agreed on by the authorities concerned or in default of agreement appointed by the Secretary of State.

(2) Where a determination required by article 10(2), (3), (4) or (5), 19(1), 20(3) or 25(1) has not been made by the transferor authority before 1st April 1974 notice that a question exists may be given before 1st April 1975 by any authority concerned.

(3) Where—

(*a*) at 1st April 1974—

(i) notice has been given by any authority under article 10(6), 19(5), 20(3), 21, 22(3) or 25(1) or paragraph 3(*c*) of Schedule 2,

(ii) notice has been given by any authority that the provisions of this paragraph are to have effect in relation to any property within paragraph (3), (4) or (5) of article 12 specified in the notice; or

(iii) notice has been given by any authority that the interpretation of any provision of this order as to the transfer of any property is in dispute,

and the question has not been determined; or

(*b*) thereafter, but before 1st April 1975—

(i) notice is given by any authority under any provision specified in (*a*)(i);

(ii) notice is so given under paragraph (2);

(iii) notice is so given that the provisions of this paragraph are to have effect in relation to any property within paragraph (3), (4) or (5) of article 12 specified in the notice; or

(iv) notice is so given that the interpretation of any provision of this order as to the transfer of any property is in dispute,

then from 1st April 1974 or from the later date on which notice is given, as the case may be—

(*k*) any provisions of this order as to the transfer and vesting of property shall cease to have effect in relation to the property;

(*l*) article 16 shall apply to the property, and article 18 shall apply to any liabilities incurred, contracts, deeds, bonds, agreements and other instruments subsisting, notices given, actions and proceedings pending and causes of action or proceeding existing in relation thereto, as temporary provision pending the determination of the question;

Provided that the authorities concerned may by instrument in writing agree that any authority may in such application be substituted for the authority specified in column (2) of Part I or II of Schedule 4 in respect of the transferor authority;

(*m*) where notice has been given under paragraph (2), the question shall be determined by agreement between the authorities concerned or failing such agreement by the decision of a person agreed on by such authorities or in default of agreement appointed by the Secretary of State; and

(*n*) on the determination of the question whether under (*m*) or otherwise—

(*x*) the determination shall specify the authority to whom the property is to be transferred; and

(*y*) the provisions described in (*l*) shall cease to have effect, the property shall by virtue of the determination be transferred to and vest in the authority specified in the determination, and the provisions of this order which would have applied to the property if the transfer had been effected by this order shall apply to it.

(4) Any reference in any provision of this order for the decision of any question by a person shall be construed as including a reference to three persons.

(5) Section 31 of the Arbitration Act 1950(a) shall have effect for the purposes of the determination of any question by any person or persons under any provision of this order as if such determination were an arbitration under any other Act within the meaning of that section.

(a) 1950 c. 27.

SCHEDULE 1

Article 7

TRANSFER OF PARTICULAR PROPERTIES

Paragraph (3) of article 10, and paragraph (6) in so far as it applies thereto, shall apply to any question whether any property is historic or ceremonial property

(1) Transferor authority	(2) Property	(3) Transferee authority
The corporation or council of any county borough comprised in a metropolitan county	Any road passenger transport undertaking of the corporation or council	The Passenger Transport Executive for the county
The corporation or council of the borough of Todmorden	Any interest in the Calderdale Joint Omnibus Committee's undertaking	The West Yorkshire Passenger Transport Authority
The corporation or council of the borough of Teesside	The Teesside passenger transport undertaking	The District Council of Middlesbrough
The corporation or council of any borough or the council of any urban or rural district	Any water undertaking of the transferor authority, other than any land, buildings or works in Wales	The water authority within whose area for water supply purposes the limits of supply of the transferor authority are comprised
The council of the urban district of Billinge-and-Winstanley, Lakes or Turton	Historic and ceremonial property, and in particular the insignia and plate, of the urban district	The Parish Council of Billinge Chapel End, Lakes or Turton North
The corporation of the borough of Teesside	Historic and ceremonial property other than land and buildings, and in particular the charters, insignia and plate, of any area comprised in the district of Langbaurgh or Stockton-on-Tees	The District Council of Langbaurgh or Stockton-on-Tees

The corporation of any borough for the whole of the area of which charter trustees are constituted	Historic and ceremonial property other than land and buildings, and in particular the charters, insignia and plate, of the borough	The charter trustees
The council of the borough of Teesside	The council's consolidated loans fund	The County Council of Cleveland
The corporations and councils of the boroughs of Dudley and Wolverhampton	Himley Hall	The District Councils of Dudley and Wolverhampton
The council of the rural district of Tavistock	Manorial rights in respect of Whitchurch Down	The Parish Council of Tavistock
The parish council of Newton Longville	Rights in respect of Newton Longville Common	The Parish Council of Newton Longville

Article 9

SCHEDULE 2

TRANSFER OF SPECIFIED CLASSES OF PROPERTY, ETC.

1. In the following table—

(*a*) "county matters" and "district matters", in relation to any transferor authority, and "parish matters", in relation to the council of the rural district of Alston with Garrigill, Disley or Tintwistle, mean—

(i) in the case of property, property (not being excepted property) held for the purposes of functions not exercisable on and after 1st April 1974 by an authority of the relevant class in relation to the transferor authority but so exercisable by the authority specified in respect of the matters transferred in column (4) of the table in this Schedule;

(ii) in the case of liabilities, liabilities incurred in relation to such functions;

(iii) in the case of contracts, deeds, bonds, agreements and other instruments, and notices, such instruments subsisting and notices given in relation to such functions;

(iv) in the case of actions and proceedings and causes of action or proceeding, such actions and proceedings pending or causes existing in relation to such functions;

but if specified as such matters in relation to any area include only such matters being local matters in respect of such area, and "parish matters" includes, in the case of property—

(i) parish property within the meaning of the Local Government Act 1933, the proceeds of sale of such property and any securities in which such proceeds have been invested;

(ii) public walks and pleasure grounds, recreation grounds, seats and shelters, public clocks, allotments (within the meaning of the Allotments Act 1925(a)), baths and washhouses, and village halls;

(iii) property held for burial purposes; and

(iv) property held for street lighting purposes, except any such property falling within article 6;

(*b*) "parish matters", in relation to the corporation or council of any non-county borough or the council of any urban district, means—

(i) in the case of property—

(*a*) property held for the purposes of functions not exercisable on and after 1st April 1974 by county or district councils; and

(*b*) parish property within the meaning of the Local Government Act 1933, the proceeds of sale of such property and any securities in which such proceeds have been invested;

(ii) in the case of liabilities, liabilities incurred in relation to such functions or parish property;

(iii) in the case of contracts, deeds, bonds, agreements and other instruments, and notices, such instruments subsisting and notices given in relation to such functions or parish property;

(iv) in the case of actions and proceedings and causes of action or proceeding, such actions and proceedings pending or causes existing in relation to such functions or parish property,

but if specified as such matters in relation to any area includes only such matters being local matters in respect of such area;

(*c*) "burial matters", "national park matters", "police matters" and "sewerage and sewage disposal matters" mean—

(a) 1925 c. 61.

(i) in the case of property, property held for the purposes of the relevant functions;

(ii) in the case of liabilities, liabilities incurred in relation to such functions;

(iii) in the case of contracts, deeds, bonds, agreements and other instruments, and notices, such instruments subsisting and notices given in relation to such functions; and

(iv) in the case of actions and proceedings and causes of action or proceeding, such actions and proceedings pending or causes existing in relation to such functions,

but if specified as such matters in relation to any area include only such matters being local matters in respect of such area, and for the purposes of the foregoing definitions "the relevant functions" means—

(i) in the case of burial matters, functions under the Burial Acts 1852 to 1906;

(ii) in the case of national park matters, functions which under Schedule 17 to the Act are to be exercised by a National Park Committee;

(iii) in the case of police matters, functions exercisable for police purposes, including the purposes of section 81 of the Road Traffic Regulation Act 1967;

(iv) in the case of sewerage and sewage disposal matters, functions exercisable for the purposes of sewerage and sewage disposal;

(*d*) "local matters", in relation to any area, means—

(i) in the case of property—

(*a*) subject to the provision of paragraph 3, sited property situated in; and

(*b*) other property held exclusively in respect of,

the area;

(ii) in the case of liabilities, liabilities incurred exclusively in respect of the area;

(iii) in the case of contracts, deeds, bonds, agreements and other instruments, and notices, such instruments subsisting and notices given exclusively in respect of the area;

(iv) in the case of actions and proceedings and causes of action or proceeding, such actions and proceedings pending or causes existing exclusively in respect of the area;

(*e*) any reference to an area of a county included in a new county or a new district includes any county borough—

(i) lying within the extent of such area; or

(ii) the boundaries of which, other than boundaries with any other county (including the county of Flintshire) or county borough or the sea, are wholly boundaries with such area.

2. In paragraph 1, "excepted property" means any property within article 20(1) which is not covered by the provision of article 20(2) and "exercisable" means exercisable otherwise than by virtue of section 101 or 110 of the Act

3. (*a*) In this Schedule, "sited property" means—

(i) land;

(ii) buildings;

(iii) fittings, furniture, equipment and stores supplied in respect of a voluntary school or a controlled community home;

(iv) subject to the provision of article 6, lamps, lamp posts and other apparatus for public lighting.

(*b*) The transferor authority may determine that any sited property shall, by reason of the fact that it is used wholly or mainly for an area other than the one in which it is situated, constitute local matters in respect of such other area.

(*c*) If notice is given by any authority concerned that they are dissatisfied with any determination under sub-paragraph (*b*) or that a determination should have been made thereunder, the question of the area which is to be the relevant area in relation to any sited property in the application of this Schedule shall be determined by agreement between the authorities concerned or failing such agreement by the decision of a person agreed on by such authorities or in default of agreement appointed by the Secretary of State.

4. Article 12 has effect, within the meaning of items 5, 10, 11, 12, 14 and 15 in the table in this Schedule, in relation to any property, where before 1st April 1974, in respect of such property—

an agreement has been entered into under paragraph (3), (4) or (5) of that article;

a determination has been given under paragraph (7) of that article;

notice has been given under paragraph (3) of article 39.

and in relation to any liabilities incurred, contracts, deeds, bonds, agreements and other instruments subsisting, notices given, actions and proceedings pending and causes of action or proceeding existing in relation to such property.

TABLE

(1) Item No.	(2) Transferor authority	(3) Matters transferred	(4) Transferee authority
1	The county council of any county	Property acquired by the county council in the exercise of their functions under the Rural Water Supplies and Sewerage Act 1944(**a**) or in making contributions to a county district council in respect of works of water supply or sewerage or sewage disposal in any area	The water authority in whose area for sewerage and sewage disposal purposes the area described in column (3) is situated
2	The County Council of Devon	National park matters in respect of the Exmoor National Park	The County Council of Somerset
3	The County Council of Yorkshire, West Riding	National park matters in relation to the area of the Yorkshire Dales National Park in Cumbria	The County Council of North Yorkshire
4	The County Council of Yorkshire, North Riding	National park matters in relation to the area of the North York Moors National Park in Cleveland	The County Council of North Yorkshire
5	The county council of Berkshire, Buckingham, Chester, Durham, East Suffolk, East Sussex, Gloucestershire, Hampshire, Lancaster, Lincoln, Parts of Lindsey, Northumberland, Nottinghamshire, Somerset, Staffordshire, Surrey, Warwickshire, Worcestershire, Yorkshire, East Riding, Yorkshire, North Riding or Yorkshire, West Riding	District matters in relation to any area of the county included in a new district	The council of the district in which the area is comprised
		Other local matters (not being police matters, matters as to which article 12 has effect or matters provided for in items 1, 3 and 4) in relation to any area of the county included in a new county	The council of the county in which the area is comprised

(a) 1944 c. 26.

(1) Item No.	(2) Transferor authority	(3) Matters transferred	(4) Transferee authority
6.	The county council of Rutland	District matters	The District Council of Rutland
7.	The county council of any county not included in items 5 and 6	District matters in relation to any area of the county included in a new district	The council of the district in which the area is comprised
8.	The county council of any county other than Rutland	Land situated outside the county falling within the definition of district matters	The council of the district specified in respect of the county council in column (3) of Part I of Schedule 4
9.	The corporation or council of any county borough	County matters	The council of the county in which the area of the county borough is comprised
10.	The corporation or council of the county borough of Teesside	Local matters other than county matters, police matters, sewerage and sewage disposal matters or matters as to which article 12 has effect in relation to any area of the county borough included in a new district	The council of the district in which the area is comprised
11.	The corporation or council of the borough of Whitley Bay or the council of the urban district of Ashton-in-Makerfield, Billinge-and-Winstanley, Golborne, Ramsbottom, Seaton Valley or Turton	County matters in relation to any area of the borough or district included in a new county	The council of the county in which the area is comprised
		Parish matters in relation to any area of the borough or district constituting a parish	The parish council of the parish
		Other local matters (not being sewerage and sewage disposal matters or matters as to which article 12 has effect) in relation to any area of the borough or district included in a new district	The council of the district in which the area is comprised

		Land situated outside the borough or district falling within the definition of county matters	The council of the county in which the district specified in respect of the corporation or council in Part II of Schedule 4 is comprised
12.	The council of the urban district of Lakes, Queensbury and Shelf or Thurrock	County matters	The council of the county in which the area of the urban district is comprised
		Parish matters in relation to any area of the urban district constituting a parish	The parish council of the parish
		Other local matters (not being sewerage and sewage disposal matters or matters as to which article 12 has effect) in relation to any area of the urban district included in a new district	The council of the district in which the area is comprised
13.	The corporation or council of any non-county borough or the council of any urban district not included in items 11 and 12	County matters	The council of the county in which the area of the borough or district is comprised
		Where a parish is constituted under Part V of Schedule 1 to the Act, parish matters, and the historic and ceremonial property, and in particular the charters, insignia and plate, of the borough or district	The parish council of the parish

(1) Item No.	(2) Transferor authority	(3) Matters transferred	(4) Transferee authority
14.	The council of the rural district of Axbridge, Bridlington, Bucklow, Castle Ward, Chester-le-Street, Clutton, Dorking and Horley, Easington, East Retford, Eton, Hemsworth, Lothingland, Meriden, Osgoldcross, Ringwood and Fordingbridge, Skipton, Sodbury, Stokesley, Stratford-on-Avon, Tadcaster, Thornbury, Wantage, West Lancashire, Wetherby, Wharfedale, Whiston, Wigan or Worksop	County matters in relation to any area of the district included in a new county	The council of the county in which the area is comprised
		Other local matters (not being sewerage and sewage disposal matters or matters in respect of which article 12 has effect) in relation to any area of the district included in a new district	The council of the district in which the area is comprised
		Land situated outside the rural district falling within the definition of county matters	The council of the county in which the district of the council specified in respect or the council of the rural district in column (2) of Part II of Schedule 4 is comprised
15.	The council of the rural district of Basford, Blackburn, Blofield and Flegg, Brixworth, Burnley, Chelmsford, Chesterfield, Chichester, Croft, Cuckfield, Darlington, Dartford, Droitwich, Eastry, Epping and Ongar, Gloucester, Hertford, Kettering, Lichfield, Market Bosworth, Norman Cross, Northampton, Pershore, Preston, Runcorn, St. Albans, St. Thomas, Shifnal, South East Derbyshire, Stockton, Strood, Thirsk, Tonbridge, Watford, Wellingborough, Winchester, Winslow, Worthing or Wortley	County matters	The council of the county in which the area of the rural district is comprised
		Other local matters (not being sewerage and sewage disposal matters or matters in respect of which article 12 has effect) in relation to any area of the district included in a new district	The council of the district in which the area is comprised
16.	The council of the rural district of Alston with Garrigill, Disley or Tintwistle	County matters	The council of the county in which the area of the district is comprised
		Parish matters	The parish council of the parish co-extensive with the district

17.	The council of any rural district not included in items 14-16	County matters	The council of the county in which the area of the district is comprised
18.	The parish authority of any divided parish		
	In the case of the divided parish of Abbots Langley, Birtley, Blagdon, Brafield-on-the Green, Burrington, Great Houghton, Harworth, Milton Malsor, Rothersthorpe, Shifnal or Sopley	(*a*) Burial matters	The parish councils of the parishes, or where there is no parish the council of the district, in which parts of the area of the parish are comprised
	In all cases	(*b*) Subject to (*a*), local matters in relation to any area of the parish included in any parish	The parish authority of the parish in which the area is comprised
		(*c*) Subject to (*a*), local matters in relation to any other area of the parish	The council of the district in which the area is comprised
19.	The corporation or council of any borough or the council of any urban district or rural district	(*a*) Rights acquired or liabilities incurred in relation to the cost of construction in any area of any public sewer or sewage disposal works constructed under powers other than the Public Health Act 1936 or enactments replaced by that Act prior to its declaration as a public sewer or sewage disposal works	The authority exercising such powers in that area on and after 1st April 1974
		(*b*) Subject to (*a*), where the area of the borough, urban district or rural district is comprised in the area for sewerage and sewage disposal purposes of one water authority, sewerage and sewage disposal matters	The water authority

(1) Item No.	(2) Transferor authority	(3) Matters transferred	(4) Transferee authority
		(*c*) Subject to (*a*), where the area of the borough, urban district or rural district is comprised in the area for sewerage and sewage disposal purposes of two or more water authorities, sewerage and sewage disposal matters being local matters in relation to any area of the borough, urban district or rural district comprised in the area of a water authority	The water authority
20.	The Avon and Dorset River Authority	Local matters in relation to any part of the area of the Authority included in the Wessex or South West Water Authority's area	The Wessex or South West Water Authority
21.	The Essex River Authority	Local matters in relation to any part of the area of the Authority included in the Anglian or Thames Water Authority's area	The Anglian or Thames Water Authority
22.	The Kent River Authority	Local matters in respect of functions other than land drainage in relation to any part of the area of the Authority included in the Southern or Thames Water Authority's area	The Southern or Thames Water Authority
23.	The Severn River Authority	Local matters in respect of functions other than land drainage and fisheries in relation to any part of the area of the Authority included in the Severn-Trent or Wessex Water Authority's area	The Severn-Trent or Wessex Water Authority

SCHEDULE 3

Article 12

AGREEMENTS AS TO THE TRANSFER OF PROPERTY OTHER THAN LAND NOT TRANSFERRED BY ARTICLES 6–11

PART I

(1)	(2)
The county council of any county other than Rutland	The councils of the districts in which any areas of the county are comprised
The corporation or council of the borough of Whitley Bay or the council of the urban district of Ashton-in-Makerfield, Billinge-and-Winstanley, Golborne, Ramsbottom, Seaton Valley or Turton or the rural district of Axbridge, Bridlington, Bucklow, Castle Ward, Chester-le-Street, Clutton, Dorking and Horley, Easington, East Retford, Eton, Hemsworth, Lothingland, Meriden, Osgoldcross, Ringwood and Fordingbridge, Skipton, Sodbury, Stokesley, Stratford-on-Avon, Tadcaster, Thornbury, Wantage, West Lancashire, Wetherby, Wharfedale, Whiston, Wigan or Worksop	The councils of the counties in which any areas of the borough or district are comprised
The corporation or council of any borough, or the council of any urban district or rural district, which is comprised in the areas for sewerage and sewage disposal purposes of two or more water authorities	The water authorities

PART II

(1)	(2)
The county council of Berkshire, Buckingham, Chester, Durham, East Suffolk, East Sussex, Gloucestershire, Hampshire, Lancaster, Lincoln, Parts of Lindsey, Northumberland, Nottinghamshire, Somerset, Staffordshire, Surrey, Warwickshire, Worcestershire, Yorkshire, East Riding, Yorkshire, North Riding, or Yorkshire, West Riding	The councils of the counties and metropolitan districts in which any areas of the county are comprised
The corporation or council of the borough of Teesside or Whitley Bay, or the council of any urban district or rural district named in the second entry in Part I of this Schedule or of the urban district of Lakes, Queensbury and Shelf or Thurrock or the rural district of Basford, Blackburn, Blofield and Flegg, Brixworth, Burnley, Chelmsford, Chesterfield, Chichester, Croft, Cuckfield, Darlington, Dartford, Droitwich, Eastry, Epping and Ongar, Gloucester, Hertford, Kettering, Lichfield, Market Bosworth, Norman Cross, Northampton, Pershore, Preston, Runcorn, St. Albans, St. Thomas, Shifnal, South East Derbyshire, Stockton, Strood, Thirsk, Tonbridge, Watford, Wellingborough, Winchester, Winslow, Worthing or Wortley	The councils of the districts and non-metropolitan counties in which any areas of the borough or district are comprised
The Avon and Dorset, Essex, Kent or Severn River Authority	The water authorities in whose areas any parts of the area of the Authority are comprised

SCHEDULE 4

Article 16

Residual Transfer of Property, Etc

Part I

(1) Transferor authority	(2) Transferee county council	(3) Most populous district
The county council of Bedford	The County Council of Bedfordshire	Luton
The county council of Berkshire	The County Council of Berkshire	Reading
The county council of Buckingham	The County Council of Buckinghamshire	Wycombe
The county council of Cambridgeshire and Isle of Ely or Huntingdon and Peterborough	The County Council of Cambridgeshire	Peterborough
The county council of Chester	The County Council of Cheshire	Warrington
The county council of Cornwall	The County Council of Cornwall	Kerrier
The county council of Cumberland or Westmorland	The County Council of Cumbria	Carlisle
The county council of Derbyshire	The County Council of Derbyshire	Derby
The county council of Devon	The County Council of Devon	Plymouth
The county council of Dorset	The County Council of Dorset	Bournemouth
The county council of Durham	The County Council of Durham	Easington
The county council of East Suffolk or West Suffolk	The County Council of Suffolk	Ipswich
The county council of East Sussex	The County Council of East Sussex	Brighton
The county council of Essex	The County Council of Essex	Southend-on-Sea

(1) Transferor authority	(2) Transferee county council	(3) Most populous district
The county council of Gloucestershire	The County Council of Gloucestershire	Gloucester
The county council of Hampshire	The County Council of Hampshire	Southampton
The county council of Herefordshire or Worcestershire	The County Council of Hereford and Worcester	Wyre Forest
The county council of Hertfordshire	The County Council of Hertfordshire	St. Albans
The county council of the Isle of Wight	The County Council of Isle of Wight	Medina
The county council of Kent	The County Council of Kent	Medway
The county council of Lancaster	The County Council of Lancashire	Blackpool
The county council of Leicestershire	The County Council of Leicestershire	Leicester
The county council of Lincoln. Parts of Holland, Lincoln Parts of Kesteven or Lincoln, Parts of Lindsey	The County Council of Lincolnshire	East Lindsey
The county council of Norfolk	The County Council of Norfolk	Norwich
The county council of Northamptonshire	The County Council of Northamptonshire	Northampton
The county council of Northumberland	The County Council of Northumberland	Wansbeck
The county council of Nottinghamshire	The County Council of Nottinghamshire	Nottingham
The county council of Oxford	The County Council of Oxfordshire	South Oxfordshire
The county council of Salop	The County Council of Salop	Wrekin
The county council of Somerset	The County Council of Somerset	Yeovil

The county council of Staffordshire	The County Council of Staffordshire	Stoke-on-Trent
The county council of Surrey	The County Council of Surrey	Guildford
The county council of Warwickshire	The County Council of Warwickshire	Warwick
The county council of West Sussex	The County Council of West Sussex	Arun
The county council of Wiltshire	The County Council of Wiltshire	Thamesdown
The county council of Yorkshire, East Riding	The County Council of Humberside	Kingston upon Hull
The county council of Yorkshire, North Riding	The County Council of North Yorkshire	Harrogate
The county council of Yorkshire, West Riding	The County Council of West Yorkshire	Leeds

PART II

(1) Transferor authority	(2) Transferee authority
The county council of Rutland	The County Council of Leicestershire
The Lincolnshire County Committee	The County Council of Lincolnshire
The Yorkshire County Committee	The County Council of North Yorkshire
The corporation or council of the county borough of Teesside	The District Council of Middlesbrough
The corporation or council of any other county borough	The council of the district in which the area of the county borough is comprised
The corporation or council of the borough of Whitley Bay	The District Council of North Tyneside
The council of the urban district of Ashton-in-Makerfield	The District Council of Wigan
The council of the urban district of Billinge-and-Winstanley	The District Council of St. Helens
The council of the urban district of Golborne	The District Council of Wigan
The council of the urban district of Lakes	The District Council of South Lakeland
The council of the urban district of Queensbury and Shelf	The District Council of Bradford
The council of the urban district of Ramsbottom	The District Council of Bury
The council of the urban district of Seaton Valley	The District Council of Blyth Valley
The council of the urban district of Thurrock	The District Council of Thurrock
The council of the urban district of Turton	The District Council of Bolton
The council of the rural district of Axbridge	The District Council of Sedgemoor
The council of the rural district of Basford	The District Council of Broxtowe
The council of the rural district of Blackburn	The District Council of Ribble Valley
The council of the rural district of Blofield and Flegg	The District Council of Broadland
The council of the rural district of Bridlington	The District Council of North Wolds
The council of the rural district of Brixworth	The District Council of Daventry

(1) Transferor authority	(2) Transferee authority
The council of the rural district of Bucklow	The District Council of Macclesfield
The council of the rural district of Burnley	The District Council of Burnley
The council of the rural district of Castle Ward	The District Council of Castle Morpeth
The council of the rural district of Chelmsford	The District Council of Chelmsford
The council of the rural district of Chesterfield	The District Council of North East Derbyshire
The council of the rural district of Chester-le-Street	The District Council of Chester-le-Street
The council of the rural district of Chichester	The District Council of Chichester
The council of the rural district of Clutton	The District Council of Wansdyke
The council of the rural district of Croft	The District Council of Richmondshire
The council of the rural district of Cuckfield	The District Council of Mid Sussex
The council of the rural district of Darlington	The District Council of Sedgefield
The council of the rural district of Dartford	The District Council of Sevenoaks
The council of the rural district of Dorking and Horley	The District Council of Mole Valley
The council of the rural district of Droitwich	The District Council of Wychavon
The council of the rural district of Easington	The District Council of Easington
The council of the rural district of East Retford	The District Council of Bassetlaw
The council of the rural district of Eastry	The District Council of Dover
The council of the rural district of Epping and Ongar	The District Council of Epping Forest
The council of the rural district of Eton	The District Council of Beaconsfield
The council of the rural district of Gloucester	The District Council of Tewkesbury
The council of the rural district of Hemsworth	The District Council of Wakefield
The council of the rural district of Hertford	The District Council of East Hertfordshire
The council of the rural district of Kettering	The District Council of Kettering

(1) Transferor authority	(2) Transferee authority
The council of the rural district of Lichfield	The District Council of Lichfield
The council of the rural district of Lothingland	The District Council of Waveney
The council of the rural district of Market Bosworth	The District Council of Bosworth
The council of the rural district of Meriden	The District Council of Solihull
The council of the rural district of Norman Cross	The District Council of Huntingdon
The council of the rural district of Northampton	The District Council of South Northamptonshire
The council of the rural district of Osgoldcross	The District Council of Selby
The council of the rural district of Pershore	The District Council of Wychavon
The council of the rural district of Preston	The District Council of South Ribble
The council of the rural district of Ringwood and Fordingbridge	The District Council of New Forest
The council of the rural district of Runcorn	The District Council of Vale Royal
The council of the rural district of St. Albans	The District Council of St. Albans
The council of the rural district of St. Thomas	The District Council of East Devon
The council of the rural district of Shifnal	The District Council of Bridgnorth
The council of the rural district of Skipton	The District Council of Craven
The council of the rural district of Sodbury	The District Council of Northavon
The council of the rural district of South East Derbyshire	The District Council of Erewash
The council of the rural district of Stockton	The District Council of Stockton-on-Tees
The council of the rural district of Stokesley	The District Council of Hambleton
The council of the rural district of Stratford-on-Avon	The District Council of Stratford-on-Avon
The council of the rural district of Strood	The District Council of Medway
The council of the rural district of Tadcaster	The District Council of Selby
The council of the rural district of Thirsk	The District Council of Hambleton

(1) Transferor authority	(2) Transferee authority
The council of the rural district of Thornbury	The District Council of Northavon
The council of the rural district of Tonbridge	The District Council of Tunbridge Wells
The council of the rural district of Wantage	The District Council of Vale of White Horse
The council of the rural district of Watford	The District Council of Three Rivers
The council of the rural district of Wellingborough	The District Council of Wellingborough
The council of the rural district of West Lancashire	The District Council of West Lancashire
The council of the rural district of Wetherby	The District Council of Leeds
The council of the rural district of Wharfedale	The District Council of Leeds
The council of the rural district of Whiston	The District Council of Knowsley
The council of the rural district of Wigan	The District Council of Wigan
The council of the rural district of Winchester	The District Council of Winchester
The council of the rural district of Winslow	The District Council of Aylesbury Vale
The council of the rural district of Worksop	The District Council of Bassetlaw
The council of the rural district of Worthing	The District Council of Arun
The council of the rural district of Wortley	The District Council of Sheffield
The corporation or council of any other non-county borough or the council of any other urban or rural district	The council of the district in which the area of the borough or district is comprised
The corporation or council of any borough included in a rural district	The parish council of the parish replacing the borough
The parish council of Abbots Langley	The Parish Council of Abbots Langley
The parish council of Altcar	The Parish Council of Altcar
The parish council of Aston	The Parish Council of Aston
The parish council of Birtley	The Parish Council of Birtley
The parish council of Blagdon	The Parish Council of Blagdon
The parish council of Bold	The Parish Council of Bold
The parish council of Brafield-on-the-Green	The Parish Council of Brafield on the Green

(1) Transferor authority	(2) Transferee authority
The parish council of Burnham	The Parish Council of Burnham
The parish council of Burrington	The Parish Council of Burrington
The parish council of Charlwood	The Parish Council of Charlwood
The parish council of Christchurch East	The Parish Council of Bransgore
The parish council of Collingtree	Thr Parish Council of Collingtree
The parish council of Compton Martin	The Parish Council of Compton Martin
The parish council of Corton	The Parish Council of Corton
The parish council of Datchworth	The Parish Council of Datchworth
The parish council of East Harptree	The Parish Council of East Harptree
The parish council of Ecton	The Parish Council of Ecton
The parish council of Great Houghton	The Parish Council of Great Houghton
The parish council of Harraton	The Parish Council of North Lodge
The parish council of Harworth	The Parish Council of Harworth Bircotes
The parish council of Heighington	The Parish Council of Heighington
The parish council of Horley	The Parish Council of Horley
The parish council of Kislingbury	The Parish Council of Kislingbury
The parish council of Little Houghton	The Parish Council of Little Houghton
The parish council of Lydiate	The Parish Council of Lydiate
The parish council of Milton Malsor	The Parish Council of Milton Malsor
The parish council of Newton Longville	The Parish Council of Newton Longville
The parish council of Orton Longueville	The Parish Council of Orton Longueville
The parish council of Orton Waterville	The Parish Council of Orton Waterville
The parish council of Overstone	The Parish Council of Overstone
The parish council of Redbourn	The Parish Council of Redbourn
The parish council of Reedham	The Parish Council of Reedham
The parish council of Rothersthorpe	The Parish Council of Rothersthorpe
The parish council of St. Michael Rural	The Parish Council of St. Michael
The parish council of Shenley Brook End	The Parish Council of Shenley Brook End
The parish council of Shifnal	The Parish Council of Shifnal

(1) Transferor authority	(2) Transferee authority
The parish council of Slaugham	The Parish Council of Slaugham
The parish council of Sopley	The Parish Council of Sopley
The parish council of Thorpe St. Andrew	The Parish Council of Thorpe St. Andrew
The parish council of Upton	The Parish Council of Upton
The parish council of West Harptree	The Parish Council of West Harptree
The parish council of Wexham	The Parish Council of Wexham
The parish council of Whaddon	The Parish Council of Whaddon
The parish council of Wootton	The Parish Council of Wootton
The parish council of Worth	The Parish Council of Worth
The parish meeting or the representative body of the parish of Alwalton	The Parish Council of Alwalton
The parish meeting or the representative body of the parish of Courteenhall	The Parish Meeting or the Parish Trustees, as the case may be, of Courteenhall
The parish meeting or the representative body of the parish of Herringfleet	The Parish Council of Herringfleet
The parish meeting or the representative body of the parish of Loxton	The Parish Council of Loxton
The parish meeting or the representative body of the parish of South Biddick	The Parish Council of South Biddick
The parish meeting or the representative body of the parish of Tattenhoe	The Parish Council of Shenley Brook End
The parish meeting or the representative body of the parish of Ubley	The Parish Council of Ubley
The representative body of any parish not included in the preceding items	The parish trustees of the parish
Any burial board, joint burial board or joint committee which ceases to exist by virtue of section 214(1)(*b*) of the Act	The authority or authorities exercising the functions specified in paragraph 1 of Schedule 26 of the Act in relation to the cemeteries and crematoria of the board or committee, or where such authority is a parish meeting the parish trustees of the parish
Any joint board which ceases to exist by virtue of section 263(2)(*b*) of the Act	The authority in whom the functions of the board are vested by section 263(2)(*a*) of the Act

(1) Transferor authority	(2) Transferee authority
Any joint board which ceases to exist by virtue of section 263(3) of the Act	The local authority which becomes the port health authority for the district of the board under the said section 263(3)
The Lake District Planning Board	The Lake District Special Planning Board
The Peak Park Planning Board	The Peak Park Joint Planning Board
Any joint board who are statutory water undertakers other than a joint water board within the meaning of the Water Act 1973	The water authority within whose area for water supply purposes the limits of supply of the transferor authority are comprised
Any joint sewerage board or joint committee of sewerage authorities	The water authority within whose area for sewerage and sewage disposal purposes the area of the transferor authority is comprised
The Avon and Dorset River Authority	The Wessex Water Authority
The Essex River Authority	The Anglian Water Authority
The Kent River Authority	The Southern Water Authority
The Severn River Authority	The Severn-Trent Water Authority
Any other river authority, the Conservators of the River Thames, the Lee Conservancy Catchment Board or the Isle of Wight River and Water Authority	The water authority in whose area the area of the authority named in column (1) is comprised
Any local fisheries committee for a sea fisheries district	The committee as reconstituted

If the Charlwood and Horley Bill is enacted before 1st April 1974 the references to the Parish Councils of Charlwood and Horley shall be construed as references to the parish councils established by it.

Geoffrey Rippon,
Secretary of State for the Environment.

8th November 1973.

EXPLANATORY NOTE

(This Note is not part of the Order.)

This Order makes, in relation to England, general provision for the transfer from the existing authorities which go out of existence on 1st April 1974 to the new authorities established by or under the Local Government Act 1972 and the Water Act 1973 of property, liabilities, contracts etc., notices, and actions and proceedings and causes of action or proceeding.

1973 No. 1862

LAND CHARGES

The Local Land Charges (Amendment) Rules 1973

Made - - - -	6*th November* 1973
Coming into Operation	8*th December* 1973

The Lord Chancellor, in exercise of the powers conferred on him by section 19 of the Land Charges Act 1925**(a)**, as set out in Schedule 4 to the Land Charges Act 1972**(b)**, and sections 8(4) and 52(8) of the Land Compensation Act 1973**(c)**, hereby makes the following Rules:—

1.—(1) These Rules may be cited as the Local Land Charges (Amendment) Rules 1973 and shall come into operation on 8th December 1973.

(2) The Interpretation Act 1889**(d)** shall apply to the interpretation of these Rules as it applies to the interpretation of an Act of Parliament.

(3) In these Rules, unless the context otherwise requires—

(i) "the principal Rules" means the Local Land Charges Rules 1966**(e)**, as amended **(f)**;

(ii) a rule or schedule referred to by number means the rule or schedule so numbered in the principal Rules.

2. The principal Rules shall be amended as follows:—

(*a*) The following rule shall be substituted for rule 4:—

"4. The register shall have an index (in the form of a map or in any other form) whereby all entries in it can readily be traced."

(*b*) The following heading and paragraph shall be substituted for the heading to rule 9 and for rule 9(1) respectively:—

"*Part* 4 *of register: miscellaneous charges*

9.—(1) Part 4 of the register shall contain entries relating to the charges specified in Schedule 3 to these Rules and entries relating to charges not registrable in another part of the register."

(a) 1925 c. 22. **(b)** 1972 c. 61.
(c) 1973 c. 26. **(d)** 1889 c. 63.
(e) S.I. 1966/579 (1966 II, p. 1318).
(f) The relevant amending instrument is S.I. 1969/1152 (1969 II, p. 3406).

(*c*) The following rule shall be substituted for rule 11:—

"*Part 6 of register: compulsory purchase and land compensation*

11.—(1) Part 6 of the register shall contain—

(*a*) those entries hitherto contained in that part which are not cancellable; and

(*b*) entries relating to restrictions on compensation registered under section 8(4), and advance payments registered under section 52(8), of the Land Compensation Act 1973.

(2) Every entry in Part 6 of the register made in pursuance of section 8(4) or 52(8) of the said Act shall contain—

(*a*) sufficient particulars, by reference to a plan or otherwise, of the land affected by the charge;

(*b*) the name and address of the authority by whom particulars have been deposited for registration;

(*c*) the date of registration of the charge;

(*d*) where the charge is registered under section 8(4) of the said Act, particulars of the nature and extent of the works for the purposes of which land was acquired by the authority:

(*e*) where the charge is registered under section 52(8) of the said Act, particulars of the advance payment made under that section on account of compensation, the agreed or estimated compensation payable and the interest in land to which the compensation relates."

(*d*) In Form D in Schedule 2—

(i) in the form relating to Part 4 of the register the word "charges" shall be substituted for the words "prohibitions and restrictions" and the word "charge" shall be substituted for the words "prohibition or restriction" wherever they occur;

(ii) the form set out in the Schedule to these Rules shall be added to the form relating to Part 6 of the register.

3.—(1) Notwithstanding the provisions of rule 2(*d*) above, the form relating to Part 4 of the register may continue to be used in the form hitherto prescribed until the Lord Chancellor otherwise directs.

(2) Until 1st April 1974 local registrars may make their own arrangements regarding the supply and issue of the supplementary form set out in the Schedule to these Rules, and accordingly before that date rule 28 shall not apply to that form.

Dated 6th November 1973.

Hailsham of St Marylebone, C.

Rule 2(*d*)(ii)

SCHEDULE

Supplementary Form Relating to Part 6 of Register

Part 6 of register: restrictions under section 8(4), and advance payments under section 52(8), of the Land Compensation Act 1973

Particulars of land affected by charge and (for charge under section 52(8)) interest in that land	Name and address of authority by whom registration particulars deposited	(Charge under section 8(4) only). Nature and extent of works on land acquired	(Charge under section 52(8) only). Particulars of advance payment and agreed or estimated compensation	Date of registration
1	2	3	4	5

EXPLANATORY NOTE

(*This Note is not part of the Rules.*)

These Rules, which amend the Local Land Charges Rules 1966, remove the need for new forms of index to receive ministerial approval extend; the scope of Part 4 of the register; and provide for restrictions on, and advance payments of, compensation under the Land Compensation Act 1973 to be registered in Part 6 of the register.

STATUTORY INSTRUMENTS

1973 No. 1863

LOCAL GOVERNMENT, ENGLAND AND WALES

The Local Authorities (Wales) (Property etc.) Order 1973

Made - - - -	*8th November* 1973
Laid before Parliament	*9th November* 1973
Coming into Operation—	
For the purposes specified in Article 1(2)(*a*)	*21st December* 1973
For all other purposes	*1st April* 1974

ARRANGEMENT OF ARTICLES

SCHEDULES

The Secretary of State for Wales, in exercise of the powers conferred upon him by section 254(1) and (2)(*a*), (*b*) and (*d*) of the Local Government Act 1972**(a)** and by those provisions as extended by section 34(1) of, and paragraph 5(2)(*b*) of Schedule 6 to, the Water Act 1973**(b)** and of all other powers enabling him in that behalf, hereby makes the following order:—

Title and commencement

1.—(1) This order may be cited as the Local Authorities (Wales) (Property etc.) Order 1973.

(2) This order shall come into operation—

(*a*) for the purposes of the following provisions, namely:—

paragraphs (2) to (6) of article 10
article 11 in so far as it provides for agreements
article 12
paragraphs (1) to (3) and (5) of article 19
paragraph (3) of article 20
paragraphs (5) and (6) of article 23
paragraph (1) of article 25
articles 21, 22, 26, 36 and 38
paragraph 3(*b*) and (*c*) of Schedule 2

on 21st December 1973; and

(*b*) for all other purposes, on 1st April 1974.

(a) 1972 c. 70. **(b)** 1973 c. 37.

Territorial extent

2.—(1) Save as expressly provided in this order or in any other order made under section 254 of the Act—

(*a*) this order extends only to the transfer of matters from authorities whose areas are wholly in Wales;

(*b*) article 7(2) and (3) extend only to the councils of counties and county boroughs in Wales;

(*c*) articles 28 and 31, in so far as they refer to property described in (*a*) or (*e*) of article 9(1), articles 33(2) and 34 in so far as they deal with matters transferred by the Act, and article 37, extend only to Wales;

(*d*) article 35(1), (3) and (4) extend only to such authorities as are described in (*a*);

(*e*) article 35(2) extends only to committees established in Wales;

(*f*) article 36 extends only to such authorities as are described in (*a*).

(2) This order extends to the transfer of matters from the following authorities, namely—

The Dee and Clwyd and The Wye River Authorities
The Gwent Water Board
The Presteigne Joint Burial Committee.

(3) Article 35(1), (3) and (4) extend to the authorities named in paragraph (2) and to the Gloucester (Chepstow Division) Port Health Authority.

(4) Article 36 extends to the Welsh National Water Development Authority.

Exclusion of certain matters

3. Nothing in this order other than the express exceptions in the table in Schedule 2 and the definition in that Schedule of "police matters" applies to—

(*a*) property held by the council of any county or county borough for police purposes, including the purposes of section 81 of the Road Traffic Regulation Act 1967**(a)**;

(*b*) property held by the council of any county or any borough having a separate commission of the peace for the purposes of section 25 of the Justices of the Peace Act 1949**(b)**; or

(*c*) the land, buildings and works in England of any water undertaking,

or to any liabilities incurred, contracts, deeds, bonds, agreements and other instruments subsisting, notices given, actions and proceedings pending or causes of action or proceeding existing in relation to such matters.

Interpretation

4.—(1) The Interpretation Act 1889**(c)** shall apply for the interpretation of this order as it applies for the interpretation of an Act of Parliament.

(2) In this order—

"the Act" means the Local Government Act 1972;

"buildings", except in article 22, means buildings not within the meaning of the term "land";

"corporate land" means corporate land within the meaning of the Local Government Act 1933**(d)**;

(a) 1967 c. 76.
(b) 1949 c. 101.
(c) 1889 c. 63.
(d) 1933 c. 51.

"historic and ceremonial property" does not include any property held (or under article 19, 20, 22 or 38 deemed to be held) for the purposes of any statutory functions.

"land" includes land covered by water and any interest or right in, to or over land;

the relevant class of authorities, in relation to any authority described in column (1) of the following table, means the class specified in respect thereof in column (2).

TABLE

(1)	(2)
A county council	County councils
The corporation or council of a borough, or the council of an urban or rural district	District councils;

"Wales" means the area consisting of the counties established by section 20 of the Act (new local government areas in Wales), and "England" does not include any area included in any of those counties; and

"water authority" means an authority established in accordance with section 2 of the Water Act 1973; and any reference to the area of a water authority, without more, means the area of that authority as defined in section 2(2)(*b*) of, or Schedule 1 to, that Act.

(3) In this order, unless the context otherwise requires, references to any enactment shall be construed as references to that enactment as amended, extended or applied by or under any other enactment.

(4) Any reference in this order to a numbered article or schedule shall, unless the reference is to an article or schedule of a specified order, be construed as a reference to the article or schedule bearing that number in this order.

(5) Any reference in any article of this order to a numbered paragraph shall, unless the reference is to a paragraph of a specified article, be construed as a reference to the paragraph bearing that number in the first-mentioned article.

Other express provision

5. This order shall have effect subject to the express provision of—

(*a*) any other order made (whether before or after this order) under section 254 of the Act;

(*b*) any regulations made under section 7 or 8 of the Superannuation Act 1972**(a)**; or

(*c*) section 16, 25 or 54(2) of the National Health Service Reorganisation Act 1973**(b)** or any order made under those sections.

Ancillary provision in relation to highways

6. There shall be transferred to and vest in or attach to a county council as the highway authority for any highway—

(*a*) the interest of the former highway authority, as such, in the highway, in so far as such interest is not vested in the county council by virtue of section 226 of the Highways Act 1959**(c)**;

(a) 1972 c. 11.
(b) 1973 c. 32.
(c) 1959 c. 25.

(*b*) any land held by the former highway authority, as such, for the purposes of their functions in relation to the highway or which has been acquired by them as highway authority for the highway and not appropriated for any other purpose;

(*c*) any equipment on or near the highway belonging to the former highway authority as such, including any road lighting system within the meaning of Part III of the Local Government Act 1966**(a)** and any other lighting system belonging to the former highway authority as highway authority for the highway; and

(*d*) any traffic sign, on or near the highway, belonging to a county, county borough or county district council and not comprised in (*c*).

In this article "traffic sign" has the meaning attached to that expression in section 54(1) of the Road Traffic Regulation Act 1967.

Particular matters

7.—(1) Any property described in column (2) of Schedule 1 (or of any extension thereof effected by any further order under section 254 of the Act made before 1st April 1974) of an authority named in column (1) shall by virtue of this order be transferred to and vest in the authority specified in respect of such property in column (3).

(2) Any liability of the council of any county or county borough to repay money borrowed for the provision of financial assistance in respect of works for water supply or sewerage or sewage disposal shall be transferred to and attach to the water authority for the area in which the works are situated.

Any other liability of the council of a county, county borough or county district to repay money borrowed under any statutory provision for the provision of financial assistance in respect of any works shall be transferred to and attach to the authority who would on and after 1st April 1974 be empowered by that statutory provision to provide such financial assistance in respect of such works.

Paragraphs (3) and (4) of article 18 shall apply to the liabilities transferred by this paragraph as they apply to the liabilities transferred by paragraph (2) of that article.

(3) This paragraph applies to the liability of the council of any county or county borough to make contributions to any authority in respect of any scheme under section 2 of the Rural Water Supplies and Sewerage Act 1944**(b)**.

Any such liability shall cease in respect of any payment falling to be made on or after 1st April 1974.

Where any payment falling to be made before 1st April 1974 is in fact made on or after that date it shall be made to the authority specified in column (2) of Part I or II of Schedule 4 in respect of the authority first referred to in this paragraph.

Sewers and sewage disposal works

8.—(1) Nothing in this article applies to any matter provided for in article 7 or in article 11(2) or (3) or 18 in their application to any property or liability transferred by article 7.

(a) 1966 c. 42.
(b) 1944 c. 26.

(2) Any public sewer (within the meaning of section 20(2) of the Public Health Act 1936**(a)** as that provision has effect at the date of the making of this order) which crosses the boundaries of the areas for sewerage and sewage disposal purposes of two or more water authorities, and any other public sewer discharging thereto, shall be transferred to and vest in the water authority within whose area for such purposes is situated the sewage disposal works, or where the sewer does not discharge to sewage disposal works the outfall, to which the first-mentioned sewer discharges.

(3) Any other public sewer or any sewage disposal works vested in a local authority by virtue of the Public Health Act 1936 shall be transferred to and vest in the water authority within whose area for sewerage and sewage disposal purposes the sewer is or the sewage disposal works are situated.

(4) In this article "sewer" includes manholes, ventilating shafts, pumping stations, pumps, pumping mains, storm overflows and associated overflow pipes and outfalls, storm flow balancing installations and any other accessories belonging to the sewer.

Transfer of specified classes of property, etc.

9.—(1) Nothing in this article applies to—

(*a*) any property held as sole trustee, exclusively for charitable purposes, by an existing local authority (being property transferred by section 210 of the Act);

(*b*) any property vested in the council of an existing county or county borough which is required to be applied in accordance with a scheme under section 19 of the Welsh Church Act 1914**(b)** (being property which is vested in the council of a new county by section 211 of the Act);

(*c*) any other property held for the purposes of any charitable trust;

(*d*) any property vested in an authority described in column (1) of Part I or II of Schedule 4 transferred to the Secretary of State by section 16, 25 or 54(2) of the National Health Service Reorganisation Act 1973 or any liabilities incurred, contracts, deeds, bonds, agreements and other instruments subsisting, notices given, actions and proceedings pending or causes of action or proceeding existing in relation to such property;

(*e*) any property vested in a county council by virtue of section 226 of the Highways Act 1959;

(*f*) any matter provided for in article 6, 7 or 8;

(*g*) any matter provided for in article 11(1) in so far as it applies to rights ensured by article 23 in its application to any property transferred by article 6, 7 or 8;

(*h*) any matter provided for in article 11(2) or (3) in their application to any matter provided for in articles 7 and 8;

(*i*) any matter provided for in article 18 in its application to any matter described in the preceding items of this paragraph.

(2) Nothing in paragraphs (4) to (6) of this article applies to matters provided for in paragraphs (2) to (4) of article 18 in their application to any matters provided for in paragraph (3) of this article, and nothing in paragraphs (5) and (6) of this article applies to any matters provided for in paragraphs (3) and (4) of article 18 in their application to any liabilities provided for in paragraph (4) of this article.

(a) 1936 c. 49. **(b)** 1914 c. 91.

(3) All property vested in an authority described in column (2) of the table in Schedule 2 (or of any extension thereof effected by any further order under section 254 of the Act made before 1st April 1974) and within any description of matters specified in respect of such authority in column (3) shall by virtue of this order be transferred to and vest in the authority specified in respect of such description of matters in column (4).

(4) All liabilities attaching to an authority described in the said column (2) and within any description of matters specified in respect of such authority in column (3) shall by virtue of this order be transferred to and attach to the authority specified in respect of such description of matters in column (4).

(5) All contracts, deeds, bonds, agreements and other instruments subsisting in favour of, or against, and all notices in force which were given (or have effect as if they had been given) by, or to, an authority described in the said column (2) and within any description of matters specified in respect of such authority in column (3) shall be of full force and effect in favour of, or against, the authority specified in respect of such description of matters in column (4).

(6) Any action or proceeding or any cause of action or proceeding, pending or existing at 1st April 1974, by, or against, an authority described in the said column (2) and within any description of matters specified in respect of such authority in column (3) shall not be prejudicially affected by reason of the Act or the Water Act 1973, and may be continued, prosecuted and enforced by, or against, the authority specified in respect of such description of matters in column (4).

(7) Save in so far as express provision is made in item No. 10 of the table in Schedule 2, this article does not extend to the historic and ceremonial property other than land and buildings, and in particular to the charters, insignia and plate, of any area.

Provision supplementary to article 9

10.—(1) The provision made in this article applies in the application of article 9.

(2) Any question as to the functions for the purposes of which any property is held, any liabilities have been incurred, any contract, deed, bond, agreement or other instrument subsists, any notice has been given or any action or proceeding or cause of action or proceeding relates shall, subject to the provision of paragraph (6), be determined by the transferor authority.

(3) Any question whether any property is historic or ceremonial property shall, subject to the provision of paragraph (6), be determined by the transferor authority.

(4) (*a*) Where any land or any part of any land vested immediately before 1st April 1974 in an authority described in column (2) of the table in Schedule 2 is situated in two or more areas specified in respect of that authority in the said table, the land or the part shall be deemed to be situated in the area so specified in which the greater proportion of it is situated.

(*b*) Where part of any land vested as aforesaid is situated (or is under (*a*) deemed to be situated) in an area specified in respect of an authority described in column (2) of the said table, any part of the land situated outside the area of that authority shall be deemed to be situated within the area so specified.

(*c*) Any question as to the area in which the greater proportion of the land or the part is situated shall, subject to the provision of paragraph (6), be determined by the transferor authority.

(5) Where in relation to any land held (or under article 19, 20 or 38, deemed to be held) for the purposes of the deposit of refuse—

(*a*) deposit has been completed; and

(*b*) it has been resolved that the land shall be used (otherwise than temporarily) for the purposes of a particular function,

the land shall be deemed to be held for those purposes and shall be held by the authority to whom it is transferred for those purposes.

Any question whether the deposit of refuse has been completed, or whether it has been resolved as described in (*b*), or whether any use is temporary, shall, subject to the provision of paragraph (6), be determined by the transferor authority.

(6) If notice is given by any authority that they are dissatisfied with any determination under paragraph (2), (3), (4) or (5), the question shall be determined by agreement between the authorities concerned or failing such agreement by the decision of a person agreed on by such authorities or in default of agreement appointed by the Secretary of State.

(7) The provisions of section 187(2) and (3) of the Act shall be disregarded.

(8) The provision of off-street parking places for vehicles shall be treated as a function exercisable on and after 1st April 1974 by both county and district councils.

Fittings, furniture, equipment and stores

11.—(1) Where by paragraph (1) of article 23 any right to the use of any accommodation is ensured for any authority other than the authority in whom the accommodation is vested on and after 1st April 1974, the fittings, furniture, equipment and stores in such accommodation which have been provided exclusively for the purposes of the functions first described in the said paragraph shall, except in so far as the first-mentioned authority shall otherwise agree, by virtue of this order be transferred to and vest in such authority.

(2) Subject to paragraph (1), where by article 7, 8 or 9 any building is transferred to and vested in any authority, the fittings, furniture and equipment of such building, and the stores therein which have been provided for the discharge of functions therein, shall, except in so far as such authority shall otherwise agree, by virtue of this order be transferred to and vest in such authority.

If the value of any stores transferred by this paragraph is included in any revenue balance, the necessary adjustment shall be made in such balance.

(3) Subject to paragraph (1), where by article 7, 8 or 9 any land to which paragraph (2) does not apply is transferred to and vested in any authority, the equipment of such land shall, except in so far as such authority shall otherwise agree, by virtue of this order be transferred to and vest in such authority.

(4) For the purposes of this article—

(*a*) "equipment" includes records; and

(*b*) any vehicles or other mobile equipment used wholly or mainly in the performance of the functions carried out in any accommodation or building or on any land shall be deemed to be equipment thereof.

Agreements as to the transfer of property other than land not transferred by the preceding articles

12.—(1) Paragraph (1) of article 9 applies to this article as it applies to article 9.

(2) Nothing in this article applies to any matter provided for in article 9 or in articles 11(2) and (3) and 18 in their application to any matter provided for in article 9.

(3) Any property other than land vested in an authority named in column (1) of Part I of Schedule 3 (or of any extension thereof effected by any further order under section 254 of the Act made before 1st April 1974) for the purposes of functions—

(*a*) which are not exercisable on and after 1st April 1974 by an authority of the relevant class in relation to such authority; but

(*b*) which are so exercisable by the authorities specified in respect of such authority in column (2),

shall by virtue of this order be transferred to and vest in such one or more of the authorities specified in column (2) as may be agreed between them.

(4) Any property other than land vested in the council of any administrative county, county borough or county district for the purposes of functions which on 1st April 1974 become exercisable in any area partly by the county council and partly by the district council shall by virtue of this order be transferred to and vest in such one of those councils as may be agreed between them.

(5) Subject to the provisions of paragraphs (3) and (4), any property other than land vested in an authority named in column (1) of Part II of Schedule 3 (or of any extension thereof effected by any further order under section 254 of the Act made before 1st April 1974) shall by virtue of this order be transferred to and vest in such one or more of the authorities specified in respect of such authority in column (2) as may be agreed between them.

(6) Any agreement under paragraph (3), (4) or (5) may—

(*a*) provide for payment in respect of any property within such paragraph;

(*b*) extend to any matter arising under article 18 in its application to property within such paragraph; and

(*c*) provide that any authority concerned shall be entitled to the use of the property for such period and on such terms as may be agreed, whether for the purposes of the functions for which the property is used immediately before 1st April 1974 or for the purposes of any other functions exercisable by them.

(7) In default of agreement as to any matter arising under paragraph (3), (4), (5) or (6) or article 18 in its application to property within any such paragraph the matter shall be determined by the decision of a person agreed on by the authorities concerned or in default of agreement appointed by the Secretary of State.

(8) In this article—

"exercisable" means exercisable otherwise than by virtue of section 101, 110 or 187(2) or (3) of the Act; and

"property" does not include the balance on any fund or account.

Balances on accounts of undertakings

13.—(1) Subject to paragraph (2), nothing in articles 7 to 12, or in article 18 in its application to any undertaking transferred by any such article, shall be effective to transfer any amount standing as a balance (whether credit or debit) in respect of any undertaking in the revenue accounts of the transferor authority immediately before 1st April 1974.

(2) The provisions of this paragraph shall apply where a local authority maintain separate accounts in respect of any water undertaking transferred by article 7.

Where in such accounts for the period ending on 31st March 1974 as finally closed a credit balance is shown the transfer effected by article 7 shall include the amount shown as such balance.

Where in such accounts for such period as so closed a deficiency is shown the water authority to whom the undertaking (or the undertaking other than any land, buildings or works in England) is transferred shall as soon as practicable pay to the authority specified in respect of the local authority in column (2) of Part II of Schedule 4 the amount shown as such deficiency.

Certain county council funds

14.—(1) This article applies to the county councils of Brecon, Denbigh, Glamorgan, Merioneth and Monmouthshire.

(2) The balances on the following funds, namely—

the county fund

any capital fund

any renewal and repairs fund

any fund of substantially similar nature to a capital fund or a renewal and repairs fund

of a county council to whom this article applies shall be apportioned between the new counties in which any parts of the area of such council are comprised in the proportions which the aggregate rateable value of all the hereditaments in the several parts, as shown in the valuation lists immediately before 1st April 1974, bear to the aggregate rateable value of all the hereditaments in all such parts, and the amounts so apportioned shall be payable to the councils of such counties.

Certain county district council funds

15.—(1) This article applies to the councils of the urban districts of Bedwellty, Caerphilly and Gelligaer and the rural districts of Aled, Cardiff, Cowbridge, Crickhowell, Gwyrfai, Hawarden, Hiraethog, Magor and St Mellons, Neath, Pontypool, Wrexham and Vaynor and Penderyn.

(2) The balances on the following funds, namely—

the general rate fund, other than the housing revenue account;

any capital fund, renewal and repairs fund or fund of a similar nature to either such fund other than one maintained in connection with any undertaking transferred by article 7, of a council to whom this article applies shall be apportioned between the districts in which any parts of the area of such council are comprised in the proportions which the aggregate rateable value of all the hereditaments in the several parts, as shown in the valuation lists immediately before 1st April 1974, bear to the aggregate rateable value of all the hereditaments in all such parts, and the amounts so apportioned shall be payable to the councils of such districts.

(3) This paragraph has effect in relation to the housing revenue account of a council to whom this article applies.

The working balance on such account shall be apportioned between the districts in which dwellings of the council are situated in the proportions which the numbers of such dwellings in the several districts bear to the total number of such dwellings, and the amounts so apportioned shall be payable to the councils of such districts and shall attach to the housing revenue accounts of the councils.

In this paragraph "dwellings" means Housing Revenue Account dwellings within the meaning of the Housing Finance Act 1972(**a**).

Residual transfer of property, etc.

16.—(1) Paragraph (1) of article 9 applies to this article as it applies to article 9.

(2) Subject to the provisions of articles 9 to 15 or of articles 11(2) and (3) and 18 in their application to any matters provided for in articles 9 to 15—

(*a*) all property and liabilities vested in or attaching to an authority described in column (1) of Part I or II of Schedule 4 (or of any extension thereof effected by any further order under section 254 of the Act made before 1st April 1974) shall by virtue of this order be transferred to and vest in or attach to the authority specified in respect of such authority in column (2);

(*b*) all contracts, deeds, bonds, agreements and other instruments subsisting in favour of, or against, and all notices in force which were given (or have effect as if they had been given) by, or to, an authority described in column (1) of Part I or II of Schedule 4 (or of any extension thereof as aforesaid) shall be of full force and effect in favour of, or against, the authority specified in respect of such authority in column (2);

(*c*) any action or proceeding or any cause of action or proceeding, pending or existing at 1st April 1974, by, or against, an authority described in column (1) of Part I or II of Schedule 4 (or of any extension thereof as aforesaid) shall not be prejudicially affected by reason of the Act or the Water Act 1973, and may be continued, prosecuted, and enforced by, or against, the authority specified in respect of such authority in column (2); and

(*d*) any power to appoint any person to any body belonging to an authority described in column (1) of Part I or II of Schedule 4 (or of any extension thereof as aforesaid) in respect of any matter provided for in (*a*) or (*b*) shall be transferred to the authority specified in respect of such authority in column (2).

(**a**) 1972 c. 47.

General saving for agreements

17.—(1) The authority to whom any account or fund is transferred, or any amount of any fund is payable, by virtue of any provision of this order, may agree that any particular amount in the account or fund shall be payable to any other authority.

(2) The authority to whom any other property other than land is transferred by the preceding articles of this order other than article 7 may by resolution agree that the property shall be transferred to any other authority specified in the resolution, and paragraphs (2) to (5) of article 18 shall apply accordingly.

(3) The transferee authority in respect of any matter other than property, provided for in paragraph (4), (5) or (6) of article 9 or in (*a*), (*b*) or (*c*) of paragraph (2) of article 16, and any other authority, may agree that that other authority shall be substituted for the transferee authority in the application of any such provision.

(4) The provision made by the preceding articles of this order, other than articles 12, 14 and 15, for the transfer of any matter is without prejudice to any agreement which may be made for payment in respect of such matter.

Liabilities, contracts etc., notices and proceedings in respect of transferred property, etc.

18.—(1) This article applies to the following matters, namely—

(*a*) any property described in (*a*), (*b*) or (*e*) of article 9(1); and

(*b*) any property transferred by this order.

(2) Subject to paragraph (6), all liabilities attaching to any authority in respect of any property to which this article applies shall by virtue of this order be transferred to and attach to the authority to whom such property is transferred.

(3) All contracts, deeds, bonds, agreements and other instruments subsisting in favour of, or against, and all notices in force which were given (or have effect as if they had been given) by, or to, the authority first mentioned in paragraph (2) in respect of any property to which this article applies, or in respect of liabilities transferred by paragraph (2), shall be of full force and effect in favour of, or against, the authority to whom such property and liabilities are transferred.

(4) Any action or proceeding or any cause of action or proceeding, pending or existing at 1st April 1974, by, or against, the authority first mentioned in paragraph (2) in respect of any property to which this article applies, or in respect of liabilities transferred by paragraph (2), shall not be prejudicially affected by reason of the Act or the Water Act 1973, and may be continued, prosecuted and enforced by, or against, the authority to whom such property and liabilities are transferred.

(5) Any power to appoint any person to any body belonging to the authority first mentioned in paragraph (2) in respect of any property (other than that described in (*a*) of article 9(1)) to which this article applies or any matter provided for in paragraphs (2) and (3) shall be transferred to the authority to whom such property or matter is transferred.

(6) Paragraph (2) shall not apply to the rights and liabilities described in entry (*a*) in item No. 14 in the table in Schedule 2, but paragraphs (3) to (5) shall apply in respect of such rights and liabilities.

Land held for several purposes

19.—(1) Where any land, not being a property described otherwise than as an undertaking in column (2) of Schedule 1 or of any extension thereof described in article 7, is held by an authority for the purposes of functions exercisable on and after 1st April 1974 by two or more authorities, or for the purposes of a function which will then be so exercisable, the land shall, subject to the provision of paragraphs (2) to (6), for the purposes of this order be deemed to be held for the purposes of the function exercisable by such one of those authorities as shall be determined by the first-mentioned authority to be the function for which the land is, immediately before that date, used to the greatest extent.

In such determination the first-mentioned authority shall disregard any use of the land which is temporary.

(2) In the application of paragraph (1), where any function is exercisable on and after 1st April 1974 by an authority of the relevant class in relation to the authority first mentioned in that paragraph and by any other authority, the function shall be deemed to be exercisable only by the authority of the relevant class.

(3) Subject to paragraph (2), two (but not more) functions exercisable on and after 1st April 1974 by an authority shall be treated as a single function in the application of paragraph (1).

(4) Any land to which paragraph (1) applies shall be held by the authority to whom it is transferred for the purposes of the function determined under that paragraph, or where two functions have been treated as a single function under paragraph (3) for the purposes of such one of those functions as is determined by the authority to whom the land is transferred.

(5) If notice is given by any authority that they are dissatisfied with the determination in paragraph (1) the purposes therein described shall be determined by agreement between the two or more authorities so described or failing such agreement by the decision of a person agreed on by such authorities or in default of agreement appointed by the Secretary of State, and paragraphs (1) and (4) shall have effect accordingly. Paragraphs (2) and (3) shall apply in the application of this paragraph.

(6) In this article, "exercisable" means exercisable otherwise than by virtue of section 101, 110 or 187(2) or (3) of the Act.

(7) In the application of this article, any reference to the purposes of functions includes a reference to the purposes of an undertaking transferred by article 7.

Property to be deemed to be held for the purposes of statutory functions

20.—(1) This article applies to—

(*a*) any property held under section 125 of the Local Government Act 1933;

(*b*) any land acquired under section 112, 114 or 119(1)(*a*) of the Town and Country Planning Act 1971**(a)** or any earlier provision corresponding to any such enactment;

(*c*) any corporate land;

(*d*) any land acquired under any provision empowering the acquisition of land for the benefit, improvement or development of any area and not allocated or appropriated for any statutory purpose; and

(*e*) any property acquired by a local authority as a gift otherwise than for charitable purposes.

(a) 1971 c. 78.

(2) (*a*) Where any property to which this article applies is, immediately before 1st April 1974—

(i) in the case of property referred to in paragraph (1)(*a*), used wholly or substantially so for the purposes of a particular function being purposes authorised by enactments other than the said section 125;

(ii) in the case of property referred to in paragraph (1)(*b*), used wholly or mainly for the purposes of statutory functions other than those exercised under the Town and Country Planning Acts 1971 and 1972; or

(iii) in the case of property referred to in paragraph (1)(*c*), (*d*) and (*e*), used wholly or mainly for the purposes of any statutory function,

it shall for the purposes of this order be deemed to be held for the purposes of the function for which it is so used.

In the application of this sub-paragraph any temporary use of the property shall be disregarded.

(*b*) Two (but not more) functions shall be treated as a single function in the application of this paragraph.

(*c*) Any property to which this paragraph applies shall be held by the authority to whom it is transferred for the purposes of the function described in (i), (ii) or (iii) of sub-paragraph (*a*) or where two functions have been treated as a single function for the purposes of such one of those functions as is determined by the authority to whom the property is transferred.

(3) Any question whether any property to which this article applies is, immediately before 1st April 1974, used as described in (i), (ii) or (iii) of paragraph (2)(*a*) shall, subject to the following provision of this paragraph, be determined by the authority in whom the property is, before 1st April 1974, vested.

If notice is given by any authority that they are dissatisfied with any such determination the question shall be determined by agreement between the authorities concerned or failing such agreement by the decision of a person agreed on by such authorities or in default of agreement appointed by the Secretary of State, and sub-paragraph (*c*) of paragraph (2) shall apply accordingly. Sub-paragraph (*b*) of paragraph (2) shall apply in the application of this paragraph.

(4) In the application of this article, any reference to the purposes of functions includes a reference to the purposes of an undertaking transferred by article 7.

Questions as to appropriations

21. The provisions of this article shall have effect in relation to any land appropriated between 9th November 1973 and 1st April 1974 and to any financial adjustment made on the appropriation.

Any such land shall for the purposes of this order be treated as held for the purpose for which it has been appropriated, and any financial adjustment made on the appropriation shall be of full effect, unless a local authority or water authority give notice that the land falls to be treated for the purposes of this order as being held for the purpose for which it was held before the appropriation, or that the financial adjustment falls to be varied. If such notice is given the question of the purpose for which the land is held or, as the case may be the adjustment to be made, shall be determined by agreement between the authorities concerned or failing such agreement by the decision of a person agreed on by such authorities or in default of agreement appointed by the Secretary of State.

Buildings to be replaced

22.—(1) The provisions of this article shall apply where—

(*a*) any building or part of a building is to be wholly or substantially so replaced by another building which at 1st April 1974 is completed or in course of erection or for the erection of which a contract has been entered into or by part of such building;

(*b*) it has been resolved by the transferor authority before the date of the making of this order that the first-mentioned building or part of a building or the site thereof is to be used for the purposes of some function other than the one for which it is held;

(*c*) the nature of the building or the location of its site is such as to make it peculiarly suited for use for the purposes of such function rather than other local government purposes,

and apart from the provisions of this article the two buildings or parts of buildings would be transferred to the same authority.

(2) The transferor authority may determine that for the purposes of this order the land on which the building or part of a building first mentioned in paragraph (1) is erected shall be deemed to be held for the purposes for which by the resolution described in item (*b*) of that paragraph it is to be used.

(3) If notice is given by any authority concerned that they question whether (*a*), (*b*) or (*c*) in paragraph (1) is satisfied, the determination shall be of no effect and the question of the purpose for which the land is to be deemed to be held shall be determined by agreement between the authorities concerned or failing such agreement by the decision of a person agreed on by such authorities or in default of agreement appointed by the Secretary of State.

User rights

23.—(1) Where, immediately before 1st April 1974, accommodation in any property transferred to and vested in any authority by virtue of this order is used (or in the case of accommodation not yet in occupation proposed to be used) otherwise than temporarily for the purposes of any functions which, on and after that date, are not exercisable (or not exercisable as regards any part of the area served from the accommodation) by the authority to whom the property is transferred, the authority exercising those functions in the area served by the accommodation or, as the case may be, the part thereof shall be entitled to the use of such accommodation, whether for the purposes of such functions or for the purposes of any other functions exercisable by them.

(2) Where—

(*a*) any property is immediately before 1st April 1974 used (or in the case of property not yet in use proposed to be used) otherwise than temporarily for the purposes of functions exercisable by one authority in relation to any area;

(*b*) the functions become exercisable on and after that day by two or more authorities; and

(*c*) the property is by virtue of this order transferred to and vested in one of the authorities described in (*b*),

any other of the authorities described in (*b*) shall be entitled to the use of such property, whether for the purposes of such functions or for the purposes of any other functions exercisable by them.

(3) Where—

(*a*) any property to which paragraph (2) does not apply is immediately before 1st April 1974 held by the council of a county, county borough or county district under section 125 of the Local Government Act 1933; and

(*b*) the property is by virtue of this order transferred to and vested in the council of any relevant area,

the council of any other relevant area shall be entitled to the use of the property.

In this paragraph, "relevant areas" means—

in relation to a county, new counties;

in relation to a county borough or county district,

new counties and districts,

being areas in which the area of the county, county borough or county district is comprised.

(4) Where—

(*a*) any property is immediately before 1st April 1974 used (or in the case of property not yet in use proposed to be used) otherwise than temporarily for the purposes of functions exercisable by two or more authorities;

(*b*) the property is by virtue of this order transferred to and vested in one authority;

any other authority exercising any of the functions described in (*a*) shall be entitled to the use of such property whether for the purposes of such functions or for the purposes of other functions exercisable by them.

(5) Any question—

(*a*) whether any accommodation in any property to which paragraph (1) applies is used (or proposed to be used) for the purposes described in that paragraph;

(*b*) whether any property to which paragraph(2) applies is used (or proposed to be used) as described in (a) thereof;

(*c*) whether any property to which paragraph (4) applies is used (or proposed to be used) as described in (*a*) thereof; or

(*d*) without prejudice to (*c*), whether any use (or proposed use) is temporary,

shall, subject to the following provision of this paragraph, be determined by the authority in whom the property is, before 1st April 1974, vested.

If, before 1st April 1975, notice is given by any authority that they are dissatisfied with any such determination (or, no determination having been made, that a question exists) the question shall be determined by agreement between the authorities concerned or failing such agreement by the decision of a person agreed on by such authorities or in default of agreement appointed by the Secretary of State.

(6) The use of any accommodation or property by virtue of this article shall be for such period and on such terms as may be determined by agreement between the authority entitled under this article to use the accommodation or property and the authority to whom the property is transferred or failing such agreement by the decision of a person agreed on by such authorities or in default of agreement appointed by the Secretary of State.

(7) In this article "exercisable" means exercisable otherwise than by virtue of section 101, 110 or 187(2) or (3) of the Act.

Charter trustees

24.—(1) It shall be the duty of the council of a district in which a city or town for which there are charter trustees is situated to provide accommodation for the proper discharge of the functions of the charter trustees.

(2) The accommodation to be provided and the terms on which it is provided shall be determined by agreement between the district council and the charter trustees, or failing such agreement by the decision of a person agreed on by them or in default of agreement appointed by the Secretary of State.

Corporate land

25.—(1) Any question whether any land vested in the corporation of a borough is corporate land shall, subject to the following provision of this paragraph, be determined by the council of the borough.

If notice is given by any authority that they are dissatisfied with any such determination the question shall be determined by agreement between the authorities concerned or failing such agreement by the decision of a person agreed on by such authorities or in default of agreement appointed by the Secretary of State.

(2) Any corporate land to which article 20(2) does not apply and which is transferred by this order to any authority shall be held by that authority as if it had been acquired by that authority under section 120(1)(*b*) or 124(1)(*b*), as the case may be, of the Act.

Inventories of property transferred to water authorities

26.—(1) Any authority from whom any water undertaking, or any water undertaking other than any land, buildings or works in England, will be transferred to a water authority by article 7 shall, not later than 31st January 1974, supply to such water authority—

(*a*) an inventory of the land, buildings, water mains, plant and other vehicles (other than any land, buildings or works in England) comprised in the undertaking;

(*b*) a statement of the financial position of the undertaking;

(*c*) a statement of any appropriations subsequent to 9th November 1973 of land held for the purposes of water supply.

(2) Any authority from whom any public sewer or any sewage disposal works will be transferred to a water authority by article 8 shall, not later than 31st January 1974, supply to such water authority an inventory of the sewers and sewage disposal works which will be transferred to such water authority.

Property and liabilities to attach to whole areas

27.—(1) Subject to paragraph (2), any interest in any property or any liability transferred by the preceding articles of this order to the authority for any county, district or community shall be held or discharged by them in respect of the whole of such area.

(2) Paragraph (1)—

(*a*) shall not apply in respect of any interest in any property or any liability which by reason of agreements made by authorities abolished by the Act falls to be held or discharged in respect of any specific area; and

(*b*) shall have effect subject to the provision of subsections (4) and (5) of section 248 of the Act (freemen and inhabitants of existing boroughs).

Byelaws, etc.

28.—(1) Any byelaws in force for the regulation of any property described in (*a*) or (*b*) of article 9(1) or transferred by the preceding articles of this order shall have effect as if they had been made by the authority to whom such property is transferred.

(2) Any provision of any local Act or of any order made under or confirmed by any Act which applies to any property described in (*a*) or (*b*) of article 9(1) or transferred by the preceding articles of this order shall have effect with the substitution for any references to (or having effect as references to) the authority from whom such property is transferred of references to the authority to whom the property is transferred.

Vehicle Licences

29. Any excise licence, operators' licence, public service vehicle licence, road service licence, plating certificate or other document issued in respect of any vehicle transferred by the preceding articles of this order shall have effect as if it had been issued to the authority to whom such vehicle is transferred, and any reference to the authority from whom the vehicle is transferred in any such licence or certificate or in any registration book or other document issued in respect of such vehicle shall have effect as a reference to the authority to whom the vehicle is transferred.

Markets

30. The expression "market authority" in Part III of the Food and Drugs Act 1955**(a)** shall include any district council to whom such a market as is described in section 49(2) of that Act is transferred by this order.

Loan sanctions

31. Any authorisation of the borrowing of money in force in respect of any property or liability described in (*a*), (*b*) or (*e*) of article 9(1) or transferred by the preceding articles of this order to the council of any county, district or community may, subject to the terms applicable thereto, be acted on by such council.

Security for loans

32. Where under this order any liability or part of a liability charged indifferently on all the revenues of a public body or on any particular revenues or fund of such body is transferred to another public body, the liability or part of the liability shall be charged indifferently on all the revenues of the public body to whom it is transferred and shall cease to be a charge on any revenues or fund of the public body from whom it is transferred.

(a) 1955 c. 16.

Capital and renewal and repairs funds

33.—(1) A local authority may transfer the balance of any capital fund or renewal and repairs fund transferred to them under article 16 or the amount of any such fund received by them under article 14 or 15 to the credit of a capital fund or a renewal and repairs fund, as the case may be, established by them under Schedule 13 to the Act.

(2) Where any matter in respect of which a repayable advance which has not been fully repaid has been made from a capital fund or a renewal and repairs fund is transferred by the Act or this order to any authority, that authority may treat the outstanding amount of the advance as an advance from a capital fund or a renewal and repairs fund established by them under Schedule 13 to the Act and make such payments to such fund as the authority consider appropriate, but otherwise any liability to make repayments in respect of the advance shall cease.

Loans pools and consolidated loans funds

34.—(1) This article applies where, if the Act had not been passed and this order had not been made, advances from a loans pool or consolidated loans fund would have fallen to be repaid in respect of any matter, and the matter is by virtue of the Act or this order transferred to an authority other than the authority to whom the pool or fund is transferred by article 16.

(2) Sums which would have become due and owing to the pool or fund in respect of such advances shall be paid by the authority first mentioned in paragraph (1) to the authority last mentioned therein:

Provided that the said authorities and the lender may agree for the transfer to the first-mentioned authority of the liability with respect to any outstanding loan.

(3) The outstanding amount in respect of any such advances shall be shown in the accounts of the authority first mentioned in paragraph (1) as loans from other local authorities and as advances to the appropriate borrowing account.

(4) The outstanding amount in respect of any such advances shall be shown in the accounts of the authority last mentioned in paragraph (1) as loans to other authorities.

Audit of accounts

35.—(1) The repeal effected by section 272 of, and Schedule 30 to, the Act of Part X of the Local Government Act 1933 shall not affect—

(*a*) any audit of accounts for any period preceding 1st April 1974; or

(*b*) any disallowance, surcharge, appeal, application or disqualification arising from any audit of such accounts by a district auditor (whether an audit completed before the said date or an audit falling within (*a*)),

but nothing in sections 154 to 167, 196(3) and 197(4) of, or in section 251(1) in so far as it extends to paragraph 7(1) of Schedule 29 to, the Act shall apply to any accounts which are subject to district audit under the said Part X.

(2) The said Part X shall apply to the accounts of any committee established under section 264 of the Act, and of the sub-committees and officers thereof, as if the committee had been established under Part III of the Local Government Act 1933.

(3) In relation to the accounts of any authority described in column (1) of Part I or II of Schedule 4 (or of any extension thereof described in article 16) to whom Part X of the said Act of 1933 applied or of the committees or officers thereof, any action which had the Act not been passed would have fallen to be taken by such authority shall be taken by the authority specified in respect of such authority in column (2).

(4) If at any audit of the accounts of an authority described in column (1) of Part I or II of Schedule 4 (or of any extension thereof described in article 16) to whom Part X of the said Act of 1933 applied or of the committees and officers thereof any sum is certified by a district auditor as due from any person, that sum shall be paid to the authority specified in respect of that authority in column (2).

Inspection of documents

36. Any officer of the council of any county or district or of a water authority, duly authorised in that behalf, shall, for the purposes of the functions of the authority by whom he is employed, be entitled during ordinary office hours to inspect and take extracts from any books or documents of any council dissolved by section 1(10) or 20(6) of the Act not in the custody of such authority.

Legal proceedings

37. All legal proceedings pending at 1st April 1974 may be amended in such manner as may be necessary or proper in consequence of the Act or the Water Act 1973 or the preceding articles of this order.

General provision as to disputes

38.—(1) Any question as to the interpretation of this order may be determined by the decision of a person agreed on by the authorities concerned or in default of agreement appointed by the Secretary of State.

(2) Where a determination required by article 10(2), (3), (4) or (5), 19(1), 20(3) or 25(1) has not been made by the transferor authority before 1st April 1974 notice that a question exists may be given before 1st April 1975 by any authority concerned.

(3) Where—

(*a*) at 1st April 1974—

(i) notice has been given by any authority under article 10(6), 19(5), 20(3), 21, 22(3) or 25(1) or paragraph 3(*c*) of Schedule 2,

(ii) notice has been given by any authority that the provisions of this paragraph are to have effect in relation to any property within paragraph (3), (4) or (5) of article 12 specified in the notice; or

(iii) notice has been given by any authority that the interpretation of any provision of this order as to the transfer of any property is in dispute,

and the question has not been determined; or

(*b*) thereafter, but before 1st April 1975—

(i) notice is given by any authority under any provision specified in (*a*)(i);

(ii) notice is so given under paragraph (2);

(iii) notice is so given that the provisions of this paragraph are to have effect in relation to any property within paragraph (3), (4) or (5) of article 12 specified in the notice; or

(iv) notice is so given that the interpretation of any provision of this order as to the transfer of any property is in dispute,

then from 1st April 1974 or from the later date on which notice is given, as the case may be—

(*k*) any provisions of this order as to the transfer and vesting of property shall cease to have effect in relation to the property;

(*l*) article 16 shall apply to the property, and article 18 shall apply to any liabilities incurred, contracts, deeds, bonds, agreements and other instruments subsisting, notices given, actions and proceedings pending and causes of action or proceeding existing in relation thereto, as temporary provision pending the determination of the question;

Provided that the authorities concerned may by instrument in writing agree that any authority may in such application be substituted for the authority specified in column (2) of Part I or II of Schedule 4 in respect of the transferor authority;

(*m*) where notice has been given under paragraph (2), the question shall be determined by agreement between the authorities concerned or failing such agreement by the decision of a person agreed on by such authorities or in default of agreement appointed by the Secretary of State; and

(*n*) on the determination of the question whether under (*m*) or otherwise—

(*x*) the determination shall specify the authority to whom the property is to be transferred; and

(*y*) the provision described in (*l*) shall cease to have effect, the property shall by virtue of the determination be transferred to and vest in the authority specified in the determination, and the provisions of this order which would have applied to the property if the transfer had been effected by this order shall apply to it.

(4) Any reference in any provision of this order for the decision of any question by a person shall be construed as including a reference to three persons.

(5) Section 31 of the Arbitration Act 1950**(a)** shall have effect for the purposes of the determination of any question by any person or persons under any provision of this order as if such determination were an arbitration under any other Act within the meaning of that section.

(a) 1950 c. 27.

SCHEDULE 1

Transfer of Particular Properties

Article 7

Paragraph (3) of article 10, and paragraph (6) in so far as it applies thereto, shall apply to any question whether any property is historic or ceremonial property

(1) Transferor authority	(2) Property	(3) Transferee authority
The council of the urban district of Gelligaer	Historic and ceremonial property, and in particular the insignia and plate, of the urban district	The Community Council of Gelligaer
The corporation of any borough for the whole of the area of which charter trustees are constituted	Historic and ceremonial property other than land and buildings, and in particular the charters, insignia and plate, of the borough	The charter trustees
The council of the rural district of Ceiriog	The water undertaking of the council other than any land, buildings or works in the area for water supply purposes of the Severn-Trent Water Authority	The Welsh National Water Development Authority
	Any land, buildings or works of the water undertaking in the area for water supply purposes of the Severn-Trent Water Authority	The Severn-Trent Water Authority
The county council of Anglesey, the corporation or council of any borough or the council of any urban district or rural district other than Ceiriog	Any water undertaking of the transferor authority, other than any land, buildings or works in England	The Welsh National Water Development Authority

SCHEDULE 2

Article 9

TRANSFER OF SPECIFIED CLASSES OF PROPERTY, ETC.

1. In the following table—

(*a*) "county matters" and "district matters", in relation to any transferor authority, mean—

(i) in the case of property, property (not being excepted property) held for the purposes of functions not exercisable on and after 1st April 1974 by an authority of the relevant class in relation to the transferor authority but so exercisable by the authority specified in respect of the matters transferred in column (4) of the table in this Schedule;

(ii) in the case of liabilities, liabilities incurred in relation to such functions;

(iii) in the case of contracts, deeds, bonds, agreements and other instruments, and notices, such instruments subsisting and notices given in relation to such functions;

(iv) in the case of actions and proceedings and causes of action or proceeding, such actions and proceedings pending or causes existing in relation to such functions;

but if specified as such matters in relation to any area include only such matters being local matters in respect of such area;

(*b*) "community matters", in relation to any transferor authority, means—

(i) in the case of property—

(*a*) property held for the purposes of functions not exercisable on and after 1st April 1974 by county or district councils; and

(*b*) parish property within the meaning of the Local Government Act 1933, the proceeds of sale of such property and any securities in which such proceeds have been invested;

(ii) in the case of liabilities, liabilities incurred in relation to such functions or parish property;

(iii) in the case of contracts, deeds, bonds, agreements and other instruments, and notices, such instruments subsisting and notices given in relation to such functions or parish property;

(iv) in the case of actions and proceedings and causes of action or proceeding, such actions and proceedings pending or causes existing in relation to such functions or parish property;

but if specified as such matters in relation to any area includes only such matters being local matters in respect of such area;

(*c*) "police matters", "port health matters" and "sewerage and sewage disposal matters" mean—

(i) in the case of property, property held for the purposes of the relevant functions;

(ii) in the case of liabilities, liabilities incurred in relation to such functions;

(iii) in the case of contracts, deeds, bonds, agreements and other instruments, and notices, such instruments subsisting and notices given in relation to such functions; and

(iv) in the case of actions and proceedings and causes of action or proceeding, such actions and proceedings pending or causes existing in relation to such functions, but if specified as such matters in relation to any area include only such matters being local matters in respect of such area, and for the purposes of the foregoing definitions "the relevant functions" means—

(i) in the case of police matters, functions exercisable for police purposes, including the purposes of section 81 of the Road Traffic Regulation Act 1967;

(ii) in the case of port health matters, functions exercisable by the transferor authority as port health authority;

(iii) in the case of sewerage and sewage disposal matters, functions exercisable for the purposes of sewerage and sewage disposal;

(*d*) "local matters", in relation to any area, means—

(i) in the case of property—

(*a*) subject to the provision of paragraph 3, sited property situated in; and

(*b*) other property held exclusively in respect of,

the area;

(ii) in the case of liabilities, liabilities incurred exclusively in respect of the area;

(iii) in the case of contracts, deeds, bonds, agreements and other instruments, and notices, such instruments subsisting and notices given exclusively in respect of the area;

(iv) in the case of actions and proceedings and causes of action or proceeding, such actions and proceedings pending or causes existing exclusively in respect of the area.

2. In paragraph 1, "excepted property" means any property within article 20(1) which is not covered by the provision of article 20(2) and "exercisable" means exercisable otherwise than by virtue of section 101 or 110 of the Act.

3. (*a*) In this Schedule "sited property" means—

(i) land;

(ii) buildings;

(iii) fittings, furniture, equipment and stores supplied in respect of a voluntary school or a controlled community home;

(iv) subject to the provision of article 6, lamps, lamp posts and other apparatus for public lighting.

(*b*) The transferor authority may determine that any sited property shall, by reason of the fact that it is used wholly or mainly for an area other than the one in which it is situated, constitute local matters in respect of such other area.

(*c*) If notice is given by any authority concerned that they are dissatisfied with any determination under sub-paragraph (*b*) or that a determination should have been made thereunder, the question of the area which is to be the relevant area in relation to any sited property in the application of this Schedule shall be determined by agreement between the authorities concerned or failing such agreement by the decision of a person agreed on by such authorities or in default of agreement appointed by the Secretary of State.

4. Article 12 has effect, within the meaning of items 2, 7, 8, 9, 11 and 12 in the table in this Schedule, in relation to any property, where before 1st April 1974, in respect of such property—

an agreement has been entered into under paragraph (3), (4) or (5) of that article;

a determination has been given under paragraph (7) of that article;

notice has been given under paragraph (3) of article 38

and in relation to any liabilities incurred, contracts, deeds, bonds, agreements and other instruments subsisting, notices given, actions and proceedings pending and causes of action or proceeding existing in relation to such property.

TABLE

(1) Item No.	(2) Transferor authority	(3) Matters transferred	(4) Transferee authority
1	The county council of any county	Property acquired by the county council in the exercise of their functions under the Rural Water Supplies and Sewerage Act 1944 or in making contributions to a county district council in respect of works of water supply or sewerage or sewage disposal, in any area	The water authority for sewerage and sewage disposal purposes for the area in which the area described in column (3) is situated
2	The county council of Brecon, Denbigh, Glamorgan, Merioneth or Monmouthshire	District matters in relation to any area of the county included in a new district	The council of the district in which the area is comprised
		Other local matters (not being police matters, matters as to which article 12 has effect or matters provided for in item 1) in relation to any area of the county included in a new county	The council of the county in which the area is comprised
3	The county council of Anglesey, Cardiganshire, Montgomeryshire or Radnorshire	District matters	The council of the district in which the area of the county is comprised
4	The county council of Caernarvon, Carmarthenshire, Flintshire or Pembroke	District matters in relation to any area of the county included in a new district	The council of the district in which the area is comprised

(1) Item No.	(2) Transferor authority	(3) Matters transferred	(4) Transferee authority
5	The county council of Brecon, Caernarvon, Carmarthenshire, Denbigh, Flintshire, Glamorgan, Merioneth, Monmouthshire or Pembroke	Land situated outside the county falling within the definition of district matters	The council of the district specified in respect of the county council in column (3) of Part I of Schedule 4
6	The corporation or council of the county borough of Cardiff, Merthyr Tydfil, Newport or Swansea	County matters	The council of the county in which the area of the county borough is comprised
7	The council of the urban district of Gelligaer	County matters	The County Council of Mid Glamorgan
		Community matters in relation to any area of the urban district included in a community	The community council of the community
		Other local matters (not being sewerage or sewage disposal matters or matters as to which article 12 has effect) in relation to any area of the urban district included in a new district	The council of the district in which the area is comprised
8	The council of the urban district of Bedwellty	County matters in relation to any area of the urban district included in a new county	The council of the county in which the area is comprised
		Other local matters (not being sewerage or sewage disposal matters or matters as to which article 12 has effect) in relation to any area of the urban district included in a new district	The council of the district in which the area is comprised

		Land situated outside the urban district falling within the definition of county matters	The County Council of Gwent
9	The council of the urban district of Caerphilly	County matters	The County Council of Mid Glamorgan
		Other local matters (not being sewerage or sewage disposal matters or matters as to which article 12 has effect) in relation to any area of the urban district included in a new district	The council of the district in which the area is comprised
10	The corporation or council of any non-county borough or the council of any urban district not included in items 7, 8 and 9	County matters	The council of the county in which the area of the borough or urban district is comprised
		Where a community council is established for the area of the borough or urban district under section 27(3) or (4) of the Act, community matters and the historic and ceremonial property, and in particular the charters, insignia and plate, of the borough or district	The community council
11	The council of the rural district of Gwyrfai, Hawarden, Pontypool or Wrexham	County matters	The council of the county in which the area of the rural district is comprised
		Other local matters (not being sewerage or sewage disposal matters or matters as to which article 12 has effect) in relation to any area of the rural district included in a new district	The council of the district in which the area is comprised

(1) Item No.	(2) Transferor authority	(3) Matters transferred	(4) Transferee authority
12	The council of the rural district of Aled, Cardiff, Cowbridge, Crickhowell, Hiraethog, Magor and St Mellons, Neath or Vaynor and Penderyn	County matters in relation to any area of the rural district included in a new county	The council of the county in which the area is comprised
		Other local matters (not being sewerage or sewage disposal matters or matters as to which article 12 has effect) in relation to any area of the rural district included in a new district	The council of the district in which the area is comprised
		Land situated outside the rural district falling within the definition of county matters	The council of the county comprising the district whose council is specified in respect of the council of the rural district in column (2) of Part II of Schedule 4
13	The council of any rural district not included in items 11 and 12	County matters	The council of the county in which the area of the rural district is comprised
14	The corporation or council of any borough or the council of any urban district or rural district	(*a*) Rights acquired or liabilities incurred in relation to the cost of construction in any area of any public sewer or sewage disposal works constructed under powers other than the Public Health Act 1936 or enactments replaced by that Act prior to its declaration as a public sewer or sewage disposal works	The authority exercising such powers in that area on and after 1st April 1974

	(*b*) Subject to (*a*), where the area of the borough, urban district or rural district is comprised in the area for sewerage and sewage disposal purposes of one water authority, sewerage and sewage disposal matters	The water authority
	(*c*) Subject to (*a*), where the area of the borough, urban district or rural district is comprised in the area for sewerage and sewage disposal purposes of two or more water authorities, sewerage and sewage disposal matters being local matters in relation to any area of the borough, urban district or rural district comprised in the area of a water authority	The water authority
15 The urban district council of Chepstow	Port health matters in respect of the Gloucester (Chepstow Division) Port Health District	The District Council of Monmouth

SCHEDULE 3

Article 12

Agreements as to the Transfer of Property other than Land not Transferred by Articles 6 to 11

Part I

(1)	(2)
The county council of Brecon, Caernarvon, Carmarthenshire, Denbigh, Flintshire, Glamorgan, Merioneth, Monmouthshire or Pembroke	The councils of the districts in which any areas of the county are comprised
The council of the urban district of Bedwellty or the rural district of Aled, Cardiff, Cowbridge, Crickhowell, Hiraethog, Magor and St Mellons, Neath or Vaynor and Penderyn	The councils of the counties in which any areas of the urban district or rural district are comprised
The corporation or council of any borough, or the council of any urban district or rural district, which is comprised in the areas for sewerage and sewage disposal purposes of two or more water authorities	The water authorities

Part II

(1)	(2)
The county council of Brecon, Denbigh, Glamorgan, Merioneth or Monmouthshire	The councils of the counties in which any areas of the county are comprised
The council of the urban district of Bedwellty, Caerphilly or Gelligaer, or the rural district of Aled, Cardiff, Cowbridge, Crickhowell, Gwyrfai, Hawarden, Hiraethog, Magor and St Mellons, Neath, Pontypool, Vaynor and Penderyn or Wrexham	The councils of the districts in which any areas of the urban or rural district are comprised

SCHEDULE 4

Article 16

Residual Transfer of Property, etc.

Part I

(1) Transferor authority	(2) Transferee county council	(3) District specified for the purposes of item 5 of the table in Schedule 2
The county council of Brecon	The County Council of Powys	Brecknock
The county council of Caernarvon	The County Council of Gwynedd	Arfon
The county council of Carmarthenshire	The County Council of Dyfed	Llanelli
The county council of Denbigh	The County Council of Clwyd	Wrexham Maelor
The county council of Flintshire	The County Council of Clwyd	Alyn and Deeside
The county council of Glamorgan	The County Council of Mid Glamorgan	Ogwr
The county council of Merioneth	The County Council of Gwynedd	Meirionnydd
The county council of Monmouthshire	The County Council of Gwent	Torfaen
The county council of Pembroke	The County Council of Dyfed	Preseli

Part II

(1) Transferor authority	(2) Transferee authority
The county council of Anglesey	The County Council of Gwynedd
The county council of Cardiganshire	The County Council of Dyfed
The county council of Montgomeryshire	The County Council of Powys
The county council of Radnorshire	The County Council of Powys
The corporation or council of the county borough of Cardiff, Merthyr Tydfil, Newport or Swansea	The council of the district in which the area of the county borough is comprised
The council of the urban district of Bedwellty	The District Council of Islwyn
The council of the urban district of Caerphilly	The District Council of Rhymney Valley
The council of the urban district of Gelligaer	The District Council of Rhymney Valley
The council of the rural district of Aled	The District Council of Colwyn
The council of the rural district of Cardiff	The District Council of Vale of Glamorgan
The council of the rural district of Cowbridge	The District Council of Vale of Glamorgan
The council of the rural district of Crickhowell	The District Council of Brecknock

(1) Transferor authority	(2) Transferee authority
The council of the rural district of Gwyrfai	The District Council of Arfon
The council of the rural district of Hawarden	The District Council of Alyn and Deeside
The council of the rural district of Hiraethog	The District Council of Colwyn
The council of the rural district of Magor and St Mellons	The District Council of Newport
The council of the rural district of Neath	The District Council of Neath
The council of the rural district of Pontypool	The District Council of Monmouth
The council of the rural district of Vaynor and Penderyn	The District Council of Brecknock
The council of the rural district of Wrexham	The District Council of Wrexham Maelor
The corporation or council of any non-county borough or the council of any urban or rural district not included in the preceding items	The council of the district in which the area of the borough, urban district or rural district is comprised
Any separate parish council	The community council which replaces the parish council
In any group of parishes, the common parish council and the parish meeting and representative body of every parish in the group	The community council which replaces the parish council
The parish meeting and representative body of any parish not included in the last preceding item	The council of the district in which the area of the parish is comprised
Any burial board, joint burial board or joint committee which ceases to exist by virtue of section 214(1) of the Act	The authority or authorities exercising the functions specified in paragraph 1 of Schedule 26 to the Act in relation to the cemeteries and crematoria of the board or committee
Any joint board which ceases to exist by virtue of section 263(2)(*b*) of the Act	The authority in whom the functions of the board are vested by section 263(2)(*a*) of the Act
Any joint board which ceases to exist by virtue of section 263(3) of the Act	The local authority which becomes the port health authority for the district of the board under the said section 263(3)
The Dee and Clwyd, Glamorgan, Gwynedd, South West Wales, Usk or Wye River Authority	The Welsh National Water Development Authority
Any joint board who are statutory water undertakers other than a joint water board within the meaning of the Water Act 1973	The water authority within whose area for water supply purposes the limits of supply of the transferor authority are comprised
Any joint sewerage board or joint committee of sewerage authorities	The water authority within whose area for sewerage and sewage disposal purposes the area of the transferor authority is comprised
The local fisheries committee for the South Wales Sea Fisheries District	The committee as reconstituted

Peter Thomas,
Secretary of State for Wales.

8th November 1973.

EXPLANATORY NOTE

(This Note is not part of the Order.)

This Order makes, in relation to Wales, general provision for the transfer from the existing authorities which go out of existence on 1st April 1974 to the new authorities established by or under the Local Government Act 1972 and the Water Act 1973 of property, liabilities, contracts etc., notices, and actions and proceedings and causes of action or proceeding.

STATUTORY INSTRUMENTS

1973 No. 1864

ROAD TRAFFIC

The Motor Vehicles (Construction and Use) (Amendment) (No. 4) Regulations 1973

Made - - -	8*th November* 1973
Laid before Parliament	9*th November* 1973
Coming into Operation	19*th November* 1973

The Secretary of State for the Environment, in exercise of his powers under section 40(1) of the Road Traffic Act 1972**(a)** and of all other enabling powers, and after consultation with representative organisations in accordance with the provisions of section 199(2) of that Act, hereby makes the following Regulations:—

1.—(1) These Regulations may be cited as the Motor Vehicles (Construction and Use) (Amendment) (No. 4) Regulations 1973 and shall come into operation on 19th November 1973.

(2) The Interpretation Act 1889**(b)** shall apply for the interpretation of these Regulations as it applies for the interpretation of an Act of Parliament.

2. The Motor Vehicles (Construction and Use) Regulations 1973**(c)**, as amended**(d)**, shall have effect as though:—

(1) in Regulation 99(1) for the words "paragraph (2)" there were substituted the words "paragraphs (1A) and (2)";

(2) in Regulation 99, after paragraph (1), there were inserted the following paragraph:—

"(1A) Paragraph (1) of this Regulation shall not prohibit the use on a road of a motor vehicle or trailer by reason only of the fact that a wheel of the vehicle or trailer is fitted with a tyre which is deflated or not fully inflated and which has any of the defects described in sub-paragraph (*c*), (*d*) or (*e*) of paragraph (1) of this Regulation, if the tyre and the wheel to which it is fitted are so constructed as to make the tyre in that condition fit for the use to which the motor vehicle or trailer is being put and the outer sides of the wall of the tyre are so marked as to enable the tyre to be identified as having been constructed to comply with the requirements of this paragraph."; and

(3) in Regulation 99(2) for the words "the foregoing paragraph" there were substituted the words "paragraph (1) of this Regulation".

(a) 1972 c.20. **(b)** 1889 c.63. **(c)** S.I. 1973/24 (1973 I, p. 93).

(d) There is no relevant amending instrument.

Signed by authority of the Secretary of State.

John Peyton,

Minister for Transport Industries,
Department of the Environment.

8th November 1973.

EXPLANATORY NOTE

(This Note is not part of the Regulations.)

Regulation 99 of the Motor Vehicles (Construction and Use) Regulations 1973 provides that no person shall use or cause or permit to be used on a road any motor vehicle or trailer, a wheel of which is fitted with a pneumatic tyre, if the tyre is deflated, or damaged or worn in certain respects.

These Regulations amend Regulation 99 so as to permit the use on a road of a motor vehicle or trailer a wheel of which is fitted with a tyre in a damaged and deflated condition if the tyre and the wheel to which it is fitted are so constructed as to make the tyre in that condition safe for use in some circumstances, and the tyre is suitably marked.

1973 No. 1865

ECCLESIASTICAL LAW

The Church Representation Rules (Amendment) Resolution 1973

Made (passed by the General Synod with the requisite majority in each House) - - -	8*th November* 1973
Laid before Parliament -	15*th November* 1973
Coming into Operation -	1*st January* 1974

In pursuance of the power conferred by section 7(1) of the Synodical Government Measure 1969(**a**) to amend by a resolution of the General Synod the Church Representation Rules, that is to say, the rules contained in Schedule 3 to the said Measure, the General Synod hereby resolves that the said rules shall be amended as follows:—

Formation of church electoral roll

1.—(1) In rule 1(2) the word "electoral" shall be omitted and for sub-paragraph (*b*) of that paragraph there shall be substituted the following sub-paragraph:—

"(*b*) is a member of the Church of England or of a Church in communion with the Church of England;"

(2) For rule 1(3) there shall be substituted the following paragraph:—

"(3) A person shall be entitled to have his name on the roll of each of any number of parishes if he is entitled by virtue of paragraph (2) of this rule to have his name entered on each roll; but a person whose name is entered on the roll of each of two or more parishes must choose one of those parishes for the purpose of the provisions of these rules which prescribe the qualifications for election to a deanery synod, a diocesan synod or the General Synod or for membership of a deanery synod under rule 19(3)(*b*)."

(3) In rule 1(5), for the words "an electoral roll officer" there shall be substituted the words "a church electoral roll officer".

(4) In rule 1(7), sub-paragraphs (*d*) and (*g*) shall be omitted and the present sub-paragraphs (*e*), (*f*) and (*h*) shall be re-lettered (*d*), (*e*) and (*f*) respectively.

(5) In rule 1(8), for the words "is entitled to do so" there shall be substituted the words "has or acquires that right".

Revision of roll and preparation of new roll

2.—(1) At the end of rule 2(4) there shall be inserted the following paragraph:—

"At every service held on each of the two Sundays within the period of fourteen days beginning with the date of the affixing of the notice or,

(**a**) 1969 No. 2.

in the case of a church in which no service is held on either of those Sundays, at every service held in that church on the first Sunday after that date the person conducting the service shall inform the congregation of the preparation of the new roll."

(2) For rule 2(5) there shall be substituted the following paragraph:—

"(5) The parochial church council shall take reasonable steps to inform every person whose name is entered on the previous roll that a new roll is being prepared and that if he wishes to have his name entered on the new roll he must apply for enrolment. No such steps need be taken with respect to any person whose name could be removed from the previous roll under rule 1(7)."

Procedural provisions relating to entry and removal of names

3. In rule 3, paragraphs (3), (4) and (5) shall be omitted.

Certification of numbers on rolls

4. In rule 4—

(*a*) in paragraph (1), after the words "secretary or" there shall be inserted the word "church";

(*b*) paragraphs (3) and (4) shall be omitted and paragraph (5) shall be renumbered (3).

Provision with respect to person whose name is on guild church roll

5. After rule 4 there shall be inserted the following rule:—

"4A.—(1) A person whose name is entered on the roll of a guild church shall for the purpose of the provisions of these rules which prescribe the qualifications for election to a deanery synod, a diocesan synod or the House of Laity of the General Synod, or for membership of a deanery synod under rule 19(3)(*b*), be deemed to be a person whose name is on the roll of the parish in which the guild church is, and references in those provisions or in rule 1(3) to a person whose name is on the roll of a parish or on the roll of each of two or more parishes, and in rule 37 to entry on the roll of a parish, shall be construed accordingly.

(2) In this rule "guild church" means a church in the City of London designated and established as a guild church under the City of London (Guild Churches) Acts 1952 and 1960(**a**)."

Chairman of annual meeting

6. In rule 7, after the words "casting vote" there shall be inserted the words "unless it is a case where rule 10(8) applies."

Qualification of persons to be chosen, etc., by annual meetings

7. In rule 9(1)—

(*a*) at the beginning there shall be inserted the words "Subject to the provisions of rule 1(3)";

(*b*) in sub-paragraph (*b*) for the words from "of any" to "overseas" there shall be substituted the words "an actual communicant member of any";

(**a**) 15 & 16 Geo. 6 & 1 Eliz. 2 c. xxxviii; 8 & 9 Eliz. 2 c. xxx.

(*c*) in sub-paragraph (*c*) for the words " of age to vote at a Parliamentary election " there shall be substituted the words " eighteen years or upwards " ; and

(*d*) paragraph (i) of the proviso shall be omitted.

Members of parochial church council

8. For rule 12(1)(*d*) there shall be substituted the following sub-paragraph:—

" (*d*) such, if any, of the readers whose names are on the roll of the parish as the annual meeting may determine ; ".

Parochial church councils : term of office

9. Rule 14 shall become paragraph (1) of that rule and after that paragraph there shall be inserted the following paragraph:—

" (2) Persons who are members of a parochial church council by virtue of their election as lay members of a deanery synod shall hold office for a term beginning with the date of their election and ending with the 31st May next following the election of their successors.".

Parishes with more than one place of worship

10. In rule 16—

(*a*) in paragraph (1), for the word " either " there shall be substituted the words " which makes provision for either or both of the following purposes, that is to say " ;

(*b*) in paragraph (1)(*a*), for the word " or ", where last occurring, there shall be substituted the word " and " ;

(*c*) in paragraph (1)(*b*), the words " (other than the parish church) " shall be omitted.

Membership of deanery synods

11.—(1) In rule 19(3)—

(*a*) there shall be inserted at the beginning the words " Subject to the provisions of rule 1(3) " ;

(*b*) after the words " consist of " there shall be inserted the words " the following persons, that is to say " ;

(*c*) after sub-paragraph (*b*) there shall be inserted the following sub-paragraph :—

" (*c*) if in the opinion of the bishop of the diocese any community of persons in the deanery who are in the spiritual care of a chaplain licensed by the bishop should be represented in that house, one lay person, being an actual communicant member of the Church of England of eighteen years or upwards, chosen in such manner as may be approved by the bishop by and from among the members of that community " ;

(*d*) the present sub-paragraph (*c*) shall be re-lettered (*d*).

(2) In rule 19(4) for the words " age to vote at a Parliamentary election " there shall be substituted the words " eighteen years or upwards " and for the proviso to rule 19(4) there shall be substituted the following provision:—

" Provided that the number of members co-opted by either house shall not exceed five per cent. of the total number of members of that house or three, whichever is the greater."

Election, etc., of members of deanery synods

12.—(1) In rule 20(2), for the words " 1st December " there shall be substituted the words " 31st December ", and the words " and adjusted " shall be omitted.

(2) After rule 20(3) there shall be inserted the following paragraph:—

" (4) Any person to be chosen as mentioned in rule 19(3)(*c*) shall be so chosen every three years and shall hold office for a term of three years beginning with the 1st June next following the date on which he is so chosen."

(3) Paragraph (4) of rule 20 shall be re-numbered (5) and in that paragraph for the letter " (*c*) " there shall be substituted the letter " (*d*) ".

(4) Paragraph (5) of rule 20 shall be re-numbered (6) and at the end of that paragraph there shall be inserted the following paragraph:—

" For the avoidance of doubt it is hereby declared that the number 150 specified in this paragraph includes the maximum number of members who may be co-opted by each house."

Variation of membership of deanery synods by scheme

13. In rule 21(1) the proviso shall be omitted.

Membership of diocesan synods

14.—(1) In rule 24(2)(*a*)(i), for the words " any full-time assistant bishop or bishops " there shall be substituted the words " any assistant bishop or bishops nominated by the bishop of the diocese ".

(2) In rule 24(2)(*a*)(iv), for the words " for this purpose " there shall be substituted the words " treated for this purpose as being ".

(3) In rule 24(2)(*a*), after head (iv) there shall be inserted the following head:—

" (v) any other member of that House, being the person chosen by and from among the clerical members of religious communities in the Province, who resides in the diocese ; "

and the present heads (v) and (vi) shall be renumbered (vi) and (vii) respectively.

(4) In rule 24(3)(*a*), there shall be inserted at the end:—

" (iv) any other member of that House, being the person chosen by and from among the lay members of religious communities in the Province, who resides in the diocese ; ".

Elections of members of diocesan synods by deanery synods

15.—(1) In rule 25(1), for the words " ending with the election of their successors " there shall be substituted the words " of three years beginning with the 1st September next following their election ".

(2) At the beginning of rule 25(3) there shall be inserted the words " Subject to the provisions of rule 1(3) ", for the words " age to vote at a Parliamentary election " there shall be substituted the words " eighteen years or upwards ", and the proviso to rule 25(3) shall be omitted.

(3) In rule 25(4), for the words " 1st December " there shall be substituted the words " 31st December " and the words " and adjusted " in sub-paragraph (*b*) shall be omitted.

(4) In the proviso to rule 25(6) for the word "two" there shall be substituted the word "five" and at the end of rule 25(6) there shall be inserted the following paragraph: —

"For the avoidance of doubt it is hereby declared that the numbers 270 and 500 specified in this paragraph include the maximum number of members who may be co-opted by each house or nominated by the bishop."

(5) In rule 26(7) for the word "him" there shall be substituted the words "the presiding officer".

Variation of membership of diocesan synods by scheme

16. In rule 27(1) the proviso shall be omitted.

House of Laity of General Synod

17. In rule 29(2) the proviso shall be omitted.

Number of elected members of House of Laity

18. In rule 30(2), the words "as adjusted under rule 4" shall be omitted.

Qualification of elected members

19.—(1) Rule 31 shall become paragraph (1) of that rule.

(2) At the beginning of rule 31 there shall be inserted the words "Subject to the provisions of rule 1(3)" and for the words "age to vote at a Parliamentary election" there shall be substituted the words "eighteen years or upwards".

(3) In rule 31(1) the proviso shall be omitted, and at the end of rule 31(1) there shall be inserted the following paragraph:—

"(2) Where a diocese is divided into two or more areas in accordance with rule 32(2), any person who under this rule is qualified for election for the diocese shall be qualified for election for any such area whether or not the parish on whose roll his name is entered, or the cathedral church at which he is a habitual worshipper, is situated in that area, but no person shall be nominated for more than one such area at the same time."

Electoral areas

20.—(1) In rule 32(2), after the words "following rule" there shall be inserted the words "and subject to paragraph (3) of this rule", and at the end of rule 32 there shall be inserted the following paragraph:—

"(3) If a diocesan synod decides to divide the diocese into two or more areas in pursuance of this rule the division shall be made in such manner that the number of members to be elected in any such area will be not less than three."

(2) Nothing in paragraph (1) above shall affect any division of a diocese made before this resolution comes into operation and any division so made shall continue in force until the next dissolution of the General Synod. Accordingly, if a casual vacancy among persons elected for any such division occurs before that dissolution the vacancy shall be filled in accordance with the Church Representation Rules by the election of a member for that division.

Conduct of elections

21.—(1) In rule 33(2), after the word "him" there shall be inserted the words "with the approval of the registrar of the province".

(2) In rule 33(3), for the words "on or before a date to be specified by the presiding officer" there shall be substituted the words "within such period, being a period of not less than 28 days ending on a date specified by the presiding officer, as that officer may specify".

(3) In rule 33(4) the words from "(unless" to "three)" shall be omitted and at the end of that paragraph there shall be inserted the following sentence:—

"Every voting paper marked and signed by the elector shall be returnable to the presiding officer within such period, being a period of not less than 21 days after the date on which the voting paper is issued, as that officer may specify."

(4) In rule 33(5), after the words "present at" there shall be inserted the words "but shall take no part in".

(5) At the end of rule 33 there shall be inserted the following paragraph:—

"(7) The presiding officer in each area shall ensure that the valid voting papers received by him for the purposes of any election to the House of Laity are preserved for a period of not less than two years beginning with the date of the election."

Duties and payment of presiding officers

22. After rule 33 there shall be inserted the following rule:—

"33A.—(1) Rules defining the duties to be undertaken by the presiding officers in connection with elections to the House of Laity shall be prepared by the provincial registrars acting jointly, but no such rules shall have effect unless approved by the Standing Committee of the General Synod.

(2) A presiding officer shall be entitled to such fees for the performance by him of the duties aforesaid as may be specified in any order for the time being in force made under section 1 of the Ecclesiastical Fees Measure 1962(**a**); and where with the prior agreement in writing of the bishop's council and standing committee the presiding officer or any other person performs any other duties in connection with elections to the House of Laity he shall be entitled to such fees as may be specified in the agreement."

Ex-officio etc., members of the House of Laity

23.—(1) In rule 35(1), after sub-paragraph (*a*) there shall be inserted the following sub-paragraph:—

"(*b*) the Vicar-General of the Province of Canterbury;",

and the present sub-paragraphs (*b*), (*c*) and (*d*) shall be re-lettered (*c*), (*d*) and (*e*) respectively.

(2) In rule 35(2) for the words "age to vote at a Parliamentary election" there shall be substituted the words "eighteen years or upwards".

(**a**) 1962 No. 1.

Appeals

24.—(1) In rule 36(1), the words " Subject to the provisions of rule 1(3) of these rules " shall be omitted.

(2) In rule 36(4), for the words " be referred " there shall be substituted the words " unless the parties agree to a settlement of their dispute, be referred by the bishop ", and for the words " two or more " there shall be substituted the words " three or a greater number, being an odd number ".

(3) In rule 36(5), for the words " two or more " there shall be substituted the words " three or a greater number, being an odd number ".

Vacation of seat by member ceasing to be qualified for election

25.—(1) Rule 37 with the omission of the proviso shall become paragraph (1) of that rule.

(2) In rule 37(1), after the words " his seat shall " there shall be inserted the words " subject to the following provisions of this rule " and for the proviso to rule 37 there shall be substituted the following paragraphs:—

" (2) If the name of a person to whom sub-paragraph (*a*) or (*c*) of paragraph (1) of this rule applies is entered on the roll of any parish in the diocese other than that of the parish mentioned in sub-paragraph (*a*) or (*c*), as the case may be, or if he is declared under rule 22 to be a habitual worshipper at the cathedral church of the diocese and, in the case of a person to whom sub-paragraph (*c*) applies, is declared by the dean to be associated with a deanery in the diocese, his seat shall not be vacated under this rule unless he resigns.

(3) If a person to whom paragraph (1)(*b*) of this rule applies continues to work or reside in the diocese, his seat shall not be vacated under this rule unless he resigns.

(4) If the bishop's council and standing committee has determined that a person to whom paragraph (1)(*d*) of this rule applies should remain a member of the House of Laity, his seat shall not be vacated under this rule."

Ex-officio membership not to disqualify for election

26. In rule 38, the word " lay ", wherever occurring, shall be omitted.

Casual vacancies

27.—(1) For rule 39(1) there shall be substituted the following paragraphs:—

" (1) Where a casual vacancy among the parochial representatives elected to the parochial church council or deanery synod occurs, the vacancy may be filled by the election by the parochial church council of a person qualified to be so elected.

(2) Where a casual vacancy among the members of a diocesan synod elected by either house of a deanery synod occurs, the vacancy may be filled by the election by that house of a person qualified to be so elected, and a meeting of the members of that house who are electors may be held for that purpose.

(3) Subject to paragraphs (1), (2) and (6) of this rule, casual vacancies among persons elected under these rules shall be filled by elections conducted in the same manner as ordinary elections.

(4) Elections to fill casual vacancies shall, where possible, be held at such times as will enable all casual vacancies among representatives of the laity who are electors to be filled at the time of every election to the House of Laity of the General Synod, but no such election shall be invalid by reason of any casual vacancies not having been so filled."

(2) The present paragraph (2) of rule 39 shall be re-numbered (5), and for the proviso to that paragraph there shall be substituted the following provision:—

" Provided that where a casual vacancy occurs in any of these three houses and the period for holding a general election to that house is due to begin, in the case of a general election to the House of Laity, within twelve months of the vacancy, and, in the case of a general election to either house of the diocesan synod, within nine months of the vacancy, the vacancy shall not be filled unless, in the first-mentioned case, the bishop's council and standing committee acting in accordance with any directions of the diocesan synod, otherwise direct or, in the last-mentioned case, the bishop otherwise directs."

(3) After paragraph (5) of rule 39 there shall be inserted the following paragraphs:—

" (6) If a casual vacancy in the House of Laity of the General Synod occurs within the period of two years beginning with the date of the last preceding general election to that House or the date of any subsequent election to fill a casual vacancy and that election was conducted by voting papers upon the principle of proportional representation in the same manner as a general election, then, provided that the bishop's council and standing committee acting in accordance with any directions of the diocesan synod agree, the election to fill the casual vacancy shall be conducted by those papers in accordance with paragraph (1) of this rule.

(7) The presiding officer for the area in question shall ask every candidate not elected in the preceding election who is still qualified for election for the diocese in question if he consents to serve. If there is only one such candidate and he so consents or only one of those candidates so consents he shall be elected to fill the casual vacancy. If two or more of those candidates so consent the votes validly cast in the preceding election shall be recounted from the beginning in accordance with the rules mentioned in rule 33(4)."

(4) The present paragraphs (3) and (4) of rule 39 shall be re-numbered (8) and (9) respectively.

Resignations

28. For rule 40 there shall be substituted the following rule:

" 40. Any person holding any office under these rules or being a member of any body constituted by or under these rules may resign his office or membership by notice in writing signed by him and sent or given to the secretary of the body of which he is an officer or member, as the case may be; and his resignation shall take effect on the date specified in the notice or, if no date is so specified, on the receipt of the notice by the secretary of that body."

Delegation of functions

29. For paragraphs (6) and (7) of rule 43 there shall be substituted the following paragraphs:—

"(6) During a vacancy in an archbishopric or where by reason of illness an archbishop is unable to exercise his functions under these rules or to appoint a commissary under paragraph (10) of this rule the functions of an archbishop under these rules shall be exercisable by the other archbishop.

(7) During a vacancy in a diocesan bishopric the functions of a diocesan bishop under these rules, including his functions as one of the authorities which together constitute the diocesan synod, shall be exercisable by such person, being a person in episcopal orders, as the archbishop of the province may appoint.

(8) Where by reason of illness a diocesan bishop is unable to exercise his functions under these rules or to appoint a commissary under paragraph (10) of this rule, the archbishop of the province may, if he thinks it necessary or expedient to do so, appoint a person in episcopal orders to exercise the functions mentioned in paragraph (7) of this rule during the period of the bishop's illness.

(9) If a person appointed in pursuance of paragraph (7) or (8) of this rule becomes unable by reason of illness to act under the appointment, the archbishop may revoke the appointment and make a fresh one.

(10) An archbishop or diocesan bishop may appoint a commissary and delegate to him all or any of the functions of the archbishop or bishop under these rules, but if a bishop proposes to delegate to a commissary his functions as one of the authorities which together constitute the diocesan synod he shall appoint a person in episcopal orders as commissary.

(11) If a person appointed in pursuance of paragraph (7) or (8) of this rule, or a person to whom the functions of a bishop as one of the authorities referred to in paragraph (10) thereof are delegated under that paragraph, is a member of the house of clergy of the diocesan synod, his membership of that house shall be suspended during the period for which the appointment or delegation has effect".

Interpretation

30.—(1) In rule 44(1) for the definition of "actual communicant member" there shall be substituted the following definitions:—

"actual communicant member of the Church of England" means a member of the Church of England who is confirmed or ready and desirous of being confirmed and has received Communion according to the use of the Church of England or of a Church in communion with the Church of England at least three times during the twelve months preceding the date of his election or appointment;

"actual communicant member of a Church in communion with the Church of England" means a communicant member of a Church in communion with the Church of England who has received Communion according to the use of the Church of England or of a Church in communion with the Church of England at least three times during the twelve months preceding the date of his election or appointment.

(2) In rule 44(4) the words "as to" and the words "Church of the Anglican Communion or an overseas" shall be omitted.

Forms

31. In Appendix I, for the form set out in Section 1 there shall be substituted the form set out in the Schedule to this resolution.

32. In Appendix I, in Sections 2 and 3—

(*a*) in sub-paragraph (ii) for the words from " another " to the end there shall be substituted the words " of any Church in communion with the Church of England " ;

(*b*) the words from " Entry " to " parishes at once " shall be omitted ;

(*c*) immediately before the word " Electoral ", where last occurring, there shall be inserted the word " Church ".

33.—(1) In Appendix I, Section 4 shall be amended in accordance with this paragraph.

(2) The words " To the Parochial Church Council . . . representatives " shall be transferred to follow immediately after the words " To the Deanery Synod . . . representatives ".

(3) The paragraph beginning " Such persons " shall be omitted.

(4) For the next following paragraph there shall be substituted the following paragraphs:—

" A person is qualified to be elected a parochial representative of the laity to the deanery synod if—

(*a*) his name is entered on the church electoral roll of the parish ;

(*b*) he is a member of the Church of England who is confirmed or ready and desirous of being confirmed and has received Communion according to the use of the Church of England or a Church in communion with the Church of England at least three times during the twelve months preceding the date of the election ; and

(*c*) he is of 18 years or upwards.

A person is qualified to be elected a parochial representative of the laity to the parochial church council if—

(*a*) his name is entered on the church electoral roll of the parish ; and

(*b*) he is a member of the Church of England who is confirmed or ready and desirous of being confirmed or a communicant member of a Church in communion with the Church of England and has received Communion according to the use of the Church of England or a Church in communion with the Church of England at least three times during the twelve months preceding the date of the election."

34. In Appendix I, in Section 5, at the end of paragraph 2 there shall be inserted the following paragraph:—

" All members, other than co-opted members, of the House of Clergy/Laity of the deanery synod are qualified electors."

35. In Appendix I, in Section 6, for the words " Other Names " there shall be substituted the words " Christian Names ", for the word " Description " there shall be substituted the words " Profession or Occupation " and at the end of the Note there shall be inserted the following paragraph:—

" All members, other than co-opted members, of the House of Clergy/Laity of the deanery synod are qualified electors."

Proceedings of parochial church councils

36. In Appendix II, in paragraph 8, after the word " three " there shall be inserted the word " clear ".

Citation, commencement and interpretation

37.—(1) This resolution may be cited as the Church Representation Rules (Amendment) Resolution 1973 and shall come into operation on 1st January 1974.

(2) Any reference in this resolution to a numbered rule or Appendix is a reference to the rule or Appendix, as the case may be, bearing that number in the Church Representation Rules.

(3) The Interpretation Measure 1925(a) shall apply for the interpretation of this resolution as it applies for the interpretation of Measures passed by the General Synod.

Approved by the General Synod of the Church of England the eighth November 1973.

W. D. Pattinson,

Secretary General.

(a) 1925 No. 1.

SCHEDULE

APPLICATION FOR ENROLMENT ON CHURCH ELECTORAL ROLL

(Full Christian name and surname)

I ....

(Full postal address)

of ....

am baptised and am a member of the Church of England or of a Church in communion with it. I am seventeen years or over and am either resident in the parish or have habitually attended public worship there for at least the past six months.

I apply for entry on the church electoral roll of the parish of . . . .

Signed ....

Date ....

NOTES

1. The only Churches at present in communion with the Church of England are other Anglican Churches and certain foreign Churches. Members of other Churches in England are usually admitted to communion as individuals, but their Churches are not yet in communion with the Church of England. Such persons would naturally take part in the government of their own Churches.

2. Every six years a new roll is prepared and those on the previous roll are informed so that they can re-apply. If you are not resident in the parish but were on the roll as an habitual worshipper and have been prevented by sickness or absence or other essential reason from worshipping for the past six months, you may write "would" before "have habitually attended" in the form and add "but was prevented from doing so because . . . ." and then state the reason.

3. If you have any problems over this form, please approach the clergy or lay people responsible for the parish, who will be pleased to help you.

EXPLANATORY NOTE

(*This Note is not part of the Resolution.*)

This Resolution of the General Synod of the Church of England, which was passed in accordance with section 7(1) of the Synodical Government Measure 1969, makes a number of miscellaneous amendments of the Church Representation Rules contained in Schedule 3 to that Measure. The principal changes are:

1. The requirement that a person who wishes to have his name entered on the electoral roll of a parish must declare that he is not a member of any religious body which is not in communion with the Church of England is abolished (paragraph 1(1) and Schedule).

2. The provisions relating to entry of a person's name on the electoral roll of two or more parishes have been simplified and clarified (paragraph 1(2)).

3. Provision is made to ensure that entry on the roll of a guild church is equivalent to entry on the roll of the parish in which the guild church is for the purpose of qualification for election to a deanery or diocesan synod or the House of Laity of the General Synod (paragraph 5).

4. Provision is made for additional members of the House of Laity of a deanery synod to represent communities of persons in the deanery who are in the spiritual care of a chaplain licensed by the bishop (paragraph 11(1)(c)).

5. The duties to be undertaken by presiding officers in connection with elections to the House of Laity of the General Synod are to be defined and provision is made for fixing the fees to be paid for the performance of such duties (paragraph 22).

6. The number of cases in which it will be necessary to hold an election to fill a casual vacancy among the elected members of a deanery or diocesan synod or the House of Laity of the General Synod is reduced (paragraphs 25(2) and 27).

7. The functions of an archbishop or diocesan bishop under the rules will, during a vacancy, be exercisable by the other archbishop or, in the case of a vacancy in a bishopric, by a person in episcopal orders appointed by the archbishop of the province and not (in either case) by the guardian of the spiritualities ; and provision is made for the case where by reason of illness an archbishop or a diocesan bishop is unable to exercise his functions under the rules (paragraph 29).

1973 No. 1866

WAGES COUNCILS

The Wages Regulation (Perambulator and Invalid Carriage) (Amendment) Order 1973

Made - - - -	*7th November* 1973
Coming into Operation	*31st December* 1973

Whereas the Secretary of State has received from the Perambulator and Invalid Carriage Wages Council (Great Britain) the wages regulation proposals set out in the Schedule hereto;

Now, therefore, the Secretary of State in exercise of powers conferred by section 11 of the Wages Councils Act 1959**(a)**, as modified by Article 2 of the Counter-Inflation (Modification of Wages Councils Act 1959) Order 1973**(b)**, and now vested in him**(c)**, and of all other powers enabling him in that behalf, hereby makes the following Order:—

1. This Order may be cited as the Wages Regulation (Perambulator and Invalid Carriage) (Amendment) Order 1973.

2.—(1) In this Order the expression "the specified date" means the 31st December 1973, provided that where, as respects any worker who is paid wages at intervals not exceeding seven days, that date does not correspond with the beginning of the period for which the wages are paid, the expression "the specified date" means, as respects that worker, the beginning of the next such period following that date.

(2) The Interpretation Act 1889**(d)** shall apply to the interpretation of this Order as it applies to the interpretation of an Act of Parliament.

3. The wages regulation proposals set out in the Schedule hereto shall have effect as from the specified date.

Signed by order of the Secretary of State.

7th November 1973.

W. H. Marsh,
Assistant Secretary,
Department of Employment.

(a) 1959 c. 69. **(b)** S.I. 1973/661 (1973 I, p. 2141).
(c) S.I. 1959/1769, 1968/729 (1959 I, p. 1795; 1968 II, p. 2108).
(d) 1889 c. 63.

Article 3

SCHEDULE

STATUTORY MINIMUM REMUNERATION

The Wages Regulation (Perambulator and Invalid Carriage) Order, 1973**(a)** (Order I. (87)), shall have effect as if in the Schedule thereto:—

for Parts II and III there were substituted the following Parts:—

"PART II

GENERAL MINIMUM TIME RATES

2. Subject to the provisions of paragraph 3, the general minimum time rates applicable in any week to the workers specified in Column 1 of the next following Table, employed on time work, are the rates set out in Column 2 as follows:—

Column 1	Column 2		
Class of workers	Males	Females	
		Up to and including 30th December 1973	On and after 31st December 1973
	Per hour	Per hour	Per hour
MALE OR FEMALE WORKERS	p	p	p
(1) Aged 18 years or over			
I Class I: skilled workers, i.e. workers in the occupations specified in (1) to (6) below	44·5	36·0	*38·83*
(1) woodworking machinists;			
(2) metallic platers;			
(3) fitters and turners;			
(4) varnishers or fine liners of wood and/or metal bodies;			
(5) upholsterers as distinct from upholstery assemblers;			
(6) workers employed on prototype or development work.			
II Class II: higher semi-skilled workers, i.e. workers in the occupations specified in (1) to (14) below ...	43·0	35·5	*38·0*
(1) woodworking machinists who are not required to set and sharpen their own tools;			
(2) wood body assemblers;			
(3) metallic platers who are not required to make and maintain plating solutions;			
(4) painters and finishers by brush or spray (other than priming, filling in coats, brush or dip stove enamelling);			
(5) fine liners of chassis;			
(6) hand welders (excepting automatic, spot or butt welding);			
(7) metal polishers and finishers;			
(8) cold spring bending;			
(9) wheel trueing by hand ;			
(10) machinists (other than those specified in (1) and (11) of this Class) who are able to operate at least two classes of machine;			
(11) sewing machinists, hood coverers and cloth cutters;			
(12) fork lift drivers;			
(13) packing case makers;			
(14) inspectors, including patrol inspectors.			

(a) S.I. 1973/342 (1973 I, p. 1203).

Column 1	Column 2		
Class of workers	Males	Females	
		Up to and including 30th December 1973	On and after 31st December 1973
	Per hour	Per hour	Per hour
	p	p	p
III Class III: lower semi-skilled workers, i.e. workers in the occupations specified in (1) to (10) below ...	42·0	35·0	*37·33*
(1) stove enamellers—brush, spray or dip; (2) automatic, spot or butt welders; (3) cold bending, rivetting and striking (other than those specified in Class II (8)); (4) painters of priming or filling in coats; (5) tyre fitters and jointers; (6) wiring and racking in plating shop; (7) machinists (other than those specified in Class II(1), (10) and (11)); (8) packers engaged in boxing, wrapping, cleaning and casual inspection of perambulators, invalid carriages, bed folders and pushchairs; (9) storekeepers; (10) assemblers (other than those specified in Class I(5) and in Class II(2)).			
IV Class IV: unskilled workers, i.e. workers in the occupations specified in (1) to (3) below	42·0	35·0	*37·33*
(1) general labourers; (2) assistants to storekeepers; (3) warehouse assistants; (4) any other workers not provided for in Classes I, II and III and in (1) to (3) of this class.			
(2) The minimum rate applicable to a worker aged under 18 years shall be as follows:—			
aged 17 and under 18 years	28·0	28·0	28·0
aged under 17 years	26·3	26·3	26·3

3. Where in any week, a worker of a class specified in paragraph 2 is employed for any part of the week on work entitling him to be treated as a worker of any one of the other classes so specified, the rate applicable to all work performed by that worker in that week shall be the higher of the rates applicable in respect of the work on which he is employed.

PART III

PIECE WORK BASIS TIME RATES

4. The piece work basis time rate applicable to any male or female worker employed on piece work is the rate applicable to that worker, specified in Column 2 of the Table below, increased by 20 per cent.:—

Column 1	Column 2		
Class of workers	Males	Females	
		Up to and including 30th December 1973	On and after 31st December 1973
	Per hour	Per hour	Per hour
	p	p	p
(*a*) Male or female workers aged 18 years or over of the classes specified in paragraph 2(1) of this Schedule:			
Class I	39·0	32·9	*34·93*
Class II	37·3	32·3	*33·97*
Class III	36·2	31·7	*33·2*
Class IV	36·2	31·7	*33·2*
(*b*) Male or female workers aged under 18 years:			
aged 17 and under 18 years	24·1	24·1	24·1
aged under 17 years	22·0	22·0	22·0"

EXPLANATORY NOTE

(*This Note is not part of the Order.*)

This Order which has effect from 31st December 1973, sets out the increased statutory minimum remuneration payable from 31st December 1973 to female workers aged 18 years and over in relation to whom the Perambulator and Invalid Carriage Wages Council (Great Britain) operates in substitution for that fixed by the Wages Regulation (Perambulator and Invalid Carriage) Order 1973. (Order I. (87)).

New provisions are printed in italics.

1973 No. 1867

WAGES COUNCILS

The Wages Regulation (Sack and Bag) (No. 2) Order 1973

Made - - - *7th November* 1973

Coming into Operation 31*st December* 1973

Whereas the Secretary of State has received from the Sack and Bag Wages Council (Great Britain) the wages regulation proposals set out in the Schedule hereto;

Now, therefore, the Secretary of State in exercise of powers conferred by section 11 of the Wages Councils Act 1959(**a**), as modified by Article 2 of the Counter-Inflation (Modification of Wages Councils Act 1959) Order 1973(**b**), and now vested in him(**c**), and of all other powers enabling him in that behalf, hereby makes the following Order:—

1. This Order may be cited as the Wages Regulation (Sack and Bag) (No. 2) Order 1973.

2.—(1) In this Order the expression "the specified date" means the 31st December 1973, provided that where, as respects any worker who is paid wages at intervals not exceeding seven days, that date does not correspond with the beginning of the period for which the wages are paid, the expression "the specified date" means, as respects that worker, the beginning of the next such period following that date.

(2) The Interpretation Act 1889(**d**) shall apply to the interpretation of this Order as it applies to the interpretation of an Act of Parliament and as if this Order and the Order hereby revoked were Acts of Parliament.

3. The wages regulation proposals set out in the Schedule hereto shall have effect as from the specified date and as from that date the Wages Regulation (Sack and Bag) Order 1973(**e**) shall cease to have effect.

Signed by Order of the Secretary of State.
7th November 1973.

W. H. Marsh,
Assistant Secretary,
Department of Employment.

(**a**) 1959 c. 69.
(**b**) S.I. 1973/661 (1973 I, p. 2141).
(**c**) S.I. 1959/1769, 1968/729 (1959 I, p. 1795; 1968 II, p. 2108).
(**d**) 1889 c. 63.
(**e**) S.I. 1973/1016 (1973 II, p. 3076).

Article 3

SCHEDULE

The following minimum remuneration shall be substituted for the statutory minimum remuneration fixed by the Wages Regulation (Sack and Bag) Order 1973 (Order S.B. (75)).

STATUTORY MINIMUM REMUNERATION

PART I

GENERAL

1. The minimum remuneration payable to a worker to whom this Schedule applies for all work except work to which a minimum overtime rate applies under Part IV of this Schedule is:—

(1) in the case of a time worker, the general minimum time rate payable to the worker under Part II or Part III of this Schedule;

(2) *in the case of a worker employed on piece work, piece rates each of which would yield, in the circumstances of the case, to an ordinary worker at least the same amount of money as the general minimum time rate which would be payable under Part II or Part III of this Schedule if he were a time worker.*

PART II

MALE WORKERS

GENERAL MINIMUM TIME RATES

2. The general minimum time rates payable to male workers are as follows:—

	Per hour p
(1) Workers aged 21 years or over and employed during the whole or part of their time:—	
(*a*) as superintendents of packing presses (hand or machine) or as press foremen (hand or machine), or	
(*b*) in setting up or minding or in setting up and minding, branding or printing machines or both such machines	40·5
Provided that the general minimum time rate payable during his first six months' employment in the trade to a worker who enters, or who has entered, the trade for the first time at or over the age of 21 years shall be	40·2
(2) All other workers aged—	
21 years or over ...	39·4
20 and under 21 years	36·0
19 " " 20 "	35·5
18 " " 19 "	35·0
17 " " 18 "	28·7
under 17 years	25·3

Provided that the general minimum time rate payable during his first two months' employment in the trade to a worker who enters, or who has entered, the trade for the first time at or over the age of 18 years shall be 0·2p per hour less than the minimum rate otherwise payable under this sub-paragraph.

PART III

FEMALE WORKERS

GENERAL MINIMUM TIME RATES

3. The general minimum time rates payable to female workers are as follows:—

	Per hour p
(1) Workers aged 18 years or over and employed as examiners of mended work, allocators, forewomen, selectors or graders of mixed loads or setters-up on branding machines	*37·3*
Provided that the general minimum time rate payable during her first six months' employment in the trade to a worker who enters, or who has entered, the trade for the first time at or over the age of 18 years shall be	*36·8*
(2) All other workers aged—	
21 years or over	*36·5*
20 and under 21 years	*36·0*
19 ,, ,, 20	*35·5*
18 ,, ,, 19 ,, ...	35·0
17 ,, ,, 18 ,, ...	28·7
under 17 years	25·3

Provided that the general minimum time rate payable during her first two months' employment in the trade to a worker who enters, or who has entered, the trade for the first time at or over the age of 16 years shall be 0·2p per hour less than the minimum rate otherwise payable under this sub-paragraph.

PART IV

OVERTIME AND WAITING TIME

MINIMUM OVERTIME RATES

4. Minimum overtime rates are payable to any worker, not being a male worker employed on piece work, as follows:—

(1) on any day other than a Saturday, Sunday or customary holiday—

(*a*) for the first two hours worked in excess of 8½ hours time-and-a-quarter

(*b*) thereafter ... ... time-and-a-half

Provided that, where the employer normally requires the worker's attendance on five days only in the week, the foregoing minimum overtime rates of time-and-a-quarter and time-and-a-half shall be payable after 9 and 11 hours' work respectively.

(2) on a Saturday, not being a customary holiday—

(*a*) where the worker is normally required to attend on six days in the week—
for the first 2 hours worked in excess of 4 hours ... time-and-a-quarter
thereafter ... ... time-and-a-half

(*b*) where the worker is normally required to attend on five days only in the week—

for the first 2 hours worked ... ... time-and-a-quarter
thereafter ... ... time-and-a-half

(3) on a Sunday or a customary holiday—
for all time worked ... ... double time

(4) in any week exclusive of any time for which a minimum overtime rate is payable under the foregoing provisions of this paragraph—
for all time worked in excess of 40 hours ... ... time-and-a-quarter.

5. In this Part of this Schedule—

(1) the expressions "time-and-a-quarter", "time-and-a-half" and "double time" means respectively—

(a) in the case of a time worker, one and a quarter times, one and a half times and twice the general minimum time rate otherwise payable to the worker.

(b) in the case of a female worker employed on piece work—

(i) a time rate equal respectively to one-quarter, one-half and the whole of the time rate otherwise applicable to the worker under Part III of this Schedule and, in addition thereto—

(ii) the piece rates otherwise applicable to the worker under paragraph 1(2).

(2) the expression "customary holiday" means

(*a*) (i) in England and Wales—

Christmas Day;

26th December if it be not a Sunday;
27th December in a year when 25th or 26th December is a Sunday;

Good Friday;
Easter Monday;

the last Monday in May;
the last Monday in August;
or where a day is substituted for any of the above days by national proclamation, that day;

(ii) in Scotland—

New Year's Day and the following day:

Provided that if New Year's Day falls on a Sunday the holidays shall be the following Monday and Tuesday, and if New Year's Day falls on a Saturday the holidays shall be New Year's Day and the following Monday;

the local Spring holiday;

the local Autumn holiday; and

two other days (being days on which the worker would normally work) in the course of a calendar year, to be fixed by the employer and notified to the worker not less than three weeks before the holiday;

or (*b*) in the case of each of the said days (other than a day fixed by the employer in Scotland and notified to the worker as aforesaid) such weekday as may be substituted therefor by the employer being either—

(i) a day which is by local custom recognised as a day of holiday, or

(ii) a day (being a day on which the worker would normally work) which falls within three weeks of the day for which it is substituted and is mutually agreed between the employer and the worker.

WAITING TIME

6.—(1) A worker is entitled to payment of the minimum remuneration specified in this Schedule for all time during which he is present on the premises of his employer unless he is present thereon in any of the following circumstances:—

(*a*) without the employer's consent, express or implied;

(*b*) for some purpose unconnected with his work and other than that of waiting for work to be given to him to perform;

(*c*) by reason only of the fact that he is resident thereon;

(*d*) during normal meal times in a room or place in which no work is being done and he is not waiting for work to be given to him to perform.

(2) The minimum remuneration payable under sub-paragraph (1) of this paragraph to a piece worker when not engaged on piece work is that which would be payable if he were a time worker.

PART V

APPLICATION

7. This Schedule applies to workers in relation to whom the Sack and Bag Wages Council (Great Britain) operates, namely, workers employed in Great Britain in the trade specified in the Schedule to the Trade Boards (Sack and Bag Trade, Great Britain) (Constitution and Proceedings) Regulations 1933**(a)**, that is to say:—

The making from woven fabrics of corn sacks, flour sacks, coal sacks, sugar sacks, cement bags, sand bags, nail bags, potato bags, seed bags and similar sacks or bags, or the repairing thereof:

including:—

(*a*) the following and similar operations (whether performed by hand or machine) known in the trade as:—

(i) Folding (or hooking), cutting, machining, turning;

(ii) Brushing, selecting, mending;

(iii) Branding, tarring, bundling;

(*b*) the warehousing of, the packing of, and similar operations in regard to sacks or bags of the kind mentioned above when carried on in association with or in conjunction with the making or repairing thereof;

(*c*) the warehousing of, the packing of, and similar operations in regard to any other articles when carried on in or in association with or in conjunction with any business, establishment, branch or department mainly engaged in any of the operations mentioned in paragraph (*b*) above;

excluding:—

(i) any of the operations mentioned above when carried on in association with or in conjunction with the weaving of jute, flax or hemp, or the dyeing, bleaching or finishing of jute, flax or hemp yarn or cloth;

(ii) any of the operations mentioned above when carried on in or in association with or in conjunction with any business, establishment, branch or department mainly engaged in a business in which the sacks or bags are used as containers for other articles the production or sale of which forms part of the business;

(iii) the making of rope-bound coal or coke sacks when carried on in association with or in conjunction with any business, establishment, branch or department engaged in the making of made-up textile articles other than sacks or bags, whether rope-bound or not, of the kind mentioned;

(iv) any of the operations mentioned in paragraph (*b*) above when carried on in or in association with or in conjunction with any business, establishment, branch or department mainly engaged in the warehousing of, the packing of, and similar operations in regard to made-up textile articles other than sacks or bags, whether rope-bound or not, of the kind mentioned;

(v) operations included in the Trade Boards (Waste Materials Reclamation) Order 1920**(b)**.

(a) S.R. & O. 1933/1157 (1933, p. 2052). **(b)** S.R. & O. 1920/305 (1920 II, p. 794).

EXPLANATORY NOTE

(*This Note is not part of the Order.*)

This Order, which has effect from 31st December 1973, sets out the increased statutory minimum remuneration payable to certain female workers in relation to whom the Sack and Bag Wages Council (Great Britain) operates in substitution for that fixed by the Wages Regulation (Sack and Bag) Order 1973 (Order S.B. (75)), which Order is revoked.

New provisions are printed in italics.

1973 No. 1868

FRIENDLY SOCIETIES

The Friendly Societies (Limits of Benefits) Order 1973

Made - - -	8*th November* 1973
Laid before Parliament	15*th November* 1973
Coming into Operation	15*th December* 1973

The Chief Registrar of Friendly Societies, with the consent of the Treasury, pursuant to the powers conferred upon him by paragraph 5(3) of Schedule 8 to the Finance Act 1966(**a**) and to all other powers enabling him in that behalf, hereby makes the following Order:—

1.—(1) This Order may be cited as the Friendly Societies (Limits of Benefits) Order 1973 and shall come into operation on 15th December 1973.

(2) The Interpretation Act 1889(**b**) shall apply to the interpretation of this Order as it applies to the interpretation of an Act of Parliament.

2. The limits in paragraphs (1)(*c*) and (1)(*d*) of paragraph 5 of Schedule 8 of the Finance Act 1966, as increased by the Friendly Societies (Limits of Benefits) Order 1970(**c**), (which govern the amount which members of registered friendly societies and branches may be entitled to receive under life or endowment business which is not tax exempt) shall be further increased as follows:—

(*a*) the limit of £3,500 shall be increased to £5,000;

(*b*) the limit of £5,000 (relating to mortgage protection policies) shall be increased to £7,250;

(*c*) the limit of £350 (relating to annuities) shall be increased to £500.

K. Brading,
Chief Registrar of Friendly Societies.

Dated 8th November 1973.

We consent to this Order.

P. L. Hawkins,
Hugh Rossi,
Two of the Lords Commissioners of Her Majesty's Treasury.

Dated 8th November 1973

(**a**) 1966 c. 18.
(**b**) 1889 c. 63.
(**c**) S.I. 1970/1618 (1970 III, p. 5367).

EXPLANATORY NOTE

(This Note is not part of the Order.)

This Order raises the limits of the amounts which a member of a registered friendly society or branch may be entitled to receive from any one or more of such societies or branches under non tax exempt business. The new limits are (i) £5,000 by way of life or endowment business or £7,250 if the entitlement, so far as it exceeds £5,000, is under any mortgage protection policy or policies and (ii) £500 by way of annuity.

STATUTORY INSTRUMENTS

1973 No. 1879

FAIR TRADING

The Restriction of Merger (No. 4) Order 1973

Made - - -	13*th November* 1973
Laid before Parliament	13*th November* 1973
Coming into Operation	14*th November* 1973

Whereas the Secretary of State in exercise of powers conferred on him by sections 69(2) and 75 of the Fair Trading Act 1973(**a**) has referred to the Monopolies and Mergers Commission for investigation and report the matter of the proposed acquisition by London and County Securities Group Limited of Inveresk Group Limited:

Now, therefore, the Secretary of State with a view to preventing action which may prejudice the reference or impede the taking of any action under the Fair Trading Act 1973 which may be warranted by the Commission's Report on the reference and in exercise of powers conferred on him by section 74(1)(*d*) of, and paragraph 12 of Schedule 8 to, that Act hereby orders as follows:—

1.—(1) This Order may be cited as the Restriction of Merger (No. 4) Order 1973 and shall come into operation on 14th November 1973.

(2) The Interpretation Act 1889(**b**) shall apply to the interpretation of this Order as it applies to the interpretation of an Act of Parliament.

2. It shall be unlawful for London and County Securities Group Limited or any subsidiary thereof to acquire any shares or any interest in shares of Inveresk Group Limited if such acquisition would or might result in London and County Securities Group Limited and Inveresk Group Limited becoming interconnected bodies corporate:

Provided that this Article shall not apply to anything done in pursuance of a legally enforceable agreement to acquire shares made before the commencement of this Order other than an agreement made in pursuance of any general offer addressed to the members of Inveresk Group Limited by London and County Securities Limited on behalf of London and County Securities Group Limited.

Geoffrey Howe,
Minister for Trade and Consumer Affairs,
Department of Trade and Industry.

13th November 1973.

(**a**) 1973 c. 41. (**b**) 1889 c. 63.

EXPLANATORY NOTE

(*This Note is not part of the Order.*)

This Order imposes a standstill on any acquisition by London and County Securities Group Limited or its subsidiaries of shares of Inveresk Group Limited which would or might result in Inveresk Group Limited becoming a subsidiary of London and County Securities Group Limited. The proposed merger of these two companies has been referred to the Monopolies and Mergers Commission.

An exemption is provided for any acquisition of shares in pursuance of an agreement made before the commencement of this Order other than an agreement resulting from a general offer to acquire shares of Inveresk Group Limited made by London and County Securities Limited on behalf of London and County Securities Group Limited.

The Order, unless previously revoked, will cease to have effect—

(*a*) 40 days after the report of the Commission on the proposed merger is laid before Parliament; or

(*b*) on the failure of the Commission to report within the period allowed.

STATUTORY INSTRUMENTS

1973 No. 1880

NORTHERN IRELAND

The Northern Ireland (Emergency Provisions) Act Proscribed Organisations (Amendment) Order 1973

Made - - - -	12*th November* 1973
Laid before Parliament	13*th November* 1973
Coming into Operation	12*th November* 1973

Whereas the Secretary of State may, under section 19(4) of the Northern Ireland (Emergency Provisions) Act 1973(**a**) (hereinafter referred to as " the said Act ") add to Schedule 2 to that Act any organisation that appears to him to be concerned in terrorism or in promoting or encouraging it:

And Whereas it appears to me that by reason of urgency it is necessary to make this Order without a draft thereof having been approved by resolution of each House of Parliament:

Now, therefore, I, the Right Honourable William Whitelaw, M.C., M.P., one of Her Majesty's Principal Secretaries of State, in exercise of the powers conferred upon me by sections 19(4) and 29 of the said Act and all other powers enabling me in that behalf do hereby order as follows:—

1. This Order may be cited as the Northern Ireland (Emergency Provisions) Act Proscribed Organisations (Amendment) Order 1973 and shall come into operation forthwith.

2. In Schedule 2 to the said Act the following organisations shall be added to the list of organisations contained therein:

" Ulster Freedom Fighters
Red Hand Commando ".

Dated this 12th day of November 1973.

W. Whitelaw,
One of Her Majesty's Principal
Secretaries of State.

EXPLANATORY NOTE

(*This Note is not part of the Order.*)

This Order adds the organisations known as the Ulster Freedom Fighters and the Red Hand Commando to the list of proscribed organisations contained in Schedule 2 to the Northern Ireland (Emergency Provisions) Act 1973.

(**a**) 1973 c. 53.

1973 No. 1881

EMERGENCY POWERS

The Emergency Regulations 1973

Made - - - -	*13th November* 1973
Laid before Parliament	*13th November* 1973
Coming into Operation	*14th November* 1973

ARRANGEMENT OF REGULATIONS

At the Court at Buckingham Palace, the 13th day of November 1973

Present,

The Queen's Most Excellent Majesty in Council

Whereas a proclamation of emergency has this day been made under section 1 of the Emergency Powers Act 1920(a), as amended by the Emergency Powers Act 1964(b), and that proclamation is now in force:

Now, therefore, Her Majesty, in pursuance of section 2 of the said Act of 1920, is pleased, by and with the advice of Her Privy Council, to order, and it is hereby ordered, as follows:—

PRELIMINARY

Title and commencement

1. (1) These Regulations may be cited as the Emergency Regulations 1973.

(2) These Regulations shall come into operation on 14th November 1973.

(a) 1920 c. 55. (b) 1964 c. 38.

Interpretation

2.—(1) In these Regulations, except so far as the context otherwise requires, the following expressions have the meanings hereby respectively assigned to them, that is to say:—

"air transport licence" and "air transport service" have the same meanings as in the Civil Aviation Act 1971(**a**);

"animal feeding stuffs" includes any substance used in the composition or preparation of animal feeding stuffs;

"chattel", in relation to Scotland, means corporeal moveable;

"district", in relation to a sewerage authority, includes any area in which the authority exercise functions with respect to the reception of foul or surface water into their sewers;

"Electricity Board" has the same meaning as in the Electricity Act 1947(**b**);

"essential goods" means food, water, fuel, animal feeding stuffs and other necessities;

"essential services" means services essential to the life of the community;

"food" includes any substance used in the composition or preparation of food;

"hovercraft" has the same meaning as in the Hovercraft Act 1968(**c**);

"land" includes (without prejudice to any of the provisions of section 3 of the Interpretation Act 1889(**d**)) parts of houses or buildings;

"liquid fuel" means any liquid used as fuel, whether for the propulsion of vehicles or for industrial, domestic or any other purposes;

"port" includes any dock, harbour, pier, quay, wharf, mooring, anchorage or other similar place;

"port authority" means the authority or person having the control or management of a port;

"regional water board" has the same meaning as in the Water (Scotland) Act 1967(**e**);

"requisition" means, in relation to any chattel, take possession of the chattel or require the chattel to be placed at the disposal of the requisitioning authority;

"river authority" includes—

(*a*) the Conservators of the River Thames,

(*b*) the Lee Conservancy Catchment Board, and

(*c*) the Isle of Wight River and Water Authority;

"sewerage authority" means an authority which is a sewerage authority for the purposes of Part II of the Public Health Act 1936(**f**), the Common Council of the City of London, the council of a county in Scotland, the town council of a burgh, any combination of such county or town councils constituted for the purposes of the provision of sewerage works or sewage disposal services, a development corporation

(**a**) 1971 c. 75. (**b**) 1947 c. 54. (**c**) 1968 c. 59.
(**d**) 1889 c. 63. (**e**) 1967 c. 78. (**f**) 1936 c. 49.

established under the New Towns Act 1946(**a**), the New Towns Act 1965(**b**), or the New Towns (Scotland) Act 1968(**c**), and the Commission for the New Towns;

"solid fuel" means coal, anthracite and coke and other manufactured fuel of which coal or anthracite is the principal constituent;

"statutory water undertakers" has the same meaning as in the provisions of the Water Act 1945(**d**) other than Part II of that Act;

"water development board" has the same meaning as in the Water (Scotland) Act 1967.

(2) The Interpretation Act 1889 shall apply to the interpretation of these Regulations as it applies to the interpertation of an Act of Parliament.

(3) Any reference in these Regulations to the doing of any act shall, unless the context otherwise requires, be construed as including a reference to the making of any statement.

(4) Any reference in these Regulations to any enactment shall, without prejudice to any specific provision in that behalf, be construed as a reference thereto as amended or extended, and as including a reference thereto as applied, by or under any other enactment.

(5) Any reference in any document to these Regulations or to any of them shall, unless the contrary intention appears, be construed as a reference to these Regulations or to that Regulation as amended by any subsequent Regulations made under the Emergency Powers Act 1920.

REGULATION OF PORTS

Control of port traffic

3.—(1) The Secretary of State may, in the case of any port, give such directions to the port authority or any other person as appear to him to be necessary or expedient for securing that the most advantageous use is made in the public interest of the facilities provided at the port, and such directions may, in particular, make provision for excluding or removing from the port ships of any class or a specified ship and for all or any of the following matters, that is to say:—

(*a*) the berthing and movement of ships;

(*b*) the movement and use of tugs, lighters, barges, floating cranes and elevators and other floating apparatus;

(*c*) the loading and unloading of ships and the use of appliances therefor;

(*d*) the movement and use of vehicles;

(*e*) the prevention of entry by unauthorised persons; and

(*f*) in connection with the loading and unloading of ships or the storage and warehousing of goods, the priority that should be given to particular cargoes or to particular operations;

and such directions shall have effect notwithstanding any lease or appropriation of berths and storage or warehouse accommodation.

(2) The Secretary of State may give directions under the foregoing paragraph requiring goods lying at the port to be removed within such period as may be specified in the directions, and, in default of compliance with those directions and without prejudice to the taking of proceedings in

(**a**) 1946 c. 68. (**b**) 1965 c. 59. (**c**) 1968 c. 16. (**d**) 1945 c. 42.

respect of the default, the Secretary of State may remove, or authorise the removal of, the goods to such place, and by such means, as he thinks fit, and the owner or consignee of the goods shall pay to the Secretary of State such reasonable charges in respect of the removal and storage thereof by or on the authority of the Secretary of State as may be agreed or as may, in default of agreement, be determined by arbitration.

(3) All occupiers of public warehouses at or in the neighbourhood of the port shall, if so required by directions given by the Secretary of State, furnish to the Secretary of State from time to time information of vacant accommodation at their warehouses, and shall, to the extent of the accommodation available, accept for storage any goods removed by or on the authority of the Secretary of State under the last foregoing paragraph:

Provided that the Secretary of State shall, in exercising his power to require the storage of goods removed as aforesaid, have regard to the suitability of the accommodation for storing those goods.

(4) The Secretary of State may appoint for any port or group of ports a body of persons, to be known as the Port Emergency Committee for the port or, as the case may be, the group, and may authorise that Committee and persons designated by them for the purpose to exercise on his behalf in relation to the port or, as the case may be, each port comprised in the group all or any of his functions under this Regulation.

(5) Where the Secretary of State appoints a Port Emergency Committee under paragraph (4) of this Regulation, he—

(*a*) may appoint a member of the Committee to be chairman of the Committee, and

(*b*) may give (whether in the instrument of appointment of the Committee or otherwise) any general or special instructions as to the proceedings of the Committee and as to the exercise by the Committee of such of his functions under this Regulation as the Committee are authorised to exercise; and any such Committee, and any person designated by them under that paragraph, shall comply with any instructions of the Secretary of State given under this paragraph.

(6) Paragraphs (1) to (5) of this Regulation shall have effect in relation to hovercraft as they have effect in relation to ships, and any reference in those paragraphs to ships shall be construed accordingly.

Default powers relating to port traffic

4.—(1) Where any directions have been given under paragraph (1) of the foregoing Regulation, other than any such directions as are mentioned in paragraph (2) of that Regulation, and those directions are not complied with within the time specified in the directions or, if no time is so specified, are not complied with within a reasonable time, the Secretary of State may take, or may authorise any other person to take, such steps as the Secretary of State may consider appropriate in the circumstances for effecting anything which would have been effected if the directions had been complied with.

(2) Without prejudice to the generality of the foregoing paragraph, the steps which may be taken by virtue of this Regulation in respect of any directions shall include entering upon, taking possession of, moving or using any ship, hovercraft or other vessel, apparatus, vehicle, premises or other property to which the directions related by such means as the Secretary of State or other person taking those steps may determine to be appropriate.

(3) Where any steps are taken by virtue of this Regulation in respect of any directions, the person to whom the directions were given shall pay to the Secretary of State or other person taking those steps such reasonable charges in respect of expenses incurred by the Secretary of State or person in taking those steps, or in consequence of having taken them, as may be agreed or as may, in default of agreement, be determined by arbitration.

(4) In Part VIII of the Merchant Shipping Act 1894(**a**) (liability of shipowners) " owner ", in relation to any ship, shall be construed as including the Secretary of State or other person by whom any steps are taken in relation to the ship by virtue of this Regulation.

In this paragraph " ship " has the same meaning as in Part VIII of that Act.

(5) The provisions of this Regulation shall have effect without prejudice to any power exercisable by virtue of paragraph (2) or paragraph (3) of the foregoing Regulation ; and the exercise of any power by virtue of this Regulation in respect of any directions shall be without prejudice to the taking of proceedings in respect of any contravention of, or failure to comply with, the directions.

(6) Paragraphs (4) and (5) of the foregoing Regulation shall have effect in relation to functions under this Regulation as they have effect in relation to functions under that Regulation.

Employment in ports

5.—(1) This Regulation shall apply to any port, or part of a port, specified in a direction given by the Secretary of State for Employment and for the time being in force, but not otherwise.

(2) Notwithstanding anything in any dock labour scheme or in section 1 of the Docks and Harbours Act 1966(**b**) (additional control of employment of dock workers), any employer, whether registered under such a scheme or not, and whether he holds a licence under that Act or not, may at any port—

(*a*) employ on dock work any person whom he has been requested by the Secretary of State to employ on such work ;

(*b*) employ any person on any such dock work, or dock work of any such class, as may be approved by the Secretary of State for the purposes of this Regulation ;

and such employment shall not constitute a contravention, either on the part of the employer or of the person employed, of any provision of any dock labour scheme or section 1 of that Act.

(3) Where the Secretary of State gives to an employer notice in writing that this paragraph is to apply to him, all earnings properly due to any person employed by that employer in the circumstances mentioned in sub-paragraph (*a*) of the last foregoing paragraph shall be paid to him by the Secretary of State as agent of the employer, and the employer shall, in such manner and at such time and place as may be directed by the Secretary of State,—

(*a*) furnish a statement of the gross wages (including overtime and allowances and without deductions of any kind) due to that person from the employer and of the period in respect of which they are due ; and

(**a**) 1894 c. 60. (**b**) 1966 c. 28.

(*b*) pay to the Secretary of State the total amount of the gross wages so due, and such further amount, calculated either by way of percentage of the gross wages or otherwise, as the Secretary of State may by notice require as a contribution towards the administrative expenses of the Secretary of State under this Regulation.

(4) If under Regulation 3 of these Regulations the Secretary of State appoints a Port Emergency Committee for a port to which this Regulation applies in whole or in part or for a group of ports of which that port is one, he may authorise that Committee to exercise on his behalf in relation to that port all or any of his functions under this Regulation; and paragraph (5) of that Regulation shall have effect in relation to functions under this Regulation as it has effect in relation to functions under that Regulation.

(5) Where any person employed by the National Dock Labour Board for the purpose of the administration of a dock labour scheme performs services for the Secretary of State or a Port Emergency Committee under this Regulation, the performance of those services shall be deemed to have been authorised by the Board as part of his employment, and the Secretary of State shall pay to the Board such sums as may, in default of agreement, be determined by arbitration in respect of—

(*a*) the remuneration and allowances payable to that person by the Board for the period during which that person performs such services for the Secretary of State or Committee; and

(*b*) the amount of the employer's contribution in respect of that person for that period and in respect of payments of his remuneration for that period.

(6) The Secretary of State, and, if any of his functions under this Regulation are delegated to a Port Emergency Committee for a port or for a group of ports, that Committee, shall be furnished by the National Dock Labour Board with such office accommodation and equipment as appears to the Secretary of State to be requisite for the proper exercise and performance of his functions under this Regulation, and the Secretary of State shall pay to the Board in respect of the use of that accommodation and equipment such sums as may, in default of agreement, be determined by arbitration.

(7) A direction given by the Secretary of State for Employment with respect to any port under paragraph (1) of this Regulation may be revoked by a subsequent direction given by him, and thereupon this Regulation shall cease to apply to that port, without prejudice to the giving of a new direction in relation thereto:

Provided that the revocation of such a direction with respect to any port or part thereof shall not affect the previous operation of this Regulation in relation to that port or part thereof, or the validity of any action taken thereunder, or any penalty or punishment incurred in respect of any contravention or failure to comply therewith, or any proceeding or remedy in respect of any such punishment or penalty.

(8) In this Regulation "dock labour scheme" means a scheme for the time being in force under the Dock Workers (Regulation of Employment)

Act 1946(**a**), "dock work", in relation to a port, means work which is treated for the purposes of a dock labour scheme as dock work at that port, and "the employer's contribution" means the employer's contribution (including any graduated contribution) under the National Insurance Act 1965(**b**), the National Insurance (Industrial Injuries) Act 1965(**c**), the National Health Service Contributions Act 1965(**d**) and section 27 of the Redundancy Payments Act 1965(**e**).

RELAXATION OF RESTRICTIONS AS TO USE OF ROAD VEHICLES

Goods vehicle licences

6. A goods vehicle with respect to which an operator's licence under Part V of the Transport Act 1968(**f**) is required, but no such licence is in force, may, notwithstanding anything in that Act, be used on a road for the carriage of goods for hire or reward, or for or in connection with any trade or business carried on by any person, so long as the use of the vehicle is under, and in accordance with, any general or special authority granted for the purposes of this paragraph by or on behalf of the Secretary of State.

Public service vehicle licences, road service licences, &c.

7.—(1) Notwithstanding anything in section 127 of the Road Traffic Act 1960(**g**), no public service vehicle licence shall be necessary for the use of a motor vehicle on a road as a stage carriage, an express carriage or a contract carriage so long as the use of the vehicle is under, and in accordance with, any general or special authority granted for the purposes of this paragraph by or on behalf of the Secretary of State.

(2) Notwithstanding anything in section 134 of the Road Traffic Act 1960, a vehicle may be used as a stage carriage or an express carriage otherwise than under a road service licence or a permit granted under section 30 of the Transport Act 1968, so long as the use of the vehicle is under, and in accordance with, any general or special authority granted for the purposes of this paragraph by or on behalf of the Secretary of State.

(3) So much of section 101 of the Road Traffic Act 1930(**h**) as requires the consent of a dock authority or a harbour authority to the running by a local authority of a public service vehicle on a road vested in a dock authority or harbour authority shall not apply so long as the running of the vehicle is under, and in accordance with, any general or special authority granted for the purposes of this paragraph by or on behalf of the Secretary of State.

(4) Notwithstanding anything in section 23 of the Transport (London) Act 1969(**i**), a vehicle may be used to provide a London bus service (as defined by subsection (7) of that section) otherwise than in pursuance of an agreement with, or consent granted by, the London Transport Executive, so long as the use of the vehicle is under, and in accordance with, any general or special authority granted for the purposes of this paragraph by or on behalf of the Secretary of State.

(**a**) 1946 c. 22. (**b**) 1965 c. 51. (**c**) 1965 c. 52. (**d**) 1965 c. 54. (**e**) 1965 c. 62.
(**f**) 1968 c. 73. (**g**) 1960 c. 16. (**h**) 1930 c. 43. (**i**) 1969 c. 35.

Other provisions as to road passenger vehicles

8.—(1) Nothing in section 144 of the Road Traffic Act 1960, in section 10 of the London Hackney Carriages Act 1843(**a**), in section 8 of the Metropolitan Public Carriage Act 1869(**b**), in section 48 of the Tramways Act 1870(**c**) or any rules or regulations thereunder, in Schedule 5 to the Burgh Police (Scotland) Act 1892(**d**) or in any local Act or any regulations or other instrument made or issued under any local Act shall apply so as to prevent any person from driving or acting as conductor of a vehicle although he is not licensed for the purpose so long as he is doing so under, and in accordance with, any general or special authority granted for the purposes of this paragraph by or on behalf of the Secretary of State.

(2) Notwithstanding anything in any enactment (whether public general or local) or in any regulations or other instrument made or issued under any enactment (whether public general or local) or in any condition of any road service licence—

(*a*) passengers may be carried (whether standing or otherwise) on any public service vehicle, tramcar or trolley vehicle without limit of number, and

(*b*) any public service vehicle, tramcar or trolley vehicle may be operated without a conductor's being carried thereon,

so long as the carriage of the passengers or, as the case may be, the operation of the vehicle is under, and in accordance with, any general or special authority granted for the purposes of this paragraph by or on behalf of the Secretary of State.

Construction and use regulations

9. Notwithstanding anything in section 40 of the Road Traffic Act 1972(**e**), a person may use on a road, or cause or permit to be so used, a motor vehicle or trailer which does not comply with regulations made or having effect as if made under the said section 40 so long as the use of the vehicle is under, and in accordance with, a special authority granted for the purposes of this Regulation by or on behalf of the Secretary of State.

Test and plating certificates

10.—(1) Notwithstanding anything in section 44 of the Road Traffic Act 1972, a person may use on a road, or cause or permit to be so used, a motor vehicle to which that section applies, and in respect of which no test certificate has been issued as therein mentioned, so long as the use of the vehicle is under, and in accordance with, any general or special authority granted for the purposes of this paragraph by or on behalf of the Secretary of State.

(2) Nothing in regulations made or having effect as if made under section 52(1) of the Road Traffic Act 1972 (which require the production of an effective test certificate or the making of a prescribed declaration on application for a vehicle excise licence for a vehicle) shall apply where the Secretary of State is satisfied that the vehicle is being used, or is to be used, under and in accordance with any general or special authority granted for the purposes of paragraph (1) of this Regulation.

(3) Notwithstanding anything in section 46 of the Road Traffic Act 1972, a person may use on a road, or cause or permit to be so used,—

(*a*) a goods vehicle which is of a class required by regulations under section 45 of that Act to have been submitted for examination for plating, and in respect of which no plating certificate is for the time being in force, or

(**a**) 1843 c. 86. (**b**) 1869 c. 115. (**c**) 1870 c. 78. (**d**) 1892 c. 55. (**e**) 1972 c. 20.

(*b*) a goods vehicle which is of a class required by such regulations to have been submitted for a goods vehicle test, and in respect of which no goods vehicle test certificate is for the time being in force,

so long as (in either case) the use of that vehicle is under, and in accordance with, any general or special authority granted for the purposes of this paragraph by or on behalf of the Secretary of State.

(4) Notwithstanding anything in section 51 of the Road Traffic Act 1972, a person may use a goods vehicle on a road for drawing a trailer, or cause or permit a goods vehicle to be so used, where the plating certificate issued for the goods vehicle does not specify a maximum laden weight for the vehicle together with any trailer which may be drawn by it, so long as the use of the vehicle for drawing the trailer is under, and in accordance with, any general or special authority granted for the purposes of this paragraph by or on behalf of the Secretary of State.

(5) Nothing in regulations made or having effect as if made under section 52(2) of the Road Traffic Act 1972 (which require the production of an effective goods vehicle test certificate, or a certificate of temporary exemption, or the making of a prescribed declaration, on application for a vehicle excise licence for a vehicle) shall apply where the Secretary of State is satisfied that the vehicle is being used, or is to be used, under and in accordance with any general or special authority granted for the purposes of paragraph (3) of this Regulation.

(6) Section 162(1) of the Road Traffic Act 1972 (which imposes requirements with respect to the production of certain documents) shall not, so far as it relates to the production of a test certificate, a plating certificate or a goods vehicle test certificate, apply in the case of a motor vehicle used under, and in accordance with, any general or special authority granted under this Regulation.

(7) In this Regulation " test certificate " has the meaning assigned to it by section 43(2) of the Road Traffic Act 1972, and " plating certificate " and " goods vehicle test certificate " have the meanings assigned to them by section 45(1) of that Act.

Drivers' hours

11.—(1) Nothing in subsections (1) to (6) of section 96 of the Transport Act 1968 (which relate to a driver's permitted hours and periods of duty and rest) shall apply to a driver so long as he is acting under, and in accordance with, any general or special authority granted for the purposes of this paragraph by or on behalf of the Secretary of State.

(2) Nothing in regulations under section 98 of the said Act—

(*a*) which concerns the entering of a current record in a driver's record book, or

(*b*) which requires a driver to have such a book in his possession,

shall apply to a driver so long as he is acting under, and in accordance with, any general or special authority granted for the purposes of this paragraph by or on behalf of the Secretary of State.

(3) An authority under paragraph (1) or paragraph (2) above may, instead of conferring all of the exemptions specified in the paragraph, confer only such exemptions as are specified in the authority.

Drivers' licences

12.—(1) Notwithstanding anything in section 4 of the Road Traffic Act 1972 or in Part III or Part IV of that Act, a person who holds a valid licence granted under Part III of that Act authorising him to drive a motor car may drive on a road, and may be employed by another person so to drive, a vehicle to which this Regulation applies, so long as he drives it under, and in accordance with, a general or special authority granted for the purposes of this Regulation by or on behalf of the Secretary of State.

(2) The vehicles to which this Regulation applies are—

(*a*) heavy locomotives ;

(*b*) light locomotives ;

(*c*) motor tractors ;

(*d*) heavy motor cars ; and

(*e*) motor cars so constructed that a trailer may by partial superimposition be attached thereto in such a manner as to cause a substantial part of the weight of the trailer to be borne thereby.

(3) So much of any regulations for the time being in force and having effect as if made under section 119 of the Road Traffic Act 1972 as requires any person, or enables any person to be required, to produce a heavy goods vehicle driver's licence shall not apply in the case of a vehicle driven under, and in accordance with, any general or special authority granted under this Regulation.

(4) In this Regulation " heavy goods vehicle driver's licence " means a licence under Part IV of the Road Traffic Act 1972, and any expression which is defined in section 190 of that Act has the meaning assigned to it by that section.

Excise licences

13.—(1) Notwithstanding anything in the Vehicles (Excise) Act 1971(**a**), a person may use or keep on a public road a mechanically propelled vehicle without there being in force and fixed to and exhibited on that vehicle a licence issued under that Act for or in respect of the use of that vehicle, so long as the use or keeping of the vehicle is under, and in accordance with, any general or special authority granted for the purposes of this paragraph by or on behalf of the Secretary of State.

(2) Where an excise licence issued or having effect under the Vehicles (Excise) Act 1971 is in force with respect to any mechanically propelled vehicle, the uses of that vehicle which are authorised by the licence shall be deemed to extend to any use made of the vehicle under, and in accordance with, any general or special authority granted for the purposes of this paragraph by or on behalf of the Secretary of State, and the provisions of section 18 of that Act shall not apply to any use of any vehicle in respect of which such a licence is in force so long as that use of that vehicle is under, and in accordance with, any such general or special authority.

Third-party insurance

14.—(1) Notwithstanding anything in section 143(1) of the Road Traffic Act 1972, a person may use, or cause or permit another person to use, a motor vehicle on a road without there being in force in relation to the use thereof by that person or that other person, as the case may be, a policy of insurance or security in respect of third-party risks issued or given for the purposes of Part VI of that Act so long as—

(*a*) there is in force in relation to some other use of the vehicle a policy of insurance or security issued or given for those purposes and the use of the vehicle by that person or that other person, as the case may be,—

(**a**) 1971 c. 10.

(i) is one to which, as respects the period of the emergency, the policy or security is, by arrangement between the Secretary of State and the issuer or giver of the policy or security or some person acting on his behalf, treated as also relating, and

(ii) is under, and in accordance with, any general or special authority granted for the purposes of this paragraph by or on behalf of the Secretary of State ; or

(*b*) the use of the vehicle by that person or that other person, as the case may be, is under, and in accordance with, any such general or special authority and there is in force in relation to the use of the vehicle such an agreement to insure or make good failures to discharge liability in respect of third-party risks as may be specified in the authority ;

and sections 162(1) and 166(1) of the said Act of 1972 (which impose requirements with respect to the furnishing of the names and addresses of the driver and the owner of a motor vehicle and to the production of certificates of insurance or security) shall not, so far as they relate to the production of such certificates, apply in the case of a motor vehicle driven under, and in accordance with, any such general or special authority.

(2) So much of any regulations made or having effect as if made by virtue of section 153 of the Road Traffic Act 1972 as, on an application for a vehicle excise licence requires the production of a certificate of insurance, or evidence that the necessary security has been given or that the vehicle is exempt from the provisions of section 143 of the said Act, shall not apply where the Secretary of State is satisfied that the vehicle is being used, or is to be used, under, and in accordance with, any general or special authority granted for the purposes of paragraph (1) of this Regulation.

Transport of petroleum-spirit and other substances

15.—(1) Regulations made under section 6 of the Petroleum (Consolidation) Act 1928(a) (regulations as to the conveyance of petroleum-spirit by road) shall not have effect in relation to any vehicle, so long as the use of the vehicle is under, and in accordance with, any general or special authority granted for the purposes of this paragraph by or on behalf of the Secretary of State.

(2) Without prejudice to the foregoing paragraph, regulations made under that section, in so far as they are made for any of the purposes specified in subsection (1)(*d*) of that section, shall not have effect in relation to the loading or unloading of vehicles at any place, so long as that place is used under, and in accordance with, any general or special authority granted for the purposes of this paragraph by or on behalf of the Secretary of State.

(3) In this Regulation any reference to section 6 of the Petroleum (Consolidation) Act 1928 shall be construed as including a reference to that section as read with section 19 of that Act (which confers power to apply the Act to substances other than petroleum-spirit) and any Order in Council made thereunder which is for the time being in force, and any reference in this Regulation to regulations under section 6 of that Act shall be construed accordingly.

PUBLIC SERVICES AND FACILITIES

Transport services and facilities

16. The British Railways Board and the London Transport Executive may respectively, to such extent as appears to them to be necessary or expedient for providing or maintaining railway services and facilities in a manner

(a) 1928 c. 32.

best calculated to promote the public interest, disregard any obligation imposed by or under any enactment—

(*a*) to carry goods or passengers or to provide transport services or facilities ;

(*b*) to employ or provide a person for any particular purpose or to perform any particular duty ; or

(*c*) to keep gates on a level crossing over a public road closed across the road ;

so long as, in so doing, they are acting under, and in accordance with, any general or special authority granted for the purposes of this Regulation by or on behalf of the Secretary of State.

Electricity supply

17.—(1) Any Electricity Board may, to such extent as appears to them to be necessary or expedient for maintaining or making the best use of supplies of electricity available for distribution or for conserving and making the best use of supplies of fuel or power available for the generation of electricity, disregard or fall short in discharging any obligation imposed by or under any enactment, or any contractual obligation—

(*a*) to give or continue to give supplies of electricity ; or

(*b*) to supply electricity in accordance with standards prescribed by or under the enactment or contract in question ;

so long as, in so doing, they are acting under, and in accordance with, any general or special authority granted for the purposes of this Regulation by or on behalf of the Secretary of State.

(2) If and so far as it appears to the Secretary of State necessary or expedient for maintaining or making the best use of supplies of electricity available for distribution—

(*a*) he may give to the person carrying on business at, or appearing to be in charge of, or occupying, any premises, directions for regulating or prohibiting consumption of electricity on the premises ; and

(*b*) he may take, or authorise any person acting on his behalf to take, such steps as appear appropriate to cut off any supply of electricity.

(3) Without prejudice to the generality of the provisions of Regulation 40(2) below, the power of giving directions conferred by paragraph (2)(*a*) above may be exercised by means of an order—

(*a*) applicable to premises of any class or description specified in the order, or premises used for purposes of any class or description specified in the order, or

(*b*) where previous directions have been given otherwise than by order, applicable to the persons or premises as respects which the previous directions had effect, or such of them as may be specified in the order.

(4) If any person, without authority duly given by or on behalf of the Secretary of State, reconnects a supply cut off in pursuance of this Regulation, he shall be guilty of an offence against this Regulation.

(5) The Secretary of State may authorise any person acting on his behalf to enter any premises, if necessary by force, for the purpose—

(*a*) of ascertaining whether there has been any contravention of a direction under this Regulation, or

(*b*) of cutting off any supply of electricity in pursuance of this Regulation, or of ascertaining whether it remains duly cut off.

(6) The provisions of this Regulation are without prejudice to the generality of Regulation 21 below (regulation of consumption and supply of electricity and other products).

(7) The powers of the Secretary of State under paragraph (2) of this Regulation shall also be exercisable by such persons, being either servants of the Crown or persons acting on behalf of Her Majesty, as may be designated for the purposes of that paragraph by the Secretary of State, and references in that paragraph to the Secretary of State shall be construed accordingly.

Gas supply

18.—(1) The British Gas Corporation may, to such extent as appears to them to be necessary or expedient—

(*a*) for maintaining or making the best use of supplies of gas available for distribution ; or

(*b*) for conserving and making the best use of supplies of fuel or other material available for the manufacture of gas ; or

(*c*) for preserving public safety ;

disregard or fall short in discharging any obligation imposed by or under any enactment, or any contractual obligation—

(i) to give or continue to give supplies of gas ; or

(ii) to supply, transmit or distribute gas in accordance with standards prescribed by or under the enactment or contract in question ;

so long as, in so doing, they are acting under, and in accordance with, any general or special authority granted for the purposes of this paragraph by or on behalf of the Secretary of State.

(2) If and so far as it appears to the Secretary of State necessary or expedient for any of the purposes set out in sub-paragraphs (*a*), (*b*) and (*c*) of paragraph (1) above—

(*a*) he may give to the person carrying on business at, or appearing to be in charge of, or occupying, any premises, directions for regulating or prohibiting the consumption of gas on the premises ; and

(*b*) he may take, or authorise any person acting on his behalf to take, such steps as appear appropriate to cut off any supply, or means of supply, of gas by disconnecting any service pipe or by any other means.

(3) If any person, without authority duly given by or on behalf of the Secretary of State, reconnects a supply, or means of supply, cut off in pursuance of this Regulation, he shall be guilty of an offence against this Regulation.

(4) The Secretary of State may authorise any person acting on his behalf to enter any premises, if necessary by force, for the purpose—

(*a*) of ascertaining whether there has been any contravention of a direction under this Regulation,

(*b*) of cutting off any supply, or means of supply, of gas in pursuance of this Regulation, or of ascertaining whether it remains duly cut off, or

(*c*) of inspecting, examining or testing any plant or equipment for the supply or consumption of gas with a view to ensuring the preservation of public safety.

(5) The provisions of this Regulation are without prejudice to the generality of Regulation 21 below (regulation of consumption and supply of gas and other products).

(6) The powers of the Secretary of State under paragraphs (2) to (4) above shall also be exercisable by such persons, being either servants of the Crown or persons acting on behalf of Her Majesty, as may be designated for the purposes of those paragraphs by the Secretary of State, and references in those paragraphs to the Secretary of State shall be construed accordingly.

Water supply and resources

19.—(1) Any statutory water undertakers, regional water board or water development board may, for the purpose of maintaining supplies of water in any locality, disregard any restriction imposed by or under any enactment or rule of law with respect to the taking of water from any source or any obligation so imposed with respect to the discharge of compensation water, and may for that purpose take water from any source, so long as, in either case, in so doing, they are acting under, and in accordance with, any general or special authority granted for the purposes of this paragraph by or on behalf of the Secretary of State.

(2) Any statutory water undertakers, regional water board or water development board may, to such extent as appears to them to be necessary or expedient for conserving and making the best use of supplies of water in any locality, disregard or fall short in discharging any obligation imposed by or under any enactment or rule of law with respect to the provision by them of supplies of water (including, in particular, but without prejudice to the generality of the foregoing words, any obligation with respect to the filtration or other treatment of water or the pressure at which water is to be supplied) so long as, in so doing, they are acting under, and in accordance with, any general or special authority granted for the purposes of this paragraph by or on behalf of the Secretary of State.

(3) In the exercise of their new functions under the Water Resources Act 1963(a), any river authority may, for the purpose of maintaining supplies of water in any locality, disregard any restriction or obligation imposed by or under any enactment or rule of law with respect to—

(*a*) the taking or impounding of water from any source,

(*b*) the discharge of water into any inland water or underground strata, or

(*c*) in connection with their functions, the construction or alteration of any works,

and may for that purpose take or impound water from any source, or discharge water into any inland water or underground strata ; but the powers conferred by this paragraph shall only be exercisable so long as in exercising them the authority are acting under, and in accordance with, any general or special authority granted for the purposes of this paragraph by or on behalf of the Secretary of State.

(4) The Secretary of State may give any river authority, statutory water undertakers, regional water board or water development board or any other person managing an undertaking or business which is directly or indirectly concerned with the supply, abstraction or impounding of water such directions as appear to him to be necessary or expedient for maintaining and making the best use in the public interest of supplies of water, and, without prejudice to the generality of the foregoing, directions under this paragraph may—

(*a*) require the provision or continued provision, or regulate or prohibit the provision, of supplies of water by any such person to any person or class of persons specified in the directions ;

(*b*) require, regulate or prohibit the carrying out of any works or class of works so specified, either generally or during or within a time so specified.

(5) Where any directions have been given under paragraph (4) above and those directions are not complied with within the time specified in the directions or, if no time is so specified, are not complied with within a reasonable

(a) 1963 c. 38.

time, the Secretary of State may take such steps as he considers appropriate in the circumstances for effecting anything which would have been effected if the directions had been complied with.

(6) Without prejudice to the generality of paragraph (5) above, the steps which may be taken by virtue of that paragraph in respect of any directions shall include entering upon, taking possession of, moving or using any apparatus, vehicle, premises or other property to which the directions related by such means as the Secretary of State determines to be appropriate.

(7) Where any steps are taken by virtue of paragraph (5) or (6) above in respect of any directions, the Secretary of State may recover from the person to whom the directions were given such reasonable charges in respect of expenses incurred by him in taking those steps, or in consequence of having taken them, as may be agreed or as may, in default of agreement, be determined by arbitration.

(8) The powers of the Secretary of State under paragraphs (4) to (7) above shall also be exercisable by such persons, being either servants of the Crown or persons acting on behalf of Her Majesty, as may be designated for the purposes of those paragraphs by the Secretary of State, and references in these paragraphs to the Secretary of State shall be construed accordingly.

Sewerage and sewage disposal

20.—(1) Any sewerage authority may, for the purpose of effectively draining their district and dealing with the contents of their sewers, disregard any prohibition or restriction imposed by or under any enactment or rule of law with respect to the discharge of foul or surface water into any natural or artificial stream, watercourse, canal, pond or lake, so long as, in so doing, they are acting under, and in accordance with, any general or special authority granted for the purposes of this Regulation by or on behalf of the Secretary of State.

(2) The Secretary of State may give any sewerage authority or any other person managing an undertaking or business which is directly or indirectly concerned in sewerage or sewage disposal in a sewerage authority's district such directions as appear to him to be necessary or expedient for securing the most effective draining of the sewerage authority's district or of dealing with the contents of the sewers there and, without prejudice to the generality of the foregoing, directions under this paragraph may require, regulate or prohibit the carrying out of any works or class of works specified in the directions, either generally or during or within a time so specified.

(3) Where any directions have been given under paragraph (2) above and those directions are not complied with within the time specified in the directions or, if no time is so specified, are not complied with within a reasonable time, the Secretary of State may take such steps as he considers appropriate in the circumstances for effecting anything which would have been effected if the directions had been complied with.

(4) Without prejudice to the generality of paragraph (3) above, the steps which may be taken by virtue of that paragraph in respect of any directions shall include entering upon, taking possession of, moving or using any ship or other vessel, apparatus, vehicle, premises or other property to which the directions related by such means as the Secretary of State determines to be appropriate.

(5) Where any steps are taken by virtue of paragraph (3) or (4) above in respect of any directions, the Secretary of State may recover from the person to whom the directions were given such reasonable charges in respect of

expenses incurred by him in taking those steps, or in consequence of having taken them, as may be agreed or as may, in default of agreement, be determined by arbitration.

(6) The powers of the Secretary of State under paragraphs (2) to (5) above shall also be exercisable by such persons, being either servants of the Crown or persons acting on behalf of Her Majesty, as may be designated for the purposes of those paragraphs by the Secretary of State, and references in those paragraphs to the Secretary of State shall be construed accordingly.

(7) In Part VIII of the Merchant Shipping Act 1894 (liability of ship-owners) " owner ", in relation to any ship, shall be construed as including the Secretary of State or other person by whom any steps are taken in relation to the ship by virtue of paragraphs (3) to (6) above.

In this paragraph " ship " has the same meaning as in Part VIII of that Act.

CONSUMPTION AND SUPPLY

Supply, &c., of fuel, refinery products, electricity, gas and water

21.—(1) The Secretary of State may by order provide for regulating or prohibiting—

(*a*) the supply, acquisition or consumption of solid or liquid fuel or refinery products ;

(*b*) the supply or consumption of electricity or gas ; or

(*c*) the supply, acquisition, abstraction, impounding or consumption of water.

(2) References in this Regulation to consumption are references to consumption for any purposes whatsoever, whether domestic, industrial or other.

Directions as to solid or liquid fuel or refinery products

22.—(1) The Secretary of State—

(*a*) may give to any person carrying on business as a supplier of liquid fuel or as a supplier of solid fuel directions as to the supply by him of any such solid or liquid fuel as may be specified in the directions, and

(*b*) may give to any person carrying on business as a refiner of liquid fuel directions as to the production of any liquid fuel, or other refinery products, or as to the use, disposal or supply of any refinery products, including those forming part of any stock held by him for the purposes of his business.

(2) Directions under paragraph (1) of this Regulation may in particular—

(*a*) require any fuel or refinery product to be supplied, in accordance with such requirements as may be specified in the directions, to such persons as may be so specified, or

(*b*) prohibit or restrict the supply of any fuel or refinery product to persons so specified, or to persons other than those to be supplied in accordance with the directions,

and directions may be given under paragraph (1)(*b*) of this Regulation for securing that the liquid fuel produced is, or is to any extent, of a description specified in the direction.

(3) Where any fuel or refinery product is supplied to any person in pursuance of a direction under this Regulation, that person shall pay such price in respect thereof as may be reasonable.

(4) The foregoing provisions of this Regulation shall apply in relation to any person carrying on a trade or business (otherwise than as a supplier of fuel) for the purposes of which he is in possession of a stock of solid fuel, as if, in respect of that fuel, he were carrying on business as such a supplier; and any directions to such a person under this Regulation may include directions prohibiting the consumption of such fuel by him:

Provided that in relation to any such person any reference in this Regulation to supply shall be construed as a reference to delivery at the place where the fuel is kept.

Maximum prices for food and animal feeding stuffs

23. The Minister of Agriculture, Fisheries and Food may by order provide for regulating, to such extent and in such manner as may be specified in the order, the maximum prices which may be charged for such foods or animal feeding stuffs as may be so specified.

Distribution of food and animal feeding stuffs

24.—(1) The Minister of Agriculture, Fisheries and Food may give to any person carrying on business as a supplier of food or animal feeding stuffs directions as to the persons to whom he is to supply any such food or animal feeding stuffs as may be specified in the directions; and any such directions may in particular require any food or animal feeding stuffs to be supplied to such persons as may be specified in the directions in accordance with such requirements as may be so specified or may, to such extent as may be specified in the directions, prohibit the supply of food or animal feeding stuffs to persons so specified.

(2) Where anything is supplied to any person in pursuance of directions under this Regulation, that person shall pay such price in respect thereof as may be reasonable.

Supply of medicines

25.—(1) The restrictions and prohibitions imposed by or under the following provisions of the Medicines Act 1968(**a**), that is to say—

(*a*) Part II (licences and certificates relating to medicinal products),

(*b*) Part III (dealings with medicinal products), and

(*c*) Part V (containers, packages and identification of medicinal products),

shall not apply to a person so long as he is acting under, and in accordance with, any general or special authority granted for the purposes of this paragraph by or on behalf of the Secretary of State, or the Minister of Agriculture, Fisheries and Food.

(2) Nothing in any regulations made, or having effect, under the Medicines Act 1971(**b**) shall require the payment of a fee on an application made under, and in accordance with, any general or special authority granted for the purposes of this paragraph by or on behalf of the Secretary of State, or the Minister of Agriculture, Fisheries and Food.

(3) An authority under paragraph (1) above may, instead of conferring exemptions from all the restrictions and prohibitions specified in the paragraph, confer only such exemptions as are specified in the authority.

(**a**) 1968 c. 67. (**b**) 1971 c. 69.

REGULATION OF TRANSPORT SERVICES

Transport of goods by road or rail

26.—(1) The Secretary of State may give to any person carrying on business as a carrier of goods by road or by rail for hire or reward directions as to the goods which are to be carried by him ; and any such directions may in particular require any essential goods to be carried for such persons, from and to such places, and in accordance with such requirements, as may be specified in the directions or may, to such extent as may be so specified, prohibit the carriage of goods for persons, or from or to places, so specified.

(2) Where in pursuance of directions given under this Regulation any goods are carried for the benefit of any person, that person shall pay such charge in respect of the carriage as may be reasonable.

(3) The powers of the Secretary of State under this Regulation shall also be exercisable by such persons, being either servants of the Crown or persons acting on behalf of Her Majesty, as may be designated for the purposes of this Regulation by the Secretary of State.

(4) The foregoing provisions of this Regulation shall apply in relation to any person carrying on a trade or business (otherwise than as a carrier of goods by road for hire or reward) for or in connection with which he uses any goods vehicles, as if, in respect of those vehicles, he were carrying on business as such a carrier of goods ; and any directions to such a person under this Regulation may include directions prohibiting the carriage of goods in the course of his own trade or business.

Transport of passengers by road or rail

27.—(1) The Secretary of State may give to any person carrying on the business of operating public service vehicles directions as to the passengers who are to be carried, or the road services which are to be provided, by him ; and any such directions may in particular require persons to be carried from and to places specified in the directions or may, to such extent as may be so specified, prohibit the carriage of persons from or to places so specified and may also specify requirements in accordance with which passengers are to be carried or, as the case may be, road services are to be provided.

(2) The Secretary of State may give to any person carrying on business as a carrier of passengers by rail directions as to the passengers who are to be carried by him, and any such directions may in particular require persons to be carried from and to places specified in the directions or may, to such extent as may be so specified, prohibit the carriage of persons from or to places so specified.

(3) Where in pursuance of directions given under this Regulation any passengers are carried for the benefit of any other person otherwise than at separate fares, that person shall pay such charge in respect of the carriage as may be reasonable.

(4) The powers of the Secretary of State under this Regulation shall also be exercisable by such persons, being either servants of the Crown or persons acting on behalf of Her Majesty, as may be designated for the purposes of this Regulation by the Secretary of State.

(5) The reference in this Regulation to public service vehicles shall be construed in accordance with sections 117 and 118 of the Road Traffic Act 1960.

Air transport

28.—(1) The Secretary of State may give to any person providing air transport services (being a person whose sole or principal place of business is in Great Britain) directions as to the passengers or cargo which are to be carried by him ; and any such directions in particular—

(*a*) may require any persons engaged in the performance of essential services to be carried from and to such places, and in accordance with such requirements, as may be specified in the directions or may, to such extent as may be so specified, prohibit the carriage of passengers from or to places so specified ;

(*b*) may require any essential goods to be carried for such persons, from and to such places, and in accordance with such requirements, as may be so specified or may, to such extent as may be so specified, prohibit the carriage of goods for persons, or from or to places, so specified.

(2) No air transport licence shall be required for a flight undertaken for the purpose of complying with directions given under this Regulation.

(3) Where in pursuance of directions given under this Regulation any passenger is carried, he (or, if he is carried for the benefit of any other person, that person) shall pay such charge in respect of the carriage as may be reasonable ; and where in pursuance of any such directions any goods are carried for the benefit of any person, that person shall pay such charge in respect of the carriage as may be reasonable.

(4) The powers of the Secretary of State under this Regulation shall also be exercisable by such persons, being either servants of the Crown or persons acting on behalf of Her Majesty, as may be designated for the purposes of this Regulation by the Secretary of State.

Transport by sea

29.—(1) The Secretary of State may give to any person having the management of a ship to which this Regulation applies (being a person in Great Britain or a person whose sole or principal place of business is in Great Britain) directions prohibiting that ship from proceeding to sea from any port in Great Britain except upon such voyages, or subject to such conditions as to the cargoes or classes of cargoes which may be carried in the ship, or as to the passengers who may be so carried, as may be specified in the directions.

(2) This Regulation applies to any ship registered in the United Kingdom, the Channel Islands or the Isle of Man.

(3) The powers of the Secretary of State under this Regulation shall also be exercisable by such persons, being either servants of the Crown or persons acting on behalf of Her Majesty, as may be designated for the purposes of this Regulation by the Secretary of State.

REQUISITIONING OF CHATTELS AND TAKING POSSESSION OF LAND

Requisitioning of chattels

30.—(1) A competent authority, if it appears to that authority to be necessary or expedient so to do for any of the purposes specified in section 2(1) of the Emergency Powers Act 1920, may requisition any chattel in Great Britain (including any vehicle, vessel or aircraft or anything on board a vehicle, vessel or aircraft and including also any detachable part of any vehicle or aircraft) and may give such directions as appear to the competent authority to be necessary or expedient in connection with the requisition.

(2) Where a competent authority requisitions any chattel under this Regulation, the competent authority may use or deal with, or authorise the use of, or dealing with, the chattel for such purpose and in such manner as the competent authority thinks expedient for any of the purposes specified in the said section 2(1) and may hold, or sell or otherwise dispose of, the chattel as if the competent authority were the owner thereof and as if the chattel were free from any mortgage, pledge, lien or other similar obligation.

(3) The powers conferred by the foregoing provisions of this Regulation on a competent authority shall also be exercisable by such persons, being either servants of the Crown or persons acting on behalf of Her Majesty, as may be designated for the purposes of those provisions by the competent authority, and references in those provisions to the competent authority shall be construed accordingly.

(4) Where a chattel is requisitioned under this Regulation, the competent authority shall pay to the owner of the chattel and to any other person interested in the chattel who suffers damage owing to the requisition such compensation as may be agreed or as may, in default of agreement, be determined by arbitration to be just having regard to all the circumstances of the particular case, so, however, that in assessing the compensation no account shall be taken of any appreciation of the value of the chattel due to the emergency.

(5) For the purposes of this Regulation, any of the following Ministers and authorities shall be a competent authority, that is to say, the Secretary of State, the Minister of Agriculture, Fisheries and Food and the Minister of Posts and Telecommunications.

Taking possession of land

31.—(1) The Secretary of State, if it appears to him to be necessary or expedient so to do for any of the purposes specified in section 2(1) of the Emergency Powers Act 1920, may take possession of any land in Great Britain, and may give such directions as appear to him to be necessary or expedient in connection with the taking of possession of that land.

(2) While any land is in the possession of the Secretary of State by virtue of this Regulation, the land may, notwithstanding any restriction imposed on the use thereof (whether by any Act or other instrument or otherwise), be used by, or under the authority of, the Secretary of State for such purpose, and in such manner, as he thinks expedient for any of the purposes specified in the said section 2(1).

(3) Without prejudice to the last foregoing paragraph, the Secretary of State may, so far as appears to him to be necessary or expedient in connection with the taking of possession of any land in pursuance of this Regulation, or with the use of any land in the possession of the Secretary of State by virtue of this Regulation, do, or authorise persons using the land under the authority of the Secretary of State to do, in relation to the land anything which any person having an interest in the land would be entitled to do by virtue of that interest.

(4) In respect of land of which possession is taken under this Regulation, the Secretary of State shall pay to the person who would otherwise be entitled to possession of the land, and to any other person having an estate or interest in the land who suffers damage by reason of the taking of possession or of anything done in relation to the land while in the possession of the Secretary of State, such compensation as may be agreed or as may, in default of agreement, be determined by arbitration to be just having regard to all the circumstances of the particular case.

OFFENCES

Sabotage

32.—(1) No person shall do any act with intent to impair the efficiency or impede the working or movement of any vessel, aircraft, hovercraft, vehicle, machinery, apparatus or other thing used or intended to be used in the performance of essential services, or to impair the usefulness of any works, structure or premises used or intended to be used as aforesaid.

(2) The foregoing provisions of this Regulation shall apply in relation to any omission on the part of a person to do anything which he is under a duty, either to the public or to any person, to do, as they apply in relation to the doing of any act by a person.

Trespassing and loitering

33.—(1) No person shall trespass on, or on premises in the vicinity of, any premises used or appropriated for the purposes of essential services; and if any person is found trespassing on any premises in contravention of this paragraph, then, without prejudice to any proceedings which may be taken against him, he may be removed by the appropriate person from the premises.

(2) No person shall, for any purpose prejudicial to the public safety, be in, or in the vicinity of, any premises used or appropriated for the purposes of essential services; and where, in any proceedings taken against a person by virtue of this paragraph, it is proved that at the material time he was present in, or in the vicinity of, the premises concerned, the prosecution may thereupon adduce such evidence of the character of that person (including evidence of his having been previously convicted of any offence) as tends to show that he was so present for a purpose prejudicial to the public safety.

(3) No person loitering in the vicinity of any premises used or appropriated for the purposes of essential services shall continue to loiter in that vicinity after being requested by the appropriate person to leave it.

(4) In this Regulation the expression "the appropriate person" means—

(*a*) any person acting on behalf of Her Majesty,

(*b*) any constable,

(*c*) the occupier of the premises or any person authorised by the occupier.

Interference with Her Majesty's forces, constables and other persons performing essential services

34.—(1) No person shall do any act having reasonable cause to believe that it would be likely to endanger the safety of any member of Her Majesty's forces or of any constable or of any person who is charged with the exercise or performance of any power or duty under any of these Regulations or is performing essential services.

(2) No person shall—

(*a*) wilfully obstruct any person acting in the course of his duty as a constable, or exercising or performing any power or duty under any of these Regulations, or performing essential services; or

(*b*) do any act having reasonable cause to believe that it would be likely to prevent any person from, or mislead or interfere with any person in, performing his duty as a constable, or exercising or performing any power or duty under any of these Regulations, or performing essential services.

Inducing persons to withhold services

35. No person shall—

(*a*) do any act calculated to induce any member of Her Majesty's forces or constable to withhold his services or commit breaches of discipline; or

(*b*) with intent to contravene, or to aid, abet, counsel or procure a contravention of, paragraph (*a*) of this Regulation, have in his possession or under his control any document of such a nature that the dissemination of copies thereof among members of Her Majesty's forces or constables would constitute such a contravention.

SUPPLEMENTAL

Power to arrest without warrant

36. Where a constable, with reasonable cause, suspects that an offence against any of these Regulations has been committed, he may arrest without warrant anyone whom he, with reasonable cause, suspects to be guilty of the offence.

Attempts to commit offences and assisting offenders

37.—(1) Without prejudice to the operation of section 8 of the Accessories and Abettors Act 1861(**a**) and section 35 of the Magistrates' Courts Act 1952(**b**), any person who attempts to commit, conspires with any other person to commit, or does any act preparatory to the commission of, an offence against any of these Regulations shall be guilty of an offence against that Regulation.

(2) Any person who, knowing or having reasonable cause to believe that another person is guilty of an offence against any of these Regulations, gives that other person any assistance with intent thereby to prevent, hinder or interfere with the apprehension, trial or punishment of that person for the said offence shall be guilty of an offence against that Regulation.

(3) This Regulation shall, in its application to Scotland, have effect as if, for the references to section 8 of the Accessories and Abettors Act 1861 and section 35 of the Magistrates' Courts Act 1952, there were substituted a reference to any rule of law relating to art and part guilt.

Penalties and place of trial

38.—(1) If any person contravenes or fails to comply with any of these Regulations or any order made, direction given or requirement imposed under any of these Regulations, he shall be guilty of an offence against that Regulation; and a person guilty of an offence against any of these Regulations shall, on summary conviction, be liable to imprisonment for a term not exceeding three months or to a fine not exceeding £100, or to both:

Provided that a person shall not be guilty of an offence against any of these Regulations by reason only of his taking part in, or peacefully persuading any other person or persons to take part in, a strike.

(2) Proceedings in respect of an offence alleged to have been committed by a person against any of these Regulations may be taken before the appropriate court in Great Britain having jurisdiction in the place where that person is for the time being.

(**a**) 1861 c. 94. (**b**) 1952 c. 55.

Arbitrations

39. An arbitration under these Regulations shall, unless otherwise agreed, be the arbitration, in England and Wales, of a single arbitrator to be appointed by the Lord Chancellor and, in Scotland, of a single arbiter to be appointed by the Lord President of the Court of Session.

Provisions as to orders and directions

40.—(1) Any power conferred by these Regulations to make an order includes power to revoke or vary the order by a subsequent order.

(2) Any power of giving directions conferred by any provision of these Regulations may be exercised by means of an order applicable to all persons to whom directions may be given under that provision, or to such of them as fall within any class or description specified in the order.

W. G. Agnew.

1973 No. 1882

VALUE ADDED TAX

The Value Added Tax (General) (Amendment) (No. 2) Regulations 1973

Made - - - -	12*th November* 1973
Laid before the House of Commons -	20*th November* 1973
Coming into Operation	11*th December* 1973

The Commissioners of Customs and Excise, in exercise of the powers conferred on them by sections 3(4) and (5), 12(7) and 33(3) and (4) of the Finance Act, 1972**(a)** and of all other powers enabling them in that behalf, hereby make the following Regulations:—

1. These Regulations may be cited as the Value Added Tax (General) (Amendment) (No. 2) Regulations 1973 and shall come into operation on 11th December 1973.

2.—(1) In these Regulations "the Principal Regulations" means the Value Added Tax (General) Regulations 1972**(b)**.

(2) The Interpretation Act 1889**(c)** shall apply for the interpretation of these Regulations as it applies for the interpretation of an Act of Parliament.

3. Regulation 25 of the Principal Regulations shall be amended by deleting paragraph (*c*) thereof and substituting therefor the following—

"(*c*) that part of the value of any supply of goods on which output tax is not chargeable by virtue of any order made by the Treasury under section 3(6) of the Act unless he acquired or imported the goods for the purpose of selling them;".

4. Regulation 27 of the Principal Regulations shall be amended as follows—

(*a*) in paragraph (2) after the words "Regulation 25(*a*), (*d*) or (*e*)" in the last line thereof there shall be inserted the words "and that part of the value of any supply which is excluded by Regulation 25(*c*) from any calculation made by a person for the purpose of using a method";

(*b*) in paragraph (3) after the word "paragraph" in line 8 thereof there shall be inserted the words "the input tax attributable to".

(a) 1972 c. 41.
(b) S.I. 1972/1147 (1972 II, p. 3362).
(c) 1889 c. 63.

5. Regulation 29(1) of the Principal Regulations shall be amended by deleting the word "of" in line 3 thereof and substituting the words ", or such other period as the Commissioners may allow, from".

6. Regulation 30(1) of the Principal Regulations shall be amended by deleting the words "not being a manufacturer" in lines 1 and 2 thereof.

7. Regulation 41(*a*) of the Principal Regulations shall be amended by the insertion after the words "for immediate shipment" in the second line thereof, the words "or to an export packer, not being the export house to whom the goods are supplied, for delivery direct to a port, Customs airport or approved inland clearance depot for immediate shipment to the order of the export house".

8. The form numbered 5 in the Schedule to the Principal Regulations shall be deleted and the form numbered 5 in the Schedule to these Regulations substituted therefor.

9. Regulation 46(3) of the Principal Regulations shall be deleted and there shall be substituted therefor the following—

"(3) Except as the Commissioners may otherwise allow, a body corporate acting as a representative member of a group as provided by section 21 of the Act, shall, on or before the 30th September in every year, make a return in the form numbered 5 in the Schedule to these Regulations giving such information as is specified therein.".

10. Regulation 49 of the Principal Regulations shall be amended by deleting the full stop after the word "thereafter" in the last line thereof and adding the words "or in such later period as the Commissioners may allow.".

11. Regulation 50(2) of the Principal Regulations shall be amended by deleting the full stop after the word "thereafter" in the last line thereof and adding the words "or in such later period as the Commissioners may allow.".

12. Regulation 51 of the Principal Regulations shall be amended as follows—

(*a*) after the words "correct it" in line 2 thereof there shall be inserted the words "in such manner and within such time";

(*b*) after the words "may require" in the penultimate line thereof there shall be inserted a full stop and the words "but in no case later than on the return furnished next after its discovery" shall be deleted.

13. Regulation 52(1) of the Principal Regulations shall be amended by deleting "21" in the penultimate line thereof and substituting "30" therefor.

14. Regulation 53 of the Principal Regulations shall be amended as follows—

(*a*) in paragraph (*a*) the words "or sheriff substitute for the county" shall be deleted;

(*b*) in paragraph (*b*) the words "sheriff officers of the county" shall be deleted and the words "sheriff officers of the sheriffdom" substituted;

(*c*) in paragraph (*e*) the word "new" shall be inserted before the word "pence";

(*d*) in paragraph (*g*) the words "of the county, or his substitute," and the words "or sheriff substitute" shall be deleted and the word "new" inserted before the word "pence"; and

(*e*) in paragraph (*h*) the words "or sheriff substitute" shall be deleted.

F. R. Frost,
Commissioner of Customs and Excise.

12th November 1973.

King's Beam House,
Mark Lane,
London EC3R 7HE.

Form No. 5 SCHEDULE Regulation 46(3)

Value Added Tax

RETURN OF

TRADING FIGURES FOR ASSOCIATED BUSINESSES IN A GROUP REGISTRATION

H.M. Customs and Excise

PART A.

Mark an 'X' in this box if all companies in the group registration have the same Trade Classification

Mark an 'X' in this box if the total turnover of all companies in the group registration is less than £1,000,000

PART B.

If you are electing to enter Total Outputs and Total Inputs as on the VAT 100 form mark an 'X' in this box and do not complete Column 9 of Part C.

VAT Registration number of the representative member of the group.

The registered person named here (i.e. the representative member) should complete and return this form before the 30th September..........

to H M Customs and Excise
Alexander House
21 Victoria Avenue
Southend on Sea
Essex SS99 1AA

A pre-paid envelope for this purpose is enclosed.

PART C

1	2	3	4	5	6	7	8	9
Name of Company	Trade Classification	Day, Month and Year of Start of Accounting Period	Day, Month and Year of End of Accounting Period	Enter an 'X' against any member with a turnover less than £250,000	Total turnover or Total Output	Any amount of VAT included in Total turnover figure	Total Purchases or Total Inputs	Total Capital expenditure
Representative member								

Signed ....
*(Director, secretary, or authorised signatory)

Date ....
*Delete as necessary

VAT 101

EXPLANATORY NOTE

(*This Note is not part of the Regulations.*)

These Regulations amend various provisions of the Value Added Tax (General) Regulations 1972.

Regulations 1 and 2 are formal.

Regulation 3 provides that when a partly exempt person sells an article, and accounts for output tax on his margin in accordance with one of the second-hand goods relief schemes, he may include the whole value of the supply in partial exemption calculations instead of including only the margin. This involves no change of practice, but removes a legal barrier to deduction of input tax in connection with second-hand dealers' overhead expenses.

Regulation 4(*a*) provides that the value of taxable supplies which is excluded from calculations of deductible input tax by partly exempt persons shall also be excluded from calculations for the purpose of deciding whether a partly exempt person may be treated as fully taxable, and therefore entitled to deduct all his input tax, subject to the normal rules. Regulation 4(*b*) provides, for the removal of doubt, that it is the input tax attributable to exempt supplies which is to be disregarded for the purpose of the 5 per cent *de minimis* rule in Regulation 27(3), not the exempt supplies themselves.

Regulation 5 provides that the Commissioners may extend the period within which a newly-registered person may make any claim for relief from value added tax on goods which he acquired or imported before the effective date of his registration. This is to ensure that a person who is registered with effect from a date more than six months in the past will not be debarred from making a claim, on the ground that the time limit has already expired.

Regulation 6 provides that a manufacturer may be regarded as an export house for the purposes of Principal Regulation 41 which provides for the zero-rating of supplies to export houses.

Regulation 7 provides that supplies to export houses under Principal Regulation 41 may be zero-rated notwithstanding that they are delivered to an export packer in the course of exportation.

Regulations 8 and 9 alter the return of trading figures required to be made by the representative member of a registered group of companies to conform to information required already under the Companies Act 1967 (c. 81) and for the return to be made annually.

Regulations 10, 11 and 12 introduce greater flexibility to Regulations 49, 50(2) and 51 of the Principal Regulations dealing respectively with the estimation of output tax and deductible input tax, and with the correction of errors by registered persons.

Regulation 13 provides that distress shall not be levied in respect of an amount due under section 31(*b*) of the Act during the period in which there is a right of appeal against the assessment to a Value Added Tax Tribunal.

Regulation 14 brings various references into line with the provisions of The Sheriff Courts (Scotland) Act 1971 (c. 58) and the terms of section 1(1) of the Decimal Currency Act 1967 (c. 47).

STATUTORY INSTRUMENTS

1973 No. 1883

WAGES COUNCILS

The Wages Regulation (Laundry) Order 1973

Made - - - -	12*th November* 1973
Coming into Operation	10*th December* 1973

Whereas the Secretary of State has received from the Laundry Wages Council (Great Britain) the wages regulation proposals set out in Schedules 1 and 2 hereof;

Now, therefore, the Secretary of State in exercise of powers conferred by section 11 of the Wages Councils Act 1959**(a)**, as modified by Article 2 of the Counter-Inflation (Modification of Wages Councils Act 1959) Order 1973**(b)**, and now vested in him **(c)**, and of all other powers enabling him in that behalf, hereby makes the following Order:—

1. This Order may be cited as the Wages Regulation (Laundry) Order 1973.

2.—(1) In this Order the expression "the specified date" means the 10th December 1973, provided that where, as respects any worker who is paid wages at intervals not exceeding seven days, that date does not correspond with the beginning of the period for which the wages are paid, the expression "the specified date" means, as respects that worker, the beginning of the next such period following that date.

(2) The Interpretation Act 1889**(d)** shall apply to the interpretation of this Order as it applies to the interpretation of an Act of Parliament and as if this Order and the Order hereby revoked were Acts of Parliament.

3. The wages regulation proposals set out in Schedules 1 and 2 hereof shall have effect as from the specified date and as from that date the Wages Regulation (Laundry) Order 1972**(e)** shall cease to have effect.

Signed by order of the Secretary of State.

12th November 1973.

W. H. Marsh,
Assistant Secretary,
Department of Employment.

(a) 1959 c. 69. **(b)** S.I. 1973/661 (1973 I, p. 2141).
(c) S.I. 1959/1769, 1968/729 (1959 I, p. 1795; 1968 II, p. 2108).
(d) 1889 c. 63. **(e)** S.I. 1972/1606 (1972 III, p. 4721).

Article 3

SCHEDULE 1

The following minimum remuneration shall be substituted for the statutory minimum remuneration fixed by the Wages Regulation (Laundry) Order 1972 (Order W. (117)).

STATUTORY MINIMUM REMUNERATION

PART I

GENERAL

1.—(1) Subject to the provisions of paragraph 14 relating to guaranteed weekly remuneration, and to the provisions of sub-paragraphs (2) and (3) of this paragraph, the minimum remuneration payable to a worker to whom this Schedule applies is as follows:—

(*a*) (i) in the case of a time worker, the hourly general minimum time rate applicable to the worker under the provisions of this Schedule;

(ii) in the case of a worker employed on piece work, piece rates each of which would yield, in the circumstances of the case, to an ordinary worker, at least the same amount of money as the hourly piece work basis time rate applicable to the worker;

(iii) in the case of a worker regularly remunerated on a system of payment by results, not being a piece worker, such time rates with the addition of bonus rates as would yield to an ordinary worker, in the circumstances of the case, at least the same amount of money as one and one-eighth times the hourly general minimum time rate which would be applicable to the worker under Part II or Part III of this Schedule if the worker were a time worker;

(*b*) for all work to which a minimum overtime rate applies under Part V of this Schedule, that rate.

(2) The minimum remuneration specified in sub-paragraph (1) of this paragraph shall be increased as follows:—

(*a*) in respect of any time to which the supplemental shift work rate applies under paragraph 12, by that rate;

(*b*) in respect of any time to which the supplemental night work rate applies under paragraph 13, by that rate.

(3) Notwithstanding any other provision of this Schedule, the general minimum time rate payable to a female worker aged 19 years or over to whom paragraph 4 applies shall be increased by the following amounts:—

	Per hour	Per week of 40 hours
(*a*) with effect from 24th December 1973	1·25p	50p
(*b*) with effect from 23rd December 1974	1·25p	50p
(*c*) with effect from 22nd December 1975	1·25p	50p

2. In this Schedule—

(1) "System of payment by results" means a system of payment which, in addition to remuneration related to time worked, includes an amount related to output or saving of time over a standard time, whether such amount is calculated on an individual or a collective basis.

(2) "time worker" means any worker who is not a piece worker and who is not remunerated on any other system of payment by results.

Part II

GENERAL MINIMUM TIME RATES

MALE WORKERS INCLUDING TRANSPORT WORKERS

3. The general minimum time rates payable to all male workers, other than workers employed, wholly or mainly, as enginemen or stokers, are as follows:—

	Per hour	Per week of 40 hours
	p	£
Aged 20 years or over	*39·65*	*15·86*
,, 19 and under 20 years	*33·51*	*13·40*
,, 18 ,, ,, 19 ,, ...	*28·82*	*11·53*
,, 17 ,, ,, 18 ,, ...	*25·22*	*10·09*
,, under 17 years	*23·73*	*9·49*

FEMALE WORKERS (OTHER THAN WORKERS TO WHOM PART III APPLIES)

4. The general minimum time rates payable to all female workers (other than workers to whom Part III of this Schedule applies) are as follows:—

	Per hour	Per week of 40 hours
	p	£
Aged 19 years or over	*35·90*	*14·36*
,, 18 and under 19 years	*30·64*	*12·26*
,, 17 ,, ,, 18 ,, ...	*25·81*	*10·32*
,, under 17 years	*23·21*	*9·28*

Part III

GENERAL MINIMUM TIME RATES

FEMALE WORKERS EMPLOYED AS SUBSTITUTES FOR MALE WORKERS

WASHHOUSE OR GENERAL INSIDE WORKERS

5. The general minimum time rates payable to female workers employed in substitution for male washhouse or general inside workers is *39·65p* per hour where the worker performs in full either the duties of an adult male worker whom she replaces or the duties which prior to the war were normally undertaken in the laundry undertaking by an adult male worker:

Provided that where the laundry, prior to replacement of male by female workers, worked a night shift on a shift system, the foregoing provisions of this paragraph shall apply only to workers engaged in machine washing and hydro extraction processes.

DRIVERS

6. The general minimum time rates payable to female workers employed, in substitution for male workers, as drivers is *39·65p* per hour where the worker performs in full either the duties of a male driver whom she replaces or the duties which prior to the war were normally undertaken in the laundry undertaking by a male driver.

7. In this Part of this Schedule the expression "prior to the war" means during the period of six months immediately preceding 3rd September 1939.

PART IV

PIECE WORK BASIS TIME RATE
MALE OR FEMALE WORKERS

8. The hourly piece work basis time rate applicable to a worker employed on piece work is one and one-eighth times the hourly general minimum time rate which would be applicable to the worker under paragraph 3, 4 or 5 if the worker were a time worker.

PART V

OVERTIME AND WAITING TIME
MINIMUM OVERTIME RATES—ALL WORKERS

9.—(1) Subject to sub-paragraph (2) of this paragraph, minimum overtime rates are payable to any worker as follows:—

(*a*) On any day other than a Sunday or customary holiday or a day on which a rest period occurs—
  (i) for the first $1\frac{1}{2}$ hours worked in excess of 9 hours ... time-and-a-quarter
  (ii) thereafter ... ... time-and-a-half

(*b*) In any week, for time worked during rest periods—
  (i) for the first 4 hours worked ... ... time-and-a-quarter
  (ii) thereafter ... ... time-and-a-half

(*c*) On a Sunday or customary holiday—
  for all time worked ... ... double time

(*d*) In any week, for all time worked in excess of 40 hours, exclusive of any time for which overtime is payable under the foregoing provisions of this paragraph ... ... time-and-a-quarter

(2) Notwithstanding the provisions of sub-paragraph (1) of this paragraph, not more than an aggregate of 5 overtime hours worked in any week shall be payable at the minimum rate of time-and-a-quarter under (*a*)(i), (*b*)(i) and (*d*) of that sub-paragraph and any such overtime hours in excess of 5 shall be payable at the minimum rate of time-and-a-half.

INTERPRETATION

10. In this Part of this Schedule:—

(1) The expression "customary holiday" means the under-mentioned days (of which at least three shall be fixed between 15th March and 1st October in each year), that is to say:—

(*a*) (i) In England and Wales—

Christmas Day, 26th December, if it be not a Sunday, 27th December, in a year in which 25th or 26th December is a Sunday, Good Friday, Easter Monday, the last Monday in May, the last Monday in August and any day proclaimed as an additional Bank Holiday or a general holiday;

(ii) In Scotland—

six weekdays in the course of a calendar year, to be fixed by the employer and notified to the worker not less than three weeks before the holiday, and any day proclaimed as an additional Bank Holiday or a general holiday, provided that in a burgh two of the said weekdays, which shall not be less than three months apart, shall be the days fixed by the town council for the purposes of section 94(3) of the Factories Act 1961(a); or

(*b*) in the case of each of the said days, such weekday as may be substituted therefor, being a day mutually agreed between the employer and the worker or his representative.

(a) 1961 c. 34.

(2) The expressions "time-and-a-quarter", "time-and-a-half" and "double time" mean respectively—

(*a*) in the case of a time worker, one and a quarter times, one and a half times and twice the hourly general minimum time rate otherwise applicable to the worker;

(*b*) in the case of a worker employed on piece work, or a worker regularly remunerated on a system of payment by results, not being a piece worker—

(i) a time rate equal respectively to one quarter, one half and the whole of the hourly general minimum time rate which would be applicable to the worker if he were a time worker and a minimum overtime rate did not apply and, in addition thereto,

(ii) the minimum remuneration applicable to the worker under paragraph 1(1)(*a*).

(3) The expression "rest period" means Saturday except where the employer has appointed—

(*a*) some other weekday in each week of employment as the day on which the worker will not normally be required to work, or

(*b*) any two weekdays one of which may be a Saturday in each week of employment as days on which the worker will not normally be required to work for more than 5 hours,

in which cases the expression "rest period" means either the day described in (*a*) or, as the case may require, each of the periods on the days described in (*b*) during which a worker will not normally be required to work.

(4) For the purposes of sub-paragraph (3) of this paragraph the employer shall appoint any rest period by notice to the worker at the commencement of the employment or as the case may require on or before the date upon which this Schedule comes into operation and may vary any arrangements in respect of any rest period or periods by a notice to have effect after a period of not less than 3 weeks.

(5) In the case of a worker of the Jewish religion who is normally employed on Sunday and not on Saturday (except where as respects a woman or young person such substitution is unlawful) the expression "Sunday" in paragraph 9 means Saturday and likewise for the purposes of sub-paragraph (3) of this paragraph the expression "Saturday" means Sunday.

WAITING TIME

11.—(1) A worker is entitled to payment of the minimum remuneration specified in Part I of this Schedule for all time during which he is present on the premises of his employer unless he is present thereon in any of the following circumstances:—

(*a*) without the employer's consent, express or implied;

(*b*) for some purpose unconnected with his work and other than that of waiting for work to be given to him to perform;

(*c*) by reason only of the fact that he is resident thereon;

(*d*) during normal meal times in a room or place in which no work is being done, and he is not waiting for work to be given to him to perform.

(2) The minimum remuneration payable under sub-paragraph (1) of this paragraph to a piece worker when not engaged on piece work is that which would be payable if the worker were a time worker.

Part VI

SUPPLEMENTAL SHIFT WORK RATE

12.—(1) A supplemental rate of 1p per hour is payable to a shift worker employed on a daily two-shift system, and the said rate is payable in addition to the minimum remuneration payable to the worker under the provisions of this or any preceding Part of this Schedule.

(2) A shift worker on a daily two-shift system is a worker who is employed on either a morning or an afternoon shift in an undertaking in which a daily two-shift system is operated.

SUPPLEMENTAL NIGHT WORK RATE

13. The supplemental night work rate is payable to a worker for any time worked between the hours of 10 p.m. and 6 a.m. and the said rate is payable in addition to the minimum remuneration payable to the worker for the said work under the provisions of this or any preceding Part of this Schedule. The amount of the supplemental night work rate is one-fifth of the hourly general minimum time rate applicable to the worker, or which would be applicable if the worker were a time worker.

Part VII

GUARANTEED WEEKLY REMUNERATION

14.—(1) Subject to the provisions of this paragraph, a worker who ordinarily works for the employer at least 39 hours weekly (or 32 hours weekly in a case where the proviso to the next following sub-paragraph applies) on work to which this Schedule applies shall be paid, in respect of any week in which he works for less than 39 hours (or 32 hours where the said proviso applies) on such work, not less than the guaranteed weekly remuneration.

(2) The guaranteed weekly remuneration is 39 hours' pay calculated at the hourly general minimum time rate ordinarily applicable to the worker under the provisions of Part II or Part III of this Schedule:

Provided that where the business of a laundry undertaking is subject in the course of the year to fluctuation by reason of changes in population of a seasonal nature and in consequence in any 12 months ending on 31st March there is, as between a period of not less than 10 consecutive weeks and any other such period, a reduction of at least 20 per cent. in the average of the weekly hours of all the workers, working at or from the laundry undertaking, in relation to whom the Council operates, the guaranteed weekly remuneration shall, in respect of the next ensuing period of 12 months, be 32 hours' pay calculated as aforesaid.

(3) The guaranteed weekly remuneration in any week shall be reduced by the amount of any holiday remuneration paid, or payable, by the employer to the worker in respect of any holiday allowed to, and taken by, the worker in that week under the provisions of the Wages Councils Act 1959.

(4) In calculating the number of hours worked in any week for the purposes of this paragraph, a worker shall be treated as though he had worked on any holiday allowed to, and taken by, him in that week under the provisions of the Wages Councils Act 1959, the number of hours ordinarily worked by him on that day of the week, provided that a worker shall not be treated as having worked in any week throughout which he is on holiday.

(5) Payment of the guaranteed weekly remuneration in any week is subject to the condition that the worker throughout the period of his ordinary employment in that week, excluding any day allowed him as a holiday, is:—

(*a*) capable of and available for work; and

(*b*) willing to perform such duties outside his normal occupation as the employer may reasonably require, if his normal work is not available to him in the establishment in which he is employed.

(6) The guaranteed weekly remuneration shall not be payable to a worker (*a*) in any week in which work is not available to him by reason of a strike or lock-out or circumstances outside the employer's control, if he has given the worker not less than four days' notice of his inability to provide such employment and the notice has expired; or (*b*) in respect of any week if the worker's employment is terminated before the end of that week.

(7) The guaranteed weekly remuneration applicable to a piece worker or a worker regularly remunerated on a system of payment by results, not being a piece worker, shall be the sum to which he would be entitled if he were a time worker.

Part VIII

APPLICABILITY OF STATUTORY MINIMUM REMUNERATION

15. This Schedule does not apply to male workers employed, wholly or mainly, as enginemen or stokers or (except in the case of the workers specified in Part III of this Schedule) to female workers employed in any of the operations specified in clause 2 of the definition of the Trade set out below, but save as aforesaid, this Schedule applies to workers in relation to whom the Laundry Wages Council (Great Britain) operates, that is to say, workers employed in Great Britain in the trade specified in the Schedule to the Laundry Wages Council (Great Britain) (Variation) Order 1971**(a)**, which Schedule reads as follows:—

"The Laundry Trade

1. The laundering of articles of every description and all processes and operations incidental thereto performed by way of trade or for the purpose of gain.

2. The following work when done in connection with a laundry undertaking by persons in the employment of the undertaking:—

(*a*) the transport of articles to be laundered and of laundered articles including the collection, loading, unloading and delivery of the articles, and attending to the articles during transport:

(*b*) driving and assisting in driving or control of, and acting as attendant to, any goods vehicle while being used for the purpose of any of the work specified in (*a*) above;

(*c*) operations performed by persons engaged on any work specified in sub-paragraph (*a*) or (*b*) above which are incidental to such work.

3. The Laundry Trade shall not include the following processes, operations and employment and such processes, operations and employment shall not constitute a laundry undertaking for the purpose of this definition, that is to say:—

(*a*) processes and operations specified in the Trade Boards (Women's Clothing) Order 1919**(b)**, the Trade Boards (Shirtmaking) Order 1920**(c)**, or the Trade Boards (Linen and Cotton Handkerchief and Household Goods and Linen Piece Goods) Order 1920**(d)**.

(*b*) the employment of any workers employed by British Transport Hotels Limited.".

(a) S.I. 1971/998 (1971 II, p. 2945).
(b) S.R. & O. 1919/1263 (1919 II, p. 531).
(c) S.R. & O. 1920/711 (1920 II, p. 790).
(d) S.R. & O. 1920/103 (1920 II, p. 780).

Article 3

SCHEDULE 2

HOLIDAYS AND HOLIDAY REMUNERATION

The Wages Regulation (Laundry) (Holidays) Order 1970(a) (Order W. (113)) shall have effect as if in the Schedule thereto for sub-paragraph (2) of paragraph 2 (which relates to customary holidays) there were substituted the following:—

"(2) The said customary holidays (of which at least three shall be fixed between the 15th March and the 1st October in each year) are:—

(*a*) (i) In England and Wales—

Christmas Day, 26th December, if it be not a Sunday, 27th December, in a year in which 25th or 26th December is a Sunday, Good Friday, Easter Monday, the last Monday in May, the last Monday in August and any day proclaimed as an additional Bank Holiday or a general holiday;

(ii) In Scotland—

six weekdays in the course of a calendar year to be fixed by the employer and notified to the worker not less than three weeks before the holiday, and any day proclaimed as an additional Bank Holiday or a general holiday, provided that in a burgh two of the said weekdays, which shall not be less than three months apart, shall be the days fixed by the town council for the purposes of section 94(3) of the Factories Act 1961; or

(*b*) in the case of each of the said days, such weekday as may be substituted therefor, being a day mutually agreed between the employer and the worker or his representative."

EXPLANATORY NOTE

(*This Note is not part of the Order.*)

This Order, which has effect from 10th December 1973, sets out in Schedule 1 the increased statutory minimum remuneration payable in substitution for that fixed by the Wages Regulation (Laundry) Order 1972 (Order W.(117)) which Order is revoked. New provisions are printed in italics.

Schedule 2 repeats without alteration the amendment to the Wages Regulation (Laundry) (Holidays) Order 1970 (Order W.(113)) relating to customary holidays which was contained in Order W.(117).

New provisions are printed in italics.

(a) S.I. 1970/1211 (1970 II, p. 4023).

STATUTORY INSTRUMENTS

1973 No. 1884

WAGES COUNCILS

The Wages Regulation (Aerated Waters) (Scotland) (Amendment) Order 1973

Made - - -	13*th November* 1973
Coming into Operation	10*th December* 1973

Whereas the Secretary of State has received from the Aerated Waters Wages Council (Scotland) the wages regulation proposals set out in Schedules 1 and 2 hereto;

Now, therefore, the Secretary of State in exercise of powers conferred by section 11 of the Wages Councils Act 1959**(a)**, as modified by Article 2 of the Counter-Inflation (Modification of Wages Councils Act 1959) Order 1973**(b)**, and now vested in him **(c)**, and of all other powers enabling him in that behalf, hereby makes the following Order:—

1. This Order may be cited as the Wages Regulation (Aerated Waters) (Scotland) (Amendment) Order 1973.

2.—(1) In this Order the expression "the specified date" means the 10th December 1973, provided that where, as respects any worker who is paid wages at intervals not exceeding seven days, that date does not correspond with the beginning of the period for which the wages are paid, the expression "the specified date" means, as respects that worker, the beginning of the next such period following that date.

(2) The Interpretation Act 1889**(d)** shall apply to the interpretation of this Order as it applies to the interpretation of an Act of Parliament.

3. The wages regulation proposals set out in Schedules 1 and 2 hereto shall have effect as from the specified date.

Signed by order of the Secretary of State.
13th November 1973.

W. H. Marsh,
Assistant Secretary,
Department of Employment.

(a) 1959 c. 69. **(b)** S.I. 1973/661 (1973 I, p. 2141).
(c) S.I. 1959/1769, 1968/729 (1959 I, p. 1795; 1968 II, p. 2108).
(d) 1889 c. 63.

Article 3

SCHEDULE 1

STATUTORY MINIMUM REMUNERATION

The Wages Regulation (Aerated Waters) (Scotland) Order 1973**(a)** (Order A.S. (77)), shall have effect as if in the Schedule thereto:—

for Part II there were substituted the following Part:—

"PART II

GENERAL MINIMUM TIME RATES

2. The general minimum time rates payable to all male and female workers are as follows:—

	Per hour	Per week of 40 hours
	p	£
(1) Male workers aged 19 years or over	*44·50*	*17·80*
(2) Female workers aged 19 years or over—		
(*a*) Up to and including 31st March 1974	*42·50*	*17·00*
(*b*) From 1st April 1974 up to and including 30th September 1974	*43·50*	*17·40*
(*c*) On and after 1st October 1974	*44·50*	*17·80*
(3) All workers aged—		
18 and under 19 years	*32·81*	*13·12*
17 ,, ,, 18 ,, ...	*28·32*	*11·33*
Under 17 years	*23·82*	*9·53*"

SCHEDULE 2

HOLIDAYS AND HOLIDAY REMUNERATION

The Wages Regulation (Aerated Waters) (Scotland) (Holidays) Order 1973**(b)** (Order A.S. (78)) shall have effect as if in the Schedule thereto for paragraph 5 which relates to long service annual holiday there were substituted the following:—

"LONG SERVICE ANNUAL HOLIDAY

5. Subject to the provisions of this paragraph, in addition to the holidays specified in paragraphs 2 and 3, an employer shall—

(1) during the 12 months commencing on 1st April 1973, allow a further annual holiday (hereinafter referred to as a "long service annual holiday") amounting to the number of days constituting the workers normal working week to every worker to whom this Schedule applies and whose contract of employment shall have existed continuously throughout the 2 years immediately preceding 1st April 1973;

(2) during the 12 months commencing on 1st April 1974 and on 1st April in each succeeding year, allow such a long service annual holiday to every such worker whose contract of employment shall have existed continuously throughout the *12 months* immediately preceding 1st April 1974 and 1st April in each succeeding year."

(a) S.I. 1973/43 (1973 I, p. 358). **(b)** S.I. 1973/44 (1973 I,p. 362).

EXPLANATORY NOTE

(*This Note is not part of the Order.*)

This Order, which has effect from 10th December 1973 amends the Wages Regulation (Aerated Waters) (Scotland) Order 1973 (Order A.S. (77)), by substituting for the statutory minimum remuneration payable to workers in relation to whom the Aerated Waters Wages Council (Scotland) operates, fixed by that Order, the increased statutory minimum remuneration set out in Schedule 1.

Schedule 2 amends the provisions of the Wages Regulation (Aerated Waters) (Scotland) (Holidays) Order 1973 (Order A.S. (78)) relating to the qualifying period for a long service annual holiday.

New provisions are printed in italics.

STATUTORY INSTRUMENTS

1973 No. 1886 (C.57) (S.150)

LOCAL GOVERNMENT, SCOTLAND

The Local Government (Scotland) Act 1973 (Commencement No. 1) Order 1973

Made - - - *9th November* 1973

In exercise of the powers conferred on me by section 238(2) of the Local Government (Scotland) Act 1973(**a**), I hereby make the following order:—

1. This order may be cited as the Local Government (Scotland) Act 1973 (Commencement No. 1) Order 1973.

2. Sections 7 (except in subsection (1) the words from "and accordingly" to the end of the subsection), 11 (except subsection (3)), 218, 224 and 233 of, and Schedule 2 to, the Local Government (Scotland) Act 1973 shall come into operation on 12th November 1973.

Gordon Campbell,
One of Her Majesty's Principal
Secretaries of State.

St. Andrew's House,
Edinburgh.
9th November 1973.

EXPLANATORY NOTE

(*This Note is not part of the Order.*)

This Order brings into operation those provisions of the Local Government (Scotland) Act 1973 which enables the Secretary of State to make rules for the conduct of local government elections (sections 7 and 233), to issue directions in connection with the first elections to the new local authorities (section 11 and Schedule 2), and to set up a Staff Commission (section 218) and Property Commission (section 224) not later than one month after the passing of the Act.

(**a**) 1973 c. 65.

STATUTORY INSTRUMENTS

1973 No. 1887

SEA FISHERIES

BOATS AND METHODS OF FISHING

The Sea Fish (Conservation) (Isle of Man) (No. 2) Order 1973

Made - - -	13*th November* 1973
Coming into Operation	1*st January* 1974

At the Court at Buckingham Palace, the 13th day of November 1973

Present,

The Queen's Most Excellent Majesty in Council

Her Majesty, in exercise of the powers conferred upon Her by section 24(2) and (3) of the Sea Fish (Conservation) Act 1967(**a**), is pleased, by and with the advice of Her Privy Council, to order, and it is hereby ordered, as follows:—

1. This Order may be cited as the Sea Fish (Conservation) (Isle of Man) (No. 2) Order 1973 and shall come into operation on 1st January 1974.

2. Section 4 of the Sea Fish (Conservation) Act 1967 (which relates to the licensing of British fishing boats) shall extend to the Isle of Man subject to the adaptations and modifications specified in the Schedule to this Order.

3. The Schedule to the Sea Fish (Conservation) (Isle of Man) Order 1973(**b**) shall be varied as follows:—

(*a*) in paragraph 15, for the words "section 5" there shall be substituted the words "sections 4 and 5";

(*b*) in paragraph 18, for the words "section 1, 3 or 5" in both places where they occur there shall be substituted the words "section 1, 3, 4 or 5";

(*c*) paragraph 19 shall be omitted;

(*d*) in paragraph 20, sub-paragraphs (*a*) and (*b*) shall be omitted;

(*e*) in paragraph 21, for sub-paragraph (*c*) there shall be substituted the following sub-paragraph:—

"(*c*) for the words after "the enforcement of" there shall be substituted the words "section 1, 3, 4 or 5 of this Act or any order made thereunder.".

W. G. Agnew.

(**a**) 1967 c. 84.

(**b**) S.I. 1973/237 (1973 I, p. 890).

SCHEDULE

Adaptations and Modifications in the Extension of Section 4 to the Isle of Man and the Fishery Limits adjacent thereto

1. For section 4(1) there shall be substituted the following provisions:—

'(1) As from such day as may be appointed by an order made by the Ministers and subject to such exceptions as may be made by such order no British fishing boat registered in the Isle of Man shall be used by way of trade or business for fishing in any area specified in the order and no fishing boat which is British-owned but not registered under the Merchant Shipping Act 1894(**a**) (where the owner is resident, or if a body corporate has its principal place of business, in the Isle of Man) shall be used by way of trade or business for fishing for salmon or migratory trout in any area so specified except under the authority of a licence granted by the Isle of Man Board of Agriculture and Fisheries (hereinafter called "the Board") and for the time being in force.

(1A) The preceding subsection shall apply to British fishing boats registered in the United Kingdom and to British-owned fishing boats which are not registered under the Merchant Shipping Act 1894 but whose owner is resident or, if a body corporate, has its principal place of business in the United Kingdom with the following modifications:—

(*a*) the insertion after the words "specified in the order" and "so specified" of the words "and within the fishery limits of the British Islands adjacent to the Isle of Man (but outside the territorial waters)";

(*b*) the substitution for the words "the Isle of Man Board of Agriculture and Fisheries" of the words "one of the Ministers by virtue of section 4(1) of the Sea Fish (Conservation) Act 1967 as it applies in the United Kingdom." '.

2. In section 4(3)—

(*a*) after the words "any licence granted" there shall be inserted the words "by the Board";

(*b*) for the words "Minister granting the licence" there shall be substituted the word "Board".

3. For section 4(5) there shall be substituted the following provision:—

"(5) The licensing powers conferred on the Board by this section may be exercised in consultation with the Ministers so as to limit the number of British fishing boats, or any class of such boats, engaged in fishing in any area for any description of fish to such extent as appears to the Ministers and the Board to be necessary or expedient for preventing overfishing, but the Board shall exercise those powers in such a way as appears to it to be likely to cause the least possible hardship.".

4. For section 4(6) there shall be substituted the following provision:—

"(6) The Board may, with the approval of the Finance Board, make charges for the granting of a licence under this section and may make different charges in relation to different classes of licence.".

5. In section 4(9)(*b*) for the words "Great Britain" there shall be substituted the words "the Isle of Man".

6. After section 4(9) there shall be inserted the following provision:—

"(10) The definitions set out in sections 1(7) and 3(8) of this Act and the definition of the words "British-owned" in section 5(9) of this Act shall have effect for the purposes of this section.".

(a) 1894 c. 60.

EXPLANATORY NOTE

(This Note is not part of the Order.)

This Order applies section 4 of the Sea Fish (Conservation) Act 1967 to the Isle of Man with exceptions, adaptations and modifications and makes consequential amendments to the Sea Fish (Conservation) (Isle of Man) Order 1973.

1973 No. 1888

SEA FISHERIES

BOATS AND METHODS OF FISHING

The Sea Fish (Conservation) (Manx Boats) (No. 2) Order 1973

Made - - - - 13*th November* 1973

Coming into Operation 1*st January* 1974

At the Court at Buckingham Palace, the 13th day of November 1973

Present,

The Queen's Most Excellent Majesty in Council

Her Majesty, in exercise of the powers conferred upon Her by section 24(1) of the Sea Fish (Conservation) Act 1967(**a**), is pleased, by and with the advice of Her Privy Council, to order, and it is hereby ordered, as follows:—

1. This Order may be cited as the Sea Fish (Conservation) (Manx Boats) (No. 2) Order 1973 and shall come into operation on 1st January 1974.

2. Section 4 of the Sea Fish (Conservation) Act 1967 (which relates to the licensing of British fishing boats) shall apply in relation to British fishing boats registered in the Isle of Man as it applies in relation to British fishing boats registered in the United Kingdom.

W. G. Agnew.

EXPLANATORY NOTE

(*This Note is not part of the Order.*)

This Order applies section 4 of the Sea Fish (Conservation) Act 1967 to British fishing boats registered in the Isle of Man.

(**a**) 1967 c. 84.

STATUTORY INSTRUMENTS

1973 No. 1889

EUROPEAN COMMUNITIES

The European Communities (Designation) Order 1973

Made - - -	13*th November* 1973
Laid before Parliament	19*th November* 1973
Coming into Operation	11*th December* 1973

At the Court at Buckingham Palace, the 13th day of November 1973

Present,

The Queen's Most Excellent Majesty in Council

Her Majesty, in exercise of the powers conferred on Her by section 2(2) of the European Communities Act 1972(**a**), is pleased, by and with the advice of Her Privy Council, to order, and it is hereby ordered, as follows:—

Citation, interpretation and commencement

1.—(1) This Order may be cited as the European Communities (Designation) Order 1973 and shall come into operation on 11th December 1973.

(2) The Interpretation Act 1889(**b**) shall apply for the interpretation of this Order as it applies for the interpretation of an Act of Parliament.

Designations of Ministers or departments

2.—(1) For the purposes of section 2(2) of the European Communities Act 1972 the Ministers or government departments specified in column 1 of the Schedule to this Order are hereby designated in relation to the matters respectively specified in column 2 of that Schedule.

(2) Where the Minister or government department is designated in relation to any item in column 2 of the said Schedule, then, for the purposes of the said section 2(2), that Minister or government department is also hereby designated in relation to anything supplemental or incidental to the matters specified in that item.

(3) Where more than one Minister or government department is designated by this Order in relation to any matter, the designation has effect as respects the making of regulations by any of them, or by more than one of them acting jointly.

(4) Regulations made by a Minister or department of the Government of Northern Ireland in pursuance of this Order shall form part of the law of Northern Ireland, and not of any other part of the United Kingdom.

W. G. Agnew.

(**a**) 1972 c. 68. (**b**) 1889 c. 63.

SCHEDULE

Column 1 *Ministers or departments*	Column 2 *Matters in relation to which the Ministers or departments are designated*
The Minister of Agriculture, Fisheries and Food and the Secretary of State	The exploitation and marketing of natural mineral waters.
The Secretary of State	The authorisation of unit trust schemes where persons who are managers or trustees under the scheme are or include corporations incorporated under the law of a Member State.
The Secretary of State	Measures to give effect to the Economic Community's rules on competition applying to undertakings.
The Secretary of State	The regulation of weights for marketing cocoa and chocolate products.
The Secretary of State	Measures for the maintenance of stocks of crude oil and petroleum products and the collection of information concerning such stocks.
Any Minister or department of the Government of Northern Ireland	All the preceding items in this column.

EXPLANATORY NOTE

(*This Note is not part of the Order.*)

This Order designates Ministers who may exercise powers to make regulations conferred by section 2(2) of the European Communities Act 1972 and specifies the matters in relation to which those powers may be exercised.

1973 No. 1891

CIVIL AVIATION

The Civil Aviation Act 1971 (Overseas Territories) Order 1973

Made - - - -	13*th November* 1973
Coming into Operation	10*th December* 1973

At the Court at Buckingham Palace, the 13th day of November 1973

Present,

The Queen's Most Excellent Majesty in Council

Her Majesty, in exercise of the powers conferred on Her by section 66(1) of the Civil Aviation Act 1971(**a**), is pleased, by and with the advice of Her Privy Council, to order, and it is hereby ordered, as follows:

Citation, commencement and interpretation

1.—(1) This Order may be cited as the Civil Aviation Act 1971 (Overseas Territories) Order 1973 and shall come into operation on 10th December 1973.

(2) The Interpretation Act 1889(**b**) shall apply, with the necessary adaptations, for the purpose of interpreting this Order, and otherwise in relation thereto, as it applies for the purpose of interpreting, and in relation to, Acts of Parliament.

Extension of s. 57(1) *of Act of* 1971

2. Section 57(1) of the Civil Aviation Act 1971, modified as in Schedule 1 hereto, shall extend to the territories specified in Schedule 2 hereto.

W. G. Agnew.

(**a**) 1971 c. 75. (**b**) 1889 c. 63.

Article 2

SCHEDULE 1

SECTION 57(1) OF THE CIVIL AVIATION ACT 1971 AS EXTENDED TO THE TERRITORIES SPECIFIED IN SCHEDULE 2

Dissolution of the corporations.

57.—(1) If the report last made in pursuance of section 39 of this Act includes a statement that in the opinion of the Board either of the British Overseas Airways Corporation or the British European Airways Corporation should be dissolved, the Secretary of State may make an order

(*a*) transferring to the Board all property, rights and liabilities which immediately before the order comes into force are property, rights and liabilities of that corporation ; and . . .

(*c*) making such modifications of the provisions of any enactment (including this Act and any enactment of the legislature of any territory to which this section extends) or any instrument made thereunder relating to either of those corporations as he considers are appropriate in consequence of the dissolution.

Article 2

SCHEDULE 2

Belize

Bermuda

British Solomon Islands Protectorate

British Virgin Islands

Cayman Islands

Falkland Islands (Colony and Dependencies)

Gilbert and Ellice Islands Colony

Hong Kong

Montserrat

Seychelles

Turks and Caicos Islands

EXPLANATORY NOTE

(*This Note is not part of the Order.*)

This Order extends with modifications s. 57(1) of the Civil Aviation Act 1971 (which relates to the dissolution of the British Overseas Airways Corporation and the British European Airways Corporation) to the territories specified in Schedule 2 of the Order.

STATUTORY INSTRUMENTS

1973 No. 1892

DIPLOMATIC SERVICE

The Consular Fees (Amendment) (No. 3) Order 1973

Made - - - - 13*th November* 1973
Coming into Operation 1*st January* 1974

At the Court at Buckingham Palace, the 13th day of November 1973

Present,

The Queen's Most Excellent Majesty in Council

Her Majesty, by virtue and in exercise of the powers conferred upon Her by section 2(1) of the Consular Salaries and Fees Act 1891(**a**) and section 8(1) of the Fees (Increase) Act 1923(**b**), or otherwise in Her Majesty vested, is pleased, by and with the advice of Her Privy Council, to order, and it is hereby ordered, as follows:—

1. This Order shall come into operation on 1st January 1974 and may be cited as the Consular Fees (Amendment) (No. 3) Order 1973.

2. Part II of the table of consular fees in the Schedule annexed to the Consular Fees Order 1971(**c**) as amended(**d**) is hereby amended by substituting for Fee 14 the following:—

	£
" 14. Issuing a British Visitors' passport	2.00 "

W. G. Agnew.

EXPLANATORY NOTE

(*This Note is not part of the Order.*)

This Order increases the fee for issuing a British Visitors' passport fixed by the Consular Fees Order 1971.

(**a**) 1891 c. 36. (**b**) 1923 c. 4. (**c**) S.I. 1971/211 (1971 I, p. 601).
(**d**) The amendments do not relate expressly to the subject matter of this Order.

1973 No. 1893

CIVIL AVIATION
FUGITIVE CRIMINAL

The Hijacking Act 1971 (Overseas Territories) (Amendment) Order 1973

Made - - - -	13*th November* 1973
Laid before Parliament	19*th November* 1973
Coming into Operation	10*th December* 1973

At the Court at Buckingham Palace, the 13th day of November 1973

Present,

The Queen's Most Excellent Majesty in Council

Her Majesty, in exercise of the powers conferred on Her by subsection (3) of section 6 of the Hijacking Act 1971(**a**), by the Foreign Jurisdiction Act 1890(**b**), by section 17 of the Fugitive Offenders Act 1967(**c**) as extended by subsection (1) of the said section 6 and of all other powers enabling Her in that behalf, is pleased, by and with the advice of Her Privy Council, to order, and it is hereby ordered as follows:—

1.—(1) This Order may be cited as the Hijacking Act 1971 (Overseas Territories) (Amendment) Order 1973 and shall come into operation on 10th December 1973.

(2) This Order shall be construed as one with the Hijacking Act 1971 (Overseas Territories) Order 1971(**d**) (hereinafter referred to as " the principal Order ") and the principal Order and this Order may be cited together as the Hijacking Act 1971 (Overseas Territories) Orders 1971 and 1973.

2. Article 4 of the principal Order is revoked and replaced by the following Article:—

" 4. The amendments specified in Schedule 3 hereto shall be made to the Pacific (Fugitive Criminals Surrender) Order in Council 1914(**e**)."

3. Section 3 in Schedule 1 to the principal Order is revoked and replaced by the following section :—

" 3. There shall be deemed to be included among the descriptions of offences set out in Schedule 1 to the Fugitive Offenders Act 1967 as extended to the Territory any offence under this Act and any attempt to commit such an offence."

4. Schedule 3 to the principal Order is revoked and replaced by the following Schedule :—

(**a**) 1971 c. 70. (**b**) 1890 c. 37. (**c**) 1967 c. 68.
(**d**) S.I. 1971/1739 (1971 III, p.4737).
(**e**) S.R. & O. 1914/152 (Rev. VIII, p. 699: 1914 I, p.640).

"SCHEDULE 3

Article 4

Amendments to the Pacific (Fugitive Criminals Surrender) Order in Council 1914

1. There shall be deemed to be included in the list of offences in respect of which surrender may be granted contained in the First Schedule to the Pacific (Fugitive Criminals Surrender) Order in Council 1914 (hereinafter in this Schedule referred to as "the Order") any offence under the Hijacking Act 1971 (hereinafter in this Schedule referred to as "the Act") and (so far as not so included by virtue of the foregoing) any attempt to commit such an offence.

2. The Order shall be applied as if an Order in Council made under section 2 of the Extradition Act 1870(**a**) as extended by section 3(2) of the Act were such an arrangement as is referred to in Article 3 of the Order, but where the Order is so applied it shall have effect as if the only offences in respect of which surrender may be granted within the meaning of the Order were offences under the Act and attempts to commit such offences.

3. For the purposes of the Order any act, wherever committed, which—

(*a*) is an offence under the Act or an attempt to commit such an offence or would be such an offence or attempt but for section 1(2) of the Act; and

(*b*) is an offence against the law of any State in the case of which the Order has been directed to apply by notice under Article 3 thereof;

shall be deemed to be an offence committed within the jurisdiction of that State."

W. G. Agnew.

EXPLANATORY NOTE

(This Note is not part of the Order.)

The Hijacking Act 1971 (Overseas Territories) Order 1971 was inadvertently not laid before Parliament, although Article 4 and Schedule 3 were made under the Foreign Jurisdiction Act 1890, section 11 of which provides for Orders to be laid, and section 3 in Schedule 1 was made under section 17 of the Fugitive Offenders Act 1967 (as extended by section 6(1) of the Hijacking Act 1971), subsection (3) of which provides for Orders to be subject to annulment. The remainder of the Order was made under section 6(2) of the Hijacking Act 1971, Orders under which are subject to no Parliamentary procedure. Accordingly this Order revokes Article 4 of, and section 3 in Schedule 1 to, and Schedule 3 to, the Hijacking Act 1971 (Overseas Territories) Order 1971, and replaces them with identical provisions. The present Order is not retrospective.

(**a**) 1870 c. 52.

1973 No. 1894

JUDGMENTS

The Reciprocal Enforcement of Foreign Judgments (Italy) Order 1973

Made - - - - 13*th November* 1973
Coming into Operation 16*th January* 1974

At the Court at Buckingham Palace, the 13th day of November 1973

Present,

The Queen's Most Excellent Majesty in Council

Whereas a Convention, a copy whereof is set out in Schedule 1 to this Order, relating to the Reciprocal Recognition and Enforcement of Judgments in Civil and Commercial Matters signed at Rome on 7th February 1964, was ratified on 15th October 1973 by Her Majesty and the President of the Republic of Italy and will enter into force on 16th January 1974:

And whereas a Protocol, a copy whereof is set out in Schedule 2 to this Order, amending the said Convention was concluded at Rome on 14th July 1970:

And whereas Her Majesty is satisfied that, in the event of Part I of the Foreign Judgments (Reciprocal Enforcement) Act 1933(**a**) being extended to judgments given in the superior courts of the Republic of Italy, substantial reciprocity of treatment will, under the terms of the said Convention and Protocol, be assured as respects the enforcement in the Republic of Italy of judgments given in the superior courts of the United Kingdom:

And whereas it is necessary in order to give effect to the said Convention and Protocol to make the provisions contained in sections 4, 5 and 6 of this Order in relation to matters with respect to which there is power to make rules of court for the purposes of Part I of the said Act:

Now, therefore, Her Majesty, by virtue and in exercise of the powers conferred on Her by sections 1 and 3 of the said Act, and of all other powers enabling Her in that behalf, is pleased, by and with the advice of Her Privy Council, to order, and it is hereby ordered, as follows:—

1.—(1) This Order shall come into operation on 16th January 1974 and may be cited as the Reciprocal Enforcement of Foreign Judgments (Italy) Order 1973.

(2) The Interpretation Act 1889(**b**) shall apply for the interpretation of this Order as it applies for the interpretation of an Act of Parliament.

2. Part I of the Foreign Judgments (Reciprocal Enforcement) Act 1933 shall extend to the Republic of Italy.

(**a**) 1933 c.13. (**b**) 1889 c.63.

3. The following courts of the Republic of Italy shall be deemed superior courts of the Republic of Italy for the purposes of Part I of the Foreign Judgments (Reciprocal Enforcement) Act 1933, that is to say:—

The Corte d'Appello
The Tribunale

4. No security for costs shall be required to be given by any person making application for the registration of a judgment of a superior court of the Republic of Italy.

5. A judgment of a superior court of the Republic of Italy shall, in the absence of proof to the contrary, be deemed to be capable of execution in the Republic of Italy if there is produced a certified copy of the judgment issued by the court and bearing the following executory formula:

"Comandiamo a tutti gli ufficiali giudiziari che ne siano richiesti e a chiunque spetti, di mettere a esecuzione il presente titolo, al pubblico ministero di darvi assistenza, e a tutti gli ufficiali della forza pubblica di concorrervi, quando ne siano legalmente richiesti."

6. The rate of interest due under the law of the Republic of Italy upon the sum in respect of which a judgment of a superior court of the Republic of Italy is given shall be deemed to be that ordered in the judgment and, if no rate is so ordered, no interest shall be deemed to be due thereon under the law of the Republic of Italy unless the contrary is shown.

W. G. Agnew.

SCHEDULE 1

CONVENTION BETWEEN THE UNITED KINGDOM OF GREAT BRITAIN AND NORTHERN IRELAND AND THE REPUBLIC OF ITALY FOR THE RECIPROCAL RECOGNITION AND ENFORCEMENT OF JUDGMENTS IN CIVIL AND COMMERCIAL MATTERS.

Her Majesty The Queen of the United Kingdom of Great Britain and Northern Ireland and of Her other Realms and Territories, Head of the Commonwealth, and the President of the Republic of Italy,

Desiring to provide on the basis of reciprocity for the recognition and enforcement of judgments in civil and commercial matters;

Have resolved to conclude a Convention for this purpose and to that end have appointed as their Plenipotentiaries:

Her Majesty The Queen of the United Kingdom of Great Britain and Northern Ireland and of Her other Realms and Territories, Head of the Commonwealth (hereinafter referred to as Her Majesty):

For the United Kingdom of Great Britain and Northern Ireland:

H.E. Sir John Guthrie WARD, Her Majesty's Ambassador Extraordinary and Plenipotentiary at Rome,

The President of the Republic of Italy:

H.E. the Hon. Giuseppe LUPIS, Under-Secretary for Foreign Affairs,
who, having communicated to each other their respective Full Powers found in good and due form, have agreed as follows:

General

Article I

For the purposes of the present Convention:

(1) The territory of one (or of the other) High Contracting Party means

(*a*) in relation to the United Kingdom, England and Wales, Scotland, Northern Ireland, and any territories to which the Convention shall have been extended under Article X; and

(*b*) in relation to the Republic of Italy, Italy.

(2) The word "judgment" means any decision of a court, however described (judgment, order and the like), which is final and conclusive as between the parties thereto notwithstanding that it may still be subject to appeal.

(3) The words "original court" mean in relation to any judgment the court by which the judgment was given; and the words "court applied to", the court in which it is sought to obtain recognition of a judgment or to which an application for the registration of a judgment or for the grant of a *dichiarazione di efficacia* is made.

(4) The words "judgment debtor" mean the person against whom the judgment was given in the original court and include, where necessary, any person against whom such judgment is enforceable under the law of the country of the original court; and the words "judgment creditor", the person in whose favour the judgment was given, and include, where necessary, any other person in whom the rights under the judgment have become vested.

(5) The word "appeal" includes any proceeding by way of discharging or setting aside a judgment or an application for a new trial or a stay of execution.

Article II

(1) Subject to the provisions of paragraph (2) the present Convention shall apply to judgments in civil and commercial matters, pronounced after the date of the entry into force of the present Convention, by the following courts:

(*a*) In the case of the United Kingdom, the House of Lords; for England and Wales, the Supreme Court of Judicature (Court of Appeal and High Court of Justice) and the Courts of Chancery of the Counties Palatine of Lancaster and Durham; for Scotland, the Court of Session and the Sheriff Court; and for Northern Ireland, the Supreme Court of Judicature; and

(*b*) in the case of Italy, the Corte d'Appello and the Tribunale.

(2) The present Convention shall not apply to:

(*a*) judgments given on appeal from courts not referred to in paragraph (1) of this Article;

(*b*) judgments given in proceedings for the recovery of any form of taxation (state or municipal);

(*c*) judgments given in proceedings for the recovery of fines or penalties due to public authorities.

(3) The present Convention shall not preclude the recognition and enforcement of judgments given in circumstances where the present Convention does not contemplate recognition or enforcement.

Recognition of Judgments

Article III

(1) Judgments in civil and commercial matters, pronounced in the territory of one High Contracting Party, shall, whatever the nationality of the judgment creditor or debtor, be recognised in the courts of the territory of the other High Contracting Party, except where it can be established that:

(*a*) in the case in question, the jurisdiction of the original court is not recognised under the provisions of Article IV ;

(*b*) the judgment was given by default and the judgment debtor, being the defendant in the proceedings in the original court, did not (notwithstanding that process may have been duly served on him in accordance with the law of the country of the original court) receive notice of those proceedings in sufficient time to enable him to defend the proceedings ;

(*c*) the judgment was obtained by fraud ;

(*d*) the recognition of the judgment would be contrary to public policy in the country of the court applied to ;

(*e*) the judgment debtor, being a defendant in the original proceedings, was a person who, in the opinion of the court applied to, was entitled under the rules of public international law to immunity from the jurisdiction of the original court and did not submit to the jurisdiction of that court ; or the judgment debtor, in the opinion of the court applied to, is entitled under the rules of public international law to immunity from the jurisdiction of that court at the time of application for registration or for a *dichiarazione di efficacia* ;

(*f*) the judgment debtor satisfies the court applied to that proceedings by way of appeal have been instituted against the judgment in the country of the original court. It is understood that if such proceedings have not been actually instituted but it appears that the judgment debtor is entitled and intends to appeal, the court applied to may adjourn its decision on the recognition of the judgment, so as to allow the judgment debtor a reasonable opportunity of instituting such proceedings, or may accord it recognition on such terms as it may think fit including the imposition of a payment into court.

(2) Where the court applied to is satisfied that the matter in dispute in the proceedings in the original court

(*a*) had before the date of the judgment in the original court been the subject of a final and conclusive judgment between the same parties by a court having jurisdiction in the matter, or

(*b*) is the subject of proceedings between the same parties in the country of the court applied to which were commenced before the date of the judgment in the original court,

the court applied to may refuse to recognise the judgment of the original court.

(3) For the purposes of the present Convention, the effect of the recognition of a judgment shall be that such judgment shall be treated as conclusive as to the matter thereby adjudicated upon in any further action as between the same parties, and shall constitute a defence in any further action between them in respect of the same cause of action.

Article IV

(1) For the purposes of sub-paragraph (*a*) of paragraph (1) of Article III, the original court shall be recognised as possessing jurisdiction in all cases:

(*a*) where the judgment debtor, being a defendant in the proceedings in the original court, submitted to the jurisdiction of that court by voluntarily appearing in the proceedings upon the merits and not only for the purpose of protecting, or obtaining the release of, property seized, or threatened with seizure, in the proceedings, or of contesting the jurisdiction of that court ; or

(*b*) where the judgment debtor was plaintiff in, or counterclaimed in, the proceedings in the original court ; or

(*c*) where in a matter relating to contract the judgment debtor, being a defendant in the proceedings in the original court, had before the commencement of the proceedings agreed in the form required by the law of the country of the original court to submit himself in respect of the subject matter of the proceedings to the jurisdiction of the courts of the country of the original court ; or

(*d*) where the judgment debtor, being a defendant in the original court, was, at the time when the proceedings were instituted, resident in, or being a body corporate had its registered or head office in, the country of that court ; or

(*e*) where the judgment debtor, being a defendant in the original court, had an office or place of business in the country of that court and the proceedings in that court were in respect of a transaction effected through or at that office or place.

(2) The provisions of paragraph (1) of this Article shall not apply to judgments where the subject matter of the proceedings is immovable property, or to judgments in actions *in rem* in respect of movable property. Nevertheless the jurisdiction of the original court shall be recognised if the immovable property was situated in the country of the original court or if the movable property was so situated at the time of the commencement of the proceedings in the original court.

(3) The provisions of paragraph (1) of this Article shall not apply:

(*a*) to judgments in matters of family law or status (including divorce decrees or other judgments in matrimonial causes) ;

(*b*) to judgments in matters of succession, or the administration of the estates of deceased persons ;

(*c*) to judgments in bankruptcy proceedings ;

(*d*) to judgments in proceedings for the winding up of companies or other bodies corporate.

In the case of judgments given in proceedings of the kind referred to in the present paragraph, the jurisdiction of the original court shall be recognised in all cases where such recognition is in accordance with the law of the country of the court applied to.

(4) In the cases specified in sub-paragraphs (*d*) and (*e*) of paragraph (1) and in paragraph (2) of this Article the jurisdiction of the original court need not be recognised, if recognition is contrary to the laws of the country of the court applied to, where the bringing of the proceedings in the original court was contrary to a compromise or other agreement under which the dispute in question was to be settled otherwise than by proceedings in the courts of the country of that court.

Enforcement of Judgments

Article V

(1) Judgments in civil and commercial matters, pronounced in the territory of one High Contracting Party, shall, whatever the nationality of the judgment creditor or debtor, be enforced in the territory of the other High Contracting Party in the manner provided in Articles VI, VII and VIII of the present Convention provided that the following conditions are fulfilled:

(*a*) none of the objections set out in Article III (read in conjunction with Article IV) to the recognition of the judgment can be established ;

(*b*) it can be established under the provisions of paragraph (3) of this Article that they could be enforced by execution in the country of the original court ;

(*c*) there is payable thereunder a sum of money ;

(*d*) the judgment debt has not been wholly satisfied ; and provided that, where the judgment debtor satisfies the court applied to that proceedings by way of appeal have been instituted against the judgment in the country of the original court or, if such proceedings have not been instituted, that he is entitled and intends to appeal, such a judgment need not be enforced and the court applied to may take such measures in regard thereto as are permitted by its own law. However, such a judgment may be enforced on such terms as the court applied to thinks fit including the imposition of a payment into court.

(2) If the amount of the costs to be paid under a judgment is not fixed by the judgment itself but by a separate order, such order shall be deemed to be part of the judgment for the purposes of the present Convention.

(3) A judgment in respect of which a certified copy has been issued by the original court shall, in the absence of proof to the contrary, be deemed to be capable of being enforced by execution in the country of the original court within the meaning of sub-paragraph (*b*) of paragraph (1) of this Article. A certified copy of a judgment issued by an Italian court shall bear the executory formula set out in the Annex to the present Convention.

Article VI

(1) In order that any judgment of a court of the Republic of Italy should be enforced in the United Kingdom, an application by a judgment creditor for its registration, accompanied by a certified copy of the judgment by the original court, should be made:

(*a*) In England and Wales, to the High Court of Justice ;

(*b*) In Scotland, to the Court of Session ; and

(*c*) In Northern Ireland, to the Supreme Court of Judicature ;

in accordance with the procedure of the court applied to.

(2) If such application is made in respect of a judgment fulfilling the conditions laid down in Article V, registration shall be granted.

Article VII

(1) In order that any judgment of a court in a territory of the United Kingdom should be enforced in Italy, an application by a judgment creditor for the grant of a *dichiarazione di efficacia* should, in accordance with the procedure of the court applied to, be made to the Corte d'Appello in whose jurisdiction the judgment is to be enforced. Such application should be accompanied by a certified copy of the judgment issued by the original court.

(2) If such application is made in respect of a judgment fulfilling the conditions laid down in Article V, a *dichiarazione di efficacia* shall be granted.

Article VIII

(1) Where any judgment has been registered under Article VI, or where a *dichiarazione di efficacia* has been granted in respect of a judgment under Article VII, such judgment shall, as from the date of registration or grant of a *dichiarazione di efficacia*, and as regards all questions relating to its execution in the country of the court applied to, be of the same effect as if it had been a judgment originally given by the court applied to at the date of the registration or of the grant of the *dichiarazione di efficacia* ; and the court applied to shall have the same jurisdiction over the execution of the judgment as it has over the execution of judgments given by itself.

(2) A copy of any judgment certified by the original court shall be accepted without legislation, but certified translations of the judgment and other documents shall be required in accordance with the procedure of the court applied to.

(3) The procedure for the registration of a judgment under Article VI and the procedure for the grant of a *dichiarazione di efficacia* under Article VII shall be made as simple and rapid as possible, and no deposit by way of security for costs shall be required of any person making application for such registration, or for the grant of a *dichiarazione di efficacia.*

(4) A period of six years, unless the law of the court applied to allows a longer period, running from the date of the judgment of the original court or, where there have been proceedings by way of appeal against the judgment, from the date of the last judgment given in the appeal proceedings, shall be allowed by the court applied to for the purpose of making any application for registration or the grant of a *dichiarazione di efficacia.*

(5) If it is found by the court applied to that the judgment in respect of which an application is made for registration or for the grant of a *dichiarazione di efficacia* has been, at the date of such application partly but not wholly satisfied by payment, registration or a *dichiarazione di efficacia* shall be granted in respect of the balance remaining payable at that date provided that the judgment is one which would be enforceable under the provisions of the present Convention.

(6) If it is found by the court applied to that the judgment in respect of which an application is made for registration or for the grant of a *dichiarazione di efficacia* contains more than one provision and that some, but not all, of the provisions of the judgment are such that if those provisions had been contained in separate judgments those judgments could properly have been registered or could have been granted a *dichiarazione di efficacia,* the judgment may be registered or granted a *dichiarazione di efficacia* in respect of those provisions of which enforcement is permitted by the present Convention.

(7) If under a judgment a sum of money is payable which is expressed in a currency other than that of the country of the court applied to, the law of the country of the court applied to shall determine if, and if so, how, the amount payable under the judgment may or shall be converted into the currency of the country of the court applied to for the purposes of the satisfaction or enforcement of the judgment debt.

(8) When granting registration or a *dichiarazione di efficacia,* the court applied to shall, if so requested by the judgment creditor, include the costs of and incidental to registration or the grant of a *dichiarazione di efficacia* and the amount due by way of interest up to the date of the grant of registration or a *dichiarazione di efficacia.*

Final Provisions

Article IX

Any difficulties which may arise in connexion with the interpretation or application of the present Convention shall be settled through the diplomatic channel, or through any other means agreed upon by the High Contracting Parties.

Article X

(1) Her Majesty may, by a notification given through the diplomatic channel, at any time while the present Convention is in force, and provided that an agreement has been concluded by an Exchange of Notes on the points mentioned in paragraph (2) of this Article, extend the operation of the present Convention to any territory for whose international relations Her Majesty's Government in the United Kingdom of Great Britain and Northern Ireland are responsible.

(2) Prior to any notification of extension in respect of any territory under paragraph (1) of this Article, an agreement shall be concluded between the High Contracting Parties by an Exchange of Notes as to the judgments of the courts of the territory concerned to which the present Convention shall apply and the courts to which application for registration of any judgment shall be made.

(3) Any extension of the present Convention under this Article shall come into force three months from the date of the notification given under paragraph (1) of this Article.

(4) At any time after the expiry of three years from the coming into force of an extension of the present Convention to any of the territories referred to in paragraph (1) of this Article, either of the High Contracting Parties may terminate such extension on giving six months' notice of termination through the diplomatic channel.

(5) The termination of the present Convention under Article XI shall, unless otherwise expressly agreed by both High Contracting Parties, terminate it in respect of any territory to which it has been extended under paragraph (1) of this Article.

Article XI

The present Convention shall be subject to ratification. Instruments of Ratification shall be exchanged at London. The Convention shall come into force three months after the date on which the Instruments of Ratification are exchanged, and shall remain in force for three years. If neither of the High Contracting Parties shall have given notice through the diplomatic channel to the other, not less than six months before the expiration of the said period of three years, of intention to terminate the present Convention, it shall remain in force until the expiration of six months from the date on which either of the High Contracting Parties shall have given notice to terminate it.

In witness whereof the above-mentioned Plenipotentiaries have signed the present Convention.

Done in duplicate at Rome the 7th day of February, 1964, in the English and Italian languages, both texts being equally authoritative.

For the United Kingdom of Great Britain and Northern Ireland	For the Republic of Italy
J. G. WARD.	G. LUPIS.

Annex

The Executory Formula referred to in paragraph (3) of Article V is as follows:

"Comandiamo a tutti gli ufficiali giudiziari che ne siano richiesti e a chiunque spetti, di mettere a esecuzione il presente titolo, al pubblico ministero di darvi assistenza, e a tutti gli ufficiali della forza pubblica di concorrervi, quando ne siano legalmente richiesti."[1]

[1] *Translation:* " We order all officers of the judiciary who may be required and anyone who is concerned, to give effect to the present document, the Public Prosecutor to render assistance, and all officers of the police to comply therewith when they may be legally required."

SCHEDULE 2

PROTOCOL AMENDING THE CONVENTION BETWEEN THE UNITED KINGDOM OF GREAT BRITAIN AND NORTHERN IRELAND AND THE ITALIAN REPUBLIC FOR THE RECIPROCAL RECOGNITION AND ENFORCEMENT OF JUDGMENTS IN CIVIL AND COMMERCIAL MATTERS, SIGNED AT ROME ON THE 7TH FEBRUARY, 1964.

Her Majesty The Queen of the United Kingdom of Great Britain and Northern Ireland and of Her other Realms and Territories, Head of the Commonwealth (hereinafter referred to as "Her Britannic Majesty ") and the President of the Italian Republic ;

Desiring to amend the Convention between the United Kingdom of Great Britain and Northern Ireland and the Italian Republic providing for the Reciprocal Recognition and Enforcement of Judgments in Civil and Commercial Matters signed at Rome on the 7th February, 1964 (hereinafter referred to as " The Convention ") ;

Have resolved to conclude a Protocol for that purpose, and to that end have appointed as their Plenipotentiaries:

Her Britannic Majesty:

H.E. Sir Patrick Hancock, Her Majesty's Ambassador Extraordinary and Plenipotentiary at Rome

The President of the Italian Republic:

H.E. the Hon. Angelo Salizzoni, Under-Secretary of State for Foreign Affairs

who, having communicated to each other their respective Full Powers, found in good and due form, have agreed as follows:

ARTICLE 1

A new paragraph shall be inserted at the end of Article II of the Convention, to read as follows:

" (4) A High Contracting Party shall not be obliged to apply the present Convention to any judgment given in respect of injury or damage of a description which is the subject of a convention with respect to third party liability in the field of nuclear energy to which that Party is also a Party."

ARTICLE 2

At the beginning of paragraph (1) of Article II of the Convention, the words: " Subject to the provisions of paragraph (2) " shall be replaced by the words " Subject to the provisions of paragraphs (2) and (4) of this Article ".

ARTICLE 3

The present Protocol shall enter into force on the same date as the Convention and shall have the same duration as the Convention.

IN WITNESS WHEREOF the above-named Plenipotentiaries have signed the present Protocol and have affixed thereto their seals.

DONE in duplicate at Rome this 14th day of July 1970, in the English and Italian languages, both texts being equally authoritative.

For the United Kingdom of Great Britain and Northern Ireland:

P. F. HANCOCK.

For the Italian Republic:

ANGELO SALIZZONI.

EXPLANATORY NOTE

(*This Note is not part of the Order.*)

This Order extends Part I of the Foreign Judgments (Reciprocal Enforcement) Act 1933 to the judgments of the superior courts of the Republic of Italy and makes certain provisions regarding the registration and enforcement of such judgments.

Relevant judgments given after the 15th January 1974 will be enforceable in the United Kingdom upon registration in the High Court, the Court of Session or the Supreme Court of Judicature in Northern Ireland.

1973 No. 1895

SOUTHERN RHODESIA

The Southern Rhodesia Act 1965 (Continuation) Order 1973

Laid before Parliament in draft

Made - - - - *13th November* 1973

At the Court at Buckingham Palace, the 13th day of November 1973

Present,

The Queen's Most Excellent Majesty in Council

Whereas a draft of the following Order has been laid before Parliament and approved by resolution of each House of Parliament:

Now, therefore, Her Majesty, in exercise of the powers conferred on Her by section 3(2) of the Southern Rhodesia Act 1965(**a**), is pleased, by and with the advice of Her Privy Council, to order, and it is hereby ordered, as follows:—

Continuation in force of section 2 *of Act of* 1965

1. Section 2 of the Southern Rhodesia Act 1965 shall continue in force for a period of one year beginning with 16th November 1973.

Citation

2. This Order may be cited as the Southern Rhodesia Act 1965 (Continuation) Order 1973.

W. G. Agnew.

EXPLANATORY NOTE

(*This Note is not part of the Order.*)

This Order continues in force for a further year the powers conferred by section 2 of the Southern Rhodesia Act 1965 to make Orders in Council in relation to Southern Rhodesia.

(**a**) 1965 c. 76.

STATUTORY INSTRUMENTS

1973 No. 1897

PETROLEUM

The Petroleum (Organic Peroxides) Order 1973

Made - - - - 13*th November* 1973

Coming into Operation 1*st January* 1974

At the Court at Buckingham Palace, the 13th day of November 1973

Present,

The Queen's Most Excellent Majesty in Council

Her Majesty, in exercise of the powers conferred on Her by section 19 of the Petroleum (Consolidation) Act 1928(**a**), is pleased, by and with the advice of Her Privy Council, to order, and it is hereby ordered, as follows:—

1.—(1) This Order may be cited as the Petroleum (Organic Peroxides) Order 1973 and shall come into operation on 1st January 1974, except that, for the purpose of making any regulations under section 6 of the Petroleum (Consolidation) Act 1928 as applied by this Order to come into operation on or after that day, this Order shall come into operation forthwith.

(2) The Interpretation Act 1889(**b**) shall apply for the interpretation of this Order as it applies for the interpretation of an Act of Parliament.

(3) In this Order, "mixture" includes mixtures of two or more solids, mixtures of two or more liquids, mixtures of solids with liquids and solids dissolved in liquids.

2.—(1) Sections 6, 13(2) and (3), 14, 15, 16 and 18 of the Petroleum (Consolidation) Act 1928 shall apply to—

(*a*) any substance specified in the first column of Part I of the Schedule to this Order, (in respect of which alternative names are in some cases set out in the second column thereof); and

(*b*) subject to paragraph (2) of this Article, any mixture, containing in aggregate 5 per cent. or more by weight of substances so specified.

(2) Sub-paragraph (*b*) of paragraph (1) above shall not apply to any mixture specified in Part II of the Schedule to this Order.

(3) In the application of the provisions of the said section 13(2) by virtue of this Order, those provisions shall have effect subject to the following modification, that is to say:—

the words "where the petroleum-spirit carried or loaded on, or unloaded from, the ship or vehicle is or was for use only on that ship or vehicle or" shall be omitted.

W. G. Agnew.

(**a**) 1928 c. 32. (**b**) 1889 c. 63.

Article 2

SCHEDULE

Part I

Organic Peroxides to which Sections 6, 13(2) and (3), 14, 15, 16 and 18 Apply

Name of substance	*Alternative name or names*
Acetyl acetone peroxide	3, 5-Dimethyl-3, 5-dihydroxydioxolane-1, 2
Acetyl benzoyl peroxide	
Acetyl cyclohexane sulphonyl peroxide	
Acetyl peroxide	Diacetyl peroxide
Benzoyl peroxide	Dibenzoyl peroxide
n-Butyl-4,4-*bis*(*tert* butylperoxy) valerate	3, 3-Di(*tert* butylperoxy) butane carboxylic acid *n*-butyl ester
tert Butyl cumyl peroxide	*tert* Butyl cumene peroxide *tert* Butyl dimethyl benzyl peroxide *tert* Butyl peroxy*iso*propyl benzene
bis(4-*tert* Butyl cyclohexyl) perdicarbonate	*bis*(4-*tert* Butyl cyclohexyl) percarbonate
tert Butyl diperphthalate	Di*tert* butyl diperphthalate
tert Butyl hydroperoxide	2-Hydroperoxy *iso*butane
tert Butyl monoperphthalate	
tert Butyl peracetate	
tert Butyl perbenzoate	
tert Butyl per*iso*butyrate	
n-Butyl perdicarbonate	*n*-Butyl percarbonate
tert Butyl perdiethylacetate	*tert* Butyl peroxydiethylacetate
tert Butyl permaleate	*tert* Butyl monopermaleate *tert* Butylperoxy maleic acid Mono*tert* butyl permaleate
tert Butyl peroxide	Di*tert* butyl peroxide
2,2-*bis*(*tert* Butylperoxy)butane	2,2-Di(*tert* butylperoxy) butane
tert Butyl peroxy-2-ethyl hexanoate	*tert* Butyl peroctoate *tert* Butyl peroxy-2-ethyl hexoate
1-3*bis*(*tert* Butyl peroxy*iso*propyl) benzene	
1,4-*bis*(*tert* Butyl peroxy*iso*propyl) benzene	
1,1-*bis*(*tert* Butylperoxy)3,3,5-trimethyl-cyclohexane	1,1-Di(*tert* butylperoxy)3,3,5-trimethyl-cyclohexane
tert Butylperoxy-3,5,5-trimethyl hexanoate	*tert* Butyl per*iso*nonanoate *tert* Butylperoxy-3, 5, 5-trimethyl hexoate
tert Butyl perpivalate	
tert Butyl *iso*propyl percarbonate	
*para*Chlorobenzoyl peroxide	Di(4-chlorobenzoyl) peroxide p,p-Dichlorobenzoyl peroxide
Cumene hydroperoxide	Cumyl hydroperoxide a,a-Dimethylbenzyl hydroperoxide 2-Phenyl*iso*propyl hydroperoxide

SCHEDULE—*continued*

PART I—*continued*

Name of substance	*Alternative name or names*
Cyclohexanone peroxide	Dicyclohexanone peroxide
Decanoyl peroxide	Di-*n*-decanoyl peroxide
Diacetone alcohol peroxide	Acetone alcohol peroxide
Di*tert* amyl peroxide	
Dibenzyl perdicarbonate	Dibenzyl peroxydicarbonate
Di-*sec*butyl perdicarbonate	Di-*sec*butyl peroxydicarbonate
2,2-*bis*(4,4-Di*tert*butylperoxy cyclohexyl) propane	
Dicetyl perdicarbonate	Dicetyl peroxydicarbonate
2,4-Dichlorobenzoyl peroxide	*bis*-2,4-Dichlorobenzoyl peroxide
Dicumyl peroxide	Di-a,a-dimethyl benzyl peroxide
Dicyclohexyl perdicarbonate	*bis*-Dicyclohexyl peroxydicarbonate
2,5-Dimethyl-2,5-*bis*(*tert*butylperoxy) hexyne-3	
2,5-Dimethyl-2,5-dihydroperoxy hexane	2, 5-Dimethylhexane-2, 5-dihydroperoxide
2,5-Dimethylhexane-2,5-diperbenzoate	2,5-Di (benzoylperoxy)2,5-dimethyl hexane 2,5-Dimethyl-2,5,-*bis*(benzoylperoxy) hexane
Di*iso*propyl benzene hydroperoxide	*iso*Propylcumyl hydroperoxide
Di-*n*-propyl perdicarbonate	Di-*n*-propyl peroxydicarbonate
2-Ethyl hexyl perdicarbonate	Di-2-ethyl hexyl perdicarbonate
3,3,6,6,9,9-Hexamethyl-1,2,4,5-tetroxonane	
bis(1-Hydroxy cyclohexyl) peroxide	1,1-Dihydroxy dicyclohexyl peroxide
Lauroyl peroxide	Dilauroyl peroxide *bis*Dodecanoyl peroxide
*para*Menthane hydroperoxide	*para*Menthanyl hydroperoxide
Methyl *iso*butyl ketone peroxide	*iso*Butyl methyl ketone peroxide 4-Methylpentane-2-one peroxide
Methyl ethyl ketone peroxide	Butanone peroxide Ethyl methyl ketone peroxide
Nonanoyl peroxide	*iso*Nonanoyl peroxide *bis*(3,5,5-Trimethyl hexanoyl) peroxide
Octanoyl peroxide	Capryloyl peroxide Caprylyl peroxide Octoyl peroxide
Pelargonyl peroxide	*n*-Nonanoyl peroxide
Peracetic acid	Acetyl hydroperoxide
Propionyl peroxide	Dipropionyl peroxide
*iso*Propyl perdicarbonate	Di*iso*propyl peroxydicarbonate
Succinic acid peroxide	Disuccinic acid peroxide Peroxy disuccinic acid Succinoyl peroxide
2,6,6-Trimethyl norpinanyl hydroperoxide	Pinane hydroperoxide

PART II

ORGANIC PEROXIDE MIXTURES EXCLUDED FROM ARTICLE 2(1)(*b*)

Benzoyl peroxide in a mixture containing not more than 35 per cent. by weight of that substance, the remainder being inert solids.

1,3-*bis*(*tert*Butyl peroxy*iso*propyl) benzene and 1,4-*bis*(*tert*butyl peroxy*iso*propyl) benzene in a mixture containing in total not more than 40 per cent. by weight of those substances, the remainder being inert solids.

Cumene hydroperoxide in a solution consisting of inert solvent and not more than 82 per cent. by weight of that substance.

Cyclohexanone peroxide in a mixture containing not more than 30 per cent. by weight of that substance, the remainder being inert solids.

Dicumyl peroxide in a mixture containing not more than 40 per cent. by weight of that substance, the remainder being inert solids.

Pelargonyl peroxide in a solution consisting of inert solvent and not more than 75 per cent. by weight of that substance.

EXPLANATORY NOTE

(*This Note is not part of the Order.*)

This Order applies certain provisions of the Petroleum (Consolidation) Act 1928 to the organic peroxides specified in Part I of the Schedule, and also, with certain exceptions, to any solution or mixture containing 5% or more by weight of any of those substances.

Under the provisions as applied the Secretary of State is empowered to make Regulations as to the conveyance of the organic peroxides by road and for protecting persons and property from danger in connection with such conveyance. In addition, the provisions as applied require notice of certain accidents in connection with the organic peroxides to be given to the Secretary of State, empower him to direct an inquiry to be made in regard thereto, make provision in regard to inquests and confer certain powers on magistrates' courts and on government inspectors in relation to the organic peroxides.

STATUTORY INSTRUMENTS

1973 No. 1898

JURIES

The Jurors' (Coroners' Courts) Allowances (Amendment) (No. 3) Regulations 1973

Made - - - -	12*th November* 1973
Coming into Operation	3*rd December* 1973

In exercise of the powers conferred on me by section 1 of the Juries Act 1949**(a)**, as amended by section 1 of the Juries Act 1954**(b)**, section 36 of the Courts Act 1971**(c)** and section 27 of the Criminal Justice Act 1972**(d)**, I hereby, with the consent of the Minister for the Civil Service, make the following Regulations:—

1. These Regulations may be cited as the Jurors' (Coroners' Courts) Allowances (Amendment) (No. 3) Regulations 1973 and shall come into operation on 3rd December 1973.

2. Regulation 6 of the Jurors' (Coroners' Courts) Allowances Regulations 1972**(e)**, as amended **(f)**, shall be amended by the substitution of the words "62p", "£1·35", "£2·40", "£3·40", "£4·05" and "£8·65" for the words "57p", "£1·25", "£2·20", "£3·12", "£3·75" and "£8·00" respectively.

3. Paragraph 3 of the Schedule to the said Regulations shall be amended as follows:—

(*a*) in sub-paragraph (*b*) the words "4·4p", "5·5p" and "6·0p" shall be substituted for the words "4·1p", "5·1p" and "5·6p" respectively;

(*b*) in sub-paragraph (*c*) the words "2·7p" shall be substituted for the words "2·6p".

Robert Carr,
One of Her Majesty's Principal
Secretaries of State.

9th November 1973.

Consent of the Minister for the Civil Service given under his official seal on 12th November 1973.

(L.S.)

J. C. Leeming,
Authorised by the Minister
for the Civil Service.

(a) 1949 c. 27.
(b) 1954 c. 41.
(c) 1971 c. 23.
(d) 1972 c. 71.
(e) S.I. 1972/1001 (1972 II, p. 3084).
(f) The relevant amending instrument is S.I. 1973/935 (1973 II, p. 2814)

EXPLANATORY NOTE

(*This Note is not part of the Regulations.*)

These Regulations provide for an increase in certain allowances in respect of jury service in a coroner's court, namely, allowances for subsistence and certain forms of travel, including, in particular, travel by private motor car.

STATUTORY INSTRUMENTS

1973 No. 1899

CORONERS

EXPENSES

The Coroners (Fees and Allowances) (Amendment) (No. 3) Rules 1973

Made - - - - *9th November* 1973

Coming into Operation *3rd December* 1973

In exercise of the powers conferred upon me by section 1(1) of the Coroners Act 1954(**a**), I hereby make the following Rules:—

1. These Rules may be cited as the Coroners (Fees and Allowances) (Amendment) (No. 3) Rules 1973 and shall come into operation on 3rd December 1973.

2. Rule 4(3) of the Coroners (Fees and Allowances) Rules 1971 (**b**), as amended(**c**), shall be amended by the substitution of the words "6p" for the words "5·6p".

3. Rule 8 of the said Rules shall be amended by the substitution of the words "62p", "£1·35", "£2·40", "£3·40", "£4·05", "£8·65", and "80p" for the words "57p", "£1·25", "£2·20", "£3·12", "£3·75", "£8·00" and "75p" respectively.

4. Rule 9 of the said Rules shall be amended by the substitution of the words "£6·25" and "80p" for the words "£5·80" and "75p" respectively.

5. Rule 10(3) of the said Rules shall be amended as follows:—

(*a*) in sub-paragraph (*b*) the words "4·4p", "5·5p" and "6·0p" shall be substituted for the words "4·1p", "5·1p" and "5·6p" respectively;

(*b*) in sub-paragraph (*c*) the words "2·7p" shall be substituted for the words "2·6p".

Robert Carr,
One of Her Majesty's Principal
Secretaries of State.

Home Office,
Whitehall.
9th November 1973.

(**a**) 1954 c. 31. (**b**) S.I. 1971/108 (1971 I, p. 200).
(**c**) The relevant amending instrument is S.I. 1973/921 (1973 II, p. 2795).

EXPLANATORY NOTE

(This Note is not part of the Rules.)

These Rules provide for an increase in certain allowances payable to witnesses attending at an inquest, namely, allowances for subsistence and certain forms of travel including, in particular, travel by private motor car.

1973 No. 1900

EMERGENCY POWERS

ELECTRICITY

The Electricity (Heating) (Restriction) Order 1973

Made - - - *14th November* 1973

Coming into Operation *15th November* 1973

The Secretary of State, in exercise of his powers under Regulation 21 of the Emergency Regulations 1973 (**a**) and of all other powers in that behalf enabling him, hereby orders as follows:—

1. This Order shall come into operation on 15th November 1973 and may be cited as the Electricity (Heating) (Restriction) Order 1973.

2.—(1) In this Order " electricity " means electricity supplied by an Electricity Board.

(2) The Interpretation Act 1889(**b**) shall apply to the interpretation of this Order as it applies to the interpretation of an Act of Parliament.

3.—(1) Subject to paragraph (2) of this Article, and except under a licence granted by the Secretary of State under this Order, no person shall consume or permit the consumption of electricity for the purpose of heating—

(*a*) any premises used wholly or mainly—

(i) as an office or showroom;

(ii) as a retail shop, bank or petrol station;

(iii) as a restaurant or catering establishment (whether or not licensed for the sale of intoxicating liquor) or for the sale or consumption of intoxicating liquor;

(iv) as a film, television or photographic studio;

(v) as a library, museum, art gallery, exhibition hall or other public hall;

(vi) as a school, college or other place of education;

(vii) as a church, chapel or other place of public worship; or

(viii) for recreation, entertainment or sport; or

(*b*) any part so used of any premises, not otherwise so used, if the heating for that part is controlled separately from the heating for the other part of the premises.

(2) Nothing in paragraph (1) of this Article shall apply to the consumption of electricity—

(*a*) on any part of any such premises which is used as living accommodation;

(*b*) on any part of any such premises to the extent that such consumption is necessary for the maintenance of the health of any person on those premises who is ill, disabled or infirm;

(*c*) for the purpose of operating any fan, circulating pump or controlling mechanism installed in any central plant used for heating any such premises by means of solid fuel, gas or oil;

(*d*) for the purpose of preventing damage to any central heating plant on any such premises;

(**a**) S.I. 1973/1881 (1973 III, p. 6516). (**b**) 1889 c. 63.

(*e*) for the purpose of operating apparatus for heating, cooling or air-conditioning on any such premises to the extent necessary to prevent damage to any apparatus, goods or material on the premises which is sensitive to changes in temperature or humidity;

(*f*) for preserving the health of any livestock on any such premises;

(*g*) on any part of such premises used as a registered pharmacy or used for the purpose of his practice or business by a registered medical practitioner, a registered dentist, a registered pharmacist, a registered optician, a registered veterinary surgeon or a registered veterinary practitioner; or

(*h*) on any part of such premises used for the purpose of dispensing hearing aids by any person registered as a dispenser of hearing aids under the Hearing Aid Council Act 1968(**a**).

4. Any licence granted under this Order may be subject to conditions and may be revoked without prior notice.

Tom Boardman,

Minister for Industry,
Department of Trade and Industry.

14th November 1973.

EXPLANATORY NOTE

(*This Note is not part of the Order.*)

This Order prohibits the consumption of electricity for space heating, except under a licence granted by the Secretary of State, in premises used for certain purposes specified in Article 3(1) of the Order. These include offices, show-rooms, shops, banks, petrol stations, restaurants, bars, studios, public halls, schools, churches and places of recreation, entertainment or sport. The prohibition does not apply to living accommodation, or where heating is necessary for the preservation of health. The premises of doctors, dentists, pharmacists, opticians, veterinary surgeons and practitioners and dispensers of hearing aids are excluded from the prohibition, in so far as they are used for the purpose of the practice or business. The use of electricity for certain specified purposes (including the operation or control of central heating plant consuming other fuels) is permitted.

(**a**) 1968 c. 50.

1973 No. 1901

EMERGENCY POWERS

ELECTRICITY

The Electricity (Advertising, Display, etc.) (Restriction) Order 1973

Made - - - - *14th November* 1973
Coming into Operation *15th November* 1973

The Secretary of State, in exercise of his powers under Regulation 21 of the Emergency Regulations 1973(**a**) and of all other powers in that behalf enabling him, hereby orders as follows:—

1. This Order shall come into operation on 15th November 1973 and may be cited as the Electricity (Advertising, Display, etc.) (Restriction) Order 1973.

2.—(1) In this Order " electricity " means electricity supplied by an Electricity Board.

(2) The Interpretation Act 1889(**b**) shall apply to the interpretation of this Order as it applies to the interpretation of an Act of Parliament.

3.—(1) Subject to paragraphs (2) and (3) of this Article, and except under a licence granted by the Secretary of State under this Order, no person shall consume or permit the consumption of electricity for the purpose of—

(*a*) advertising any article, product or service;

(*b*) the display of any article, building or structure or any part thereof; or

(*c*) lighting (whether by means of floodlights or any other form of illumination) any area in the open air for the purpose of recreation, entertainment or sport.

(2) Nothing in paragraph (1) of this Article shall apply to the consumption of electricity for the purpose of—

(*a*) broadcasting any advertisement from an authorised broadcasting station; or

(*b*) projecting any advertisement by means of any film or slide on to a screen in any premises licensed under the Cinematograph Act 1909(**c**) or the Theatres Act 1968(**d**); or

(*c*) displaying any article or structure which is a traffic sign within the meaning of section 54(1) of the Road Traffic Regulation Act 1967(**e**); or

(**a**) S.I. 1973/1881 (1973 III, p. 6516). (**b**) 1889 c. 63. (**c**) 1909 c. 30. (**d**) 1968 c. 54.
(**e**) 1967 c. 76.

(*d*) displaying any sign indicating the nature of the premises at any of the following:—

(i) ambulance stations;

(ii) fire stations;

(iii) first aid stations;

(iv) police stations;

(v) hospitals;

(vi) the premises of a registered dentist;

(vii) the premises of a fully registered medical practitioner;

(viii) the premises of a registered pharmacist;

(ix) the premises of a registered optician;

(x) the premises of a registered veterinary surgeon or registered veterinary practitioner;

(xi) the premises of a registered dispenser of hearing aids; or

(*e*) illuminating any telephone which is intended for public use.

(3) Nothing in paragraph (1) of this Article shall apply to the consumption of electricity at any premises used for the purpose of any railway undertaking.

4. Any licence granted under this Order may be subject to conditions and may be revoked without prior notice.

Tom Boardman,
Minister for Industry,
Department of Trade and Industry.

14th November 1973.

EXPLANATORY NOTE

(*This Note is not part of the Order.*)

This Order prohibits the consumption of electricity supplied by an Electricity Board for purposes of advertising or display, or lighting any area in the open air for the purpose of recreation, entertainment or sport, except under a licence granted by the Secretary of State or for certain purposes specified in the Order, including advertising on television or by radio, or in cinemas or theatres, and the illumination of traffic signs, public telephones and signs indicating hospitals, police and fire stations and other specified premises. The prohibition does not apply to railway premises.

STATUTORY INSTRUMENTS

1973 No. 1910

REPRESENTATION OF THE PEOPLE

The Local Elections (Parishes and Communities) Rules 1973

Made - - - -	12*th November* 1973
Laid before Parliament	3*rd December* 1973
Coming into Operation	1*st January* 1974

In exercise of the powers conferred upon me by sections 42, 83 and 89(6) of the Local Government Act 1972(**a**) and by section 78 and by section 165(1) (as amended by paragraph 11 of Schedule 6 to the Local Government Act 1972) of the Representation of the People Act 1949(**b**), I hereby make the following Rules:—

1.—(1) These Rules may be cited as the Local Elections (Parishes and Communities) Rules 1973 and shall come into operation on 1st January 1974.

(2) The Interpretation Act 1889(**c**) shall apply to the interpretation of these Rules as it applies to the interpretation of an Act of Parliament.

2.—(1) The Parish Council Election Rules 1973(**d**) shall be revoked as from 1st January 1974.

(2) Section 38 of the Interpretation Act 1889 shall apply as if the Rules revoked by these Rules were Acts of Parliament.

3. In the application of the parliamentary elections rules in Schedule 2 to the Representation of the People Act 1949 to the elections of parish or community councillors adaptations, alterations and exceptions shall be made therein so that the elections shall be conducted in accordance with the rules set out in Schedule 1 hereto.

4. In the application of those provisions of the Representation of the People Act 1949 referred to in section 165(1) of that Act to an election of the chairman of a parish or community council and of parish or community councillors the following modification shall have effect:—

In section 119(2)(*b*) of the said Act for the words "such amount not exceeding five hundred pounds" there shall be substituted the words "an amount of fifty pounds or such smaller amount or such larger amount not exceeding three hundred pounds".

5.—(1) The declaration of acceptance of office by the chairman of a parish or community council or by a parish or community councillor shall be in the form in Part I of Schedule 2 hereto or a form to the like effect.

(**a**) 1972 c. 70.
(**b**) 1949 c. 68.
(**c**) 1889 c. 63.
(**d**) S.I. 1973/166 (1973 I, p. 670).

(2) In relation to an election of parish or community councillors a declaration as to election expenses shall be in the form in Part II of Schedule 2 hereto, or a form to the like effect.

Robert Carr,
One of Her Majesty's Principal
Secretaries of State.

Home Office,
Whitehall.
12th November 1973.

SCHEDULE 1

Election Rules

Arrangement of rules

Part I

Provisions as to Time

Part II

Stages Common to Contested and Uncontested Elections

Part III

Contested Elections

General provisions

Part VI

Supplemental

Appendix

Forms

Part I

Provisions as to Time

Timetable

1. The proceedings at the election shall be conducted in accordance with the following Table.

Timetable

Proceeding	*Time*
Publication of notice of election ...	Not later than the twenty-fifth day before the day of election.
Delivery of nomination papers... ...	Not later than noon on the nineteenth day before the day of election.
Publication of statement as to persons nominated	Not later than noon on the seventeenth day before the day of election.
Delivery of notices of withdrawals of candidature	Not later than noon on the sixteenth day before the day of election.
Notice of poll	Not later than the sixth day before the day of election.
Notice of appointment of polling or counting agents	Not later than the fifth day before the day of election.
Polling	On the day of election.

Computation of time

2.—(1) In computing any period of time for the purposes of the timetable in rule 1 a Sunday, day of the Christmas break, of the Easter break or of a bank holiday break or day appointed for public thanksgiving or mourning shall be disregarded and any such day shall not be treated as a day for the purpose of any proceedings up to the completion of the poll nor shall the returning officer be obliged to proceed with the counting of the votes thereon.

(2) In this rule "the Christmas break" means the period beginning with the last week day before Christmas Day and ending with the first week day after Christmas Day which is not a bank holiday, "the Easter break" means the period beginning with the Thursday before and ending with the Tuesday after Easter Day, and "a bank holiday break" means any bank holiday not included in the Christmas break or the Easter break and the period beginning with the last week day before that bank holiday and ending with the next week day which is not a bank holiday.

Hours of poll

3. The poll shall commence at eight o'clock in the morning and be kept open till nine o'clock in the evening of the same day and no longer.

PART II

STAGES COMMON TO CONTESTED AND UNCONTESTED ELECTIONS

Notice of election

4.—(1) Notice of the election in the form in the Appendix, or a form to the like effect, shall be prepared, signed and published by the returning officer.

(2) The notice shall be published by causing a copy to be exhibited conspicuously in the electoral area; and—

(*a*) at the offices, if any, of the parish or community council; and

(*b*) at the principal offices of the council for any district which includes the whole or part of the electoral area;

(*c*) at such other places as the returning officer thinks best calculated to bring the notice to the attention of those concerned.

Nomination of candidates

5.—(1) Each candidate shall be nominated by a separate nomination paper in the form in the Appendix, or a form to the like effect, delivered at the place fixed for the purpose by the returning officer.

(2) The nomination paper shall state the full names, home address and (if desired) description of the candidate and the surname shall be placed first in the list of his names.

(3) The description (if any) shall not exceed six words in length, and need not refer to his rank, profession or calling so long as, with the other particulars of the candidate, it is sufficient to identify him.

Subscription of nomination paper

6.—(1) The nomination paper shall be subscribed by two electors for the electoral area as proposer and seconder.

(2) Where a nomination paper bears the signatures of more than the required number of persons as proposing or seconding the nomination of a candidate, the signature appearing first on the paper in each category shall be taken into account to the exclusion of any others in that category.

(3) The nomination paper shall give the electoral number of each person subscribing it.

(4) The returning officer shall provide nomination papers and forms of consent to nomination and shall supply any elector for the electoral area with as many nomination papers and forms of consent to nomination as may be required and shall, at the request of any such elector, prepare for signature a nomination paper.

(5) No person shall—

(*a*) subscribe more nomination papers than there are vacancies to be filled in the electoral area; or

(*b*) subscribe a nomination paper for more than one ward of a parish or a community divided into wards; or

(*c*) subscribe more than one nomination paper in respect of the same candidate:

Provided that a person shall not be prevented from subscribing a nomination paper by reason only of his having subscribed that of a candidate who has died or withdrawn before delivery of the first-mentioned paper.

(6) If any person subscribes nomination papers in contravention of the last foregoing paragraph, his signature shall be inoperative in all but those papers (up to the permitted number) which are first delivered.

(7) In this rule—

the expression "elector for the electoral area" means a person who is registered as a local government elector for the electoral area in the register to be used at the election or who, pending the publication of that register, appears from the electors lists therefor as corrected by the registration officer to be entitled to be so registered (and accordingly includes a person shown in the register or electors lists as below voting age if it appears therefrom that he will be of voting age on the day fixed for the poll, but not otherwise);

the expression "electoral number" means the distinctive letter or letters of the parliamentary polling district in which a person is registered together with his number in the said register, or pending the publication of the register, the distinctive letter or letters of the parliamentary polling district in which he is entitled to be registered together with his number (if any) in the electors lists therefor.

Consent to nomination

7.—(1) A person shall not be validly nominated unless his consent to nomination, given in writing in the form in the Appendix, or a form to the like effect, on or within one month before the last day for the delivery of nomination papers, and attested by one witness, is delivered at the place and within the time appointed for the delivery of nomination papers.

(2) A candidate's consent given under this rule shall contain a statement declaring, with reference to the date of his nomination, that to the best of his belief he will be or is qualified as required by law to be elected to and hold the office in question, and the statement shall give particulars of his qualification.

Decisions as to validity of nomination papers

8.—(1) Where a nomination paper and the candidate's consent thereto are delivered in accordance with these rules, the candidate shall be deemed to stand nominated unless and until the returning officer decides that the nomination paper is invalid, or proof is given to the satisfaction of the returning officer of the candidate's death, or the candidate withdraws.

(2) The returning officer shall be entitled to hold a nomination paper invalid only on one of the following grounds, that is to say:—

(*a*) that the particulars of the candidate or the persons subscribing the paper are not as required by law; or

(*b*) that the paper is not subscribed as so required.

(3) The returning officer shall examine the nomination papers, and decide whether the candidates have been validly nominated in accordance with these rules and shall do so as soon as practicable after each paper is delivered.

(4) Where he decides that a nomination paper is invalid, he shall endorse and sign on the paper the fact and the reasons for his decision.

(5) The returning officer shall send notice of his decision to each candidate at his home address as stated on his nomination paper.

(6) The decision of the returning officer that a nomination paper is valid shall be final and shall not be questioned in any proceeding whatsoever.

(7) Subject to the last foregoing paragraph, nothing in this rule shall prevent the validity of a nomination being questioned on an election petition.

Publication of nominations

9.—(1) The returning officer shall prepare and publish a statement in the form in the Appendix, or a form to the like effect, showing the persons who have been and stand nominated and any other persons who have been nominated, with the reason why they no longer stand nominated.

(2) The statement shall show the names, addresses and descriptions (if any) of the persons nominated as given in their nomination papers.

(3) The statement shall show the persons standing nominated arranged alphabetically in the order of their surnames and, if there are two or more of them with the same surname, of their other names; and if there are two or more of them with the same surname and other names, the order in which those persons shall be shown shall be determined by lot drawn by the returning officer.

(4) In the case of a person nominated by more than one nomination paper, the returning officer shall take the particulars required by the foregoing provisions of this rule from such one of the papers as the candidate or the returning officer in default of the candidate may select.

(5) The statement as to persons nominated shall be published by causing it to be affixed to the place appointed for the delivery of nominated papers.

Inspection of nomination papers and consents to nomination

10. Any person may, at all reasonable times after the latest time for delivery of nomination papers and before the day of election, inspect and take copies of, and extracts from, nomination papers and consents to nomination.

Withdrawal of candidates

11.—(1) A candidate may withdraw from his candidature by notice of withdrawal signed by him and attested by one witness and delivered at the place appointed for the delivery of nomination papers.

(2) In the case of a candidate who is outside the United Kingdom, a notice of withdrawal signed by his proposer and accompanied by a written declaration also so signed of the candidate's absence from the United Kingdom shall be of the same effect as a notice of withdrawal signed by the candidate:

Provided that where the candidate stands nominated by more than one nomination paper a notice of withdrawal under this paragraph shall be effective if, but only if—

(*a*) it and the accompanying declaration are signed by all the proposers, except any who is, and is stated in the said declaration to be, outside the United Kingdom; or

(*b*) it is accompanied, in addition to the said declaration, by a written statement signed by the candidate that the proposer giving the notice is authorised to do so on the candidate's behalf during his absence from the United Kingdom.

Nomination in more than one ward

12. A candidate who is validly nominated for more than one ward of a parish or a community must duly withdraw from his candidature in all those wards except one, and

if he does not so withdraw he shall be deemed to have withdrawn from his candidature in all those wards.

Method of election

13.—(1) If the number of persons remaining validly nominated for the electoral area after any withdrawals under these rules exceeds the number of vacancies, the councillors shall be elected from among them at a poll under Part III of these rules.

(2) If the said number does not exceed the number of vacancies, the person or persons (if any) remaining validly nominated for the electoral area after any withdrawals under these rules shall be declared elected in accordance with Part IV of these rules.

PART III

CONTESTED ELECTIONS

GENERAL PROVISIONS

Poll to be taken by ballot

14. The votes at the poll shall be given by ballot, the result shall be ascertained by counting the votes given to each candidate, and the candidate or candidates to whom the majority of votes have been given shall be declared to have been elected.

The ballot papers

15.—(1) The ballot of every voter shall consist of a ballot paper and the persons remaining validly nominated for the electoral area after any withdrawals under these rules, and no others, shall be entitled to have their names inserted in the ballot paper.

(2) Every ballot paper shall be in the form in the Appendix, and shall be printed in accordance with the directions therein, and—

(*a*) shall contain the names and other particulars of the candidates as shown in the statement of persons nominated;

(*b*) shall be capable of being folded up;

(*c*) shall have a number printed on the back;

(*d*) shall have attached, either at the side or at the top, a counterfoil with the same number printed on the face or the back;

(*e*) shall be of a different colour from that of any ballot papers used in an election of district councillors held on the same date and for the same area.

(3) The order of the names in the ballot paper shall be the same as in the statement as to persons nominated.

The official mark

16.—(1) Every ballot paper shall be marked with an official mark, which shall be either embossed or perforated.

(2) The official mark shall be kept secret.

Prohibition of disclosure of vote

17. No person who has voted at the election shall, in any legal proceeding to question the election, be required to state for whom he voted.

Use of schools and public rooms

18.—(1) The returning officer may use, free of charge, for the purpose of taking the poll or counting the votes—

(*a*) a room in a school maintained or assisted by a local education authority or a school in respect of which grants are made out of moneys provided by Parliament to the person or body of persons responsible for the management of the school;

(*b*) a room the expense of maintaining which is payable out of any rate.

(2) The returning officer shall make good any damage done to, and defray any expense incurred by the persons having control over, any such room as aforesaid by reason of its being used for the purpose of taking the poll or of counting the votes.

(3) The use of a room in an unoccupied house for the purpose of taking the poll or of counting the votes shall not render a person liable to be rated or to pay any rate for that house.

Action to be taken before the Poll

Notice of poll

19.—(1) Notice of the poll shall be published by the returning officer at the places at which the notice of election is required to be published under rule 4 of these rules.

(2) Notice of the poll shall specify—

(*a*) the day and hours fixed for the poll;

(*b*) the number of councillors to be elected;

(*c*) the particulars of each candidate remaining validly nominated (the names and other particulars of the candidates, and the order of the names of the candidates, being the same as in the statement as to persons nominated);

(*d*) the names of the proposer and seconder signing a candidate's nomination paper; and

(*e*) the situation of each polling station and the description of the persons entitled to vote thereat.

(3) In the case of a candidate nominated by more than one nomination paper, the nomination paper mentioned in sub-paragraph (*d*) of paragraph (2) of this rule shall be that from which the names and other particulars of the candidate shown in the statement as to persons nominated are taken.

Provision of polling stations

20.—(1) The returning officer shall provide a sufficient number of polling stations and, subject to the following provisions of this rule, shall allot the electors to the polling stations in such manner as he thinks most convenient.

(2) One or more polling stations may be provided in the same room.

(3) The polling station allotted to electors from any parliamentary polling district wholly or partly within the electoral area shall, in the absence of special circumstances, be in the parliamentary polling place for that district, unless the polling place is outside the electoral area.

(4) The returning officer shall provide each polling station with such number of compartments as may be necessary in which the voters can mark their votes screened from observation.

Appointment of presiding officers and clerks

21.—(1) The returning officer shall appoint and may pay a presiding officer to attend at each polling station and such clerks as may be necessary for the purposes of the election, but he shall not appoint any person who has been employed by or on behalf of a candidate in or about the election.

(2) The returning officer may, if he thinks fit, preside at a polling station and the provisions of these rules relating to a presiding officer shall apply to a returning officer so presiding with the necessary modifications as to things to be done by the returning officer to the presiding officer or by the presiding officer to the returning officer.

(3) A presiding officer may do, by the clerks appointed to assist him, any act (including the asking of questions) which he is required or authorised by these rules to do at a polling station except order the arrest, exclusion or removal of any person from the polling station.

List of proxies

22. The registration officer shall as soon as practicable prepare a special list (in these rules referred to as "the list of proxies") giving—

(*a*) the names and numbers on the register of the electors for whom proxies have been appointed;

(*b*) the names and addresses of the persons appointed.

Equipment of polling stations

23.—(1) The returning officer shall provide each presiding officer with such number of ballot boxes and ballot papers as in the opinion of the returning officer may be necessary.

(2) Where the poll at an election of parish or community councillors is taken together with the poll at an election of district councillors, one ballot box may, if the returning officer thinks fit, be used for the two elections; but, if separate ballot boxes are used, no vote for any parish or community councillor shall be rendered invalid by the ballot paper being placed in the box intended for the reception of ballot papers for district councillors.

(3) Every ballot box shall be so constructed that the ballot papers can be put therein, but cannot be withdrawn therefrom, without the box being unlocked.

(4) The returning officer shall provide each polling station with—

(*a*) materials to enable voters to mark the ballot papers;

(*b*) instruments for stamping thereon the official mark;

(*c*) copies of the register of electors for the electoral area or such part thereof as contains the names of the electors allotted to the station;

(*d*) the parts of the list of proxies prepared for the election corresponding to the register of electors for the electoral area or part thereof provided under the last foregoing paragraph.

(5) A notice in the form in the Appendix, giving directions for the guidance of the voters in voting, shall be printed in conspicuous characters and exhibited inside and outside every polling station.

(6) In every compartment of every polling station there shall be exhibited a notice as follows:—"The voter may vote for not more than candidate(s)"; so however that the notice may be adapted as far as circumstances require.

Appointment of polling and counting agents

24.—(1) Each candidate may, before the commencement of the poll, appoint polling agents to attend at polling stations for the purpose of detecting personation and one or more counting agents up to the number he may be authorised by the returning officer to appoint to attend at the counting of the votes:

Provided that—

(*a*) the number of counting agents authorised by the returning officer shall be the same in the case of each candidate;

(*b*) the appointment of an agent may be on behalf of more than one candidate;

(*c*) not more than four polling agents shall be appointed to attend at any polling station.

(2) If the number of polling agents appointed to attend at a polling station exceeds the permitted number, only those agents, up to the permitted number whose appointments are signed by or on behalf of the greater number of candidates, or, in the event of an equality in the number of signatures, only such of those agents as may be determined by the returning officer, shall be deemed to have been duly appointed.

(3) Notice in writing of the appointment, stating the names and addresses of the persons appointed, shall be given by the candidate to the returning officer and shall be so given not later than the time appointed for that purpose in rule 1 of these rules.

(4) If an agent dies, or becomes incapable of acting, the candidate may appoint another agent in his place, and shall forthwith give to the returning officer notice in writing of the name and address of the agent appointed.

(5) In the following provisions of these rules references to polling and counting agents shall be taken as references to agents whose appointments have been duly made and notified and who are within the permitted number.

(6) Any notice required to be given to a counting agent by the returning officer may be delivered at, or sent by post to, the address stated in the notice of appointment.

(7) A candidate may himself do any act or thing which any polling or counting agent of his, if appointed, would have been authorised to do, or may assist his agent in doing any such act or thing.

(8) Where by these rules any act or thing is required or authorised to be done in the presence of the polling or counting agents, the non-attendance of any agents or agent at the time and place appointed for the purpose shall not, if the act or thing is otherwise duly done, invalidate the act or thing done.

Declaration of secrecy

25.—(1) Before the opening of the poll a declaration of secrecy in the form in paragraph (4) of this rule, or in a form as near thereto as circumstances admit, shall be made by—

(*a*) the returning officer and the presiding officers;

(*b*) every clerk authorised to attend at a polling station or the counting of the votes;

(*c*) every candidate attending at a polling station or at the counting of the votes;

(*d*) every candidate's wife or husband attending at the counting of the votes;

(*e*) every polling agent and counting agent;

(*f*) every person permitted by the returning officer to attend at the counting of the votes, though not entitled as of right to do so.

(2) Notwithstanding anything in the foregoing paragraph, the following persons attending at the counting of the votes, that is to say:—

(*a*) any candidate;

(*b*) any candidate's wife or husband attending by virtue of the rule authorising candidates' wives or husbands to attend as such;

(*c*) any person permitted by the returning officer to attend, though not entitled as of right to do so;

(*d*) any clerk making the declaration in order to attend at the counting of the votes;

need not make the declaration before the opening of the poll but shall make it before he or she is permitted to attend the counting, and a person becoming obliged to make a declaration by reason of his appointment after the opening of the poll shall make the declaration before acting under that appointment.

(3) The returning officer shall make the declaration in the presence of a Justice of the Peace, and any other person shall make the declaration in the presence either of a Justice of the Peace or of the returning officer, and subsections (1), (2), (3) and (6) of section 53 of the Representation of the People Act 1949 shall be read to the declarant by the person taking the declaration or shall be read by the declarant in the presence of that person:

Provided that the declaration may be made by the returning officer or any other person before a person who is chairman of the Greater London Council, a county council or a district council or mayor of a London borough, and may be made by a person other than the returning officer before the proper officer of any such council.

(4) The declaration shall be as follows:—

"I solemnly promise and declare that I will not do anything forbidden by subsections (1), (2), (3) and (6) of section 53 of the Representation of the People Act 1949, which have been read to [by] me.".

THE POLL

Admission to polling station

26.—(1) The presiding officer shall regulate the number of voters to be admitted to the polling station at the same time, and shall exclude all other persons except—

(*a*) the candidates;

(*b*) the polling agents appointed to attend at the polling station;

(*c*) the clerks appointed to attend at the polling station;

(*d*) the constables on duty; and

(*e*) the companions of blind voters.

(2) Not more than one polling agent shall be admitted at the same time to a polling station on behalf of the same candidate.

(3) A constable or person employed by a returning officer shall not be admitted to vote in person elsewhere than at his own polling station under the provisions of the Representation of the People Act 1949 in that behalf, except on production and surrender of a certificate as to his employment which shall be in the form in the Appendix, or a form to the like effect, and signed by an officer of police of or above the rank of inspector or by the returning officer, as the case may be.

(4) Any certificate surrendered under this rule shall forthwith be cancelled.

Keeping of order in station

27.—(1) It shall be the duty of the presiding officer to keep order at his polling station.

(2) If a person misconducts himself in a polling station, or fails to obey the lawful orders of the presiding officer, he may immediately, by order of the presiding officer, be removed from the polling station by a constable in or near that station or by any other person authorised in writing by the returning officer to remove him, and the person so removed shall not, without the permission of the presiding officer, again enter the polling station during the day.

(3) Any person so removed may, if charged with the commission in the polling station of an offence, be dealt with as a person taken into custody by a constable for an offence without a warrant.

(4) The powers conferred by this rule shall not be exercised so as to prevent a voter who is otherwise entitled to vote at a polling station from having an opportunity of voting at that station.

Sealing of ballot boxes

28. Immediately before the commencement of the poll, the presiding officer shall show the ballot box empty to such persons, if any, as are present in the polling station, so that they may see that it is empty, and shall then lock it up and place his seal on it in such manner as to prevent it being opened without breaking the seal, and shall place it in his view for the receipt of ballot papers, and keep it so locked and sealed.

Questions to be put to voters

29.—(1) The presiding officer may, and if required by a candidate or his polling agent shall, put to any person applying for a ballot paper at the time of his application, but not afterwards, the following questions, or either of them, that is to say:—

(*a*) in the case of a person applying as an elector—

(i) Are you the person registered in the register of local government electors now in force for this electoral area as follows [*read the whole entry from the register*]?

(ii) Have you already voted at the present election [*adding in the case of an election for several wards,* in this or any other ward] otherwise than as proxy for some other person?

(*b*) in the case of a person applying as proxy—

(i) Are you the person whose name appears as A.B. in the list of proxies for this election as entitled to vote as proxy on behalf of C.D.?

(ii) Have you already voted here or elsewhere at the present election as proxy on behalf of C.D.?

(2) A ballot paper shall not be delivered to any person required to answer the above questions or any of them unless he has answered the questions or question satisfactorily.

(3) Save as by this rule authorised, no inquiry shall be permitted as to the right of any person to vote.

Challenge of voter

30.—(1) If at the time a person applies for a ballot paper for the purpose of voting in person, or after he has applied for a ballot paper for that purpose and before he has left the polling station, a candidate or his polling agent declares to the presiding officer that he has reasonable cause to believe that the applicant has committed an offence of personation and undertakes to substantiate the charge in a court of law, the presiding officer may order a constable to arrest the applicant, and the order of the presiding officer shall be sufficient authority for the constable so to do.

(2) A person against whom a declaration is made under this rule shall not by reason thereof be prevented from voting.

(3) A person arrested under the provisions of this rule shall be dealt with as a person taken into custody by a constable for an offence without a warrant.

Voting procedure

31.—(1) A ballot paper shall be delivered to a voter who applies therefor, and immediately before delivery—

(*a*) the ballot paper shall be stamped with the official mark, either embossed or perforated;

(*b*) the number, name and description of the elector as stated in the copy of the register of electors shall be called out;

(*c*) the number of the elector shall be marked on the counterfoil;

(*d*) a mark shall be placed in the register of electors against the number of the elector to denote that a ballot paper has been received but without showing the particular ballot paper which has been received; and (*e*) in the case of a person applying for a ballot paper as proxy, a mark shall also be placed against his name in the list of proxies.

(2) The voter, on receiving the ballot paper, shall forthwith proceed into one of the compartments in the polling station and there secretly mark his paper and fold it up so as to conceal his vote, and shall then show to the presiding officer the back of the paper so as to disclose the official mark, and put the ballot paper so folded up into the ballot box in the presence of the presiding officer.

(3) The voter shall vote without undue delay, and shall leave the polling station as soon as he has put his ballot paper into the ballot box.

Votes marked by presiding officer

32.—(1) The presiding officer, on the application of—

(*a*) a voter who is incapacitated by blindness or other physical cause from voting in manner directed by these rules; or

(*b*) if the poll is taken on a Saturday, a voter who declares that he is a Jew, and objects on religious grounds to voting in manner directed by these rules; or

(*c*) a voter who declares orally that he is unable to read;

shall, in the presence of the polling agents, cause the vote of the voter to be marked on a ballot paper in manner directed by the voter, and the ballot paper to be placed in the ballot box.

(2) The name and number in the register of electors of every voter whose vote is marked in pursuance of this rule, and the reason why it is so marked, shall be entered on a list (in these rules called "the list of votes marked by the presiding officer").

In the case of a person voting as proxy for an elector, the number to be entered together with the name of the voter shall be the number of the elector.

Voting by blind persons

33.—(1) If a voter makes an application to the presiding officer to be allowed on the ground of blindness to vote with the assistance of another person by whom he is accompanied (in these rules referred to as "the companion"), the presiding officer shall require the voter to declare orally whether he is so incapacitated by his blindness as to be unable to vote without assistance.

(2) If the presiding officer is satisfied that the voter is so incapacitated and is also satisfied by a written declaration made by the companion (in these rules referred to as "the declaration made by the companion of a blind voter") that the companion is a qualified person within the meaning of this rule and has not previously assisted more than one blind person to vote at the election, the presiding officer shall grant the application, and thereupon anything which is by these rules required to be done to or by the said voter in connection with the giving of his vote may be done to, or with the assistance of, the companion.

(3) For the purposes of this rule, a person shall be qualified to assist a blind voter to vote, if that person is either—

(*a*) a person who is entitled to vote as an elector at the election; or

(*b*) the father, mother, brother, sister, husband, wife, son or daughter of the blind voter and has attained the age of eighteen years.

(4) The name and number in the register of electors of every voter whose vote is given in accordance with this rule and the name and address of the companion shall be entered on a list (in these rules referred to as "the list of blind voters assisted by companions").

In the case of a person voting as proxy for an elector, the number to be entered together with the name of the voter shall be the number of the elector.

(5) The declaration made by the companion—

(*a*) shall be in the form in the Appendix;

(*b*) shall be made before the presiding officer at the time when the voter applies to vote with the assistance of a companion and shall forthwith be given to the presiding officer who shall attest and retain it.

(6) No fee or other payment shall be charged in respect of the declaration.

Tendered ballot papers

34.—(1) If a person, representing himself to be—

(*a*) a particular elector named in the register; or

(*b*) a particular person named in the list of proxies as proxy for an elector,

applies for a ballot paper after another person has voted in person either as the elector or his proxy, the applicant shall, on satisfactorily answering the questions permitted by law to be asked at the poll, be entitled, subject to the following provisions of this rule, to mark a ballot paper (in these rules referred to as "a tendered ballot paper") in the same manner as any other voter.

(2) A tendered ballot paper shall—

(*a*) be of a colour differing from the other ballot papers;

(*b*) instead of being put into the ballot box, be given to the presiding officer and endorsed by him with the name of the voter and his number in the register of electors, and set aside in a separate packet.

(3) The name of the voter and his number in the register of electors shall be entered on a list (in these rules referred to as the "tendered votes list").

(4) In the case of a person voting as proxy for an elector, the number to be endorsed or entered together with the name of the voter shall be the number of that elector.

Spoilt ballot papers

35. A voter who has inadvertently dealt with his ballot paper in such manner that it cannot be conveniently used as a ballot paper may, on delivering it to the presiding officer and proving to his satisfaction the fact of the inadvertence, obtain another ballot paper in the place of the ballot paper so delivered (in these rules referred to as "a spoilt ballot paper"), and the spoilt ballot paper shall be immediately cancelled.

Adjournment of poll in case of riot

36.—(1) Where the proceedings at any polling station are interrupted or obstructed by riot or open violence, the presiding officer shall adjourn the proceedings until the following day and shall forthwith give notice to the returning officer.

(2) Where the poll is adjourned at any polling station—

(*a*) the hours of polling on the day to which it is adjourned shall be the same as for the original day; and

(*b*) reference in these rules to the close of the poll shall be construed accordingly.

Procedure on close of poll

37.—(1) As soon as practicable after the close of the poll, the presiding officer shall, in the presence of the polling agents, make up into separate packets, sealed with his own seal and the seals of such polling agents as desire to affix their seals—

(*a*) each ballot box in use at the station, sealed so as to prevent the introduction of additional ballot papers and unopened, but with the key attached;

(*b*) the unused and spoilt ballot papers placed together;

(*c*) the tendered ballot papers;

(*d*) the marked copies of the register of electors and of the list of proxies;

(*e*) the counterfoils of the used ballot papers and the certificates as to employment on duty on the day of the poll;

(*f*) the tendered votes list, the list of blind voters assisted by companions, the list of votes marked by the presiding officer, a statement of the number of voters whose votes are so marked by the presiding officer under the heads "physical incapacity", "Jews", and "unable to read", and the declarations made by the companions of blind voters;

and shall deliver the packets or cause them to be delivered to the returning officer to be taken charge of by him:

Provided that if the packets are not delivered by the presiding officer personally to the returning officer, the arrangements for their delivery shall require the approval of the returning officer.

(2) The marked copies of the register of electors and of the list of proxies shall be in one packet but shall not be in the same packet as the counterfoils of the used ballot papers and the certificates as to employment on duty on the day of the poll.

(3) The packets shall be accompanied by a statement (in these rules referred to as "the ballot paper account") made by the presiding officer showing the number of ballot papers entrusted to him, and accounting for them under the heads of ballot papers issued and not otherwise accounted for, unused, spoilt and tendered ballot papers.

COUNTING OF VOTES

Attendance at counting of votes

38.—(1) The returning officer shall make arrangements for counting the votes in the presence of the counting agents as soon as practicable after the close of the poll, and shall give to the counting agents notice in writing of the time and place at which he will begin to count the votes.

(2) No person other than—

(*a*) the returning officer and his clerks;

(*b*) the candidates and their wives or husbands;

(*c*) the counting agents;

may be present at the counting of the votes, unless permitted by the returning officer to attend.

(3) A person not entitled as of right to attend at the counting of the votes shall not be permitted to do so by the returning officer unless the returning officer is satisfied that the efficient counting of the votes will not be impeded, and the returning officer has either consulted the candidates or is satisfied that it is impracticable to consult them.

(4) The returning officer shall give the counting agents all such reasonable facilities for overseeing the proceedings, and all such information with reference thereto, as he can give them consistently with the orderly conduct of the proceedings and the discharge of his duties in connection therewith.

(5) In particular, where the votes are counted by sorting the ballot papers according to the candidate for whom the vote is given and then counting the number of ballot papers for each candidate, the counting agents shall be entitled to satisfy themselves that the ballot papers are correctly sorted.

The count

39.—(1) Before the returning officer proceeds to count the votes, he shall—

(*a*) in the presence of the counting agents open each ballot box and, taking out the ballot papers therein, count and record the number thereof and verify each ballot paper account;

(b) if polls have been taken together for the election of parish or community councillors and district councillors, separate the ballot papers relating to the election of parish or community councillors from those relating to district councillors and count and record the numbers relating to each election; and

(c) then mix together the whole of the ballot papers relating to the election of parish or community councillors contained in the ballot boxes.

(2) The returning officer shall not count any tendered ballot paper.

(3) The returning officer, while separating, counting, and recording the number of ballot papers and counting the votes, shall keep the ballot papers with their faces upwards and take all proper precautions for preventing any person from seeing the numbers printed on the back of the papers.

(4) The returning officer shall verify each ballot paper account by comparing it with the number of ballot papers recorded by him, and if necessary or if so required by a candidate the unused and spoilt ballot papers in his possession and the tendered votes list (opening and resealing the packets containing the unused and spoilt ballot papers and the tendered votes list) and shall draw up a statement as to the result of the verification which any counting agent may copy.

(5) The returning officer shall, so far as practicable, proceed continuously with counting the votes, allowing only time for refreshment:

Provided that he may, in so far as he thinks necessary, exclude the hours between nine o'clock in the evening and nine o'clock on the following morning.

(6) During the excluded time the returning officer shall place the ballot papers and other documents relating to the election under his own seal and the seals of such of the counting agents as desire to affix their seals and shall otherwise take proper precautions for the security of the papers and documents.

Re-count

40.—(1) A candidate may, if present when the counting or any re-count of the votes is completed, require the returning officer to have the votes re-counted or again re-counted but the returning officer may refuse to do so if in his opinion the request is unreasonable.

(2) No step shall be taken on the completion of the counting or any re-count of votes until the candidates present at the completion thereof have been given a reasonable opportunity to exercise the right conferred by this rule.

Rejected ballot papers

41.—(1) Any ballot paper—

(a) which does not bear the official mark; or

(b) on which votes are given for more candidates than the voter is entitled to vote for; or

(c) on which anything is written or marked by which the voter can be identified except the printed number on the back; or

(d) which is unmarked or void for uncertainty;

shall, subject to the provisions of this rule, be void and not counted.

(2) Where the voter is entitled to vote for more than one candidate, a ballot paper shall not be deemed to be void for uncertainty as respects any vote as to which no uncertainty arises and that vote shall be counted.

(3) A ballot paper on which a vote is marked—

(a) elsewhere than in the proper place; or

(b) otherwise than by means of a cross; or

(c) by more than one mark;

shall not by reason thereof be deemed to be void (either wholly or as respects that vote), if an intention that the vote shall be for one or other of the candidates clearly appears and the way the paper is marked does not of itself identify the voter and it is not shown that he can be identified thereby.

(4) The returning officer shall endorse—

(*a*) the word "rejected" on any ballot paper which under this rule is not to be counted; and

(*b*) in the case of a ballot paper on which any vote is counted under paragraph (2) of this rule, the words "rejected in part" and a memorandum specifying the votes counted;

and shall add to the endorsement the words "rejection objected to" if an objection is made by a counting agent to his decision.

(5) The returning officer shall draw up a statement showing the number of ballot papers rejected, including those rejected in part, under the several heads of—

(*a*) want of official mark;

(*b*) voting for more candidates than voter is entitled to;

(*c*) writing or mark by which voter could be identified;

(*d*) unmarked or wholly void for uncertainty;

(*e*) rejected in part.

Decisions on ballot papers

42. The decision of the returning officer on any question arising in respect of a ballot paper shall be final, but shall be subject to review on an election petition.

Equality of votes

43. Where, after the counting of the votes (including any re-count) is completed an equality of votes is found to exist between any candidates and the addition of a vote would entitle any of those candidates to be declared elected, the returning officer shall forthwith decide between those candidates by lot, and proceed as if the candidate on whom the lot falls had received an additional vote.

PART IV

FINAL PROCEEDINGS IN CONTESTED AND UNCONTESTED ELECTIONS

Declaration of result

44.—(1) In a contested election, when the result of the poll has been ascertained the returning officer shall forthwith declare to be elected the candidate or candidates to whom the majority of votes have been given and shall as soon as possible publish the name or names of the candidate or candidates elected and the total number of votes given to each candidate, whether elected or not, together with the number of rejected ballot papers under each head shown in the statement of rejected ballot papers.

(2) In an uncontested election, the returning officer shall, not later than eleven o'clock in the morning on the day of election, publish the name or names of the person or persons elected.

The return

45. The returning officer shall forthwith upon declaration of the result of the election return the name of each person elected to the proper officer of the parish or community council or, if there is no such proper officer, to the chairman of the council or, if there is no such chairman, to the proper officer of the district in which the parish or community is situate.

Part V

Disposal of Documents

Sealing of ballot papers

46.—(1) On the completion of the counting at a contested election the returning officer shall seal up in separate packets the counted and rejected ballot papers, including ballot papers rejected in part.

(2) The returning officer shall not open the sealed packets of tendered ballot papers or of counterfoils and certificates as to employment on duty on the day of the poll, or of marked copies of the register of electors and lists of proxies.

Delivery of documents

47. The returning officer shall then forward to the proper officer of the district in which the parish or community is situate the following documents, that is to say:—

(*a*) the packets of ballot papers in his possession;

(*b*) the ballot paper accounts and the statements of rejected ballot papers and of the result of the verification of the ballot paper accounts;

(*c*) the tendered votes lists, the lists of blind voters assisted by companions, the lists of votes marked by the presiding officer and the statements relating thereto, and the declarations made by the companions of blind voters;

(*d*) the packets of counterfoils and certificates as to employment on duty on the day of the poll;

(*e*) the packets containing marked copies of registers and of lists of proxies,

endorsing on each packet a description of its contents, the date of the election to which they relate and the name of the electoral area for which the election was held.

Orders for production of documents

48.—(1) An order—

(*a*) for the inspection or production of any rejected ballot papers, including ballot papers rejected in part; or

(*b*) for the opening of a sealed packet of counterfoils and certificates as to employment on duty on the day of the poll or for the inspection of counted ballot papers,

may be made by either a county court or an election court if the court is satisfied by evidence on oath that the order is required for the purpose of instituting or maintaining a prosecution for an offence in relation to ballot papers, or for the purpose of an election petition.

(2) The order may be made subject to such conditions as to persons, time, place and mode of inspection, production or opening as the court making the order may think expedient and may direct the proper officer of the district council having custody of the ballot papers and the sealed packets of counterfoils and certificates to retain them intact for such period as may be specified in the order:

Provided that in making and carrying into effect the order, care shall be taken that the way in which the vote of any particular elector has been given shall not be disclosed until it has been proved that his vote was given and the vote has been declared by a competent court to be invalid.

(3) An appeal shall lie to the High Court from any order of a county court made under this rule.

(4) Any power given under this rule to a county court may be exercised by any judge of the court otherwise than in open court.

(5) Where an order is made for the production by the proper officer of the district council of any document in his possession relating to any specified election, the

production by him or his agent of the document ordered in such manner as may be directed by that order shall be conclusive evidence that the document relates to the specified election; and any endorsement on any packet of ballot papers so produced shall be prima facie evidence that the ballot papers are what they are stated to be by the endorsement.

(6) The production from proper custody of a ballot paper purporting to have been used at any election, and of a counterfoil marked with the same printed number and having a number marked thereon in writing, shall be prima facie evidence that the elector whose vote was given by that ballot paper was the person who at the time of the election had affixed to his name in the register of electors the same number as the number written on the counterfoil.

(7) Save as by this rule provided, no person shall be allowed to inspect any rejected or counted ballot papers in the possession of the proper officer of the district council or to open any sealed packets of counterfoils and certificates.

Retention and public inspection of documents

49.—(1) The proper officer of the district council shall retain for six months among the records of the district council all documents relating to an election which are, in pursuance of these rules, forwarded to him by a returning officer or held by him and then, unless otherwise directed by an order under the last foregoing rule, shall cause them to be destroyed.

(2) The said documents, except ballot papers, counterfoils and certificates as to employment on duty on the day of the poll, shall during a period of six months from the day of election be open to public inspection at such time and in such manner as may be determined by the district council.

(3) The proper officer of the district council shall, on request, supply copies of or extracts from the documents open to public inspection on payment of such fees, and subject to such conditions, as may be determined by the district council.

Supplemental provisions as to documents

50. Subject to the provisions of these rules, the proper officer of the district council shall, in respect of the custody and destruction of ballot papers and other documents coming into his possession in pursuance of these rules, be subject to the directions of the district council.

PART VI

SUPPLEMENTAL

Countermand or abandonment of poll on death of candidate

51.—(1) If at a contested election proof is given to the satisfaction of the returning officer before the result of the election is declared that one of the persons named or to be named as candidate in the ballot papers has died, then the returning officer shall countermand the poll for the election of parish or community councillors or, if polling has begun, direct that the poll be abandoned, and the provisions of section 36(2) of the Representation of the People Act 1949 shall apply to any further election ordered under the Local Government Act 1972.

(2) Where the poll is abandoned by reason of the death of a candidate, the proceedings at or consequent on that poll shall be interrupted, and the presiding officer at any polling station shall take the like steps (so far as not already taken) for the delivery to the returning officer of ballot boxes and of ballot papers and other documents as he is required to take on the close of the poll in due course, and the returning officer shall dispose of ballot papers and other documents in his possession as he is required to do on the completion in due course of the counting of the votes; but—

(*a*) it shall not be necessary for any ballot paper account to be prepared or verified; and

(*b*) the returning officer, without taking any step or further step for the counting of the ballot papers or of the votes, shall seal up all the ballot papers, whether the votes on them have been counted or not, and it shall not be necessary to seal up counted and rejected ballot papers in separate packets.

(3) The foregoing provisions of these rules as to the inspection, production, retention and destruction of ballot papers and other documents relating to a poll at an election shall apply to any such documents relating to a poll abandoned by reason of the death of a candidate, with the following modifications:—

(*a*) ballot papers on which the votes were neither counted nor rejected shall be treated as counted ballot papers; and

(*b*) no order shall be made for the production or inspection of any ballot papers or for the opening of a sealed packet of counterfoils or certificates as to employment on duty on the day of the poll unless the order is made by a court with reference to a prosecution.

Filling of casual vacancies

52.—(1) On a casual vacancy occurring in the office of councillor of a community or on a casual vacancy occurring in the office of councillor of a parish after 31st December 1975, an election to fill the vacancy shall be held if, within fourteen days (computed in accordance with rule 2) after public notice of the vacancy has been given in accordance with section 87(2) of the Local Government Act 1972, notice in writing of a request for such an election has been given to the proper officer of the council of the district within which the parish or community is situate by two electors for the electoral area:

Provided that where a casual vacancy occurs within six months before the day on which the councillor whose office is vacant would regularly have retired, an election shall not be held.

(2) In the case of such a casual vacancy which is filled by election, the election shall be—

(*a*) held on a day appointed by the returning officer, being a day falling within a period of sixty days (so computed) beginning with the day on which public notice of the vacancy was given;

(*b*) conducted in the manner prescribed by the foregoing provisions of these rules.

(3) In this rule the expression "elector for the electoral area" means a person who is registered as a local government elector for the electoral area in the register to be used at the election or who, pending the publication of that register, appears from the electors lists therefor as corrected by the registration officer to be entitled to be so registered.

(4) In the case of a casual vacancy occurring in the office of councillor of a parish before 1st January 1976 or of any other casual vacancy occurring in the office of councillor of a parish or community which is not filled by election in accordance with the foregoing provisions of this rule, the vacancy shall be filled by the parish or community council within a period of sixty days beginning with the day on which public notice of the vacancy was given.

General duty of returning officer

53. It shall be the general duty of the returning officer to do any act or thing that may be necessary for effectually conducting the election under these rules.

Notices

54. Any notice required to be given by these rules may relate to more than one electoral area and, at elections of district councillors and parish or community councillors, the polls of which are taken together, to both elections.

Interpretation

55.—(1) The expression "electoral area" means the parish or community or, if the parish or community is divided into wards, a ward.

(2) Any reference in these rules to a proper officer shall, in relation to any purpose and any local authority or other body or any area, be construed as a reference to an officer appointed for that purpose by that body or for that area, as the case may be.

(3) A reference in this Schedule to a rule shall be construed as a reference to a rule contained in this Schedule.

(4) Any reference in this Schedule to any enactment shall be taken as a reference to that enactment as amended or replaced by any other enactment.

APPENDIX

Note.—The forms contained in this Appendix may be adapted so far as circumstances require.

Rule 4.

NOTICE OF ELECTION

PARISH/COMMUNITY OF

ELECTION OF PARISH/COMMUNITY COUNCILLORS for the [Ward of the] [Wards of the] Parish/Community

If the notice relates to more than one election, adapt form accordingly.

1. An election is to be held of Parish/Community Councillors for the said [ward] [wards] [parish] [community].

2. Nomination papers must be delivered at on any day after the date of this notice, but not later than noon on the day of .

3. Forms of nomination paper may be obtained from the undersigned at or from at . Either will at the request of any local government elector for the said electoral area prepare a nomination paper for signature.

4. If the election is contested, the poll will take place on the day of .

(Signed)..
Returning Officer.

day of , 19 .

Rule 5.

NOMINATION PAPER

ELECTION OF PARISH/COMMUNITY COUNCILLORS for the [Ward of the] Parish/Community of

Day of election..

We, the undersigned, being local government electors for the said [ward] [parish] [community], do hereby nominate the undermentioned person as a candidate at the said election.

Candidate's surname	Other names in full	Description (if any)	Home Address in full

Signatures	Electoral Number (*see* note 3) Distinctive Letter(s)	Number
Proposer..	....	....
Seconder..	....	....

NOTE 1.—The attention of candidates and local government electors is drawn to the rules for filling up nomination papers and other provisions relating to nomination contained in the Local Elections (Parishes and Communities) Rules 1973.

NOTE 2.—Where a candidate is commonly known by some title he may be described by his title as if it were his surname.

NOTE 3.—A person's electoral number consists of the distinctive letter or letters of the parliamentary polling district in which he is registered together with his number in the register to be used at the election except that before publication of the register the distinctive letter or letters of the parliamentary polling district in which he is entitled to be registered together with his number (if any) in the electors list for that register shall be used instead.

NOTE 4.—An elector may not—

(*a*) subscribe more nomination papers than there are vacancies to be filled in the electoral area; or

(*b*) subscribe a nomination paper for more than one ward of a parish or a community divided into wards; or

(*c*) subscribe more than one nomination paper in respect of the same candidate.

NOTE 5.—A person whose name is entered in the register or electors lists may not subscribe a nomination paper if the entry gives as the date on which he will become of voting age a date later than the day fixed for the poll.

CANDIDATE'S CONSENT TO NOMINATION

Rule 7.

I, (name in full)..
of (home address in full)..
....hereby consent to my nomination as a candidate for election as councillor for the...[ward of] the parish/community of...

I declare, with reference to the day of my nomination as a candidate, that I am qualified, and if there is a poll will be qualified on the day of election, to be so elected; that I have attained the age of twenty-one years and am a British subject or citizen of the Republic of Ireland; and that

*(*a*) I am registered as a local government elector for the parish/community of ....in respect of the following address..
..................................and my electoral number is...................................
(*see* Note below)

Rule 13.

DIRECTIONS FOR THE GUIDANCE OF THE VOTERS IN VOTING WHERE THE POLL IS ON A QUESTION OF APPOINTMENT TO AN OFFICE

1. The voter should see that the ballot paper, before it is handed to him, is stamped with the official mark.

2. The voter will go into one of the compartments and, with the pencil provided in the compartment, place a cross on the right-hand side of the ballot paper, opposite the name of each candidate for whom he votes, thus X.

3. The voter will then fold up the ballot paper so as to show the official mark on the back, and leaving the compartment will, without showing the front of the paper to any person, show the official mark on the back to the presiding officer, and then, in the presence of the presiding officer, put the paper into the ballot box, and forthwith leave the polling station.

4. If the voter inadvertently spoils a ballot paper he can return it to the officer, who will, if satisfied of such inadvertence, give him another paper.

5. If the voter votes for more than candidate(s), or places any mark on the paper by which he may be afterwards identified, his ballot paper will be void, and will not be counted.

Rule 23.

DECLARATION TO BE MADE BY THE COMPANION OF A BLIND VOTER

I, A.B., of , having been requested to assist C.D., who is numbered on the register of local government electors for the electoral area for which the poll is being held, to record his vote at the poll now being held for the said area, do hereby declare that [I am entitled to vote at the said poll] [I am the* of the said voter and have attained the age of eighteen years], and that I have not previously assisted any blind person [except E.F., of], to vote at the said poll.

*State the relationship of the companion to the voter.

(Signed) A.B.

Date....................

I, the undersigned, being the presiding officer for the polling station for the electoral area for which the poll is being held, do hereby certify that the above declaration, having been first read to the above-named declarant, was signed by the declarant in my presence.

(Signed) X.Y.

day of , 19 , at minutes past o'clock.

NOTE.—If the person making the above declaration knowingly and wilfully makes therein a statement false in a material particular, he will be guilty of an offence.

Rule 15.

BALLOT PAPER

Form of Front of Ballot Paper

ELECTION OF PARISH [COMMUNITY] COUNCILLORS

1	**BROWN** JOHN EDWARD Brown, 2 The Cottages, Barlington, Grayshire Labour	
2	**BROWN** THOMAS WILLIAM Brown, 15 Barchester Road, Barlington, Grayshire Liberal	
3	**JONES** William David Jones, The Grange, Barlington, Grayshire Conservative	
4	**MERTON** Hon. George Travis, commonly called Viscount Merton, Barlington, Grayshire	
5	**SMITH** Mary Smith, School House, Barlington, Grayshire Progressive	
6	**WILLIAMS** Elizabeth Williams, 3 Ivy Lane, Barlington, Grayshire Housewife	

Form of Back of Ballot Paper

No.
Election for the [Parish/Community of] [Ward of the Parish/Community of] day of 19 .
Note—The number on the ballot paper is to correspond with that on the counterfoil.

Directions as to printing the ballot paper

1. Nothing is to be printed on the ballot paper except in accordance with these directions.

2. So far as practicable, the following arrangements shall be observed in the printing of the ballot paper:—

(*a*) no word shall be printed on the face except the particulars of the candidates and a heading "ELECTION OF PARISH [COMMUNITY] COUNCILLORS";

(*b*) no rule shall be printed on the face except the horizontal rules separating the particulars of the candidates from one another and the vertical rules separating those particulars from the numbers on the left-hand side and the spaces on the right where the vote is to be marked;

(*c*) the whole space beneath the heading shall be equally divided between the candidates by the rules separating their particulars;

(*d*) the particulars of each candidate shall be printed one below the other in the order shown in the statement as to persons nominated;

(*e*) the spacing, layout and style and size of type face shall be as nearly as may be the same as in the specimen form in this Appendix.

3. The surname of each candidate shall in all cases be printed by itself in large capitals, and his full particulars shall be set out below it and shall be printed in ordinary type except that small capitals shall be used—

(*a*) if his surname is the same as another candidate's, for his other names; and

(*b*) if his other names are also the same as the other candidate's, either for his residence or for his description unless each of them is the same as that of another candidate with the same surname and other names.

4. The number on the back of the ballot paper shall be printed in ordinary type.

Rule 23.

DIRECTIONS FOR THE GUIDANCE OF THE VOTERS IN VOTING

1. The voter should see that the ballot paper, before it is handed to him, is stamped with the official mark.

2. The voter will go into one of the compartments and, with the pencil provided in the compartment, place a cross on the right-hand side of the ballot paper, opposite the name of each candidate for whom he votes, thus X.

3. The voter will then fold up the ballot paper so as to show the official mark on the back, and leaving the compartment will, without showing the front of the paper to any person, show the official mark on the back to the presiding officer, and then, in the presence of the presiding officer, put the paper into the ballot box, and forthwith leave the polling station.

4. If the voter inadvertently spoils a ballot paper he can return it to the officer, who will, if satisfied of such inadvertence, give him another paper.

5. If the voter votes for more than candidate(s) or places any mark on the paper by which he may afterwards be identified, his ballot paper will be void, and will not be counted.

6. If the voter fraudulently takes a ballot paper out of a polling station or fraudulently puts into the ballot box any paper other than the one given to him by the officer he will be liable on conviction to imprisonment for a term not exceeding six months or to a fine not exceeding twenty pounds or to both such imprisonment and such fine.

Certificate of employment

Rule 26.

Election in the [Ward of the] Parish/Community of

I certify that (name)................................ who is numbered...................... in the register of electors for the electoral area named above, is likely to be unable to go in person to the polling station allotted to him at the election on (date of poll)......... ....by reason of the particular circumstances of his employment on that date—

*(*a*) as a constable,

*(*b*) by me for a purpose connected with the election.

Signature ....

*Police rank..
(Inspector or above)

*Returning Officer

Date............................

*Delete whichever is inapplicable.

NOTE.—The person named above is entitled to vote at any polling station of the above electoral area on production and surrender of this certificate to the presiding officer.

Declaration to be made by the Companion of a Blind Voter

Rule 33.

I, A. B., of , having been requested to assist C. D. [*in the case of a blind person voting as proxy add* voting as proxy for G. H.], who is numbered on the register of local government electors for the [Parish/Community of] [Ward of the Parish/Community of], to record his vote at the election now being held for the said [parish] [community] [ward], do hereby declare that [I am entitled to vote as an elector at the said election] [I am the* of the said voter and have attained the age of eighteen years], and that I have not previously assisted any blind person [except E. F., of], to vote at the said election.

*State the relationship of the companion to the voter

(Signed) A. B.

day of , 19 .

I, the undersigned, being the presiding officer for the polling station for the [Parish of] [Community of] [Ward of the Parish/Community of], do hereby certify that the above declaration, having been first read to the above-named declarant, was signed by the declarant in my presence.

(Signed) X. Y.

day of , 19 , at minutes past o'clock. [a.m.] [p.m.].

NOTE.—If the person making the above declaration knowingly and wilfully makes therein a statement false in a material particular, he will be guilty of an offence.

SCHEDULE 2

PART I

DECLARATION OF ACCEPTANCE OF OFFICE

*Insert description of office.

I, A. B., having been elected to the office of * hereby declare that I take the said office upon myself, and will duly and faithfully fulfil the duties thereof to the best of my judgment and ability.

Dated this day of , 19 .

Signature ....

This declaration was made and subscribed before me.

....
†Proper officer of the Council of the parish/community of...........

†If the declaration is made and subscribed before any other person authorised by section 83(4) of the Local Government Act 1972, adapt form accordingly.

PART II

DECLARATION AS TO EXPENSES

Election for the [Ward of the] Parish/Community of

Day of election ....

Full name of candidate..

I declare as follows:—

1. The amount paid by me or on my behalf for my election expenses at the above election was £ .

2. To the best of my knowledge and belief no other election expenses have been paid or incurred by me or by any other person or organization in connection with my candidature.

3. To the best of my knowledge and belief the accompanying return of election expenses is complete and correct as required by law.

4. I understand that the law does not allow any election expenses not mentioned in the return to be defrayed except in pursuance of a court order.

Signature of candidate....................................

EXPLANATORY NOTE

(*This Note is not part of the Rules.*)

These Rules revoke and replace the Parish Council Election Rules 1973. They apply to community council elections as well as to parish council elections. A casual vacancy, other than one occurring in the office of councillor of a parish before 1st January 1976, may be filled by election if two electors so request: otherwise it is filled by co-option (Rule 52 in Schedule 1).

1973 No. 1911

REPRESENTATION OF THE PEOPLE

The Parish and Community Meetings (Polls) Rules 1973

Made - - -	12*th November* 1973
Laid before Parliament	3*rd December* 1973
Coming into Operation	1*st April* 1974

In exercise of the powers conferred upon me by paragraph 18(5) of Part III and paragraph 34(5) of Part V of Schedule 12 to the Local Government Act 1972(**a**), I hereby make the following Rules:—

1.—(1) These Rules may be cited as the Parish and Community Meetings (Polls) Rules 1973 and shall come into operation on 1st April 1974:

Provided that they shall not have effect in relation to a poll consequent on a parish meeting which has been demanded before that date.

(2) The Interpretation Act 1889(**b**) shall apply to the interpretation of these Rules as it applies to the interpretation of an Act of Parliament.

2.—(1) The Parish Meetings (Polls) Rules 1970(**c**) are hereby revoked.

(2) Notwithstanding paragraph (1) of this Rule, the Rules therein mentioned shall apply to any poll which has been demanded before these Rules come into operation.

(3) Section 38 of the Interpretation Act 1889 shall apply as if the Rules revoked by this Instrument were Acts of Parliament.

3.—(1) At a poll consequent on a parish or community meeting the returning officer shall be an officer appointed by the district council in which the parish or community is situate.

(2) The returning officer shall appoint an office for the purpose of the poll.

(3) If a poll consequent on a parish or community meeting is required to be taken, the chairman of the meeting shall notify the district council of the fact and shall give the returning officer such particulars as will enable him to give notice of the poll.

4. In the application of those provisions of the Representation of the People Act 1949(**d**) referred to in section 165(1) of that Act, other than section 53 thereof, to the election of the chairman of a parish meeting at a parish meeting or to a poll consequent on a parish or community meeting the following adaptations, modifications and exceptions shall have effect:—

(**a**) 1972 c. 70.
(**b**) 1889 c. 63.
(**c**) S.I. 1970/189 (1970 I, p. 814).
(**d**) 1949 c. 68.

(*a*) where the poll is to be taken on any question other than that of the election of the chairman of the parish meeting or of an appointment to any other office only the following of the aforesaid provisions shall apply, namely, sections 47, 99, 100, 101, 146, 151 (other than paragraph (*b*) thereof), 154, 156, 158, 159 and 163;

(*b*) references to the proper officer of the authority for which the election was held shall be taken as references to the returning officer;

(*c*) references to the authority for which the election was held shall be taken as references to the parish and references to the area thereof shall be construed accordingly except in section 115(7) of the said Act where the expression "the area of the authority for which the election was held" means the district (as defined in section 270 of the Local Government Act 1972) in which the parish is situate;

(*d*) in sections 47(2), 86(1) and 87(1) for the expression "local government election" there shall be substituted the expression "election under the Local Government Act";

(*e*) in section 119(2)(*b*) for the words "such amount not exceeding five hundred pounds" there shall be substituted the words "an amount of fifty pounds or such smaller amount or such larger amount not exceeding three hundred pounds";

(*f*) references to an election under the Local Government Act shall be deemed to include a reference to the election of the chairman of a parish meeting at a parish meeting and to a poll consequent on a parish or community meeting.

5. In the application of section 53 of the Representation of the People Act 1949 and the Local Elections (Parishes and Communities) Rules 1973(**a**) to a poll consequent on a parish or community meeting, adaptations, alterations and exceptions shall be made therein so that they shall read as set out in the Schedule hereto.

Robert Carr,
One of Her Majesty's Principal
Secretaries of State.

Home Office,
Whitehall.
12th November 1973.

(a) S.I. 1973/1910 (1973 III, p. 6591).

SCHEDULE

Arrangement of rules

APPENDIX

Forms

Notice of abandonment of poll.

Notice of poll on a question other than a question of appointment to an office.

Notice of poll on a question of appointment to an office.

Ballot paper on a question other than a question of appointment to an office.

Ballot paper on a question of appointment to an office.

Directions for the guidance of the voters in voting where the poll is on a question other than a question of appointment to an office.

Directions for the guidance of the voters in voting where the poll is on a question of appointment to an office.

Declaration to be made by the companion of a blind voter.

Declaration of result of poll on a question other than a question of appointment to an office.

Declaration of result of poll on a question of appointment to an office.

Timetable

1. The proceedings at the poll shall be conducted in accordance with the following Table.

TIMETABLE

Proceeding	*Time*
Delivery of notices of withdrawals of candidature	Not later than noon on the fourth day after the day on which the poll was demanded.
Notice of poll	Not later than the fifth day before the day of the poll.
Notice of appointment of polling or counting agents	Not later than the third day before the day of the poll.
Polling	On the day of the poll which shall be such day as shall be fixed by the returning officer not earlier than the fourteenth day nor, unless for special reasons the Secretary of State otherwise directs, later than the twenty-fifth day after the day on which the poll was demanded.

Computation of time

2.—(1) In computing any period of time for the purposes of the Timetable, a Sunday, day of the Christmas break, of the Easter break or of a bank holiday break or day appointed for public thanksgiving or mourning shall be disregarded and any such day shall not be treated as a day for the purpose of any proceedings up to the completion of the poll nor shall the returning officer be obliged to proceed with the counting of the votes thereon.

(2) In this rule "the Christmas break" means the period beginning with the last week day before Christmas Day and ending with the first week day after Christmas Day which is not a bank holiday, "the Easter break" means the period beginning with the Thursday before and ending with the Tuesday after Easter

Day, and "a bank holiday break" means any bank holiday not included in the Christmas break or the Easter break and the period beginning with the last week day before that bank holiday and ending with the next week day which is not a bank holiday.

Hours of poll

3. The poll shall commence at four o'clock in the afternoon and be kept open till nine o'clock in the evening of the same day and no longer.

Withdrawal of candidates

4.—(1) A candidate may not later than the time appointed for that purpose in rule 1 withdraw from his candidature by a notice of withdrawal signed by him and attested by one witness and delivered at the office appointed by the returning officer.

(2) If by reason of any withdrawal under this rule the number of remaining candidates becomes equal to or less than the number of persons to be elected, a poll shall not be taken and those candidates shall be deemed to be elected and the returning officer shall as soon as possible publish notice of the abandonment of the poll in the form in the Appendix, or in a form to the like effect, stating that no poll will be taken and giving a list of the persons elected and shall send a copy to each of those candidates and to the chairman of the meeting at which the poll was demanded.

Poll to be taken by ballot

5. The votes at the poll shall be given by ballot, and the poll shall be conducted in accordance with these rules.

The ballot papers

6.—(1) The ballot of every voter shall consist of a ballot paper.

(2) Every ballot paper shall be in the appropriate form in the Appendix, and shall be printed in accordance with the appropriate directions therein and—

(*a*) (i) if the poll is taken on a question of appointment to any office, shall contain the full names, home addresses and (if required) descriptions of the candidates arranged alphabetically in the order of their surnames and, if there are two or more of them with the same surname, of their other names; and if there are two or more of them with the same surname and other names, the order in which those persons shall be shown shall be determined by lot drawn by the returning officer;

(ii) if the poll is taken on any other question, shall state the question or questions on which the poll is to be taken;

(*b*) shall be capable of being folded up;

(*c*) shall have a number printed on the back;

(*d*) shall have attached either at the side or at the top, a counterfoil with the same number printed on the face or the back.

(3) Where a poll on a question of appointment to any office and a poll on any other question are taken together, ballot papers of a different colour shall be used for each poll.

The official mark

7.—(1) Every ballot paper shall be marked with an official mark, which shall be either embossed or perforated.

(2) The official mark shall be kept secret.

Prohibition of disclosure of vote

8. No person who has voted at the poll shall, in any legal proceeding to question the poll, be required to state how or for whom he voted.

Use of schools and public rooms

9.—(1) The returning officer may use, free of charge, for the purpose of taking the poll or counting the votes—

(*a*) a room in a school maintained or assisted by a local education authority or a school in respect of which grants are made out of moneys provided by Parliament to the person or body of persons responsible for the management of the school;

(*b*) a room the expense of maintaining which is payable out of any rate.

(2) The returning officer shall make good any damage done to, and defray any expense incurred by the persons having control over, any such room as aforesaid by reason of its being used for the purpose of taking the poll or of counting the votes.

(3) The use of a room in an unoccupied house for the purpose of taking the poll or of counting the votes shall not render a person liable to be rated or to pay any rate for that house.

Notice of poll

10.—(1) Notice of the poll in the appropriate form in the Appendix shall be published by the returning officer—

(*a*) by posting a notice of the poll in some conspicuous place or places in the parish or community, and

(*b*) in such other manner, if any, as appears to the returning officer to be desirable for giving publicity to the poll.

(2) Notice of the poll shall specify—

(*a*) the day and hours fixed for the poll;

(*b*) if the poll is taken on a question of appointment to any office, the name of the office, the number of vacancies, the particulars of each candidate who has not withdrawn (the order of the names of the candidates and the particulars being the same as in the ballot paper) and the name of the proposer of each candidate;

(*c*) if the poll is taken on any question other than the question of an appointment, the particulars of the question and the name of the proposer of the resolution in respect of which the poll is being taken; and

(*d*) the situation of each polling station and the description of the persons entitled to vote thereat.

Provision of polling stations

11.—(1) The returning officer shall provide one polling station or such other number of polling stations as he considers sufficient, and shall, if more than one polling station is provided, allot the voters to the polling stations in such manner as he thinks most convenient.

(2) One or more polling stations may be provided in the same room.

(3) The polling station allotted to electors from any parliamentary polling district wholly or partly within the parish or community shall, in the absence of special circumstances, be in the parliamentary polling place for that district, unless the polling place is outside the parish or community.

(4) The returning officer shall provide each polling station with such number of compartments as may be necessary in which the voters can mark their votes screened from observation.

Appointment of presiding officers and clerks

12.—(1) The returning officer shall appoint and may pay a presiding officer to attend at each polling station and such clerks as may be necessary for taking the poll and counting the votes.

(2) The returning officer may, if he thinks fit, preside at a polling station and the provisions of these rules relating to a presiding officer shall apply to a returning officer so presiding with the necessary modifications as to things to be done by the returning officer to the presiding officer or by the presiding officer to the returning officer.

(3) A presiding officer may do, by the clerks appointed to assist him, any act (including the asking of questions) which he is required or authorised by these rules to do at a polling station except order the arrest, exclusion or removal of any person from the polling station.

Equipment of polling stations

13.—(1) The returning officer shall provide each presiding officer with such number of ballot boxes and ballot papers as in the opinion of the returning officer may be necessary.

(2) Every ballot box shall be so constructed that the ballot papers can be put therein, but cannot be withdrawn therefrom, without the box being unlocked.

(3) The returning officer shall provide each polling station with—

(*a*) materials to enable voters to mark the ballot papers;

(*b*) instruments for stamping thereon the official mark;

(*c*) copies of the register of electors for the parish or community or such part thereof as contains the names of the voters allotted to the station.

(4) A notice in the appropriate form in the Appendix, giving directions for the guidance of the voters in voting, shall be printed in conspicuous characters and exhibited inside and outside every polling station.

(5) Where the poll is taken on a question of appointment to any office there shall be exhibited in every compartment of every polling station a notice as follows:—"The voter may vote for not more than   candidate(s) as [*insert name of office*]"; so however that if the poll is taken on questions of appointment to two or more offices, the notice may be adapted accordingly.

Appointment of polling and counting agents

14.—(1) Each candidate may appoint one polling agent to attend at each polling station for the purpose of detecting personation and one counting agent to attend at the counting of the votes.

(2) Notice in writing of the appointment, stating the names and addresses of the persons appointed, shall be given by the candidate to the returning officer and shall be so given not later than the time appointed for that purpose in rule 1 of these rules.

(3) If an agent dies, or becomes incapable of acting, the candidate may appoint another agent in his place, and shall forthwith give to the returning officer notice in writing of the name and address of the agent appointed.

(4) In the following provisions of these rules references to polling and counting agents shall be taken as references to agents whose appointments have been duly made and notified and who are within the permitted number.

(5) Any notice required to be given to a counting agent by the returning officer may be delivered at, or sent by post to, the address stated in the notice of appointment.

(6) A candidate may himself do any act or thing which any polling or counting agent of his, if appointed, would have been authorised to do, or may assist his agent in doing any such act or thing.

(7) Where by these rules any act or thing is required or authorised to be done in the presence of the polling or counting agents, the non-attendance of any agents or agent at the time and place appointed for the purpose, shall not, if the act or thing is otherwise duly done, invalidate the act or thing done.

Declaration of secrecy

15.—(1) Before the opening of the poll a declaration of secrecy in the form in paragraph (4) of this rule, or in a form as near thereto as circumstances admit, shall be made by—

(*a*) the returning officer and the presiding officers;

(*b*) every clerk authorised to attend at a polling station or the counting of the votes;

(*c*) every candidate attending at a polling station or at the counting of the votes;

(*d*) every candidate's wife or husband attending at the counting of the votes;

(*e*) every polling agent and counting agent;

(*f*) where the poll is taken on a question other than a question of appointment to any office, the proposer of the resolution in respect of which the poll is taken who attends at the counting of the votes;

(*g*) every person permitted by the returning officer to attend at the counting of the votes, though not entitled as of right to do so.

(2) Notwithstanding anything in the foregoing paragraph, the following persons attending at the counting of the votes, that is to say:—

(*a*) any candidate or, where the poll is taken on a question other than a question of appointment to any office, the proposer of the resolution in respect of which the poll is taken;

(*b*) any candidate's wife or husband attending by virtue of rule 28 of these rules, authorising candidates' wives or husbands to attend as such;

(*c*) any person permitted by the returning officer to attend, though not entitled as of right to do so;

(*d*) any clerk making the declaration in order to attend at the counting of the votes;

need not make the declaration before the opening of the poll but shall make it before he or she is permitted to attend the counting, and a person becoming obliged to make a declaration by reason of his appointment after the opening of the poll shall make the declaration before acting under the appointment.

(3) The returning officer shall make the declaration in the presence of a Justice of the Peace, and any other person shall make the declaration in the presence either of a Justice of the Peace or of the returning officer, and paragraphs (5), (6), (7) and (9) of this rule shall be read to the declarant by the person taking the declaration, or shall be read by the declarant in the presence of that person:

Provided that the declaration may be made by the returning officer or any other person before a person who is chairman of the Greater London Council, a county council or a district council or mayor of a London borough, and may be made by a person other than the returning officer before a person who is the proper officer of any such council.

(4) The declaration shall be as follows:—

"I solemnly promise and declare that I will not do anything forbidden by paragraphs (5), (6), (7) and (9) of rule 15 of the Schedule to the Parish and Community Meetings (Polls) Rules 1973 which have been read to [by] me.".

(5) The following persons, that is to say:—

(*a*) the returning officer and every presiding officer or clerk attending at a polling station;

(*b*) every candidate or polling agent so attending,

shall maintain and aid in maintaining the secrecy of voting and shall not, except for some purpose authorised by law, communicate to any person before the poll is closed any information as to—

(i) the name of any voter who has or has not applied for a ballot paper or voted at a polling station;

(ii) the number on the register of electors of any voter who has or has not applied for a ballot paper or voted at a polling station; or

(iii) the official mark.

(6) Every person attending at the counting of the votes shall maintain and aid in maintaining the secrecy of voting and shall not—

(*a*) ascertain or attempt to ascertain at the counting of the votes the number on the back of any ballot paper;

(*b*) communicate any information obtained at the counting of the votes as to the candidate for whom or the manner in which any vote is given on any particular ballot paper.

(7) No person whatsoever shall—

(*a*) interfere with or attempt to interfere with a voter when recording his vote;

(*b*) otherwise obtain or attempt to obtain in a polling station information as to the candidate for whom or the manner in which a voter in that station is about to vote or has voted;

(*c*) communicate at any time to any person any information obtained in a polling station as to the candidate for whom or the manner in which a voter in that station is about to vote or has voted, or as to the number on the back of the ballot paper given to a voter at that station;

(*d*) directly or indirectly induce a voter to display his ballot paper after he has marked it so as to make known to any person the name of the candidate for whom or the manner in which he has or has not voted.

(8) No person having undertaken to assist a blind voter to vote shall communicate at any time to any person any information as to the candidate for whom or the manner in which that voter intends to vote or has voted, or as to the number on the back of the ballot paper given for the use of that voter.

(9) If any person acts in contravention of paragraph (5), (6), (7) or (8) of this rule, he shall be liable on summary conviction to imprisonment for a term not exceeding six months.

Admission to polling station

16. The presiding officer shall regulate the number of voters to be admitted to the polling station at the same time, and shall exclude all other persons except—

(*a*) the candidates;

(*b*) the polling agents appointed to attend at the polling station;

(*c*) the clerks appointed to attend at the polling station;

(*d*) the constables on duty; and

(*e*) the companions of blind voters.

Keeping of order in station

17.—(1) It shall be the duty of the presiding officer to keep order at his polling station.

(2) If a person misconducts himself in a polling station, or fails to obey the lawful orders of the presiding officer, he may immediately, by order of the presiding officer, be removed from the polling station by a constable in or near that station or by any other person authorised in writing by the returning officer to remove him, and the person so removed shall not, without the permission of the presiding officer, again enter the polling station during the day.

(3) Any person so removed may, if charged with the commission in the polling station of an offence, be dealt with as a person taken into custody by a constable for an offence without a warrant.

(4) The powers conferred by this rule shall not be exercised so as to prevent a voter who is otherwise entitled to vote at a polling station from having an opportunity of voting at that station.

Sealing of ballot boxes

18. Immediately before the commencement of the poll, the presiding officer shall show the ballot box empty to such persons, if any, as are present in the polling station, so that they may see that it is empty, and shall then lock it up and place his seal on it in such manner as to prevent it being opened without breaking the seal, and shall place it in his view for the receipt of ballot papers, and keep it so locked and sealed.

Questions to be put to voters

19.—(1) The presiding officer may, and if required by a candidate or his polling agent shall, put to any person applying for a ballot paper at the time of his application, but not afterwards, the following questions, or either of them that is to say:—

(i) Are you the person registered in the register of local government electors now in force for this parish or community as follows (*read the whole entry from the register*)?

(ii) Have you already voted at the present poll?

(2) A ballot paper shall not be delivered to any person required to answer the above questions or either of them unless he has answered the questions or question satisfactorily.

(3) Save as by this rule authorised, no inquiry shall be permitted as to the right of any person to vote.

Challenge of voter

20.—(1) If at the time a person applies for a ballot paper, or after he has applied for a ballot paper and before he has left the polling station, a candidate or his polling agent declares to the presiding officer that he has reasonable cause to believe that the applicant has committed an offence of personation and undertakes to substantiate the charge in a court of law, the presiding officer may order a constable to arrest the applicant, and the order of the presiding officer shall be sufficient authority for the constable so to do.

(2) A person against whom a declaration is made under this rule shall not by reason thereof be prevented from voting.

(3) A person arrested under the provisions of this rule shall be dealt with as a person taken into custody by a constable for an offence without a warrant.

Voting procedure

21.—(1) A ballot paper shall be delivered to a voter who applies therefor, and immediately before delivery—

(*a*) the ballot paper shall be stamped with the official mark, either embossed or perforated;

(*b*) the number, name and description of the voter as stated in the copy of the register of electors shall be called out;

(*c*) the number of the voter shall be marked on the counterfoil; and

(*d*) a mark shall be placed in the register of electors against the number of the voter to denote that a ballot paper has been received but without showing the particular ballot paper which has been received.

(2) The voter, on receiving the ballot paper, shall forthwith proceed into one of the compartments in the polling station and there secretly mark his paper and fold it up so as to conceal his vote, and shall then show to the presiding officer the back of the paper so as to disclose the official mark, and put the ballot paper so folded up into the ballot box in the presence of the presiding officer.

(3) The voter shall vote without undue delay, and shall leave the polling station as soon as he has put his ballot paper into the ballot box.

Votes marked by presiding officer

22.—(1) The presiding officer, on the application of—

(*a*) a voter who is incapacitated by blindness or other physical cause from voting in manner directed by these rules; or

(*b*) if the poll is taken on a Saturday, a voter who declares that he is a Jew, and objects on religious grounds to vote in manner directed by these rules; or

(*c*) a voter who declares orally that he is unable to read,

shall, in the presence of the polling agents, cause the vote of the voter to be marked on a ballot paper in manner directed by the voter, and the ballot paper to be placed in the ballot box.

(2) The name and number in the register of electors of every voter whose vote is marked in pursuance of this rule, and the reason why it is so marked, shall be entered on a list (in these rules called "the list of votes marked by the presiding officer").

Voting by blind persons

23.—(1) If a voter makes an application to the presiding officer to be allowed on the ground of blindness to vote with the assistance of another person by whom he is accompanied (in these rules referred to as "the companion"), the presiding officer shall require the voter to declare orally whether he is so incapacitated by his blindness as to be unable to vote without assistance.

(2) If the presiding officer is satisfied that the voter is so incapacitated and is also satisfied by a written declaration made by the companion (in these rules referred to as "the declaration made by the companion of a blind voter") that the companion is a qualified person within the meaning of this rule and has not previously assisted more than one blind person to vote at the poll, the presiding officer shall grant the application, and thereupon anything which is by these rules required to be done to or by the said voter in connection with the giving of his vote may be done to, or with the assistance of, the companion.

(3) For the purposes of this rule, a person shall be qualified to assist a blind voter to vote, if that person is either—

(*a*) a person who is entitled to vote at the poll; or

(*b*) the father, mother, brother, sister, husband, wife, son or daughter of the blind voter and has attained the age of eighteen years.

(4) The name and number in the register of electors of every voter whose vote is given in accordance with this rule and the name and address of the companion shall be entered on a list (in these rules referred to as "the list of blind voters assisted by companions").

(5) The declaration made by the companion—

(a) shall be in the form in the Appendix;

(b) shall be made before the presiding officer at the time when the voter applies to vote with the assistance of a companion and shall forthwith be given to the presiding officer who shall attest and retain it.

(6) No fee or other payment shall be charged in respect of the declaration.

Tendered ballot papers

24.—(1) If a person, representing himself to be a particular voter named in the register, applies for a ballot paper after another person has voted as the voter, the applicant shall, on satisfactorily answering the questions permitted by law to be asked at the poll, be entitled, subject to the following provisions of this rule, to mark a ballot paper (in these rules referred to as "a tendered ballot paper") in the same manner as any other voter.

(2) A tendered ballot paper shall—

(a) be of a colour differing from the other ballot papers;

(b) instead of being put into the ballot box, be given to the presiding officer and endorsed by him with the name of the voter and his number in the register of electors, and set aside in a separate packet.

(3) The name of the voter and his number on the register of electors shall be entered on a list (in these rules referred to as the "tendered votes list").

Spoilt ballot papers

25. A voter who has inadvertently dealt with his ballot paper in such manner that it cannot be conveniently used as a ballot paper may, on delivering it to the presiding officer and proving to his satisfaction the fact of the inadvertence, obtain another ballot paper in the place of the ballot paper so delivered (in these rules referred to as "a spoilt ballot paper"), and the spoilt ballot paper shall be immediately cancelled.

Adjournment of poll in case of riot

26.—(1) Where the proceedings at any polling station are interrupted or obstructed by riot or open violence, the presiding officer shall adjourn the proceedings until the following day and shall forthwith give notice to the returning officer.

(2) Where the poll is adjourned at any polling station—

(a) the hours of polling on the day to which it is adjourned shall be the same as for the original day; and

(b) references in these rules to the close of the poll shall be construed accordingly.

Procedure on close of poll

27.—(1) As soon as practicable after the close of the poll, the presiding officer shall, in the presence of the polling agents, make up into separate packets, sealed with his own seal and the seals of such polling agents as desire to affix their seals—

(a) each ballot box in use at the station, sealed so as to prevent the introduction of additional ballot papers and unopened, but with the key attached;

(b) the unused and spoilt ballot papers placed together;

(c) the tendered ballot papers;

(d) the marked copy of the register of electors;

(e) the counterfoils of the used ballot papers;

(f) the tendered votes list, the list of blind voters assisted by companions, the list of votes marked by the presiding officer, a statement of the number of voters whose votes are so marked by the presiding officer under the heads "physical incapacity", "Jews", and "unable to read", and the declarations made by the companions of blind voters;

and shall deliver the packets or cause them to be delivered to the returning officer to be taken charge of by him:

Provided that if the packets are not delivered by the presiding officer personally to the returning officer, the arrangements for their delivery shall require the approval of the returning officer.

(2) The marked copy of the register of electors shall not be in the same packet as the counterfoils of the used ballot papers.

(3) The packets shall be accompanied by a statement (in these rules referred to as "the ballot paper account") made by the presiding officer showing the number of ballot papers entrusted to him, and accounting for them under the heads of ballot papers issued and not otherwise accounted for, and unused, spoilt and tendered ballot papers.

Attendance at counting of votes

28.—(1) The returning officer shall make arrangements for counting the votes in the presence of the counting agents as soon as practicable after the close of the poll, and shall give to the counting agents notice in writing of the time and place at which he will begin to count the votes.

(2) No person other than—

(*a*) the returning officer and his clerks;

(*b*) the candidates and their wives or husbands;

(*c*) where the poll is taken on a question other than a question of appointment to any office, the proposer of the resolution in respect of which the poll is taken;

(*d*) the counting agents,

may be present at the counting of the votes, unless permitted by the returning officer to attend.

(3) A person not entitled as of right to attend at the counting of the votes shall not be permitted to do so by the returning officer unless the returning officer is satisfied that the efficient counting of the votes will not be impeded.

(4) The returning officer shall give the counting agents all such reasonable facilities for overseeing the proceedings, and all such information with reference thereto, as he can give them consistently with the orderly conduct of the proceedings and the discharge of his duties in connection therewith.

(5) In particular, where the votes are counted by sorting the ballot papers according to the candidate for whom the vote is given and then counting the number of ballot papers for each candidate, the counting agents shall be entitled to satisfy themselves that the ballot papers are correctly sorted.

The count

29.—(1) Before the returning officer proceeds to count the votes, he shall—

(*a*) in the presence of the counting agents open each ballot box and, taking out the ballot papers therein, count and record the number thereof and verify each ballot paper account;

(*b*) where a poll on a question of appointment to any office and a poll on any other question have been taken together, separate the ballot papers relating to each poll and count and record the numbers relating to each poll; and

(*c*) then mix together the whole of the ballot papers relating to the poll or each poll, as the case may be, which are contained in the ballot boxes.

(2) The returning officer shall not count any tendered ballot paper.

(3) The returning officer, while separating, counting and recording the number of ballot papers and counting the votes, shall keep the ballot papers with their faces upwards and take all proper precautions for preventing any person from seeing the numbers printed on the back of the papers.

(4) The returning officer shall verify each ballot paper account by comparing it with the number of ballot papers recorded by him, and the unused and spoilt ballot papers in his possession and the tendered votes list (opening and resealing the packets containing the unused and spoilt ballot papers and the tendered votes list) and shall draw up a statement as to the result of the verification which any counting agent may copy.

(5) The returning officer shall, so far as practicable, proceed continuously with counting the votes, allowing only time for refreshment:

Provided that he may, in so far as he thinks necessary, exclude the hours between nine o'clock in the evening and nine o'clock on the following morning.

(6) During the excluded time the returning officer shall place the ballot papers and other documents relating to the poll under his own seal and the seals of such of the counting agents as desire to affix their seals and shall otherwise take proper precautions for the security of the papers and documents.

Re-count

30.—(1) A candidate may, if present when the counting or any re-count of the votes is completed, require the returning officer to have the votes re-counted or again re-counted but the returning officer may refuse to do so if in his opinion the request is unreasonable.

(2) No steps shall be taken on the completion of the counting or any re-count of votes until the candidates present at the completion thereof have been given a reasonable opportunity to exercise the right conferred by this rule.

Rejected ballot papers

31.—(1) Any ballot paper—

(*a*) which does not bear the official mark; or

(*b*) on which votes are given for more candidates than the voter is entitled to vote for; or

(*c*) on which anything is written or marked by which the voter can be identified except the printed number on the back; or

(*d*) which is unmarked or void for uncertainty,

shall, subject to the provisions of this rule, be void and not counted.

(2) Where the voter is entitled to vote for more than one candidate or on more than one question, as the case may be, a ballot paper shall not be deemed to be void for uncertainty as respects any vote as to which no uncertainty arises and that vote shall be counted.

(3) A ballot paper on which a vote is marked—

(*a*) elsewhere than in the proper place; or

(*b*) otherwise than by means of a cross; or

(*c*) by more than one mark,

shall not by reason thereof be deemed to be void (either wholly or as respects that vote), if an intention that the vote shall be for one or other of the candidates or for or against any question clearly appears, and the way the paper is marked does not of itself identify the voter and it is not shown that he can be identified thereby.

(4) The returning officer shall endorse—

(*a*) the word "rejected" on any ballot paper which under this rule is not to be counted; and

(*b*) in the case of a ballot paper on which any vote is counted under paragraph (2) of this rule, the words "rejected in part" and a memorandum specifying the votes counted;

and shall add to the endorsement the words "rejection objected to" if an objection is made by a counting agent to his decision.

(5) The returning officer shall draw up a statement showing the number of ballot papers rejected, including those rejected in part, under the several heads of—

(*a*) want of official mark;

(*b*) voting for more candidates than voter is entitled to;

(*c*) writing or mark by which voter could be identified;

(*d*) unmarked or wholly void for uncertainty;

(*e*) rejected in part.

Decisions on ballot papers

32. The decision of the returning officer on any question arising in respect of a ballot paper shall be final, but shall be subject to review on an election petition.

Equality of votes

33. Where, after the counting of the votes (including any re-count) is completed, an equality of votes is found to exist between any candidates or for and against any question and the addition of a vote would entitle any of those candidates to be declared elected or would decide the question, the returning officer shall forthwith decide either between those candidates or that question by lot, and proceed as if the candidate or the answer in favour of or against the question on whom or on which the lot falls had received an additional vote.

Declaration of result

34. When the result of the poll has been ascertained the returning officer shall forthwith—

(*a*) in the case of a poll on a question of appointment to any office, declare to be elected the candidate or candidates for whom the majority of votes have been given and shall as soon as possible publish a notice in the appropriate form in the Appendix, or a form to the like effect, showing the name or names of the candidate or candidates elected and the total number of votes given to each candidate whether elected or not, together with the number of rejected ballot papers under each head shown in the statement of rejected ballot papers;

(*b*) in the case of a poll on any other question, declare the number of votes given for and against the question and whether the proposal to which the question relates has been carried or lost and shall as soon as possible publish a notice in the appropriate form in the Appendix, or a form to the like effect, showing the result as declared together with the number of rejected ballot papers under each head shown in the statement of rejected ballot papers.

The return

35. The returning officer shall forthwith upon declaration of the result of the poll return the name of each person elected or the result of the poll, as the case may be, to the chairman of the meeting at which the poll was demanded.

Sealing of ballot papers

36.—(1) On the completion of the counting the returning officer shall seal up in separate packets the counted and rejected ballot papers, including ballot papers rejected in part.

(2) The returning officer shall not open the sealed packets of tendered ballot papers or of counterfoils or of marked copies of the register of electors.

Delivery of documents to the district council

37. The returning officer shall then forward to the proper officer of the council of the district in which the parish or community is situate the following documents, that is to say:—

(*a*) the packets of ballot papers in his possession;

(*b*) the ballot paper accounts and the statements of rejected ballot papers and of the result of the verification of the ballot paper accounts;

(*c*) the tendered votes lists, the lists of blind voters assisted by companions, the lists of votes marked by the presiding officer and the statements relating thereto, and the declarations made by the companions of blind voters;

(*d*) the packets of counterfoils;

(*e*) the packets containing marked copies of the register of electors,

endorsing on each packet a description of its contents, the date of the poll to which they relate and the name of the parish or community for which the poll was held.

Orders for production of documents

38.—(1) An order for—

(*a*) the inspection or production of any rejected ballot papers, including ballot papers rejected in part; or

(*b*) the opening of a sealed packet of counterfoils or for the inspection of counted ballot papers,

may be made by either a county court or an election court if the court is satisfied by evidence on oath that the order is required for the purpose of instituting or maintaining a prosecution for an offence in relation to ballot papers, or for the purpose of an election petition.

(2) The order may be made subject to such conditions as to persons, time, place and mode of inspection, production or opening as the court making the order may think expedient and may direct the proper officer of the district council having custody of the ballot papers and the sealed packets of counterfoils to retain them intact for such period as may be specified in the order:

Provided that in making and carrying into effect the order, care shall be taken that the way in which the vote of any particular voter has been given shall not be disclosed until it has been proved that his vote was given and the vote has been declared by a competent court to be invalid.

(3) An appeal shall lie to the High Court from any order of a county court made under this rule.

(4) Any power given under this rule to a county court may be exercised by any judge of the court otherwise than in open court.

(5) Where an order is made for the production by the proper officer of the district council of any document in his possession relating to any specified poll, the production by him or his agent of the document ordered in such manner as may be directed by that order shall be conclusive evidence that the document relates to the specified poll; and any endorsement on any packet of ballot papers so produced shall be prima facie evidence that the ballot papers are what they are stated to be by the endorsement.

(6) The production from proper custody of a ballot paper purporting to have been used at any poll, and of a counterfoil marked with the same printed number and having a number marked thereon in writing shall be prima facie evidence that the voter whose vote was given by that ballot paper was the person who at the time of the poll had affixed to his name in the register of electors the same number as the number written on the counterfoil.

(7) Save as by this rule provided, no person shall be allowed to inspect any rejected or counted ballot papers in the possession of the proper officer of the district council or to open any sealed packets of counterfoils.

Retention and public inspection of documents

39.—(1) The proper officer of the district council shall retain for six months among the records of the district all documents relating to a poll which are, in pursuance of these rules, forwarded to him by a returning officer or held by him and then, unless otherwise directed by an order under the last foregoing rule, shall cause them to be destroyed.

(2) The said documents, except ballot papers and counterfoils, shall during a period of six months from the day of the poll be open to public inspection at such time and in such manner as may be determined by the district council.

(3) The proper officer of the district council shall, on request, supply copies of or extracts from the documents open to public inspection on payment of such fees, and subject to such conditions, as may be determined by the district council.

Supplemental provisions as to documents

40. Subject to the provisions of these rules, the proper officer of the district council shall, in respect of the custody and destruction of ballot papers and other documents coming into his possession in pursuance of these rules, be subject to the directions of the district council.

Countermand or abandonment of poll on death of candidate

41.—(1) If before the result of the poll is declared proof is given to the satisfaction of the returning officer that a candidate who has not withdrawn has died, then the returning officer shall countermand the poll or, if polling has begun, direct that the poll be abandoned.

(2) Where the poll is abandoned by reason of the death of a candidate, the proceedings at or consequent on that poll shall be interrupted, and the presiding officer at any polling station shall take the like steps (so far as not already taken) for the delivery to the returning officer of ballot boxes and of ballot papers and other documents as he is required to take on the close of the poll in due course, and the returning officer shall dispose of ballot papers and other documents in his possession as he is required to do on the completion in due course of the counting of the votes; but—

(*a*) it shall not be necessary for any ballot paper account to be prepared or verified; and

(*b*) the returning officer, without taking any step or further step for the counting of the ballot papers or of the votes, shall seal up all the ballot papers, whether the votes on them have been counted or not, and it shall not be necessary to seal up counted and rejected ballot papers in separate packets.

(3) The foregoing provisions of these rules as to the inspection, production, retention and destruction of ballot papers and other documents relating to a poll shall apply to any such documents relating to a poll abandoned by reason of the death of a candidate, with the following modifications:—

(*a*) ballot papers on which the votes were neither counted nor rejected shall be treated as counted ballot papers; and (*b*) no order shall be made for the production or inspection of any ballot papers or for the opening of a sealed packet of counterfoils unless the order is made by a court with reference to a prosecution.

(4) Where a poll is countermanded or abandoned by reason of the death of a candidate, the district council may by order make any appointment or make provision for the holding of a parish meeting or do such other thing as appears to them to be expedient in the circumstances.

General duty of returning officer

42. It shall be the general duty of the returning officer to do any act or thing that may be necessary for effectually conducting the poll under these rules.

Interpretation

43.—(1) In these rules unless the context otherwise requires, the expression "appointment to any other office" includes the election of the chairman of the parish meeting.

(2) For any reference in these rules to a parish or a community there shall, if the poll is held for part of a parish or a community, be substituted a reference to part of a parish or part of a community.

(3) Any reference in these rules to a proper officer shall, in relation to any purpose and any local authority or other body or any area, be construed as a reference to an officer appointed for that purpose by that body or for that area, as the case may be.

(4) A reference in this Schedule to a rule shall be construed as a reference to a rule contained in this Schedule.

(5) Any person before whom a declaration is authorised to be made under these rules may take the declaration.

APPENDIX

Note.—The forms contained in this Appendix may be adapted as far as circumstances require.

Rule 4.

NOTICE OF ABANDONMENT OF POLL

Parish of .

Whereas at a Parish Meeting for the Parish of held on the day of , 19 , a demand was made for a poll as to which of the following candidates should be appointed as [*insert name of office*] for the said parish, and such demand was not withdrawn:—

[*insert names, home address, and description of each candidate*.]

And whereas the said [*insert name*] has since withdrawn his candidature and the number of the remaining candidates does not exceed the number of persons to be appointed to the said office, I hereby give notice that the poll demanded will not take place, and I hereby declare that the said [*insert names*] are appointed to the said office.

Dated this day of , 19 .

....
Returning Officer.

NOTICE OF POLL ON A QUESTION OTHER THAN A QUESTION OF APPOINTMENT TO AN OFFICE

Rule 10.

Parish/Community of .

Whereas at a Parish/Community Meeting for the Parish/Community of held on the day of , 19 , a poll was demanded on the following question, namely,

NOTICE IS HEREBY GIVEN THAT—

*1. A poll on the said question will be taken on the day of , 19 , between the hours of 4 p.m. and 9 p.m.

*If the poll relates to two or more questions, adapt form accordingly.

*2 The names and address of the proposer of the resolution in respect of which the poll is taken are as follows:—

Surname 1	Other names in full 2	Home address in full 3

†3. The situation of the polling stations and the description of the persons entitled to vote at each are as follows:—

†If there is only one polling station, adapt form accordingly.

Polling Station	Persons entitled to vote thereat

Dated this day of , 19 .

....

Returning Officer.

NOTICE OF POLL ON A QUESTION OF APPOINTMENT TO AN OFFICE

Rule 10.

Parish of .

Whereas at a Parish Meeting for the Parish of held on the day of , 19 , a poll was demanded on the question of the appointment to the following office, namely,

NOTICE IS HEREBY GIVEN THAT—

1. A poll on the said appointment will be taken on the day of , 19 , between the hours of 4 p.m. and 9 p.m.

2. The number of persons to be appointed as [*insert name of office*] is .

*Insert particulars as to each candidate with respect to whom the poll is to be taken, in the alphabetical order of the candidates' surnames.

3. The following is a statement as to the persons nominated for election to the said appointment:—

*Persons nominated				
Surname 1	Other names in full 2	Description (if any) 3	Home address in full 4	Proposer's name 5

†If there is only one polling station, adapt form accordingly.

†4. The situation of the polling stations and the description of the persons entitled to vote at each are as follows:—

Polling Station	Persons entitled to vote thereat

Dated this day of , 19 .

....
Returning Officer.

Rule 6.

BALLOT PAPER ON A QUESTION OTHER THAN A QUESTION OF APPOINTMENT TO AN OFFICE

Form of Front of Ballot Paper

Questions	Answers	
	Yes	No
[should the parish/community be grouped with the parish/community of under a common parish/community council?]		
[should a parish/community council be established for the parish/community?]		
[should section 3(1) of the Parish Councils Act 1957 (which empowers a parish/community meeting to light roads and public places) be adopted for the parish/community?]		

Form of Back of Ballot Paper

No.

Poll consequent on Parish/Community Meeting for the Parish/Community of .

day of . 19 .

Note.—The number on the ballot paper is to correspond with that on the counterfoil.

Directions as to printing ballot paper

1. Nothing is to be printed on the ballot paper except in accordance with these directions.

2. So far as practicable, the following arrangements shall be observed in the printing of the ballot paper:—

(*a*) no rule shall be printed on the face except the vertical and horizontal rules separating the answers from the questions and the answers from each other;

(*b*) an equal amount of space for the answer "Yes" and the answer "No" to each question shall be allocated;

(*c*) the spacing, layout and style and size of type face shall be as nearly as may be the same as in the specimen form in this Appendix.

3. The number on the back of the ballot paper shall be printed in ordinary type.

Rule 6

BALLOT PAPER ON A QUESTION OF APPOINTMENT TO AN OFFICE

Form of Front of Ballot Paper

1	**BROWN** JOHN EDWARD Brown, 2 The Cottages, Barlington, Grayshire Labour	
2	**BROWN** THOMAS WILLIAM Brown, 15 Barchester Road, Barlington, Grayshire Liberal	
3	**JONES** William David Jones, The Grange, Barlington, Grayshire Conservative	
4	**MERTON** Hon. George Travis, commonly called Viscount Merton, Barlington, Grayshire	
5	**SMITH** Mary Smith, School House, Barlington, Grayshire Schoolteacher, Progressive	
6	**WILLIAMS** Elizabeth Williams, 3 Ivy Lane, Barlington, Grayshire Housewife	

Form of Back of Ballot Paper

No.

Poll on appointment of [*insert name of office*] for the Parish of
day of , 19 .

Note.—The number on the ballot paper is to correspond with that on the counterfoil.

Directions as to printing the ballot paper

1. Nothing is to be printed on the ballot paper except in accordance with these directions.

2. So far as practicable, the following arrangements shall be observed in the printing of the ballot paper:—

(*a*) no word shall be printed on the face except the particulars of the candidates;

(*b*) no rule shall be printed on the face except the horizontal rules separating the particulars of the candidates from one another and the vertical rules separating those particulars from the numbers on the left-hand side and the spaces on the right where the vote is to be marked;

(*c*) the whole space between the top and bottom of the paper shall be equally divided between the candidates by the rules separating their particulars;

(*d*) the spacing, layout and style and size of type face shall be as nearly as may be the same as the specimen form in this Appendix.

3. The surname of each candidate shall in all cases be printed by itself in large capitals, and his full particulars shall be set out below and shall be printed in ordinary type except that small capitals shall be used—

(a) if his surname is the same as another candidate's, for his other names; and

(*b*) if his other names are also the same as the other candidate's, either for his residence or for his description unless each of them is the same as that of another candidate with the same surname and other names.

4. The number on the back of the ballot paper shall be printed in ordinary type.

DIRECTIONS FOR THE GUIDANCE OF THE VOTERS IN VOTING WHERE THE POLL IS ON A QUESTION OTHER THAN A QUESTION OF APPOINTMENT TO AN OFFICE

Rule 13.

1. The voter should see that the ballot paper, before it is handed to him, is stamped with the official mark.

2. The voter will go into one of the compartments and, with the pencil provided in the compartment, place a cross thus X in the column of the ballot paper headed "Yes" or in that headed "No" according to whether he wishes to vote in favour of or against the question opposite to which he places the cross.

Where the ballot paper refers to more than one question the voter may vote in the manner described on each question in the ballot paper.

3. The voter will then fold up the ballot paper so as to show the official mark on the back, and leaving the compartment will, without showing the front of the paper to any person, show the official mark on the back to the presiding officer, and then, in the presence of the presiding officer, put the paper into the ballot box, and forthwith leave the polling station.

4. If the voter inadvertently spoils a ballot paper, he can return it to the officer, who will, if satisfied of such inadvertence, give him another paper.

5. If the voter places any mark on the paper by which he may afterwards be identified, his ballot paper will be void, and will not be counted.

Rule 13.

DIRECTIONS FOR THE GUIDANCE OF THE VOTERS IN VOTING WHERE THE POLL IS ON A QUESTION OF APPOINTMENT TO AN OFFICE

1. The voter should see that the ballot paper, before it is handed to him, is stamped with the official mark.

2. The voter will go into one of the compartments and, with the pencil provided in the compartment, place a cross on the right-hand side of the ballot paper, opposite the name of each candidate for whom he votes, thus X.

3. The voter will then fold up the ballot paper so as to show the official mark on the back, and leaving the compartment will, without showing the front of the paper to any person, show the official mark on the back to the presiding officer, and then, in the presence of the presiding officer, put the paper into the ballot box, and forthwith leave the polling station.

4. If the voter inadvertently spoils a ballot paper he can return it to the officer, who will, if satisfied of such inadvertence, give him another paper.

5. If the voter votes for more than candidate(s), or places any mark on the paper by which he may be afterwards identified, his ballot paper will be void, and will not be counted.

Rule 23.

DECLARATION TO BE MADE BY THE COMPANION OF A BLIND VOTER

*State the relationship of the companion to the voter.

I, A.B., of , having been requested to assist C.D., who is numbered on the register of local government electors for the electoral area for which the poll is being held, to record his vote at the poll now being held for the said area, do hereby declare that [I am entitled to vote at the said poll] [I am the* of the said voter and have attained the age of eighteen years], and that I have not previously assisted any blind person [except E.F., of], to vote at the said poll.

(Signed) A.B.

Date..................

I, the undersigned, being the presiding officer for the polling station for the electoral area for which the poll is being held, do hereby certify that the above declaration, having been first read to the above-named declarant, was signed by the declarant in my presence.

(Signed) X.Y.

day of , 19 , at minutes past o'clock.

NOTE.—If the person making the above declaration knowingly and wilfully makes therein a statement false in a material particular, he will be guilty of an offence.

DECLARATION OF RESULT OF POLL ON A QUESTION OTHER THAN A QUESTION OF APPOINTMENT TO AN OFFICE

Rule 34.

Parish/Community of .

Whereas a poll of the local government electors of the [Parish/Community] [electoral areas of of the Parish/Community] was taken on the day of , 19 , on the following question[s], namely [*state the question or questions upon which the poll was taken*].

I, the undersigned, being the returning officer at the said poll, hereby give notice that the number of votes given thereat was as follows:—

For the question .. .. votes.

Against the question .. .. votes.

Majority for [or against] .. .. ..

‡REJECTED BALLOT PAPERS

‡If no ballot papers rejected omit this part of form.

........ballot papers were rejected for the following reason(s):—

§(*a*) want of official mark........[*insert number*]

§(*b*) writing or mark by which voter could be identified........[*insert number*]

§(*c*) unmarked or wholly void for uncertainty........[*insert number*]

§........ballot papers were rejected in part.

§Delete if inapplicable.

And I hereby declare that the said question was carried [or lost].

Dated this day of , 19 .

....

Returning Officer.

DECLARATION OF RESULT OF POLL ON A QUESTION OF APPOINTMENT TO AN OFFICE

Rule 34.

Parish of

Whereas a poll of the local government electors of the parish of was taken on the day of , 19 , as to the person[s] to be appointed as [*insert name of office*] for the parish;

I, the undersigned, being the returning officer at the said poll, hereby give notice that the number of votes given for each candidate at the poll was as follows:—

Names of Candidate		Home address in full	Number of Votes given
Surname	Other Names in full		

‡If no ballot papers rejected omit this part of form.

§Delete if inapplicable.

‡REJECTED BALLOT PAPERS

........ballot papers were rejected for the following reason(s):—

§(*a*) want of official mark........[*insert number*]

§(*b*) voting for more candidates than voter is entitled to........[*insert number*]

§(*c*) writing or mark by which voter could be identified........[*insert number*]

§(*d*) unmarked or wholly void for uncertainty........[*insert number*]

§........ballot papers were rejected in part.

And I hereby declare that the said are duly appointed to the said office.

Dated this day of , 19 .

....

Returning Officer.

EXPLANATORY NOTE

(*This Note is not part of the Rules.*)

These Rules revoke and replace the Parish Meetings (Polls) Rules 1970. They apply to a poll consequent on a community meeting as well as to a poll consequent on a parish meeting.

1973 No. 1913

EMERGENCY POWERS

ELECTRICITY

The Electricity (Heating) (Restriction) Variation Order 1973

Made - - - -	15*th November* 1973
Coming into Operation	16*th November* 1973

The Secretary of State, in exercise of his powers under Regulations 21(1) and 40(1) of the Emergency Regulations 1973(**a**) and of all other powers in that behalf enabling him, hereby orders as follows:—

1. This Order shall come into operation on 16th November 1973, and may be cited as the Electricity (Heating) (Restriction) Variation Order 1973.

2. The Electricity (Heating) (Restriction) Order 1973(**b**) shall be varied as follows:—

(1) Subparagraph (*a*)(vi) of Article 3(1) shall be deleted.

(2) Nothing in Article 3(1) shall apply to the consumption of electricity between 00.30 a.m. and 07.30 a.m. on any day.

Tom Boardman,
Minister for Industry,
Department of Trade and Industry.

15th November 1973.

EXPLANATORY NOTE

(*This Note is not part of the Order.*)

This Order varies the Electricity (Heating) (Restriction) Order 1973—which prohibits (with certain exceptions) the consumption of electricity for space heating in certain kinds of non-domestic premises specified in that Order—by removing the prohibition on such consumption—

(*a*) in schools, colleges and other places of education; and

(*b*) between 00.30 a.m. and 07.30 a.m. in all premises to which the Order applies.

(**a**) S.I. 1973/1881 (1973 III, p. 6516). (**b**) S.I. 1973/1900 (1973 III, p. 6587).

1973 No. 1919

WATER, ENGLAND AND WALES

The Anglian Water Authority (Regional Land Drainage Committee) Order 1973

Made - - -	12*th November* 1973
Coming into Operation	20*th November* 1973

Whereas—

(1) the Anglian Water Authority (hereafter in this Order referred to as "the Water Authority") are required by paragraph 1(1) of Schedule 5 to the Water Act 1973(**a**) to establish a committee to be known as a regional land drainage committee and, in accordance with paragraph 1(7) and (9) of the said Schedule, have submitted to the Minister of Agriculture, Fisheries and Food (hereafter in this Order referred to as "the Minister") a determination that the total number of members of their regional land drainage committee (hereafter in this Order referred to as "the committee") shall be seventeen;

(2) the constituent councils for the committee are the councils of the counties and London borough specified in the first column of the Schedule to this Order;

(3) the Minister, having had regard to the appropriate penny rate product and proportion mentioned in paragraph 3(1) of the said Schedule 5 relating to each of the said constituent councils,—

(*a*) considers it to be inappropriate that the councils of the counties of Leicestershire, Oxfordshire and Nottinghamshire and the London borough of Havering (being four of the said constituent councils) should appoint a member of the committee; and

(*b*) considers that one member of the committee should be appointed jointly by the councils of the counties of Buckinghamshire and Hertfordshire (being two of the said constituent councils):

Now, therefore, the Minister, in exercise of the powers conferred on him by paragraphs 1(12) and 3(1) of Schedule 5 to the Water Act 1973, and of every other power enabling him in that behalf, and having had regard to the appropriate penny rate product and proportion mentioned in the said paragraph 3(1) relating to each of the said constituent councils, hereby orders as follows:—

Citation and commencement

1. This Order may be cited as the Anglian Water Authority (Regional Land Drainage Committee) Order 1973 and shall come into operation on 20th November 1973.

(**a**) 1973 c. 37.

Interpretation

2.—(1) In this Order—

"the Act of 1972" means the Local Government Act 1972(**a**);

"constituent council" means the council of any county established by the Act of 1972 any part of which is in the Water Authority area and the council of any London borough wholly or partly within that area;

"the Water Authority area" means the area of the Water Authority for the purposes of their functions relating to land drainage.

(2) Any reference in this Order to a specified county or to the council thereof is a reference to the county of that name established by the Act of 1972 or to the council so established for that county, as the case may be.

(3) The Interpretation Act 1889(**b**) shall apply for the interpretation of this Order as it applies for the interpretation of an Act of Parliament.

Constituent councils appointments of committee members

3.—(1) The number of members to be appointed to the committee by or on behalf of constituent councils for the committee shall be nine.

(2) The number of members of the committee to be appointed by each of the councils of the counties and the London borough specified in the first column of the Schedule to this Order or by or on behalf of the councils of the group of counties so specified shall be the number specified in relation to that county or London borough or to that group in the second column of that Schedule.

(3) Where in the said Schedule the number to be appointed is specified in relation to a group of counties that number shall be appointed jointly by the councils of the counties comprising the group.

In witness whereof the Official Seal of the Minister of Agriculture, Fisheries and Food is hereunto affixed on 12th November 1973.

(L.S.)

Joseph Godber,
Minister of Agriculture,
Fisheries and Food.

SCHEDULE

Article 3

Counties and London borough	*Number of Members*
The county of Bedfordshire	One
The counties of Buckinghamshire and Hertfordshire	One jointly
The county of Cambridgeshire	One
The county of Essex	One
The London borough of Havering	None
The county of Humberside	One
The county of Leicestershire	None
The county of Lincolnshire	One
The county of Norfolk	One
The county of Northamptonshire	One
The county of Nottinghamshire	None
The county of Oxfordshire	None
The county of Suffolk	One

(**a**) 1972 c. 70. (**b**) 1889 c. 63.

EXPLANATORY NOTE

(This Note is not part of the Order.)

Paragraph 1 of Schedule 5 to the Water Act provides that each water authority shall establish a regional land drainage committee consisting of:—

(*a*) a Chairman and a number of other members appointed by the Minister of Agriculture, Fisheries and Food;

(*b*) two members appointed by the water authority; and

(*c*) a number of members appointed by or on behalf of constituent councils being, in the case of the Anglian Water Authority, councils of counties or of London boroughs any part of whose area is in the water authority area.

When the total number of members of a water authority's regional land drainage committee, being not less than eleven nor more than seventeen, has been fixed by them, the Minister is required by paragraph 1(12) of the Schedule by Order to specify the number of members to be appointed to the committee by or on behalf of the constituent councils, their number being required by paragraph 1(13) of the Schedule to exceed by one the number of the other members. In determining the number of such members to be appointed by or on behalf of each constituent council, the Minister is required by paragraph 3(1) of the Schedule to have regard to the appropriate penny rate product and proportion mentioned in that paragraph and where, having regard thereto, the Minister considers it inappropriate that a constituent council should appoint a member of the committee, or considers that one or more members should be appointed jointly by that council and one or more other constituent councils, he may by the Order so provide.

The Anglian Water Authority, established on 1st August 1973, has determined that the total number of the members of their regional land drainage committee should be seventeen and this Order specifies the number of members of that committee which are to be appointed by or on behalf of constituent councils and by which of those councils such members are to be appointed.

1973 No. 1920

WATER, ENGLAND AND WALES

The North West Water Authority (Regional Land Drainage Committee) Order 1973

Made - - -	12*th November* 1973
Coming into Operation	20*th November* 1973

Whereas—

(1) the North West Water Authority (hereafter in this Order referred to as "the Water Authority") are required by paragraph 1(1) of Schedule 5 to the Water Act 1973(**a**) to establish a committee to be known as a regional land drainage committee and, in accordance with paragraph 1(7) and (9) of the said Schedule, have submitted to the Minister of Agriculture, Fisheries and Food (hereafter in this Order referred to as "the Minister") a determination that the total number of members of their regional land drainage committee (hereafter in this Order referred to as "the committee") shall be fifteen;

(2) the constituent councils for the committee are the councils of the counties specified in the first column of the Schedule to this Order;

(3) the Minister, having had regard to the appropriate penny rate product and proportion mentioned in paragraph 3(1) of the said Schedule 5 relating to each of the said constituent councils, considers it to be inappropriate that the councils of the counties of Derbyshire, Northumberland, North Yorkshire, Salop and Staffordshire (being five of the said constituent councils) should appoint a member of the committee:

Now, therefore, the Minister, in exercise of the powers conferred on him by paragraphs 1(12) and 3(1) of Schedule 5 to the Water Act 1973, and of every other power enabling him in that behalf, and having had regard to the appropriate penny rate product and proportion mentioned in the said paragraph 3(1) relating to each of the said constituent councils, hereby orders as follows:—

Citation and commencement

1. This Order may be cited as the North West Water Authority (Regional Land Drainage Committee) Order 1973 and shall come into operation on 20th November 1973.

Interpretation

2.—(1) In this Order—

"the Act of 1972" means the Local Government Act 1972(**b**);

"constituent council" means the council of any county established by the Act of 1972 any part of which is in the Water Authority area;

(**a**) 1973 c. 37. (**b**) 1972 c. 70.

"the Water Authority area" means the area of the Water Authority for the purposes of their functions relating to land drainage.

(2) Any reference in this Order to a specified county or to the council thereof is a reference to the county of that name established by the Act of 1972 or to the council so established for that county, as the case may be.

(3) The Interpretation Act 1889(**a**) shall apply for the interpretation of this Order as it applies for the interpretation of an Act of Parliament.

Constituent councils appointments of committee members

3.—(1) The number of members to be appointed to the committee by or on behalf of constituent councils for the committee shall be eight.

(2) The number of members of the committee to be appointed by each of the councils of the counties specified in the first column of the Schedule to this Order shall be the number specified in relation to that county in the second column of that Schedule.

In witness whereof the Official Seal of the Minister of Agriculture, Fisheries and Food is hereunto affixed on 12th November 1973.

(L.S.)

Joseph Godber,
Minister of Agriculture,
Fisheries and Food.

Article 3

SCHEDULE

Counties	*Number of Members*
Cheshire	One
Cumbria	One
Derbyshire	None
Greater Manchester	Three
Lancashire	One
Merseyside	Two
Northumberland	None
North Yorkshire	None
Salop	None
Staffordshire	None

(**a**) 1889 c. 63.

EXPLANATORY NOTE

(This Note is not part of the Order.)

Paragraph 1 of Schedule 5 to the Water Act provides that each water authority shall establish a regional land drainage committee consisting of:—

(*a*) a Chairman and a number of other members appointed by the Minister of Agriculture, Fisheries and Food;

(*b*) two members appointed by the water authority; and

(*c*) a number of members appointed by constituent councils being, where no part of Greater London is in the water authority area, councils of counties any part of whose area is in the water authority area.

When the total number of members of a water authority's regional land drainage committee, being not less than eleven nor more than seventeen, has been fixed by them, the Minister is required by paragraph 1(12) of the Schedule by Order to specify the number of members to be appointed to the committee by the constituent councils, their number being required by paragraph 1(13) of the Schedule to exceed by one the number of the other members. In determining the number of such members to be appointed by each constituent council, the Minister is required by paragraph 3(1) of the Schedule to have regard to the appropriate penny rate product and proportion mentioned in that paragraph and where, having regard thereto, the Minister considers it inappropriate that a constituent council should appoint a member of the committee he may by the Order so provide.

The North West Water Authority, established on 26th July 1973, has determined that the total number of the members of their regional land drainage committee should be fifteen and this Order specifies the number of members of that committee which are to be appointed by constituent councils and by which of those councils such members are to be appointed.

1973 No. 1921

WATER, ENGLAND AND WALES

The Severn-Trent Water Authority (Regional Land Drainage Committee) Order 1973

Made - - -	12*th November* 1973
Coming into Operation	15*th November* 1973

Whereas—

(1) the Severn-Trent Water Authority (hereafter in this Order referred to as "the Water Authority") are required by paragraph 1(1) of Schedule 5 to the Water Act 1973(**a**) to establish a committee to be known as a regional land drainage committee and, in accordance with paragraph 1(7) and (9) of the said Schedule, have submitted to the Minister of Agriculture, Fisheries and Food (hereafter in this Order referred to as "the Minister") a determination that the total number of members of their regional land drainage committee (hereafter in this Order referred to as "the committee") shall be seventeen;

(2) the constituent councils for the committee are the councils of the counties specified in the first column of the Schedule to this Order;

(3) the Minister, having had regard to the appropriate penny rate product and proportion mentioned in paragraph 3(1) of the said Schedule 5 relating to each of the said constituent councils,—

(*a*) considers it to be inappropriate that the councils of the counties of Avon, Clwyd, Humberside, Lincolnshire, Northamptonshire, Oxfordshire, Powys and South Yorkshire (being eight of the said constituent councils) should appoint a member of the committee; and

(*b*) considers that one member of the committee should be appointed jointly by the councils of the counties of Gloucestershire and Warwickshire (being two of the said constituent councils) and that one member of the committee should be appointed jointly by the councils of the county of Hereford and Worcester and the county of Salop (being two of the said constituent councils):

Now, therefore, the Minister, in exercise of the powers conferred on him by paragraphs 1(12) and 3(1) of Schedule 5 to the Water Act 1973, and of every other power enabling him in that behalf, and having had regard to the appropriate penny rate product and proportion mentioned in the said paragraph 3(1) relating to each of the said constituent councils, hereby orders as follows:—

Citation and commencement

1. This Order may be cited as the Severn-Trent Water Authority (Regional Land Drainage Committee) Order 1973 and shall come into operation on 15th November 1973.

(a) 1973 c.37.

Interpretation

2.—(1) In this Order—

"the Act of 1972" means the Local Government Act 1972(**a**);

"constituent council" means the council of any county established by the Act of 1972 any part of which is in the Water Authority area;

"the Water Authority area" means the area of the Water Authority for the purposes of their functions relating to land drainage.

(2) Any reference in this Order to a specified county or to the council thereof is a reference to the county of that name established by the Act of 1972 or to the council so established for that county, as the case may be.

(3) The Interpretation Act 1889(**b**) shall apply for the interpretation of this Order as it applies for the interpretation of an Act of Parliament.

Constituent councils appointments of committee members

3.—(1) The number of members to be appointed to the committee by or on behalf of constituent councils for the committee shall be nine.

(2) The number of members of the committee to be appointed by each of the councils of the counties specified in the first column of the Schedule to this Order or by or on behalf of the councils of each group of counties so specified shall be the number specified in relation to that county or to that group in the second column of that Schedule.

(3) Where in the said Schedule the number to be appointed is specified in relation to a group of counties that number shall be appointed jointly by the councils of the counties comprising the group.

In witness whereof the Official Seal of the Minister of Agriculture, Fisheries and Food is hereunto affixed on 12th November 1973.

(L.S.)

Joseph Godber,
Minister of Agriculture,
Fisheries and Food.

(**a**) 1972 c. 70.
(**b**) 1889 c. 63.

Article 3

SCHEDULE

Counties	*Number of Members*
Avon	None
Clwyd	None
Derbyshire	One
Gloucestershire, Warwickshire	One jointly
Hereford and Worcester, Salop	One jointly
Humberside	None
Leicestershire	One
Lincolnshire	None
Northamptonshire	None
Nottinghamshire	One
Oxfordshire	None
Powys	None
South Yorkshire	None
Staffordshire	One
West Midlands	Three

EXPLANATORY NOTE

(*This Note is not part of the Order.*)

Paragraph 1 of Schedule 5 to the Water Act provides that each water authority shall establish a regional land drainage committee consisting of:—

(*a*) a Chairman and a number of other members appointed by the Minister of Agriculture, Fisheries and Food;

(*b*) two members appointed by the water authority; and

(c) a number of members appointed by or on behalf of constituent councils being, where no part of Greater London is in the water authority area, councils of counties any part of whose area is in the water authority area.

When the total number of members of a water authority's regional land drainage committee, being not less than eleven nor more than seventeen, has been fixed by them, the Minister is required by paragraph 1(12) of the Schedule by Order to specify the number of members to be appointed to the committee by or on behalf of the constituent councils, their number being required by paragraph 1(13) of the Schedule to exceed by one the number of the other members. In determining the number of such members to be appointed by or on behalf of each constituent council, the Minister is required by paragraph 3(1) of the Schedule to have regard to the appropriate penny rate product and proportion mentioned in that paragraph and where, having regard thereto, the Minister considers it inappropriate that a constituent council should appoint a member of the committee, or considers that one or more members should be appointed jointly by that council and one or more other constituent councils, he may by the Order so provide.

The Severn-Trent Water Authority, established on 14th August 1973, has determined that the total number of the members of their regional land drainage committee should be seventeen and this Order specifies the number of members of that committee which are to be appointed by or on behalf of constituent councils and by which of those councils such members are to be appointed.

1973 No. 1922

WATER, ENGLAND AND WALES

The South West Water Authority (Regional Land Drainage Committee) Order 1973

Made - - - *12th November* 1973

Coming into Operation *20th November* 1973

Whereas—

(1) the South West Water Authority (hereafter in this Order referred to as "the Water Authority") are required by paragraph 1(1) of Schedule 5 to the Water Act 1973(**a**) to establish a committee to be known as a regional land drainage committee and, in accordance with paragraph 1(7) and (9) of the said Schedule, have submitted to the Minister of Agriculture, Fisheries and Food (hereafter in this Order referred to as "the Minister") a determination that the total number of members of their regional land drainage committee (hereafter in this Order referred to as "the committee") shall be thirteen;

(2) the constituent councils for the committee are the councils of the counties specified in the first column of the Schedule to this Order;

(3) the Minister, having had regard to the appropriate penny rate product and proportion mentioned in paragraph 3(1) of the said Schedule 5 relating to each of the said constituent councils, considers it to be inappropriate that the councils of the counties of Dorset and Somerset (being two of the said constituent councils) should appoint a member of the committee:

Now, therefore, the Minister, in exercise of the powers conferred on him by paragraphs 1(12) and 3(1) of Schedule 5 to the Water Act 1973, and of every other power enabling him in that behalf, and having had regard to the appropriate penny rate product and proportion mentioned in the said paragraph 3(1) relating to each of the said constituent councils, hereby orders as follows:—

Citation and commencement

1. This Order may be cited as the South West Water Authority (Regional Land Drainage Committee) Order 1973 and shall come into operation on 20th November 1973.

Interpretation

2.—(1) In this Order—

"the Act of 1972" means the Local Government Act 1972(**b**);

(**a**) 1973 c. 37. (**b**) 1972 c. 70.

"constituent council" means the council of any county established by the Act of 1972 any part of which is in the Water Authority area;

"the Water Authority area" means the area of the Water Authority for the purposes of their functions relating to land drainage.

(2) Any reference in this Order to a specified county or to the council thereof is a reference to the county of that name established by the Act of 1972 or to the council so established for that county, as the case may be.

(3) The Interpretation Act 1889(**a**) shall apply for the interpretation of this Order as it applies for the interpretation of an Act of Parliament.

Constituent councils appointments of committee members

3.—(1) The number of members to be appointed to the committee by or on behalf of constituent councils for the committee shall be seven.

(2) The number of members of the committee to be appointed by each of the councils of the counties specified in the first column of the Schedule to this Order shall be the number specified in relation to that county in the second column of that Schedule.

In witness whereof the Official Seal of the Minister of Agriculture, Fisheries and Food is hereunto affixed on 12th November 1973.

(L.S.)

Joseph Godber,
Minister of Agriculture,
Fisheries and Food.

SCHEDULE

Article 3

Counties	*Number of Members*
Cornwall	Two
Devon	Five
Dorset	None
Somerset	None

(**a**) 1889 c. 63.

EXPLANATORY NOTE

(This Note is not part of the Order.)

Paragraph 1 of Schedule 5 to the Water Act provides that each water authority shall establish a regional land drainage committee consisting of:—

(*a*) a Chairman and a number of other members appointed by the Minister of Agriculture, Fisheries and Food;

(*b*) two members appointed by the water authority; and

(*c*) a number of members appointed by constituent councils being, where no part of Greater London is in the water authority area, councils of counties any part of whose area is in the water authority area.

When the total number of members of a water authority's regional land drainage committee, being not less than eleven nor more than seventeen, has been fixed by them, the Minister is required by paragraph 1(12) of the Schedule by Order to specify the number of members to be appointed to the committee by the constituent councils, their number being required by paragraph 1(13) of the Schedule to exceed by one the number of the other members. In determining the number of such members to be appointed by each constituent council, the Minister is required by paragraph 3(1) of the Schedule to have regard to the appropriate penny rate product and proportion mentioned in that paragraph and where, having regard thereto, the Minister considers it inappropriate that a constituent council should appoint a member of the committee he may by the Order so provide.

The South West Water Authority, established on 26th July 1973, has determined that the total number of the members of their regional land drainage committee should be thirteen and this Order specifies the number of members of that committee which are to be appointed by constituent councils and by which of those councils such members are to be appointed.

STATUTORY INSTRUMENTS

1973 No. 1923

WATER, ENGLAND AND WALES

The Southern Water Authority (Regional Land Drainage Committee) Order 1973

Made - - -	*12th November* 1973
Coming into Operation	*20th November* 1973

Whereas—

(1) the Southern Water Authority (hereafter in this Order referred to as "the Water Authority") are required by paragraph 1(1) of Schedule 5 to the Water Act 1973(**a**) to establish a committee to be known as a regional land drainage committee and, in accordance with paragraph 1(7) and (9) of the said Schedule, have submitted to the Minister of Agriculture, Fisheries and Food (hereafter in this Order referred to as "the Minister") a determination that the total number of members of their regional land drainage committee (hereafter in this Order referred to as "the committee") shall be seventeen;

(2) the constituent councils for the committee are the councils of the counties and London boroughs specified in the first column of the Schedule to this Order;

(3) the Minister, having had regard to the appropriate penny rate product and proportion mentioned in paragraph 3(1) of the said Schedule 5 relating to each of the said constituent councils,—

(*a*) considers it to be inappropriate that the councils of the counties of Berkshire, Surrey and Wiltshire (being three of the said constituent councils) should appoint a member of the committee; and

(*b*) considers that one member of the committee should be appointed jointly by the councils of the London boroughs of Bexley, Bromley and Greenwich (being three of the said constituent councils):

Now, therefore, the Minister, in exercise of the powers conferred on him by paragraphs 1(12) and 3(1) of Schedule 5 to the Water Act 1973, and of every other power enabling him in that behalf, and having had regard to the appropriate penny rate product and proportion mentioned in the said paragraph 3(1) relating to each of the said constituent councils, hereby orders as follows:—

Citation and commencement

1. This Order may be cited as the Southern Water Authority (Regional Land Drainage Committee) Order 1973 and shall come into operation on 20th November 1973.

(**a**) 1973 c. 37.

Interpretation

2.—(1) In this Order—

"the Act of 1972" means the Local Government Act 1972(**a**);

"constituent council" means the council of any county established by the Act of 1972 any part of which is in the Water Authority area and the council of any London borough wholly or partly within that area;

"the Water Authority area" means the area of the Water Authority for the purposes of their functions relating to land drainage.

(2) Any reference in this Order to a specified county or to the council thereof is a reference to the county of that name established by the Act of 1972 or to the council so established for that county, as the case may be.

(3) The Interpretation Act 1889(**b**) shall apply for the interpretation of this Order as it applies for the interpretation of an Act of Parliament.

Constituent councils appointments of committee members

3.—(1) The number of members to be appointed to the committee by or on behalf of constituent councils for the committee shall be nine.

(2) The number of members of the committee to be appointed by each of the councils of the counties specified in the first column of the Schedule to this Order or by or on behalf of the councils of the group of London boroughs so specified shall be the number specified in relation to that county or to that group in the second column of that Schedule.

(3) Where in the said Schedule the number to be appointed is specified in relation to a group of London boroughs that number shall be appointed jointly by the councils of the London boroughs comprising the group.

In witness whereof the Official Seal of the Minister of Agriculture, Fisheries and Food is hereunto affixed on 12th November 1973.

(L.S.)

Joseph Godber,
Minister of Agriculture,
Fisheries and Food.

Article 3

SCHEDULE

Counties and London boroughs	*Number of Members*
The county of Berkshire	None
The county of East Sussex	One
The county of Hampshire	Two
The county of Isle of Wight	One
The county of Kent	Three
The London boroughs of Bexley, Bromley and Greenwich	One jointly
The county of Surrey	None
The county of West Sussex	One
The county of Wiltshire	None

(**a**) 1972 c. 70. (**b**) 1889 c. 63.

EXPLANATORY NOTE

(*This Note is not part of the Order.*)

Paragraph 1 of Schedule 5 to the Water Act provides that each water authority shall establish a regional land drainage committee consisting of:—

(*a*) a Chairman and a number of other members appointed by the Minister of Agriculture, Fisheries and Food;

(*b*) two members appointed by the water authority; and

(*c*) a number of members appointed by or on behalf of constituent councils being, in the case of the Southern Water Authority, councils of counties or of London boroughs any part of whose area is in the water authority area.

When the total number of members of a water authority's regional land drainage committee, being not less than eleven nor more than seventeen, has been fixed by them, the Minister is required by paragraph 1(12) of the Schedule by Order to specify the number of members to be appointed to the committee by or on behalf of the constituent councils, their number being required by paragraph 1(13) of the Schedule to exceed by one the number of the other members. In determining the number of such members to be appointed by or on behalf of each constituent council, the Minister is required by paragraph 3(1) of the Schedule to have regard to the appropriate penny rate product and proportion mentioned in that paragraph and where, having regard thereto, the Minister considers it inappropriate that a constituent council should appoint a member of the committee, or considers that one or more members should be appointed jointly by that council and one or more other constituent councils, he may by the Order so provide.

The Southern Water Authority, established on 1st August 1973, has determined that the total number of the members of their regional land drainage committee should be seventeen and this Order specifies the number of members of that committee which are to be appointed by or on behalf of constituent councils and by which of those councils such members are to be appointed.

1973 No. 1924

WATER, ENGLAND AND WALES

The Welsh National Water Development Authority (Regional Land Drainage Committee) Order 1973

Made - - - 12*th November* 1973

Coming into Operation 20*th November* 1973

Whereas—

(1) the Welsh National Water Development Authority (hereafter in this Order referred to as "the Welsh Authority") are required by paragraph 1(1) of Schedule 5 to the Water Act 1973(**a**) to establish a committee to be known as a regional land drainage committee and, in accordance with paragraph 1(7), (9) and (10) of the said Schedule, have submitted to the Minister of Agriculture, Fisheries and Food (hereafter in this Order referred to as "the Minister") a determination (which has provisional effect only until confirmed by the Minister) that the total number of members of their regional land drainage committee (hereafter in this Order referred to as "the committee") shall be nineteen;

(2) the constituent councils for the committee are the councils of the counties specified in the first column of the Schedule to this Order;

(3) the Minister, having had regard to the appropriate penny rate product and proportion mentioned in paragraph 3(1) of the said Schedule 5 relating to each of the said constituent councils, considers it to be inappropriate that the councils of the counties of Gloucestershire and Salop (being two of the said constituent councils) should appoint a member of the committee:

Now, therefore, the Minister, in exercise of the powers conferred on him by paragraphs 1(11), (12) and 3(1) of Schedule 5 to the Water Act 1973, and of every other power enabling him in that behalf, and having had regard to the appropriate penny rate product and proportion mentioned in the said paragraph 3(1) relating to each of the said constituent councils, hereby orders as follows:—

Citation and commencement

1. This Order may be cited as the Welsh National Water Development Authority (Regional Land Drainage Committee) Order 1973 and shall come into operation on 20th November 1973.

Interpretation

2.—(1) In this Order—

"the Act of 1972" means the Local Government Act 1972(**b**);

"constituent council" means the council of any county established by the Act of 1972 any part of which is in the Welsh Authority area;

(**a**) 1973 c. 37.

(**b**) 1972 c. 70.

"the Welsh Authority area" means the area of the Welsh Authority for the purposes of their functions relating to land drainage.

(2) Any reference in this Order to a specified county or to the council thereof is a reference to the county of that name established by the Act of 1972 or to the council so established for that county, as the case may be.

(3) The Interpretation Act 1889(**a**) shall apply for the interpretation of this Order as it applies for the interpretation of an Act of Parliament.

Confirmation of determination

3. The determination of the Welsh Authority that the total number of members of the committee shall be nineteen is hereby confirmed.

Constituent councils appointments of committee members

4.—(1) The number of members to be appointed to the committee by or on behalf of constituent councils for the committee shall be ten.

(2) The number of members of the committee to be appointed by each of the councils of the counties specified in the first column of the Schedule to this Order shall be the number specified in relation to that county in the second column of that Schedule.

In witness whereof the Official Seal of the Minister of Agriculture, Fisheries and Food is hereunto affixed on 12th November 1973.

(L.S.)

Joseph Godber,
Minister of Agriculture,
Fisheries and Food.

SCHEDULE

Article 4

Counties	*Number of Members*
Cheshire	One
Clwyd	One
Dyfed	One
Gloucestershire	None
Gwent	One
Gwynedd	One
Hereford and Worcester	One
Mid Glamorgan	One
Powys	One
Salop	None
South Glamorgan	One
West Glamorgan	One

(**a**) 1889 c. 63.

EXPLANATORY NOTE

(This Note is not part of the Order.)

Paragraph 1 of Schedule 5 to the Water Act provides that each water authority (including the Welsh National Water Development Authority) shall establish a regional land drainage committee consisting of:—

(*a*) a Chairman and a number of other members appointed by the Minister of Agriculture, Fisheries and Food;

(*b*) two members appointed by the water authority; and

(*c*) a number of members appointed by constituent councils being, where no part of Greater London is in the water authority area, councils of counties any part of whose area is in the water authority area.

That paragraph also provides that the total membership of the regional land drainage committee shall be determined by the water authority within the limits of eleven and seventeen. The water authority may determine a membership in excess of seventeen, but under paragraph 1(11) such a determination is provisional until confirmed by the Minister by Order

When the total number of members of a water authority's regional land drainage committee has been finally determined, the Minister is required by paragraph 1(12) of the Schedule by Order to specify the number of members to be appointed to the committee by the constituent councils, their number being required by paragraph 1(13) of the Schedule to exceed by one the number of the other members. In determining the number of such members to be appointed by each constituent council, the Minister is required by paragraph 3(1) of the Schedule to have regard to the appropriate penny rate product and proportion mentioned in that paragraph and where, having regard thereto, the Minister considers it inappropriate that a constituent council should appoint a member of the committee he may by the Order so provide.

The Welsh National Water Development Authority, established on 6th August 1973, having provisionally determined that the total number of the members of their regional land drainage committee should be nineteen, this Order confirms that number and specifies the number of members of that committee which are to be appointed by constituent councils and by which of those councils such members are to be appointed.

STATUTORY INSTRUMENTS

1973 No. 1925

WATER, ENGLAND AND WALES

The Wessex Water Authority (Regional Land Drainage Committee) Order 1973

Made - - - 12*th November* 1973

Coming into Operation 20*th November* 1973

Whereas—

(1) the Wessex Water Authority (hereafter in this Order referred to as "the Water Authority") are required by paragraph 1(1) of Schedule 5 to the Water Act 1973(**a**) to establish a committee to be known as a regional land drainage committee and, in accordance with paragraph 1(7) and (9) of the said Schedule, have submitted to the Minister of Agriculture, Fisheries and Food (hereafter in this Order referred to as "the Minister") a determination that the total number of members of their regional land drainage committee (hereafter in this Order referred to as "the committee") shall be thirteen;

(2) the constituent councils for the committee are the councils of the counties specified in the first column of the Schedule to this Order;

(3) the Minister, having had regard to the appropriate penny rate product and proportion mentioned in paragraph 3(1) of the said Schedule 5 relating to each of the said constituent councils, considers it to be inappropriate that the councils of the counties of Devon and Gloucestershire (being two of the said constituent councils) should appoint a member of the committee:

Now, therefore, the Minister, in exercise of the powers conferred on him by paragraphs 1(12) and 3(1) of Schedule 5 to the Water Act 1973, and of every other power enabling him in that behalf, and having had regard to the appropriate penny rate product and proportion mentioned in the said paragraph 3(1) relating to each of the said constituent councils, hereby orders as follows:—

Citation and commencement

1. This Order may be cited as the Wessex Water Authority (Regional Land Drainage Committee) Order 1973 and shall come into operation on 20th November 1973.

Interpretation

2.—(1) In this Order—

"the Act of 1972" means the Local Government Act 1972(**b**);

"constituent council" means the council of any county established by the Act of 1972 any part of which is in the Water Authority area;

"the Water Authority area" means the area of the Water Authority for the purposes of their functions relating to land drainage.

(**a**) 1973 c. 37. (**b**) 1972 c. 70.

(2) Any reference in this Order to a specified county or to the council thereof is a reference to the county of that name established by the Act of 1972 or to the council so established for that county, as the case may be.

(3) The Interpretation Act 1889(**a**) shall apply for the interpretation of this Order as it applies for the interpretation of an Act of Parliament.

Constituent councils appointments of committee members

3.—(1) The number of members to be appointed to the committee by or on behalf of constituent councils for the committee shall be seven.

(2) The number of members of the committee to be appointed by each of the councils of the counties specified in the first column of the Schedule to this Order shall be the number specified in relation to that county in the second column of that Schedule.

In witness whereof the Official Seal of the Minister of Agriculture, Fisheries and Food is hereunto affixed on 12th November 1973.

(L.S.)

Joseph Godber,
Minister of Agriculture,
Fisheries and Food.

Article 3

SCHEDULE

Counties	*Number of Members*
Avon	Three
Devon	None
Dorset	Two
Gloucestershire	None
Somerset	One
Wiltshire	One

(**a**) 1889 c. 63.

EXPLANATORY NOTE

(*This Note is not part of the Order.*)

Paragraph 1 of Schedule 5 to the Water Act provides that each water authority shall establish a regional land drainage committee consisting of:—

(*a*) a Chairman and a number of other members appointed by the Minister of Agriculture, Fisheries and Food;

(*b*) two members appointed by the water authority; and

(*c*) a number of members appointed by constituent councils being, where no part of Greater London is in the water authority area, councils of counties any part of whose area is in the water authority area.

When the total number of members of a water authority's regional land drainage committee, being not less than eleven nor more than seventeen, has been fixed by them, the Minister is required by paragraph 1(12) of the Schedule by Order to specify the number of members to be appointed to the committee by the constituent councils, their number being required by paragraph 1(13) of the Schedule to exceed by one the number of the other members. In determining the number of such members to be appointed by each constituent council, the Minister is required by paragraph 3(1) of the Schedule to have regard to the appropriate penny rate product and proportion mentioned in that paragraph and where, having regard thereto, the Minister considers it inappropriate that a constituent council should appoint a member of the committee he may by the Order so provide.

The Wessex Water Authority, established on 26th July 1973, has determined that the total number of the members of their regional land drainage committee should be thirteen and this Order specifies the number of members of that committee which are to be appointed by constituent councils and by which of those councils such members are to be appointed.

1973 No. 1926

WATER, ENGLAND AND WALES

The Yorkshire Water Authority (Regional Land Drainage Committee) Order 1973

Made - - - 12*th November* 1973

Coming into Operation 20*th November* 1973

Whereas—

(1) the Yorkshire Water Authority (hereafter in this Order referred to as "the Water Authority") are required by paragraph 1(1) of Schedule 5 to the Water Act 1973(**a**) to establish a committee to be known as a regional land drainage committee and, in accordance with paragraph 1(7) and (9) of the said Schedule, have submitted to the Minister of Agriculture, Fisheries and Food (hereafter in this Order referred to as "the Minister") a determination that the total number of members of their regional land drainage committee (hereafter in this Order referred to as "the committee") shall be thirteen;

(2) the constituent councils for the committee are the councils of the counties specified in the first column of the Schedule to this Order;

(3) the Minister, having had regard to the appropriate penny rate product and proportion mentioned in paragraph 3(1) of the said Schedule 5 relating to each of the said constituent councils,—

(*a*) considers it to be inappropriate that the councils of the counties of Cleveland, Lancashire and Nottinghamshire (being three of the said constituent councils) should appoint a member of the committee; and

(*b*) considers that one member of the committee should be appointed jointly by the councils of the counties of Derbyshire and South Yorkshire (being two of the said constituent councils):

Now, therefore, the Minister, in exercise of the powers conferred on him by paragraphs 1(12) and 3(1) of Schedule 5 to the Water Act 1973, and of every other power enabling him in that behalf, and having had regard to the appropriate penny rate product and proportion mentioned in the said paragraph 3(1) relating to each of the said constituent councils, hereby orders as follows:—

Citation and commencement

1. This Order may be cited as the Yorkshire Water Authority (Regional Land Drainage Committee) Order 1973 and shall come into operation on 20th November 1973.

Interpretation

2.—(1) In this Order—

"the Act of 1972" means the Local Government Act 1972(**b**);

(**a**) 1973 c. 37. (**b**) 1972 c. 70.

"constituent council" means the council of any county established by the Act of 1972 any part of which is in the Water Authority area;

"the Water Authority area" means the area of the Water Authority for the purposes of their functions relating to land drainage.

(2) Any reference in this Order to a specified county or to the council thereof is a reference to the county of that name established by the Act of 1972 or to the council so established for that county, as the case may be.

(3) The Interpretation Act 1889(a) shall apply for the interpretation of this Order as it applies for the interpretation of an Act of Parliament.

Constituent councils appointments of committee members

3.—(1) The number of members to be appointed to the committee by or on behalf of constituent councils for the committee shall be seven.

(2) The number of members of the committee to be appointed by each of the councils of the counties specified in the first column of the Schedule to this Order or by or on behalf of the councils of the group of counties so specified shall be the number specified in relation to that county or to that group in the second column of that Schedule.

(3) Where in the said Schedule the number to be appointed is specified in relation to a group of counties that number shall be appointed jointly by the councils of the counties comprising the group.

In witness whereof the Official Seal of the Minister of Agriculture, Fisheries and Food is hereunto affixed on 12th November 1973.

(L.S.)

Joseph Godber,
Minister of Agriculture,
Fisheries and Food.

SCHEDULE

Article 3

Counties	*Number of Members*
Cleveland	None
Derbyshire, South Yorkshire	One jointly
Humberside	One
Lancashire	None
Nottinghamshire	None
North Yorkshire	One
South Yorkshire	One
West Yorkshire	Three

(a) 1889 c. 63.

EXPLANATORY NOTE

(This Note is not part of the Order.)

Paragraph 1 of Schedule 5 to the Water Act provides that each water authority shall establish a regional land drainage committee consisting of:—

(*a*) a Chairman and a number of other members appointed by the Minister of Agriculture, Fisheries and Food;

(*b*) two members appointed by the water authority; and

(*c*) a number of members appointed by or on behalf of constituent councils being, where no part of Greater London is in the water authority area, councils of counties any part of whose area is in the water authority area.

When the total number of members of a water authority's regional land drainage committee, being not less than eleven nor more than seventeen, has been fixed by them, the Minister is required by paragraph 1(12) of the Schedule by Order to specify the number of members to be appointed to the committee by or on behalf of the constituent councils, their number being required by paragraph 1(13) of the Schedule to exceed by one the number of the other members. In determining the number of such members to be appointed by or on behalf of each constituent council, the Minister is required by paragraph 3(1) of the Schedule to have regard to the appropriate penny rate product and proportion mentioned in that paragraph and where, having regard thereto, the Minister considers it inappropriate that a constituent council should appoint a member of the committee, or considers that one or more members should be appointed jointly by that council and one or more other constituent councils, he may by the Order so provide.

The Yorkshire Water Authority, established on 26th July 1973, has determined that the total number of members of their regional land drainage committee should be thirteen and this Order specifies the number of members of that committee which are to be appointed by or on behalf of constituent councils and by which of those councils such members are to be appointed.

STATUTORY INSTRUMENTS

1973 No. 1928

HOUSING, ENGLAND AND WALES
HOUSING, SCOTLAND

The Assistance for House Purchase and Improvement (Increase of Subsidy) Order 1973

Laid before the House of Commons in draft

Made - - - -	15*th November* 1973
Coming into Operation	1*st December* 1973

The Secretary of State for the Environment, the Secretary of State for Wales and the Secretary of State for Scotland, acting jointly in exercise of their powers under subsections (3), (4) and (5) of section 28 of the Housing Subsidies Act 1967**(a)** (added to that section by section 78 of the Housing Act 1969**(b)**)**(c)** and of all other powers enabling them in that behalf, with the approval of the Treasury, hereby make the following order in the terms of a draft which has been laid before the Commons House of Parliament and has been approved by a resolution of that House:—

1. This order may be cited as the Assistance for House Purchase and Improvement (Increase of Subsidy) Order 1973 and shall come into operation on 1st December 1973.

2.—(1) In this order "the Act" means the Housing Subsidies Act 1967.

(2) The Interpretation Act 1889**(d)** shall apply for the interpretation of this order as it applies for the interpretation of an Act of Parliament.

3. With respect to interest payable for any period beginning on or after 1st January 1974 under a contract requiring repayment of a loan subsidised under Part II of the Act, the Assistance for House Purchase and Improvement (Increase of Subsidy) Order 1969**(e)** shall be varied and have effect as follows:—

(*a*) in article 4, for the date "1st January 1970" there shall be substituted the date "1st January 1974"; and

(*b*) for the Schedule, there shall be substituted the following Schedule—

(a) 1967 c. 29. **(b)** 1969 c. 33.
(c) The powers conferred on the Minister of Housing and Local Government are now exercisable by the Secretary of State for the Environment under S.I. 1970/1681 (1970 III, p. 5551).
(d) 1889 c. 63 **(e)** S.I. 1969/1626 (1969 III, p. 5120).

SCHEDULE

(1) Rate of Interest	(2) Higher percentage	(3) Higher percentage
Exceeding 7 per cent. per annum but not exceeding $7\frac{7}{8}$ per cent. per annum.	$2\frac{1}{4}$ per cent.	2 per cent.
Exceeding $7\frac{7}{8}$ per cent. per annum but not exceeding $8\frac{3}{4}$ per cent. per annum.	$2\frac{1}{2}$ per cent.	$2\frac{1}{4}$ per cent.
Exceeding $8\frac{3}{4}$ per cent. per annum but not exceeding $9\frac{5}{8}$ per cent. per annum.	$2\frac{3}{4}$ per cent.	$2\frac{1}{2}$ per cent.
Exceeding $9\frac{5}{8}$ per cent. per annum but not exceeding $10\frac{1}{2}$ per cent. per annum.	3 per cent.	$2\frac{3}{4}$ per cent.
Exceeding $10\frac{1}{2}$ per cent. per annum but not exceeding $11\frac{3}{8}$ per cent. per annum.	$3\frac{1}{4}$ per cent.	3 per cent.
Exceeding $11\frac{3}{8}$ per cent. per annum.	$3\frac{1}{2}$ per cent.	$3\frac{1}{4}$ per cent. "

Geoffrey Rippon,
Secretary of State for the Environment.

8th November 1973.

Peter Thomas,
Secretary of State for Wales.

9th November 1973.

Gordon Campbell,
Secretary of State for Scotland.

12th November 1973.

We approve.

Michael Joplin,
P. L. Hawkins,
Two of the Lords Commissioners
of Her Majesty's Treasury.

15th November 1973.

EXPLANATORY NOTE

(This Note is not part of the Order.)

The Assistance for House Purchase and Improvement (Increase of Subsidy) Order 1969 ("the 1969 Order") specified two scales of percentages higher than and to replace, in most cases, the two per cent. and the one and three-quarters per cent. mentioned respectively in section 28(1) and (2) of the Housing Subsidies Act 1967 (aggregate amount of subsidy for option mortgages). The 1969 Order thus increased subsidy for option mortgages with respect to interest payable for any period beginning on or after 1st January 1970, provided that the rate of interest applicable for the time being under the repayment contract exceeded seven per cent. per annum.

The present Order, which operates in respect of interest payable under option mortgages for any period beginning on or after 1st January 1974, varies the 1969 Order so as to increase the subsidy for such mortgages where the rate of interest for the time being applicable under the repayment contract exceeds 10½ per cent. per annum. The Order extends the interest rate limits set out in the Schedule to the 1969 Order and specifies two scales of percentages in relation thereto, which are higher than and replace the two per cent. and the one and three-quarters per cent. mentioned respectively in section 28(1) and (2) of the 1967 Act. The scale of higher percentages in column (2) of the Schedule to the 1969 Order (as varied by the present Order) applies where the periodical payments consist partly of repayment of capital and partly of interest on the loan. The scale of higher percentages in column (3) of the Schedule applies to periodical payments of interest on capital where, under the repayment contract, no repayment of capital is required to be made by those periodical payments. Each scale varies according to the rate of interest applicable for the time being under the repayment contract.

1973 No. 1929

CIVIL AVIATION

The Civil Aviation Authority (Amendment) Regulations 1973

Made - - - -	15*th November* 1973
Laid before Parliament	16*th November* 1973
Coming into Operation	12*th December* 1973

The Secretary of State, in exercise of his powers under section 5(2) of the Civil Aviation Act 1971**(a)** and of all other powers enabling him in that behalf, hereby makes the following Regulations:—

1. These Regulations may be cited as the Civil Aviation Authority (Amendment) Regulations 1973 and shall come into operation on 12th December 1973.

2. The Interpretation Act 1889**(b)** shall apply for the purpose of the interpretation of these Regulations as it applies for the purpose of the interpretation of an Act of Parliament.

3. The Civil Aviation Authority Regulations 1972**(c)** shall be amended as follows:

(1) After Regulation 18 there shall be added the following:—

PART IV

OTHER FUNCTIONS OF THE AUTHORITY

19.—(1) The function of the Authority of being a party to civil proceedings is hereby prescribed for the purposes of section 5(2) of the Act.

(2) In any civil proceedings to which the Authority is or becomes a party, the Authority shall disclose to the Court and any other party to the proceedings information in its possession which, apart from section 36(1) of the Act, it would have been under a duty to disclose for the purpose of those proceedings.

Michael Heseltine,
Minister for Aerospace and Shipping,
Department of Trade and Industry.

15th November 1973.

(a) 1971 c. 75. **(b)** 1889 c. 63.
(c) S.I. 1972/178 (1972 I, p. 652).

EXPLANATORY NOTE

(*This Note is not part of the Regulations.*)

These Regulations, made under section 5(2) of the Civil Aviation Act 1971, provide that the Civil Aviation Authority in any civil proceedings to which it is or becomes a party shall disclose to the Court and to any other party to such proceedings information in its possession which, apart from section 36(1) of the Act, it would have been under a duty to disclose for the purpose of those proceedings. The restriction on disclosure of information, imposed by section 36, does not apply to information required to be disclosed by Regulations made under section 5(2).

1973 No. 1935

NATIONAL HEALTH SERVICE, ENGLAND AND WALES

The Isles of Scilly (National Health Service) Order 1973

Made - - -	16*th November* 1973
Laid before Parliament	26*th November* 1973
Coming into Operation	17*th December* 1973

The Secretary of State for Social Services, in exercise of powers conferred upon him by section 58(4) of the National Health Service Reorganisation Act 1973(**a**), hereby makes the following Order:—

Citation, commencement and interpretation

1.—(1) This Order may be cited as the Isles of Scilly (National Health Service) Order 1973 and shall come into operation on 17th December 1973.

(2) The rules for the construction of Acts of Parliament contained in the Interpretation Act 1889(**b**) shall apply for the purpose of the interpretation of this Order as they apply for the purpose of the interpretation of an Act of Parliament.

Extension of National Health Service Reorganisation Act

2.—(1) The National Health Service Reorganisation Act 1973 shall extend to the Isles of Scilly with the modification specified in the following paragraph of this Article.

(2) The expression "local authority" in the said Act of 1973 shall, in relation to the said Isles, mean the Council of the Isles as constituted under the Isles of Scilly Order 1943(**c**).

16th November 1973.

Keith Joseph,
Secretary of State for Social Services.

(**a**) 1973 c. 32. (**b**) 1889 c. 63.
(**c**) S.R. & O. 1943/107 (Rev. XII, p. 558: 1943 I, p. 602).

STATUTORY INSTRUMENTS

1973 No. 1936

ANIMALS

The Diseases of Animals (Waste Food) Order 1973

Made - - -	16*th November* 1973
Coming into Operation	
Articles 1, 2 *and* 11	3*rd December* 1973
Article 4	1*st February* 1974
Remainder	1*st July* 1974

The Minister of Agriculture, Fisheries and Food and the Secretary of State acting jointly in exercise of powers conferred by sections 1(1), 20 and 85(1) of the Diseases of Animals Act 1950(**a**) and now vested in them(**b**), and all other powers enabling them in that behalf, hereby order as follows:—

Citation and commencement

1. This order, which may be cited as the Diseases of Animals (Waste Food) Order 1973, applies to Great Britain and shall come into operation as to articles 1, 2 and 11 on 3rd December 1973, as to article 4 on 1st February 1974 and as to the remainder on 1st July 1974.

2.—(1) In this order unless the context otherwise requires, the following expressions have the meanings respectively assigned to them:—

"animal" means any kind of mammal except man, and any kind of four-footed beast which is not a mammal;

"approved disinfectant" has the meaning assigned by the Diseases of Animals (Approved Disinfectants) Order 1972(**c**);

"issuing authority" means the Minister of Agriculture, Fisheries and Food or the Secretary of State;

"livestock" means cattle, sheep, pigs and goats;

"the Minister" means the Minister of Agriculture, Fisheries and Food;

"poultry" means live birds of the following species, that is to say all species of fowls, turkeys, geese, ducks, guinea fowls, pigeons, pheasants, partridges, and quails;

"processed" in relation to waste food means treated so that all of the waste food being treated was maintained for at least 60 minutes at a temperature of not less than 100°C (212°F) or treated by an alternative process which has been authorised in writing by the Minister or the Secretary of State; and the expressions "processing" and "unprocessed" shall be construed accordingly;

"waste food" means—

(*a*) any meat, bones, blood, offal or other part of the carcase of any

(**a**) 1950 c. 36.
(**b**) By the Transfer of Functions (Animal Health) Order 1955 (S.I. 1955/958 (1955 I, p. 1184)).
(**c**) S.I. 1972/1413 (1972 III, p. 4281).

livestock or of any poultry, or product derived therefrom or hatchery waste or eggs or egg shells; or

(*b*) any broken or waste foodstuffs (including table or kitchen refuse, scraps or waste) which contain or have been in contact with any meat, bones, blood, offal or with any other part of the carcase of any livestock or of any poultry;

but does not include meal manufactured from protein originating from livestock or poultry.

(2) Other expressions used in this order have, insofar as the content admits, the same meanings as in the Diseases of Animals Act 1950.

(3) The Interpretation Act 1889(**a**) applies to the interpretation of this order as it applies to the interpretation of an Act of Parliament, and as if this order and the order hereby revoked were Acts of Parliament.

Prohibitions relating to unprocessed waste food etc.

3.—(1) Subject to paragraph (4) of this article, no person shall have in his possession on any premises for the purpose of feeding to any livestock or poultry on such premises any unprocessed waste food unless he is the holder of a licence issued under the provisions of article 7 of this order.

(2) Subject to paragraph (4) of this article (but without prejudice to the provisions of article 4 of this order) no person shall feed or cause or permit to be fed to any livestock or poultry—

(*a*) any waste food, or

(*b*) any other feedingstuffs for livestock or poultry which have been in contact with unprocessed waste food,

unless such waste food or other feedingstuffs have first been processed by means of plant and equipment the operation of which is licensed under the provisions of a licence granted under article 7 of this order.

(3) Without prejudice to the provisions of article 4 of this order, no person shall feed or cause or permit to be fed to any livestock or poultry any processed waste food which has been in contact with unprocessed waste food until such processed waste food has been processed again.

(4) The prohibitions contained in paragraphs (1) and (2) of this article shall not apply to the possession by any person of waste food originating solely from his own household, or to the feeding or causing or permitting to be fed such waste food to livestock or poultry belonging to him provided such waste food has been processed.

Prohibition on feeding waste food from ships, aircraft etc.

4. Notwithstanding any provisions contained in article 3 of this order, no person shall in any circumstances feed or cause or permit to be fed to any animal or to any poultry or other birds any waste food removed from any ship, aircraft, hovercraft or road or other vehicle (being waste food which was or which originated from stores for the consumption of passengers, crew, animals, poultry or other birds carried on such ship, aircraft, hovercraft, road or other vehicle and imported into Great Britain) or any other waste food which has been in contact with imported waste food of the aforesaid description.

Restrictions on disposal of unprocessed waste food

5.—(1) No person having possession, charge or control of any unprocessed waste food intended for feeding to livestock or poultry shall move or cause or

(**a**) 1889 c. 63.

permit to be moved any such waste food from the premises where it is except to premises in respect of which a licence has been issued to the occupier under the provisions of article 7 or article 8 of this order.

(2) No person shall permit any unprocessed waste food intended for feeding to livestock or poultry to be moved onto premises which he occupies unless he is the holder in respect of the premises to which such waste food is moved of a licence issued under the provisions of article 7 or article 8 of this order:

Provided always that nothing contained in the foregoing provisions of this article shall apply to the movement of any waste food to other premises for the purpose of manufacture into meal.

Restrictions on access to unprocessed waste food

6.—(1) No person having possession, charge or control of any unprocessed waste food intended for feeding to livestock or poultry shall cause or permit any such waste food to come into contact with any other food intended for feeding to livestock or poultry or with anything intended to be used for or about livestock or poultry.

(2) No person having possession, charge or control of any unprocessed waste food shall—

(*a*) permit any livestock, or any poultry under his control, to have access to such waste food;

(*b*) in the case of unprocessed waste food intended for feeding to livestock or poultry, permit any livestock, poultry, dogs or cats to have access to such waste food.

Licensing of plant and equipment

7. A licence authorising the operation of plant and equipment for processing waste food may be granted by the issuing authority only to the occupier of premises which conform to the specifications set out in Part I of Schedule 1 to this order, or which are approved by the Minister or the Secretary of State as being of a standard substantially equivalent to those specifications, and shall contain the conditions and requirements set out in Part II of Schedule 1 to this order, or such substantially equivalent conditions and requirements as may be approved by the Minister or Secretary of State as appropriate.

Licensing of holding premises

8. A licence authorising the reception of waste food intended for feeding to livestock or poultry may be granted under this article by the issuing authority only to the occupier of premises (hereinafter referred to as "holding premises") which conform to the specifications set out in Part I of Schedule 2 to this order or which are approved by the Minister or the Secretary of State as being of a standard substantially equivalent to those specifications and shall contain the conditions and requirements set out in Part II of Schedule 2 to this order or such substantially equivalent conditions and requirements as may be approved by the Minister or the Secretary of State as appropriate.

Restrictions on movement of waste food by road

9.—(1) No person shall use or cause or permit to be used any road vehicle for the carriage of unprocessed waste food intended for feeding to livestock or poultry unless such vehicle is drip-proof, is covered and enclosed by material capable of being thoroughly disinfected and is so constructed as to prevent spillage of any waste food out of the vehicle.

(2) No person shall—

(*a*) place or convey any livestock, poultry, feedingstuffs for livestock or poultry (other than waste food) or anything intended to be used for or about livestock or poultry in any road vehicle which also contains in any part thereof processed waste food or unprocessed waste food intended for feeding to livestock or poultry;

(*b*) place or convey any unprocessed waste food in any road vehicle which also contains in any part thereof processed waste food.

(3) The person in charge of any road vehicle who uses or causes to be used that vehicle for the conveyance of unprocessed waste food intended for feeding to livestock or poultry shall, as soon as practicable after each occasion on which it is so used, and before any further use is made of such vehicle for the carriage of any animal or bird or of any thing (including unprocessed waste food), thoroughly cleanse and disinfect such vehicle with an approved disinfectant.

(4) No person shall cause or permit any road vehicle which he knows or has reasonable grounds for believing has contained unprocessed waste food intended for feeding to livestock or poultry to enter any premises where livestock or poultry are kept before it has been thoroughly cleansed and disinfected with an approved disinfectant.

Prohibition on distribution of processed waste food

10. No person shall move or cause or permit to be moved any processed waste food intended for feeding to livestock or poultry from the premises on which processing has taken place except to other premises occupied by the holder of the licence granted under article 7 of this order in respect of the premises at which the processing has taken place unless such movement is made in accordance with the conditions and requirements of an authority in writing issued by the Minister or the Secretary of State.

Applications for licences

11. An application for a licence to be granted pursuant to the provisions of article 7 or article 8 of this order shall be made in writing to the veterinary inspector appointed for the time being to receive such applications for the area in which the premises are situated.

Exemption

12. The Minister as respects England and Wales or the Secretary of State as respects Scotland, may, if he thinks fit, and subject to such conditions for preventing the spread of disease as he may think expedient, issue a certificate exempting any person from all or any of the provisions of this order.

Offences

13. If any person acting under the authority of any licence, authority or certificate granted under this order contravenes or fails to comply with any requirement or condition of any such licence, authority or certificate he shall be guilty of an offence against the Diseases of Animals Act 1950.

Enforcement

14. The provisions of this order shall, except where it is otherwise provided, be executed and enforced by the local authority.

Revocation

15. The Diseases of Animals (Waste Foods) Order 1957(**a**) is hereby revoked.

Amendment

16. For the definitions of "poultry" and "waste food" set out in article 1(2) of the Movement of Pigs (Waste Food Precautions) Order 1973(**b**) there shall be substituted respectively the definitions of "poultry" and "waste food" set out in article 2(1) of this order.

In Witness whereof the Official Seal of the Minister of Agriculture, Fisheries and Food is hereunto affixed on 16th November 1973.

(L.S.)

Joseph Godber,
Minister of Agriculture, Fisheries and Food.

Gordon Campbell,
Secretary of State for Scotland.

16th November 1973.

Article 7

SCHEDULE 1

Constructional Specifications and Operating Conditions for Processing Premises

Part I

CONSTRUCTIONAL SPECIFICATIONS

1. The processing premises must be physically separate from any premises where animals and poultry are kept and must have a separate entrance.

2. The premises must be constructed in such manner that they do not permit access to and can be maintained free from livestock, poultry, dogs and cats.

3. The processing premises must contain two areas which must be used solely and separately for the following purposes:—

(*a*) One area for the reception and storage of unprocessed waste food hereinafter referred to as the "reception area";

(*b*) One area for the handling of processed waste food hereinafter referred to as the "clean area".

In addition, if the reception area is not of adequate size to permit the cleansing and disinfection of lorries within it, there must be provided an area solely and separately for the following purpose:—

An area adjoining the reception area enclosed and of adequate size for the cleansing and disinfection of vehicles hereinafter to be referred to as the "disinfection area".

4. The entire floor area of the reception area, the clean area and disinfection area must be concreted over and rendered impervious.

(**a**) S.I. 1957/628 (1957 I, p. 148). (**b**) S.I. 1973/690 (1973 I, p. 2293).

5. The reception area and the clean area must be fully enclosed and roofed. They must be constructed of durable materials and be bird and rat proof. The walls and doors to a height of 1800 millimetres nominal (6 feet) must be of solid construction and either constructed of an impervious material or rendered impervious on interior surfaces. Doors to the reception area must be of sufficient height and width to permit the entrance of a vehicle for unloading and the reception area must be of sufficient size to permit unloading from the delivery vehicle and containers. Construction of the doorways must be such that seepage is prevented.

6. The reception area must be separated from the clean area by means of a solid brick or solid block wall with no apertures, or by such other means as will ensure that there is no direct movement of personnel or anything between the two areas except waste food through the processing plant.

7. The processing plant must be constructed and placed so as to allow it to be loaded from the reception area and discharged into the clean area.

8. There must be at all times a means acceptable to the issuing authority of showing that the waste food being processed has reached the required temperature.

9. The reception area and the disinfection area must have separate surface drainage from the clean area so that flow or seepage into the clean area cannot occur.

10. Drainage from the premises as a whole must be conducted away in such a manner as to be inaccessible to livestock and poultry. Adequate gulleys having substantial covers with apertures not exceeding 9 millimetres in width must be provided for such drainage.

11. The premises must have an adequate water supply under pressure sufficient for the operation and cleansing of the premises, all the equipment therein and all vehicles and equipment used for transporting waste food to or from the premises.

Part II

Conditions to be Contained in a Licence for Processing Premises

1. The premises to which the licence relates must be delineated in the licence.

2. The premises to which the licence relates must be used solely for the purpose for which it is licensed.

3. The licensee must at all times maintain the premises rodent free and in a good state of repair and the plant and equipment in a serviceable condition.

4. The licensee must ensure that no livestock or poultry, dogs or cats are at any time permitted on the premises.

5. The whole premises must be securely closed when no one is in attendance.

6. The licensee must ensure that all unprocessed waste food brought onto the premises is unloaded and stored within the reception part, the entrance to which must be securely closed when no one is in attendance.

7. The plant and equipment used for processing waste food must, in the opinion of the issuing authority, be adequate for processing in accordance with the requirements of this order.

8. The licensee must ensure that processed waste food is removed from the premises only from the clean area.

9. The licensee shall not permit waste food to remain in the reception area in an unprocessed state for more than 48 hours before being processed.

10. The licensee must ensure that the premises are cleansed at the end of each day on which processing of waste food has taken place.

11. The licensee must ensure that the inside surfaces of any vehicle owned or controlled by him which has been used for transporting unprocessed waste food and any other part of such a vehicle which has been soiled with unprocessed waste food are cleansed and disinfected with an approved disinfectant as soon as possible after the completion of unloading.

12. The licensee must ensure that any container which has contained unprocessed waste food is cleansed within the reception area after use and in no circumstances taken into the clean area or used for the carriage of processed waste food.

13. The licensee must ensure that no equipment (other than a container to which paragraph 12 applies) which has been used in connection with unprocessed waste food is moved from the reception area or the disinfection area unless it has been cleansed and disinfected with an approved disinfectant. Such equipment may not be taken into the clean area or used in connection with processed waste food.

14. The licensee must ensure that any floor sweepings or other waste collected in the clean area are processed again before coming into contact with livestock or poultry or are disposed of effectively.

15. The licensee and his employees must not leave the reception and disinfection areas without first washing their hands, cleansing and disinfecting their footwear and changing or cleansing and disinfecting their outer clothing.

16. The licensee must record the source and distribution of waste food and retain such records for three months.

17. The licensee must at all reasonable times permit an inspector or other officer of the issuing authority to enter the premises and to examine or test any plant, equipment, tool, vehicle, records or other thing thereon, and to take samples of any waste food found thereon.

18. If an inspector of the issuing authority has reasonable grounds for suspecting that the processing premises authorised by a licence granted under the order or its contents or the operation of any plant and equipment is such as to constitute the risk of the spread of disease, he may serve upon the licensee a notice requiring cleansing and disinfection of such processing premises, plant, equipment, vehicles, tools or other thing as necessary at the licensee's expense. Such notice may specify the method of cleansing and disinfection to be adopted, and the date by which such cleansing and disinfection is to be completed, and may prohibit forthwith the movement of waste food onto the premises until such time as the required cleansing and disinfection has been satisfactorily completed and may specify the method of disposal of any waste food remaining on the processing premises.

19. These conditions may be extended or additional conditions may be included at the discretion of the issuing authority.

20. The licence shall be valid for such period not exceeding one year from the date of its granting as may be specified therein but may be previously revoked or suspended by the issuing authority in the event of the licensee failing to comply with one or more of the conditions of the licence or with the requirements of a notice issued under the provisions of paragraph 18 above.

Article 8

SCHEDULE 2

Constructional Specifications and Operating Conditions for Holding Premises

Part I

CONSTRUCTIONAL SPECIFICATIONS

1. The holding premises must be physically separate from premises where livestock and poultry are kept and have no direct access to such premises.

2. The holding premises must be constructed in such a manner that they do not permit entry to and can be maintained free from livestock, poultry, dogs and cats.

3. The holding premises must be fully enclosed and roofed. They must be constructed of durable materials and be bird and rat proof. The walls and doors to a minimum height of 1800 millimetres nominal (6 feet) shall be of solid construction and either constructed of impervious material or rendered impervious on interior surfaces. The floor area contained between the walls must be concreted and rendered impervious. Doors must be of sufficient height and width to permit the entrance of a vehicle for unloading. Construction of the doorways must be such that seepage is prevented.

4. The holding premises must be of sufficient size to permit unloading of containers and the cleansing and disinfection of delivery vehicles within it.

5. Drainage from the premises as a whole must be conducted away in such a manner as to be inaccessible to livestock and poultry. Adequate gulleys, having substantial covers, with apertures not exceeding 9 millimetres in width must be provided for such drainage.

6. The premises must have an adequate water supply under pressure sufficient for the operation and cleansing of the premises, all the equipment therein, and all the vehicles, containers and equipment used for transporting waste food to or from the premises.

PART II

CONDITIONS TO BE CONTAINED IN A LICENCE FOR HOLDING PREMISES

1. The holding premises to which the licence relates must be delineated in the licence.

2. The premises to which the licence relates must be used solely for the purpose for which it is licensed.

3. The licensee must ensure that the holding premises are kept rodent free and in a good state of cleanliness and repair.

4. The licensee must ensure that no livestock, poultry, dogs or cats are at any time permitted on the holding premises.

5. The licensee must ensure that the holding premises are securely closed at all times when no one is in attendance.

6. The licensee must ensure that all waste food brought onto the holding premises is unloaded and stored within the holding premises.

7. The licensee must ensure that the inside surfaces of any vehicle owned or controlled by him which has been used for transporting waste food and any other part of such a vehicle which has been soiled with waste food is cleansed and disinfected with an approved disinfectant as soon as possible after the completion of unloading.

8. The licensee must ensure that any receptacle which has contained unprocessed waste food is cleansed within the holding premises after use.

9. The licensee and his employees must not leave the premises without first washing their hands, cleansing and disinfecting their footwear and changing or cleansing and disinfecting their outer clothing.

10. The licensee must record the source and distribution of waste food and shall retain such records for three months.

11. The licensee must at all reasonable times permit an inspector or other officer of the issuing authority to enter the holding premises and to examine or test any equipment, tool, vehicle, records or other thing thereon, and to take samples of any waste food found thereon.

12. If an inspector of the issuing authority has reasonable grounds for suspecting that any holding premises authorised by a licence granted under the order or its contents is such as to constitute the risk of the spread of disease, he may serve upon the licensee a notice requiring cleansing and disinfection of such holding premises, equipment, vehicles, tools or other things as necessary at the licensee's expense. Such notice may specify the method of cleansing and disinfection to be adopted, and the date by which such cleansing and disinfection is to be completed, and may prohibit forthwith the movement of waste food onto the holding premises until such time as the cleansing and disinfection required has been satisfactorily completed and may specify the method of disposal of any waste food remaining on the holding premises.

13. These conditions may be extended or additional conditions may be added at the discretion of the issuing authority.

14. The licence shall be valid for such period not exceeding one year from the date of issue as may be specified therein but may be previously revoked or suspended by the Minister or the Secretary of State in the event of the licensee failing to comply with one or more of the conditions of the licence or with the requirements of a notice issued under the provisions of paragraph 12 above.

EXPLANATORY NOTE

(This Note is not part of the Order.)

This Order revokes and re-enacts, with amendments, the Diseases of Animals (Waste Foods) Order 1957.

The definition of waste food is extended to comprise—

(*a*) meat, or any other part of the carcase of any livestock or poultry, or any product derived therefrom or hatchery waste, eggs or egg shells, or

(*b*) broken or waste foodstuffs which contain or have been in contact with meat or any other part of the carcase of any livestock or poultry.

Meal manufactured from protein originating from livestock or poultry is, however, excluded from the definition of waste food.

The principal requirements of the Order are:—

(1) A prohibition on the possession of waste food which has not been processed as required by the Order on any premises for the purpose of feeding to livestock or poultry on those premises, unless a licence granted under Article 7 of the Order is held, or the feeding to livestock or poultry of waste food, or any feedingstuffs which have been in contact with waste food, unless such waste food or such feedingstuffs have first been processed by means of plant and equipment operated under a licence granted under Article 7. (Article 3.)

(These prohibitions do not, however, apply to the possession by any person of waste food originating from his own household, or to the use of such waste food provided it has first been processed as required by the Order.)

(2) A complete prohibition is imposed upon the feeding to any animal, poultry or other birds of any waste food brought into Great Britain as part of the stores on a ship, aircraft etc. or of any other waste food which has been in contact with such imported stores. (Article 4.)

(3) Restrictions are placed upon the movement of unprocessed waste food intended for livestock or poultry except onto premises in respect of which a licence is held under Article 7 or Article 8 (except in the case of waste food intended for manufacture into meal) and upon access to or contact with unprocessed waste food. (Articles 5 and 6.)

Restrictions are also imposed in respect of movement of waste food by road, and as to the distribution of processed waste food. (Articles 9 and 10.)

The Schedules to the Order set out specifications for premises on which processing of waste food is licensed or on which unprocessed waste food may be collected for further distribution, and also operating conditions required at premises of both types.

1973 No. 1939

LOCAL GOVERNMENT, ENGLAND AND WALES

The Local Government (Successor Parishes) (No. 2) Order 1973

Made - - -	16*th November* 1973
Laid before Parliament	26*th November* 1973
Coming into Operation	17*th December* 1973

The Secretary of State for the Environment, upon consideration of proposals made to him by the Local Government Boundary Commission for England and in exercise of the powers conferred upon him by paragraph 2(1) of Part V of Schedule 1 to the Local Government Act 1972(**a**) and of all other powers enabling him in that behalf, hereby makes the following order:—

Title, commencement and interpretation

1. This order may be cited as the Local Government (Successor Parishes) (No. 2) Order 1973 and shall come into operation on 17th December 1973.

2. The Interpretation Act 1889(**b**) shall apply for the interpretation of this order as it applies for the interpretation of an Act of Parliament.

Successor parishes

3. There shall be constituted the parishes named in column (1) of the Schedule to this order, the boundaries of which are coterminous with the boundaries of the existing urban districts or boroughs respectively specified in respect of such parishes in column (2).

Parish councillors

4. In relation to the parishes named in the said column (1), 17th December 1973 is hereby specified as the date for the purposes of sub-paragraphs (2) (aldermen and councillors of boroughs or councillors of urban districts to be parish councillors) and (5) (cessation of provision suspending elections, and filling of casual vacancies) of paragraph 13 of Schedule 3 to the Local Government Act 1972.

(**a**) 1972 c. 70. (**b**) 1889 c. 63.

SCHEDULE

(1) Parishes	(2) Existing urban districts or boroughs
County of Cambridgeshire	
Wisbech	The borough of Wisbech
County of Cheshire	
Winsford	The urban district of Winsford
County of Cornwall	
Falmouth	The borough of Falmouth
Truro	The city of Truro
County of Cumbria	
Kendal	The borough of Kendal
County of Devon	
Barnstable	The borough of Barnstable
Bideford	The borough of Bideford
Tiverton	The borough of Tiverton
Newton Abbot	The urban district of Newton Abbot
County of Greater Manchester	
Horwich	The urban district of Horwich
Saddleworth	The urban district of Saddleworth
County of Hertfordshire	
Bishop's Stortford	The urban district of Bishop's Stortford
Harpenden	The urban district of Harpenden
County of Lancashire	
Clitheroe	The borough of Clitheroe
County of North Yorkshire	
Skipton	The urban district of Skipton
County of Staffordshire	
Kidsgrove	The urban district of Kidsgrove
County of Suffolk	
Felixstowe	The urban district of Felixstowe
County of Tyne and Wear	
Hetton	The urban district of Hetton
County of West Sussex	
Chichester	The city of Chichester
County of West Yorkshire	
Denby Dale	The urban district of Denby Dale
Featherstone	The urban district of Featherstone
Holmfirth	The urban district of Holmfirth
Ilkley	The urban district of Ilkley
Kirkburton	The urban district of Kirkburton
Meltham	The urban district of Meltham
Normanton	The urban district of Normanton
County of Wiltshire	
Trowbridge	The urban district of Trowbridge

Geoffrey Rippon,

16th November 1973.

Secretary of State for the Environment.

EXPLANATORY NOTE

(*This Note is not part of the Order.*)

Part V of Schedule 1 to the Local Government Act 1972 makes provision for the constitution of parishes for areas of existing boroughs and urban districts in England. A number of parishes were constituted by the Local Government (Successor Parishes) Order 1973 (S.I. 1973/1110). This Order gives effect to further proposals made by the Local Government Boundary Commission for England. It also specifies a date for certain electoral provisions of the 1972 Act (*see* Article 4).

1973 No. 1943

EMERGENCY POWERS

PETROLEUM

The Motor Fuel (Restriction of Supplies) Order 1973

Made - - - - 20*th November* 1973

Coming into Operation 21*st November* 1973

The Secretary of State, in exercise of his powers under Regulation 21 of the Emergency Regulations 1973(**a**) and all other powers in that behalf enabling him, hereby orders as follows:

Citation and commencement

1. This Order may be cited as the Motor Fuel (Restriction of Supplies) Order 1973 and shall come into operation on 21st November 1973.

Interpretation

2.—(1) In this Order—

" business " includes a trade, profession or employment and includes any activity carried on by a body of persons whether corporate or unincorporate and the performance by a local or public authority of its functions ;

" dealer " means a person carrying on an undertaking for the supply of motor fuel by retail ;

" motor fuel " means—

(*a*) light oil (within the meaning of the Hydrocarbon Oil (Customs & Excise) Act 1971(**b**)) of a kind intended for use as fuel for propelling a motor vehicle ; or

(*b*) heavy oil (within the meaning of that Act) of a kind intended for use as fuel for propelling a motor vehicle other than heavy oil in respect of which rebate of duty has been allowed under Section 9 of that Act ;

" motor vehicle " means a mechanically propelled vehicle intended or adapted for use on roads ;

" normal quantity ", in relation to the acquisition of motor fuel, means a quantity not exceeding the greatest quantity acquired by the acquirer from his normal supplier on any single occasion during the 6 months immediately preceding the commencement of this Order ;

" normal supplier ", in relation to the acquisition of motor fuel by a person, means the dealer or other supplier from whom that person has acquired motor fuel on at least 3 occasions within the 6 months immediately preceding the commencement of this Order ;

(**a**) S.I. 1973/1881(1973 III, p.6516). (**b**) 1971 c. 12.

"two-stroke mixture" means a mixture of motor fuel being light oil within the meaning of the Hydrocarbon Oil (Customs & Excise) Act 1971 and other oil consisting of not less than 16 nor more than 100 parts of motor fuel of that description to one part of other oil.

(2) The Interpretation Act 1889(**a**) shall apply for the interpretation of this Order as it applies for the interpretation of an Act of Parliament.

(3) This Order is subject to any directions given by the Secretary of State under Regulation 22 of the Emergency Regulations 1973.

Restriction of supplies

3.—(1) Subject to this Article, no person shall acquire motor fuel unless—

(*a*) it is supplied by a dealer directly into the ordinary fuel tank of a motor vehicle ; or

(*b*) it is acquired in a normal quantity from the acquirer's normal supplier for use within a reasonable time—

(i) in a motor vehicle which is an agricultural machine within the meaning of Schedule 3 to the Vehicles (Excise) Act 1971(**b**) or in respect of which no duty is chargeable under that Act ;

(ii) otherwise than in a motor vehicle ; or

(iii) in the course of the acquirer's business.

(2) Nothing in paragraph (1) of this Article shall prevent—

(*a*) the acquisition of two-stroke mixture in a normal quantity from the acquirer's normal supplier or the acquisition of motor fuel in a normal quantity from the acquirer's normal supplier for making two-stroke mixture within a reasonable time ; or

(*b*) where motor fuel is supplied to an acquirer under subparagraph (*b*) of that paragraph—

(i) the subsequent issue or distribution of that fuel by the acquirer for use by any officer, servant or agent of the acquirer in the course of the acquirer's business ;

(ii) the acquisition by any such officer, servant or agent of any such fuel for such use when it has been so issued or distributed.

Records

4. Every person shall keep a record of any motor fuel supplied by him under Article 3(1)(*b*) of this Order showing—

(*a*) the quantity supplied ;

(*b*) the date of the supply ; and

(*c*) the identity of the acquirer.

Licences

5.—(1) Nothing in this Order shall prevent the acquisition of motor fuel under the authority of a licence granted by the Secretary of State under this Order.

(2) Any licence granted under this Order may be subject to conditions and may be revoked without prior notice.

(**a**) 1889 c. 63. (**b**) 1971 c. 10.

(3) Every licence granted under this Order shall be the property of the Secretary of State and any person being in possession of any such licence shall, if requested to do so by the Secretary of State, produce or deliver it to such a person or to a person of such class or description, and within such time, as may be specified in or at the time of the request.

Tom Boardman,
Minister for Industry,
Department for Trade and Industry.

20th November 1973.

EXPLANATORY NOTE

(*This Note is not part of the Order.*)

This Order restricts the acquisition of motor fuel by requiring it to be supplied directly into the fuel tank of a motor vehicle or, if it is for use in an agricultural motor vehicle or in a motor vehicle not chargeable with vehicle excise duty or for use otherwise than in a motor vehicle or for business use, by requiring it to be supplied in normal quantities from the acquirer's normal supplier.

STATUTORY INSTRUMENTS

1973 No. 1944

LOCAL GOVERNMENT, ENGLAND AND WALES

The Police (Retirement of Senior Officers) Regulations 1973

Made - - - -	19*th November* 1973
Laid before Parliament	28*th November* 1973
Coming into Operation	24*th December* 1973

In exercise of the powers conferred on me by section 260 of the Local Government Act 1972**(a)**, I hereby make the following Regulations:—

Citation and operation

1. These Regulations may be cited as the Police (Retirement of Senior Officers) Regulations 1973 and shall come into operation on 24th December 1973.

Interpretation

2.—(1) In these Regulations the following expressions have the meanings hereby respectively assigned to them, that is to say:—

"the Act" means the Local Government Act 1972;

"the Pensions Regulations" means the Police Pensions Regulations 1973**(b)**;

"a senior officer to whom these Regulations apply" means a chief constable or deputy chief constable of, or an assistant chief constable in, a police force in England and Wales who retires from service as such on or before 1st April 1974 and to whom section 260 of the Act applies by virtue of Regulation 3.

(2) Part II of the Pensions Regulations shall apply for the interpretation of these Regulations as it applies for the interpretation of the Pensions Regulations.

Application of section 260 *of the Act*

3.—(1) For the purposes of subsection (1) of section 260 of the Act (which provides that a person who holds a prescribed office, attains or has attained the age of 50 years on or before 31st March 1974 and fulfills prescribed conditions may by notice given before the prescribed date and in the prescribed manner elect that section 260 shall, and section 259 of the Act shall not, apply to him) the office of constable shall be a prescribed office and in relation to a person holding that office the prescribed conditions shall be that—

(*a*) he is, on 1st January 1974—

(i) the chief constable or deputy chief constable of a police force in England or Wales, or

(ii) an assistant chief constable in such a police force whose annual pensionable pay on the date on which he gives notice under section 260(1) of the Act is not less than two thirds of that of the chief constable of that force calculated, however, where either officer is on an incremental scale of pay, by reference to the minimum of his scale;

(a) 1972 c. 70.

(b) S.I. 1973/428 (1973 I, p. 1401).

(*b*) where he retires before 1st April 1974, he does so with the agreement of the police authority and, before the date of his retirement, has or will have attained the age of 50 years;

(*c*) he does not, before the date of his retirement, accept an offer of appointment as chief constable or deputy chief constable of, or as an assistant chief constable in, another police force in Great Britain;

(*d*) he will not have attained the age of 65 years on or before 31st March 1974, and

(*e*) where on retirement he is entitled to an award under Regulation 23 of the Pensions Regulations (deferred pension and award where no other award payable), under paragraph (2) thereof he relinquishes his entitlement to a deferred pension or, as the case may be, he repays to the police authority any award paid to him under paragraph (4) thereof,

and the notice given by such a person under section 260(1) of the Act shall be given in writing to the police authority before 28th February 1974.

(2) For the purposes of subsection (2) of the said section 260 (which provides that, unless notice of objection has been given in accordance therewith, where a person has elected under subsection (1) section 260 shall, and section 259 of the Act shall not, apply to him on his retirement within the prescribed period and before attaining the normal retiring age) the prescribed period shall be the period ending on 1st April 1974.

Benefits payable

4.—(1) Subject to the provisions of these Regulations, there shall be payable to or in respect of a senior officer to whom these Regulations apply benefits by way of pension or allowance corresponding in all respects to the pensions or allowances which, subject to paragraph (3), would be payable to or in respect of him under the Pensions Regulations were those Regulations subject to the modifications set out in the Schedule to these Regulations.

(2) Where a benefit hereunder by way of pension or allowance is payable to or in respect of a senior officer to whom these Regulations apply and a pension or allowance under the Pensions Regulations is also so payable to the same beneficiary, the amount of the pension or allowance hereunder shall be reduced by, subject to paragraph (3), the amount of that under the Pensions Regulations.

(3) For the purposes of this Regulation, in determining the pension or allowance which would be, or is, payable under the Pensions Regulations, the following provisions thereof shall be disregarded, namely—

(*a*) Regulation 24 (commutation);

(*b*) Regulation 25 (allocation);

(*c*) Regulation 31 (gratuity in lieu of widow's pension) and

(*d*) Regulation 41 (gratuity in lieu of child's allowance).

Application of Pensions Regulations

5.—(1) Subject to any necessary adaptations and subject to the modifications set out in the Schedule to these Regulations, the provisions of the Pensions Regulations (including, subject to paragraph (2), those mentioned in Regulation 4(3)) shall apply in relation to a benefit payable under these Regulations as though they were set out in these Regulations.

(2) Separate notice of commutation or of allocation shall be given under Regulation 24 or 25 of the Pensions Regulations for the purposes of those Regulations and of these Regulations and, where such a notice has been given for the purposes hereof—

(*a*) the said Regulation 24 or 25 shall have effect in relation to the benefit by way of pension under these Regulations as reduced in accordance with Regulation 4(2); and

(*b*) the lump sum or pension provided for in the said Regulation 24 or 25 shall, subject to the provisions of these Regulations, be payable as benefit thereunder but nothing in Regulation 4(2) shall apply in relation thereto.

Robert Carr.
One of Her Majesty's Principal
Secretaries of State.

Home Office,
Whitehall.
19th November 1973.

SCHEDULE

MODIFICATION OF PENSIONS REGULATIONS IN THEIR APPLICATION FOR THE PURPOSES OF THESE REGULATIONS

1. Regulation 19(2)(*b*) of the Pensions Regulations shall be omitted.

2. There shall be reckonable as pensionable service the period of pensionable service reckonable by the senior officer concerned under Part V of the Pensions Regulations together with the period beginning with the date of his retirement and ending with the date on which he would, if he had continued to serve, have become entitled to reckon 30 years' pensionable service or have attained the age of 65 years, whichever is the earlier, except that the total period so reckonable shall not exceed twice the period first mentioned in this paragraph.

3. For the purpose of calculating an award to or in respect of a senior officer to whom these Regulations apply, he shall be deemed to have served as a regular policeman for the period mentioned in the preceding paragraph and to have paid pension contributions accordingly and the additional pensionable service reckonable thereunder shall be deemed to be reckonable by virtue of that service.

EXPLANATORY NOTE

(*This Note is not part of the Regulations.*)

Regulation 3 (read with section 260(1) and (2) of the Local Government Act 1972) provides that a chief constable, deputy chief constable or assistant chief constable in England or Wales who will be aged 50 years or over on 31st March 1974 and fulfills the conditions set out in paragraph (1) of the Regulation may, by written notice given to the police authority before 28th February 1974, elect that section 260 (provision for early retirement) shall, and section 259 (compensation for loss of office) shall not, apply to him; subject, however, to the right of the police authority to object within a month of their being given the notice.

Where, by virtue of such an election, section 260 applies to such a senior officer, Regulations 4 and 5 provide for the payment to or in respect of him of benefits by way of pension or allowance corresponding, as near as may be, to those which would have so been payable under the Police Pensions Regulations 1973 had his pensionable service been that provided for in paragraph 2 of the Schedule (in the case of most senior officers, 30 years' pensionable service). Provision to prevent overlapping benefits is made by paragraph (2) of Regulation 4.

1973 No. 1945

HORTICULTURE

HORTICULTURAL GRANTS

The Horticulture Capital Grant Scheme 1973

Made - - - -	20*th November* 1973
Laid before Parliament	29*th November* 1973
Coming into Operation	1*st January* 1974

The Minister of Agriculture, Fisheries and Food, the Secretary of State for Scotland and the Secretary of State for Wales, acting jointly, in exercise of the powers conferred upon them by section 29 of the Agriculture Act 1970**(a)**, and of all their other enabling powers, with the approval of the Treasury, hereby make the following scheme:—

Citation, extent and commencement

1. This scheme, which may be cited as the Horticulture Capital Grant Scheme 1973, shall apply throughout the United Kingdom, and shall come into operation on 1st January 1974.

Interpretation

2.—(1) In this scheme, unless the context otherwise requires—

"the Act" means the Agriculture Act 1970;

"agricultural business" means a business consisting in, or such part of any business as consists in, the pursuit of agriculture;

"the appropriate Minister" means—

(*a*) in relation to England or Northern Ireland, and in relation to Wales for the purpose of the making, receipt or recovery of any payment, the Minister of Agriculture, Fisheries and Food;

(*b*) in relation to Wales, save for the purpose of the making, receipt or recovery of any payment, the Minister of Agriculture, Fisheries and Food and the Secretary of State, acting jointly;

(*c*) in relation to Scotland, the Secretary of State;

"approved" means approved by the appropriate Minister in writing, and "approve" and "approval" shall be construed accordingly;

(a) 1970 c. 40.

"glasshouse" means a fixed or mobile structure, used for the production of horticultural produce for sale, which is mounted on durable foundations, is not less than 5½ feet high at the ridge, and of which more than half the total area of the sides, ends and roof is of glass or of such other translucent material as will, to the satisfaction of the appropriate Minister, give a durability and transparency similar to that of glass;

"horticultural produce" means—

(*a*) fruit,

(*b*) vegetables of a kind grown for human consumption, including fungi, but not including maincrop potatoes or peas grown for seed, for harvesting dry or for vining,

(*c*) flowers, pot plants and decorative foliage,

(*d*) herbs,

(*e*) seeds, other than pea seeds, and bulbs and other material, being seeds, bulbs or material for sowing or planting for production of fruit, of such vegetables, flowers, plants or foliage as aforesaid, or of herbs, or for reproduction of the seeds, bulbs or other material planted, or

(*f*) trees and shrubs, other than trees grown for the purposes of afforestation,

but does not include hops;

"horticultural production business" means an agricultural business which consists in, or such part of an agricultural business as consists in, the growing in the United Kingdom of horticultural produce for sale, or the growing of such produce and its storage, preparation for market or transport;

"preparation for market", in relation to horticultural produce, does not include canning, bottling, pulping or cooking, or preserving by sterilisation, by freezing, by dehydrating, by heat or by chemical process.

(2) Except in so far as the context otherwise requires, any reference in this scheme to a numbered paragraph or Schedule shall be construed as a reference to the paragraph or Schedule bearing that number in this scheme.

(3) The Interpretation Act 1889(**a**) applies to the interpretation of this scheme as it applies to the interpretation of an Act of Parliament.

Eligible expenditure

3. Subject to the provisions of this scheme, the appropriate Minister may make to any person a grant towards expenditure incurred, or to be incurred, by him for the purposes of, or in connection with, the carrying on of a horticultural production business, being expenditure which—

(*a*) has been or is to be incurred in respect of the provision of any facility, or the carrying out of any work, or any part thereof, of a kind specified in Schedule 1;

(*b*) appears to the appropriate Minister to be of a capital nature or incurred in connection with expenditure of a capital nature; and

(*c*) is approved for the purposes of a grant under this scheme.

Basic conditions of eligibility for a grant

4.—(1) A grant shall not be payable under paragraph 3 unless the appropriate Minister is satisfied that—

(**a**) 1889 c. 63.

(*a*) at all times during the period of 24 months ending with the date of application for approval there has been occupied for the purposes of the horticultural production business not less than four acres of land calculated, as appropriate, in accordance with the provisions of sub-paragraph (2) below; and

(*b*) the business will, after the proposals in respect of which expenditure is to be or has been incurred have been carried out, be capable of yielding a sufficient livelihood to any person carrying it on with reasonable efficiency.

(2) For the purposes of sub-paragraph (1)(*a*) above, there shall be added to the actual area of the land occupied for the purposes of the horticultural production business any area given by multiplying—

(*a*) by 20 the area of land in any building so occupied for the production of rhubarb or mushrooms; and

(*b*) by 20 the area of land so occupied which is or can at any one time be covered by any glasshouse in use or available for use thereon; and

(*c*) by 5 the area of any watercress bed on the land so occupied; and

(*d*) by 5 the area of any land so occupied which is or can at any one time be covered by any structure (not being a glasshouse) in use or available for use thereon, and clad with glass or other translucent material, including lights, cloches and plastic tunnels designed and used to give all round protection to crops; and

(*e*) by 5 any part of the land so occupied which is necessary for access to horticultural produce growing or to be grown on any area mentioned in paragraphs (*c*) or (*d*) of this sub-paragraph.

(3) The area referred to in sub-paragraph (2)(*a*) above includes the superficial area of the soil or other material used for growing mushrooms in trays or on shelves.

Applications for, and conditions of payment of, grants

5.—(1) It shall be a condition of the making of payment of a grant to any person under this scheme that—

(*a*) there is an application in writing for the approval of the appropriate Minister stating the facility in respect of the provision of which, or the work in respect of the carrying out of which, expenditure towards which a grant is claimed has been or is to be incurred, and furnishing such other information as that Minister may reasonably require;

(*b*) the appropriate Minister has approved the proposals in respect of the carrying out of which the expenditure has been or is to be incurred, whether or not subject to conditions specified by him in writing;

(*c*) no modification of the approved proposals has been carried out, except with the approval of the appropriate Minister, and subject to such conditions (if any) as may have been specified by him in writing;

(*d*) the appropriate Minister is satisfied that the approved proposals have been carried out in a proper manner, and completed without avoidable delay, and any condition subject to which an approval has been given has been complied with.

(2) The appropriate Minister may either refuse to approve expenditure, or approve it in whole or in part, for the purposes of a grant under this scheme, and any such grant may be made, and any such approval may be given, subject to such conditions as the appropriate Minister may think fit.

Duration of scheme

6. Expenditure shall only qualify for consideration for a grant under this scheme if application for its approval for the purposes of such a grant is made before 1st January 1981.

Amounts of grant

7. The amounts of grant payable under this scheme shall be determined in accordance with the provisions of Schedule 2.

Restrictions on expenditure in respect of which grant may be payable

8.—(1) Where at the date on which a claim for a grant under this scheme is received by the appropriate Minister—

(*a*) the amount of the expenditure included in the claim and towards which grant is payable, or

(*b*) the aggregate of the amount of that expenditure and any other expenditure towards which a grant has been paid or is payable in respect of the same agricultural business under this scheme or any other scheme made under section 29 of the Act which comes into operation on or after 1st January 1974, or under any regulations made under section 2(2) of the European Communities Act 1972**(a)** which provide for the payment of grant to a person carrying on an agricultural business as therein defined in accordance with an approved development plan, being expenditure in respect of which a claim for payment of grant has been received during the two years immediately preceding the date of the present claim,

exceeds 40,000 units of account per labour unit appearing to the appropriate Minister to be required in the carrying on of the agricultural business to which the claim relates, the appropriate Minister shall not pay grant towards so much of that expenditure or, as the case may be, the aggregate of that expenditure as exceeds that figure.

(2) For the purposes of sub-paragraph (1) above—

(*a*) "unit of account" means a unit of account of the European Economic Community, and the reference to "40,000 units of account" shall be taken to be a reference to the sterling equivalent of that number of units of account on the date on which the claim for grant is received, calculated at such rate as may appear to the appropriate Minister to be appropriate, having regard to any relevant provisions of any instrument issued by that Community; and

(*b*) "labour unit" means the amount of work, other than work done by contractors, which would, in the opinion of the appropriate Minister, occupy the full time (not exceeding 2,300 hours per year) of a full-time adult male worker.

(3) Where it appears to the appropriate Minister that the facility in respect of the provision of which, or the work in respect of the carrying out of which, expenditure towards which a grant under this scheme is claimed has been or is to be incurred is partly for the purposes of a horticultural production business and partly for other purposes, and is, so far as it is for the purposes of that business, a facility or work of a kind specified in Schedule 1, grant may be paid towards such proportion of the expenditure reasonably incurred in carrying out approved proposals for the provision of that facility or the carrying out of that work as appears to that Minister to be referable to the purposes of the horticultural production business.

(a) 1972 c. 68.

Restriction on grant

9. The appropriate Minister may reduce or withhold grant payable under this scheme in any case where—

(*a*) assistance in respect of the expenditure towards which grant is claimed is or may be given otherwise than under this scheme; or

(*b*) the provision of the facility or the carrying out of the work in respect of which the expenditure towards which grant is claimed is or is to be incurred appears to the appropriate Minister to frustrate the purposes served by assistance previously given out of money provided by Parliament or the European Economic Community.

In Witness whereof the Official Seal of the Minister of Agriculture, Fisheries and Food is hereunto affixed on 19th November 1973.

(L.S.)

Joseph Godber,
Minister of Agriculture, Fisheries and Food.

20th November 1973.

Gordon Campbell,
Secretary of State for Scotland.

20th November 1973.

Peter Thomas,
Secretary of State for Wales.

We approve.

20th November 1973.

Hugh Rossi,
P. L. Hawkins,
Two of the Lords Commissioners of Her Majesty's Treasury.

Paragraphs 3, 8(3)

SCHEDULE 1

FACILITIES FOR WHICH GRANT MAY BE PAID

IMPROVEMENTS TO LAND

1. Reclamation of waste land.

2. Grubbing up of orchards.

3. Removal of hedges and banks, filling in of ditches, removal of boulders, tree roots and other obstructions to efficient production.

4. Land levelling work, including filling in of ponds and depressions.

5. Provision, replacement and improvement of roads, paths and other permanent ways, railway crossings, bridges, under-passes, fords and hard-standings.

6. Provision, replacement, improvement and renewal of cattle grids.

7. Provision, replacement and improvement (but not repair) of permanent fences (including hedges), walls and gates.

8. Provision, replacement or improvement of shelter belts.

9. Provision, replacement, reconstruction, alteration, enlargement or other improvement of watercress beds.

BUILDINGS (other than dwelling houses)

10. Provision or enlargement of permanent buildings (other than buildings designed and intended for the production of horticultural produce).

11. Replacement, improvement, alteration or reconditioning of permanent buildings, of permanently sited frames and of durable structures for cladding with film plastic.

12. Provision, replacement or improvement of permanent yards, loading platforms and ramps.

13. Supply and installation of permanent thermal insulation, vapour sealing or gas sealing, for the control of temperature or atmosphere in buildings.

PROVISION OF SERVICES FOR BUILDINGS (other than dwelling houses)

14. Provision, replacement or improvement of systems for the disposal of sewage, effluent and waste.

15. Provision of water, gas or electricity supply.

PLANT AND EQUIPMENT FOR PRODUCTION AND HARVESTING

16. Supply and installation of the following kinds of new plant and equipment to be used for, or in connection with, the production and harvesting of horticultural produce:—

(i) Plant and equipment for the control of environment in buildings and in durable structures clad with film plastic, including:—

ventilation equipment, irradiation equipment, day length control equipment, mist-spray equipment, irrigation equipment, equipment for changing and controlling the composition or humidity of the atmosphere, automatic glasshouse shading equipment, power-operated equipment for washing down glasshouses, soil and bench warming equipment, equipment for the conditioning of bulbs and other planting material, equipment for measuring soil conductivity, instruments for the measurement. recording and control of environment, water meters, dilutors and instruments for the measurement and control of plant nutrients used in conjunction with irrigation systems.

(ii) Irrigation equipment for use in the open or in structures other than permanent buildings, including:—

equipment for the automatic or semi-automatic control of irrigation, water meters, dilutors and instruments for the measurement and control of plant nutrients used in conjunction with irrigation systems.

(iii) Plant and equipment for the handling, preparation or treatment (other than the sterilisation by heat or cultivation) of soil, compost or other media for growing horticultural produce.

(iv) Plant and equipment for the control (other than by cultivation) of pests and diseases of, and weeds among, horticultural produce, including:—

plant pot and box cleansing and sterilising machines, thermostatically-controlled warm-water baths, thermostatically-controlled cabinets, dilutors and instruments for the measurement and control of substances for the control of pests and diseases used in conjunction with irrigation systems, water meters, power-operated equipment for horticultural spraying and dusting, and power-operated herbicide sprayers.

(v) Plant and equipment for the movement of horticultural produce, or for the movement of materials and equipment used in connection with the growing of horticultural produce, being:—

conveyors and elevators, fork-lift trucks, fork lifts and pallet and bin transporters for use with tractors, power-operated self-loading pallet trucks, manually-propelled power-operated stackers, self-actuating lifters, power-operated winches for mobile glasshouses and purpose built self-loading produce transporters.

(vi) Miscellaneous plant and equipment, being:—

equipment for planting, potting or cleaning growing plants and bulbs, precision seed-drills, polythene and straw laying machines, power-operated pruners, pruning pulverisers, heading machines and equipment for the protection of horticultural crops against frost.

(vii) Equipment and containers specifically designed for the growing of horticultural produce, being:—

beds, troughs, racks, benches and like equipment of a durable nature.

17. Supply of new equipment for the harvesting of horticultural produce (other than peas and potatoes) including mobile orchard lifts, mobile fruit harvesters and mobile harvesting and packing platforms for use in orchards.

18. Supply and installation, or reconstruction, alteration or other improvement, of systems for the production and distribution of heat in buildings (including parts of buildings) other than dwelling houses, or in permanently sited frames, or in durable structures clad with film plastic.

19. Supply and installation of plant and equipment for the sterilisation of soil by heat.

PLANT AND EQUIPMENT FOR STORAGE AND PREPARATION FOR MARKET

20. Supply and installation of the following items of new plant and equipment for the storage of horticultural produce or of containers for such produce or for the preparation for market of horticultural produce:—

(i) Plant and equipment for control of temperature or atmosphere, being:— scrubbers, coolers, circulation fans, extractor fans, humidifiers, compressors, condensers (for cooling gas in stores), coolant tanks and pumps, pipework installations and instruments for the measurement, recording and control of temperature or atmosphere.

(ii) Plant and equipment for movement of produce or containers, being:—

loading and feed tables, automatic feed units, conveyors, elevators, fork-lift trucks, fork lifts and pallet transporters for use with tractors, power-operated self-loading pallet trucks, manually-propelled power-operated stackers, self-actuating lifters and bulk bins for use in temperature-controlled stores.

(iii) Plant and equipment for size, weight and quality grading, being:—

sorting tables, return flow tables, grading machines, cull eliminators, automatic loaders, trays, mercury switches and other ancillary equipment or separate components for use with plant and equipment in this group.

(iv) Plant and equipment for preparation for market, being:—

cleaners, brushers and polishers (for fruit or vegetables), machinery for washing bulbs, horticultural plants, fruit or vegetables (including soak tanks), driers (contact and air), trough installations (for flowers), dipping tank installations and sprinkler installations, hydro-cooling installations, equipment for cleaning, sorting and testing of seeds, equipment for the hot or cold treatment of bulbs and defoliating machines.

(v) Plant and equipment for packing, being:—

packing tables, packing benches, packing stands, automatic or semi-automatic fruit packers or box fillers, power-operated equipment for stapling or stitching of containers, power-operated equipment for tying or strapping of produce and containers, shrub or tree bundlers and bulb and seed counting machines.

(vi) Plant and equipment for pre-packaging.

(vii) Miscellaneous plant and equipment, being:—

heating equipment (other than portable heaters), settling tanks and silt traps, and, where essential to and installed as part of a system for preparation for market, chlorinating equipment, circulating pumps and filters, racks and benches, compressors, electric motors and internal combustion engines and weighing machines.

GENERAL PROVISION

21. Any operation incidental to the provision of any of the facilities specified in this Schedule, and necessary or proper in carrying out the work or for securing the full benefit of the said facilities.

SCHEDULE 2

Paragraph 7

AMOUNTS OF GRANT

1. Subject to the provisions of this scheme, the amount of any grant payable under the scheme towards approved expenditure in respect of any work or facility of a kind specified in—

(*a*) any of paragraphs 1 to 15 of Schedule 1 shall be 25 per cent. of that expenditure;

(*b*) any of paragraphs 16 to 20 of Schedule 1 shall be 15 per cent. of that expenditure;

(*c*) paragraph 21 of Schedule 1 shall be at the rate of grant appropriate to the facility to which the operation applies.

2. In such cases and subject to such conditions as the appropriate Minister may from time to time determine, the amount of any expenditure towards which grant is payable under this scheme shall, if the applicant for grant so elects, be taken for the purpose of determining the amount of the grant as such standard amount as the appropriate Minister may from time to time fix with the approval of the Treasury.

EXPLANATORY NOTE

(This Note is not part of the Scheme.)

This Scheme, which applies throughout the United Kingdom, is made under section 29 of the Agriculture Act 1970, and authorises the payment of grant towards prescribed capital expenditure for the purposes of, or in connection with, a horticultural production business as defined in the Scheme. The rate of grant is 25 per cent. of approved expenditure where it relates to land or buildings and the provision of services to buildings, and 15 per cent. where it relates to plant and equipment. Provision is made for the use of standard costs.

The Scheme lays down the conditions of eligibility, including a minimum acreage requirement over a period of two years and a sufficient livelihood test. Provision is made for the approval of proposals by the appropriate Minister, who can impose conditions. Proposals must be properly carried out without avoidable delay, and any conditions must be observed.

The Scheme restricts the total amount of expenditure which may qualify for grant, taking into account similar grant-aided expenditure during the preceding two years, and makes provision for the apportionment of expenditure which is incurred partly for the purposes of the business, and partly for other purposes. It also provides that grant which would otherwise have been payable may be reduced or withheld altogether if financial assistance for the facility or work is available from another source, or if the provision of that facility or the carrying out of that work would frustrate other work in respect of which expenditure has been grant-aided. The Scheme comes into operation on 1st January 1974 and the last date for applications is 31st December 1980.

1973 No. 1946

CUSTOMS AND EXCISE

The Customs Duties and Drawbacks (Revenue Duties) Order 1973

Made - - - -	*20th November* 1973
Laid before the House of Commons - -	*28th November* 1973
Coming into Operation	*1st January* 1974

The Treasury, by virtue of the powers conferred upon them by section 1(4) and (5) of the Finance Act 1973**(a)**, and of all other powers enabling them in that behalf, hereby make the following Order:—

1.—(1) This Order may be cited as the Customs Duties and Drawbacks (Revenue Duties) Order 1973.

(2) The Interpretation Act 1889**(b)** shall apply for the interpretation of this Order as it applies for the interpretation of an Act of Parliament.

(3) This Order shall come into operation on 1st January 1974 and shall cease to have effect on 1st January 1975.

2. In this Order—

"the Agreements" means—

(*a*) the Agreements, signed on 22nd July 1972, between the European Economic Community (hereinafter referred to as "the Community") and, respectively, Austria**(c)**, Iceland**(d)**, Portugal**(e)**, Sweden**(f)** and Switzerland**(g)**,

(*b*) the Agreement, signed on 14th May 1973, between the Community and Norway**(h)**,

---

(a) 1973 c. 51. **(b)** 1889 c. 63.
(c) Annexed to Regulation (EEC) No. 2836/72OJ No. L300 31.12.1972, p.1 (OJ/SE 1972 (31 Dec.) p. 3).
(d) Annexed to Regulation (EEC) No. 2842/72 OJ No. L301 31.12.1972, p. 1 (OJ/SE 1972 (31 Dec.) p. 3).
(e) Annexed to Regulation (EEC) No. 2844/72 OJ No. L301 31.12.1972, p.164 (OJ/SE 1972 (31 Dec.) p. 166).
(f) Annexed to Regulation (EEC) No. 2838/72 OJ No. L300 31.12.1972, p.96 (OJ/SE 1972 (31 Dec.) p. 98).
(g) Annexed to Regulation (EEC) No. 2840/72 OJ No. L300 31.12.1972, p. 188 (OJ/SE 1972 (31 Dec.) p. 190).
(h) Annexed to Regulation (EEC) No. 1691/73 OJ No. L171 27.6.1973, p. 1.

(*c*) the Agreement, signed on 5th October 1973, between the Community and Finland:

"Treaty of Accession" means the treaty relating to the accession of the United Kingdom to the European Economic Community and to the European Atomic Energy Community, signed at Brussels on the 22nd January 1972;

"unit of account" shall for the purposes of this Order be converted into sterling at the rate of 2·4 units of account to one pound, or at such rate as, for the purposes of the Customs Tariff 1959, may be fixed under any Order made by the Treasury under sections 1 and 13 of the Import Duties Act 1958(**a**); and

references to a heading or subheading other than a column heading are references to a heading or subheading of the Customs Tariff 1959; and the description of goods in the Schedules hereto shall be interpreted and applied in accordance with the Interpretative Rules of the said Tariff.

3.—(1) This Order applies to goods of the descriptions specified in the Schedules hereto.

(2) This Order does not increase duties of customs otherwise than in pursuance of a Community obligation.

4. In the case of goods to which this Order applies, for the column headings applicable to rates of customs duty and of drawback set out in Schedules 1, 2, 3, 5, 6 and 7 of the Finance Act 1973 and Table 2 of Schedule 1 to the Finance Act 1964(**b**) (hereinafter referred to as the "original schedules") and for the descriptions of goods specified in those Schedules there shall be substituted the column headings and descriptions of goods set out in Schedules 1 to 6 hereto (hereinafter referred to as the "new schedules") and, except as is provided by Articles 8 to 11 and 13 of this Order, for the rates of customs duty chargeable and of drawback, if any, allowable on goods specified under the column headings in the original schedules there shall be substituted the rates specified in the new schedules.

5. Where a rate provided under this Order is expressed as plus a figure "UA" or plus a percentage, "UA" refers to units of account and the percentage refers to a percentage of the value of the goods.

6.—(1) In the new schedules the rates shown in the columns headed as follows apply to goods of the following categories and if no rate is shown for any particular description, then, unless otherwise provided for, the Full rate shall be applicable.

Column heading	*Goods*
Commonwealth 1	Goods qualifying for Commonwealth preference.
Commonwealth 2	Goods qualifying for Commonwealth preference of the part of the Commonwealth preference area formed by the countries named in Part 1 of Schedule 8 hereto.

(**a**) 1958 c. 6. (**b**) 1964 c. 49.

Column heading	*Goods*
FTA	Goods which satisfy the provisions of Article 25(1) to the Agreements, or goods to which the Convention rate would have been applicable under the provisions of the Finance Act 1973.
Republic of Ireland	Goods of the Republic of Ireland consigned to the United Kingdom from that country.
EEC	Goods originating or in free circulation in a state which is a member of the Community.
Full	Other goods.

(2) Where goods qualify for a rate under more than one category the lower or lowest rate shall be applicable.

7.—(1) The substitution by or under this Order of a rate of drawback for a rate previously in force shall apply only in relation to goods in respect of which duty at the corresponding rate has been paid.

(2) Notwithstanding that this Order shall cease to have effect on 1st January 1975, it shall be without prejudice to any claim to drawback on goods imported before that date.

8. In respect of the following goods originating in Denmark the rates of customs duty chargeable and of drawback, if any, allowable shall—

(*a*) for goods described in Schedules 1 and 2 hereto, be reduced to the rates applicable under the column headings "Commonwealth 2", and

(*b*) for goods described in that part of Schedule 4 hereto relating to tobacco of heading 24.02 description 2 "Manufactured; extracts and essences", other than goods in subheading C.1.a) of that heading, be reduced to the rates applicable under the column heading "Republic of Ireland", and for goods of the last mentioned subheading be at a rate of £4·4300 per pound.

9.—(1) For all goods of the countries and territories listed in Part 1 of Schedule 8 hereto being originating products entitled to the benefit of special rates under either Articles 109(3) or 119(2) of the Treaty of Accession, the rates of customs duty chargeable and of drawback, if any, allowable shall be those shown under the column headings "Commonwealth 1" in the new schedules if they are lower than all other rates applicable thereto.

(2) For all goods of the countries and territories listed in Part 2 of Schedule 8 hereto being originating products entitled to special rates under either Articles 109(2) or 119(2) of the Treaty of Accession the rates of customs duty chargeable and of drawback, if any, allowable shall be those shown in the appropriate column of the original schedules if they are lower than all other rates applicable thereto.

10. The rates of customs duty chargeable and of drawback, if any, allowable on the following goods which, notwithstanding that the goods do not satisfy the provisions of Article 25(1) of Protocol No. 3 to the Agreements, are nevertheless entitled, under the Agreements, to the benefit of reduced rates of duty as originating products within the meaning of the Agreements, shall not be those shown under the column headings "FTA" in Schedules 1 to 7 hereto but shall be charged as follows:

(*a*) beer of subheading 22.03A., at the rate shown under the column heading "EEC" in Schedule 2 hereto plus 4%,

(*b*) spirits to which Article 11 applies, at the rate shown in the column heading "Article 10" in Schedule 7 hereto, and

(*c*) perfumed spirits of subheading 33.06 B., matches of subheadings 36.05 B.I. and 36.06 and mechanical lighters of subheadings 98.10 A.I.a) 2. and 98.10 B.I.b) at the respective rates shown under the column headings "EEC" in Schedules 1, 5 and 6 hereto.

11.—(1) In the case of spirits of subheading 22.09 C.V. (Spirituous beverages other than rum, arrack and tafia, gin, whisky, vodka or plum, pear or cherry brandy) which contain eggs, egg yolk or sugar (sucrose or invert sugar) and are entitled to the benefit of reduced rates of duty under the Agreements, the rates shown in Schedule 7 hereto shall apply in place of those shown in Schedule 1 hereto.

(2) For the purposes of this Article, the description of goods in column 1 to the said Schedule shall be taken to include all goods which it would include if it were a heading or subheading and were accordingly subject to the Interpretative Rules of the Customs Tariff 1959.

12.—(1) Where the presence of total dry extract in the products falling within subheading 22.05 C. in Table 1 of Schedule 3 hereto, other than products with a registered designation of origin falling within subheadings 22.05 C.III. a) and 22.05 C.IV.a), exceeds the maximum quantities shown in column 2 of Table 2 to that Schedule but does not exceed 330 grammes per litre, then the rates of customs duty applicable to products on which duty falls to be paid at the Full or Commonwealth 1 rates shall, in place of those shown in the said Table 1, be those shown in columns 3 and 4, and, where it exceeds 330 grammes per litre, then the rates shall be those shown in columns 5 and 6 of the said Table 2.

(2) In this Article and in Schedule 3 "total dry extract" means the content in grammes per litre, determined densimetrically at 20°C, of all substances in the product which do not volatilise.

13. Until such time as the Agreement with Finland referred to in Article 2(*c*) is ratified and in full force the following provisions shall apply to the goods of Finland:

(*a*) Article 11 shall not apply;

(*b*) in Schedules 1 to 4 hereto the rates of customs duty chargeable and of drawback, if any, allowable shall be those shown under the column headings as follows:

Schedule	*Goods*		*Column heading*
1	Spirits	22.08 22.09	FTA
	Perfumed spirits	33.06 B.	Full
2	Beer	22.03 A.	Commonwealth 1
		22.07	FTA
3	Vermouth	22.06	Full
4	Unmanufactured tobacco	24.01	Full
	Manufactured tobacco	24.02	FTA

and (*c*) for matches and mechanical lighters described in Schedules 5 and 6 hereto the rates of customs duty shall be as follows:

Schedule	*Goods*		*Rate of duty*
5	Matches	36.05 B.I. 36·06	£0·4900 plus 4·4% per 7,200 matches
6	Mechanical lighters	98.10 A.I.a)2.	£0·2000 plus 3% per lighter
		98.10 B.I.b)	£0·2000 plus 4·4% per lighter

Hugh Rossi,
P. L. Hawkins,
Two of the Lords Commissioners of Her Majesty's Treasury.

20th November 1973.

SCHEDULE 1

Spirits (Rates of Customs Duties)

Table 1: Spirits other than Imported Perfumed Spirits

Description of Spirits Including heading and subheading	Rates of customs duties				
	Unit of Quantity	Full	Commonwealth 1 and FTA	Commonwealth 2 and Republic of Ireland	EEC
	per	£	£	£	£
22.08 Ethyl alcohol or neutral spirits, undenatured, of a strength of 140° proof or higher; denatured spirits (including ethyl alcohol and neutral spirits) of any strength:					
A. Denatured spirits (including ethyl alcohol and neutral spirits) of any strength:					
I. If warehoused 3 years or more	proof gallon	15·5250 plus 0·2909 UA per liquid gallon	15·4500 plus 0·2909 UA per liquid gallon	15·4500	15·5250
II. If not warehoused, or warehoused less than 3 years	proof gallon	15·6000 plus 0·2909 UA per liquid gallon	15·5250 plus 0·2909 UA per liquid gallon	15·5250	15·6000
B. Ethyl alcohol or neutral spirits, undenatured, of a strength of 140° proof or higher:					
I. If warehoused 3 years or more	proof gallon	15·5250 plus 0·5455 UA per liquid gallon	15·4500 plus 0·5455 UA per liquid gallon	15·4500	15·5250
II. If not warehoused, or warehoused less than 3 years	proof gallon	15·6000 plus 0·5455 UA per liquid gallon	15·5250 plus 0·5455 UA per liquid gallon	15·5250	15·6000
22.09 Spirits (other than those of Heading No. 22.08); liqueurs and other spirituous beverages; compound alcoholic preparations (known as "concentrated extracts") for the manufacture of beverages:					

A. Spirits (other than those of heading No. 22.08) in containers holding:					
I. 2 litres or less:					
a) If warehoused 3 years or more	proof gallon	15·5125 plus 1·6592 UA plus 0·1818 UA per liquid gallon	15·4500 plus 1·6592 UA plus 0·1818 UA per liquid gallon	15·4500	15·5125
b) If not warehoused, or warehoused less than 3 years	proof gallon	15·5875 plus 1·6592 UA plus 0·1818 UA per liquid gallon	15·5250 plus 1·6592 UA plus 0·1818 UA per liquid gallon	15·5250	15·5875
II. More than 2 litres:					
a) If warehoused 3 years or more	proof gallon	15·5125 plus 1·6592 UA	15·4500 plus 1·6592 UA	15·4500	15·5125
b) If not warehoused, or warehoused less than 3 years	proof gallon	15·5875 plus 1·6592 UA	15·5250 plus 1·6592 UA	15·5250	15·5875
B. Compound alcoholic preparations (known as "concentrated extracts") for the manufacture of beverages:					
I. Aromatic bitters of an alcoholic strength of 77·2° proof to 86° proof containing from 1·5% to 6% by weight of gentian, spices and various ingredients and from 4% to 10% of sugar, in containers of a capacity of 0·5 litre or less:					
a) If warehoused 3 years or more	proof gallon	15·5125	15·4500	15·4500	15·5125
b) If not warehoused, or warehoused less than 3 years	proof gallon	15·5875	15·5250	15·5250	15·5875
C. Spirituous beverages:					
I. Rum, arrack and tafia, in containers holding:					
a) 2 litres or less:					
1. Entered in such a manner as to indicate that the strength is not to be tested:					
aa) If warehoused 3 years or more	liquid gallon	20·9450 plus 1·4908 UA	20·8575 plus 1·4908 UA	20·8575	20·9450
bb) If not warehoused, or warehoused less than 3 years	liquid gallon	21·0450 plus 1·4908 UA	20·9575 plus 1·4908 UA	20·9575	21·0450

Description of Spirits Including heading and subheading	Unit of Quantity	Rates of customs duties			
		Full	Commonwealth 1 and FTA	Commonwealth 2 and Republic of Ireland	EEC
22.09 C.I. a) (*cont.*)	per	£	£	£	£
2. Other:					
aa) If warehoused 3 years or more:					
11. Rum	proof gallon	15·5250 plus 1·0370 UA plus 0·0909 UA per liquid gallon	15·4500 plus 1·0370 UA plus 0·0909 UA per liquid gallon	15·4500	15·5250
22. Arrack and tafia	proof gallon	15·5125 plus 1·0370 UA plus 0·0909 UA per liquid gallon	15·4500 plus 1·0370 UA plus 0·0909 UA per liquid gallon	15·4500	15·5125
bb) If not warehoused, or warehoused less than 3 years:					
11. Rum	proof gallon	15·6000 plus 1·0370 UA plus 0·0909 UA per liquid gallon	15·5250 plus 1·0370 UA plus 0·0909 UA per liquid gallon	15·5250	15·6000
22. Arrack and tafia	proof gallon	15·5875 plus 1·0370 UA plus 0·0909 UA per liquid gallon	15·5250 plus 1·0370 UA plus 0·0909 UA per liquid gallon	15·5250	15·5875
b) More than 2 litres:					
1. In bottle, entered in such a manner as to indicate that the strength is not be to tested:					
aa) If warehoused 3 years or more	liquid gallon	20·9450 plus 1·3999 UA	20·8575 plus 1·3999 UA	20·8575	20·9450
bb) If not warehoused, or warehoused less than 3 years	liquid gallon	21·0450 plus 1·3999 UA	20·9575 plus 1·3999 UA	20·9575	21·0450
2. Other:					
aa) If warehoused 3 years or more:					
11. Rum	proof gallon	15·5250 plus 1·0370 UA	15·4500 plus 1·0370 UA	15·4500	15·5250

22. Arrack and tafia	proof gallon	15·5125 plus 1·0370 UA	15·4500 plus 1·0370 UA	15·4500	15·5125
bb) If not warehoused, or warehoused less than 3 years:					
11. Rum	proof gallon	15·6000 plus 1·0370 UA	15·5250 plus 1·0370 UA	15·5250	15·6000
22. Arrack and tafia	proof gallon	15·5875 plus 1·0370 UA	15·5250 plus 1·0370 UA	15·5250	15·5875
11. Gin, in containers holding:					
a) 2 litres or less:					
1. Entered in such a manner as to indicate that the strength is not to be tested:					
aa) If warehoused 3 years or more	liquid gallon	20·9450 plus 1·4908 UA	20·8575 plus 1·4908 UA	20·8575	20·9450
bb) If not warehoused, or warehoused less than 3 years	liquid gallon	21·0450 plus 1·4908 UA	20·9575 plus 1·4908 UA	20·9575	21·0450
2. Other:					
aa) If warehoused 3 years or more	proof gallon	15·5125 plus 1·0370 UA plus 0·0909 UA per liquid gallon	15·4500 plus 1·0370 UA plus 0·0909 UA per liquid gallon	15·4500	15·5125
bb) If not warehoused, or warehoused less than 3 years	proof gallon	15·5875 plus 1·0370 UA plus 0·0909 UA per liquid gallon	15·5250 plus 1·0370 UA plus 0·0909 UA per liquid gallon	15·5250	15·5875
b) More than 2 litres:					
1. In bottle, entered in such a manner as to indicate that the strength is not to be tested:					
aa) If warehoused 3 years or more	liquid gallon	20·9450 plus 1·3999 UA	20·8575 plus 1·3999 UA	20·8575	20·9450
bb) If not warehoused, or warehoused less than 3 years	liquid gallon	21·0450 plus 1·3999 UA	20·9575 plus 1·3999 UA	20·9575	21·0450
2. Other:					
aa) If warehoused 3 years or more	proof gallon	15·5125 plus 1·0370 UA	15·4500 plus 1·0370 UA	15·4500	15·5125
bb) If not warehoused, or warehoused less than 3 years	proof gallon	15·5875 plus 1·0370 UA	15·5250 plus 1·0370 UA	15·5250	15·5875

Description of Spirits Including heading and subheading	Rates of customs duties				
	Unit of Quantity	Full	Commonwealth 1 and FTA	Commonwealth 2 and Republic of Ireland	EEC
22.09 C. (*cont.*)	per	£	£	£	£
III. Whisky:					
a) Bourbon whiskey, in containers holding:					
1. 2 litres or less:					
aa) Entered in such a manner as to indicate that the strength is not to be tested:					
11. If warehoused 3 years or more	liquid gallon	20·9450 plus 1·0708 UA	—	—	—
22. If not warehoused or warehoused less than 3 years	liquid gallon	21·0450 plus 1·0708 UA	—	—	—
bb) Other:					
11. If warehoused 3 years or more	proof gallon	15·5125 plus 0·7259 UA plus 0·0909 UA per liquid gallon	—	—	—
22. If not warehoused, or warehoused less than 3 years	proof gallon	15·5875 plus 0·7259 UA plus 0·0909 UA per liquid gallon	—	—	—
2. More than 2 litres:					
aa) In bottle, entered in such a manner as to indicate that the strength is not to be tested:					
11. If warehoused 3 years or more	liquid gallon	20.9450 plus 0·9799 UA	—	—	—
22. If not warehoused, or warehoused less than 3 years	liquid gallon	21·0450 plus 0·9799 UA	—	—	—
bb) Other:					
11. If warehoused 3 years or more	proof gallon	15·5125 plus 0·7259 UA	—	—	—
22. If not warehoused, or warehoused less than 3 years	proof gallon	15·5875 plus 0·7259 UA	—	—	—

b) Other, in containers holding:					
1. 2 litres or less:					
aa) Entered in such a manner as to indicate that the strength is not to be tested:					
11. If warehoused 3 years or more	liquid gallon	20·9450 plus 1·2108 UA	20·8575 plus 1·2108 UA	20·8575	20·9450
22. If not warehoused. or warehoused less than 3 years	liquid gallon	21·0450 plus 1·2108 UA	20·9575 plus 1·2108 UA	20·9575	21·0450
bb) Other:					
11. If warehoused 3 years or more	proof gallon	15·5125 plus 0·8296 UA plus 0·0909 UA per liquid gallon	15·4500 plus 0·8296 UA plus 0·0909 UA per liquid gallon	15·4500	15·5125
22. If not warehoused, or warehoused less than 3 years	proof gallon	15·5875 plus 0·8296 UA plus 0·0909 UA per liquid gallon	15·5250 plus 0·8296 UA plus 0·0909 UA per liquid gallon	15·5250	15·5875
2. More than 2 litres:					
aa) In bottle. entered in such a manner as to indicate that the strength is not to be tested:					
11. If warehoused 3 years or more	liquid gallon	20·9450 plus 1·1199 UA	20·8575 plus 1·1199 UA	20·8575	20·9450
22. If not warehoused, or warehoused less than 3 years	liquid gallon	21·0450 plus 1·1199 UA	20·9575 plus 1·1199 UA	20·9575	21·0450
bb) Other:					
11. If warehoused 3 years or more	proof gallon	15·5125 plus 0·8296 UA	15·4500 plus 0·8296 UA	15·4500	15·5125
22. If not warehoused, or warehoused less than 3 years	proof gallon	15·5875 plus 0·8296 UA	15·5250 plus 0·8296 UA	15·5250	15·5875
IV. Vodka with an ethyl alcohol content of 79·3° proof or less and plum, pear or cherry brandy in containers holding:					
a) 2 litres or less:					
1. Entered in such a manner as to indicate that the strength is not to be tested:					
aa) If warehoused 3 years or more	liquid gallon	20·9450 plus 1·9108 UA	20·8575 plus 1·9108 UA	20·8575	20·9450
bb) If not warehoused, or warehoused less than 3 years	liquid gallon	21·0450 plus 1·9108 UA	20·9575 plus 1·9108 UA	20·9575	21·0450

Description of Spirits Including heading and subheading	Rates of customs duties				
	Unit of Quantity	Full	Commonwealth 1 and FTA	Commonwealth 2 and Republic of Ireland	EEC
22.09 C. IV. a) *(cont.)*	per	£	£	£	£
2. Other:					
aa) If warehoused 3 years or more	proof gallon	15·5125 plus 1·3481 UA plus 0·0909 UA per liquid gallon	15·4500 plus 1·3481 UA plus 0·0909 UA per liquid gallon	15·4500	15·5125
bb) If not warehoused, or warehoused less than 3 years	proof gallon	15·5875 plus 1·3481 UA plus 0·0909 UA per liquid gallon	15·5250 plus 1·3481 UA plus 0·0909 UA per liquid gallon	15·5250	15·5875
b) More than 2 litres:					
1. In bottle, entered in such a manner as to indicate that the strength is not to be tested:					
aa) If warehoused 3 years or more	liquid gallon	20·9450 plus 1·8199 UA	20·8575 plus 1·8199 UA	20·8575	20·9450
bb) If not warehoused, or warehoused less than 3 years	liquid gallon	21·0450 plus 1·8199 UA	20·9575 plus 1·8199 UA	20·9575	21·0450
2. Other:					
aa) If warehoused 3 years or more	proof gallon	15·5125 plus 1·3481 UA	15·4500 plus 1·3481 UA	15·4500	15·5125
bb) If not warehoused, or warehoused less than 3 years	proof gallon	15·5875 plus 1·3481 UA	15·5250 plus 1·3481 UA	15·5250	15·5875
V. Other, in containers holding:					
a) 2 litres or less:					
1. Entered in such a manner as to indicate that the strength is not to be tested:					
aa) If warehoused 3 years or more	liquid gallon	20·9450 plus 2·4217 UA	20·8575 plus* 2·4217 UA	20·8575	20·9450
bb) If not warehoused, or warehoused less than 3 years	liquid gallon	21·0450 plus 2·4217 UA	20·9575 plus* 2·4217 UA	20·9575	21·0450

2. Other:					
aa) If warehoused 3 years or more	proof gallon	15·5125 plus 1·6592 UA plus 0·1818 UA per liquid gallon	15·4500 plus* 1·6592 UA plus 0·1818 UA per liquid gallon	15·4500	15·5125
bb) If not warehoused, or warehoused less than 3 years	proof gallon	15·5875 plus 1·6592 UA plus 0·1818 UA per liquid gallon	15·5250 plus* 1·6592 UA plus 0·1818 UA per liquid gallon	15·5250	15·5875
b) More than 2 litres:					
1. In bottle, entered in such a manner as to indicate that the strength is not to be tested:					
aa) If warehoused 3 years or more	liquid gallon	20·9450 plus 2·2399 UA	20·8575 plus* 2·2399 UA	20·8575	20·9450
bb) If not warehoused, or warehoused less than 3 years	liquid gallon	21·0450 plus 2·2399 UA	20·9575 plus* 2·2399 UA	20·9575	21·0450
2. Other:					
aa) If warehoused 3 years or more	proof gallon	15·5125 plus 1·6592 UA	15·4500 plus* 1·6592 UA	15·4500	15·5125
bb) If not warehoused, or warehoused less than 3 years	proof gallon	15·5875 plus 1·6592 UA	15·5250 plus* 1·6592 UA	15·5250	15·5875

* For FTA spirits containing eggs or egg yolk and/or sugar of these descriptions see Article 11 and Schedule 7.

TABLE 2: IMPORTED PERFUMED SPIRITS

Description of Spirits Including heading and subheading	Rates of customs duty		
	Unit of Quantity	Full Commonwealth 1	Commonwealth 2 EEC FTA Republic of Ireland
	per	£	£
33.06 Perfumery, Cosmetics and Toilet Preparations:			
B. Other than shaving cream:			
1. Perfumed spirits:			
a) In cask:			
1. If warehoused 3 years or more	liquid gallon	9·6000 plus 4·4%	9·6000
2. If warehoused 2 and less than 3 years	liquid gallon	9·6750 plus 4·4%	9·6750
3. If not warehoused, or warehoused less than 2 years	liquid gallon	9·7200 plus 4·4%	9·7200
b) In bottle:			
1. If warehoused 3 years or more	liquid gallon	9·6500 plus 4·4%	9·6500
2. If warehoused 2 and less than 3 years	liquid gallon	9·7250 plus 4·4%	9·7250
3. If not warehoused, or warehoused less than 2 years	liquid gallon	9·7700 plus 4·4%	9·7700

SCHEDULE 2

BEER (RATES OF CUSTOMS DUTIES AND DRAWBACKS)

Description of beer	Heading and subheading	Rates of customs duty and drawback per 36 gallons				
		Full	EEC	Commonwealth 1	Commonwealth 2 and Republic of Ireland	FTA
		£	£	£	£	£
Beer made from Malt	22·03A.	7·5000 plus 9·6%	7·5000	6·9000 plus 9·6%	6·9000	6·9000 plus 4%
Beer of Tariff heading 22·07 (other fermented beverages):	22·07B.					
In containers holding 2 litres or less		7·5000 plus 7·8552 UA	7·5000	6·9000 plus 7·8552 UA	6·9000	6·9000 plus 7·8552 UA
In containers holding more than 2 litres		7·5000 plus 5·8896 UA	7·5000	6·9000 plus 5·8896 UA	6·9000	6·9000 plus 5·8896 UA
		Each of the above rates of duty and drawback being, in the case of beer of an original gravity exceeding 1,030 degrees, increased by £0·2900 for each additional degree.				

Supplementary provision as to drawback

As respects beer the worts whereof before fermentation were of a specific gravity of less than 1,030 degrees the amount of drawback allowable shall not exceed the amount of the customs duty shown to the satisfaction of the Commissioners to have been paid.

SCHEDULE 3

WINE (RATES OF CUSTOMS DUTIES)

TABLE 1 (NORMAL RATES)

Description of Wine Including heading and subheading	Rates of Duty (per gallon)					
	Full	Common-wealth 1	Common-wealth 2	EEC	FTA	Republic of Ireland
	£	£	£	£	£	£
22.05 Wine of Fresh Grapes: Grape Must with fermentation arrested by the addition of Alcohol:						
A. Sparkling wine:						
I. Light wine	1·4600 plus 0·7273 UA	1·4000 plus 0·7273 UA	1·4000	1·4600	—	1·0500
II., III. and IV. Other wine	2·4000 plus* 0·7273 UA	2·1000 plus* 0·7273 UA	2·1000*	2·4000*	—	1·3000/2·1000*
B. Wine in bottles with "mushroom" corks held in place by ties or fastenings, and wine in other containers having an excess pressure of not less than 1 atmosphere but less than 3 atmospheres, measured at a temperature of 20°C:						
I. Light wine	1·4600 plus 0·7273 UA	1·4000 plus 0·7273 UA	1·4000	1·4600	—	1·0500
II., III. and IV. Other wine	2·4000 plus* 0·7273 UA	2·1000 plus* 0·7273 UA	2·1000*	2·4000*	—	1·3000/2·1000*
C. Other:						
I. Of an actual alcoholic strength not exceeding 13° (22·7° of proof spirit) in containers holding:						
a) 2 litres or less	0·7500 plus 0·5455 UA	0·8100 plus 0·2182 UA	0·8500	0·9000	—	0·7500
b) More than 2 litres:						
1. Not in bottle	0·8250 plus 0·1636 UA	0·7650 plus 0·1636 UA	0·7750	0·8250	—	0·7500
2. In bottle	0·9000 plus 0·1636 UA	0·8100 plus 0·1636 UA	0·8500	0·9000	—	0·7500

II. Of an actual alcoholic strength exceeding 13° (22·7° of proof spirit) but not exceeding 15° (26·2° of proof spirit), in containers holding:						
a) 2 litres or less:						
1. Light wine	0·9000 plus 0·2545 UA	0·8100 plus 0·2545 UA	0·8500	0·9000		0·7500
2. Other wine	1·8500 plus 0·2545 UA	—	—	1·8500		—
b) More than 2 litres:						
1. Light wine:						
aa) Not in bottle	0·8250 plus 0·2000 UA	0·7650 plus 0·2000 UA	0·7750	0·8250	—	0·7500
bb) In bottle	0·7500 plus 0·5000 UA	0·8100 plus 0·2000 UA	0·8500	0·9000	—	0·7500
2. Other wine:						
aa) Not in bottle	1·7750 plus 0·2000 UA	—	—	1·7750	—	—
bb) In bottle	1·8500 plus 0·2000 UA	—	—	1·8500	—	—
III. Of an actual alcoholic strength exceeding 15° (26·2° of proof spirit) but not exceeding 18° (31·5° of proof spirit):						
a) With a registered designation of origin, in containers holding:						
1. 2 litres or less	1·8500 plus 0·2454 UA	0·8100/1·5200 plus 0·2454 UA in each case	0·8500/1·5500	1·8500	—	0·7500 but 1·0000 if exceeding 27° of proof spirit
2. More than 2 litres:						
aa) Port, Madeira, sherry and Setubal muscatel:						
11. Not in bottle	1·7750 plus 0·2000 UA	—	—	1·7750	—	—
22. In bottle	1·8500 plus 0·2000 UA	—	—	1·8500	—	—
bb) Other:						
11. Not in bottle	1·7750 plus 0·2182 UA	0·7650/1·4750 plus 0·2182 UA in each case	0·7750/1·4750	1·7750	—	0·7500 but 1·0000 if exceeding 27° of proof spirit

Description of Wine Including heading and subheading	Rates of Duty (per gallon)					
	Full	Commonwealth 1	Commonwealth 2	EEC	FTA	Republic of Ireland
	£	£	£	£	£	£
22·05 C.III. a) 2. bb) (*cont.*) 22. In bottle	1·8500 plus 0·2182 UA	0·8100/1·5200 plus 0·2182 UA in each case	0.8500/1·5500	1·8500	—	0·7500 but 1·0000 if exceeding 27° of proof spirit
b) Other, in containers holding:						
1. 2 litres or less:						
aa) Wine admitted to Commonwealth preference and Irish Republic rates, not exceeding 27° of proof spirit	—	0·8100 plus 0·3091 UA	0·8500	—	—	0·7500
bb) and cc) Other	1·8500 plus 0·3091 UA	1·5200 plus 0·3091 UA	1·5500	1·8500	—	1·0000
2. More than 2 litres:						
aa) Wine admitted to Commonwealth preference and Irish Republic rates, not exceeding 27° of proof spirit:						
11. Not in bottle	—	0·7650 plus 0·2545 UA	0·7750	—	—	0·7500
22. In bottle	—	0·8100 plus 0·2545 UA	0·8500	—	—	0·7500
bb) and cc) Other:						
11. Not in bottle	1·7750 plus 0·2545 UA	1·4750 plus 0·2545 UA	1·4750	1·7750	—	1·0000
22. In bottle	1·8500 plus 0·2545 UA	1·5200 plus 0·2545 UA	1·5500	1·8500	—	1·0000
IV. Of an actual alcoholic strength exceeding 18° (31·5° of proof spirit) but not exceeding 22° (38·4° of proof spirit):						
a) With a registered designation of origin, in containers holding:						

1. 2 litres or less	1·8500 plus 0·2636 UA	1·5200 plus 0·2636 UA	1·5500	1·8500	—	1·0000/1·4750
2. More than 2 litres:						
aa) Port, Madeira, sherry and Setubal muscatel:						
11. Not in bottle	1·7750 plus 0·2182 UA	—	—	1·7750	—	—
22. In bottle	1·8500 plus 0·2182 UA	—	—	1·8500	—	—
bb) Other:						
11. Not in bottle	1·7750 plus 0·2363 UA	1·4750 plus 0·2363 UA	1·4750	1·7750	—	1·0000/1·4750
22. In bottle	1·8500 plus 0·2363 UA	1·5200 plus 0·2363 UA	1·5500	1·8500	—	1·0000/1·4750
b) Other:						
1. and 2. aa) Not in bottle	1·7750 plus 0·3454 UA	1·4750 plus 0·3454 UA	1·4750	1·7750	—	1·0000/1·4750
1. and 2. bb) In bottle	1·8500 plus 0·3454 UA	1·5200 plus 0·3454 UA	1·5500	1·8500	—	1·0000/1·4750
V. Of an actual alcoholic strength exceeding 22° (38·4° of proof spirit) in containers holding:						
a) 2 litres or less	1·8500 plus 0·1818 UA plus 0·0165 UA per degree proof*	1·5200 plus 0·1818 UA plus 0·0165 UA per degree proof*	1·5500*	1·8500*	—	1·4750*
b) More than 2 litres:						
1. and 2. aa) Not in bottle	1·7750 plus 0·0165 UA per degree proof*	1·4750 plus 0·0165 UA per degree proof*	1·4750*	1·7750*	—	1·4750*
1. and 2. bb) In bottle	1·8500 plus 0·0165 UA per degree proof*	1·5200 plus 0·0165 UA per degree proof*	1·5500*	1·8500*	—	1·4750*
22.06 Vermouths, and other Wines of Fresh Grapes flavoured with Aromatic Extracts:						
A. Of an actual alcoholic strength of 18° (31·5° of proof spirit) or less, in containers holding:						

Description of Wine Including heading and subheading	Rates of Duty (per gallon)					
	Full	Common-wealth 1	Common-wealth 2	EEC	FTA	Republic of Ireland
22·06 A. (*cont.*)	£	£	£	£	£	£
I. 2 litres or less:						
a) Light Wine:						
1. Still	0·9000 plus 0·3091 UA	0·8100 plus 0·3091 UA	0·8500	0·9000	0·9000	0·7500
2. Other	1·4600 plus 0·3091 UA	1·4000 plus 0·3091 UA	1·4000	1·4600	1·4600	1·0500
b) and						
c) Other wine:						
1. Still	1·8500 plus 0·3091 UA	1·5200 plus 0·3091 UA	1·5500	1·8500	1·8500	1·0000
2. Other	2·4000 plus 0·3091 UA	2·1000 plus 0·3091 UA	2·1000	2·4000	2·4000	1·3000
II. More than 2 litres:						
a) Light wine:						
1. Still:						
aa) Not in bottle	0·8250 plus 0·2545 UA	0·7650 plus 0·2545 UA	0·7750	0·8250	0·8250	0·7500
bb) In bottle	0·9000 plus 0·2545 UA	0·8100 plus 0·2545 UA	0·8500	0·9000	0·9000	0·7500
2. Other	1·4600 plus 0·2545 UA	1·4000 plus 0·2545 UA	1·4000	1·4600	1·4600	1·0500
b) and						
c) Other wine:						
1. Still:						
aa) Not in bottle	1·7750 plus 0·2545 UA	1·4750 plus 0·2545 UA	1·4750	1·7750	1·7750	1·0000
bb) In bottle	1·8500 plus 0·2545 UA	1·5200 plus 0·2545 UA	1·5500	1·8500	1·8500	1·0000
2. Other	2·4000 plus 0·2545 UA	2·1000 plus 0·2545 UA	2·1000	2·4000	2·4000	1·3000
B. Of an actual alcoholic strength exceeding 18° (31·5° of proof spirit) but not exceeding 22° (38·4° of proof spirit) in containers holding:						

I. 2 litres or less: a) and b)						
1. Still	1·8500 plus 0·3454 UA	1·5200 plus 0·3454 UA	1·5500	1·8500	1·8500	1·0000/1·4750
2. Other	2·4000 plus 0·3454 UA	2·1000 plus 0·3454 UA	2·1000	2·4000	2·4000	1·3000/2·1000
II. More than 2 litres: a) and b) 1. Still:						
aa) Not in bottle	1·7750 plus 0·2909 UA	1·4750 plus 0·2909 UA	1·4750	1·7750	1·7750	1·0000/1·4750
bb) In bottle	1·8500 plus 0·2909 UA	1·5200 plus 0·2909 UA	1·5500	1·8500	1·8500	1·0000/1·4750
2. Other	2·4000 plus 0·2909 UA	2·1000 plus 0·2909 UA	2·1000	2·4000	2·4000	1·3000/2·1000
C. Of an actual alcoholic strength exceeding 22° (38·4° of proof spirit), in containers holding: I. 2 litres or less: a) and b)						
1. Still	1·8500 plus 0·1818 UA plus 0·0165 UA per de-ree proof*	1·5200 plus 0·1818 UA plus 0·0165 UA per degree proof*	1·5500*	1·8500*	1·8500*	1·4750*
2. Other	2·4000 plus 0·1818 UA plus 0·0165 UA per de-gree proof*	2.1000 plus 0·1818 UA plus 0·0165 UA per degree proof*	2·1000*	2·4000*	2·4000*	2·1000*
II. More than 2 litres: a) and b) 1. Still:						
aa) Not in bottle	1·7750 plus 0·0165 UA per degree proof*	1·4750 plus 0·0165 UA per degree proof*	1·4750*	1·7750*	1·7750*	1·4750*
bb) In bottle	1·8500 plus 0·0165 UA per degree proof*	1·5200 plus 0·0165 UA per degree proof*	1·5500*	1·8500*	1·8500*	1·4750*

Description of Wine Including heading and subheading	Rates of Duty (per gallon)					
	Full	Common-wealth 1	Common-wealth 2	EEC	FTA	Republic of Ireland
22.06 C. II. a) and b) (*cont.*) 2. Other	£ 2·4000 plus 0·0165 UA per degree proof*	£ 2·1000 plus 0·0165 UA per degree proof*	£ 2·1000*	£ 2·4000*	£ 2·4000*	£ 2·1000*
22.07 Other Fermented Beverages: A. Piquette: I. Not in bottle	0·8250 plus whichever is the greater of 0·1636 UA or 0·0165 UA per degree of proof spirit	0·7650 plus whichever is the greater of 0·1636 UA or 0·0165 UA per degree of proof spirit	0·7750	0·8250	—	0·7500
II. In bottle	0·9000 plus whichever is the greater of 0·1636 UA or 0·0165 UA per degree of proof spirit	0·8100 plus whichever is the greater of 0·1636 UA or 0·0165 UA per degree of proof spirit	0·8500	0·9000	—	0·7500
B. Other: I. Sparkling: a) Light wine	1·4600 plus 0·5455 UA	1·4000 plus 0·5455 UA	1·4000	1·4600	—	1·0500
b), c) and d) Other wine	2·4000 plus 0·5455 UA*	2·1000 plus 0·5455 UA*	2·1000*	2·4000*	—	1·3000/2·1000*
II. Still, in containers holding: a) 2 litres or less: 2. Other than beer: aa) Light wine	0·7500 plus 0·5455 UA	0·8100 plus 0·2182 UA	0·8500	0·9000	—	0·7500

bb), cc) and dd) Other wine:	1·8500 plus 0·2182 UA*	1·5200 plus 0·2182 UA*	1·5500*	1·8500*	—	1·0000/1·4750*
b) More than 2 litres:						
2. Other than beer:						
aa) Light wine:						
11. Not in bottle	0·8250 plus 0·1636 UA	0·7650 plus 0·1636 UA	0·7750	0·8250	—	0·7500
22. In bottle	0·9000 plus 0·1636 UA	0·8100 plus 0·1636 UA	0·8500	0·9000	—	0·7500
bb), cc) and dd) Other wine:						
11. Not in bottle	1·7750 plus 0·1636 UA*	1·4750 plus 0·1636 UA*	1·4750*	1·7750*	—	1·0000/1·4750*
22. In bottle	1·8500 plus 0·1636 UA*	1·5200 plus 0·1636 UA*	1·5500*	1·8500*	—	1·0000/1·4750*
23.05 Residues and Waste from the Food Industries						
A. Wine Lees:						
I. Having total alcoholic content not exceeding 10 litres of pure alcohol per 100 kg and dry matter content not less than 25% by weight:						
b) Light wine	0·8250	0·7650	0·7750	0·8250	—	0·7500
c), d) and e) Other wine	1·7750*	1·4750*	1·4750*	1·7750*	—	1·0000/1·4750*
II. Other:						
a) Light wine	0·8250 plus 1·6592 UA per proof gallon	0·7650 plus 1·6592 UA per proof gallon	0·7750	0·8250	—	0·7500
b), c) and d) Other wine	1·7750* plus 1·6592 UA per proof gallon	1·4750* plus 1·6592 UA per proof gallon	1·4750*	1·7750*	—	1·0000/1·4750*
*Together, in the case of wine exceeding 42 degrees of proof spirit, with an addition for each additional degree or fraction of a degree of	0·1440	0·1200	0·1200	0·1440	0·1440	0·1200

TABLE 2

(SPECIAL RATES FOR WINE OF SUBHEADING 22.05 C. WITH EXCESSIVE DRY EXTRACT)

(Article 12)

Normal Classification Including heading and subheading	Rates of customs duty for wine with excessive total dry extract but not exceeding 330 grammes per litre			Rates of customs duty for wine with total dry extract exceeding 330 grammes per litre	
	Total dry extract not in excess of 330 but exceeding:	per liquid gallon		Per liquid gallon plus in every case 0·0165 UA per degree of proof spirit	
		Full	Commonwealth 1	Full	Commonwealth 1
		£	£	£	£
C. I. Of an actual alcoholic strength not exceeding 13° (22·7° of proof spirit), in containers holding:					
a) 2 litres or less	90 g. per litre	0·9000 plus 0·2545 UA	0·8100 plus 0·2545 UA	0·9000 plus 0·1818 UA	0·8100 plus 0·1818 UA
b) More than 2 litres:					
1. Not in bottle	90 g. per litre	0·8250 plus 0·2000 UA	0·7650 plus 0·2000 UA	0·8250	0·7650
2. In bottle	90 g. per litre	0·7500 plus 0·5000 UA	0·8100 p!us 0·2000 UA	0·9000	0·8100
C. II. Of an actual alcoholic strength exceeding 13° (22·7° of proof spirit) but not exceeding 15° (26·2° of proof spirit), in containers holding:					
a) 2 litres or less:					
1. Light wine	130 g. per litre	0·9000 plus 0·3091 UA	0·8100 plus 0·3091 UA	0·9000 plus 0·1818 UA	0·8100 plus 0·1818 UA
2. Other wine	130 g. per litre	1·8500 plus 0·3091 UA	—	1·8500 plus 0·1818 UA	—
b) More than 2 litres:					
1. Light wine:					
aa) Not in bottle	130 g. per litre	0·8250 plus 0·2545 UA	0·7650 plus 0·2545 UA	0·8250	0·7650
bb) In bottle	130 g. per litre	0·9000 plus 0·2545 UA	0·8100 plus 0·2545 UA	0·9000	0·8100

Normal Classification Including heading and subheading	Rates of customs duty for wine with excessive total dry extract but not exceeding 330 grammes per litre			Rates of customs duty for wine with total dry extract exceeding 330 grammes per litre	
	Total dry extract not in excess of 330 but exceeding:	per liquid gallon		Per liquid gallon plus in every case 0·0165 UA per degree of proof spirit	
		Full	Commonwealth 1	Full	Commonwealth 1
		£	£	£	£
C. II. b) (*cont.*) 2. Other wine: aa) Not in bottle	130 g. per litre	1·7750 plus 0·2545 UA	—	1·7750	—
bb) In bottle	130 g. per litre	1·8500 plus 0·2545 UA	—	1·8500	—
C. III. Of an actual alcoholic strength exceeding 15° (26·2° of proof spirit) but not exceeding 18° (31·5° of proof spirit): b) Other than wines with a registered designation of origin, in containers holding: 1. 2 litres or less: aa) Wine admitted to Commonwealth preference not exceeding 27° of proof spirit	130 g. per litre	—	0·8100 plus 0·3454 UA	—	0·8100 plus 0·1818 UA
cc) Other	130 g. per litre	1·8500 plus 0·3454 UA	1·5200 plus 0·3454 UA	1·8500 plus 0·1818 UA	1·5200 plus 0·1818 UA
2. More than 2 litres: aa) Wine admitted to Commonwealth preference not exceeding 27° of proof spirit: 11. Not in bottle	130 g. per litre	—	0·7650 plus 0·3454 UA	—	0·7650
22. In bottle	130 g. per litre	—	0·8100 plus 0·3454 UA	—	0·8100
cc) Other: 11. Not in bottle	130 g. per litre	1·7750 plus 0·3454 UA	1·4750 plus 0·3454 UA	1·7750	1·4750
22. In bottle	130 g. per litre	1·8500 plus 0·3454 UA	1·5200 plus 0·3454 UA	1·8500	1·5200

Normal Classification Including heading and subheading	Rates of customs duty for wine with excessive total dry extract but not exceeding 330 grammes per litre			Rates of customs duty for wine with total dry extract exceeding 330 grammes per litre	
	Total dry extract not in excess of 330 but exceeding:	per liquid gallon		Per liquid gallon plus in every case 0·0165 UA per degree of proof spirit	
		Full	Commonwealth 1	Full	Commonwealth 1
	£	£	£	£	£
C IV. Of an actual alcoholic strength exceeding 18° (31·5° of proof spirit) but not exceeding 22° (38·4° of proof spirit):					
b) 2. Other than wines with a registered designation of origin:					
aa) Not in bottle	—	—	—	1·7750	1·4750
bb) In bottle	—	—	—	1·8500 plus 0·1818 UA	1·5200 plus 0·1818 UA

For the purposes of both Tables to this Schedule, "Light wine" means wine not exceeding 25 degrees or, in the case of wine qualifying for Commonwealth preference and shown below the column headings "Commonwealth 1", "Commonwealth 2" and "Republic of Ireland", 27 degrees of proof spirit.

Where two rates are shown in Table 1 below the heading "Republic of Ireland", separated by a diagonal stroke (/) the lower rate refers to wine exceeding 27 degrees but not exceeding 32 degrees and the higher rate to wine exceeding 32 degrees of proof spirit.

Where two rates are shown in Table 1 below the heading "Commonwealth 1" or "Commonwealth 2", separated by a diagonal stroke (/) the lower rate refers to wine not exceeding 27 degrees and the higher rate to wine exceeding 27 degrees of proof spirit.

SCHEDULE 4

Tobacco (Rates of Customs Duties and Drawbacks)

Table 1

Description of Tobacco, including subheading	Heading	Rates per pound					
		Full	EEC	Common-wealth 1	Common-wealth 2	FTA	Republic of Ireland
		£	£	£	£	£	£
1. *Unmanufactured and refuse*							
A. Of a value, per package, not less than 280 UA per 100 Kg net weight:	24·01						
I. Containing 10% or more by weight of moisture:							
a) Of a value not more than 466 UA per 100 Kg		4·2710 plus 6%	4·2710	4·2248 plus 6%	4·2280	4·2710 plus 6%	4·2248
b) Other		4·2710 plus 0·1270 UA	4·2710	4·2248 plus 0·1270 UA	4·2280	4·2710 plus 0·1270 UA	4·2248
II. Containing less than 10% by weight of moisture:							
a) Of a value not more than 466 UA per 100 Kg		4·3174 plus 6%	4·3174	4·2664 plus 6%	4·2700	4·3174 plus 6%	4·2664
b) Other		4·3174 plus 0·1270 UA	4·3174	4·2664 plus 0·1270 UA	4·2700	4·3174 plus 0·1270 UA	4·2664
B. Other:							
I. Containing 10% or more by weight of moisture:							
a) Of a value less than 121·8 UA per 100 Kg		4·2710 plus 0·0508 UA	4·2710	4·2248 plus 0·0508 UA	4·2280	4·2710 plus 0·0508 UA	4·2248
b) Of a value of 121·8 UA or more per 100 Kg but less than 143·4 UA per 100 Kg		4·2710 plus 9·2%	4·2710	4·2248 plus 9·2%	4·2280	4·2710 plus 9·2%	4·2248
c) Of a value of 143·4 UA or more per 100 Kg		4·2710 plus 0·0598 UA	4·2710	4·2248 plus 0·0598 UA	4·2280	4·2710 plus 0·0598 UA	4·2248

Description of Tobacco, including subheading	Heading	Rates per pound					
		Full	EEC	Common-wealth 1	Common-wealth 2	FTA	Republic of Ireland
24·01 B. (*cont.*)		£	£	£	£	£	£
II. Containing less than 10% by weight of moisture:							
a) Of a value less than 121·8 UA per 100 Kg		4·3174 plus 0·0508 UA	4·3174	4·2664 plus 0·0508 UA	4·2700	4·3174 plus 0·0508 UA	4·2664
b) Of a value of 121·8 UA or more per 100 Kg but less than 143·4 UA per 100 Kg		4·3174 plus 9·2%	4·3174	4·2664 plus 9·2%	4·2700	4·3174 plus 9·2%	4·2664
c) Of a value of 143·4 UA or more per 100 Kg		4·3174 plus 0·0598 UA	4·3174	4·2664 plus 0·0598 UA	4·2700	4·3174 plus 0·0598 UA	4·2664
2. *Manufactured; extracts and essences*	24.02						
A. Cigarettes		4·4926 plus 36%	4·4926	4·4215 plus 36%	4·4615	4·3615 plus 36%	4·3615
B. Cigars		4·6900 plus 20·8%	4·6900	4·6015 plus 20·8%	4·6015	4·6015 plus 20·8%	4·6015
C. Smoking Tobacco:							
I. Cavendish or negrohead:							
a) Manufactured in bond		4·3910 plus 46·8%	4·3910	4·3325 plus 46·8%	4·3325	4·3910 plus 46·8%	4·3325
b) Other		4·4852 plus 46·8%	4·4852	4·4180 plus 46·8%	4·4180	4·4180 plus 46·8%	4·4180
II. Other		4·3875 plus 46·8%	4·3875	4·3290 plus 46·8%	4·3450	4·3050 plus 46·8%	4·3050
D. Chewing Tobacco and Snuff:							
I. Chewing tobacco		4·3875 plus 26%	4·3875	4·3290 plus 26%	4·3450	4·3050 plus 26%	4·3050
II. Snuff		4·4228 plus 26%	4·4228	4·3616 plus 26%	4·3660	4·3550 plus 26%	4·3550
E. Other, including agglomerated tobacco in the form of sheets or strip:							
I. Snuffwork (including tobacco dust or powder stalk flour and ground tobacco)		4·4228 plus 10·4%	4·4228	4·3616 plus 10·4%	4·3660	4·3550 plus 10·4%	4·3550
II. Other manufactured tobacco		4·3875 plus 10·4%	4·3875	4·3290 plus 10·4%	4·3450	4·3050 plus 10·4%	4·3050

TABLE 2

Description of tobacco	Rates of drawback per pound weight			
	in respect of tobacco on which customs duty at the Full rate has been paid	in respect of tobacco on which customs duty at Commonwealth 1 rate has been paid	in respect of tobacco on which customs duty at the EEC rate has been paid	in respect of tobacco on which customs duty at Commonwealth 2 or Republic of Ireland rate has been paid
	£	£	£	£
Cigars	4·4912	4·4450	4·4912	4·4450
Cigarettes	4·3242	4·2780	4·3242	4·2780
Cut, roll, cake or other manufactured tobacco	4·3122	4·2660	4·3122	4·2660
Snuff (not being offal snuff)	4·3372	4·2910	4·3372	4·2910
Stalks and Tobacco refuse	4·2872	4·2410	4·2872	4·2410
	Each of the above rates of drawback being increased by a rate equivalent to any duty paid being either ad valorem duty or expressed in UA.			

SCHEDULE 5

Matches (Rates of Customs Duties)

Heading and subheading	Rates for every 7,200 matches (and so in proportion for any less number of matches)			
	Full Commonwealth 1	Commonwealth 2	EEC	FTA Republic of Ireland
	£	£	£	£
36.05 B.I. and 36.06	0·5095 plus 4·4%	Full rate or 0·5255 whichever is the less	0·5095	0·4900

SCHEDULE 6

Mechanical Lighters (Rates of Customs Duties)

Lighters: Incomplete as well as complete chargeable with a duty of customs under the Finance Acts	Heading and subheading	Rates per lighter		
		Full Commonwealth 1	EEC Commonwealth 2	FTA Republic of Ireland
		£	£	£
Parts of base metal, obtained by turning bars, angles, shapes, sections or wire, of solid section, the greatest diameter of which does not exceed 25 mm; being incomplete lighters	98.10 A. I. a) 2.	0·2250 plus 3%	0·2250	0·2000
Other	98.10 B. I. b)	0·2250 plus 4·4%	0·2250	0·2000

SCHEDULE 7

SPECIAL RATES OF CUSTOMS DUTIES ON SPIRITS (ARTICLE 11)

Description of Spirit Including heading and subheading	Rates of Customs Duty		
	Unit of quantity	FTA	Article 10
	per	£	£
22.09 C. V. Spirituous beverages other than C.I. (Rum), C.II. (Gin), C.III. (Whisky) or C.IV. (Vodka and plum, pear or cherry brandy) containing eggs or egg yolk and/or sugar (sucrose or invert sugar); in containers holding:			
a) 2 litres or less:			
1. Entered in such a manner as to indicate that the strength is not to be tested:			
aa) If warehoused 3 years or more	liquid gallon	20·8575 plus 1·5090 UA	20·9450 plus 1·5090 UA
bb) If not warehoused, or warehoused less than 3 years	liquid gallon	20·9575 plus 1·5090 UA	21·0450 plus 1·5090 UA
2. Other:			
aa) If warehoused 3 years or more	proof gallon	15·4500 plus 1·0370 UA plus 0·1091 UA per liquid gallon	15·5125 plus 1·0370 UA plus 0·1091 UA per liquid gallon
bb) If not warehoused, or warehoused less than 3 years	proof gallon	15·5250 plus 1·0370 UA plus 0·1091 UA per liquid gallon	15·5875 plus 1·0370 UA plus 0·1091 UA per liquid gallon
b) More than 2 litres:			
1. In bottle, entered in such a manner as to indicate that the strength is not to be tested:			
aa) If warehoused 3 years or more	liquid gallon	20·8575 plus 1·3999 UA	20·9450 plus 1·3999 UA
bb) If not warehoused, or warehoused less than 3 years	liquid gallon	20·9575 plus 1·3999 UA	21·0450 plus 1·3999 UA
2. Other:			
aa) If warehoused 3 years or more	proof gallon	15·4500 plus 1·0370 UA	15·5125 plus 1·0370 UA
bb) If not warehoused, or warehoused less than 3 years	proof gallon	15·5250 plus 1·0370 UA	15·5875 plus 1·0370 UA

SCHEDULE 8

PART I

(Articles 6(1) and 9(1))

Anguilla
The Bahamas
Barbados
Bermuda
Botswana
British Antarctic Territory
British Honduras
British Indian Ocean Territory
British Solomon Islands
British Virgin Islands
Brunei
Associated States in the Caribbean:
Antigua, Dominica, Grenada, St. Lucia, St. Vincent, St. Kitts-Nevis
Cayman Islands
Central and Southern Line Islands
Falkland Islands and Dependencies
Fiji
The Gambia
Ghana
Gilbert and Ellice Islands
Guyana
Jamaica
Kenya
Lesotho
Malawi
Mauritius
Montserrat
Nigeria
Papua—New Guinea
Pitcairn
The Seychelles
Sierra Leone
St. Helena and Dependencies
Swaziland
Tanzania
Tonga
Trinidad and Tobago
Turks and Caicos Islands
Uganda
Western Samoa
Zambia

Part II

(Article 9(2))

Republic of Burundi
Federal Republic of the Cameroon
Comoro Archipelago
Republic of Chad
Central African Republic
People's Republic of the Congo (Brazzaville)
Republic of Dahomey
French Polynesia
The French Settlements in Oceania, Southern and Antarctic Territories
French Territories of the Afars and Issas
Gabonese Republic
Republic of the Ivory Coast
Republic of Kenya
Malagasy Republic
Mauritius
Republic of Mali
Islamic Republic of Mauritania
New Caledonia and Dependencies
Anglo French Condominium of the New Hebrides
Netherlands Antilles
Republic of Niger
Republic of Rwanda
Republic of Senegal
Somali Democratic Republic
St. Pierre and Miquelon
Surinam
Republic of Tanzania
Republic of Togo
Republic of Uganda
Republic of Upper Volta
Wallis and Futuna Islands
Zaire

EXPLANATORY NOTE

(This Note is not part of the Order.)

This Order, which comes into operation on 1st January 1974, implements obligations of the United Kingdom under the Treaty of Accession to the European Economic Community and under the Agreements between the European Community and Austria, Iceland, Norway, Portugal, Sweden and Switzerland, in relation to all customs revenue duties other than those on hydrocarbon oil. In detail:

1. It provides in the case of the full rates of duty for the transitional tariff moves which have to be made towards the duties in the common customs tariff (CCT) at 1st January 1974. In general, these moves reduce by 2/5 the difference between the protective element in the revenue duties applied in the United Kingdom at 1st January 1972 and the duties in the CCT. (Article 4).

2. It continues the process begun by section 1 of the Finance Act 1973 by providing a second reduction of 1/5 in the protective elements in the revenue duties on goods entitled to benefit from the eventual abolition of customs duties in trade between the UK and other Member States of the European Communities. (Article 4).

3. It provides in the case of goods qualifying for Commonwealth preference

(*a*) for the transitional tariff moves which have to be made towards the CCT at 1st January 1974. In general, these moves reduce by 2/5 the difference between the protective element in the revenue duty applicable to these goods in the UK at 1st January 1972 and the duty in the CCT. (Article 4).

(*b*) for goods of certain developing Commonwealth countries (listed in Part 1 of Schedule 8), that the Commonwealth Preference rate applied before accession shall continue in force if lower than the rate chargeable under (*a*) above. (Articles 4 and 9(1)).

4. It provides that in the case of goods of certain countries and territories associated with the European Economic Community (listed in Part 2 of Schedule 8) the protective element in the full rate of revenue duty applied before accession shall continue in force if lower than the protective element in the full rate chargeable under this Order. (Article 9(2)).

5. It provides for the maintenance of pre-accession duty treatment for goods of Denmark and the Republic of Ireland. (Article 8 and Sch. 4).

6. It provides that goods of the EFTA countries shall continue to benefit from the absence of any protective element in the customs duty, if they are entitled to such treatment under the terms of the Agreements between those countries and the Community or, if they are not so entitled under the Agreements, for the duties to be increased by 2/5 of the CCT duty. Preferential rates of duty are prescribed for certain other goods which are not wholly free of protective duty under the Agreements or which do not satisfy the full origin conditions. (Articles 4, 10 and 11).

7. It provides the method for the conversion of sums expressed in Units of Account of the Community into pounds sterling where duties are expressed by reference to such Units of Account. (Article 2).

8. It provides that, if the necessary agreement between Finland and the European Economic Community has entered into force before 1st January 1974, goods originating in Finland will be dealt with in the same way as goods of the EFTA countries under item 6 above. But, if no such agreement is then in force, it provides for the appropriate transitional move towards the CCT. (Article 13).

The Schedules to the Order set out the rates of duty (and drawback where appropriate) for each class of goods. A special table of rates is provided in respect of certain sweet wines, where the rules of the CCT for tariff classification may affect the rate of duty. (Table 2, Schedule 3). This table reduces by 2/5 the difference between the protective element in the UK revenue duty chargeable under the normal classification rules and the CCT duty resulting from this re-classification rule. (Article 12). A special schedule (Schedule 7) is also provided in relation to certain spirits originating in EFTA countries and containing eggs, egg yolk or sugar. (Article 11).

1973 No. 1947

CUSTOMS AND EXCISE

The Customs Duties and Drawbacks (Revenue Duties) (Algeria, Cyprus, Egypt, Morocco, Tunisia and Turkey) Order 1973

Made - - - -	20*th November* 1973
Laid before the House of Commons	28*th November* 1973
Coming into Operation	1*st January* 1974

The Treasury, by virtue of the powers conferred upon them by section 1(4) and (5) of the Finance Act 1973**(a)**, and of all other powers enabling them in that behalf, hereby make the following Order:—

1.—(1) This Order may be cited as the Customs Duties and Drawbacks (Revenue Duties) (Algeria, Cyprus, Egypt, Morocco, Tunisia and Turkey) Order 1973.

(2) The Interpretation Act 1889**(b)** shall apply for the interpretation of this Order as it applies for the interpretation of an Act of Parliament.

(3) This Order shall come into operation on 1st January 1974 and shall cease to have effect on 1st January 1975 in relation to Articles 6 to 9 and Schedule 1.

2. In this Order—

"the Agreements" means:

(*a*) the Agreement signed on 19th December 1972 between the European Economic Community (hereinafter referred to as "the Community") and Cyprus**(c)**, and

(*b*) the Agreement signed on 18th December 1972 between the Community and Egypt**(d)**;

"Principal Order" means the Customs Duties and Drawbacks (Revenue Duties) Order 1973**(e)**;

(a) 1973 c. 51. **(b)** 1889 c. 63.

(c) Annexed to Regulation (EEC) No. 1246/73 OJ No. L133, 21.5.1973, p. 1.

(d) Annexed to Regulation (EEC) No. 2409/73 OJ No. L251, 7.9.1973, p. 1.

(e) 1973/1946(1973 III, p. 6707).

"unit of account" shall for the purposes of this Order be converted into sterling at the rate of 2·4 units of account to one pound, or at such rate as, for the purposes of the Customs Tariff 1959, may be fixed under any Order made by the Treasury under sections 1 and 13 of the Import Duties Act 1958**(a)**; and

reference to a heading or subheading other than a column heading are references to a heading or subheading of the Customs Tariff 1959; and the description of goods in Schedules 1 and 2 hereto shall be interpreted and applied in accordance with the Interpretative Rules of the said Tariff.

3. This Order does not increase duties of customs otherwise than in pursuance of a Community obligation.

4. Where a rate provided under this Order is expressed as plus a figure "UA" or plus a percentage, "UA" refers to units of account and the percentage refers to a percentage of the value of the goods.

5.—(1) The substitution by or under this Order of a rate of drawback for a rate previously in force shall apply only in relation to goods in respect of which duty at the corresponding rate has been paid.

(2) Notwithstanding that Articles 6 to 9 and Schedule 1 shall cease to have effect on 1st January 1975, it shall be without prejudice to any claim to drawback on goods imported before that time.

6. Except as provided by Article 7 of this Order and notwithstanding the provisions of Article 4 of the Principal Order, in the case of goods of Cyprus which would have benefited under the rules of origin for rates of customs duty applicable at the Commonwealth rate under the provisions of the Finance Act 1973, the rates of customs duty chargeable and of drawback, if any, allowable shall on all description of goods for which rates are provided by Schedules 1 to 7 to the Principal Order, be the lower of the rates shown under the column headings "Commonwealth 1" and "Commonwealth 2" in the Schedules to the Principal Order.

7. Subject to the provisions of Article 9 of this Order and notwithstanding the provisions of Article 4 of the Principal Order, in the case of goods of Cyprus described under the headings and subheadings of column 1 of Schedule 1 hereto, the rates of customs duty chargeable and of drawback, if any, allowable shall be—

(*a*) where the rate shown under the column heading "EEC" of the Schedules to the Principal Order does not exceed the rate shown under the column heading "Agreement rate (Cyprus)" in Schedule 1 hereto, the lower of the said Agreement rate (Cyprus) rate and the rate provided for by Article 6 of this Order;

(*b*) where the rate shown under the column headings "EEC" of the Schedules to the Principal Order exceeds the rate shown under the column heading "Agreement rate (Cyprus)" in Schedule 1 hereto, the lower of the said EEC rate and the rate provided for by Article 6 of this Order.

(a) 1958 c. 6.

8. Subject to the provisions of Article 9 of this Order but notwithstanding the provisions of Article 4 of the Principal Order, in the case of goods of Egypt described under the headings and subheadings of column 1 of Schedule 1 hereto, the rates of customs duty chargeable and of drawback, if any, allowable shall be the higher of the rates applicable shown under the column headings "Agreement rate (Egypt)" in Schedule 1 hereto and those shown under the column headings "EEC" of the Schedules to the Principal Order.

9.—(1) In Articles 7 and 8 of this Order the rates referred to as shown under the column headings "Agreement rate (Cyprus)", "Agreement rate (Egypt)" and "EEC" shall not apply unless the goods qualify for benefit as originating products under the Agreements.

(2) Articles 7 and 8 of this Order shall not apply to spirits of subheadings 22.08 and 22.09A. obtained from agricultural products listed in Annex II to the EEC Treaty.

10. The rates of customs duty chargeable on wines of heading 22.05 originating in Algeria, Morocco, Tunisia and Turkey shall where the conditions set out in the second subparagraph of Article 9(3) of Regulation (EEC) No. 816/70(**a**) (relating to guarantees that prices will not be lower than the reference price fixed under the Regulation) are fulfilled and notwithstanding the provisions of Article 4 of the Principal Order but subject to the provisions of Article 11 of this Order, be those shown in Table 1 of Schedule 2 hereto.

11.—(1) Where the presence of total dry extract in the products falling within subheading 22.05 in Table 1 of Schedule 2 hereto, other than products with a registered designation of origin falling within subheadings 22.05 C.III.a) and 22.05 C.IV.a), exceeds the maximum quantities shown in column 2 of Table 2 to that Schedule but does not exceed 330 grammes per litre, then the rates of customs duty applicable shall, in place of those shown in the said Table 1, be those shown in column 3 and, where it exceeds 330 grammes per litre, then the rates shall be those shown in column 4 of the said Table 2.

(2) In this Article and in Schedule 2 "total dry extract" means the content in grammes per litre, determined densimetrically at 20°C, of all substances in the product which do not volatilise.

Hugh Rossi,
P. L. Hawkins,

Two of the Lords Commissioners of Her Majesty's Treasury.

20th November 1973.

(**a**) OJ No. L99, 5.5.1970, p. 1 (OJ/SE 1970(1) p. 234).

SCHEDULE 1

Description of goods by heading and subheading	Schedule No. in Principal Order	Units of quantity per	Agreement Rate (Cyprus)	Agreement Rate (Egypt)
			£	£
22.03 A.I.	2	36 liquid gallons	7·0800 plus 2·8%	7·1700 plus 4·3%
†22.03 A.II.	2	36 liquid gallons	7·0800 plus 2·8%	7·1700 plus 4·3%
†plus for each degree exceeding 1030 original gravity	2	36 liquid gallons	0·2900 for each additional degree	0·2900 for each additional degree
22.06 A.I.a) 1.	3 Table 1	liquid gallon	0·7950 plus 0·0927 UA	0·8175 plus 0·1390 UA
A.I.a) 2.	3 Table 1	liquid gallon	1·4180 plus 0·0927 UA	1·4270 plus 0·1390 UA
A.I.c) 1.	3 Table 1	liquid gallon	1·5875 plus 0·0927 UA	1·6437 plus 0·1390 UA
A.I.c) 2.	3 Table 1	liquid gallon	2·1900 plus 0·0927 UA	2·2350 plus 0·1390 UA
A.II.a) 1.aa)	3 Table 1	liquid gallon	0·7725 plus 0·0763 UA	0·7837 plus 0·1145 UA
A.II.a) 1.bb)	3 Table 1	liquid gallon	0·7950 plus 0·0763 UA	0·8175 plus 0·1145 UA
A.II.a) 2.	3 Table 1	liquid gallon	1·4180 plus 0·0763 UA	1·4270 plus 0·1145 UA
A.II.c) 1.aa)	3 Table 1	liquid gallon	1·5650 plus 0·0763 UA	1·6100 plus 0·1145 UA
A.II.c) 1.bb)	3 Table 1	liquid gallon	1·5875 plus 0·0763 UA	1·6437 plus 0·1145 UA
A.II.c) 2.	3 Table 1	liquid gallon	2·1900 plus 0·0763 UA	2·2350 plus 0·1145 UA
B.I.b) 1.	3 Table 1	liquid gallon	1·5875 plus 0·1036 UA	1·6437 plus 0·1554 UA
B.I.b) 2.	3 Table 1	liquid gallon	2·1900 plus 0·1036 UA	2·2350 plus 0·1554 UA
B.II.b) 1.aa)	3 Table 1	liquid gallon	1·5650 plus 0·0872 UA	1·6100 plus 0·1309 UA
B.II.b) 1.bb)	3 Table 1	liquid gallon	1·5875 plus 0·0872 UA	1·6437 plus 0·1309 UA
B.II.b) 2.	3 Table 1	liquid gallon	2·1900 plus 0·0872 UA	2·2350 plus 0·1309 UA
C.I.a) 1.	3 Table 1	liquid gallon	1·5875 plus 0·0545 UA plus 0·0049 UA per degree proof	1·6437 plus 0·0818 UA plus 0·0074 UA per degree proof
C.I.a) 2.	3 Table 1	liquid gallon	2·1900 plus 0·0545 UA plus 0·0049 UA per degree proof	2·2350 plus 0·0818 UA plus 0·0074 UA per degree proof
*C.I.b) 1.	3 Table 1	liquid gallon	1·5872 UA plus 0·0545 UA plus 0·0049 UA per degree proof	1·6437 plus 0·0818 UA plus 0·0074 UA per degree proof
*C.I.b) 2.	3 Table 1	liquid gallon	2·1900 UA plus 0·0545 UA plus 0·0049 UA per degree proof	2·2350 plus 0·0818 UA plus 0·0074 UA per degree proof

Description of goods by heading and subheading	Schedule No. in Principal Order	Units of quantity per	Agreement Rate (Cyprus)	Agreement Rate (Egypt)
			£	£
C.II.a) 1.aa)	3 Table 1	liquid gallon	1·5650 plus 0·0049 UA per degree proof	1·6100 plus 0·0074 UA per degree proof
C.II.a) 1.bb)	3 Table 1	liquid gallon	1·5875 plus 0·0049 UA per degree proof	1·6437 plus 0·0074 UA per degree proof
C.II.a) 2.	3 Table 1	liquid gallon	2·1900 plus 0·0049 UA per degree proof	2·2350 plus 0·0074 UA per degree proof
*C.II.b) 1.aa)	3 Table 1	liquid gallon	1·5650 plus 0·0049 UA per degree proof	1·6100 plus 0·0074 UA per degree proof
*C.II.b) 1.bb)	3 Table 1	liquid gallon	1·5872 plus 0·0049 UA per degree proof	1·6437 plus 0·0074 UA per degree proof
*C.II.b) 2.	3 Table 1	liquid gallon	2·1900 plus 0·0049 UA per degree proof	2·2350 plus 0·0074 UA per degree proof
*plus for each degree or fraction of a degree over 42° proof	3 Table 1	liquid gallon	0·1272 per degree proof	0·1308 per degree proof
22.08 A.I.	1 Table 1	proof gallon	15·4725 plus 0·0872 UA per liquid gallon	15·4837 plus 0·1309 UA per liquid gallon
A.II.	1 Table 1	proof gallon	15·5475 plus 0·0872 UA per liquid gallon	15·5587 plus 0·1309 UA per liquid gallon
B.I.	1 Table 1	proof gallon	15·4725 plus 0·1636 UA per liquid gallon	15·4837 plus 0·2454 UA per liquid gallon
B.II.	1 Table 1	proof gallon	15·5475 plus 0·1636 UA per liquid gallon	15·5587 plus 0·2454 UA per liquid gallon
22.09 A.I.a)	1 Table 1	proof gallon	15·4687 plus 0·4977 UA plus 0·0545 UA per liquid gallon	15·4781 plus 0·7466 UA plus 0·0818 UA per liquid gallon
A.I.b)	1 Table 1	proof gallon	15·5437 plus 0·4977 UA plus 0·0545 UA per liquid gallon	15·5531 plus 0·7466 UA plus 0·0818 UA per liquid gallon
A.II.a)	1 Table 1	proof gallon	15·4687 plus 0·4977 UA	15·4781 plus 0·7466 UA
A.II.b)	1 Table 1	proof gallon	15·5437 plus 0·4977 UA	15·5531 plus 0·7466 UA
B.I.a)	1 Table 1	proof gallon	15·4687	15·4781
B.I.b)	1 Table 1	proof gallon	15·5437	15·5531
C.I.a) 1.aa)	1 Table 1	liquid gallon	20·8837 plus 0·4472 UA	20·8968 plus 0·6708 UA
C.I.a) 1.bb)	1 Table 1	liquid gallon	20·9837 plus 0·4472 UA	20·9968 plus 0·6708 UA
C.I.a) 2.aa) 11.	1 Table 1	proof gallon	15·4725 plus 0·3111 UA plus 0·0272 UA per liquid gallon	15·4837 plus 0·4666 UA plus 0·0409 UA per liquid gallon
C.I.a) 2.aa) 22.	1 Table 1	proof gallon	15·4687 plus 0·3111 UA plus 0·0272 UA per liquid gallon	15·4781 plus 0·4666 UA plus 0·0409 UA per liquid gallon

Description of goods by heading and subheading	Schedule No. in Principal Order	Units of quantity per	Agreement Rate (Cyprus)	Agreement Rate (Egypt)
			£	£
C.1.a) 2.bb) 11.	1 Table 1	proof gallon	15·5475 plus 0·3111 UA plus 0·0272 UA per liquid gallon	15·5587 plus 0·4666 UA plus 0·0409 UA per liquid gallon
C.I.a) 2.bb) 22.	1 Table 1	proof gallon	15·5437 plus 0·3111 UA plus 0·0272 UA per liquid gallon	15·5531 plus 0·4666 UA plus 0·0409 UA per liquid gallon
C.I.b) 1.aa)	1 Table 1	liquid gallon	20·8837 plus 0·4199 UA	20·8968 plus 0·6299 UA
C.I.b) 1.bb)	1 Table 1	liquid gallon	20·9837 plus 0·4199 UA	20·9968 plus 0·6299 UA
C.I.b) 2.aa) 11.	1 Table 1	proof gallon	15·4725 plus 0·3111 UA	15·4837 plus 0·4666 UA
C.I.b) 2.aa) 22.	1 Table 1	proof gallon	15·4687 plus 0·3111 UA	15·4781 plus 0·4666 UA
C.I.b) 2.bb) 11.	1 Table 1	proof gallon	15·5475 plus 0·3111 UA	15·5587 plus 0·4666 UA
C.I.b) 2.bb) 22.	1 Table 1	proof gallon	15·5437 plus 0·3111 UA	15·5531 plus 0·4666 UA
C.II.a) 1.aa)	1 Table 1	liquid gallon	20·8837 plus 0·4472 UA	20·8968 plus 0·6708 UA
C.II.a) 1.bb)	1 Table 1	liquid gallon	20·9837 plus 0·4472 UA	20·9968 plus 0·6708 UA
C.II.a) 2.aa)	1 Table 1	proof gallon	15·4687 plus 0·3111 UA plus 0·0272 UA per liquid gallon	15·4781 plus 0·4666 UA plus 0·0409 UA per liquid gallon
C.II. a) 2.bb)	1 Table 1	proof gallon	15·5437 plus 0·3111 UA plus 0·0272 UA per liquid gallon	15·5531 plus 0·4666 UA plus 0·0409 UA per liquid gallon
C.II.b) 1.aa)	1 Table 1	liquid gallon	20·8837 plus 0·4199 UA	20·8968 plus 0·6299 UA
C.II.b) 1.bb)	1 Table 1	liquid gallon	20·9837 plus 0·4199 UA	20·9968 plus 0·6299 UA
C.II.b) 2.aa)	1 Table 1	proof gallon	15·4687 plus 0·3111 UA	15·4781 plus 0·4666 UA
C.II.b) 2.bb)	1 Table 1	proof gallon	15·5437 plus 0·3111 UA	15·5531 plus 0·4666 UA
C.III.b) 1.aa) 11.	1 Table 1	liquid gallon	20·8837 plus 0·3632 UA	20·8968 plus 0·5448 UA
C.III.b) 1.aa) 22.	1 Table 1	liquid gallon	20·9837 plus 0·3632 UA	20·9968 plus 0·5448 UA
C.III.b) 1.bb) 11.	1 Table 1	proof gallon	15·4687 plus 0·2488 UA plus 0·0272 UA per liquid gallon	15·4781 plus 0·3733 UA plus 0·0409 UA per liquid gallon
C.III.b) 1.bb) 22.	1 Table 1	proof gallon	15·5437 plus 0·2488 UA plus 0·0272 UA per liquid gallon	15·5531 plus 0·3733 UA plus 0·0409 UA per liquid gallon
C.III.b) 2.aa) 11.	1 Table 1	liquid gallon	20·8837 plus 0·3359 UA	20·8968 plus 0·5039 UA
C.III.b) 2.aa) 22.	1 Table 1	liquid gallon	20·9837 plus 0·3359 UA	20·9968 plus 0·5039 UA
C.III.b) 2.bb) 11.	1 Table 1	proof gallon	15·4687 plus 0·2488 UA	15·4781 plus 0·3733 UA
C.III.b) 2.bb) 22.	1 Table 1	proof gallon	15·5437 plus 0·2488 UA	15·5531 plus 0·3733 UA
C.IV.a) 1.aa)	1 Table 1	liquid gallon	20·8837 plus 0·5732 UA	20·8968 plus 0·8598 UA
C.IV.a) 1.bb)	1 Table 1	liquid gallon	20·9837 plus 0·5732 UA	20·9968 plus 0·8598 UA

Description of goods by heading and subheading	Schedule No. in Principal Order	Units of quantity per	Agreement Rate (Cyprus)	Agreement Rate (Egypt)
			£	£
22.09 C.IV.a) 2.aa)	1 Table 1	proof gallon	15·4687 plus 0·4044 UA plus 0·0272 UA per liquid gallon	15·4781 plus 0·6066 UA plus 0·0409 UA per liquid gallon
C.IV.a) 2.bb)	1 Table 1	proof gallon	15·5437 plus 0·4044 UA plus 0·0272 UA per liquid gallon	15·5531 plus 0·6066 UA plus 0·0409 UA per liquid gallon
C.IV.b) 1.aa)	1 Table 1	liquid gallon	20·8837 plus 0·5459 UA	20·8968 plus 0·8189 UA
C.IV.b) 1.bb)	1 Table 1	liquid gallon	20·9837 plus 0·5459 UA	20·9968 plus 0·8189 UA
C.IV.b) 2.aa)	1 Table 1	proof gallon	15·4687 plus 0·4044 UA	15·4781 plus 0·6066 UA
C.IV.b) 2.bb)	1 Table 1	proof gallon	15·5437 plus 0·4044 UA	15·5531 plus 0·6066 UA
C.V.a) 1.aa)	1 Table 1	liquid gallon	20·8837 plus 0·7256 UA	20·8968 plus 1·0897 UA
C.V.a) 1.bb)	1 Table 1	liquid gallon	20·9837 plus 0·7256 UA	20·9968 plus 1·0897 UA
C.V.a) 2.aa)	1 Table 1	proof gallon	15·4687 plus 0·4977 UA plus 0·0545 UA per liquid gallon	15·4781 plus 0·7466 UA plus 0·0818 UA per liquid gallon
C.V.a) 2.bb)	1 Table 1	proof gallon	15·5437 plus 0·4977 UA plus 0·0545 UA per liquid gallon	15·5531 plus 0·7466 UA plus 0·0818 UA per liquid gallon
C.V.b) 1.aa)	1 Table 1	liquid gallon	20·8837 plus 0·6719 UA	20·8968 plus 1·0079 UA
C.V.b) 1.bb)	1 Table 1	liquid gallon	20·9837 plus 0·6719 UA	20·9968 plus 1·0079 UA
C.V.b) 2.aa)	1 Table 1	proof gallon	15·4687 plus 0·4977 UA	15·4781 plus 0·7466 UA
C.V.b) 2.bb)	1 Table 1	proof gallon	15·5437 plus 0·4977 UA	15·5531 plus 0·7466 UA
24.02 A.	4 Table 1	pound weight	4·4008 plus 10·8%	4·4205 plus 16·2%
B.	4 Table 1	pound weight	4·6281 plus 6·2%	4·6413 plus 9·36%
C.I.a)	4 Table 1	pound weight	4·3501 plus 14%	4·3588 plus 21·06%
C.I.b)	4 Table 1	pound weight	4·4382 plus 14%	4·4482 plus 21·06%
C.II.	4 Table 1	pound weight	4·3298 plus 14%	4·3421 plus 21·06%
D.I.	4 Table 1	pound weight	4·3298 plus 7·8%	4·3421 plus 11·7%
D.II.	4 Table 1	pound weight	4·3753 plus 7·8%	4·3855 plus 11·7%
E.I.	4 Table 1	pound weight	4·3753 plus 3·1%	4·3855 plus 4·68%
E.II.	4 Table 1	pound weight	4·3298 plus 3·1%	4·3421 plus 4·68%
33.06 B.I.a) 1.	4 Table 2	liquid gallon	9·6000 plus 1·3%	9·6000 plus 1·9%
B.I.a) 2.	4 Table 2	liquid gallon	9·6750 plus 1·3%	9·6750 plus 1·9%
B.I.a) 3.	4 Table 2	liquid gallon	9·7200 plus 1·3%	9·7200 plus 1·9%
B.I.b) 1.	4 Table 2	liquid gallon	9·6500 plus 1·3%	9·6500 plus 1·9%

Description of goods by heading and subheading	Schedule No. in Principal Order	Units of quantity per	Agreement Rate (Cyprus)	Agreement Rate (Egypt)
			£	£
B.I.b) 2.	4 Table 2	liquid gallon	9·7250 plus 1·3%	9·7250 plus 1·9%
B.I.b) 3.	4 Table 2	liquid gallon	9·7700 plus 1·3%	9·7700 plus 1·9%
36.05 B.I. and 36.06	5	7,200 matches	0·4958 plus 1·3%	0·4987 plus 2%
98.10 A.I.a) 2.	6	per lighter	0·2075 plus 0·9%	0·2112 plus 1·3%
B.I.b)	6	per lighter	0·2075 plus 1·3%	0·2112 plus 1·9%

SCHEDULE 2

Preferential Rates of Duty on Wine from Algeria, Morocco, Tunisia and Turkey

TABLE 1

(Normal Rates of Customs Duty)

Description by heading & subheading	Rates of customs duty per gallon	
	£	
22.05 A.I.	1·4600 plus 0·4363 UA	
A.III. and IV.	2·4000 plus 0·4363 UA*	
B.I.	1·4600 plus 0·4363 UA	
B.III. and IV.	2·4000 plus 0·4363 UA*	
C.I. a)	0·7500 plus 0·3273 UA	
C.I. b) 1.	0·8250 plus 0·0981 UA	
C.I. b) 2.	0·9000 plus 0·0981 UA	
C.II. a) 1.	0·9000 plus 0·1527 UA	
C.II. a) 2.	1·8500 plus 0·1527 UA	
C.II. b) 1.aa)	0·8250 plus 0·1200 UA	
C.II. b) 1.bb)	0·7500 plus 0·3000 UA	
C.II. b) 2.aa)	1·7750 plus 0·1200 UA	
C.II. b) 2.bb)	1·8500 plus 0·1200 UA	
C.III.a) 1.	1·8500 plus 0·1472 UA	
C.III.a) 2.bb) 11.	1·7750 plus 0·1309 UA	
C.III.a) 2.bb) 22.	1·8500 plus 0·1309 UA	
C.III.b) 1.cc)	1·8500 plus 0·1854 UA	
C.III.b) 2.cc) 11.	1·7750 plus 0·1527 UA	
C.III.b) 2.cc) 22.	1·8500 plus 0·1527 UA	
C.IV.a) 1.	1·8500 plus 0·1581 UA	
C.IV.a) 1.bb) 11.	1·7750 plus 0·1417 UA	
C.IV.a) 1.bb) 22.	1·8500 plus 0·1417 UA	
C.IV.b) 2.aa)	1·7750 plus 0·2072 UA	
C.IV.b) 2.bb)	1·8500 plus 0·2072 UA	
C.V. a) 1. and 2.	1·8500 plus 0·1090 UA*	Together with additional duty for all wines in subheading C.V. of 0·0099 UA per degree of proof spirit.
C.V. b) 1.aa) and 2.aa)	1·7750*	
C.V. b) 1.bb) and 2.bb)	1·8500*	
*Together, in the case of wine exceeding 42 degrees of proof spirit, with an addition for each additional degree or fraction of a degree of	0·1440 UA	

TABLE 2

(SPECIAL RATES FOR WINE OF SUBHEADING 22.05 WITH EXCESS TOTAL DRY EXTRACT)

Normal classification in heading and subheading	Rates of customs duty for wine with excessive dry extract not exceeding 330 grammes per litre		Rates of customs duty for wine with total dry extract exceeding 330 grammes per litre
	Total dry extract not in excess of	per liquid gallon	per liquid gallon plus in every case 0·0099 UA per degree of proof spirit
		£	£
C.I.a)	90 g. per litre	0·9000 plus 0·1527 UA	0·9000 plus 0·1090 UA
C.I.b) 1.		0·8250 plus 0·1200 UA	0·8250
C.I.b) 2.		0·9000 plus 0·1200 UA	0·9000
C.II. a) 1.	130 g. per litre	0·9000 plus 0·1854 UA	0·9000 plus 0·1090 UA
C.II. a) 2.		1·8500 plus 0·1854 UA	1·8500 plus 0·1090 UA
C.II. b) 1.aa)		0·8250 plus 0·1527 UA	0·8250
C.II. b) 1.bb)		0·9000 plus 0·1527 UA	0·9000
C.II. b) 2.aa)		1·7750 plus 0·1527 UA	1·7750
C.II. b) 2.bb)		1·8500 plus 0·1527 UA	1·8500
C.III.b) 1.cc)		1·8500 plus 0·2072 UA	1·8500 plus 0·1090 UA
C.III.b) 2.cc) 11.		1·7750 plus 0·2072 UA	1·7750
C.III.b) 2.cc) 22.		1·8500 plus 0·2072 UA	1·8500
C.IV.b) 2.aa)			1·7750
C.IV.b) 2.bb)			1·8500 plus 0·1090 UA

EXPLANATORY NOTE

(*This Note is not part of the Order*.)

1. This Order, which comes into operation on 1st January 1974, implements obligations of the United Kingdom under the Agreements of 18th and 19th December 1972 between the European Community and Egypt and Cyprus respectively, in relation to Customs revenue duties other than those on hydrocarbon oils. It also implements obligations of the United Kingdom under Regulation (EEC) 2012/73 (OJ L206/5 dated 27.7.73) in respect of certain wines from Algeria, Morocco, Tunisia and Turkey.

2. For Cyprus the Order provides for the protective element (generally nil) in the rates of duty on all descriptions of goods eligible for Commonwealth preference treatment to be retained at the level applicable before the protocol extending the Agreement to the United Kingdom came into force, where such rates are lower than the Commonwealth rates aligned on 1st January 1974 towards the duties in the common customs tariff (CCT). (Article 6). It also provides special reduced rates in certain circumstances for specified goods (excluding those listed in Annex II to the Treaty of Rome) satisfying the origin conditions of the Agreement. (Articles 7 and 9).

3. For Egypt the Order provides for a cut of 55% in the protective element in the duties on goods other than those listed in Annex II of the Treaty of Rome subject to such rates not being lower than the EEC rates. (Articles 8 and 9).

4. For wines from Algeria, Morocco, Tunisia and Turkey the UK protective elements in the duties are aligned to 60% of the CCT rates by reducing the difference between them by 40%. A separate table of rates is provided for certain sweet wines which under the rules of the CCT have to be classified under different tariff subheadings and thus attract a higher level of CCT duty. (Articles 10 and 11).

5. The Order provides for corresponding alterations in drawback rates, where applicable. (Article 5).

1973 No. 1948

CUSTOMS AND EXCISE

The Hydrocarbon Oil (Customs Duties) Order 1973

Made - - - -	20*th November* 1973
Laid before the House of Commons	28*th November* 1973
Coming into Operation	1*st January* 1974

The Treasury, by virtue of the powers conferred on them by section 1(4) and (5) of the Finance Act 1973**(a)** and of all other powers enabling them in that behalf, hereby make the following Order:—

1. This Order may be cited as the Hydrocarbon Oil (Customs Duties) Order 1973 and shall come into operation on 1st January 1974.

2.—(1) In this Order—

"the Act of 1971" means the Hydrocarbon Oil (Customs & Excise) Act 1971**(b)**;

"the additional duty" means any amount by which the customs duty charged under section 4(1) of the Act of 1971 on hydrocarbon oil may be increased by virtue of Article 3(2) of this Order;

"entered premises" means premises of which entry has been made pursuant to regulation 3(1) of the Hydrocarbon Oil Regulations 1973**(c)**;

"hydrocarbon oil" and "refinery" have the same meanings as in the Act of 1971;

"like hydrocarbon oil" means hydrocarbon oil which, in the opinion of the Commissioners, is sufficiently similar to imported hydrocarbon oil to be regarded for the purpose of relief under Article 4 of this Order as interchangeable with that hydrocarbon oil;

any reference to exportation and cognate expressions shall include a reference to shipment as stores;

references to subheadings are references to subheadings of the Customs Tariff 1959; those subheadings shall be interpreted and applied in accordance with the Interpretative Rules of the said Tariff;

in columns 2 and 3 of Schedule 1 to this Order, the references to rates of duty expressed as percentages are references to percentages of the value of the goods; and

(a) 1973 c. 51. **(b)** 1971 c. 12. **(c)** S.I. 1973/1311 (1973 II, p. 3984).

hydrocarbon oil shall be treated as originating in, or, as the case may be, manufactured or produced in, a country, territory or state, if it is to be so treated by virtue of any directly applicable instrument of the European Economic Community or any applicable regulation made under section 12(2) of the Import Duties Act 1958**(a)** or section 2(1) of the Finance Act 1973.

(2) The Interpretation Act 1889**(b)** shall apply for the interpretation of this Order as it applies for the interpretation of an Act of Parliament.

(3) This Order does not increase duties of customs otherwise than in pursuance of a Community obligation.

3.—(1) This Article applies to hydrocarbon oil of which entry on importation into the United Kingdom is made on or after the 1st January 1974 and which falls under the subheadings specified in Schedule 1 to this Order, but shall not apply to hydrocarbon oil—

(*a*) originating or at the time of its importation into the United Kingdom in free circulation in a state which is a member of the European Economic Community, or

(*b*) originating in, or manufactured or produced in, a country or territory named in Schedule 2 to this Order, or

(*c*) which, from the time when the Agreement signed on 5th October 1973 between the European Economic Community and Finland is ratified and in full force, is treated as originating in Finland.

(2) Subject to the provisions of Article 3(1) above the rate of customs duty chargeable under the Act of 1971 on hydrocarbon oil falling under the subheadings specified in column 1 of Schedule 1 to this Order shall—

(*a*) in the case of hydrocarbon oil originating in Egypt, be increased by the relevant rates specified in column 2 of that Schedule; and

(*b*) in the case of other hydrocarbon oil, be increased by the relevant rates specified in column 3 of that Schedule:

Provided that the additional duty

(*a*) shall be disregarded for the purpose of calculating the duty of excise chargeable under section 6 of the Act of 1971; and

(*b*) shall, in respect of pinene classifiable under subheading 29.01 C.I.a) and hydrocarbon oil of subheadings 38.07 B or 38.07 C.I. which are entered for home use on importation, removed from warehouse or taken for use or consumption within a refinery or entered premises before 1st July 1974, be chargeable at the relevant rates specified in the brackets in columns 2 and 3 of the said Schedule.

(3) Notwithstanding the provisions of section 4(2) of the Act of 1971, any additional duty on hydrocarbon oil which is taken for consumption or use within a refinery or entered premises shall be charged at the time when it is so taken for consumption or use; and, thereupon, the proprietor of the hydrocarbon oil shall deliver to the proper officer an entry thereof for such purpose in such form and manner and containing such particulars as the Commissioners may direct, and shall pay such additional duty on making the entry. This paragraph does not apply to hydrocarbon oil taken for use in any operation

(a) 1958 c. 6. **(b)** 1889 c. 63.

permitted under the Customs and Excise Act 1952(**a**) to be carried out in a warehouse.

4.—(1) The Commissioners shall have power to remit or repay any additional duty on any hydrocarbon oil imported or proposed to be imported into the United Kingdom where they are satisfied that it is intended to export the hydrocarbon oil or goods incorporating it or manufactured or produced from it:

Provided that the Commissioners shall not grant relief under this Article if they have been notified by the Department of Trade and Industry that in the opinion of that Department the granting of such relief would not conduce to the exportation of hydrocarbon oil or of goods incorporating or manufactured or produced from hydrocarbon oil or would not be in the national interest.

(2) For the purposes of this Article the Commissioners may treat any imported hydrocarbon oil as if it were intended to export that oil or goods incorporating it or manufactured or produced from it, if they are satisfied that like hydrocarbon oil or goods incorporating, or manufactured or produced from, like hydrocarbon oil have been or are intended to be exported and that in the circumstances it is proper for the imported hydrocarbon oil to be so treated:

Provided that the Commissioners shall not grant relief under this paragraph of this Article unless they are satisfied that the like hydrocarbon oil has borne or will bear any additional duty due thereon and has not been or will not be relieved from payment of that duty on exportation.

(3) Any relief from duty under this Article shall be subject to such conditions as the Commissioners see fit to impose for the protection of the revenue or for securing that the imported hydrocarbon oil or goods incorporating it or manufactured or produced from it will be exported, or that, in such circumstances as the Commissioners may require, there shall be paid by way of duty such amount as may be so required.

5. Sections 7, 9, 12, 13 and 15 of the Act of 1971 shall not apply to the amount by which any customs duty is increased by virtue of the provisions of this Order.

Hugh Rossi,
P. L. Hawkins,
Two of the Lords Commissioners
of Her Majesty's Treasury.

20th November 1973.

(**a**) 1952 c. 44.

SCHEDULE 1

Column 1 Tariff subheading	Column 2 Rate of duty %	Column 3 Rate of duty %
27.07 A.I.a)	0·7	1·6
27.07 A.II.a)	0·1	0·4
27.07 B.I.	0·9	2·0
27.07 G.II.a)	0·6	1·4
27.10 A.III.a)	2·4	2·4
27.10 A.III.b)	2·4	2·4
27.10 B.III.a)	2·4	2·4
27.10 B.III.b) 1	2·4	2·4
27.10 C.I.c) 1	1·4	1·4
27.10 C.II.c) 1	1·4	1·4
27.10 C.III.c) 1	1·6	1·6
27.10 C.III.d) 1	2·4	2·4
27.12 A.III.a)	0·8	0·8
27.12 B.I.	2·8	2·8
27.14 C.II.a)	0·8	0·8
27.16 A.I.	0·5	1·2
27.16 B.I.	0·1	0·4
29.01 A.I.b)	3·1	7·0
29.01 C.I.a)	1·7 (1·4)	3·8 (3·2)
29.01 C.II.a)	1·9	4·4
29.01 D.I.a) 1	2·8	6·4
29.01 D.VI.a)	1·8	4·1
32.09 A.II.a)	2·1	4·8
36.08 A.	2·7	6·0
38.07 A.	0·7	1·6
38.07 B.	0·7 (0·5)	1·6 (1·2)
38.07 C.I.	0·8 (0.5)	1·9 (1·2)
38.08 B.I.	0·8	1·9
38.14 B.I.a) 1	1·4	3·2
38·14 B.III.a)	1·9	4·4
38.18 A.	1·9	4·4
38.19 E.I.	1·8	4·1
38.19 T.I.	2·5	5·7
39.02 C.V.a)	3·2	7·3
39.02 C.VI.a) 1	2·8	6·4
39.02 C.XIII.a)	2·1	4·8
39.02 C.XIV.a) 1	3·0	6·7

SCHEDULE 2

Anguilla
Austria
The Bahamas
Barbados
Bermuda
Botswana
British Antarctic Territory
British Honduras
British Indian Ocean Territory
British Solomon Islands
British Virgin Islands
Brunei
Republic of Burundi
Associated States in the Caribbean:
  Antigua, Dominica, Grenada, St. Lucia, St. Vincent, St. Kitts-Nevis
Cayman Islands
The Federal Republic of the Cameroon
Comoro Archipelago
Central and Southern Line Islands
Republic of Chad
Central African Republic
People's Republic of the Congo (Brazzaville)
Cyprus
Republic of Dahomey
Falkland Islands and Dependencies
Fiji
French Polynesia
The French Settlements in Oceania, Southern and Antarctic Territories
French Territories of the Afars and Issas
Gabonese Republic
The Gambia
Ghana
Gilbert and Ellice Islands
Guyana
Iceland
Republic of the Ivory Coast
Jamaica
Kenya
Lesotho
Liechtenstein
Malagasy Republic
Malawi
Republic of Mali

Islamic Republic of Mauritania
Mauritius
Montserrat
Netherlands Antilles
New Caledonia and Dependencies
Anglo-French Condominium of the New Hebrides
Republic of Niger
Nigeria
Norway
Papua—New Guinea
Pitcairn
Portugal
Republic of Rwanda
Republic of Senegal
The Seychelles
Sierra Leone
Somali Democratic Republic
St. Helena and Dependencies
St. Pierre and Miquelon
Surinam
Swaziland
Sweden
Switzerland
Republic of Togo
Tanzania
Tonga
Trinidad & Tobago
Turks & Caicos Islands
Uganda
Republic of Upper Volta
Wallis and Futuna Islands
The Independent State of Western Samoa
Zaire
Zambia

EXPLANATORY NOTE

(This Note is not part of the Order.)

1. This Order, coming into operation on 1st January 1974, implements the first stage of the United Kingdom's obligations, under the Treaty of Accession to the European Economic Community and under the individual Agreements between the EEC and the non-acceding EFTA countries and Cyprus and Egypt, to introduce protective elements into the customs duty on certain hydrocarbon oils, and to align them progressively with the Common Customs Tariff of the EEC by 1st July 1977. The full rate of additional duty added to the existing non-protective customs duty represents the required 2/5 of Community rates.

2. Article 3(1) of the Order provides that the additional customs duty shall not apply to imported hydrocarbon oil which originates or is in free circulation in a Member State of the EEC or which qualifies under other regulations as originating in, or as manufactured or produced in, one of the countries listed in Schedule 2 to the Order.

3. Article 3(2) imposes on imported oil the additional rates of customs duty set out in Schedule 1, that Schedule containing separate rates for Egypt in accordance with an EEC Agreement with that country. It further provides that section 6 of the Hydrocarbon Oil (Customs & Excise) Act 1971 shall not have the effect of adding these additional rates to the UK excise duty on oil; and it allows certain temporary partial suspensions of CCT rates which have been prescribed by the Community. No additional rates of duty are imposed on crude petroleum oils and crude oils obtained from bituminous minerals, of Tariff heading 27.09.

4. Article 3(3) substitutes for the provisions of section 4(2) of the 1971 Act special provision for the additional duty on the hydrocarbon oil affected to be charged at the time when it is taken for consumption or use within a refinery or an oil producer's premises.

5. Article 4 makes provision for the relief of imported oil from the additional duty where that oil or goods made with or from it have been or are to be exported. This provision is in substitution for relief under section 13 of the 1971 Act.

6. Article 5 provides that the following sections of the 1971 Act, namely section 7 (reliefs for use for certain industrial purposes), sections 9 and 12 (rebates of duty for heavy and light oil), section 13 (relief for export—a substituted relief being provided by Article 4 of the Order) and section 15 (relief for horticultural use) shall not apply in regard to the additional duty. Reliefs from the basic customs revenue duty remain unaffected.

1973 No. 1949

EXCHANGE CONTROL

The Exchange Control (Authorised Dealers and Depositaries) (No. 2) Order 1973

Made - - - *20th November* 1973

Coming into Operation *20th December* 1973

The Treasury, in exercise of the powers conferred upon them by sections 42(1) and 36(5) of the Exchange Control Act 1947(**a**), hereby make the following Order:—

1.—(1) This Order may be cited as the Exchange Control (Authorised Dealers and Depositaries) (No. 2) Order 1973, and shall come into operation on 20th December 1973.

(2) In this Order, notwithstanding section 43(2) of the Exchange Control Act 1947 (which provides that references to the United Kingdom in that Act shall be construed as if the Isle of Man were part of the United Kingdom) and notwithstanding section 31 of the Interpretation Act 1889(**b**), the expression "the United Kingdom" does not include the Isle of Man.

(3) The Interpretation Act 1889 shall apply for the interpretation of this Order as it applies for the interpretation of an Act of Parliament.

2. Offices in the United Kingdom, the Channel Islands or the Isle of Man of the persons specified in Schedule 1 to this Order are authorised to act for the purposes of the said Act as authorised dealers in relation to gold.

3. The following are authorised to act for the purposes of the said Act as authorised dealers in relation to gold and all foreign currencies:—

(*a*) offices in the United Kingdom, the Channel Islands or the Isle of Man of the persons specified in paragraph 1 of Schedule 2 to this Order;

(*b*) offices in the United Kingdom of the persons specified in paragraph 2 of Schedule 2 to this Order, and

(*c*) the Head Office of United Dominions Trust Ltd.

4. The following are authorised to act as authorised depositaries for the purposes of Part III of the said Act:—

(*a*) the Bank of England, and the Quotations Department and the Official Assignee of The Stock Exchange; and

(*b*) the persons and offices specified in Schedule 3 to this Order.

(**a**) 1947 c.14. (**b**) 1889 c.63.

5. The Orders specified in Schedule 4 to this Order are hereby revoked.

6. This Order shall extend to the Channel Islands, and any reference in this Order to the Exchange Control Act 1947 includes a reference to that Act as extended by the Exchange Control (Channel Islands) Order 1947(a).

Hugh Rossi,
P. L. Hawkins,
Two of the Lords Commissioners of Her Majesty's Treasury.

20th November 1973.

SCHEDULE 1

Authorised Dealers in Gold

Offices in the United Kingdom, the Channel Islands or the Isle of Man of the following persons:—

The Bank of England.
Mocatta & Goldsmid Ltd.
Sharps, Pixley Ltd.

SCHEDULE 2

Authorised Dealers in Gold and in all Foreign Currencies

1. Offices in the United Kingdom, the Channel Islands or the Isle of Man of the following persons:—

Barclays Bank Ltd.
Coutts & Co.
Hambros (Guernsey) Ltd.
Hambros (Jersey) Ltd.
Hill Samuel & Co. (Guernsey) Ltd.
Hill Samuel & Co. (Jersey) Ltd.
Isle of Man Bank Ltd.
Kleinwort, Benson (Channel Islands) Ltd.
Kleinwort, Benson (Guernsey) Ltd.
Lloyds Bank Ltd.
Midland Bank Ltd.
National Westminster Bank Ltd.
Rothschild & Sons (C.I.) Ltd., N.M.
Standard & Chase Bank C.I. Ltd.
Williams & Glyn's Bank Ltd.

2. Offices in the United Kingdom of the following persons:—

Afghan National Bank Ltd.
African Continental Bank Ltd.
Algemene Bank Nederland N.V.

(a) S.R. & O. 1947/ 2034 (Rev VI, p.1001: 1947 I, p.660).

Allied Bank International.
Allied Irish Banks Ltd.
American Express International Banking Corporation.
American National Bank and Trust Company of Chicago.
Anglo-Israel Bank Ltd.
Anglo-Portuguese Bank Ltd.
Anglo-Romanian Bank Ltd.
Ansbacher & Co. Ltd., Henry.
Arab Bank Ltd.
Arbuthnot Latham & Co., Ltd.
Associated Japanese Bank (International) Ltd.
Atlantic International Bank Ltd.
Australia and New Zealand Banking Group Ltd.
Baer International Ltd., Julius.
Banca Commerciale Italiana.
Banca Nazionale del Lavoro.
Banco de Bilbao.
Banco do Brasil S.A.
Banco do Estado de Sao Paulo S.A.
Banco Español en Londres, S.A.
Banco Urquijo Ltd.
Bangkok Bank Ltd.
Bank Hapoalim B.M.
Bank Melli Iran.
Bank of Adelaide.
Bank of America Ltd.
Bank of America National Trust & Savings Association.
Bank of Baroda.
Bank of California, N.A., The.
Bank of Ceylon.
Bank of China.
Bank of Cyprus (London) Ltd.
Bank of India.
Bank of Ireland.
Bank of London & South America Ltd.
Bank of Montreal.
Bank of New South Wales.
Bank of New York, The.
Bank of New Zealand.
Bank of Nova Scotia.
Bank of Scotland.
Bank of Tokyo Ltd., The.
Bank of Tokyo Trust Company, The.
Bankers Trust Company.
Bankers Trust International Ltd.
Banque Belge Ltd.
Banque Belgo-Zairoise S.A.
Banque de l'Indochine.
Banque de Paris et des Pays-Bas.
Banque de Suez (U.K.) Ltd.
Barclays Bank International Ltd.
Barclays Bank (London and International) Ltd.
Baring Brothers & Co., Ltd.
Bates & Sons Ltd., Edward.
Brandt's Sons & Co., Ltd., Wm.
British and French Bank Ltd.
British Bank of the Middle East, The.
Brown Harriman & International Banks Ltd.
Brown, Shipley & Co. Ltd.
Burston & Texas Commerce Bank Ltd.
Canadian Imperial Bank of Commerce.
Central Bank of India.

Chartered Bank, The.
Charterhouse Japhet Ltd.
Chase and Bank of Ireland (International) Ltd.
Chase Manhattan Bank N.A., The.
Chemical Bank.
Citicorp International Bank Ltd.
City National Bank of Detroit.
Clydesdale Bank Ltd.
Commercial Bank of Australia, Ltd.
Commercial Bank of the Near East Ltd.
Commercial Banking Company of Sydney, Ltd.
Commerzbank A.G.
Commonwealth Trading Bank of Australia.
Continental Illinois Ltd.
Continental Illinois National Bank and Trust Company of Chicago.
Co-operative Bank Ltd.
County Bank Ltd.
Crédit Industriel et Commercial.
Crédit Lyonnais.
Crédit Suisse.
Credito Italiano.
Crocker National Bank.
Dai-Ichi Kangyo Bank, Ltd., The.
Daiwa Bank Ltd., The.
Detroit Bank & Trust Company, The.
Discount Bank (Overseas) Ltd.
Dow Banking Corporation.
Dresdner Bank A.G.
European Brazilian Bank Ltd.
Fidelity Bank, The.
First City National Bank of Houston.
First International Bancshares Ltd.
First National Bank in Dallas.
First National Bank of Boston, The.
First National Bank of Chicago, The.
First National City Bank.
First Pennsylvania Banking and Trust Company, The.
First Wisconsin National Bank of Milwaukee.
Franklin National Bank.
French Bank of Southern Africa Ltd.
Fuji Bank Ltd., The.
Ghana Commercial Bank.
Gibbs Holdings Ltd., Antony.
Girard Trust Bank.
Gray Dawes & Co. Ltd.
Guinness Mahon & Co. Ltd.
Habib Bank (Overseas) Ltd.
Hambros Bank Ltd.
Harris Trust and Savings Bank.
Havana International Bank Ltd.
Hill Samuel & Co. Ltd.
Hoare & Co., C.
Hongkong & Shanghai Banking Corporation, The.
Hungarian International Bank Ltd.
Industrial Bank of Japan Ltd., The.
International Commercial Bank Ltd.
International Marine Banking Co. Ltd.
International Westminster Bank Ltd.
Investitions—und Handels—Bank A.G.
Ionian Bank Ltd.
Irving Trust Company.
Israel-British Bank (London) Ltd.

Italian International Bank Ltd.
Japan International Bank Ltd.
Johnson Matthey Bankers Ltd.
Joseph & Sons, Ltd., Leopold.
Keyser Ullmann Ltd.
Kleinwort, Benson Ltd.
Korea Exchange Bank.
Kyowa Bank, Ltd., The.
Lazard Brothers & Co., Ltd.
Libra Bank Ltd.
Lloyds & Bolsa International Bank Ltd.
Lloyds Bank Europe Ltd.
London & Continental Bankers Ltd.
London Interstate Bank Ltd.
London Multinational Bank Ltd.
Long-Term Credit Bank of Japan, Ltd., The.
Manufacturers Hanover Ltd.
Manufacturers Hanover Trust Company.
Marine Midland Bank—New York.
Mellon Bank N.A.
Mercantile Bank Ltd.
Merrill Lynch-Brown Shipley Bank Ltd.
Midland and International Banks Ltd.
Mitsubishi Bank, Ltd., The.
Mitsui Bank, Ltd., The.
Montagu & Co., Ltd., Samuel.
Morgan Grenfell & Co. Ltd.
Morgan Guaranty Trust Company of New York.
Moscow Narodny Bank, Ltd.
National and Grindlays Bank Ltd.
National Bank of Australasia, Ltd.
National Bank of Commerce of Seattle, The.
National Bank of Detroit.
National Bank of Greece.
National Bank of New Zealand, Ltd., The.
National Bank of Nigeria Ltd.
National Bank of Pakistan.
National Commercial & Glyns Ltd.
Nedbank Ltd.
Nordic Bank Ltd.
North Carolina National Bank.
Northern Bank Ltd.
Northern Trust Company, The.
Orion Bank Ltd.
Orion Termbank Ltd.
Oversea-Chinese Banking Corporation Ltd.
Overseas Union Bank Ltd.
Provincial Bank of Ireland Ltd.
Rafidain Bank.
Rea Brothers Ltd.
Republic National Bank of Dallas.
Reserve Bank of Australia.
Rothschild & Sons Ltd., N.M.
Rothschild Intercontinental Bank Ltd.
Royal Bank of Canada, The.
Royal Bank of Scotland Ltd., The.
Sanwa Bank Ltd., The.
Scandinavian Bank Ltd.
Schroder, Wagg & Co. Ltd., J. Henry.
Scottish Co-operative Society Ltd.
Security Pacific National Bank.
Singer & Friedlander Ltd.

Slater, Walker Ltd.
Société Générale pour favoriser le développement du Commerce et de l'Industrie en France.
Standard and Chartered Banking Group Ltd.
Standard Bank Ltd., The.
State Bank of India.
Sumitomo Bank, Ltd., The.
Swiss Bank Corporation.
Swiss-Israel Trade Bank.
Taiyo Kobe Bank, Ltd., The.
Texas Commerce Bank N.A.
Tokai Bank, Ltd., The.
Toronto-Dominion Bank, The.
Trade Development Bank.
UBAF Ltd.
Ulster Bank Ltd.
Union Bank of Switzerland.
United Bank Ltd.
United Bank of Kuwait Ltd., The.
United California Bank.
United Commercial Bank.
United International Bank Ltd.
Wallace Brothers Sassoon Bank Ltd.
Warburg & Co., Ltd., S.G.
Wells Fargo Ltd.
Westdeutsche Landesbank Girozentrale.
Western American Bank (Europe) Ltd.
White, Weld & Co. Ltd.
Yorkshire Bank Ltd.
Zivnostenska Banka National Corporation.

SCHEDULE 3

Authorised Depositaries

1. Offices in the United Kingdom, the Channel Islands or the Isle of Man of the persons listed in Schedule 2 to this Order.

2. Members in the United Kingdom, the Channel Islands or the Isle of Man of:—

The Stock Exchange.
Th Association of Stock and Share Dealers.
The London Discount Market Association.
The Association of Canadian Investment Dealers and Members of the Toronto and Montreal Stock Exchanges in Great Britain.
The Association of New York Stock Exchange Member Firms having Representation in the United Kingdom.
The Issuing Houses Association.
The Association of Investment Trust Companies.
The British Insurance Association.
The Association of Trustee Savings Banks.

3. Solicitors practising in the United Kingdom, the Channel Islands or the Isle of Man, advocates practising in the Isle of Man, and advocates and écrivains of the Royal Courts of Jersey and Guernsey practising in the Channel Islands.

4. The Public Trustee and the Accountant General of the Supreme Court.

5. Persons in the United Kingdom not included in paragraphs 2, 3 or 4 of this Schedule who are holders of a principal's licence or are exempted (whether by

definition, class or name) for the purposes of the Prevention of Fraud (Investments) Act 1958(**a**) or the Prevention of Fraud (Investments) Act (Northern Ireland) 1940(**b**), and the offices in the Channel Islands or the Isle of Man of such persons.

6. (*a*) Partners in the following firms of Chartered Accountants practising in the United Kingdom, the Channel Islands or the Isle of Man:—

Bagshaw & Co.
Black, Geoghegan & Till.
J. B. Boyd, Wrigley & Co.
C. D. Bromhead & Co.
Buckley Hall Devin & Co.
Butterworth, Jones & Co.
Caldwell & Braham.
Chapman Hilton Hutchinson & Dunford.
Chater & Myhill.
Clark, Battams & Co.
W. O. Crossley & Co.
Davies & Crane.
Dearden, Lord, Annan, Morrish.
Evans, Rankin & Co.
Everett, Chettle & Co.
Finnie, Ross, Welch & Co.
J. B. Garside & Son.
Grace, Ryland & Co.
Hancock & Ashford.
Hilton, Sharp & Clarke.
Hodgson, Morris & Co.
Hogg Bullimore Gundry & Co.
Honey, Barrett & Co.
Hope, Agar & Co.
Hyland, Riches & Raw.
Kidston Jackson McBain.
Kingston Smith & Co.
P. D. Leake & Co.
Levy, Gee & Co.
Leyland & Co.
D. Lux & Co.
MacIntyre Hudson & Co.
Mallett (E. Churchill) & Co.
Maw Ellis Warne & Co.
Meston & Co.
Moore, Stephens & Co.
Morgan, Brown & Haynes.
Pike, Russell & Co.
Porter, Matthews & Marsden.
Pulleyn, Heselton & Co.
W. M. Rogers & Co.
Safferys.
Sheard, Vickers & Winder.
Shulman & Partners.
Smith & Williamson.
Stanley Holmes & Co.
R. N. Store & Co.
Stubbs, Parkin & South.
Stubbs, Parkin, South & Phillips.
Wm. Syme & Co.
Tansley Witt & Co.
Thomson McLintock & Co.
Turquands Barton Mayhew & Co.
Watts, Knowles & Co.

(**a**) 1958 c.45. (**b**) 1940 c.9. (N.I.).

(*b*) The following Chartered Accountants practising in the United Kingdom, the Channel Islands or the Isle of Man:—

G. H. Barnard (of Fuller, Jenks, Beecroft & Co.).
J. K. H. Cook (of Cook & Co.).
Ancrum F. Evans (of Rutherfords).
Michael W. Forrest (of Michael W. Forrest & Associates).
I. F. D. Hill (of Cook & Co.).
Neville A. Joseph (of Wendover, Buckinghamshire).
Helen M. Lowe (of Edinburgh).
M. C. Webb (of Uxbridge, Middlesex).
N. J. Williams (of Bertram Silcock & Co.).

7. Offices in the Channel Islands of:—
Australia and New Zealand Banking Group (Channel Islands) Ltd.
Bank of Bermuda (Guernsey) Ltd., The.
Bank of Nova Scotia Channel Islands Ltd., The.
Bank of Nova Scotia Trust Company Channel Islands Ltd., The.
Barclaytrust Channel Islands Ltd.
Barclaytrust International Ltd.
Barfield Trust Co. Ltd.
British Law Executor and Trustee Company (Channel Islands) Ltd., The.
British Law Executor and Trustee Company (Guernsey) Ltd., The.
Channel International Bank Ltd.
First National Bank of Chicago (C.I.) Ltd., The.
First National City Bank (Channel Islands) Ltd.
Hume Corporation (Guernsey) Ltd.
Italian International Bank (Channel Islands) Ltd.
Jersey International Bank of Commerce Ltd.
Joseph & Sons (Guernsey) Ltd., Leopold.
L.B.I. Finance (Guernsey) Ltd.
Lloyds Bank Executor & Trustee Company (Channel Islands) Ltd.
Midland Bank Trust Company (Channel Islands) Ltd.
Midland Bank Trust Corporation (Guernsey) Ltd.
Midland Bank Trust Corporation (Jersey) Ltd.
Morgan Grenfell (Guernsey) Ltd.
Morgan Grenfell (Jersey) Ltd.
National and Grindlays Bank (Jersey) Ltd
National Westminster Guernsey Trust Company Ltd.
National Westminster Jersey Trust Company Ltd.
New Guarantee Trust of Jersey Ltd., The.
Ocean Finance and Trust Corporation Ltd.
Orion Bank (Guernsey) Ltd.
Rea Brothers (Guernsey) Ltd.
Royal Bank of Canada (Channel Islands) Ltd., The.
Royal Trust Company of Canada (C.I.) Ltd., The.
Slater, Walker (Guernsey) Ltd.
Slater, Walker (Jersey) Ltd.
Sterling Industrial Securities (Guernsey) Ltd.
Wallace Brothers Sassoon Bank (Jersey) Ltd.
Williams & Glyn's Bank Executor & Trustee Company (Channel Islands) Ltd.
Williams & Glyn's Bank Investments (Jersey) Ltd.
Wobaco Trust (Jersey) Ltd.

8. Offices in the Isle of Man of:—
Barclaytrust Isle of Man Ltd.
International Finance & Trust Corporation Ltd.
Kleinwort, Benson (Isle of Man) Ltd.
Singer & Friedlander (Isle of Man) Ltd.
Slater, Walker (Isle of Man) Ltd.
Williams & Glyn's Bank (I.O.M.) Ltd.

9. Offices in the United Kingdom of:—

Bankers' Automated Clearing Services Ltd.

Grand Metropolitan Pension Trust Ltd.

10. The Senior Investment Manager of the Post Office Staff Superannuation Fund.

11. The Head Office of United Dominions Trust Ltd.

SCHEDULE 4

ORDERS REVOKED

The Exchange Control (Authorised Dealers and Depositaries) Order 1973	S.I. 1973/42 (1973 I, p. 351).
The Exchange Control (Authorised Dealers and Depositaries) (Amendment) Order 1973	S.I. 1973/451 (1973 I, p. 1544).
The Exchange Control (Authorised Dealers and Depositaries) (Amendment) (No. 2) Order 1973	S.I. 1973/615 (1973 I, p. 1948).
The Exchange Control (Authorised Dealers and Depositaries) (Amendment) (No. 3) Order 1973	S.I. 1973/775 (1973 I, p. 2454).
The Exchange Control (Authorised Dealers and Depositaries) (Amendment) (No. 4) Order 1973	S.I. 1973/1154 (1973 II, p. 3509).
The Exchange Control (Authorised Dealers and Depositaries) (Amendment) (No. 5) Order 1973	S.I. 1973/1623 (1973 III, p. 5067).

EXPLANATORY NOTE

(This Note is not part of the Order.)

This Order, which supersedes (with amendments) the Exchange Control (Authorised Dealers and Depositaries) Order 1973, as amended, lists:—

(*a*) the banks and other persons authorised under the Exchange Control Act 1947 to deal in gold and foreign currencies; and

(*b*) those who are entitled to act as authorised depositaries for the purpose of the deposit of securities as required by that Act.

The main change relates to the banks which were listed in Schedule 2 to that Order, under which any office opened by any of those banks in the Channel Islands or the Isle of Man automatically became an authorised dealer in gold and foreign currency and an authorised depositary. Now any office opened in the Channel Islands or the Isle of Man by the banks listed in paragraph 2 of Schedule 2 to the new Order becomes an authorised depositary, but it does not become an authorised dealer in gold or foreign currency.

1973 No. 1950

SOCIAL SECURITY

The National Insurance (Industrial Injuries) (Prescribed Diseases) Amendment Regulations 1973

Made - - - -	21*st November* 1973
Laid before Parliament	29*th November* 1973
Coming into Operation	24*th December* 1973

The Secretary of State for Social Services**(a)**, in exercise of powers conferred by sections 56 and 85 of the National Insurance (Industrial Injuries) Act 1965**(b)** and section 57 of that Act as modified by section 8 of the National Insurance Act 1966**(c)**, and section 5 of the National Insurance Act 1972**(d)**, and of all other powers enabling him in that behalf, after reference to the Industrial Injuries Advisory Council, hereby makes the following regulations:—

Citation, interpretation and commencement

1. These regulations, which may be cited as the National Insurance (Industrial Injuries) (Prescribed Diseases) Amendment Regulations 1973 shall be read as one with the National Insurance (Industrial Injuries) (Prescribed Diseases) Regulations 1959**(e)** as amended**(f)** (hereinafter referred to as "the principal regulations"), and shall come into operation on 24th December 1973.

Amendment of Part I of Schedule 1 *to the principal regulations*

2. Part I of Schedule 1 to the principal regulations shall be amended by the addition at the end of the first column of paragraph 39 of the words "or of the epithelial lining of the urethra" and the said paragraph shall accordingly have effect as set out in the Schedule to these regulations.

Transitional provisions

3.—(1) Where a person, who has been employed on or at any time after 5th July 1948 in insurable employment in any occupation referred to in the second column of paragraph 39 of Part I of Schedule 1 to the principal regulations is, as a result of primary neoplasm of the epithelial lining of the urethra, either incapable of work or suffering from a loss of faculty on the date on which these regulations come into operation, and the disease is due to the nature of the employment, the provisions of regulation 6 of the principal regulations (which relates to the date of development) shall be applied subject to the modification that the date on which these regulations come into operation shall be treated as the first day on which he was incapable of work or, as the case may be, as the day on which he first suffered from the relevant loss of faculty, and the date of development shall be determined accordingly.

(a) For transfer of functions from the Minister of Pensions and National Insurance to (eventually) the Secretary of State, *see* Ministry of Social Security Act 1966 (c. 20) and S.I. 1968/1699 (1968 III, p. 4585).
(b) 1965 c. 52.
(c) 1966 c. 6.
(d) 1972 c. 57.
(e) S.I. 1959/467 (1959 II, p. 1943).
(f) The relevant amending instruments are S.I. 1965/1264, 1966/987, 1969/619, 1972/910, 1258, 1511 (1965 II, p. 3596; 1966 II, p. 2366; 1969 I, p. 1727; 1972 II, pp. 2862, 3768; III, p. 4455).

(2) Where a person to whom the last foregoing paragraph applies is awarded disablement benefit in respect of primary neoplasm of the epithelial lining of the urethra and claims an increase of that benefit under section 14 of the National Insurance (Industrial Injuries) Act 1965 (which section relates to increases of disablement pensions in cases of special hardship), then, if at any time after having been employed as aforesaid, but before the date on which these regulations come into operation, that person has abandoned any occupation as a result of the disease, the fact that he has abandoned that occupation shall be disregarded in determining his regular occupation for the purposes of the said section 14.

Signed by authority of the Secretary of State for Social Services.

Paul Dean,
Parliamentary Under Secretary of State,
Department of Health and Social Security.

21st November 1973.

Regulation 2

SCHEDULE

Containing paragraph 39 of Schedule 1 of the Principal Regulations as amended by these Regulations.*

Description of disease or injury	Nature of occupation
39. Primary neoplasm of the epithelial lining of the urinary bladder (Papilloma of the bladder), or of the epithelial lining of the renal pelvis or of the epithelial lining of the ureter *or of the epithelial lining of the urethra.*	(*a*) Work in a building in which any of the following substances is produced for commercial purposes:— (i) alpha-naphthylamine or beta-naphthylamine; (ii) diphenyl substituted by at least one nitro or primary amino group or by at least one nitro and primary amino group; (iii) any of the substances mentioned in sub-paragraph (ii) above if further ring substituted by halogeno, methyl or methoxy groups, but not by other groups; (iv) the salts of any of the substances mentioned in sub-paragraphs (i) to (iii) above; (v) auramine or magenta; Any occupation involving: (*b*) the use or handling of any of the substances mentioned in sub-paragraphs (i) to (iv) of paragraph (*a*), or work in a process in which any such substance is used or handled or is liberated; (*c*) the maintenance or cleaning of any plant or machinery used in any such process as is mentioned in paragraph (*b*), or the cleaning of clothing used in any such building as is mentioned in paragraph (*a*) if such clothing is cleaned within the works of which the building forms a part or in a laundry maintained and used solely in connection with such works.

*The words added by these Regulations are shown in italics.

EXPLANATORY NOTE

(*This Note is not part of the Regulations.*)

These Regulations, by making an addition to the diseases prescribed in Part I of Schedule 1 to the National Insurance (Industrial Injuries) (Prescribed Diseases) Regulations 1959, extend insurance under the National Insurance (Industrial Injuries) Act 1965 to primary neoplasm of the epithelial lining of the urethra in the case of persons insurably employed in occupations involving the production of certain chemicals.

The Regulations also contain transitional provisions relating to persons covered by the amendment who are already suffering from the disease on the day on which the Regulations come into operation.

1973 No. 1951

LOCAL GOVERNMENT, ENGLAND AND WALES

The Fire Services (Retirement of Senior Officers) Regulations 1973

Made - - -	19*th November* 1973
Laid before Parliament	28*th November* 1973
Coming into Operation	24*th December* 1973

In exercise of the powers conferred on me by section 260 of the Local Government Act 1972(**a**), I hereby make the following Regulations:—

Citation and operation

1. These Regulations may be cited as the Fire Services (Retirement of Senior Officers) Regulations 1973 and shall come into operation on 24th December 1973.

Interpretation

2.—(1) In these Regulations the following expressions have the meanings hereby respectively assigned to them, that is to say:—

"the Act" means the Local Government Act 1972;

"the Pension Scheme" means the Firemen's Pension Scheme 1973 set out in Appendix 2 to the Firemen's Pension Scheme Order 1973(**b**);

"a senior officer to whom these Regulations apply" means a chief officer or deputy chief officer of, or an assistant chief officer in, a fire brigade in England and Wales who retires from service as such on or before 1st April 1974 and to whom section 260 of the Act applies by virtue of Regulation 3.

(2) Part I of the Pension Scheme shall apply for the interpretation of these Regulations as it applies for the interpretation of the Pension Scheme.

Application of section 260 *of the Act*

3.—(1) For the purposes of subsection (1) of section 260 of the Act (which provides that a person who holds a prescribed employment, attains or has attained the age of 50 years on or before 31st March 1974 and fulfills prescribed conditions may by notice given before the prescribed date and in the prescribed manner elect that section 260 shall, and section 259 of the Act

(**a**) 1972 c. 70.　　(**b**) S.I. 1973/966 (1973 II, p. 2906).

shall not, apply to him) employment as a member of a fire brigade shall be a prescribed employment and in relation to a person in such employment the prescribed conditions shall be that—

(*a*) he is, on 1st January 1974—

(i) the chief officer or deputy chief officer of a fire brigade in England or Wales, or

(ii) an assistant chief officer in such a fire brigade whose annual pensionable pay on the date on which he gives notice under section 260(1) of the Act is not less than two thirds of that of the chief officer of that brigade calculated, however, where either officer is on an incremental scale of pay, by reference to the minimum of his scale;

(*b*) where he retires before 1st April 1974, he does so with the agreement of the fire authority and, before the date of his retirement, has or will have attained the age of 50 years;

(*c*) he does not, before the date of his retirement, accept an offer of appointment as chief officer or deputy chief officer of, or as an assistant chief officer in, another fire brigade in England or Wales or as firemaster or deputy firemaster of, or as an assistant firemaster in, a fire brigade in Scotland;

(*d*) he will not have attained the age of 60 years on or before 31st March 1974, and

(*e*) where on retirement he is entitled to an award under Article 16 of the Pension Scheme (deferred pension and award where no other award payable), under paragraph (2) thereof he relinquishes his entitlement to a deferred pension or, as the case may be, he repays to the fire authority any award paid to him under paragraph (4) thereof,

and the notice given by such a person under section 260(1) of the Act shall be given in writing to the fire authority before 28th February 1974.

(2) For the purposes of subsection (2) of the said section 260 (which provides that, unless notice of objection has been given in accordance therewith, where a person has elected under subsection (1) section 260 shall, and section 259 of the Act shall not, apply to him on his retirement within the prescribed period and before attaining the normal retiring age) the prescribed period shall be the period ending on 1st April 1974.

Benefits payable

4.—(1) Subject to the provisions of these Regulations, there shall be payable to or in respect of a senior officer to whom these Regulations apply benefits by way of pension or allowance corresponding in all respects to the pensions or allowances which, subject to paragraph (3), would be payable to or in respect of him under the Pension Scheme were that Scheme subject to the modifications set out in the Schedule to these Regulations.

(2) Where a benefit hereunder by way of pension or allowance is payable to or in respect of a senior officer to whom these Regulations apply and a pension or allowance under the Pension Scheme is also so payable to the same beneficiary, the amount of the pension or allowance hereunder shall be reduced by, subject to paragraph (3), the amount of that under the Pension Scheme.

(3) For the purposes of this Regulation, in determining the pension or allowance which would be, or is, payable under the Pension Scheme, the following provisions thereof shall be disregarded, namely—

(*a*) Article 21 (commutation);

(*b*) Article 26 (gratuity in lieu of widow's pension);

(*c*) Article 37 (gratuity in lieu of child's allowance), and

(*d*) Article 41 (allocation).

Application of Pension Scheme

5.—(1) Subject to any necessary adaptations and subject to the modifications set out in the Schedule to these Regulations, the provisions of the Pension Scheme (including, subject to paragraph (2), those mentioned in Regulation 4(3)) shall apply in relation to a benefit payable under these Regulations as though they were set out in these Regulations.

(2) Separate notice of commutation or of allocation shall be given under Article 21 or 41 of the Pension Scheme for the purposes of that Scheme and of these Regulations and, where such a notice has been given for the purposes hereof—

(*a*) the said Article 21 or 41 shall have effect in relation to the benefit by way of pension under these Regulations as reduced in accordance with Regulation 4(2); and

(*b*) the lump sum or pension provided for in the said Article 21 or 41 shall, subject to the provisions of these Regulations, be payable as benefit thereunder but nothing in Regulation 4(2) shall apply in relation thereto.

Robert Carr,
One of Her Majesty's Principal
Secretaries of State.

Home Office,
Whitehall.

19th November 1973.

SCHEDULE

MODIFICATION OF PENSION SCHEME IN ITS APPLICATION FOR THE PURPOSES OF THESE REGULATIONS

1. Article 12(2) of the Pension Scheme shall be omitted.

2. There shall be reckonable as pensionable service the period of pensionable service reckonable by the senior officer concerned under Part V of the Pension Scheme together with the period beginning with the date of his retirement and ending with the date on which he would, if he had continued to serve, have become entitled to reckon 30 years' pensionable service or have attained the age of 60 years, whichever is the earlier, except that the total period so reckonable shall not exceed twice the period first mentioned in this paragraph.

3. For the purpose of calculating an award to or in respect of a senior officer to whom these Regulations apply, he shall be deemed to have served as a regular fireman for the period mentioned in the preceding paragraph and to have paid pension contributions accordingly and the additional pensionable service reckonable thereunder shall be deemed to be reckonable by virtue of that service.

EXPLANATORY NOTE

(This Note is not part of the Regulations.)

Regulation 3 (read with section 260(1) and (2) of the Local Government Act 1972) provides that a chief officer or deputy chief officer of, or an assistant chief officer in, a fire brigade in England or Wales who will be aged 50 years or over on 31st March 1974 and fulfills the conditions set out in paragraph (1) of the Regulation may, by written notice given to the fire authority before 28th February 1974, elect that section 260 (provision for early retirement) shall, and section 259 (compensation for loss of office) shall not, apply to him; subject, however, to the right of the fire authority to object within a month of their being given the notice.

Where, by virtue of such an election, section 260 applies to such a senior officer, Regulations 4 and 5 provide for the payment to or in respect of him of benefits by way of pension or allowance corresponding, as near as may be, to those which would have so been payable under the Firemen's Pension Scheme 1973 had his pensionable service been that provided for in paragraph 2 of the Schedule (in the case of most senior officers, 30 years' pensionable service). Provision to prevent overlapping benefits is made by paragraph (2) of Regulation 4.

1973 No. 1952

TRADE DESCRIPTIONS

Crystal Glass (Descriptions) Regulations 1973

Made - - - -	20*th November* 1973
Laid before Parliament	28*th November* 1973
Coming into Operation	19*th December* 1973

The Secretary of State, in exercise of powers conferred on him by section 2 of the European Communities Act 1972**(a)** and the European Communities (Designation) Order 1972**(b)**, hereby makes the following Regulations:—

1. These Regulations may be cited as the Crystal Glass (Descriptions) Regulations 1973, and shall come into operation on 19th December 1973.

2.–(1)In these Regulations "the Act of 1968" means the Trade Descriptions Act 1968**(c)**;

"glass" means glassware falling within tariff heading No. 70.13 of the Customs Tariff 1959**(d)**;

"British Standard 3828" means the British Standard of that number published by the British Standards Institution on 28th February 1973 as amended by Amendment Slip No. 1 so published on 29th June 1973.

(2) For the purposes of these Regulations a person exposing glass for supply or having glass in his possession for supply shall be deemed to offer to supply that glass.

(3) The Interpretation Act 1889**(e)**, shall apply to the interpretation of these Regulations as it applies to the interpretation of an Act of Parliament.

3. Any person who, in the course of a trade or business, supplies or offers to supply in the United Kingdom glass to which there is applied a description, symbol, trade mark, name or other inscription in contravention of any provision of these Regulations shall be guilty of an offence.

4.–(1) A description specified in the Schedule hereto shall not be applied to glass unless the glass is of the chemical composition and has the physical properties mentioned in relation to that description in columns (*d*) to (*g*) of Annex I of British Standard 3828 being composition and properties determined in accordance with the appropriate methods set out in Annex II of that Standard.

(a) 1972 c. 68.
(b) S.I. 1972 /1811 (1972 III, p. 5216).
(c) 1968 c. 29.
(d) *See* S.I. 1971/1971 (1971 III, p. 5330).
(e) 1889 c. 63.

(2) Where a description specified in paragraph 3 or 4 of the Schedule hereto other than "crystal glass" and "crystallin" is applied to glass there shall also be applied thereto the description "crystal glass" or "crystallin":

Provided that this paragraph shall not apply in relation to glass intended for supply in another Member State of the European Economic Community if the description is in the language of that Member State.

5.—(1) A symbol described in columns (*h*) and (*i*) of Annex I of the said Standard in relation to descriptions of glass shall not be applied to glass unless any of those descriptions is also lawfully applied thereto.

(2) A single label may bear both the description and the symbol.

6. A trade mark, the name of an undertaking or any other inscription containing as a main part, as an adjective or as a root one of the descriptions specified in the Schedule hereto or a description likely to be confused therewith, shall not be applied to glass unless the trade mark, name or other inscription is, in very prominent lettering, immediately preceded—

(*a*) if the glass is glass to which a description specified in the Schedule hereto may lawfully be applied, by any such description;

(*b*) in any other case, by a statement of the exact nature of the glass.

7. Nothing in these Regulations shall apply in relation to glass which is intended for export from the United Kingdom to a country other than a Member State of the European Economic Community.

8.—(1) Sections 4 and 5 of the Act of 1968 shall apply for the purposes of determining whether a description, symbol, trade mark, name or other inscription referred to in these Regulations is applied to glass as those sections apply for the purpose of determining whether a trade description is applied to goods for the purposes of the Act of 1968.

(2) The following provisions of the Act of 1968 shall (with necessary modifications) apply in relation to an offence under these Regulations as they apply in relation to an offence under that Act (modified where appropriate in relation to Northern Ireland by section 40(1) of that Act), that is to say, sections 18, 19, 20, 23, 24 and 25.

(3) The following provisions of the Act of 1968 shall (with necessary modifications) apply in relation to the enforcement of these Regulations as they apply in relation to the enforcement of that Act (modified where appropriate in relation to Northern Ireland as aforesaid), that is to say, sections 26, 27, 28, 29 and 30(1).

(4) Section 33 (modified in relation to Northern Ireland as aforesaid) of the Act of 1968 shall apply in relation to compensation for goods seized and detained under these Regulations as it applies in relation to compensation for goods seized and detained under that Act.

Anthony Grant,
Parliamentary Under Secretary of State
for Industrial Development,
Department of Trade and Industry.

20th November 1973.

SCHEDULE

Descriptions of Glass

1. Cristal superieur 30%
Cristallo superiore 30%
Hochbleikristall 30%
Volloodkristal 30%
Full lead crystal 30%
Krystal 30%

2. Cristal au plomb 24%
Cristallo al piombo 24%
Bleikristall 24%
Loodkristal 24%
Lead crystal 24%
Krystal 24%

3. Cristallin
Vetro sonoro superiore
Kristallglas
Kristallynglas
Sonoorglas
Crystal glass, crystallin
Krystallin

4. Verre sonore
Vetro sonoro
Kristallglas
Sonoorglas
Crystal glass, crystallin
Krystallin

5. The percentage figures in paragraphs 1 and 2 above refer to the lead oxide content of the glass.

EXPLANATORY NOTE

(*This Note is not part of the Regulations.*)

These Regulations implement Council Directive No. 69/493/EEC (O.J. No.L.326, 29.12.1969, p.36) (O.J./S.E.1969 (II), p. 599) relating to crystal glass.

They prohibit the supply of certain glassware to which is applied any of the descriptions specified in the Schedule to the Regulations unless the glass is of the chemical composition and has the physical properties mentioned in relation to that description in British Standard 3828 published on 28th February 1973, as amended by Amendment Slip No. 1 published on 29th June 1973. Copies of the British Standard and Amendment referred to may be obtained from British Standards Institution, British Standards House, 2 Park Street, London W1A 2BS.

STATUTORY INSTRUMENTS

1973 No. 1954

PENSIONS

The Pensions Increase (Compensation to Clerks to General Commissioners) Regulations 1973

Made - - -	*20th November* 1973
Laid before Parliament	*29th November* 1973
Coming into Operation	*21st December* 1973

The Minister for the Civil Service, in exercise of the powers conferred on him by section 5(2) and (4) of the Pensions (Increase) Act 1971(**a**) and of all other powers enabling him in that behalf, hereby makes the following Regulations:—

1. These Regulations may be cited as the Pensions Increase (Compensation to Clerks to General Commissioners) Regulations 1973, and shall come into operation on 21st December 1973.

2. The Interpretation Act 1889(**b**) shall apply for the interpretation of these Regulations as it applies for the interpretation of an Act of Parliament.

3. The Pensions (Increase) Act 1971 shall have effect in relation to a pension payable under Part IV of the Clerks to General Commissioners (Compensation) Regulations 1973(**c**) as if it were specified in Part I of Schedule 2 to that Act.

4. Any increase of pension payable by virtue of these Regulations shall take effect in respect of any period beginning on or after 1st September 1971.

Given under the official seal of the Minister for the Civil Service on 20th November 1973.

(L.S.)

Kenneth Baker,
Parliamentary Secretary to the Civil Service Department.

(**a**) 1971 c. 56. (**b**) 1889 c. 63.
(**c**) S.I. 1973/900 (1973 II, p. 2766).

EXPLANATORY NOTE

(This Note is not part of the Regulations.)

These Regulations provide for the payment of increases under the Pensions (Increase) Act 1971 on long-term compensation payable under Part IV of the Clerks to General Commissioners (Compensation) Regulations 1973 to or in respect of part-time Clerks to General Commissioners who suffer loss of employment or loss or diminution of emoluments in consequence of adjustments of the divisions for which the General Commissioners act.

The Regulations have retrospective effect from 1st September 1971 by virtue of section 5(4) of the Act.

1973 No. 1955

WAGES COUNCILS

The Wages Regulation (Retail Drapery, Outfitting and Footwear) Order 1973

Made - - - *20th November* 1973

Coming into Operation *4th February* 1974

Whereas the Secretary of State has received from the Retail Drapery, Outfitting and Footwear Trades Wages Council (Great Britain) the wages regulation proposals set out in the Schedule hereto ;

Now, therefore, the Secretary of State in exercise of powers conferred by section 11 of the Wages Councils Act 1959(**a**), as modified by Article 2 of the Counter-Inflation (Modification of Wages Councils Act 1959) Order 1973(**b**), and now vested in him (**c**), and of all other powers enabling him in that behalf, hereby makes the following Order:—

1. This Order may be cited as the Wages Regulation (Retail Drapery, Outfitting and Footwear) Order 1973.

2.—(1) In this Order the expression "the specified date" means the 4th February 1974, provided that where, as respects any worker who is paid wages at intervals not exceeding seven days, that date does not correspond with the beginning of the period for which the wages are paid, the expression "the specified date" means, as respects that worker, the beginning of the next such period following that date.

(2) The Interpretation Act 1889(**d**) shall apply to the interpretation of this Order, as it applies to the interpretation of an Act of Parliament and as if this Order and the Order hereby revoked were Acts of Parliament.

3. The wages regulation proposals set out in the Schedule hereto shall have effect as from the specified date and as from that date the Wages Regulation (Retail Drapery, Outfitting and Footwear) (No. 2) Order 1972(**e**) shall cease to have effect.

Signed by order of the Secretary of State.

20th November 1973.

W. H. Marsh,
Assistant Secretary,
Department of Employment.

(**a**) 1959 c. 69. (**b**) S.I. 1973/661 (1973 I, p. 2141).
(**c**) S.I. 1959/1769, 1968/729 (1959 I, p. 1795; 1968 II, p. 2108).
(**d**) 1889 c. 63. (**e**) S.I. 1972/1297 (1972 II, p. 3887).

ARRANGEMENT OF SCHEDULE

PART I

STATUTORY MINIMUM REMUNERATION

PART II

ANNUAL HOLIDAY AND HOLIDAY REMUNERATION

PART III

GENERAL

Article 3

SCHEDULE

The following minimum remuneration and provisions as to holidays and holiday remuneration shall be substituted for the statutory minimum remuneration and the provisions as to holidays and holiday remuneration fixed by the Wages Regulation (Retail Drapery, Outfitting and Footwear) (No. 2) Order 1972 (Order R.D.O. (62)).

Part I

STATUTORY MINIMUM REMUNERATION

APPLICATION

1. Subject to the provisions of paragraphs 2, 6 and 9, the minimum remuneration payable to workers to whom this Schedule applies shall be the remuneration set out in paragraphs 3, 4 and 5.

Any increase in remuneration payable under the provisions of paragraph 3, 4 or 5 shall become effective on the first day of the first full pay week following the date upon which the increase would otherwise become payable under those provisions.

HOURS ON WHICH REMUNERATION IS BASED

2.—(1) The minimum remuneration specified in paragraphs 3, 4 and 5 relates to a week of 40 hours exclusive of overtime and, except in the case of guaranteed weekly remuneration under paragraph 9, is subject to a proportionate reduction according as the number of hours worked is less than 40.

(2) In calculating the remuneration for the purpose of this Schedule recognised breaks for meal times shall, subject to the provisions of paragraph 7, be excluded.

WORKERS OTHER THAN TEMPORARY SHOP MANAGERS, TEMPORARY SHOP MANAGERESSES AND TRANSPORT WORKERS

3.—(1) Subject to the provisions of paragraph 1, the minimum remuneration payable to male or female workers of the classes specified in column 1 of the following table employed in the London Area, Provincial A Area or Provincial B Area, as the case may be, shall be the appropriate amount set out in Column 2.

Column 1	Column 2					
	LONDON AREA		PROVINCIAL A AREA		PROVINCIAL B AREA	
	Per week		Per week		Per week	
	Male	Female	Male	Female	Male	Female
	£	£	£	£	£	£
(*a*) SHOP MANAGERS and SHOP MANAGERESSES where the number of staff (computed in accordance with the provisions of sub-paragraph (2) of this paragraph) is:—						
1 or 2 ...	*19·80*	*19·05*	*19·50*	*18·75*	*18·95*	*18·25*
3 ...	*20·10*	*19·35*	*19·80*	*19·05*	*19·25*	*18·55*
4 ...	*20·45*	*19·70*	*20·15*	*19·40*	*19·60*	*18·90*
5 ...	*20·75*	*20·00*	*20·45*	*19·70*	*19·90*	*19·20*
6 ...	*21·10*	*20·35*	*20·80*	*20·05*	*20·25*	*19·55*
(*b*) CLERKS GRADE I, aged 22 years or over ...	*18·50*	*17·05*	*18·10*	*16·75*	*17·45*	*16·15*
(*c*) CLERKS GRADE I, aged under 22 years, CLERKS GRADE II, SALES ASSISTANTS, CASHIERS, CENTRAL WAREHOUSE WORKERS, CREDIT TRAVELLERS, STOCK HANDS—						
Aged 21 years or over ...	*18·20*	*16·80*	*17·80*	*16·45*	*17·15*	*15·90*
,, 20 and under 21 years ...	*14·70*	*13·75*	*14·40*	*13·45*	*13·80*	*13·05*
,, 19 ,, ,, 20 ,, ...	*13·70*	*13·00*	*13·45*	*12·70*	*12·85*	*12·30*
,, 18 ,, ,, 19 ,, ...	*13·05*	*12·50*	*12·80*	*12·25*	*12·25*	*11·85*
,, 17 ,, ,, 18 ,, ...	*10·90*	*10·65*	*10·65*	*10·40*	*10·25*	*10·05*
,, 16 ,, ,, 17 ,, ...	*10·45*	*10·30*	*10·20*	*10·05*	*9·85*	*9·70*
,, under 16 years ...	*10·15*	*10·05*	*9·90*	*9·75*	*9·50*	*9·40*
(*d*) ALL OTHER WORKERS (OTHER THAN THE WORKERS SPECIFIED IN PARAGRAPH 4 AND PARAGRAPH 5)—						
Aged 21 years or over ...	*17·80*	*16·50*	*17·40*	*16·15*	*16·90*	*15·65*
,, 20 and under 21 years ...	*14·55*	*13·60*	*14·25*	*13·30*	*13·70*	*12·85*
,, 19 ,, ,, 20 ,, ...	*13·65*	*12·95*	*13·40*	*12·65*	*12·80*	*12·25*
,, 18 ,, ,, 19 ,, ...	*13·00*	*12·45*	*12·75*	*12·20*	*12·20*	*11·80*
,, 17 ,, ,, 18 ,, ...	*10·85*	*10·60*	*10·60*	*10·35*	*10·20*	*10·00*
,, 16 ,, ,, 17 ,, ...	*10·40*	*10·25*	*10·15*	*10·00*	*9·80*	*9·65*
,, under 16 years ...	*10·10*	*10·00*	*9·85*	*9·70*	*9·45*	*9·35*

Provided that where a sales assistant enters, or has entered, the retail drapery, outfitting and footwear trades for the first time at or over the age of 20 years, the minimum remuneration payable shall be—

(i) during the first three months of the employment, £0·50 per week less, and

(ii) during the second three months of the employment, £0·25 per week less than the minimum remuneration otherwise applicable to the worker under (*c*) of this sub-paragraph.

(2) In the foregoing table, "number of staff" means the number of persons (including the manager or manageress) normally employed by the employer, for whose control the manager or manageress is responsible to the employer, and in computing that number both full-time workers and workers other than full-time workers shall be included, except that in the case of workers other than full-time workers the number to be counted shall be the number of such workers or the number (treating any fraction as one) obtained by dividing by 30 the aggregate of the hours normally worked in the week by all such workers whichever is the less.

TEMPORARY SHOP MANAGERS AND TEMPORARY SHOP MANAGERESSES

4.—(1) Subject to the provisions of this paragraph, the minimum remuneration payable to temporary shop managers and temporary shop manageresses, for each continuous period of employment as temporary shop manager or temporary shop manageress (reckoned in accordance with the provisions of sub-paragraph (2) of this paragraph) shall be the appropriate minimum remuneration for a shop manager or shop manageress, as the case may be, under the provisions of paragraph 3(1)(*a*).

(2) In reckoning any continuous period of employment as temporary shop manager or temporary shop manageress for the purposes of sub-paragraph (1) of this paragraph, no account shall be taken of any period of employment—

(*a*) not exceeding two consecutive working days ; or

(*b*) not exceeding a total of two weeks in any year, being a period when the shop manager or shop manageress is absent on holiday:

Provided that for the purposes of this paragraph where in any year a worker is employed by the same employer as a temporary shop manager or temporary shop manageress at more than one shop during the absence on holiday of the shop manager or shop manageress, the first period of such employment and any subsequent periods of such employment in the same year shall be treated as a continuous period of employment.

(3) The minimum remuneration payable to temporary shop managers and temporary shop manageresses for any period of employment mentioned in (*a*) or (*b*) of sub-paragraph (2) of this paragraph, shall be not less than the appropriate minimum remuneration for a sales assistant under the provisions of this Schedule.

(4) For the purposes of this paragraph "year" means the 12 months commencing with 1st January and ending with 31st December.

TRANSPORT WORKERS

5. Subject to the provisions of paragraph 1, the minimum remuneration payable to Transport Workers employed in the London Area, Provincial A Area or Provincial B Area, as the case may be, shall be the appropriate amount set out in Column 3 of the following table:—

Column 1	Column 2		Column 3		
Age of transport worker	Type of Vehicle: Mechanically propelled vehicle with carrying capacity of	Type of Vehicle: Horse-drawn vehicle	LONDON AREA	PROVINCIAL A AREA	PROVINCIAL B AREA
			Per week	Per week	Per week
			£	£	£
21 years or over	1 ton or less	one-horse	*18·20*	*17·80*	*17·10*
20 and under 21 years	1 ton or less	one-horse	*14·65*	*14·55*	*13·95*
19 " " 20 "	1 ton or less	one-horse	*14·15*	*14·05*	*13·45*
18 " " 19 "	1 ton or less	one-horse	*13·50*	*13·40*	*12·90*
under 18 years	1 ton or less	one-horse	*11·40*	*11·30*	*10·90*
All ages	Over 1 ton and up to 2 tons	two-horse	*18·40*	*18·00*	*17·30*
All ages	Over 2 tons and up to 5 tons	—	*18·60*	*18·20*	*17·50*
All ages	Over 5 tons	—	*18·80*	*18·40*	*17·70*

MINIMUM OVERTIME RATES

6.—(1) Subject to the provisions of this paragraph, overtime shall be payable to all workers at the following minimum rates:—

(*a*) For work on a Sunday or customary holiday,

(i) where time worked does not exceed 4½ hours—double time for 4½ hours

(ii) where time worked exceeds 4½ hours but does not exceed 8 hours—double time for 8 hours

(iii) where time worked exceeds 8 hours—double time for all time worked

Provided that—

(i) Where a worker performs work on a customary holiday which is a day fixed by the employer, being a day on which the worker would normally work, during the period commencing on the last day on which the worker would normally work before Christmas Day and ending in England and Wales on the next following 2nd January, and in Scotland on the next following 3rd January, overtime rates in accordance with the provisions of this sub-paragraph shall be payable to that worker only if—

(*a*) he is a worker who normally works for the employer for more than 9 hours in a week ; and

(*b*) he has been in the employment of the employer throughout the period of 8 weeks immediately preceding the week in which Christmas Day falls.

(ii) Where it is or becomes the practice in a Jewish undertaking for the employer to require attendance on Sunday instead of Saturday, the provisions of this paragraph shall apply as if in such provisions the word "Saturday" were substituted for "Sunday", except where such substitution is unlawful.

(*b*) On the weekly short day in any week during which, under sub-section (3) of section 40 of the Shops Act 1950(**a**), the employer is relieved of his obligation to allow the worker a weekly half day,

for any time worked after 1.30 p.m. .. .. .. double time

(*c*) On the weekly short day (not being a weekly short day to which (*b*) of this sub-paragraph applies),

for any time worked after 1.30 p.m. .. .. .. time-and-a-half

(*d*) In any week, exclusive of any time in respect of which a minimum overtime rate is payable under the foregoing provisions of this paragraph,

for all time worked in excess of 40 hours .. .. time-and-a-half

Provided that in any week which includes one customary holiday "33 hours" shall be substituted for "40 hours", in any week which includes two customary holidays "26 hours" shall be substituted for "40 hours" and in any week which includes three customary holidays "19 hours" shall be substituted for the said "40 hours".

(2) Overtime rates in accordance with provisions (*a*), (*c*) and (*d*) of sub-paragraph (1) of this paragraph shall be payable to a shop manager, temporary shop manager, shop manageress or temporary shop manageress only if the overtime worked is specifically authorised in writing by the employer or his representative.

(**a**) 1950 c. 28.

WAITING TIME

7. A worker is entitled to payment of the minimum remuneration specified in this Schedule for all the time during which he is present on the premises of the employer, unless he is present thereon in any of the following circumstances, that is to say—

(1) without the employer's consent, express or implied ;

(2) for some purpose unconnected with his work, and other than that of waiting for work to be given to him to perform ;

(3) by reason only of the fact that he is resident thereon ; or

(4) during normal meal times and he is not waiting for work to be given to him to perform.

WORKERS WHO ARE NOT REQUIRED TO WORK ON A CUSTOMARY HOLIDAY

8.—(1) Subject to the provisions of sub-paragraph (2) and sub-paragraph (3) of this paragraph, a worker who is not required to work on a customary holiday shall be paid for that holiday not less than the amount to which he would have been entitled under the foregoing provisions of this Schedule had the day not been a customary holiday and had he worked the number of hours ordinarily worked by him on that day of the week.

(2) A worker shall not be entitled to any payment under this paragraph unless he—

(*a*) worked for the employer throughout the last working day on which work was available for him preceding the holiday ; and

(*b*) presents himself for employment at the usual starting time on the first working day after the holiday:

Provided that (*a*) or (*b*), as the case may be, of this sub-paragraph shall be deemed to be complied with where the worker is excused by his employer or is prevented by his proved illness or injury from working or presenting himself for employment as aforesaid.

(3) A worker shall not be entitled to any payment under this paragraph in respect of a customary holiday which is a day fixed by the employer, being a day on which the worker would normally work, during the period commencing on the last day on which the worker would normally work before Christmas Day and ending in England and Wales on the next following 2nd January and in Scotland on the next following 3rd January unless—

(*a*) he is a worker who normally works for the employer for more than 9 hours in a week ; and

(*b*) he has been in the employment of the employer throughout the period of 8 weeks immediately preceding the week in which Christmas Day falls.

GUARANTEED WEEKLY REMUNERATION PAYABLE TO A FULL-TIME WORKER

9.—(1) Notwithstanding the other provisions of this Schedule, where in any week the total remuneration (including holiday remuneration but excluding the amount specified in sub-paragraph (2) of this paragraph) payable under those other provisions to a full-time worker is less than the guaranteed weekly remuneration provided under this paragraph, the minimum remuneration payable to that worker for that week shall be that guaranteed weekly remuneration with the addition of any amount excluded as aforesaid.

(2) The amount to be excluded from the total remuneration referred to in the forgoing sub-paragraph is the whole of the remuneration payable in respect of overtime.

(3) The guaranteed weekly remuneration is the remuneration to which the worker would be entitled under paragraph 3, 4 or 5 for 40 hours work in his normal occupation:

Provided that—

(*a*) where the worker normally works for the employer on work to which this Schedule applies for less than 40 hours in the week by reason only of the fact that he does not hold himself out as normally available for work for more than the number of hours he normally works in the week, and the worker has informed his employer in writing that he does not so hold himself out, the guaranteed weekly remuneration shall be the remuneration to which the worker would be entitled (calculated as in paragraph 2) for the number of hours in the week normally worked by the worker for the employer on work to which this Schedule applies;

(*b*) where in any week a worker at his request and with the written consent of his employer is absent from work during any part of his normal working hours on any day (other than a holiday allowed under Part II or a customary holiday or a holiday allowed to all persons employed in the undertaking or branch of an undertaking in which the worker is employed), the guaranteed weekly remuneration payable in respect of that week shall be reduced in respect of each day on which he is absent as aforesaid by one-sixth where the worker's normal working week is six days or by one-fifth where his normal working week is five days.

(4) Guaranteed weekly remuneration is not payable in respect of any week unless the worker throughout his normal working hours in that week (excluding any time allowed to him as a holiday or during which he is absent from work in accordance with proviso (*b*) to sub-paragraph (3) of this paragraph) is

(*a*) capable of and available for work; and

(*b*) willing to perform such duties outside his normal occupation as the employer may reasonably require if his normal work is not available in the establishment in which he is employed.

(5) Guaranteed weekly remuneration is not payable in respect of any week if the worker's employment is terminated before the end of that week.

(6) If the employer is unable to provide the worker with work by reason of a strike or other circumstances beyond his control and gives the worker four clear days' notice to that effect, guaranteed weekly remuneration shall not be payable after the expiry of such notice in respect of any week during which or during part of which the employer continues to be unable to provide work as aforesaid:

Provided that in respect of the week in which the said notice expires there shall be paid to the worker in addition to any remuneration payable in respect of time worked in that week, any remuneration that would have been payable if the worker had worked his normal hours of work on every day in the week prior to the expiry of the notice.

BENEFITS OR ADVANTAGES

10.—(1) The benefits or advantages set out in (*a*), (*b*), (*c*) and (*d*) of this sub-paragraph, being benefits or advantages provided, in pursuance of the terms and conditions of the employment of a worker to whom this Schedule applies, by the employer or by some other person under arrangements with the employer, are authorised to be reckoned as payment of wages by the employer in lieu of payment in cash in the following manner:—

(*a*) Dinner of good and sufficient quality and quantity provided on each day on which the worker normally works in the week, other than the weekly short day, as an amount of £0·70 per week except in the circumstances provided for in (*d*) of this sub-paragraph.

(*b*) Tea of good and sufficient quality and quantity provided on each day on which the worker normally works in the week, other than the weekly short day, as an amount of £0·25 per week except in the circumstances provided for in (*d*) of this sub-paragraph.

(*c*) Full board on Sunday and customary holidays, part board only on the other days of the week and lodging for the full week, as the appropriate amount set out in the table below:—

In the case of a worker aged	LONDON AREA	PROVINCIAL A AREA	PROVINCIAL B AREA
	Per week	Per week	Per week
	£	£	£
21 years or over	2·15	1·90	1·70
20 and under 21 years	2·00	1·80	1·55
19 " " 20 "	1·80	1·50	1·30
18 " " 19 "	1·65	1·40	1·20
17 " " 18 "	1·50	1·25	1·05
16 " " 17 "	1·25	1·00	0·80
under 16 years	1·15	0·90	0·65

(*d*) Full board and lodging for the full week, as the appropriate amount set out in the table below:—

In the case of a worker aged	LONDON AREA	PROVINCIAL A AREA	PROVINCIAL B AREA
	Per week	Per week	Per week
	£	£	£
21 years or over	2·80	2·50	2·35
20 and under 21 years	2·70	2·40	2·20
19 " " 20 "	2·45	2·20	2·00
18 " " 19 "	2·30	2·00	1·85
17 " " 18 "	2·15	1·90	1·65
16 " " 17 "	1·90	1·65	1·45
under 16 years	1·80	1·50	1·30

Provided that where in any week the total amount which, in accordance with the foregoing provisions of this sub-paragraph, the employer would be entitled to reckon as payment of wages to a worker in lieu of payment in cash, exceeds the appropriate amount (according to the age of the worker and the area in which he is employed) set out in (*d*) of this sub-paragraph, then in the case of that worker the employer shall not be entitled in respect of that week, so to reckon as payment of wages as aforesaid, more than such appropriate amount set out in (*d*) of this sub-paragraph:

Provided also that where a worker is employed in a shop—

(i) which is registered under section 53 of the Shops Act 1950 (which relates to persons observing the Jewish Sabbath), this sub-paragraph in relation to such a worker shall have effect as if for the word "Sunday" in (*c*) thereof, there were substituted the word "Saturday";

(ii) situated in a district in which an order is in force under section 54 of the Shops Act 1950, authorising shops to be open for the serving of customers on Sunday and which it is the practice to keep open on Sunday, this sub-paragraph in relation to such a worker shall have effect as if for the word "Sunday" there were substituted the words "the week-day upon which the shop in which the worker is employed must be closed in pursuance of an order made under section 54 of the Shops Act 1950".

(2) In this paragraph—

"PART BOARD" means breakfast and supper, being meals of good and sufficient quality and quantity;

"FULL BOARD" means breakfast, dinner, tea and supper, being meals of good and sufficient quality and quantity; and

"LODGING" means clean and adequate accommodation and clean and adequate facilities for eating, sleeping, washing and leisure.

(3) Nothing in this paragraph shall be construed as authorising the making of any deduction or the giving of remuneration in any manner which is illegal by virtue of the Truck Acts 1831 to 1940(**a**), or of any other enactment.

Part II

ANNUAL HOLIDAY AND HOLIDAY REMUNERATION

ANNUAL HOLIDAY

11.—(Subject to the provisions of paragraphs 12 and 13 an employer shall, between 1st April 1974 and 31st October 1974, and in each succeeding year between 1st April and 31st October, allow a holiday (hereinafter referred to as an "annual holiday") to every worker (other than a worker who normally works for the employer for less than 9 hours in a week) in his employment to whom this Schedule applies who has been employed by him during the 12 months immediately preceding the commencement of the holiday season for any one of the periods of employment (calculated in accordance with the provisions of paragraph 18) set out in the table below and the duration of the annual holiday shall in the case of each such worker be related to that period as follows:—

Period of employment	Duration of annual holiday — Where the worker's normal working week is			
	Six days	Five days	Four days	Three days or less
12 months...	*18 days*	*15 days*	*12 days*	*9 days*
Not less than 11 months but less than 12 months ...	*16 „*	*13 „*	*11 „*	*8 „*
„ „ „ 10 „ „ „ „ 11 „ ...	*15 „*	*12 „*	*10 „*	*7 „*
„ „ „ 9 „ „ „ „ 10 „ ...	*13 „*	*11 „*	*9 „*	*6 „*
„ „ „ 8 „ „ „ „ 9 „ ...	*12 „*	*10 „*	*8 „*	*6 „*
„ „ „ 7 „ „ „ „ 8 „ ...	*10 „*	*8 „*	*7 „*	*5 „*
„ „ „ 6 „ „ „ „ 7 „ ...	*9 „*	*7 „*	*6 „*	*4 „*
„ „ „ 5 „ „ „ „ 6 „ ...	*7 „*	*6 „*	*5 „*	*3 „*
„ „ „ 4 „ „ „ „ 5 „ ...	*6 „*	*5 „*	*4 „*	*3 „*
„ „ „ 3 „ „ „ „ 4 „ ...	*4 „*	*3 „*	*3 „*	*2 „*
„ „ „ 2 „ „ „ „ 3 „ ...	*3 „*	*2 „*	*2 „*	*1 day*
„ „ „ 1 month „ „ „ 2 „ ...	*1 day*	*1 day*	*1 day*	*nil*

(2) Notwithstanding the provisions of the last foregoing sub-paragraph—

(*a*) the number of days of annual holiday which an employer is required to allow to a worker in any holiday season shall not exceed in the aggregate *three times* the number of days constituting the worker's normal working week;

(**a**) 1831 c. 37; 1887 c. 46; 1896 c. 44; 1940 c. 38.

(*b*) where a worker does not wish to take his annual holiday or part thereof during the holiday season in any year and, before the expiration of such holiday season, enters into an agreement in writing with his employer that the annual holiday or part thereof shall be allowed, at a date or dates to be specified in that agreement, after the expiration of the holiday season but before the first day of January in the following year, then any day or days of annual holiday so allowed shall be treated as having been allowed during the holiday season ;

(3) In this Schedule the expression "holiday season" means in relation to the year 1974 the period commencing on 1st April 1974, and ending on 31st October 1974, and, in each succeeding year, the period commencing on 1st April and ending on 31st October of the same year.

12. Where at the written request of the worker at any time during the three months immediately preceding the commencement of the holiday season in any year, his employer allows him any day or days of holiday and pays him holiday remuneration in respect thereof calculated in accordance with the provisions of paragraphs 15 and 16, then—

(1) the annual holiday to be allowed in accordance with paragraph 11 in the holiday season in that year shall be reduced by the day or days of holiday so allowed prior to the commencement of that holiday season ; and

(2) for the purpose of calculating accrued holiday remuneration under paragraph 17 any day or days of holiday deducted in accordance with sub-paragraph (1) hereof shall be treated as if they had been allowed in the holiday season.

13.—(1) Subject to the provisions of this paragraph, an annual holiday shall be allowed on consecutive working days, being days on which the worker is normally called upon to work for the employer.

(2) Where the number of days of annual holiday for which a worker has qualified exceeds the number of days constituting his normal working week *but does not exceed twice that number,* the holiday may by agreement between the employer and the worker be allowed in two periods of consecutive working days; so however that when a holiday is so allowed, one of the periods shall consist of a number of such days not less than the number of days constituting the worker's normal working week.

(3) *Where the number of days of annual holiday for which a worker has qualified exceeds twice the number of days constituting his normal working week the holiday may be allowed as follows:—*

(*a*) *as to one or two periods of consecutive working days, comprising not more than twice the number of days constituting the worker's normal working week, during the holiday season; so however that one of such periods is not less than the period constituting the worker's normal working week;*

(*b*) *as to any additional days, on consecutive working days to be fixed by the employer, either during the holiday season or before the beginning of the next following holiday season.*

(4) For the purposes of this paragraph, days of annual holiday shall be treated as consecutive notwithstanding that a customary holiday on which the worker is not required to work for the employer or a day on which he does not normally work for the employer intervenes.

(5) Where a customary holiday on which the worker is not required to work for the employer immediately precedes a period of annual holiday or occurs during such a period and the total number of days of annual holiday required to be allowed in the period under the foregoing provisions of this paragraph, together with any customary holiday, exceeds the number of days constituting the worker's normal working week then, notwithstanding the foregoing provisions of this paragraph, the duration of that period of annual holiday may be reduced by one day and in such a case one day of annual holiday may be allowed on a day on which the worker normally works for the employer (not being the worker's weekly short day) in the holiday season or after the holiday season in the circumstances specified in sub-paragraph (2)(*b*) of paragraph 11.

(6) No day of annual holiday shall be allowed on a customary holiday.

(7) A day of annual holiday under this Schedule may be allowed on a day on which the worker is entitled to a day of holiday (not being a customary holiday) or to a half-holiday under any enactment other than the Wages Councils Act 1959:

Provided that where the total number of days of annual holiday allowed to a worker under this Schedule is less than the number of days in his normal working week, the said annual holiday shall be in addition to the said day of holiday or the said half-holiday.

14. An employer shall give to a worker reasonable notice of the commencing date or dates and of the duration of his annual holiday. Such notice may be given individually to the worker or by the posting of a notice in the place where the worker is employed.

REMUNERATION FOR ANNUAL HOLIDAY

15.—(1) Subject to the provisions of paragraph 16, a worker qualified to be allowed an annual holiday under this Schedule shall be paid by his employer, on the last pay day preceding such holiday, one day's holiday pay (as defined in paragraph 19) in respect of each day thereof.

(2) Where an annual holiday is taken in more than one period the holiday remuneration shall be apportioned accordingly.

16. Where any accrued holiday remuneration has been paid by the employer to the worker (in accordance with paragraph 17 of this Schedule or with Order R.D.O. (62)) in respect of employment during any of the periods referred to in that paragraph, or that Order, the amount of holiday remuneration payable by the employer in respect of any annual holiday for which the worker has qualified by reason of employment during the said period shall be reduced by the amount of the said accrued holiday remuneration unless that remuneration has been deducted from a previous payment of holiday remuneration made under the provisions of this Schedule or of Order R.D.O. (62).

ACCRUED HOLIDAY REMUNERATION PAYABLE ON TERMINATION OF EMPLOYMENT

17. Where a worker (other than a worker who normally works for the employer for less than 9 hours in a week) ceases to be employed by an employer after the provisions of this Schedule become effective the employer shall, immediately on the termination of the employment (hereinafter referred to as the "termination date"), pay to the worker as accrued holiday remuneration—

(1) in respect of employment in the 12 months up to 1st April immediately preceding the termination date, a sum equal to the holiday remuneration for any days of annual holiday for which he has qualified except days of annual holiday which he has been allowed or has become entitled to be allowed before leaving the employment ; and

(2) in respect of any employment since 1st April immediately preceding the termination date, a sum equal to the holiday remuneration which would have been payable to him if he could have been allowed an annual holiday in respect of that employment at the time of leaving it:

Provided that—

(*a*) no worker shall be entitled to the payment by his employer of accrued holiday remuneration if he is dismissed on the grounds of misconduct and is so informed by the employer at the time of dismissal;

(*b*) where during the period or periods in respect of which the said accrued holiday remuneration is payable the worker has at his written request been allowed any day or days of holiday (other than days of holiday allowed by the employer under paragraph 12) for which he had not qualified under the provisions of this Schedule, any accrued holiday remuneration payable as aforesaid may be reduced by the amount of any sum paid by the employer to the worker in respect of such day or days of holiday;

(*c*) where a worker is employed under a contract of service under which he is required to give not less than one week's notice before terminating his employment and the worker, without the consent of his employer, terminates his employment without having given not less than one week's notice or before one week has expired from the beginning of such notice, the amount of accrued holiday remuneration payable to the worker shall be the amount payable under the foregoing provisions of this paragraph less an amount equal to the statutory minimum remuneration which would be payable to him at the termination date for one week's work if working his normal working week and the normal number of daily hours worked by him.

CALCULATION OF EMPLOYMENT

18. For the purpose of calculating any period of employment qualifying a worker for an annual holiday or for any accrued holiday remuneration, the worker shall be treated as if he were employed for a month in respect of any month (as defined in paragraph 19) throughout which he has been in the employment of the employer.

Part III

GENERAL

DEFINITIONS

19. For the purposes of this Schedule—

"CARRYING CAPACITY" means the weight of the maximum load normally carried by the vehicle, and such carrying capacity when so established shall not be affected either by variations in the weight of the load resulting from collections or deliveries or emptying of containers during the course of the journey, or by the fact that on any particular journey a load greater or less than the established carrying capacity is carried.

"CASHIER" means a worker employed in a shop and engaged wholly or mainly in receiving cash or giving change.

"CENTRAL WAREHOUSE WORKER" means a worker wholly or mainly employed in a central warehouse, that is to say, a warehouse from which an undertaking in the retail drapery, outfitting and footwear trades supplies its branch shops.

"CLERK GRADE I" means a worker engaged wholly or mainly on clerical work which includes responsibility for maintaining ledgers or wages books or for preparing financial accounts of the undertaking or of a branch or department thereof.

"CLERK GRADE II" means a worker, other than a Clerk Grade I, engaged wholly or mainly on clerical work.

"CREDIT TRAVELLER" means a worker employed in an undertaking engaged in credit trading and wholly or mainly engaged in calling upon customers or prospective customers for the purpose of opening accounts, collecting payments or selling goods.

"CUSTOMARY HOLIDAY" means

(1) (*a*) In England and Wales—

(i) Christmas Day;

26th December if it be not a Sunday; 27th December in a year when 25th or 26th December is a Sunday;

Good Friday;

Easter Monday;

the last Monday in May;

the last Monday in August (*or where a day is substituted for any of the above days by national proclamation, that day*) and any day proclaimed as a public holiday throughout England and Wales; and

(ii) one other day being a day on which the worker would normally work during the period commencing on the last day on which the worker would normally work before Christmas Day and ending on the next following 2nd January, to be fixed by the employer and notified to the worker not less than three weeks before the holiday;

(*b*) In Scotland—

(i) New Year's Day (or, if New Year's Day falls on a Sunday, the following Monday);

the local Spring holiday;

the local Autumn holiday;

Christmas Day (or, if Christmas Day falls on a Sunday, the following Monday);

two other days being days on which the worker would normally work, in the course of a calendar year, to be fixed by the employer and notified to the worker not less than three weeks before the holiday, and any day proclaimed as a public holiday throughout Scotland; and

(ii) one other day being a day on which the worker would normally work during the period commencing on the last day on which the worker would normally work before Christmas Day and ending on the next following 3rd January, to be fixed by the employer and notified to the worker not less than three weeks before the holiday; or

(2) where in any undertaking it is not the custom or practice to observe such days as are specified in (1)(*a*)(i) or (1)(*b*)(i) above as holidays, such other days, not fewer in number, as may by agreement between the employer or his representative and the worker or his representative be substituted for the specified days.

"FULL-TIME WORKER" means a worker who normally works for the employer for at least 34 hours in the week on work to which this Schedule applies.

"MONTH" means the period commencing on a date of any number in one month and ending on the day before the date of the same number in the next month, or if the commencing date is the 29th, 30th or 31st day of a month, and there is no date of the same number in the next month, then on the last day of that month.

"NORMAL WORKING WEEK" means the number of days on which it has been usual for the worker to work in a week while in the employment of the employer during the 12 months immediately preceding the commencement of the holiday season, or, where accrued holiday remuneration is payable under (2) of paragraph 17, on the termination of the employment, during the 12 months immediately preceding the termination date:

Provided that—

(1) part of a day shall count as a day;

(2) no account shall be taken of any week in which the worker did not perform any work for which statutory minimum remuneration has been fixed.

"ONE DAY'S HOLIDAY PAY" means the appropriate proportion of the remuneration which the worker would be entitled to receive from his employer at the date of the annual holiday (or where the holiday is taken in more than one period at the date of the first period) or at the termination date, as the case may be, for one week's work—

(1) if working his normal working week and the number of daily hours normally worked by him (exclusive of overtime),

(2) if the employer were not providing him with meals or board and lodging, and

(3) if paid at the appropriate rate of statutory minimum remuneration for work for which statutory minimum remuneration is payable and at the same rate for any work for the same employer for which such remuneration is not payable,

and in this definition "appropriate proportion" means—

where the worker's normal working week is	six days	.. one-sixth
" " " " "	five "	.. one-fifth
" " " " "	four "	.. one-quarter
" " " " "	three "	.. one-third
" " " " "	two "	.. one-half
" " " " "	one day	.. the whole.

"SALES ASSISTANT" means a worker who is wholly or mainly engaged in the serving of customers.

"SHOP MANAGER", "SHOP MANAGERESS" means a worker who is employed at, and is normally immediately in charge of the operation of, an undertaking or branch (but not of a department of an undertaking or branch), who has the custody of cash and stock, and who has immediate control of other workers (if any) employed at that undertaking or branch ; and for the purposes of this definition a worker shall not be deemed not to be immediately in charge of the operation of an undertaking or branch by reason only of being subject to the supervision of the employer or some person acting on his behalf, being in either case a person who is not normally, during the hours when the undertaking or branch is open to the public, wholly or mainly engaged in work at that undertaking or branch.

"STOCK HAND" means a worker employed in a shop, or in a warehouse operated in connection with a shop, and wholly or mainly engaged in the custody of goods or the receiving and checking of stock or the assembly of orders.

"TEMPORARY SHOP MANAGER", "TEMPORARY SHOP MANAGERESS" means a worker who during the absence of the shop manager or shop manageress performs all the duties of the shop manager or the shop manageress, whilst he is performing the said duties.

"TIME-AND-A-HALF" and "DOUBLE TIME" mean, respectively, one and a half times and twice the hourly rate obtained by dividing by 40 the minimum weekly remuneration to which the worker is entitled under the provisions of paragraph 3, 4 or 5.

"TRANSPORT WORKER" means a worker engaged wholly or mainly in driving a mechanically propelled or horse drawn road vehicle for the transport of goods and on work in connection with the vehicle and its load (if any) while on the road.

"WATCHMAN" means a worker wholly or mainly engaged in guarding the employer's premises for the prevention of theft, fire, damage or trespass.

"WEEK" means "pay week".

"WEEKLY SHORT DAY" means:—

(1) that day in any week on which the worker is, in accordance with the provisions of section 17 of the Shops Act 1950, required not to be employed about the business of a shop after half-past one o'clock in the afternoon, or,

(2) where there is no such day, or where the day falls on a customary holiday, a working day in the week not being a customary holiday, fixed by the employer and notified to the worker not later than the Saturday preceding the week during which it is to have effect; or, failing such notification, the last working day in the week which is not a customary holiday:

Provided that where the day specified in (1) of this definition falls on Christmas Day or Boxing Day in England and Wales or Christmas Day or New Year's Day in Scotland the employer may fix as the weekly short day for that week a working day in the following week not being either a customary holiday or the weekly short day for that following week.

AREAS

20. In this Schedule:—

(1) "LONDON AREA" means the Metropolitan Police District, as defined in the London Government Act 1963(a), the City of London, the Inner Temple and the Middle Temple.

(2) "PROVINCIAL A AREA" means

(*a*) In Scotland,

(i) the following burghs:—

ABERDEEN COUNTY
Aberdeen (including part in Kincardine County)
Fraserburgh
Peterhead

ANGUS COUNTY
Arbroath
Brechin
Dundee
Forfar
Montrose

ARGYLL COUNTY
Dunoon

AYR COUNTY
Ardrossan
Ayr
Irvine
Kilmarnock
Largs
Prestwick
Saltcoats
Stevenston
Troon

DUNBARTON COUNTY
Bearsden
Clydebank
Dumbarton
Helensburgh
Kirkintilloch
Milngavie

EAST LOTHIAN COUNTY
North Berwick

FIFE COUNTY
Buckhaven and Methil
Burntisland
Cowdenbeath
Dunfermline
Kirkcaldy
Leven
Lochgelly
St. Andrews

INVERNESS COUNTY
Inverness

KINCARDINE COUNTY
Stonehaven

ORKNEY COUNTY
Kirkwall

PERTH COUNTY
Perth

RENFREW COUNTY
Barrhead
Gourock
Greenock
Johnstone
Paisley
Port Glasgow
Renfrew

ROSS AND CROMARTY COUNTY
Stornoway

ROXBURGH COUNTY
Hawick

SELKIRK COUNTY
Galashiels

(a) 1963 c. 33.

BANFF COUNTY
Buckie

BUTE COUNTY
Rothesay

CLACKMANNAN COUNTY
Alloa

DUMFRIES COUNTY
Dumfries

LANARK COUNTY
Airdrie
Coatbridge
Glasgow
Hamilton
Lanark
Motherwell and Wishaw
Rutherglen

MIDLOTHIAN COUNTY
Dalkeith
Edinburgh
Musselburgh

MORAY COUNTY
Elgin

STIRLING COUNTY
Denny and Dunipace
Falkirk
Grangemouth
Kilsyth
Stirling

WEST LOTHIAN COUNTY
Armadale
Bathgate
Bo'ness

WIGTOWN COUNTY
Stranraer

ZETLAND COUNTY
Lerwick

(ii) The following Special Lighting Districts, the boundaries of which have been defined, namely:—Vale of Leven and Renton in the County of Dunbarton; and Larbert and Airth in the County of Stirling; and

(iii) The following areas, the boundaries of which were defined as Special Lighting Districts prior to 10th March 1943, namely:—Bellshill and Mossend, Blantyre, Cambuslang, Larkhall and Holytown, New Stevenston and Carfin, all in the County of Lanark.

(*b*) In England and Wales, the areas administered by County Borough, Municipal Borough or Urban District Councils, except where they are included in the London area or are listed in (3)(*b*) of this paragraph.

(3) "PROVINCIAL B AREA" means

(*a*) in Scotland, all areas other than those listed in (2)(*a*) of this paragraph;

(*b*) in England and Wales, all areas not included in the London area administered by Rural District Councils, and the areas administered by the following Municipal Borough and Urban District Councils:—

ENGLAND (excluding Monmouthshire)

BEDFORDSHIRE
Ampthill
Sandy

BERKSHIRE
Wallingford
Wantage

BUCKINGHAMSHIRE
Buckingham
Linslade
Marlow
Newport Pagnell

CHESHIRE
Alsager
Longdendale

DORSET
Blandford Forum
Lyme Regis
Shaftesbury
Sherborne
Wareham
Wimborne Minster

DURHAM
Barnard Castle
Tow Law

ELY, ISLE OF
Chatteris

ESSEX
Brightlingsea
Burnham-on-Crouch
Saffron Walden
West Mersea
Wivenhoe

LINCOLNSHIRE
Alford
Barton-upon-Humber
Bourne
Brigg
Horncastle
Mablethorpe and Sutton
Market Rasen
Woodhall Spa

NORFOLK
Cromer
Diss
Downham Market
Hunstanton
North Walsham
Sheringham
Swaffham
Thetford
Wells-next-the-Sea
Wymondham

CORNWALL

Bodmin
Bude Stratton
Fowey
Helston
Launceston
Liskeard
Looe
Lostwithiel
Padstow
Penryn
St. Just
Torpoint

DERBYSHIRE

Bakewell
Whaley Bridge
Wirksworth

DEVON

Ashburton
Buckfastleigh
Budleigh Salterton
Crediton
Dartmouth
Great Torrington
Holsworthy
Honiton
Kingsbridge
Lynton
Northam
Okehampton
Ottery St. Mary
Salcombe
Seaton
South Molton
Tavistock
Totnes

SUFFOLK

Aldeburgh
Beccles
Bungay
Eye
Hadleigh
Halesworth
Haverhill
Leiston-cum-Sizewell
Saxmundham
Southwold
Sudbury
Stowmarket
Woodbridge

GLOUCESTERSHIRE

Nailsworth
Tewkesbury

HEREFORDSHIRE

Bromyard
Kington
Ledbury

HERTFORDSHIRE

Baldock
Chorleywood
Royston
Sawbridgeworth

HUNTINGDONSHIRE

Huntingdon and
Godmanchester
Ramsey
St. Ives
St. Neots

KENT

Lydd
New Romney
Queenborough
Sandwich
Tenterden

LANCASHIRE

Carnforth
Grange

SUSSEX

Arundel
Rye

WESTMORLAND

Appleby
Lakes

WILTSHIRE

Bradford-on-Avon
Calne
Malmesbury
Marlborough
Melksham
Westbury
Wilton

NORTHAMPTONSHIRE

Brackley
Burton Latimer
Higham Ferrers
Oundle

NORTHUMBERLAND

Alnwick
Amble

OXFORDSHIRE

Bicester
Chipping Norton
Thame
Woodstock

RUTLAND

Oakham

SHROPSHIRE

Bishop's Castle
Church Stretton
Ellesmere
Market Drayton
Newport
Wem

SOMERSET

Chard
Crewkerne
Glastonbury
Ilminster
Portishead
Shepton Mallet
Street
Watchet
Wellington

WORCESTERSHIRE

Bewdley
Droitwich

YORKSHIRE

Hedon
Hornsea
Malton
Norton
Pickering
Richmond
Tickhill
Withernsea

WALES AND MONMOUTHSHIRE

ANGLESEY
- Amlwch
- Beaumaris
- Llangefni
- Menai Bridge

BRECONSHIRE
- Builth Wells
- Hay
- Llanwrtyd Wells

CAERNARVONSHIRE
- Bethesda
- Betws-y-Coed
- Criccieth
- Llanfairfechan
- Penmaenmawr
- Portmadoc
- Pwllheli

CARDIGANSHIRE
- Aberayron
- Cardigan
- Lampeter
- New Quay

CARMARTHENSHIRE
- Cwmamman
- Kidwelly
- Llandeilo
- Llandovery
- Newcastle Emlyn

DENBIGHSHIRE
- Llangollen
- Llanrwst
- Ruthin

FLINTSHIRE
- Buckley
- Mold

GLAMORGAN
- Cowbridge

MERIONETHSHIRE
- Bala
- Barmouth
- Dolgellau
- Towyn

MONMOUTHSHIRE
- Caerleon
- Chepstow
- Usk

MONTGOMERYSHIRE
- Llanfyllin
- Llanidloes
- Machynlleth
- Montgomery
- Newtown and Llanllwchaiarn
- Welshpool

PEMBROKESHIRE
- Fishguard and Goodwick
- Narberth
- Neyland
- Tenby

RADNORSHIRE
- Knighton
- Llandrindod Wells
- Presteigne

(4) Any reference to a local government area shall be construed as a reference to that area as it was on 23rd April 1961, unless otherwise stated.

WORKERS TO WHOM THIS SCHEDULE APPLIES

21.—(1)—(i) Subject to the provisions of sub-paragraph (2) of this paragraph, the workers to whom this Schedule applies are all workers employed in Great Britain in any undertaking or any branch or department of an undertaking, being an undertaking, branch or department engaged—

(*a*) wholly or mainly in the retail drapery, outfitting and footwear trades ; or

(*b*) wholly or mainly in those trades and one or more of the groups of retail distributive trades set out in the Appendix to this paragraph, and to a greater extent in the retail drapery, outfitting and footwear trades than in any one of those groups:

Provided that if a branch or department of an undertaking is not so engaged this Schedule shall not apply to workers employed in that branch or department (notwithstanding that the undertaking as a whole is so engaged), except in the case of workers as respects their employment in a department of that branch if that department is so engaged.

(ii) For the purposes of this sub-paragraph

(*a*) in determining the extent to which an undertaking or branch or department of an undertaking is engaged in a group of trades, regard shall be had to the time spent in the undertaking, branch or department on work in that group of trades ;

(*b*) an undertaking or branch or department of an undertaking which is engaged in any operation in a group of trades shall be treated as engaged in that group of trades.

(2) This Schedule does not apply to any of the following workers in respect of their employment in any of the following circumstances, that is to say—

(i) workers employed on the making, trimming, fitting, alteration or repair of wearing apparel;

(ii) workers in relation to whom the Road Haulage Wages Council operates in respect of any employment which is within the field of operation of that Council;

(iii) workers employed on post office business;

(iv) workers employed on the maintenance or repair of buildings, plant, equipment or vehicles (but not including workers employed as cleaners);

(v) workers employed on the cutting, sewing, making up and fixing of blinds, curtains, pelmets and loose covers;

(vi) workers employed as watchmen.

(3) For the purpose of this Schedule the retail drapery, outfitting and footwear trades consist of

(i) the sale by retail of

(*a*) wearing apparel of all kinds (including footwear, headwear and handwear) and accessories, trimmings and adornments for wearing apparel (excluding jewellery and imitation jewellery);

(*b*) haberdashery;

(*c*) textile fabrics in the piece, leather cloth, plastic cloth and oil cloth (but not including carpets, linoleum and other kinds of floor covering);

(*d*) knitting, rug, embroidery, crochet and similar wools or yarns;

(*e*) made-up household textiles (but excluding mattresses and floor coverings);

(*f*) umbrellas, sunshades, walking sticks, canes and similar articles;

(ii) operations in or about the shop or other place where any of the articles included in (i) of this sub-paragraph are sold by retail, being operations carried on for the purpose of such sale or otherwise in connection with such sale;

(iii) operations in connection with the warehousing or storing of any of the articles included in (i) of this sub-paragraph for the purpose of the sale thereof by retail, or otherwise in connection with such sale, where the warehousing or storing takes place at a warehouse or store carried on in conjunction with one or more shops or other places where the said articles are sold by retail;

(iv) operations in connection with the transport of any of the articles included in (i) of this sub-paragraph when carried on in conjunction with their sale by retail or with the warehousing or storing operations specified in (iii) of this sub-paragraph; and

(v) clerical or other office work carried on in conjunction with the sale by retail of any of the articles included in (i) of this sub-paragraph and relating to such sale or to any of the operations specified in (ii) to (iv) of this sub-paragraph;

and for the purpose of this definition the sale by retail of any of the articles in (i) of this sub-paragraph includes the sale of that article to a person for use in connection with a trade or business carried on by him if such sale takes place at or in connection with a shop engaged in the retail sale to the general public of any of the articles included in (i) of this sub-paragraph.

APPENDIX TO PARAGRAPH 21

GROUPS OF RETAIL DISTRIBUTIVE TRADES

Group 1.—The Retail Food Trades, that is to say, the sale by retail of food or drink for human consumption and operations connected therewith including:—

(i) operations in or about the shop or other place where the food or drink aforesaid is sold, being operations carried on for the purpose of such sale or otherwise in connection with such sale ;

(ii) operations in connection with the warehousing or storing of such food or drink for the purpose of sale by retail, or otherwise in connection with such sale, where the warehousing or storing takes place at a warehouse or store carried on in conjunction with one or more shops or other places where such food or drink is sold by retail ;

(iii) operations in connection with the transport of such food or drink when carried on in conjunction with its sale by retail or with the warehousing or storing operations specified in (ii) above ; and

(iv) clerical or other office work carried on in conjunction with the sale by retail aforesaid and relating to such sale or to any of the operations in (i) to (iii) above ;

but not including

the sale by retail of bread, pastry or flour confectionery (other than biscuits or meat pastries) or the sale by retail of meat (other than bacon, ham, pressed beef, sausages or meat so treated as to be fit for human consumption without further preparation or cooking) or the sale by retail of milk (other than dried or condensed milk) or the sale by retail of ice-cream, aerated waters, chocolate confectionery or sugar confectionery, or the sale of food or drink for immediate consumption.

For the purpose of this definition "sale by retail" includes any sale of food or drink to a person for use in connection with a catering business carried on by him, when such sale takes place at or in connection with a shop engaged in the retail sale of food or drink to the general public.

Group 2.—The Retail Furnishing and Allied Trades, that is to say—

(1) the sale by retail of the following articles:—

(*a*) household and office furniture, including garden furniture, mattresses, floor coverings and mirrors, but excluding billiard tables, clocks, pianos, gramophones and pictures ;

(*b*) ironmongery, turnery and hardware, of kinds commonly used for household purposes, including gardening implements ;

(*c*) hand tools ;

(*d*) woodware, basketware, glassware, potteryware, chinaware, brassware, plasticware and ceramic goods, being articles or goods of kinds commonly used for household purposes or as household ornaments ;

(*e*) electrical and gas appliances and apparatus, of kinds commonly used for household purposes (excluding clocks), and accessories and component parts thereof ;

(*f*) heating, lighting and cooking appliances and apparatus, of kinds commonly used for household purposes, and accessories and component parts thereof ;

(*g*) radio and television sets and their accessories and component parts ;

(*h*) pedal cycles and their accessories and component parts;

(*i*) perambulators, push chairs and invalid carriages;

(*j*) toys, indoor games, requisites for outdoor games, gymnastics and athletics, but excluding billiard tables and sports clothing;

(*k*) saddlery, leather goods (other than articles of wearing apparel), travel goods and ladies' handbags;

(*l*) paint, distemper and wallpaper, and oils of kinds commonly used for household purposes (excluding petrol and lubricating oils);

(*m*) brushes, mops and brooms, used for household purposes, and similar articles;

(*n*) disinfectants, chemicals, candles, soaps and polishes, of kinds commonly used for household purposes;

(2) operations in or about the shop or other place where any of the articles specified in (1) above are sold by retail, being operations carried on for the purpose of such sale or otherwise in connection with such sale;

(3) operations in connection with the warehousing or storing of any of the articles specified in (1) above for the purpose of the sale thereof by retail, or otherwise in connection with such sale, where the warehousing or storing takes place at a warehouse or store carried on in conjunction with one or more shops or other places where the said articles are sold by retail;

(4) operations in connection with the transport of any of the articles specified in (1) above when carried on in conjunction with their sale by retail or with the warehousing or storing operations specified in (3) above; and

(5) clerical or other office work carried on in conjunction with the sale by retail of any of the articles specified in (1) above and relating to such sale or to any of the operations specified in (2) to (4) above;

and for the purpose of this definition the sale by retail of any of the articles specified in (1) above does not include sale by auction (except where the auctioneer sells articles by retail which are his property or the property of his master) but includes the sale of any of the articles therein specified to a person for use in connection with a trade or business carried on by him if such sale takes place at or in connection with a shop engaged in the retail sale to the general public of any of the said articles.

Group 3.—The Retail Bookselling and Stationery Trades, that is to say—

(1) the sale by retail of the following articles:—

(*a*) books (excluding printed music and periodicals);

(*b*) all kinds of stationery including printed forms, note books, diaries and similar articles, and books of kinds used in an office or business for the purpose of record;

(*c*) pens, pencils, ink, blotting paper and similar articles;

(*d*) maps and charts;

(*e*) wrapping and adhesive paper, string, paste and similar articles;

(2) operations in or about the shop or other place where any of the articles specified in (1) above are sold by retail, being operations carried on for the purpose of such sale or otherwise in connection with such sale;

(3) operations in connection with the warehousing or storing of any of the articles specified in (1) above for the purpose of the sale thereof by retail, or otherwise in connection with such sale, where the warehousing or storing takes place at a warehouse or store carried on in conjunction with one or more shops or other places where the said articles are sold by retail;

(4) operations in connection with the transport of any of the articles specified in (1) above when carried on in conjunction with their sale by retail or with the warehousing or storing operations specified in (3) above; and

(5) clerical or other office work carried on in conjunction with the sale by retail of any of the articles specified in (1) above and relating to such sale or to any of the operations specified in (2) to (4) above.

Group 4. The Retail Newsagency, Tobacco and Confectionery Trades, that is to say—

(1) the sale by retail of the following articles:—

(*a*) newspapers, magazines and other periodicals;

(*b*) tobacco, cigars, cigarettes, snuff and smokers' requisites;

(*c*) articles of sugar confectionery and chocolate confectionery and ice-cream;

(2) operations in or about the shop or other place where any of the articles specified in (1) above are sold by retail, being operations carried on for the purpose of such sale or otherwise in connection with such sale;

(3) operations in connection with the warehousing or storing of any of the articles specified in (1) above for the purpose of the sale thereof by retail, or otherwise in connection with such sale, where the warehousing or storing takes place at a warehouse or store carried on in conjunction with one or more shops or other places where the said articles are sold by retail;

(4) operations in connection with the transport of any of the articles specified in (1) above when carried on in conjunction with their sale by retail or with the warehousing or storing operations specified in (3) above; and

(5) clerical or other office work carried on in conjunction with the sale by retail of any of the articles specified in (1) above and relating to such sale or to any of the operations specified in (2) to (4) above.

EXPLANATORY NOTE

(This Note is not part of the Order.)

This Order, which has effect from 4th February 1974, sets out the increased statutory minimum remuneration payable and the holidays to be allowed to workers in relation to whom the Retail Drapery, Outfitting and Footwear Trades Wages Council (Great Britain) operates in substitution for the statutory minimum remuneration and holidays set out in the Wages Regulation (Retail Drapery, Outfitting and Footwear) (No. 2) Order 1972 (Order R.D.O. (62)). It also amends the provisions relating to customary holidays contained in Order R.D.O. (62) so as to take account of recent changes in the law and practice relating to public holidays. Order R.D.O. (62) is revoked.

New provisions are printed in italics.

1973 No. 1956

NATIONAL HEALTH SERVICE, ENGLAND AND WALES

The National Health Service Reorganisation Act 1973 (Appointed Day) Order 1973

Made - - -	21*st November* 1973
Laid before Parliament	29*th November* 1973
Coming into Operation	20*th December* 1973

The Secretary of State for Social Services, in exercise of powers conferred on him by section 55(1) of the National Health Service Reorganisation Act 1973(**a**) and of all other powers enabling him in that behalf, hereby makes the following Order:—

1. This Order may be cited as the National Health Service Reorganisation Act 1973 (Appointed Day) Order 1973 and shall come into operation on 20th December 1973.

2. The appointed day for the purposes of any provision of the National Health Service Reorganisation Act 1973 mentioned in the first column of the Schedule to this Order shall be 1st April 1974.

Keith Joseph,
Secretary of State for Social Services.

21st November 1973.

(**a**) 1973 c. 32.

SCHEDULE

Provisions of the National Health Service Reorganisation Act 1973	Subject matter
Section 14 (1) and (2)	Abolition of authorities.
Section 15 (2)	Orders preserving certain Boards of Governors of teaching hospitals.
Section 16 (1), (2) and (4)	Transfer of property, rights and liabilities from local authorities.
Section 17 (1)	Transfer of property, rights and liabilities from Executive Councils and pricing committees.
Section 18 (1), (2) and (3)	Transfer of staff to employment of new health authorities.
Section 24 (1), (2) and (3)	Transfer of trust property from abolished authorities.
Section 25 (1), (2) and (3)	Transfer of trust property held for health purposes by local health authorities.
Section 27 (1)	Application of trust property previously held for general hospital purposes.
Section 29 (1)	Special Trustees for a university or teaching hospital.
Section 34 (1)	Establishment of "relevant bodies" for purposes of investigations by Health Service Commissioner.
Section 54 (5)	Enforceability of rights and liabilities by and against health authorities.
Schedule 1:	
Paragraph 1 (3)	Consultations on appointment of members of Regional Health Authorities.
Paragraph 2 (2) (*c*)	Consultations on appointment of members of Area Health Authorities.
Paragraph 4	Consultations on appointment of additional members to Area Health Authorities (Teaching).
Paragraph 6 (4)	Consultations on appointments to Family Practitioner Committees.

EXPLANATORY NOTE

(This Note is not part of the Order.)

This Order appoints 1st April 1974 as the day that is meant by any reference to the appointed day in any provision of the National Health Service Reorganisation Act 1973.

1973 No. 1958

LICENSING (LIQUOR)

The Isles of Scilly (Sale of Intoxicating Liquor) Order 1973

Made - - - *19th November* 1973

Coming into Operation *1st January* 1974

In exercise of the powers conferred on me by section 202 of the Licensing Act 1964(**a**), I hereby make the following Order:—

Citation, commencement etc.

1.—(1) This Order may be cited as the Isles of Scilly (Sale of Intoxicating Liquor) Order 1973 and shall come into operation on 1st January 1974.

(2) Save where the context otherwise requires, this Order shall apply only to the Isles of Scilly.

2.—(1) In this Order, unless the context otherwise requires—

"the Act as modified" means the Licensing Act 1964 with the exclusions, adaptations and modifications referred to in Article 3 of this Order;

"annual permit" means a permit granted in pursuance of Article 6 of this Order;

"intoxicating liquor" has the same meaning as in the Licensing Act 1964;

"Joint Police Committee" means the Joint Police Committee for the Isles of Scilly;

"new permit" means a permit granted otherwise than by way of renewal or transfer;

"occasional permit" means a permit granted in pursuance of Article 7 of this Order;

"permit" means an annual or an occasional permit for the sale by retail of intoxicating liquor (and also, in the case of a permit granted to a club for club premises, for its supply to or to the order of members otherwise than by way of sale);

"sale by retail" means, in relation to intoxicating liquor, the sale at any one time to any one person of quantities not exceeding—

(*a*) in the case of spirits, wine or British wine, two gallons or one case;

(*b*) in the case of beer or cider, four and a half gallons or two cases;

the expressions "beer", "British wine", "case", "cider", 'spirits" and "wine" have the meanings respectively assigned to them in section 307 of the Customs and Excise Act 1952(**b**);

"transfer" has the meaning assigned to it in Article 12 of this Order.

(**a**) 1964 c. 26. (**b**) 1952 c. 44.

(2) Any reference in this Order to any enactment, including any enactment in the Licensing Act 1964 and the Gaming Act 1968(**a**), shall be construed as a reference to that enactment as amended by any other enactment.

(3) The Interpretation Act 1889(**b**) shall apply to the interpretation of this Order as it applies to the interpretation of an Act of Parliament.

3. The Isles of Scilly (Sale of Intoxicating Liquor) Order 1962(**c**) is hereby revoked.

Exclusion, modification and adaptation of Licensing Act 1964 *and other enactments*

4.—(1) In its application to the Isles of Scilly, the Licensing Act 1964 (with the exception of Part X) shall be subject to the exclusions, modifications and adaptations contained in the Schedule to this Order and in paragraph (2) of this Article.

(2) Without prejudice to the provisions of the Schedule to this Order, section 6 of the Gaming Act 1968 and any provisions in the Licensing Act 1964 or any other enactment relating to the sale or supply of intoxicating liquor shall, in its application to the Isles of Scilly, be modified and adapted as follows, except where the context otherwise requires:—

(*a*) a reference to the general annual licensing meeting or transfer sessions or licensing sessions shall be construed as a reference to a meeting of the Joint Police Committee held for the purposes of this Order;

(*b*) subject to sub-paragraphs (*c*) and (*d*) of this paragraph and except in section 83 of the Licensing Act 1964, a reference to a licence of any description or a justices' licence shall be construed as a reference to a permit of that description;

(*c*) a reference to a justices' on-licence shall be construed as a reference to an annual permit authorising the sale of intoxicating liquor on the premises specified therein for consumption either on or off those premises;

(*d*) a reference to a justices' off-licence shall be construed as a reference to an annual permit authorising the sale of intoxicating liquor on the premises specified therein for consumption off those premises only;

(*e*) a reference to the licensing district or the licensing district for which the licensing justices act, shall be construed as a reference to the Isles of Scilly;

(*f*) a reference to the licensing justices, and, except in section 188 of the Licensing Act 1964 and in the expression "clerk to the justices", a reference to justices of the peace or justices shall be construed as a reference to the Joint Police Committee and a reference to a justice or a justice of the peace shall, except in sections 54, 85, 187 and 188 of the Licensing Act 1964, be construed as a reference to a member of that committee;

(*g*) a reference to licensed premises shall be construed as a reference to premises in respect of which a permit has been granted under this Order;

(**a**) 1968 c. 65. (**b**) 1889 c. 63.
(**c**) S.I. 1962/621 (1962 I, p. 597).

(*h*) a reference to the local authority shall be construed as a reference to the Council of the Isles of Scilly.

Powers of Joint Police Committee

5.—(1) The Joint Police Committee shall be the liquor licensing authority for the Isles of Scilly.

(2) The Joint Police Committee may grant a permit to any person not disqualified under this order or under any enactment from holding such a permit or a justices' licence as they think fit and proper.

Annual permits

6.—(1) Subject to the provisions of this Order and of the Act as modified, a person shall not sell or expose for sale by retail any intoxicating liquor except as authorised by an annual permit on premises specified in the permit and in accordance with any conditions specified therein.

(2) Any such annual permit shall be one authorising the sale of intoxicating liquor on the premises specified therein—

(*a*) for consumption off those premises; or

(*b*) for consumption either on or off those premises.

(3) In the case of a permit for consumption off the premises, the permit may authorise the sale of—

(*a*) intoxicating liquor of all descriptions; or

(*b*) of beer, cider and wine only.

(4) In the case of a permit for consumption either on or off the premises, the permit may authorise the sale—

(*a*) of intoxicating liquor of all descriptions; or

(*b*) of beer, cider and wine only; or

(*c*) of beer and cider only; or

(*d*) of cider only; or

(*e*) of wine only.

(5) Any such annual permit shall have effect from the date stated therein until 31st March next following.

Occasional permits

7.—(1) Notwithstanding anything contained in Article 6 of this Order, intoxicating liquor may be sold or exposed for sale by retail in accordance with an occasional permit granted by the Joint Police Committee or, in the case of paragraph (7) of this Article, a court, in accordance with the provisions of this Article.

(2) The holder of an annual permit may be granted an occasional permit authorising the sale or exposure for sale by him of any intoxicating liquor to which his annual permit extends at such place, other than the premises in respect of which his annual permit was granted, and between such hours as may

be specified in the occasional permit; but an occasional permit unless granted under paragraphs (5) to (7) of this Article shall not authorise the sale of intoxicating liquor thereunder on Christmas Day, Good Friday or any day appointed for public fast or thanksgiving.

(3) The Joint Police Committee shall not grant an occasional permit to an applicant who holds only a residential permit granted under Part IV of the Act as modified; and if he holds only a restaurant permit or residential and restaurant permit granted under that Part, the Committee shall not grant the occasional permit unless satisfied that the sale of intoxicating liquor under the authority of the occasional permit is to be ancillary to the provision of substantial refreshment.

(4) Unless granted under paragraphs (5) to (7) of this Article, an occasional permit shall not be granted for a period exceeding three weeks at any one time.

(5) When a notice has been given under Article 12 of this Order, the person to whom it is proposed to transfer the annual permit may be granted an occasional permit to sell and expose for sale by retail intoxicating liquor until the Joint Police Committee give their decision on the application for transfer, as though the annual permit had been transferred.

(6) Where an application for the renewal of an annual permit has been refused and an appeal against the refusal has been duly made, the applicant may be granted an occasional permit to sell and expose for sale intoxicating liquor until the determination of the appeal.

(7) Where on conviction of an offence an annual permit is forfeited either by the court or by virtue of the conviction, and the person convicted appeals against the conviction, the convicting court may, on such conditions as it thinks just, grant an occasional permit to be in force until the appeal is determined.

Disqualification

8.—(1) Where under any enactment a person is disqualified for holding a justices' licence that person shall be disqualified for holding a permit.

(2) Any provision in the Licensing Act 1964 empowering a court to disqualify a person for holding a justices' licence shall, in its application to the Isles of Scilly, have effect as if it provided also for disqualification for holding a permit.

Penalty for unlawful sale of liquor

9. The provisions of section 160 of the Licensing Act 1964 shall apply as if the sale or exposure for sale of intoxicating liquor, otherwise than as authorised by a permit, were a contravention of that section.

Application for new annual permit

10.—(1) A person applying for a new annual permit shall—

(*a*) not less than twenty-one days before the application is made, give notice in writing to the clerk of the Joint Police Committee, the chief constable of the Devon and Cornwall police area, the clerk of the Council of the Isles of Scilly and the chief fire officer of his intention to apply for the permit;

(*b*) not more than twenty-eight days before the application is made, display notice of the application for a period of seven days in a place where it can conveniently be read by the public on or near the premises to which the application relates.

(2) With the notice given under paragraph (1)(*a*) of this Article there shall be deposited a plan of the premises to which the application relates, if the application is—

(*a*) for the grant of an annual permit authorising consumption on the premises; or

(*b*) for the provisional grant of an annual permit under section 6 of the Act as modified (except where the applicant complies with subsection (5) of that section).

(3) A notice under this Article shall—

(*a*) be signed by the applicant or his authorised agent;

(*b*) state the name and address of the applicant and his trade or calling during the six months preceding the giving of the notice;

(*c*) state the situation of the premises to which the application relates;

(*d*) state the kind of permit for which application is to be made.

Application for renewal of annual permit

11.—(1) A person proposing to apply to the Joint Police Committee for the renewal of an annual permit shall give notice in accordance with Article 10(1)(*a*) of this Order but shall not be required to give notice to the chief fire officer.

(2) A person intending to oppose an application by the holder of a permit for the renewal of his permit shall give notice in writing of his intention to the applicant, specifying in general terms the grounds of the opposition, not later than seven days before the meeting of the Joint Police Committee; and unless notice has been so given the Joint Police Committee shall not entertain the objection:

Provided that, on objection being made to the renewal, the Joint Police Committee may, notwithstanding that notice of intention to oppose has not been given, adjourn consideration of the application to a day of which they shall give notice to the applicant and the objector, and shall, on that day, hear the application and the objection as if notice of intention to oppose had been given.

(3) Evidence given on an application for the renewal of a permit shall be given on oath.

(4) For the purpose of this Order the renewal of an annual permit means the grant of an annual permit by way of renewal of a similar permit in respect of the same premises which is in force on the date of the application:

Provided that where such a permit is not in force at the date of the application, but was in force at some time within the period of twelve months preceding the application, the grant of a permit in pursuance of the application shall be treated as a renewal of that permit, if the Joint Police Committee are satisfied that the applicant had reasonable cause for not making the application while that permit was in force.

(5) A renewal of an annual permit may be made by endorsement on the original permit or on a copy.

Application for transfer of annual permit

12.—(1) A person applying for the transfer of an annual permit shall, not less than twenty-one days before the application is made, give notice in writing of his intention to apply for the transfer of the permit to the clerk of the Joint Police Committee, the chief constable of the Devon and Cornwall police area, the clerk of the Council of the Isles of Scilly and the holder of the permit (if any) if he is not the applicant.

(2) The Joint Police Committee shall not grant an application to transfer an annual permit—

(*a*) except in the cases and to the persons described in paragraphs (*a*) to (*e*) of section 8(1) of the Act as modified, or, in the case of a forfeiture of a permit or the personal disqualification of the holder of the permit, to the owner of the premises specified in the permit or any person applying on his behalf;

(*b*) unless the transfer is to a person who is in the opinion of the Joint Police Committee a fit and proper person to be the holder of a permit.

(3) This Article shall apply in relation to the transfer of a provisional annual permit as if the permit were in force but so that in paragraph (2)(*a*) the reference to the case of a forfeiture of a permit or the personal disqualification of the holder of the permit shall be omitted, and for the purposes of section 8(1) of the Act as modified as it applies to provisional annual permits, "occupation" shall include intended occupation, and other expressions shall be similarly construed.

(4) For the purposes of this Order, the transfer of an annual permit is the grant of an annual permit to one person in substitution for another person who holds or has held a similar permit in respect of the same premises.

Appeal to the Crown Court

13.—(1) Any person aggrieved by the refusal of the Joint Police Committee to grant a new annual permit or a renewal or transfer of an annual permit or by any decision of the Joint Police Committee as to the conditions of an annual permit or by the making of an order under section 19 of the Act as modified may appeal against that refusal, decision or order to the Crown Court.

(2) The provisions of sections 21 to 25 of the Act as modified shall apply to an appeal under paragraph (1) of this Article as they apply to an appeal under section 21(1) of the Licensing Act 1964.

Fees payable in respect of permits

14. There may be charged by the clerk to the Joint Police Committee in respect of the issue, renewal and transfer of annual permits and the issue of certified copies of annual permits such fees respectively as are for the time being chargeable by justices' clerks under the Licensing Act 1964 in respect of the issue, renewal and transfer of justices' licences and the issue of certified copies of justices' licences.

Clerk to Joint Police Committee not to act professionally in certain matters

15.—(1) A solicitor or other person being a clerk to the Joint Police Committee shall not by himself, his partner or clerk, as solicitor or agent for any person, conduct or act in any application for or in respect of a permit or any other proceedings under this Order or any of the provisions of the Licensing Act 1872(**a**), the Licensing Act 1902(**b**) or the Licensing Act 1964, before the Joint Police Committee or before any justice acting for the Isles of Scilly.

(2) The provisions of subsection (3) of section 28 of the Licensing Act 1964 shall apply as if any contravention of this Article were a contravention of that subsection.

Savings

16. Nothing contained in this Order shall prejudice or affect any rights, powers, authorities or privileges vested in or enjoyed by Her Majesty, Her Heirs or Successors in right of the Duchy of Cornwall or in or by the Duke of Cornwall for the time being.

Robert Carr,
One of Her Majesty's Principal
Secretaries of State.

Home Office,
Whitehall.

19th November 1973.

(**a**) 1872 c. 94. (**b**) 1902 c. 28.

SCHEDULE

Article 4(1)

PART I

Provisions of Licensing Act 1964 *which are excluded from applying to the Isles of Scilly*

Sections 1 to 5, 6(2), 7, 8 (except as applied by Article 12 of this Order), 9(3) and (4), 10(1) to (4), 21 to 25 (except as applied by Article 13 of this Order), 26 to 29, 36(2)(*b*), 37, 38, 56, 57(2) and (3), 61(1), 66, 67, 74(6), 75(1), 87, 93(4), 102 to 147, 180 and 189.

Schedule 1, paragraphs 1 to 5 of Schedules 2, 3, 4, 8, 9 and 11.

PART II

Provisions of Licensing Act 1964 *which are modified or adapted in their application to the Isles of Scilly*

Section	Extent of modification or adaptation
Section 9	Section 9 shall apply as if the reference in subsection (5) to subsection (3) were omitted and any reference to a licence or justices' licence included a reference to a permit.
Section 10	Section 10 shall apply as if in subsection (5) for the reference to a protection order there were substituted a reference to an occasional permit, valid for two months, authorising such sales of intoxicating liquor as might lawfully be made under the annual permit.
Section 19	Section 19 shall apply as if for subsection (1) there were substituted the following provision:— "On an application for the renewal of an annual permit authorising the sale of intoxicating liquor either on or off the premises, the Joint Police Committee, on renewing such a permit may order that, within the time fixed by the order, such structural alterations may be made in the part of the premises where intoxicating liquor is sold or consumed as they think reasonably necessary to secure the proper conduct of the business.".
Section 36	Section 36 shall apply as if in subsection (2) the reference to removal were omitted.
Section 58	In section 58 subsection (1) shall apply as if for paragraphs (*a*) and (*b*) there were substituted the words "(*a*) 'local authority' means the Council of the Isles of Scilly; (*b*) 'clerk of the local authority' means the clerk of the Council of the Isles of Scilly.".
Section 60	Section 60 shall apply as if each parish of the Isles of Scilly were a separate licensing district and the Joint Police Committee the licensing justices for that district.

Section	Extent of modification or adaptation
Section 64	Section 64 shall apply as if the reference to removal in subsection (3) were omitted.
Section 65	Section 65 shall apply as if the reference to removal in subsection (3) were omitted.
Section 69	Section 69 shall apply as if for the reference in subsection (2) to 4th April there were substituted a reference to 31st March.
Section 71	Section 71 shall apply as if the references in subsection (3) to the requirements as to notices of Schedule 2 of the Act were references to the requirements as to notices of paragraph (1) of Article 10 of this Order and a notice under that section shall be signed by the applicant or his authorised agent and shall state the situation of the premises and the nature of the application.
Section 98	Section 98 shall apply as if the authorities referred to in subsection (5) were (*a*) the Council of the Isles of Scilly, and (*b*) the chief constable of the Devon and Cornwall police area.
Section 99	Section 99 shall apply as if the references to removal in subsections (3) and (4) were omitted.
Section 183	Section 183 shall apply as if in subsection (1) for the word "licensed" in the second place where it occurs there were substituted the word "authorised".
Section 193	Section 193 shall apply to members of the Joint Police Committee as it applies to justices.
Schedule 2	In Schedule 2, paragraph 6 shall apply as if it required the clerk to the Joint Police Committee to keep a list of persons giving notice under Articles 10, 11 or 12 of this Order and paragraph 7 shall apply as if the references to the requirements of the preceding paragraphs of the Schedule were references to the requirements of those Articles.

EXPLANATORY NOTE

(This Note is not part of the Order.)

This Order applies only to the Isles of Scilly and substitutes for those provisions of the Licensing Act 1964 which prohibit the sale of intoxicating liquor except as authorised under that Act, and are applicable in England and Wales generally, a prohibition on the sale of intoxicating liquor except as authorised by permits granted by the Joint Police Committee for the Isles of Scilly. The Order also provides for the exercise by that Committee of the functions of licensing justices as to permitted hours, and makes certain ancillary provisions excluding, modifying or adapting the provisions of the 1964 Act in order to conform with the special conditions in the Isles of Scilly. The provisions of the Order are similar to those of the Isles of Scilly (Sale of Intoxicating Liquor) Order 1962, which it revokes, but take account of legislation enacted since 1962.

1973 No. 1964

POULTRY

The Poultry and Hatching Eggs (Importation) Amendment Order 1973

Made - - -	*21st November* 1973
Laid before Parliament	*23rd November* 1973
Coming into Operation	*22nd November* 1973

The Minister of Agriculture, Fisheries and Food and the Secretary of State, acting jointly in exercise of the powers conferred by sections 1(1), 33(1), 45, 49(1), 84(2) and (3) and 85(1) of the Diseases of Animals Act 1950(**a**) and now vested in them (**b**), as adapted to air transport by section 11(1) of the Agriculture (Miscellaneous Provisions) Act 1954(**c**), and all other powers enabling them in that behalf, hereby order as follows:—

Citation and commencement

1. This order may be cited as the Poultry and Hatching Eggs (Importation) Amendment Order 1973 and shall come into operation on 22nd November 1973.

Amendment of Principal Order

2. The Poultry and Hatching Eggs (Importation) Order 1972(**d**) shall be altered by the insertion at the end of Article 3 the following sentence:—

"In the application of this Article to Scotland the words "other than Northern Ireland" in Paragraph (1) shall cease to have effect."

In Witness whereof the Official Seal of the Minister of Agriculture, Fisheries and Food is hereunto affixed on 21st November 1973.

(L.S.)

Joseph Godber,
Minister of Agriculture, Fisheries and Food.

Gordon Campbell,
Secretary of State for Scotland.

21st November 1973.

(**a**) 1950 c. 36.
(**b**) By the Transfer of Functions (Animal Health) Order 1955 (S.I. 1955/958 (1955 I, p. 1184)).
(**c**) 1954 c. 39.
(**d**) S.I. 1972/2025 (1972 III, p. 6004).

EXPLANATORY NOTE

(This Note is not part of the Order.)

Article 3 of the Poultry and Hatching Eggs (Importation) Order 1972 prohibits the landing in Great Britain of poultry or poultry eggs intended for hatching from any country outside Great Britain other than Northern Ireland, the Republic of Ireland, the Channel Islands and the Isle of Man, subject to certain exceptions.

This Order, made under the Diseases of Animals Act 1950, extends this prohibition to poultry and poultry eggs brought from Northern Ireland to Scotland.

1973 No. 1965

AGRICULTURE

AGRICULTURAL GRANTS, GOODS AND SERVICES

The Farm Capital Grant Scheme 1973

Made - - -	20*th November* 1973
Laid before Parliament	3*rd December* 1973
Coming into Operation	
Paragraph 9	21*st December* 1973
Remainder	1*st January* 1974

The Minister of Agriculture, Fisheries and Food, the Secretary of State for Scotland and the Secretary of State for Wales, acting jointly, in exercise of the powers conferred on them by sections 28 and 29 of the Agriculture Act 1970(**a**), the Minister of Agriculture, Fisheries and Food also acting in exercise of the powers conferred on him by section 51(1) of the said Act and the said Ministers also acting in exercise of all other powers enabling them in that behalf, with the approval of the Treasury, hereby make the following scheme:—

Citation, commencement and extent

1. This scheme, which may be cited as the Farm Capital Grant Scheme 1973, shall come into operation on 1st January 1974, save that paragraph 9 hereof shall come into operation on 21st December 1973, and shall apply throughout the United Kingdom, save that paragraphs 3(2) and 6(2) shall not apply to Scotland or Northern Ireland.

Interpretation

2.—(1) In this scheme, unless the context otherwise requires—

"agricultural business" means a business consisting in, or such part of any business as consists in, the pursuit of agriculture;

"agriculture" and cognate expressions shall be construed, except in relation to Scotland, in accordance with section 109 of the Agriculture Act 1947(**b**) and, in relation to Scotland, in accordance with section 86 of the Agriculture (Scotland) Act 1948(**c**);

"the appropriate Minister" means—

(*a*) in relation to England or Northern Ireland, and in relation to Wales for the purpose of the making, receipt or recovery of any payment, the Minister of Agriculture, Fisheries and Food;

(**a**) 1970 c. 40.
(**b**) 1947 c. 48.
(**c**) 1948 c. 45.

(*b*) in relation to Wales, save for the purpose of the making, receipt or recovery of any payment, the Minister of Agriculture, Fisheries and Food and the Secretary of State acting jointly;

(*c*) in relation to Scotland, the Secretary of State;

"approved" means approved by the appropriate Minister in writing, and "approve" and "approval" shall be construed accordingly;

"labour unit" means the amount of work, other than work done by contractors, which would in the opinion of the appropriate Minister occupy the full time, not exceeding 2,300 hours per year, of a full-time adult male worker;

"unit of account" means a unit of account of the European Economic Community and in relation to any expenditure or approval of expenditure for the purposes of a grant under this scheme any reference in this scheme, elsewhere than in paragraph 5, to a specified number of units of account shall be taken to be a reference to the sterling equivalent of that number of units of account on the date of receipt by the appropriate Minister of a claim for payment of grant under this scheme towards that expenditure and any such reference in paragraph 5 shall be taken to be a reference to the sterling equivalent of that number of units of account on the date of receipt by the appropriate Minister of an application for such approval calculated, in either case, at such rate as may appear to the appropriate Minister to be appropriate having regard to any relevant provisions of any instrument issued by that Community;

"Wales" includes Monmouthshire and references to England shall be construed accordingly.

(2) The Interpretation Act 1889(**a**) shall apply to the interpretation of this scheme as it applies to the interpretation of an Act of Parliament.

(3) Except insofar as the context otherwise requires, any reference in this scheme—

(*a*) to an enactment shall be construed as a reference to that enactment as amended or extended by any other enactment;

(*b*) to a numbered paragraph or schedule shall be construed as a reference to the paragraph or schedule bearing that number in this scheme.

Eligible expenditure

3.—(1) Subject to the provisions of this scheme, the appropriate Minister may make to any person a grant towards expenditure incurred or to be incurred by him for the purposes of, or in connection with, the carrying on or establishment of an agricultural business, being expenditure which—

(*a*) has been or is to be incurred in respect of any work or facility, or any part thereof, of a kind specified in any of paragraphs 1 to 10 and 12 of Schedule 1 or, in relation to Scotland only, paragraph 11 of that Schedule or in respect of any work or facility certified under section 26(6) of the Agriculture Act 1967(**b**) as amended by section 32(2)(*e*) of the Agriculture Act 1970, and

(*b*) appears to the appropriate Minister to be of a capital nature or incurred in connection with expenditure of a capital nature, and

(*c*) is approved for the purposes of a grant under this scheme.

(**a**) 1889 c. 63. (**b**) 1967 c. 22.

(2) The works and facilities specified in this scheme for the purposes of section 51 of the Agriculture Act 1970 are the works and facilities (not being works and facilities with respect to which a certificate has been issued under section 26(6) of the Agriculture Act 1967) specified in paragraphs 1 to 3 and 5 to 10 of Schedule 1.

(3) Subject to the provisions of paragraphs 4 and 5, the appropriate Minister may, as that Minister thinks fit, either refuse to approve expenditure or approve it in whole or in part for the purposes of a grant under this scheme and any such grant may be made, and any such approval may be given, subject to such conditions as the appropriate Minister thinks fit.

(4) Where it appears to the appropriate Minister that expenditure in respect of which approval for the purposes of a grant under this scheme is applied for is expenditure incurred or to be incurred partly for the purposes of, or in connection with, the carrying on or establishment of an agricultural business and partly for other purposes, the appropriate Minister may for the purposes of a grant under this scheme treat as having been, or to be, incurred for the purposes of, or in connection with, the carrying on or establishment of an agricultural business so much of that expenditure as appears to that Minister to be referable to the carrying on or establishment of that agricultural business.

(5) Any approval of expenditure for the purposes of a grant under this scheme may be varied or withdrawn by the appropriate Minister with the applicant's written consent.

(6) Any application for approval of expenditure shall be made in such form and manner and at such time as the appropriate Minister may from time to time require and the applicant for grant shall furnish all such particulars and information relating to the expenditure as the appropriate Minister may require.

Restrictions on approval of expenditure

4.—(1) Subject to the provisions of sub-paragraphs (3) and (4) of this paragraph, the appropriate Minister shall not approve any expenditure for the purposes of a grant under this scheme if it appears to that Minister that the land on which there is or is to be carried on or established the agricultural business for the purposes of which, or in connection with which, the expenditure is or is to be incurred is land—

(*a*) which lacks such buildings as are, in the opinion of that Minister, necessary for agricultural production on that land, and

(*b*) all or the greater part of which has, within a period of 5 years ending on the date of the receipt by the appropriate Minister of the application for approval, reverted from being occupied as part of a larger agricultural unit capable of yielding a sufficient livelihood to an occupier reasonably skilled in husbandry.

(2) Subject to the provisions of the next following sub-paragraph, the appropriate Minister shall not approve for the purposes of a grant under this scheme expenditure in respect of any work or facility unless that Minister is satisfied that the agricultural business for the purposes of which, or in connection with which, the expenditure is or is to be incurred is capable of yielding a sufficient livelihood to a person reasonably skilled in husbandry or will be capable of doing so after the carrying out or provision of the work or facility in respect of which the expenditure is or is to be incurred.

(3) The preceding provisions of this paragraph shall not apply as respects any expenditure—

(*a*) in respect of any work or facility which is of a kind specified in any of paragraphs 4 to 11 and, insofar as it relates to any of those paragraphs, paragraph 12 of Schedule 1 and which, in the opinion of the appropriate Minister, would continue to be of benefit to the land on which the said agricultural business is or is to be carried on or established if that land were to be subsequently occupied as part of a larger agricultural unit;

(*b*) in respect of any work or facility certified under section 26(6) of the Agriculture Act 1967 as a consequence of an amalgamation or boundary adjustment proposals for which were approved in pursuance of the Farm Amalgamations and Boundary Adjustments Scheme 1967(**a**), that approval having been treated, by virtue of a subsequent scheme under section 26 of the said Act, as an approval of the amalgamation or boundary adjustment, as the case may be, given in pursuance of the latter scheme.

(4) The provisions of sub-paragraph (1) of this paragraph shall not apply as respects any expenditure if it appears to the appropriate Minister that—

(*a*) the land referred to in that sub-paragraph is newly reclaimed for, or restored to, agriculture, or

(*b*) the reverting of the land described in sub-paragraph (1)(*b*) hereof was not contrary to the interests of good estate management.

5.—(1) The appropriate Minister shall not approve for the purposes of a grant under this scheme any expenditure in connection with the breeding or keeping of poultry or the production of eggs:

Provided that this restriction shall not apply as respects any expenditure in respect of any work or facility certified under section 26(6) of the Agriculture Act 1967.

(2) The appropriate Minister shall not approve for the purposes of a grant under this scheme any expenditure in connection with the breeding or keeping of pigs—

(*a*) unless it appears to that Minister that the aggregate of the amount of that expenditure and any other expenditure of that kind which has been or is to be incurred or which has been or is to be approved in respect of the same agricultural business for the purposes of a grant under this scheme amounts or will amount to not less than 10,000 units of account and not more than 40,000 units of account, that other expenditure being expenditure in respect of which an application for approval for the purposes of grant under this scheme has been received by the appropriate Minister during the 2 years immediately preceding the day on which an application for approval of the first-mentioned expenditure has been so received, and

(*b*) unless it appears to that Minister that after completion of the works or facilities in respect of which the aforesaid aggregate expenditure has been or is to be incurred, the land on which there will be carried on the agricultural business, or at least one of the agricultural businesses, for the purposes of which or in connection with which the expenditure has been or is to be incurred will be capable of producing not less than

(**a**) S.I. 1967/1608 (1967 III, p. 4418).

35 per cent. of the feeding stuffs required for the pigs kept on the land on which that business or those businesses will be carried on:

Provided that this restriction shall not apply as respects any expenditure in respect of any work or facility certified under section 26(6) of the Agriculture Act 1967.

Duration of scheme

6.—(1) Expenditure shall qualify for consideration for a grant under this scheme if application for its approval for the purposes of such a grant is received by the appropriate Minister before 1st January 1981.

(2) For the purposes of section 51(1)(*b*) of the Agriculture Act 1970 the provisions of the last foregoing sub-paragraph shall apply as if for the reference therein to 1st January 1981 there were substituted a reference to 1st January 1976.

Amounts of grant

7. The amounts of grant payable under this scheme shall be determined in accordance with the provisions of Schedule 2.

Restrictions on grant

8.—(1) The appropriate Minister may reduce or withhold grant payable under this scheme in any case where

(*a*) assistance in respect of expenditure towards which grant is claimed is or may be given otherwise than under this scheme or under section 51 of the Agriculture Act 1970; or

(*b*) the carrying out or provision of the work or facility, towards the expenditure on which grant is claimed, appears to the appropriate Minister to frustrate the purposes served by assistance previously given out of money provided by Parliament or the European Economic Community.

(2) Where at the date on which a claim for a grant under this scheme is received by the appropriate Minister—

(*a*) the amount of the expenditure included in the claim and towards which grant is payable, or

(*b*) the aggregate of the amount of that expenditure and any other expenditure towards which a grant has been paid or is payable in respect of the same agricultural business under this scheme or any other scheme made under section 29 of the Agriculture Act 1970 which comes into operation on or after 1st January 1974, or under any regulations made under section 2(2) of the European Communities Act 1972(**a**) which provide for the payment of grant to a person carrying on an agricultural business as therein defined in accordance with an approved development plan, being expenditure in respect of which a claim for payment of grant has been received by the appropriate Minister during the 2 years immediately preceding the date of the present claim,

exceeds 40,000 units of account per labour unit appearing to the appropriate Minister to be required in the carrying on of the agricultural business to which the claim relates, the appropriate Minister shall not pay grant towards

(**a**) 1972 c. 68.

so much of that expenditure or, as the case may be, the aggregate of that expenditure as exceeds that figure.

Variation of the 1970 *schemes*

9.—(1) The Farm Capital Grant Scheme 1970(**a**), as varied(**b**), shall be further varied as follows:—

(*a*) by substituting for paragraph 5(1) thereof the following sub-paragraph:—

"5.—(1) Expenditure shall qualify for consideration for a grant under this scheme if application for its approval for the purposes of such a grant is received by the appropriate Minister—

(*a*) before 1st January 1974 or such later date, not later than 31st January 1974, as the appropriate Minister may in special circumstances permit in the case of any expenditure other than expenditure in respect of any work or facility of a kind specified in any of paragraphs 4 to 7, 9 and 13 of Schedule 2 which, in the opinion of the appropriate Minister, is for the benefit of hill land or of benefit in the farming of hill land, or

(*b*) before 1st January 1978 in the case of any expenditure in respect of any work or facility of a kind specified in any of paragraphs 4 to 7, 9, 13 and, insofar as it relates to any of the aforesaid paragraphs, 18 of Schedule 2 which, in the opinion of the appropriate Minister, is for the benefit of hill land or of benefit in the farming of hill land.";

(*b*) by substituting for paragraph 9 of Schedule 2 thereto the following paragraph:—

"9. Provision, replacement or improvement of pens, dips, stells or other facilities designed and intended for use in connection with the gathering, treatment or feeding of sheep or cattle or for sheltering them in periods of adverse weather but not for in-wintering.".

(2) The Farm Capital Grant (Scotland) Scheme 1970(**c**), as varied(**d**), shall be further varied as follows:—

(*a*) by substituting for paragraph 5 thereof the following paragraph:—

"5. Expenditure shall qualify for consideration for a grant under this scheme if application for its approval for the purposes of such a grant is received by the Secretary of State—

(*a*) before 1st January 1974 or such later date, not later than 31st January 1974, as the Secretary of State may in special circumstances permit in the case of any expenditure other than expenditure in respect of any work or facility of a kind specified in any of paragraphs 4 to 7, 9 and 13 of Schedule 1 which, in the opinion of the Secretary of State, is for the benefit of hill land or of benefit in the farming of hill land, or

(*b*) before 1st January 1978 in the case of any expenditure in respect of any work or facility of a kind specified in any of paragraphs 4 to 7, 9, 13 and, insofar as it relates to any of the aforesaid paragraphs, 16 of Schedule 1 which, in the

(**a**) S.I. 1970/1759 (1970 III, p. 5741).
(**b**) S.I. 1971/1077, 1972/368, 1973/492 (1971 II, p. 3210; 1972 I, p. 1444; 1973 I p. 1574).
(**c**) S.I. 1970/1805 (1970 III, p. 5869).
(**d**) S.I. 1971/1076, 1972/362, 1973/476 (1971 II, p. 3208; 1972 I, p. 1434; 1973 I, p. 1560).

opinion of the Secretary of State, is for the benefit of hill land or of benefit in the farming of hill land.";

(*b*) by substituting for paragraph 9 of Schedule 1 thereto the following paragraph:—

"9. Provision, replacement or improvement of pens, dips, stells or other facilities designed and intended for use in connection with the gathering, treatment or feeding of sheep or cattle or for sheltering them in periods of adverse weather but not for in-wintering.".

(3) Sub-paragraphs (1)(*b*) and (2)(*b*) of this paragraph shall have effect only as respects expenditure in respect of which an application for approval for the purposes of a grant under the Farm Capital Grant Scheme 1970, as varied, or, as the case may be, the Farm Capital Grant (Scotland) Scheme 1970, as varied, is received by the appropriate Minister on or after 1st January 1974 and before 1st January 1978.

In Witness whereof the Official Seal of the Minister of Agriculture, Fisheries and Food is hereunto affixed on 19th November 1973.

(L.S.)

Joseph Godber,
Minister of Agriculture, Fisheries and Food.

Gordon Campbell,
Secretary of State for Scotland.

20th November 1973.

Peter Thomas,
Secretary of State for Wales.

20th November 1973.

We approve.

Hugh Rossi,

P. L. Hawkins,

Two of the Lords Commissioners for Her Majesty's Treasury.

20th November 1973.

Paragraph 3(1)(*a*) and (2)

SCHEDULE 1

WORKS AND FACILITIES ELIGIBLE FOR GRANT

1. Provision, replacement, improvement, alteration, enlargement or reconditioning of permanent buildings (excluding living accommodation and buildings designed and intended for specialised horticultural use or for any use mentioned in paragraph 8 of this Schedule), silos, bulk dry stores, yards, loading platforms, ramps or banks.

2. Provision, replacement or improvement of systems for the disposal of farm waste.

3. Provision, replacement or improvement of facilities for the supply of electricity or gas for agricultural purposes.

4. Field drainage, including under-drainage and ditching.

5. Provision, replacement or improvement of facilities for the supply of water.

6. Provision or improvement of farm flood protection works; protection or improvement of river banks.

7. Provision, replacement or improvement of roads, fords, bridges, culverts, railway crossings, creeps, piers, jetties or slips.

8. Provision, replacement or improvement of pens, dips, stells or other facilities designed and intended for use in connection with the gathering, treatment or feeding of sheep or cattle or for sheltering them in periods of adverse weather but not for in-wintering.

9. Orchard grubbing.

10. Provision, replacement or improvement of wire-work for hop gardens.

11. In Scotland only, making, improvement or alteration of the banks or channels of watercourses to provide or improve the drainage of agricultural land or to prevent or mitigate the flooding or erosion of agricultural land.

12. Any work or facility incidental to the carrying out or provision of any work or facility specified in paragraphs 1 to 11 of this Schedule or necessary or proper in carrying it out or providing it or securing the full benefit thereof.

Paragraph 7

SCHEDULE 2

AMOUNTS OF GRANT

1. Subject to the provisions of this Schedule and of paragraph 8 of this scheme the amount of any grant payable under this scheme towards expenditure in respect of any work or facility of a kind specified in

(*a*) any of paragraphs 1 to 3 and 5 to 10 of Schedule 1 shall be 20 per cent. of that expenditure;

(*b*) paragraph 11 of that Schedule shall be 60 per cent. of that expenditure.

2.—(1) Subject to the provisions of this Schedule and of paragraph 8 of this scheme, the amount of any grant payable under this scheme towards expenditure in respect of field drainage, including under-drainage and ditching

(*a*) shall be 55 per cent. of that expenditure if it appears to the appropriate Minister that during the period of 2 years immediately preceding the date of receipt by the appropriate Minister of the claim for payment of grant under this scheme towards that expenditure the claimant for such grant or any other person incurred for the purposes of or in connection with the carrying on of the agricultural business to which that claim relates other expenditure which appears to the appropriate Minister to be of a capital nature or incurred in connection with expenditure of a capital nature and not to be of a kind specified in sub-paragraph (2) of this paragraph and if it appears to the appropriate Minister that the amount of any grant which may be or become payable under this scheme or any other scheme made under section 29 of the Agriculture Act 1970 which comes into operation on or after 1st January 1974 or any regulations of the kind mentioned in paragraph 8(2)(*b*) of this scheme in respect of that other expenditure together with the amount of grant which may become payable under this scheme in respect of the aforesaid expenditure on field drainage, under-drainage or ditching, as the case may be, does not in aggregate amount to more than 25 per cent. of the aggregate of that other expenditure and the said expenditure on field drainage, under-drainage or ditching, or 25 per cent. of such proportion of the aforesaid aggregate of expenditure as is equivalent to 40,000 units of account per labour unit appearing to the appropriate Minister to be required in the establishment or carrying on of the agricultural business to which the aforesaid claim relates, whichever is the less;

(*b*) in any case to which the provisions of sub-paragraph (1)(*a*) of this paragraph do not apply shall be 25 per cent. of that expenditure or 25 per cent. of the aggregate of that expenditure and any other expenditure which appears to the appropriate Minister to be of a kind referred to as other expenditure in sub-paragraph (1)(a) of this paragraph and to have been incurred within the aforesaid period of 2 years less any grant under this scheme or any other scheme made under section 29 of the Agriculture Act 1970 which comes into operation on or after 1st January 1974 or any regulations of the kind mentioned in paragraph 8(2)(*b*) of this scheme which may be or become payable in respect of that other expenditure, whichever is the greater, so however that if the aforesaid aggregate amount exceeds such amount as is equivalent to 40,000 units of account per labour unit appearing to the appropriate Minister to be required in the establishment or carrying on of the agricultural business to which the claim relates the reference to that aggregate amount shall be taken to be a reference to the last mentioned amount.

(2) The expenditure referred to as other expenditure in sub-paragraph (1)(*a*) and (*b*) of this paragraph does not include—

(*a*) any expenditure in connection with the breeding or keeping of poultry or the production of eggs;

(*b*) any expenditure in connection with the breeding or keeping of pigs which does not comply with the restriction on approval specified in paragraph 5(2) of this scheme;

(*c*) any expenditure on the purchase of pigs or on the purchase of calves intended for slaughter at less than 7 months of age;

(*d*) any expenditure on the purchase of land;

(*e*) any expenditure on the erection, alteration or improvement of any living accommodation;

(*f*) any expenditure on the purchase of livestock (other than livestock of a kind mentioned in sub-paragraph (2)(*c*) of this paragraph) unless the appropriate Minister is satisfied that the purchase is an initial purchase made in order to increase the number of animals kept for the purposes of the agricultural business to which the claim for grant relates;

(*g*) any expenditure towards which, it appears to the appropriate Minister, no grant under any scheme or regulations of a kind mentioned in the said sub-paragraph (1)(*a*) and (*b*) is or will become payable, being all or part of expenditure in respect of which a claim for such grant has been or may be made.

3. The amount of any grant payable under this scheme towards expenditure in respect of the carrying out or provision of any work or facility which is incidental to the carrying out or provision of another work or facility of any kind

specified in paragraphs 1 to 11 of Schedule 1 or necessary or proper in the carrying out or provision of that other work or facility or for securing the full benefit thereof shall be calculated at the rate of grant appropriate to that other work or facility in accordance with the provisions of this Schedule.

4. Notwithstanding the foregoing provisions of this Schedule, the amount of any grant payable under this scheme towards expenditure approved for the purposes of a grant under this scheme in respect of any work or facility certified under section 26(6) of the Agriculture Act 1967 shall be 50 per cent. of that expenditure:

Provided that if any work or facility certified as aforesaid has been so certified as a consequence of an amalgamation or boundary adjustment approved, or submitted for approval, for the purposes of a grant under section 26 of the said Act, as originally enacted or as amended by section 32(2)(*e*) of the Agriculture Act 1970, on or after 19th March 1970 and not later than 18th March 1972 in pursuance of a scheme made under the said section 26, the amount of any grant payable under this scheme towards expenditure approved for the purposes of a grant under this scheme in respect of that work or facility shall be 60 per cent. of that expenditure.

5. If an application for approval of expenditure for the purposes of a grant under this scheme in respect of any work or facility certified under section 26(6) of the Agriculture Act 1967 is, in the opinion of the appropriate Minister, in substitution for an application for such approval of expenditure in respect of some other work or facility certified as aforesaid, the amount of any grant payable under this scheme towards the first mentioned expenditure shall be calculated at the rate of grant appropriate to the last mentioned expenditure in accordance with the provisions of paragraph 4 of this Schedule.

6. In such cases and subject to such conditions as the appropriate Minister may from time to time determine, the amount of any expenditure towards which grant is payable under this scheme shall, if the applicant for grant so elects, be taken for the purpose of determining the amount of the grant as such standard amount as the appropriate Minister may from time to time fix with the approval of the Treasury.

EXPLANATORY NOTE

(This Note is not part of the Scheme.)

This Scheme, which is made under section 29 of the Agriculture Act 1970 and applies to the whole of the United Kingdom, comes into operation on 1st January 1974. It largely supersedes the Farm Capital Grant Scheme 1970 and the Farm Capital Grant (Scotland) Scheme 1970, as varied, for the purposes of approval and payment of grant in respect of applications received on or after 1st January 1974. However, the superseded schemes will remain in operation in relation to grants at special rates for the benefit of hill land farms.

The principal changes are—

(*a*) The Scheme restricts the total amount of expenditure which may qualify for grant, taking into account similar grant-aided expenditure during the preceding 2 years (paragraph 8(2)) and it also restricts the amount of expenditure on pig production enterprises which may qualify for grant and imposes a requirement as to the quantity of feeding stuffs capable of being produced from the land on which the pigs are kept (paragraph 5(2)).

(*b*) The Scheme provides that, in general, expenditure on egg production or the breeding or keeping of poultry shall not qualify for grant (paragraph 5(1)).

(*c*) The rate of grant for field drainage is reduced to a maximum of 55 per cent. This rate of grant will be payable if the total amount of grant payable under this and certain other enactments towards certain capital expenditure incurred during the preceding 2 years does not exceed 25 per cent. of the total amount of expenditure incurred. In other cases a lower rate of grant (but not lower than 25 per cent.), calculated by reference to the total amount of capital expenditure incurred during the period and to grant payable under this and the other enactments, will be payable (Schedule 2, paragraph 2).

1973 No. 1967

WEIGHTS AND MEASURES

The Weights and Measures Act 1963 (Pasta) Order 1973

Laid before Parliament in draft

Made - - - *23rd November* 1973

Coming into Operation *1st July* 1974

Whereas the Secretary of State pursuant to section 54(2) of the Weights and Measures Act 1963(**a**) (hereinafter referred to as "the Act") has consulted with organisations appearing to him to be representative of interests substantially affected by this Order and considered the representations made to him by such organisations with respect to the subject matter of this Order:

And whereas a draft of this Order has been laid before Parliament and approved by resolution of each House of Parliament pursuant to section 54(3) of the Act:

Now, therefore, the Secretary of State, in exercise of powers conferred by section 21(2), (3) and (5) of the Act and now vested in him(**b**) and of all other powers enabling him in that behalf, hereby makes the following Order:

1.—(1) This Order may be cited as the Weights and Measures Act 1963 (Pasta) Order 1973 and shall come into operation on 1st July 1974.

(2) The Interpretation Act 1889(**c**) shall apply to the interpretation of this Order as it applies to the interpretation of an Act of Parliament.

2. Part VIII of Schedule 4 to the Act shall cease to apply to the flour products described as macaroni and similar products.

3. Pasta which is not pre-packed shall be sold by retail only by net weight.

4. Subject to Article 5 of this Order pasta shall be pre-packed only if:

(*a*) it is made up in one of the following quantities by net weight, that is to say:

(i) 4 oz, 8 oz, 12 oz, 1 lb, 1½ lb, or a multiple of 1 lb; or

(ii) 125 g, 250 g, 375 g, 500 g or a multiple of 500 g; and

(*b*) the container is marked with an indication of quantity by net weight.

(**a**) 1963 c. 31.
(**b**) S.I. 1970/1537 (1970 III, p. 5293).
(**c**) 1889 c. 63.

5. Pasta shall be exempted from all requirements of Article 4(*a*) of this Order if pre-packed in a quantity not exceeding 50 g.

Geoffrey Howe,
Minister for Trade and Consumer Affairs,
Department of Trade and Industry.

23rd November 1973.

EXPLANATORY NOTE

(*This Note is not part of the Order.*)

This Order provides that Part VIII of Schedule 4 to the Weights and Measures Act 1963 shall cease to apply to macaroni and similar products and reproduces with amendments the provisions of that Part relating to pasta, a description which includes, inter alia, macaroni and similar products. Pasta may only be pre-packed in a prescribed range of imperial or metric weights where the quantity exceeds 50 g and if the container is marked with an indication of the quantity by net weight. If not pre-packed, pasta may only be sold by retail by net weight. The reference to metric units is new.

1973 No. 1968

WEIGHTS AND MEASURES

The Weights and Measures Act 1963 (Salt) Order 1973

Laid before Parliament in draft

Made - - -	*23rd November* 1973
Coming into Operation	*1st January* 1975

Whereas the Secretary of State pursuant to section 54(2) of the Weights and Measures Act 1963(**a**) (hereinafter referred to as "the Act") has consulted with organisations appearing to him to be representative of interests substantially affected by this Order and considered the representations made to him by such organisations with respect to the subject matter of this Order:

And whereas a draft of this Order has been laid before Parliament and approved by resolution of each House of Parliament pursuant to section 54(3) of the Act:

Now, therefore, the Secretary of State, in exercise of powers conferred by section 21(2), (3) and (5) of the Act and now vested in him(**b**) and of all other powers enabling him in that behalf, hereby makes the following Order:

1.—(1) This Order may be cited as the Weights and Measures Act 1963 (Salt) Order 1973 and shall come into operation on 1st January 1975.

(2) The Interpretation Act 1889(**c**) shall apply to the interpretation of this Order as it applies to the interpretation of an Act of Parliament.

2. Part VIII of Schedule 4 to the Act shall cease to apply to salt.

3. Salt which is not pre-packed shall be sold by retail only by net weight.

4. Subject to Article 5 of this Order salt, other than cut lump salt, shall be pre-packed only if:

(*a*) it is made up in one of the following quantities by net weight, that is to say:

(i) 4 oz, 8 oz, 12 oz, 1 lb, 1½ lb, or a multiple of 1 lb; or

(ii) 125 g, 250 g, 500 g, 750 g, 1 kg, 1·5 kg, or a multiple of one kg up to and including 10 kg, 12·5 kg, 25 kg or 50 kg; and

(*b*) the container is marked with an indication of quantity by net weight.

(**a**) 1963. c. 31.
(**b**) S.I. 1970/1537 (1970 III, p. 5293).
(**c**) 1889 c. 63.

5. Salt shall be exempted from all requirements of Article 4(*a*) of this Order if pre-packed in a quantity not exceeding 100 g.

Geoffrey Howe,
Minister for Trade and Consumer Affairs,
Department of Trade and Industry.

23rd November 1973.

EXPLANATORY NOTE

(This Note is not part of the Order.)

This Order provides that Part VIII of Schedule 4 to the Weights and Measures Act 1963 shall cease to apply to salt and reproduces with amendments the provisions of that Part relating to salt. Salt, other than cut lump salt, may only be pre-packed in a prescribed range of imperial or metric weights where the quantity exceeds 100 g and if the container is marked with an indication of the quantity by net weight. If not pre-packed, salt may only be sold by retail by net weight. The reference to metric units is new.

1973 No. 1969 (C.58)

SOCIAL SECURITY

The Pensioners' Payments and National Insurance Act 1973 (Commencement) Order 1973

Made - - - *23rd November* 1973

The Secretary of State for Social Services, in exercise of powers conferred by sections 8(1) and 9(3)(*a*) of the Pensioners' Payments and National Insurance Act 1973(**a**), and section 1(1) of the Northern Ireland (Temporary Provisions) Act 1972(**b**), and of all other powers enabling him in that behalf, hereby makes the following Order:—

Citation

1. This Order may be cited as the Pensioners' Payments and National Insurance Act 1973 (Commencement) Order 1973.

Appointed day

2. The day appointed for the coming into force in Great Britain and in Northern Ireland of section 5 of the Pensioners' Payments and National Insurance Act 1973 (increase in flat-rate contributions) shall be 21st January 1974.

Keith Joseph,
Secretary of State for Social Services.

23rd November 1973.

(**a**) 1973 c. 61. (**b**) 1972 c. 22.

EXPLANATORY NOTE

(This Note is not part of the Order.)

This Order brings into operation in Great Britain and in Northern Ireland on 21st January 1974 section 5 of the Pensioners' Payments and National Insurance Act 1973 which provides for increases in the weekly rate of flat-rate national insurance contributions payable by employers, self-employed persons and non-employed persons.

The remaining provisions of the Act came into operation on the passing of the Act.

1973 No. 1972 (C.59)

MATRIMONIAL CAUSES

The Matrimonial Causes Act 1973 (Commencement) Order 1973

Made - - - *26th November* 1973

The Lord Chancellor, in exercise of the powers conferred on him by section 55(2) of the Matrimonial Causes Act 1973(**a**), hereby makes the following Order:—

1.—(1) This Order may be cited as the Matrimonial Causes Act 1973 (Commencement) Order 1973.

(2) The Interpretation Act 1889(**b**) shall apply to this Order as it applies to an Act of Parliament.

2. The Matrimonial Causes Act 1973 shall come into operation on 1st January 1974.

Dated 26th November 1973.

Hailsham of St. Marylebone, C.

EXPLANATORY NOTE

(*This Note is not part of the Order.*)

This Order brings the Matrimonial Causes Act 1973 into operation on 1st January 1974.

(**a**) 1973 c. 18. (**b**) 1889 c. 63.

STATUTORY INSTRUMENTS

1973 No. 1973 (L.27)

MATRIMONIAL CAUSES

SUPREME COURT OF JUDICATURE, ENGLAND

COUNTY COURTS

The Matrimonial Causes (Amendment No. 3) Rules 1973

Made - - -	*26th November* 1973
Laid before Parliament	*30th November* 1973
Coming into Operation	*1st January* 1974

We, the authority having power to make rules of court for the purposes mentioned in section 50 of the Matrimonial Causes Act 1973(**a**), as amended by section 6(2) of the Domicile and Matrimonial Proceedings Act 1973(**b**), hereby exercise that power as follows:—

1.—(1) These Rules may be cited as the Matrimonial Causes (Amendment No. 3) Rules 1973 and shall come into operation on 1st January 1974.

(2) In these Rules a rule referred to by number means the rule so numbered in the Matrimonial Causes Rules 1971(**c**), as amended(**d**), and a form referred to by number means the form so numbered in Appendix 2 to those Rules.

(3) The Interpretation Act 1889(**e**) shall apply to the interpretation of these Rules as it applies to the interpretation of an Act of Parliament.

2. Rule 9 shall be amended as follows:—

(1) For paragraphs (2) and (3) there shall be substituted the following paragraphs:—

"(2) A petition for divorce, nullity or judicial separation—

(*a*) shall state whether or not there are to the knowledge of the petitioner any proceedings continuing in any country outside England and Wales which are in respect of the marriage to which the petition relates or are capable of affecting its validity or subsistence, and

(*b*) if there are any such proceedings, shall give particulars of them including—

(i) the court in or tribunal or authority before which they were begun,

(ii) the date when they were begun,

(iii) the names of the parties,

(**a**) 1973 c. 18. (**b**) 1973 c. 45. (**c**) S.I. 1971/953 (1971 II, p. 2713).
(**d**) The relevant amending instruments are S.I. 1971/1923, 1973/777 (1971 III, p. 5243; 1973 I, p. 2459). (**e**) 1889 c. 63.

(iv) the date, or as the case may be, the expected date of any trial in the proceedings, and

(v) such other facts as may be relevant to the question whether the proceedings on the petition should be stayed under Schedule 1 to the Domicile and Matrimonial Proceedings Act 1973.

(3) In paragraph (2) "proceedings continuing in any country outside England and Wales" includes any proceedings in that country which are not instituted in a court of law, if those proceedings are instituted before a tribunal or other authority in that country having power under the law having effect there to determine questions of status, and proceedings shall be treated as continuing in a country outside England and Wales if they have been begun and have not been finally disposed of."

(2) In paragraph (5) the letter (*a*) and the words "and (*b*)" to the end shall be omitted.

3. In rule 21 after paragraph (3) there shall be inserted the following paragraph:—

"(3A) Where an answer to any such petition as is mentioned in rule 9(2) contains a prayer for relief, it shall contain the information required by that paragraph in the case of the petition in so far as it has not been given by the petitioner."

4. After rule 36 there shall be added the following rule:—

"*Stay under Domicile and Matrimonial Proceedings Act* 1973

36A.—(1) An application to the court by the petitioner or respondent in proceedings for divorce for an order under paragraph 8 of Schedule 1 to the Domicile and Matrimonial Proceedings Act 1973 (in this rule referred to as "Schedule 1") shall be made to the registrar, who may determine the application or refer the application, or any question arising thereon, to a judge for his decision as if the application were an application for ancillary relief.

(2) An application for an order under paragraph 9 of Schedule 1 shall be made to a judge.

(3) Where, on giving directions for trial, it appears to the registrar from any information given pursuant to rule 9(2) or 21(3A) or paragraph (4) of this rule that any proceedings which are in respect of the marriage in question or which are capable of affecting its validity or subsistence are continuing in any country outside England and Wales, and he considers that the question whether the proceedings on the petition should be stayed under paragraph 9 of Schedule 1 ought to be determined by the court, he shall fix a date and time for the consideration of that question by a judge and give notice thereof to all parties.

In this paragraph "proceedings continuing in any country outside England and Wales" has the same meaning as in rule 9(2).

(4) Any party who makes a request for directions for trial in proceedings for divorce, nullity or judicial separation shall, if there has been a change in the information given pursuant to rule 9(2) or 21(3A), file a statement giving particulars of the change.

(5) An application by a party to the proceedings for an order under paragraph 10 of Schedule 1 may be made to the registrar and he may determine

the application or may refer the application, or any question arising thereon, to a judge as if the application were an application for ancillary relief."

5. Form 2 shall be amended as follows:—

(1) For paragraph (3) there shall be substituted the following paragraph:—

"(3) [*In the case of a petition for divorce, nullity, judicial separation or presumption of death and dissolution of marriage where it is alleged that the court has jurisdiction based on domicile*] The petitioner is domiciled in England and Wales [*or* The petitioner is domiciled in and the respondent is domiciled in England and Wales] [*or, where it is alleged that the court has jurisdiction based on habitual residence*] The petitioner has [*or* The respondent has] [*or* The petitioner and the respondent have] been habitually resident in England and Wales throughout the period of one year ending with the date of the presentation of the petition [*or as the case may be*] [*give details of the habitual residence relied on including the addresses of places of residence during the one year period and the length of residence at each place*]. The petitioner is a [*state occupation*] [and resides at], and the respondent is a [*state occupation*] [and resides at]."

(2) After paragraph 9 there shall be added the following paragraph:—

"(9A) There are no proceedings continuing in any country outside England and Wales which are in respect of the marriage or are capable of affecting its validity or subsistence [except [*give particulars of the proceedings, including the court in or tribunal or authority before and the date on which they were begun, the names of the parties, the date or expected date of any trial in the proceedings and such other facts as may be relevant to the question whether the proceedings on the petition should be stayed under Schedule 1 to the Domicile and Matrimonial Proceedings Act* 1973]]."

6. In Form 17 for paragraph 12 there shall be substituted the following paragraph:—

"12. This Court has jurisdiction to entertain these proceedings by reason of the fact that [*in the case of an application based on domicile* I am [*or* the respondent is] [*or* the respondent and I are] domiciled in England and Wales] [*or in the case of an application based on residence* I have been habitually resident in England and Wales throughout the period of one year ending with the date of this application [*or* the respondent is now resident in England and Wales]]."

Dated 26th November 1973.

Hailsham of St. Marylebone, C.
George Baker, P.
John Latey, J.
Ifor Lloyd.
Irvon Sunderland.
W. D. S. Caird.
J. L. Williams.
F. B. Purchas.
Margaret Puxon.
J. D. Clarke.
D. E. Morris.

EXPLANATORY NOTE

(This Note is not part of the Rules.)

These Rules, which amend the Matrimonial Causes Rules 1971, are consequential on the coming into operation of the Domicile and Matrimonial Prcceedings Act 1973.

Rules 2 and 5 alter the requirements as to information to be given in the petition, particularly those with regard to the domicile and residence of the parties, so as to reflect the new bases of the court's jurisdiction under the Act. Rule 6 makes similar provision for applications on the ground of wilful neglect to maintain. Rules 2 and 5 also require a petitioner to give details of concurrent proceedings in respect of the marriage in any other country, whether before a court or tribunal or other authority, and a respondent spouse praying for relief must supplement these details in his or her answer (Rule 3).

Rule 4 deals with staying proceedings on a petition where there are concurrent proceedings in another country. An application for an obligatory stay under paragraph 8 of Schedule 1 to the Act is to be made to a registrar. An application for a discretionary stay under paragraph 9 must be made to a judge and if the registrar, on giving directions for trial, considers that the question of imposing such a stay ought to be considered by the court, he must refer it to a judge.

STATUTORY INSTRUMENTS

1973 No. 1977

AGRICULTURAL EMPLOYMENT

SAFETY, HEALTH AND WELFARE

The Agriculture (Tractor Cabs) (Amendment) Regulations 1973

Laid before Parliament in draft

Made - - - *23rd November* 1973

Coming into Operation *28th November* 1973

The Minister of Agriculture, Fisheries and Food and the Secretary of State, acting jointly, in exercise of the powers conferred on them by subsections (1) to (4) of section 1 and by section 17 of the Agriculture (Safety, Health and Welfare Provisions) Act 1956(**a**), and of all their other enabling powers, after consultation with such organisations as appear to them to represent the interests concerned, hereby make the following regulations, a draft whereof has been laid before Parliament and has been approved by resolution of each House of Parliament:—

Citation, and extent

1. These regulations, which may be cited as the Agriculture (Tractor Cabs) (Amendment) Regulations 1973, shall apply to Great Britain.

Interpretation

2.—(1) These regulations shall be construed as one with the Agriculture (Tractor Cabs) Regulations 1967(**b**), in these regulations referred to as "the principal regulations".

(2) The Interpretation Act 1889(**c**) applies to the interpretation of these regulations as it applies to the interpretation of an Act of Parliament.

Amendment of principal regulations to provide for restrictions on noise

3. The principal regulations shall be amended as follows:—

(*a*) In regulation 2(1), for the definition of "approval mark", there shall be substituted the following definition:

" "approval mark" means one of the two marks, incorporating a crown inside a triangle, illustrated in paragraph 1 of Part I of the Schedule to these regulations, and "appropriate approval mark" means

(*a*) in relation to a safety cab fitted to a tractor which is or has

(**a**) 1956 c. 49.
(**b**) S.I. 1967/1072 (1967 II, p. 3163).
(**c**) 1889 c. 63.

been new on or after 1st September 1975, or in relation to a safety cab which itself is or has been new on or after 1st September 1977, the mark illustrated in sub-paragraph (1) of that paragraph;

(*b*) in relation to any other safety cab, either approval mark; "

(*b*) After regulation 3(2) there shall be inserted the following paragraphs:

"(2A) In the case of a certificate of approval issued on or after 1st September 1977 the Ministers shall further be satisfied, and in the case of a certificate issued before that date may be so satisfied, before issuing the certificate, that the noise levels inside safety cabs of the model to which it relates, when fitted to tractors of descriptions specified in the certificate, would not be more than 90 dBA if tested in accordance with British Standard Specification No. B.S. 4063: 1973(**a**).

(2B) Where a certificate of approval is issued for any model of safety cab in respect of which the Ministers have been satisfied as to the matters specified in regulation 3(2A) above, the fact shall be stated in the certificate.

(2C) While a safety cab is fitted to a tractor which is or has been new on or after 1st September 1975, or where a safety cab itself is or has been new on or after 1st September 1977, it shall not be an approved safety cab for the purpose of these regulations unless the Ministers have been satisfied as to the matters specified in regulation 3(2A) above in relation to safety cabs of that model, and the fact is stated in the certificate of approval."

(*c*) In Part I of the Schedule, for paragraph 1 there shall be substituted the following paragraph:

"1.—(1) Where the Ministers have been satisfied, before issuing a certificate of approval (whether issued before or on or after 1st September 1977), that the noise levels inside safety cabs of the model to which it relates, when fitted to tractors of descriptions specified in the certificate, would not be more than 90 dBA if tested in accordance with British Standard Specification No. B.S. 4063: 1973, the approval mark on an approved safety cab of that model shall be the following symbol:

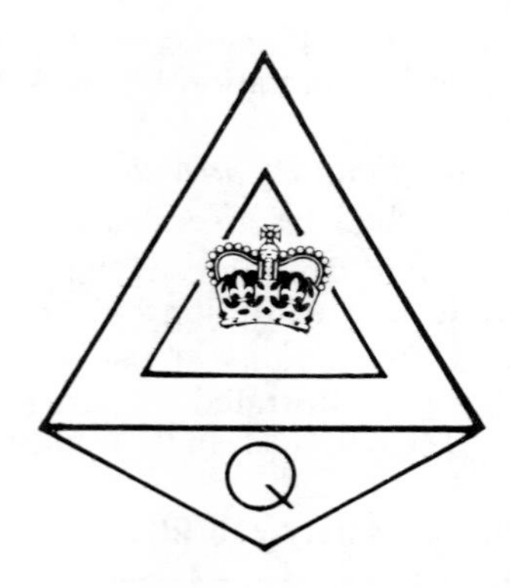

(a) Specification for requirements and testing of protective cabs and frames for agricultural wheeled tractors: published by the British Standards Institution, 2 Park Street, London, W1A 2B.

(2) In any other case the approval mark on an approved safety cab shall be the following symbol:

"

Minor consequential amendments

4. In consequence of the provisions of the preceding regulation, the principal regulations shall also be amended as follows:

(*a*) In regulation 2(3)(*a*), after the word "protection", there shall be added the words "(including protection from noise)".

(*b*) In regulation 3(7)(*a*), before the words "approval mark", there shall be added the word "correct".

(*c*) In regulations 4 and 5(1), before the words "approval mark", wherever they occur, there shall be inserted the word "appropriate".

(*d*) In paragraph (*a*) of regulation 4, after the words "supplementary marks", there shall be inserted the words "which relate to that approval mark and".

(*e*) In paragraphs (1) and (2) of regulation 7, after the end of sub-paragraph (*b*) in each case, there shall be inserted the words "or (*c*) that the safety cab has been approved as being of a particular standard"

(*f*) In Part II of the Schedule to the regulations, for sub-paragraph (*e*) there shall be substituted the following sub-paragraphs:

"(*e*) Supplementary marks relating to the same approval mark shall be as near as is reasonably practicable to the approval mark and to each other.

(*f*) Where there is more than one approval mark on a safety cab the supplementary marks relating to each shall be separate and clearly distinguishable from those relating to the other."

Miscellaneous amendments to principal regulations

5.—(1) Regulation 2(2) of the principal regulations (which deems the hire purchase of a tractor to be a sale) shall be amended by inserting after the word "tractor" the words "or a safety cab".

(2) Regulation 3(2) of the principal regulations (which provides for the testing of safety cabs in accordance with a British Standard Specification) shall be amended by substituting for the words "British Standard Specification

No. B.S. 4063: 1966" the words "the requirements relating to protective cabs set out in British Standard Specification No. B.S. 4063: 1973."

(3) Where the first letting on hire or loan of a tractor for use in agriculture by the hirer or borrower, as the case may be, occurred before 1st September 1970, regulations 4(*c*) and 5 of the principal regulations (which prohibit the letting on hire and use of tractors without safety cabs) shall cease to apply to that tractor from the commencement of these regulations until 1st September 1977, notwithstanding the provisions of regulation 1(2) of the principal regulations.

In Witness whereof the Official Seal of the Minister of Agriculture, Fisheries and Food is hereunto affixed on 22nd November 1973.

(L.S.)

Joseph Godber,
Minister of Agriculture, Fisheries and Food.

Gordon Campbell,
Secretary of State for Scotland.

23rd November 1973.

EXPLANATORY NOTE

(This Note is not part of the Regulations.)

These Regulations amend the Agriculture (Tractor Cabs) Regulations 1967 by providing for safety cabs to be tested for noise levels. A new approval mark is prescribed for cabs whose noise levels are not more than 90 dBA. From 1st September 1975 new tractors will have to be fitted with such cabs, and from 1st September 1977 all new safety cabs will have to satisfy the requirements as to noise. There is no restriction on fitting cabs which do not satisfy these requirements to tractors first sold before September 1975. Approved cabs fitted to such tractors will not have to be replaced with models which meet the noise requirements.

The Regulations apply the new British Standard Specification 4063: 1973 to the testing of safety cabs instead of B.S. 4063: 1966.

The exemption until 1st September 1977 for tractors sold for use in agriculture before 1st September 1970 is extended to include tractors let on hire or loaned for such use before the latter date.

The Regulations also provide for the hire-purchase of a safety cab to be treated as a sale.

1973 No. 1978

CIVIL AVIATION

The Civil Aviation Authority (Charges) (Third Amendment) Regulations 1973

Made - - -	*27th November* 1973
Laid before Parliament	*5th December* 1973
Coming into Operation	*1st January* 1974

The Secretary of State, in exercise of his powers under section 9(3) of the Civil Aviation Act 1971(**a**), and of all other powers enabling him in that behalf, hereby makes the following Regulations:

1. These Regulations may be cited as the Civil Aviation Authority (Charges) (Third Amendment) Regulations 1973 and shall come into operation on 1st January 1974.

2. The Interpretation Act 1889(**b**) shall apply for the purpose of the interpretation of these Regulations as it applies for the purpose of the interpretation of an Act of Parliament.

3.—(1) The Civil Aviation Authority (Charges) Regulations 1972(**c**), as amended(**d**), shall be further amended as follows:

(*a*) In regulation 2(1) the words from "and "Class 2 licence" " to the end shall be deleted;

(*b*) Regulation 4 shall be deleted;

(*c*) Schedule 2 shall be deleted.

(2) Section 38(2) of the Interpretation Act 1889 (which relates to the effect of repeals) shall apply to these Regulations as if these Regulations were an Act of Parliament and as if the provisions deleted by paragraph (1) of this Regulation were an Act of Parliament thereby repealed.

Michael Heseltine,
Minister for Aerospace and Shipping.
Department of Trade and Industry.

27th November 1973.

(**a**) 1971 c. 75.
(**b**) 1889 c. 63.
(**c**) S.I. 1972/150 (1972 I, p. 504).
(**d**) S.I. 1972/1272,1973/92 (1972 II, p. 3814; 1973 I, p. 476).

EXPLANATORY NOTE

(This Note is not part of the Regulations.)

These Regulations further amend the Civil Aviation Authority (Charges) Regulations 1972 by excluding from the scope of the Regulations charges payable in connection with air transport licences. These charges have been incorporated in a Scheme of charges made by the Authority under section 9(1) of the Civil Aviation Act 1971.

STATUTORY INSTRUMENTS

1973 No. 1979

MERCHANT SHIPPING

The Merchant Shipping (Metrication) Regulations 1973

Made - - -	*27th November* 1973
Laid before Parliament	*5th December* 1973
Coming into Operation	*1st January* 1974

The Secretary of State in exercise of powers conferred by section 90 of the Merchant Shipping Act 1970(**a**) and now vested in him (**b**) hereby makes the following Regulations:

1.—(1) These Regulations may be cited as the Merchant Shipping (Metrication) Regulations 1973 and shall come into operation on the 1st day of January 1974.

(2) The Interpretation Act 1889(**c**) shall apply to these Regulations as it applies to the interpretation of an Act of Parliament.

2.—(1) In section 7(1) of the Merchant Shipping Act 1894(**d**)—

(*a*) in paragraph (*a*), for the words "four inches" there shall be substituted the words "one decimetre";

(*b*) at the beginning of paragraph (*c*) there shall be inserted the words "In the case of every such ship registered before the 1st day of January 1974".

(2) After the said paragraph (*c*) there shall be inserted the following paragraphs—

"(*d*) In the case of every such ship registered on or after that date, a scale of decimetres, or of metres and decimetres, denoting a draught of water shall be marked on each side of her stem and of her stern post—

(i) in figures at two-decimetre intervals, if the scale is in decimetres; and

(ii) in figures at each metre interval and at intervening two-decimetre intervals, if the scale is in metres and decimetres;

the capital letter "M" being placed after each metre figure; the top figure of the scale showing both the metre and (except where it marks a full metre interval) the decimetre figure; the lower line of the figures, or figures and letters (as the case may be), coinciding with the draught

(**a**) 1970 c. 36.
(**b**) *See* S.I. 1970/1537 (1970 III, p. 5293).
(**c**) 1889 c. 63.
(**d**) 1894 c. 60.

line denoted thereby; the figures and letters being not less than one decimetre in length and being marked by being cut in and painted white or yellow on a dark ground, or in such other way as the Secretary of State approves.

(*e*) In the case of every such ship registered after that date but before the 31st day of December 1974 a scale shall be marked either in accordance with paragraph (*c*) of this sub-section, or in accordance with paragraph (*d*) of this sub-section."

(3) In section 7(3) of the said Act of 1894 the words "of feet" shall be deleted.

(4) In section 436(1) of the said Act of 1894, the words "of feet" and "in feet and inches" shall be deleted.

3. The Pilotage Act 1913(**a**) is hereby adapted as follows:

In section 39(1)(*a*) the words "one inch broad and three inches long" shall be replaced by the words "twenty-five millimetres broad and seventy-five millimetres long".

Michael Heseltine,
Minister for Aerospace and Shipping,
Department of Trade and Industry.

27th November 1973.

EXPLANATORY NOTE

(*This Note is not part of the Regulations.*)

These Regulations adapt certain measurement provisions of the Merchant Shipping Acts, dealing with the marking on ships' sides, to the metric scale.

(**a**) 2 & 3 Geo. 5. c. 31.

1973 No. 1983

SEA FISHERIES

BOATS AND METHODS OF FISHING

The Cod (North-east Arctic) Licensing Order 1973

Made - - -	*26th November* 1973
Laid before Parliament	*5th December* 1973
Coming into Operation	*1st January* 1974

The Minister of Agriculture, Fisheries and Food and the Secretaries of State respectively concerned with the sea fishing industry in Scotland and Northern Ireland, in exercise of the powers conferred on them by sections 4 and 15 of the Sea Fish (Conservation) Act 1967**(a)** as the latter section is amended by section 22(1) of, and paragraph 38 of Part II of Schedule I to, the Sea Fisheries Act 1968**(b)** and of all other powers enabling them in that behalf, being satisfied that substantially equivalent measures are being taken by governments of other countries concerned, hereby make the following Order:—

Citation and commencement

1. This Order may be cited as the Cod (North-east Arctic) Licensing Order 1973 and shall come into operation on 1st January 1974.

Interpretation

2.—(1) In this Order:

"the Act" means the Sea Fish (Conservation) Act 1967;

"North-east Arctic waters" means the area of sea described in the Schedule to this Order comprising Statistical Areas I and II of the International Council for the Exploration of the Sea.

(2) The Interpretation Act 1889**(c)** shall apply for the interpretation of this Order as it applies for the interpretation of an Act of Parliament.

Appointed day

3. The appointed day for the purposes of section 4 of the Act (which provides for the licensing of British fishing vessels in relation to fishing by way of trade or business in specified areas) in conjunction with this Order, is 1st January 1974.

Area, Fish, Period

4. This Order applies to fishing in North-east Arctic waters for cod (*Gadus morhua*) during the period 1st January 1974 to 31st December 1974, both dates inclusive.

(a) 1967 c. 84. (b) 1968 c. 77. (c) 1889 c. 63.

Enforcement

5. For the purposes of the enforcement of section 4 of the Act in conjunction with this Order there are hereby conferred on every British sea-fishery officer the powers of a British sea-fishery officer under section 8(2) and (3) of the Sea Fisheries Act 1968.

In Witness whereof the Official Seal of the Minister of Agriculture, Fisheries and Food is hereunto affixed on 22nd November 1973.

(L.S.)

Joseph Godber,
Minister of Agriculture, Fisheries and Food.

Gordon Campbell,
Secretary of State for Scotland.

22nd November 1973.

W. S. I. Whitelaw,
Secretary of State for Northern Ireland.

26th November 1973.

SCHEDULE

North-east Arctic Waters

The area of sea lying between longitude 11°W and 68°30′E, to the north of a line running from a position longitude 11°W and latitude 63°N in an easterly direction along the parallel of latitude 63°N to longitude 4°W, then south to latitude 62°N, thence east to the coast of Norway.

EXPLANATORY NOTE

(This Note is not part of the Order.)

Section 4 of the Sea Fish (Conservation) Act 1967 provides that from a day appointed by an Order, no British fishing boat registered in the United Kingdom shall be used by way of trade or business for fishing in any area specified in the Order except under the authority of a licence granted by one of the Fisheries Ministers.

This Order appoints 1st January 1974 as the day from which no such fishing boats shall fish for cod in North-east Arctic waters (comprising the International Council for the Exploration of the Sea Statistical Areas I and II) between 1st January and 31st December 1974 except under the authority of such a licence.

STATUTORY INSTRUMENTS

1973 No. 1991 (S.151)

COURT OF SESSION, SCOTLAND

Act of Sederunt (Rules of Court Amendment No. 6) 1973

Made - - - *28th November* 1973

Coming into Operation *1st January* 1974

The Lords of Council and Session, under and by virtue of the powers conferred upon them by section 16 of the Administration of Justice (Scotland) Act 1933(**a**) and of all other powers competent to them in that behalf, do hereby enact and declare as follows—

1. The Rules of Court(**b**) are hereby amended as follows:—

By adding a new Rule of Court 170B as follows:—

170B—Domicile and Matrimonial Proceedings Act 1973(**c**)

(*a*) The condescendence of the Summons, (either in its original form or as amended at any time prior to the commencement of proof) in every action of divorce, separation, declarator of marriage, or declarator of nullity of marriage, in the Court of Session shall contain a short statement of whether to the knowledge of the pursuer any proceedings are continuing in any country outside Scotland, which are in respect of the marriage to which the Summons relates or are capable of affecting its validity or subsistence.

(*b*) If there are any such proceedings said statement shall give particulars thereof including:—

(i) The Court or Tribunal or authority before which they have been commenced;

(ii) The date of commencement;

(iii) The names of the parties;

(iv) The date, or expected date of any proof in the proceedings; and

(v) Such other facts as may be relevant to the question of whether the Court of Session action should be sisted under Schedule 3 of the Domicile and Matrimonial Proceedings Act 1973.

(*c*) For the purposes of this Rule and said Schedule 3, proceedings shall be treated as 'continuing' where proceedings in respect of that marriage or capable of affecting its validity have been instituted before a Court, Tribunal or other authority in any country outside Scotland and such proceedings have not been finally disposed of.

(*d*) A short statement such as is referred to in paragraph (*a*) hereof shall in all such actions be inserted in any defences or minute lodged by

(**a**) 1933 c. 41. (**b**) S.I. 1965/321 (1965 I, p. 803). (**c**) 1973 c. 45.

any party in such action, containing the particulars referred to in paragraph (*b*) hereof in so far as these particulars are additional to or contradictory of any such particulars provided by the pursuer in the action, or in any case in which the pursuer has provided no such statement.

(*e*) Any application made by any party in an action of divorce, separation, declarator of marriage or declarator of nullity of marriage for an order in terms of Part I or Part II of Schedule 2 of said Act, or for a sist of such an action or the recall of a sist in such an action in terms of said Schedule 3 shall be made by motion enrolled and intimated in accordance with current practice.

2. This Act of Sederunt may be cited as the Act of Sederunt (Rules of Court Amendment No. 6) 1973, and shall come into operation on 1st January 1974.

And the Lords appoint this Act of Sederunt to be inserted in the Books of Sederunt.

G. C. Emslie,
I.P.D.

Edinburgh.
28th November 1973.

EXPLANATORY NOTE

(*This Note is not part of the Act of Sederunt.*)

This Act of Sederunt amends the Rules of Court by providing that a short statement shall be inserted in all Summonses of divorce, separation, declarator of marriage or declarator of nullity of marriage and in defences and minutes lodged in such actions *inter alia* averring whether other proceedings are continuing in any country other than Scotland in respect of that marriage or which may affect the validity of the marriage, and further by providing that applications to the Court under Parts I and II of Schedule 2 and Schedule 3 of the Domicile and Matrimonial Proceedings Act 1973 shall be made by way of motion.

STATUTORY INSTRUMENTS

1973 No. 1992

LOCAL GOVERNMENT, ENGLAND AND WALES

The Yorkshire Deeds Registries (Compensation to Officers) (Amendment) Regulations 1973

Made - - -	*28th November* 1973
Laid before Parliament	*11th December* 1973
Coming into Operation	*1st January* 1974

The Lord Chancellor, in exercise of the powers conferred on him by section 19 of the Law of Property Act 1969(**a**), hereby makes the following Regulations:—

1.—(1) These Regulations may be cited as the Yorkshire Deeds Registries (Compensation to Officers) (Amendment) Regulations 1973 and shall come into operation on 1st January 1974.

(2) In these Regulations "the principal Regulations" means the Yorkshire Deeds Registries (Compensation to Officers) Regulations 1970(**b**) and a reference to a regulation by number means the regulation so numbered in those Regulations.

(3) The Interpretation Act 1889(**c**) shall apply to the interpretation of these Regulations as it applies to the interpretation of an Act of Parliament.

2. For the tables in the Schedule to the principal Regulations there shall be substituted the tables set out in the Schedule to these Regulations.

Dated 28th November 1973.

Hailsham of St. Marylebone, C.

(**a**) 1969 c. 59. (**b**) S.I. 1970/1488 (1970 III, p. 4846). (**c**) 1889 c. 63.

SCHEDULE

Regulation 2(2)

TABLE 1(*a*)

The capital value of an amount of £1 per annum, payable for life, which attracts pensions increase from age 55, or retirement age if greater

Age last birthday	*Capital value*	
	Female	*Male*
	£·p	£·p
30	14·82	14·34
31	14·86	14·37
32	14·91	14·39
33	14·95	14·41
34	14·99	14·42
35	15·03	14·43
36	15·06	14·44
37	15·09	14·44
38	15·12	14·43
39	15·14	14·42
40	15·15	14·40
41	15·16	14·37
42	15·15	14·33
43	15·14	14·29
44	15·12	14·23
45	15·09	14·16
46	15·05	14·08
47	14·99	13·99
48	14·92	13·88
49	14·83	13·75
50	14·72	13·61
51	14·59	13·45
52	14·43	13·26
53	14·25	13·04
54	14·04	12·79
55	13·79	12·52
56	13·54	12·24
57	13·28	11·95
58	13·01	11·66
59	12·74	11·36
60	12·46	11·06
61	12·17	10·76
62	11·87	10·45
63	11·57	10·14
64	11·27	9·82

Table 1(*a*) (*continued*)

Age last birthday	*Capital value*	
	Female	*Male*
	£·p	£·p
65	10·96	9·51
66	10·64	9·19
67	10·32	8·87
68	10·00	8·56
69	9·68	8·25
70	9·36	7·94
71	9·03	7·63
72	8·70	7·32
73	8·38	7·02
74	8·05	6·72
75	7·73	6·43
76	7·41	6·14
77	7·09	5·86
78	6·78	5·59
79	6·47	5·32

NOTE:—This table is for use in connection with regulation 35(1) and (2) for the compounding of annual retirement compensation which a person is currently entitled to receive under regulation 19, 20, 21 or 22 and which attracts pensions increase when the person attains age 55, or retirement age if greater. Where the compensation is payable before age 60 (females), 65 (males), but will be reduced on the attainment of that age (in connection with National Insurance pension) the tables should be used in conjunction with Table 2(*a*), *i.e.*, Table 2(*a*) should be used for valuing that part of the compensation which ceases to be payable at 60 (65) and this table should be used for valuing the remainder.

TABLE 1(*b*)

The capital value of an amount of £1 per annum, payable for life, which attracts pensions increase from the outset

Age last birthday	*Capital value*	
	Female	*Male*
	£·p	£·p
23	18·59	18·24
24	18·52	18·15
25	18·44	18·05
26	18·36	17·95
27	18·28	17·85
28	18·19	17·74
29	18·10	17·63
30	18·00	17·51
31	17·90	17·38
32	17·79	17·25
33	17·68	17·12
34	17·57	16·98
35	17·45	16·83
36	17·32	16·68
37	17·19	16·52
38	17·05	16·35
39	16·91	16·18
40	16·76	16·00
41	16·61	15·81
42	16·45	15·62
43	16·29	15·42
44	16·12	15·21
45	15·94	15·00
46	15·76	14·78
47	15·57	14·56
48	15·37	14·33
49	15·17	14·09
50	14·96	13·84
51	14·74	13·59
52	14·51	13·33
53	14·28	13·07
54	14·04	12·80
55	13·79	12·52
56	13·54	12·24
57	13·28	11·95
58	13·01	11·66
59	12·74	11·36
60	12·46	11·06
61	12·17	10·76
62	11·87	10·45
63	11·57	10·14
64	11·27	9·82

Table 1(*b*) (*continued*)

Age last birthday	*Capital value*	
	Female	*Male*
	£·p	£·p
65	10·96	9·51
66	10·64	9·19
67	10·32	8·87
68	10·00	8·56
69	9·68	8·25
70	9·36	7·94
71	9·03	7·63
72	8·70	7·32
73	8·38	7·02
74	8·05	6·72
75	7·73	6·43
76	7·41	6·14
77	7·09	5·86
78	6·78	5·59
79	6·47	5·32

NOTE:—This table is for use in connection with regulation 35(1) and (2) for the compounding of annual retirement compensation which a person is currently entitled to receive under regulation 19, 20, 21 or 22 and which attracts pensions increase from the outset. Where the compensation is payable before age 60 (females), 65 (males) but will be reduced on the attainment of that age (in connection with National Insurnace pension) the tables should be used in conjunction with Table 2(*b*), *i.e.*, Table 2(*b*) should be used for valuing that part of the compensation which ceases to be payable at 60 (65) and this table should be used for valuing the remainder.

TABLE 2(*a*)

The capital value of an amount of £1 per annum, ceasing at age 60 (females), 65 (males), which attracts pensions increase from age 55, or retirement age if greater

Age last birthday	*Capital value*	
	Female	*Male*
	£·p	£·p
30	12·11	12·92
31	12·01	12·87
32	11·91	12·81
33	11·80	12·75
34	11·68	12·68
35	11·55	12·60
36	11·40	12·51
37	11·24	12·41
38	11·07	12·30
39	10·88	12·18
40	10·67	12·04
41	10·44	11·89
42	10·19	11·72
43	9·92	11·53
44	9·63	11·33
45	9·31	11·11
46	8·96	10·86
47	8·58	10·59
48	8·16	10·30
49	7·71	9·98
50	7·22	9·62
51	6·68	9·23
52	6·09	8·80
53	5·45	8·33
54	4·75	7·81
55	3·99	7·24
56	3·18	6·64
57	2·33	6·01
58	1·43	5·35
59	·49	4·65
60	—	3·91
61	—	3·13
62	—	2·30
63	—	1·42
64	—	·48

NOTE:—This table is for use in connection with regulation 35(1) and (2) for the compounding of any part of annual retirement compensation which will cease to be payable on the attainment of age 60 (female), 65 (males), and which attracts pensions increase from age 55, or retirement age if greater. Table 1(*a*) should be used in relation to the remainder of such compensation, *i.e.*, the part which is payable for life—see note on that table.

TABLE 2(*b*)

The capital value of an amount of £1 per annum, ceasing at age 60 (females), 65 (males), which attracts pensions increase from the outset

Age last birthday	*Capital value*	
	Female	*Male*
	£·p	£·p
23	16·68	17·24
24	16·51	17·10
25	16·33	16·95
26	16·14	16·79
27	15·94	16·63
28	15·74	16·46
29	15·52	16·28
30	15·29	16·09
31	15·05	15·89
32	14·80	15·68
33	14·54	15·46
34	14·26	15·23
35	13·97	15·00
36	13·66	14·75
37	13·34	14·49
38	13·01	14·22
39	12·66	13·94
40	12·29	13·64
41	11·90	13·33
42	11·49	13·01
43	11·07	12·67
44	10·63	12·31
45	10·16	11·94
46	9·67	11·56
47	9·15	11·16
48	8·61	10·74
49	8·04	10·30
50	7·45	9·85
51	6·83	9·38
52	6·17	8·88
53	5·48	8·36
54	4·75	7·81
55	3·99	7·24
56	3·18	6·64
57	2·33	6·01
58	1·43	5·35
59	·49	4·65

Table 2(*b*) (*continued*)

Age last birthday	Capital value	
	Female	Male
	£·p	£·p
60	—	3·91
61	—	3·13
62	—	2·30
63	—	1·42
64	—	·48

NOTE:—This table is for use in connection with regulation 35(1) and (2) for the compounding of any part of annual retirement compensation which will cease to be payable on the attainment of age 60 (females), 65 (males), and which attracts pensions increase from the outset. Table 1(*b*) should be used in relation to the remainder of such compensation, *i.e.*, the part which is payable for life—see note on that table.

TABLE 3

The capital value of an amount of £1 per annum, payable to a widow until death or remarriage, which attracts pensions increase from the outset

Age of widow at date of widowhood	*Capital value*	*Age of widow at date of widowhood*	*Capital value*
	£·p		£·p
20	6·00	45	13·14
21	6·00	46	13·25
22	6·00	47	13·34
23	6·00	48	13·40
24	6·13	49	13·44
25	6·58	50	13·46
26	7·01	51	13·46
27	7·41	52	13·43
28	7·78	53	13·38
29	8·11	54	13·31
30	8·41	55	13·22
31	8·72	56	13·10
32	9·06	57	12·96
33	9·42	58	12·80
34	9·82	59	12·61
35	10·24	60	12·39
36	10·65	61	12·14
37	11·04	62	11·87
38	11·40	63	11·57
39	11·73	64	11·27
40	12·04	65	10·96
41	12·33	66	10·64
42	12·59	67	10·32
43	12·81	68	10·00
44	12·99	69	9·68
		70	9·35

NOTE:—This table is for use in connection with regulation 35(1) for compounding annual compensation to a widow which attracts pensions increase from the outset under regulation 25. It should also be used, where a reduction of compensation under regulation 25(4) falls to be apportioned between the compensation payable under that regulation and under regulation 26, for ascertaining the capital value of annual compensation to a widow.

TABLE 4(*a*)

The annual amount, payable for life, and attracting pensions increase from age 55, or retirement age if greater, equal in value to a lump sum of £100

Age	*Annual amount*	
	Female	*Male*
	£·p	£·p
30	6·75	6·97
31	6·73	6·96
32	6·71	6·95
33	6·69	6·94
34	6·67	6·93
35	6·65	6·93
36	6·64	6·93
37	6·63	6·93
38	6·61	6·93
39	6·61	6·93
40	6·60	6·94
41	6·60	6·96
42	6·60	6·98
43	6·61	7·00
44	6·61	7·03
45	6·63	7·06
46	6·64	7·10
47	6·67	7·15
48	6·70	7·20
49	6·74	7·27
50	6·79	7·35
51	6·85	7·43
52	6·93	7·54
53	7·02	7·67
54	7·12	7·82
55	7·25	7·99
56	7·39	8·17
57	7·53	8·37
58	7·69	8·58
59	7·85	8·80
60	8·03	9·04
61	8·22	9·29
62	8·42	9·57
63	8.64	9.86
64	8·87	10·18
65	9·12	10·52
66	9·40	10·88
67	9·69	11·27
68	10·00	11·68
69	10·33	12·12
70	10·68	12·59

Table 4(a) (continued)

Age	Annual amount	
	Female	Male
	£·p	£·p
71	11·07	13·11
72	11·49	13·66
73	11·93	14·25
74	12·42	14·88
75	12·94	15·55
76	13·50	16·29
77	14·10	17·06
78	14·75	17·89
79	15·46	18·80

NOTE:—This table is for use in connection with regulation 23(1) for ascertaining the annual amount (which attracts pensions increase from age 55, or retirement age if greater) by which retirement compensation under regulation 19, 20 or 21 is to be reduced where a claimant has not paid to the compensating authority an amount equal to any sum paid to him by way of superannuation contributions or that amount has been repaid to him by the compensating authority at his request. It should also be used in connection with regulation 35(2) for calculating for the purposes of that paragraph the annual value of retirement compensation awarded as a lump sum.

TABLE 4(*b*)

The annual amount, payable for life, and attracting pensions increase from the outset, equal in value to a lump sum of £100

Age last birthday	*Annual amount*	
	Female	*Male*
	£·p	£·p
23	5·38	5·48
24	5·40	5·51
25	5·42	5·54
26	5·45	5·57
27	5·47	5·60
28	5·50	5·64
29	5·52	5·67
30	5·56	5·71
31	5·59	5·75
32	5·62	5·80
33	5·66	5·84
34	5·69	5·89
35	5·73	5·94
36	5·77	6·00
37	5·82	6·05
38	5·87	6·12
39	5·91	6·18
40	5·97	6·25
41	6·02	6·33
42	6·08	6·40
43	6·14	6·49
44	6·20	6·57
45	6·27	6·67
46	6·35	6·77
47	6·42	6·87
48	6·51	6·98
49	6·59	7·10
50	6·68	7·23
51	6·78	7·36
52	6·89	7·50
53	7·00	7·65
54	7·12	7·81
55	7·25	7·99
56	7·39	8·17
57	7·53	8·37
58	7·69	8·58
59	7·85	8·80

Table 4(*b*) (*continued*)

Age last birthday	*Annual amount*	
	Female	*Male*
	£·p	£·p
60	8·03	9·04
61	8·22	9·29
62	8·42	9·57
63	8·64	9·86
64	8·87	10·18
65	9·12	10·52
66	9·40	10·88
67	9·69	11·27
68	10·00	11·68
69	10·33	12·12
70	10·68	12·59
71	11·07	13·11
72	11·49	13·66
73	11·93	14·25
74	12·42	14·88
75	12·94	15·55
76	13·50	16·29
77	14·10	17·06
78	14·75	17·89
79	15·46	18·80

NOTE:—This table is for use in connection with regulation 23(1) for ascertaining the annual amount (attracting pensions increase throughout life) by which retirement compensation under regulation 19, 20 or 21 is to be reduced where a claimant has not paid to the compensating authority an amount equal to any sum paid to him by way of superannuation contributions or that amount has been repaid to him by the compensating authority at his request. It should also be used in connection with regulation 35(2) for calculating for the purposes of that paragraph the annual value of retirement compensation awarded as a lump sum.

TABLE 5

The annual amount, attracting pensions increase from the outset, payable to a widow until death or remarriage, equal in value to a lump sum of £100

Age of widow at date of widowhood	*Annual amount*	*Age of widow at date of widowhood*	*Annual amount*
	£·p		£·p
20	16·67	45	7·61
21	16·67	46	7·55
22	16·67	47	7·50
23	16·67	48	7·46
24	16·31	49	7·44
25	15·20	50	7·43
26	14·27	51	7·43
27	13·50	52	7·45
28	12·85	53	7·47
29	12·33	54	7·51
30	11·89	55	7·56
31	11·47	56	7·63
32	11·04	57	7·72
33	10·62	58	7·81
34	10·18	59	7·93
35	9·77	60	8·07
36	9·39	61	8·24
37	9·06	62	8·42
38	8·77	63	8·64
39	8·53	64	8·87
40	8·31	65	9·12
41	8·11	66	9·40
42	7·94	67	9·69
43	7·81	68	10·00
44	7·70	69	10·33
		70	10·70

NOTE:—This table is for use in connection with regulation 25(4) for ascertaining the annual amount (which attracts pensions increase from the outset) by which compensation to a widow is to be reduced in the circumstances described in that paragraph. If a reduction is required to be apportioned between compensation payable under regulations 25 and 26, the capital value of annual compensation to a widow should be ascertained by reference to Table 3.

TABLE 6

The capital value of each £100 per annum of long-term compensation, attracting pensions increase from age 55, according to the outstanding period of long-term compensation

Outstanding number of complete years of long-term compensation	*Capital value*	
	Female	*Male*
	£·p	£·p
0	98·65	98·50
1	95·95	95·50
2	93·25	92·60
3	90·65	89·80
4	88·20	87·15
5	85·90	84·70
6	83·70	82·40
7	81·60	80·25
8	79·60	78·20
9	77·70	76·30
10	75·80	74·40
11	73·85	72·45
12	71·80	70·45
13	69·75	68·40
14	67·70	66·40
15	65·65	64·40
16	63·65	62·45
17	61·70	60·55
18	59·80	58·75
19	58·00	57·00
20	56·25	55·30
21	54·55	53·65
22	59·95	52·10
23	51·40	50·60
24	49·90	49·15
25	48·45	47·75
26	47·05	46·40
27	45·75	45·10
28	44·45	43·90
29	43·20	42·75
30	42·05	41·60

NOTE:—This table is for use in connection with regulation 35(1) and (2) for compounding awards of long-term compensation which attracts pensions increase from age 55 under Part IV of these Regulations. The total amount of the annual long-term compensation which is to be compounded must first be calculated, *i.e.*, the amount which the person would receive on account of that compensation or the part of it which is to be compounded, if it were paid until "normal retiring age" (as defined in these Regulations). The capital value of that annual long-term compensation will be the total calculated multiplied by the appropriate factor.

EXPLANATORY NOTE

(This Note is not part of the Regulations.)

These Regulations amend the Yorkshire Deeds Registries (Compensation to Officers) Regulations 1970 by substituting revised commutation tables which take account of pensions increase legislation.

1973 No. 1993 (L.28)

DEEDS OF ARRANGEMENT

The Deeds of Arrangement Fees Order 1973

Made - - -	21*st November* 1973
Coming into Operation	1*st January* 1974

The Lord Chancellor, with the advice and consent of the Judges of the Supreme Court as to the court fees hereby fixed, and the Treasury, in exercise of the powers conferred on them by section 213 of the Supreme Court of Judicature (Consolidation) Act 1925(**a**), section 22(4) of the Administration of Justice Act 1925(**b**) and sections 2 and 3 of the Public Offices Fees Act 1879(**c**), hereby make and concur in the following Order:—

1.—(1) This Order may be cited as the Deeds of Arrangement Fees Order 1973 and shall come into operation on 1st January 1974.

(2) The Interpretation Act 1889(**d**) shall apply to the interpretation of this Order as it applies to the interpretation of an Act of Parliament.

2. In this Order, unless the context otherwise requires—

(*a*) "the Act" means the Deeds of Arrangement Act 1914(**e**), as amended by the Administration of Justice Act 1925, and "the Rules" means the Deeds of Arrangement Rules 1925(**f**), as amended (**g**),

"the bankruptcy fee" means the fee payable on a similar proceeding in bankruptcy under any order made under section 133(1) of the Bankruptcy Act 1914(**h**),

"the Supreme Court fee" means the fee payable on a similar document or proceeding under any order other than this one made under section 213 of the Supreme Court of Judicature (Consolidation) Act 1925;

(*b*) expressions used in this Order shall have the same meaning as in the Act or in the Rules;

(*c*) a section referred to by number means the section so numbered in the Act;

(*d*) a rule referred to by number means the rule so numbered in the Rules; and

(*e*) a fee referred to by number means the fee so numbered in the Schedule to this Order.

3.—(1) The fees set out in column 2 of the Schedule to this Order shall be taken in respect of the items in column 1 thereof, and the documents to be stamped shall be those prescribed in column 3 thereof.

(**a**) 1925 c. 49. (**b**) 1925 c. 28. (**c**) 1879 c. 58. (**d**) 1889 c. 63.
(**e**) 1914 c. 47. (**f**) S.R. & O. 1925/795 (Rev. V, p. 711: 1925, p. 210).
(**g**) S.R. & O. 1941/1253, S.I. 1962/297 (Rev. V, p. 711: 1941 I, p. 215; 1962 I, p. 286).
(**h**) 1914 c. 59.

(2) The fees in Part I of the Schedule to this Order shall be taken in the office of the Registrar of the Court, those in Part II by the Registrar and those in Part III by the Department of Trade and Industry.

(3) The fees shall be taken either by adhesive stamps or in cash.

(4) An adhesive stamp denoting payment of a fee shall be an adhesive stamp on which the word "Insolvency" has been printed.

4. The Order as to Fees for proceedings in connection with Deeds of Arrangement(**a**), the Deeds of Arrangement (Board of Trade) Fees Order 1925(**b**) and the Deeds of Arrangement (Board of Trade) Fees Amendment Order 1925(**c**) are hereby revoked save as to any fee or percentage due or payable before the commencement of this Order.

Dated 16th November 1973.

Hailsham of St. Marylebone, C.

Dated 21st November 1973.

Michael Jopling,
Hugh Rossi,
Two of the Lords Commissioners
of Her Majesty's Treasury.

We consent.

Dated 15th November 1973.

Widgery, C. J.
Denning, M. R.
Reginald Goff, J.

(**a**) S.R. & O. 1914/1829 (Rev. V, p. 730: 1914 I, p. 503).
(**b**) S.R. & O. 1925/818 (Rev. V, p. 732: 1925, p. 231).
(**c**) S.R. & O. 1925/953 (Rev. V, p. 732: 1925, p. 234).

SCHEDULE

Article 3

Column 1	*Column* 2	*Column* 3
PART I	£	
1. On an application under section 11(1) to give security under a deed of arrangement, for taking security and giving certificate—		
(*a*) where the estimated assets available for distribution amongst the unsecured creditors, as shown by the affidavit filed on registration, are less than £100;	0·50	The application
(*b*) otherwise.	1	The application
2. (*a*) On an application to the court for extension of time under section 3(1) or 3(4);	The bankruptcy fee	The application
(*b*) on an application by a creditor for a declaration under section 11(2), or an order under section 16; and	The bankruptcy fee	The application
(*c*) on an application by any person under section 23.	The bankruptcy fee	The application
3. On any other document or proceeding not otherwise provided for in this part of this Schedule.	The Supreme Court fee	The document or any document relating to the proceeding

PART II

	£	
4. On filing with the Registrar a deed where the total estimated amount of property included therein or the total amount of composition thereunder appears from the affidavit of the debtor to be—		
(*a*) £1,000 or less;	3·00	The copy deed
(*b*) over £1,000 and not over £2,500;	5·00	The copy deed
(*c*) over £2,500 and not over £5,000;	8·00	The copy deed
(*d*) over £5,000.	10·00	The copy deed
5. On filing with the Registrar any deed not covered by Fee No. 4.	4·00	The copy deed
6. On a certificate of registration of an original deed endorsed thereon.	0·50	The certificate
7. On filing with the Registrar a statutory declaration, affidavit or notice pursuant to the Act or Rules.	0·25	The declaration, affidavit or notice
8. On searching the register and on inspecting the filed copy, including taking the limited extract under section 9 and rule 9 (for every name inspected).	0·25	The search form.

PART III

	£	
9. On an account transmitted by a trustee under section 13—		
(*a*) where the gross amount of the assets realised and brought to credit, or of the composition distributed (in the case of a composition) during the period of account does not exceed £1,000, on every £100 or part thereof;	0·50	The account
(*b*) where the gross amount exceeds £1,000;	5·00	The account
and in addition for every £100 or part thereof exceeding £1,000.	0·25	The account
10. On an application to inspect the accounts of a trustee under section 13(3).	0·25	The application
11. On an application for an official audit of a trustee's accounts under section 15(1).	1·50	The application
12. On the audit of a trustee's accounts under section 15(1)—		
(*a*) where the amount brought to credit after deduction of the amount received and spent in carrying on the business, and of the amount paid to secured creditors out of the proceeds of their securities does not exceed £5,000, on every £100 or part thereof;	1·50	The account
(*b*) where the amount so brought to credit exceeds £5,000;	75·00	The account
and in addition for every £100 or part thereof exceeding £5,000.	0·75	The account
Note: The minimum fee for Fee No. 12(*a*) shall be £7·50, and in calculating Fee No. 12(*a*) or (*b*) credit shall be given for any amount paid for Fee No. 9.		
13. On copies of documents supplied—		
(*a*) per foolscap or A4 ISO page;	0·10	The copy
(*b*) all larger pages.	0·20	The copy.

EXPLANATORY NOTE

(*This Note is not part of the Order.*)

This Order replaces the Order dated the 28th December 1914 as to Fees for proceedings in connection with Deeds of Arrangement and the Deeds of Arrangement (Board of Trade) Fees Order 1925. It abolishes the use of impressed stamps and increases the fees to be taken by the Registrar of Deeds of Arrangement and the Department of Trade and Industry in connection with these proceedings.

STATUTORY INSTRUMENTS

1973 No. 1995 (C.60)

CRIMINAL PROCEDURE, NORTHERN IRELAND

The Criminal Justice Act 1972 (Commencement No. 4) Order 1973

Made - - - - *27th November* 1973

In exercise of the powers conferred upon me by subsection (6) of section 66 of the Criminal Justice Act 1972**(a)**, there having been made the rules of court**(b)** referred to in that part of the proviso to that subsection which relates to the provision set out in Schedule 4 to that Act, I hereby make the following Order:—

1. This Order may be cited as the Criminal Justice Act 1972 (Commencement No. 4) Order 1973.

2. Section 63(3) of and Schedule 4 to the Criminal Justice Act 1972 shall come into force on 1st January 1974.

Robert Carr,
One of Her Majesty's Principal
Secretaries of State.

Home Office,
Whitehall.
27th November 1973.

EXPLANATORY NOTE

(*This Note is not part of the Order.*)

This Order brings into force on 1st January 1974 so much of the Criminal Justice Act 1972 as makes provision for a reference to the Court of Criminal Appeal in Northern Ireland of a point of law following an acquittal on indictment.

(a) 1972 c.71.

(b) Criminal Appeal (Reference of Points of Law) (Northern Ireland) Rules 1973 (S.R. & O. (N.I.) 1973 No.428).

1973 No. 1996

PENSIONS

The Local Government Superannuation (Miscellaneous Provisions) (No. 2) Regulations 1973

Made - - - -	28*th November* 1973
Laid before Parliament	10*th December* 1973
Coming into Operation—	
Regulations 1 *to* 8 -	31*st December* 1973
Regulations 9 *to* 11 -	1*st April* 1974

The Secretary of State for the Environment, in exercise of the powers conferred on him by section 7 of the Superannuation Act 1972**(a)**, as read with paragraph 5(1) of Schedule 7 to that Act, and of all other powers enabling him in that behalf, after consultation with such associations of local authorities as appeared to him to be concerned, the local authorities with whom consultation appeared to him to be desirable and such representatives of other persons likely to be affected by the regulations as appeared to him to be appropriate, hereby makes the following regulations:—

Title and commencement

1.—(1) These regulations may be cited as the Local Government Superannuation (Miscellaneous Provisions) (No. 2) Regulations 1973.

(2) Regulations 1 to 8 shall come into operation on 31st December 1973; and regulations 9 to 11 shall come into operation on 1st April 1974.

Interpretation

2.—(1) In these regulations "the Act of 1937" means the Local Government Superannuation Act 1937**(b)** and words and expressions to which meanings are assigned by the Act of 1937 have the same respective meanings in these regulations.

(2) In these regulations, unless the context otherwise requires—

(*a*) any reference to any enactment or instrument shall be construed as a reference thereto as amended, modified, extended, applied or re-enacted by any other enactment or instrument (including these regulations); and

(*b*) any reference to the Act of 1937, section 15 of the Local Government Superannuation Act 1953**(c)** or section 7 of the Superannuation (Miscellaneous Provisions) Act 1948**(d)** shall, additionally, be construed as a

(a) 1972 c. 11. **(b)** 1937 c. 68. **(c)** 1953 c. 25. **(d)** 1948 c. 33.

reference thereto as having effect by virtue of paragraph 5(1) of Schedule 7 to the Superannuation Act 1972 and as amended by the Local Government Superannuation (Miscellaneous Provisions) Regulations 1973(**a**).

(3) The Interpretation Act 1889(**b**) shall apply for the interpretation of these regulations as it applies for the interpretation of an Act of Parliament and as if these regulations and the regulations revoked by regulation 11 below were Acts of Parliament.

Superannuation funds

3. In section 1 of the Act of 1937 (which relates to superannuation funds) after subsection (2A) there shall be inserted the following subsection—

"(2B) A superannuation fund shall be maintained for the purposes of this Part of this Act by the National Water Council.".

Appropriate superannuation fund

4.—(1) In section 4 of the Act of 1937 (which relates to the funds to which contributions are payable)—

(*a*) after subsection (1) there shall be inserted the following subsection—

"(1A) The appropriate superannuation fund in relation to the contributory employees of an employing authority who are a water authority within the meaning of the Water Act 1973(**c**) shall be the superannuation fund maintained by the National Water Council.";

(*b*) in subsection (2), for the word "subsection" there shall be substituted the word "subsections".

(2) Notwithstanding anything in section 4 of the Act of 1937, the appropriate superannuation fund for the purposes of the Act of 1937 in relation to the contributory employees of an employing authority who are a district council, a parish council established by or under the Local Government Act 1972(**d**) or a community council shall be the superannuation fund maintained by the council of the county established by the Local Government Act 1972 within which the area of the employing authority is situate.

Use of superannuation fund moneys

5. In section 21 of the Act of 1937 (which relates to management of a superannuation fund and use and investment of moneys)—

(*a*) in subsection (3), after the word "may", where it first occurs, there shall be inserted the words ", subject to subsection (4),";

(*b*) at the end of the section there shall be added the following subsection—

"(4) An administering authority shall not under the preceding subsection use on or after 31st December 1973—

(**a**) S.I. 1973/313 (1973 I, p. 1100).
(**b**) 1889 c. 63.
(**c**) 1973 c. 37.
(**d**) 1972 c. 70.

(*a*) any further moneys forming part of the superannuation fund maintained by them for any purpose for which they have a statutory borrowing power other than for the purpose of defraying expenses (including those payable by them to meet the expenses of other local authorities) pending the receipt of revenues receivable by them in respect of the financial year in which those expenses are chargeable, so long as the aggregate amount for the time being not repaid of any moneys so used by them before 31st December 1973 equals or exceeds 25 per cent of the value for the time being of the fund; or

(*b*) any moneys for any such purpose, so as to bring the aggregate amount of all moneys so used by them to an amount which exceeds 25 per cent of that value.".

Interpretation of Act of 1937

6. In section 40(1) of the Act of 1937 (Interpretation) in the definition of "local authority"—

(*a*) after the words "county district," there shall be inserted the words "the council of a district,";

(*b*) after the word "London,", where third occurring, there shall be inserted the words "any parish council, any community council";

(*c*) at the end of the definition there shall be added the words "the National Water Council and any water authority within the meaning of the Water Act 1973;".

Officers who are to be compulsorily superannuable

7. In Part I of Schedule 1 to the Act of 1937 (which specifies the local authorities whose whole-time officers are to be compulsorily superannuable)—

(*a*) after the paragraph beginning "The council of a county" there shall be inserted the following paragraph—

"The council of a district.";

(*b*) at the end of the part there shall be added the following paragraphs—

"The National Water Council.

A water authority within the meaning of the Water Act 1973.".

Option to pay contributions, etc.

8. Any existing employee who by virtue of the provisions of paragraph (*a*) of regulation 6 above and paragraph (*a*) of regulation 7 above or of paragraph (*c*) of the said regulation 6 and paragraph (*b*) of the said regulation 7 becomes a contributory employee on the coming into operation of those regulations may, by notice in writing given to his employing authority before 1st April 1974, elect to pay contributions to the appropriate superannuation fund in respect of the period beginning with the day on which he entered upon his employment under that authority and ending with the day immediately before the date on which those regulations come into operation as if he had during that period been a contributory employee under that authority and to reckon service rendered by him to that authority during that period accordingly.

Dissolution, etc., of joint committees

9. Every joint committee established by a scheme of combination made under section 2 of the Act of 1937 and in force immediately before 1st April 1974 shall cease to exist and where any person is a trustee of a superannuation fund maintained by such a committee he shall cease to be a trustee thereof.

Transfer of superannuation funds and consequential matters

10.—(1) The superannuation fund maintained under Part I of the Act of 1937 by any authority or other body specified in column (1) of the schedule to these regulations (in this regulation referred to as a "transferor authority") shall by virtue of these regulations be transferred to and vest in the authority specified opposite thereto in column (2) of that schedule (in this regulation referred to as the "successor authority") and any such fund shall be carried by the successor authority to the fund which they are required to maintain under Part I of the Act of 1937.

(2) Any admission agreement made, or having effect as if made, under section 15 of the Local Government Superannuation Act 1953, section 7 of the Superannuation (Miscellaneous Provisions) Act 1948 or any corresponding local Act provision, whereby the employees of any body are or can be admitted to participate in the benefits of the superannuation fund maintained by a transferor authority shall have effect in all respects as an agreement on the like terms and conditions between that body and the successor authority and, in the case of an agreement made under a local Act provision, as if it had been made under the said section 15 with the approval of the Secretary of State.

(3) All liabilities attaching to a transferor authority in respect of their superannuation fund shall, subject to provisions of this regulation, attach to the successor authority in respect of their superannuation fund.

(4) Any liability of any authority or other body or of any person to make payments into the superannuation fund of a transferor authority shall become a liability to make payments into the superannuation fund of the successor authority.

(5) Subject to paragraph (2), all contracts, deeds, bonds, agreements and other instruments subsisting in favour of, or against, and all notices in force which were given by or to a transferor authority or any other body on their behalf for the purposes of their superannuation fund shall be of full force and effect in favour of, or against, the successor authority.

(6) Any action or proceeding or cause of action or proceeding pending or existing at 1st April 1974 by or against a transferor authority in respect of their superannuation fund shall not be prejudicially affected by reason of the Local Government Act 1972 or these regulations and may be continued, prosecuted and enforced by or against the successor authority.

(7) Where a transferor authority would have become liable, or would have been empowered, on the happening of any event, to make a payment out of their superannuation fund or take any other action in respect of any person who has ceased to participate in the benefits of the fund before 1st April 1974, then on the happening of that event such payment or action shall, or as the case may be

may, be made out of the superannuation fund of the successor authority or taken by that authority.

(8) Where a person has ceased to contribute to the superannuation fund of a transferor authority before 1st April 1974 and has not become a contributor to any other superannuation fund maintained under Part I of the Act of 1937 or a local Act, the superannuation fund of the successor authority shall on and after that date be deemed to be the fund to which he was last a contributor.

(9) The accounts of any authority or other body or of their committees or officers relating to any superannuation fund transferred by this regulation shall be made up to 31st March 1974 and shall be audited in like manner and subject to the like incidents and consequences as if these regulations had not been made:

Provided that any sum certified by a district auditor at any such audit as due from any person shall be paid to the successor authority.

(10) All legal proceedings pending on 1st April 1974 may be amended in such manner as may be necessary or proper in consequence of this regulation.

(11) The successor authority in relation to any superannuation fund transferred by this regulation shall send to any person entitled to a benefit payable out of the fund a notification in writing of the name and address of the authority which is liable under this regulation to make the payment.

Revocations

11. The following provisions of the Act of 1937 shall cease to have effect—

(*a*) in section 1—

(i) in subsection (1)(*a*), the words "county, county borough and";

(ii) subsections (1)(*b*) to (*d*) and (2);

(*b*) section 2;

(*c*) in section 4—

(i) in subsection (1), the words from "or are" to the words "admitting authority", where they first occur, and the words from "or, as" to the end of that subsection;

(ii) in subsection (2), proviso (*a*);

(iii) subsection (3);

(*d*) in section 40(1)—

(i) the definition of "combination scheme";

(ii) in the definition of "local authority", the words "county borough or county district" and the words from "joint committee", where they first occur, to the word "other";

(*e*) in Part I of Schedule 1, the words "county borough or county district" and the words "a joint committee established by a combination scheme.".

SCHEDULE

Regulation 10

TRANSFER OF SUPERANNUATION FUNDS

(1) Transferor authority	(2) Successor authority
The council of the administrative county of Glamorgan The Mid Glamorgan (Superannuation) Joint Committee	The County Council of Mid Glamorgan
The council of the administrative county of Yorkshire, West Riding The West Riding (Local Authorities) Superannuation Joint Committee	The County Council of West Yorkshire
The Bucklow (Superannuation) Joint Committee	The County Council of Cheshire
The Central Lancashire (Local Authorities) Joint Superannuation Committee The East Cheshire (Local Authorities) Joint Superannuation Committee The South-East Lancashire (Local Authorities) Superannuation Joint Committee	The County Council of Greater Manchester
The Cotswold District Joint Superannuation Committee	The County Council of Gloucestershire
The Durham (Local Authorities) Superannuation Joint Committee	The County Council of Durham
The Lichfield (Superannuation) Joint Committee	The County Council of Staffordshire
The Northumberland (Local Authorities) Superannuation Joint Committee	The County Council of Northumberland
The West Lancashire (Superannuation) Joint Committee	The County Council of Merseyside
The council of any other administrative county, any other joint committee established by a scheme of combination made under section 2 of the Act of 1937 and the council of a county borough or county district	The council of the county within which the area, or the greater part of the area, of the authority specified in column (1) is situate or, in the case of a joint committee so specified, the areas, or the greater part of the areas, of the constituent authorities thereof are situate
The Upper Tame Drainage Authority The Derwent Valley Water Board The Durham County Water Board The Fylde Water Board The Staffordshire Potteries Water Board The West Lancashire Water Board The Wirral Water Board	The National Water Council

Geoffrey Rippon,
Secretary of State for the Environment.

28th November 1973.

EXPLANATORY NOTE

(This Note is not part of the Regulations.)

These Regulations make amendments to the enactments constituting the local government superannuation scheme consequential on the Local Government Act 1972 ("the Act of 1972") and the Water Act 1973 ("the Act of 1973").

Although repealed by the Superannuation Act 1972, the enactments constituting that scheme have effect by virtue of paragraph 5(1) of Schedule 7 to that Act as Regulations made under section 7 of that Act.

The principal amendments—

(1) place on the National Water Council a duty to maintain a superannuation fund for the purposes of the local government superannuation scheme (**Regulation** 3);

(2) determine, by way of amendment to section 1 of the Local Government Superannuation Act 1937, the bodies which on and after 1st April 1974 are to maintain superannuation funds for the purposes of that scheme, namely, every county council, the Greater London Council and every London borough council (all of which at present maintain such funds) and the National Water Council (**Regulation** 11(*a*) and (*b*));

(3) make whole-time employees of district councils and whole-time employees of the National Water Council or of water authorities within the meaning of the Act of 1973 compulsorily superannuable (**Regulations** 6(*a*) and 7(*a*) and **Regulations** 6(*c*) and 7(*b*) respectively) and provide for the participation by the first-mentioned employees in the superannuation funds of the county councils constituted under the Act of 1972 (**Regulation** 4(2)) and by the last-mentioned employees in the superannuation fund of the National Water Council (**Regulation** 4(1)(*a*)).

Provision is made enabling certain whole-time employees of any body mentioned in paragraph (3) above to opt to pay contributions in respect of previous service with that body and to reckon that service accordingly (**Regulation** 8).

In addition the **Regulations**—

(*a*) provide for the abolition on 1st April 1974 of joint superannuation committees (**Regulation** 9) and for the transfer on that date of superannuation funds maintained for the purposes of the scheme by those committees or by bodies which by virtue of the Act of 1972 or the Act of 1973 cease to exist on that date (Regulation 10 and the Schedule);

(*b*) restrict the use by a body maintaining a superannuation fund of its fund moneys for the purposes of its own undertakings (**Regulation** 5).

1973 No. 1997

EXCHANGE CONTROL

The Exchange Control (Purchase of Foreign Currency) (Amendment) Order 1973

Made - - -	*28th November* 1973
Laid before Parliament	*7th December* 1973
Coming into Operation	*31st December* 1973

The Treasury, in exercise of the powers conferred upon them by sections 31 and 36(5) of the Exchange Control Act 1947(**a**), hereby make the following Order:—

1.—(1) This Order may be cited as the Exchange Control (Purchase of Foreign Currency) (Amendment) Order 1973, and shall come into operation on 31st December 1973.

(2) The Interpretation Act 1889(**b**) shall apply for the interpretation of this Order as it applies for the interpretation of an Act of Parliament.

2. The Exchange Control (Purchase of Foreign Currency) Order 1970(**c**), as amended (**d**), shall be further amended by deleting the Schedule thereto and substituting the following:—

"SCHEDULE

The banks specified for the purposes of articles 3 and 5 of this Order are the offices in the United Kingdom or the Channel Islands of the following banks, namely:—

Allied Irish Banks Ltd.
Bank of England.
Bank of Ireland.
Bank of Scotland.
Barclays Bank International Ltd.
Barclays Bank Ltd.
Clydesdale Bank Ltd.
Coutts & Co.
Hambros Bank Ltd.
Hambros (Guernsey) Ltd.
Hambros (Jersey) Ltd.
Hoare & Co., C.

(**a**) 1947 c.14. (**b**) 1889 c.63.
(**c**) S.I. 1970/789 (1970 II, p.2499).
(**d**) S.I.1970/1312, 1972/137 (1970 III, p.4390; 1972 I, 494).

Isle of Man Bank Ltd.
Lewis's Bank Ltd.
Lloyds Bank Ltd.
Midland Bank Ltd.
Morris Wigram Ltd.
National Westminster Bank Ltd.
Northern Bank Ltd.
Royal Bank of Scotland Ltd., The.
Ulster Bank Ltd.
Williams & Glyn's Bank Ltd.
Yorkshire Bank Ltd."

3. This Order shall extend to the Channel Islands, and any reference in this Order to the Exchange Control Act 1947 includes a reference to that Act as extended by the Exchange Control (Channel Islands) Order 1947(**a**).

28th November 1973.

Michael Jopling,
P. L. Hawkins,
Two of the Lords Commissioners
of Her Majesty's Treasury.

EXPLANATORY NOTE

(*This Note is not part of the Order.*)

The Exchange Control (Purchase of Foreign Currency) Order 1970 inter alia exempts from section 1(1) of the Exchange Control Act 1947 the purchase abroad by travellers resident here of foreign currency for travel expenditure if the traveller holds a cheque card issued by a bank named in the Schedule to that Order and encashes his cheque within the limits imposed on the use of his cheque card by the bank which issued it.

This Order consolidates, with amendments, the Schedule to the 1970 Order. The Bank of England and three other banks are added to the list. The other amendments are to take account of mergers etc. and changes of name.

(**a**) S.R. & O. 1947/2034 (Rev. VI, p.1001: 1947 I, p.660).

1973 No. 1998

SEA FISHERIES

BOATS AND METHODS OF FISHING

The Foreign Sea-Fishery Officers Order 1973

Made - - -	*27th November* 1973
Laid before Parliament	*30th November* 1973
Coming into Operation	*1st December* 1973

The Minister of Agriculture, Fisheries and Food and the Secretaries of State respectively concerned with the sea fishing industry in Scotland and Northern Ireland in exercise of the powers conferred on them by section 7(4) of the Sea Fisheries Act 1968(**a**) and of all other powers enabling them in that behalf, hereby make the following order:—

Citation and commencement

1. This order may be cited as the Foreign Sea-Fishery Officers Order 1973 and shall come into operation on 1st December 1973.

Interpretation

2.—(1) In this order—

"the Act" means the Sea Fisheries Act 1968;

"the baselines" means the lines drawn round the coast of Iceland so as to join successively, in the order in which they are there set out, the points identified by the co-ordinates of latitude and longitude in Schedule 1 to this order;

"the Convention" means the Interim Agreement between Her Majesty's Government in the United Kingdom and the government of Iceland constituted by the Exchange of Notes of 13th November 1973(**b**);

"the Convention area" means the area to which the Convention applies being the area described in Schedule 2 to this order;

"mile" means nautical mile;

"the 12 mile line" means a line drawn round the coast of Iceland 12 miles from the baselines and extended seawards by lines drawn 12 miles from and around the Island of Grimsey (from its outermost headlands and skerries) and around Hvalbakur (64° 35.8′ north latitude 13° 16.7′ west longitude);

(**a**) 1968 c. 77. (**b**) Cmnd. 5484.

"the 50 mile line" means a line drawn round the coast of Iceland 50 miles from the baselines and extended seawards by lines drawn 50 miles around Hvalbakur (64° 35.8′ north latitude 13° 16.7′ west longitude) and Kolbeinsey (67° 07.5′ north latitude 18° 36′ west longitude).

(2) The Interpretation Act 1889(**a**) shall apply for the interpretation of this order as it applies for the interpretation of an Act of Parliament.

Foreign Sea-Fishery Officers

3. In relation to the Convention there are hereby specified as foreign sea-fishery officers, entitled to exercise in relation to British fishing boats anywhere within the Convention area the powers referred to in section 9 of the Act, coastguard officers duly appointed by the government of Iceland to enforce the provisions of the Convention.

In witness whereof the Official Seal of the Minister of Agriculture, Fisheries and Food is hereunto affixed on 27th November 1973.

(L.S.)

Joseph Godber,
Minister of Agriculture, Fisheries and Food.

Gordon Campbell,
26th November 1973. Secretary of State for Scotland.

W. S. I. Whitelaw,
26th November 1973. Secretary of State for Northern Ireland.

SCHEDULE 1

THE BASELINES

The baselines defined in Article 2(1) of this order are drawn by joining together successively, in the order in which they are set out below, the points identified by the following co-ordinates of latitude and longitude:—

1.	Horn	66° 27.4′ north	22° 24.5′ west
2.	Asbudarrif	66° 08.1′ north	20° 11.2′ west
3.	Siglunes	66° 11.9′ north	18° 50.1′ west
4.	Flatey	66° 10.3′ north	17° 50.5′ west
5.	Lagey	66° 17.8′ north	17° 07.0′ west
6.	Raudinupur	66° 30.7′ north	16° 32.5′ west
7.	Rifstangi	66° 32.3′ north	16° 11.9′ west
8.	Hraunhafnartangi	66° 32.3′ north	16° 01.6′ west
9.	Langanes	66° 22.6′ north	14° 32.0′ west
10.	Glettinganes	65° 30.6′ north	13° 36.4′ west
11.	Nordfjardarhorn	65° 10.0′ north	13° 31.0′ west
12.	Gerpir	65° 04.7′ north	13° 29.8′ west
13.	Holmur	64° 58.9′ north	13° 30.7′ west
14.	Setusker	64° 57.7′ north	13° 31.6′ west

(**a**) 1889 c. 63.

15.	Thursasker	64° 54.1′ north	13° 36.9′ west
16.	Yztibodi	64° 35.2′ north	14° 01.6′ west
17.	Selsker	64° 32.8′ north	14° 07.1′ west
18.	Hvitingar	64° 23.8′ north	14° 28.1′ west
19.	Stokksnes	64° 14.1′ north	14° 58.5′ west
20.	Hrollaugseyjar	64° 01.7′ north	15° 58.8′ west
21.	Tvisker	63° 55.6′ north	16° 11.4′ west
22.	Ingolfshofdi	63° 47.8′ north	16° 38.6′ west
23.	Hvalsiki	63° 44.1′ north	17° 33.7′ west
24.	Medallandssandur I	63° 32.4′ north	17° 56.0′ west
25.	Medallandssandur II	63° 30.6′ north	18° 00.0′ west
26.	Myrnatangi	63° 27.4′ north	18° 12.0′ west
27.	Kotlutangi	63° 23.4′ north	18° 43.0′ west
28.	Lundadrangur	63° 23.5′ north	19° 07.6′ west
29.	Geirfuglasker	63° 19.0′ north	20° 30.1′ west
30.	Eldeyjardrangur	63° 43.8′ north	22° 59.6′ west
31.	Geirfugladrangur	63° 40.6′ north	23° 17.3′ west
32.	Skalasnagi	64° 51.3′ north	24° 02.6′ west
33.	Bjargtangar	65° 32.2′ north	24° 32.3′ west
34.	Kopanes	65° 48.3′ north	24° 06.3′ west
35.	Bardi	66° 03.7′ north	23° 47.6′ west
36.	Straumnes	66° 25.7′ north	23° 08.5′ west
37.	Kogur	66° 28.3′ north	22° 55.8′ west
38.	Horn	66° 27.9′ north	22° 28.5′ west

SCHEDULE 2

The area between the 12 mile line and the 50 mile line but excluding therefrom the area within a radius of 12 miles from Kolbeinsey (67° 07.5′ north latitude 18° 36′ west longitude).

EXPLANATORY NOTE

(This Note is not part of the Order.)

This Order specifies the class of persons who are to be foreign sea-fishery officers for the purpose of enforcing a specified Convention between the United Kingdom Government and the government of Iceland relating to the conduct of fishing in the area specified in the Order.

1973 No. 1999

SEA FISHERIES

BOATS AND METHODS OF FISHING

The Sea Fishing (Specified Northern Waters) Prohibition Order 1973

Made - - -	*27th November* 1973
Laid before Parliament	*30th November* 1973
Coming into Operation	*1st December* 1973

Whereas it appears to the Minister of Agriculture, Fisheries and Food and the Secretaries of State respectively concerned with the sea fishing industry in Scotland and Northern Ireland necessary or expedient to make this order for the purpose of giving effect to an Interim Agreement made on 13th November 1973 and now in force between Her Majesty's Government in the United Kingdom and the government of Iceland(**a**):

NOW, therefore, the Ministers in exercise of the powers conferred on them by sections 5(1) and 15 of the Sea Fish (Conservation) Act 1967(**b**) (as the last mentioned section is amended by section 22(1) of, and paragraph 38 of Schedule 1 to, the Sea Fisheries Act 1968(**c**)), as together read with section 22(2) thereof, and of all other powers enabling them in that behalf, hereby order as follows:—

Citation and commencement

1. This order may be cited as the Sea Fishing (Specified Northern Waters) Prohibition Order 1973 and shall come into operation on 1st December 1973.

Interpretation

2.—(1) In this order—

"the baselines" means the lines drawn round the coast of Iceland so as to join successively, in the order in which they are there set out, the points identified by the co-ordinates of latitude and longitude in Schedule 1 to this order;

"mile" means nautical mile;

"the 12 mile line" means a line drawn round the coast of Iceland 12 miles from the baselines and extended seawards by lines drawn 12 miles from and around the Island of Grimsey (from its outermost headlands and skerries) and around Hvalbakur (64° 35.8′ north latitude 13° 16.7′ west longitude);

(a) Cmnd 5484. (b) 1967 c.84. (c) 1968 c.77.

"the 50 mile line" means a line drawn round the coast of Iceland 50 miles from the baselines and extended seawards by lines drawn 50 miles around Hvalbakur (64° 35.8′ north latitude 13° 16.7′ west longitude) and Kolbeinsey (67° 07.5′ north latitude 18° 36′ west longitude).

(2) The Interpretation Act 1889(**a**) shall apply for the interpretation of this order as it applies for the interpretation of an Act of Parliament.

Prohibition

3.—(1) There is hereby prohibited, in relation to any area defined in column 1 of Part I of Schedule 2 to this order, for the period specified in column 2 of that Part opposite the area so defined, all fishing for sea fish within that area.

(2) Without prejudice to paragraph (1) of this Article, there is hereby also prohibited in relation to any area defined in column 1 of Part II of Schedule 2 (being an area included in, or partly included in, an area as defined in column 1 of Part I of Schedule 2) for the period specified in column 2 of the said Part II opposite the area so defined, all fishing for sea fish within that area.

Enforcement

4. For the purpose of the enforcement of this order there are hereby conferred on every British sea-fishery officer the powers of a British sea-fishery officer under section 8(2) and (3) of the Sea Fisheries Act 1968.

In Witness whereof the Official Seal of the Minister of Agriculture, Fisheries and Food is hereunto affixed on 27th November 1973.

(L.S.)

Joseph Godber,
Minister of Agriculture, Fisheries and Food.

Gordon Campbell,
26th November 1973. Secretary of State for Scotland.

W. S. I. Whitelaw,
26th November 1973. Secretary of State for Northern Ireland.

(**a**) 1889 c. 63.

SCHEDULE 1

THE BASELINES

The baselines defined in Article 2(1) of this order are drawn by joining together successively, in the order in which they are set out below, the points identified by the following co-ordinates of latitude and longitude:—

1.	Horn	66° 27.4′ north	22° 24.5′ west
2.	Asbudarrif	66° 08.1′ north	20° 11.2′ west
3.	Siglunes	66° 11.9′ north	18° 50.1′ west
4.	Flatey	66° 10.3′ north	17° 50.5′ west
5.	Lagey	66° 17.8′ north	17° 07.0′ west
6.	Raudinupur	66° 30.7′ north	16° 32.5′ west
7.	Rifstangi	66° 32.3′ north	16° 11.9′ west
8.	Hraunhafnartangi	66° 32.3′ north	16° 01.6′ west
9.	Langanes	66° 22.6′ north	14° 32.0′ west
10.	Glettinganes	65° 30.6′ north	13° 36.4′ west
11.	Nordfjardarhorn	65° 10.0′ north	13° 31.0′ west
12.	Gerpir	65° 04.7′ north	13° 29.8′ west
13.	Holmur	64° 58.9′ north	13° 30.7′ west
14.	Setusker	64° 57.7′ north	13° 31.6′ west
15.	Thursasker	64° 54.1′ north	13° 36.9′ west
16.	Yztibodi	64° 35.2′ north	14° 01.6′ west
17.	Selsker	64° 32.8′ north	14° 07.1′ west
18.	Hvitingar	64° 23.8′ north	14° 28.1′ west
19.	Stokksnes	64° 14.1′ north	14° 58.5′ west
20.	Hrollaugseyjar	64° 01.7′ north	15° 58.8′ west
21.	Tvisker	63° 55.6′ north	16° 11.4′ west
22.	Ingolfshofdi	63° 47.8′ north	16° 38.6′ west
23.	Hvalsiki	63° 44.1′ north	17° 33.7′ west
24.	Medallandssandur I	63° 32.4′ north	17° 56.0′ west
25.	Medallandssandur II	63° 30.6′ north	18° 00.0′ west
26.	Myrnatangi	63° 27.4′ north	18° 12.0′ west
27.	Kotlutangi	63° 23.4′ north	18° 43.0′ west
28.	Lundadrangur	63° 23.5′ north	19° 07.6′ west
29.	Geirfuglasker	63° 19.0′ north	20° 30.1′ west
30.	Eldeyjardrangur	63° 43.8′ north	22° 59.6′ west
31.	Geirfugladrangur	63° 40.6′ north	23° 17.3′ west
32.	Skalasnagi	64° 51.3′ north	24° 02.6′ west
33.	Bjargtangar	65° 32.2′ north	24° 32.3′ west
34.	Kopanes	65° 48.3′ north	24° 06.3′ west
35.	Bardi	66° 03.7′ north	23° 47.6′ west
36.	Straumnes	66° 25.7′ north	23° 08.5′ west
37.	Kogur	66° 28.3′ north	22° 55.8′ west
38.	Horn	66° 27.9′ north	22° 28.5′ west

SCHEDULE 2

Part I

Column 1	Column 2
Area	Period
An area off the north-west coast of Iceland between the 12 mile line and the 50 mile line, and between the meridian of 22° 24′ west longitude anti-clockwise to the parallel of 65° 30′ north latitude.	The months of September and October in the years 1974 and 1975.
An area off the south-west coast of Iceland between the 12 mile line and the 50 mile line, and between the parallel of 65° 30′ north latitude anti-clockwise to the meridian of 20° 30′ west longitude.	From the date of the coming into operation of this order until 31st December 1973 (both dates inclusive); the months of November and December in the year 1974; 1st November 1975 to 13th November 1975 (both dates inclusive).
An area off the south coast of Iceland between the 12 mile line and the 50 mile line, and between the meridian of 20° 30′ west longitude anti-clockwise to the meridian of 14° 30′ west longitude.	The months of May and June in the years of 1974 and 1975.
An area off the south-east coast of Iceland between the 12 mile line and the 50 mile line, and between the meridian of 14° 30′ west longitude anti-clockwise to a line drawn 045 from Bjarnarey (65° 47.1′ north latitude 14° 18.2′ west longitude).	The months of January and February in the years 1974 and 1975.
An area off the north-east coast of Iceland between the 12 mile line and the 50 mile line, and between a line drawn 045° from Bjarnarey anti-clockwise to the meridian of 16° 11.8′ west longitude.	The months of July and August in the years 1974 and 1975.
An area off the north coast of Iceland between the 12 mile line and the 50 mile line, and between the meridian of 16° 11.8′ west longitude anti-clockwise to the meridian of 22° 24′ west longitude, but excluding therefrom the area within a radius of 12 miles from Kolbeinsey (67° 07.5′ north latitude 18° 36′ west longitude).	The months of March and April in the years 1974 and 1975.

PART II

Column 1	Column 2
Area	Period
An area off the north-west coast of Iceland demarcated by— —a line drawn between the positions 66° 57′ north latitude 23° 36′ west longitude and 67° 01′ north latitude 22° 24′ west longitude; —a line drawn 340° from the position 66° 57′ north latitude 23° 36′ west longitude; —the meridian of 22° 24′ west longitude; —the 50 mile line.	From the date of the coming into operation of this order until 13th November 1975 (both dates inclusive).
An area off the south coast of Iceland demarcated by— —the meridian of 22° 00′ west longitude; —the parallel of 63° 00′ north latitude; —the meridian of 21° 25′ west longitude; —the 12 mile line.	20th March to 20th April (both dates inclusive) in the years 1974 and 1975.
An area off the north-east coast of Iceland demarcated by— —the meridian of 16° 11.8′ west longitude; —the 12 mile line; —a line drawn 045° from Langanes (66° 22.7′ north latitude 14° 31.9′ west longitude); —the 50 mile line.	1st April to 1st June (both dates inclusive) in the years 1974 and 1975.
An area off the north-west coast of Iceland between the 12 mile line and a line drawn 20 miles from the baselines, and between the meridian of 22° 24′ west longitude anti-clockwise to the parallel of 65° 30′ north latitude.	From the date of the coming into operation of this order until 13th November 1975 (both dates inclusive).
An area off the east coast of Iceland between the 12 mile line and a line drawn 20 miles from the baselines, and demarcated in the south by the 12 mile line around Hvalbakur (64° 35.8′ north latitude 13° 16.7′ west longitude) and in the north by a line drawn 045° from Bjarnarey (65° 47.1′ north latitude 14° 18.2′ west longitude).	From the date of the coming into operation of this order until 13th November 1975 (both dates inclusive).
An area off the north coast of Iceland demarcated by— —a line drawn between the positions 66° 39.7′ north latitude 22° 24′ west longitude and 66° 23.8′ north latitude 18° 50′ west longitude; —the 12 mile line.	From the date of the coming into operation of this order until 13th November 1975 (both dates inclusive).

EXPLANATORY NOTE

(This Note is not part of the Order.)

This Order, made in implementation of an Agreement between Her Majesty's Government in the United Kingdom and the government of Iceland, prohibits all fishing for sea fish in specified areas in the vicinity of Iceland during the periods mentioned in the Order.

By virtue of section 5(8) of the Sea Fish (Conservation) Act 1967 the prohibition applies to all British fishing boats registered in the United Kingdom and to fishing boats which are British owned but not registered under the Merchant Shipping Act 1894 (c.60).

1973 No. 2000

SEA FISHERIES

BOATS AND METHODS OF FISHING

The Sea Fishing (Specified Northern Waters) Licensing Order 1973

Made - - -	*29th November* 1973
Laid before Parliament	*30th November* 1973
Coming into Operation	*1st December* 1973

The Minister of Agriculture, Fisheries and Food and the Secretaries of State respectively concerned with the sea fishing industry in Scotland and Northern Ireland, being satisfied that substantially equivalent measures are being taken by governments of other countries concerned, in exercise of the powers conferred on them by section 4(1), (2) and (8) and section 15 of the Sea Fish (Conservation) Act 1967(**a**) (as the last mentioned section is amended by section 22(1) of, and paragraph 38 of Schedule 1 to, the Sea Fisheries Act 1968(**b**)) as together read with section 22(2) thereof, and of all other powers enabling them in that behalf, hereby order as follows:—

Citation and commencement

1. This order may be cited as the Sea Fishing (Specified Northern Waters) Licensing Order 1973, and shall come into operation on 1st December 1973.

Interpretation

2.—(1) In this order—

"the Act" means the Sea Fish (Conservation) Act 1967;

"the baselines" means the lines drawn round the coast of Iceland so as to join successively, in the order in which they are there set out, the points identified by the co-ordinates of latitude and longitude in Schedule 1 to this order;

"mile" means nautical mile;

(**a**) 1967 c. 84. (**b**) 1968 c. 77.

"the 12 mile line" means a line drawn round the coast of Iceland 12 miles from the baselines and extended seawards by lines drawn 12 miles from and around the Island of Grimsey (from its outermost headlands and skerries) and around Hvalbakur (64° 35.8′ north latitude 13° 16.7′ west longitude);

"the 50 mile line" means a line drawn round the coast of Iceland 50 miles from the baselines and extended seawards by lines drawn 50 miles around Hvalbakur (64° 35.8′ north latitude 13° 16.7′ west longitude) and Kolbeinsey (67° 07.5′ north latitude 18° 36′ west longitude).

"the specified area" means the area described in Schedule 2 to this Order.

(2) The Interpretation Act 1889(**a**) shall apply for the interpretation of this order as it applies for the interpretation of an Act of Parliament, and as if this order and the order hereby revoked were Acts of Parliament.

Revocation of previous Order

3. The Sea Fishing (Specified Northern Waters) Licensing Order 1972(**b**) is hereby revoked.

Appointed Day

4. The appointed day for the purpose of section 4 of the Act (which provides for the licensing of British fishing vessels in relation to fishing by way of trade or business in specified areas) in conjunction with this order is the day on which this order comes into operation.

Area and Period

5. This order applies to fishing for sea fish in the specified area for the period beginning with the day on which this order comes into operation and ending on 13th November 1975 (both dates inclusive).

Provided that nothing in this order shall authorise a licence under section 4 of the Act to be granted in respect of any part of the specified area in any period in which fishing for sea fish in such part is prohibited by the Sea Fishing (Specified Northern Waters) Prohibition Order 1973(**c**).

Enforcement

6. For the purposes of the enforcement of section 4 of the Act in conjunction with this order there are hereby conferred on every British sea-fishery officer the powers of a British sea-fishery officer under section 8(2) and (3) of the Sea Fisheries Act 1968.

In witness whereof the Official Seal of the Minister of Agriculture, Fisheries and Food is hereunto affixed on 28th November 1973.

(L.S.)

Joseph Godber,
Minister of Agriculture, Fisheries and Food.

Gordon Campbell,
28th November 1973. Secretary of State for Scotland.

W. S. I. Whitelaw,
29th November 1973. Secretary of State for Northern Ireland.

(**a**) 1889 c. 63.
(**b**) S.I. 1972/1477 (1972 III, p. 4380).
(**c**) S.I.1973/1999 (1973 III, p.6884).

SCHEDULE 1

THE BASELINES

The baselines defined in Article 2(1) of this order are drawn by joining together successively, in the order in which they are set out below, the points identified by the following co-ordinates of latitude and longitude:

1.	Horn	66° 27.4′ north	22° 24.5′ west
2.	Asbudarrif	66° 08.1′ north	20° 11.2′ west
3.	Siglunes	66° 11.9′ north	18° 50.1′ west
4.	Flatey	66° 10.3′ north	17° 50.5′ west
5.	Lagey	66° 17.8′ north	17° 07.0′ west
6.	Raudinupur	66° 30.7′ north	16° 32.5′ west
7.	Rifstangi	66° 32.3′ north	16° 11.9′ west
8.	Hraunhafnartangi	66° 32.3′ north	16° 01.6′ west
9.	Langanes	66° 22.6′ north	14° 32.0′ west
10.	Glettinganes	65° 30.6′ north	13° 36.4′ west
11.	Nordfjardarhorn	65° 10.0′ north	13° 31.0′ west
12.	Gerpir	65° 04.7′ north	13° 29.8′ west
13.	Holmur	64° 58.9′ north	13° 30.7′ west
14.	Setusker	64° 57.7′ north	13° 31.6′ west
15.	Thursasker	64° 54.1′ north	13° 36.9′ west
16.	Yztibodi	64° 35.2′ north	14° 01.6′ west
17.	Selsker	64° 32.8′ north	14° 07.1′ west
18.	Hvitingar	64° 23.8′ north	14° 28.1′ west
19.	Stokksnes	64° 14.1′ north	14° 58.5′ west
20.	Hrollaugseyjar	64° 01.7′ north	15° 58.8′ west
21.	Tvisker	63° 55.6′ north	16° 11.4′ west
22.	Ingolfshofdi	63° 47.8′ north	16° 38.6′ west
23.	Hvalsiki	63° 44.1′ north	17° 33.7′ west
24.	Medallandssandur I	63° 32.4′ north	17° 56.0′ west
25.	Medallandssandur II	63° 30.6′ north	18° 00.0′ west
26.	Myrnatangi	63° 27.4′ north	18° 12.0′ west
27.	Kotlutangi	63° 23.4′ north	18° 43.0′ west
28.	Lundadrangur	63° 23.5′ north	19° 07.6′ west
29.	Geirfuglasker	63° 19.0′ north	20° 30.1′ west
30.	Eldeyjardrangur	63° 43.8′ north	22° 59.6′ west
31.	Geirfugladrangur	63° 40.6′ north	23° 17.3′ west
32.	Skalasnagi	64° 51.3′ north	24° 02.6′ west
33.	Bjargtangar	65° 32.2′ north	24° 32.3′ west
34.	Kopanes	65° 48.3′ north	24° 06.3′ west
35.	Bardi	66° 03.7′ north	23° 47.6′ west
36.	Straumnes	66° 25.7′ north	23° 08.5′ west
37.	Kogur	66° 28.3′ north	22° 55.8′ west
38.	Horn	66° 27.9′ north	22° 28.5′ west

SCHEDULE 2

The area of sea between the 12 mile line and the 50 mile line but excluding therefrom the area within a radius of 12 miles from Kolbeinsey (67° 07.5′ north latitude 18° 36′ west longitude).

EXPLANATORY NOTE

(This Note is not part of the Order.)

Section 4 of the Sea Fish (Conservation) Act 1967 provides that from a day appointed by an Order, no British fishing boat registered in the United Kingdom shall be used by way of trade or business for fishing in any area specified in the Order except under the authority of a licence granted by one of the Fisheries Ministers.

This Order appoints 1st December 1973 as the day from which no such fishing boat shall fish for sea fish in a specified area in the vicinity of Iceland except under the authority of such a licence.

1973 No. 2004

SEA FISHERIES

LANDING AND SALE OF SEA FISH

The Haddock (Restrictions on Landing) Order 1973

Made - - - *29th November* 1973

Laid before Parliament *7th December* 1973

Coming into Operation *1st January* 1974

The Minister of Agriculture, Fisheries and Food and the Secretaries of State respectively concerned with the sea fishing industry in Scotland and Northern Ireland, in exercise of the powers conferred on them by sections 6 and 15 of the Sea Fish (Conservation) Act 1967(**a**) as the latter section is amended by section 22(1) of, and paragraph 38 of Part II of Schedule 1 to, the Sea Fisheries Act 1968(**b**) and of all other powers enabling them in that behalf, after consultation with the Secretary of State for Trade and Industry(**c**), hereby make the following Order:—

Citation and Commencement

1. This Order may be cited as the Haddock (Restrictions on Landing) Order 1973 and shall come into operation on 1st January 1974.

Interpretation

2.—(1) In this Order:—

'the specified waters' means the waters described in Schedule 1 to this Order.

(2) The Interpretation Act 1889(**d**) shall apply for the interpretation of this Order as it applies for the interpretation of an Act of Parliament.

Prohibition on Landing

3. Except as hereinafter provided, the landing in the United Kingdom of haddock (*Melanogrammus aeglefinus*) caught in the specified waters is hereby prohibited.

Exception from the Prohibition on Landing

4.—(1) There shall be excepted from the prohibition contained in Article 3 of this Order the landing in the United Kingdom of haddock caught in the specified waters provided that:—

(**a**) 1967 c. 84. (**b**) 1968 c. 77.
(**c**) For transfer of function from the Board of Trade to the Secretary of State for Trade and Industry *see* the Secretary of State for Trade and Industry Order 1970 (S.I. 1970/1537 (1970 III, p. 5293)). (**d**) 1889 c. 63.

(i) the haddock were caught in the course of fishing for sea fish of any description other than haddock; and

(ii) the haddock so caught are comprised in a catch the whole or part of which was taken in the specified waters and do not exceed in weight one-tenth of the total weight of the catch landed in the United Kingdom or, if only part of the catch was taken in the specified waters, one-tenth of the total weight of that part landed as aforesaid.

(2) Notwithstanding the exception contained in Article 4(1) of this Order the prohibition contained in Article 3 of this Order shall apply to the landing in the United Kingdom of haddock caught during the period 1st March 1974 to 31st May 1974 (both dates inclusive):—

(*a*) in those parts of the specified waters described in Part I of Schedule 2 to this Order; or

(*b*) in that part of the specified waters described in Part II of Schedule 2 to this Order with hooks having a gape of less than 3 centimetres.

Powers of British Sea-Fishery Officers

5. For the purpose of the enforcement of this Order there are hereby conferred on every British sea-fishery officer the powers of a British sea-fishery officer under section 8(2) and (3) of the Sea Fisheries Act 1968.

In Witness whereof the Official Seal of the Minister of Agriculture, Fisheries and Food is hereunto affixed on 26th November 1973.

(L.S.)

Joseph Godber,
Minister of Agriculture, Fisheries and Food.

Gordon Campbell,
27th November 1973. Secretary of State for Scotland.

W. S. I. Whitelaw,
29th November 1973. Secretary of State for Northern Ireland.

SCHEDULE 1

The area bounded by the coasts of Nova Scotia, west of Halifax; New Brunswick; Maine; New Hampshire; Massachusetts and Rhode Island, to a point 71° 40′ west longitude; and thence by straight lines connecting the following co-ordinates in the order listed:—

39° 00′ north, 71° 40′ west.

39° 00′ north, 63° 20′ west:

44° 20′ north, 63° 20′ west:

Halifax, Nova Scotia.

SCHEDULE 2

Part I

Those two parts of the Northwest Atlantic Ocean which are respectively bounded by straight lines connecting the following co-ordinates in the order listed:—

(*a*) 42° 20′ north, 67° 00′ west;
41° 15′ north, 67° 00′ west;
41° 15′ north, 65° 40′ west;
42° 00′ north, 65° 40′ west;
42° 20′ north, 66° 00′ west.

(*b*) 42° 04′ north, 65° 44′ west;
42° 40′ north, 64° 30′ west;
43° 00′ north, 64° 30′ west;
43° 00′ north, 66° 32′ west;
42° 20′ north, 66° 32′ west;
42° 20′ north, 66° 00′ west.

Part II

That part of the Northwest Atlantic Ocean bounded by straight lines connecting the following co-ordinates in the order listed:—

42° 10′ north, 69° 55′ west;
41° 10′ north, 69° 10′ west;
41° 35′ north, 68° 30′ west;
41° 50′ north, 68° 45′ west;
41° 50′ north, 69° 00′ west.

EXPLANATORY NOTE

(This Note is not part of the Order.)

This Order which is made under sections 6 and 15 of the Sea Fish (Conservation) Act 1967 implements a recommendation of the International Commission for the Northwest Atlantic Fisheries.

The Order prohibits the landing in the United Kingdom of haddock caught in a specified area of the Northwest Atlantic. It excepts from the prohibition the landing of such haddock caught whilst fishing for any other species of fish provided the haddock do not exceed 10% of the total weight of the catch (or that part of the catch) taken in the specified area. However the exception does not apply to the landing of haddock caught during the period 1st March to 31st May 1974 in certain defined parts of the specified area of the Northwest Atlantic.

STATUTORY INSTRUMENTS

1973 No. 2005

INDUSTRIAL TRAINING

The Industrial Training (Electricity Supply Board) (Revocation) Order 1973

Made - - -	*27th November* 1973
Laid before Parliament	*10th December* 1973
Coming into Operation	
Article 3	*1st March* 1974
Remainder	*1st January* 1974

The Secretary of State after consultation with the Electricity Supply Industry Training Board, with the employers in the electricity supply industry, and organisations and associations of organisations appearing to be representative of substantial numbers of persons employed in the activities of the electricity supply industry and in exercise of his powers under section 9 of the Industrial Training Act 1964(**a**) and of all other powers enabling him in that behalf hereby makes the following order:—

Citation, commencement and interpretation

1.—(1) This Order may be cited as the Industrial Training (Electricity Supply Board) (Revocation) Order 1973.

(2) Article 3 of this Order shall come into operation on 1st March 1974.

(3) The provisions of this Order, other than Article 3, shall come into operation on 1st January 1974.

(4) In this Order—

(*a*) "the Act" means the Industrial Training Act 1964 and references in this Order to sections are references to sections in the Act;

(*b*) "the Board" means the Electricity Supply Industry Training Board;

(*c*) "the electricity supply industry" means the industry described in the Industrial Training Order;

(*d*) "employer in the electricity supply industry" means any of the following, that is to say—

(**a**) 1964 c. 16.

(i) the Electricity Council;

(ii) the Central Electricity Generating Board;

(iii) an Area Electricity Board;

(iv) the North of Scotland Hydro-Electric Board;

(v) the South of Scotland Electricity Board;

(vi) the London Transport Executive;

(*e*) "the Industrial Training Order" means the Industrial Training (Electricity Supply Board) Order 1965(**a**);

(*f*) "the remaining assets" means any amount by which the assets of the Board immediately before 1st March 1974 may exceed the amount which has been required to meet the liabilities of the Board and the expenses of the winding up.

(5) The Interpretation Act 1889(**b**) shall apply to the interpretation of this Order as it applies to the interpretation of an Act of Parliament and as if this Order and the Industrial Training Order were Acts of Parliament.

Winding up of the Board

2.—(1) The Board shall be wound up in accordance with the provisions of this Article.

(2) On the coming into operation of this Article the Board shall cease to exercise its functions except insofar as continued exercise of those functions may be necessary or expedient for the purpose of the winding up.

(3) Between the coming into operation of this Article and 1st March 1974 the Board shall discharge its liabilities.

(4) Immediately before 1st March 1974 the Board shall transfer to, or to the order of, the Secretary of State in such manner as he may direct the remaining assets of the Board and those assets shall be applied by the Secretary of State for the purpose specified in paragraph (5) of this Article.

(5) The specified purpose shall be the repayment (as the case may allow in whole or in part) of levies paid by employers in the electricity supply industry.

(6) The accounts of the Board up to 1st March 1974 shall be prepared and audited in accordance with section 8 and those accounts and the final report of the Board shall be laid before Parliament in accordance with that section.

Revocation of Industrial Training Order

3. The Industrial Training Order is hereby revoked.

Signed by order of the Secretary of State.
27th November 1973.

R. Chichester-Clark,
Minister of State,
Department of Employment.

(**a**) S.I. 1965/1256 (1965 II, p. 3548). (**b**) 1889 c. 63.

EXPLANATORY NOTE

(This Note is not part of the Order.)

This Order provides with effect from 1st January 1974 for the winding up of the Electricity Supply Industry Training Board, which was established by the Industrial Training (Electricity Supply Board) Order 1965, and for the revocation of that Order with effect from 1st March 1974. Any assets remaining on the completion of the winding up are to be applied for the purpose of repaying levy to employers in the electricity supply industry.

1973 No. 2006

INDUSTRIAL TRAINING

The Industrial Training (Gas Industry Board) (Revocation) Order 1973

Made - - -	27*th November* 1973
Laid before Parliament	10*th December* 1973
Coming into Operation	
Article 3	1*st April* 1974
Remainder	1*st January* 1974

The Secretary of State after consultation with the Gas Industry Training Board, with the British Gas Corporation, being the sole employer engaged in the activities of the gas industry, and with organisations and associations of organisations appearing to be representative of substantial numbers of persons employed in the activities of the gas industry and in the exercise of his powers under section 9 of the Industrial Training Act 1964(**a**) and of all other powers enabling him in that behalf hereby makes the following order:—

Citation, commencement and interpretation

1.—(1) This Order may be cited as the Industrial Training (Gas Industry Board) (Revocation) Order 1973.

(2) Article 3 of this Order shall come into operation on 1st April 1974.

(3) The provisions of this Order, other than Article 3, shall come into operation on 1st January 1974.

(4) In this Order—

(*a*) "the Act" means the Industrial Training Act 1964 and references in this Order to sections are references to sections in the Act;

(*b*) "the Board" means the Gas Industry Training Board;

(*c*) "the Corporation" means the body established under the Gas Act 1948 by the name of the Gas Council and named the British Gas Corporation by section 1 of the Gas Act 1972(**b**);

(*d*) "the former employers in the gas industry" means the Area Gas Boards, whose property, rights, liabilities and obligations were vested in the Corporation on 1st January 1973 by section 1(1) of the Gas Act 1972;

(*e*) "the gas industry" means the industry described in the Industrial Training Order;

(*f*) "the Industrial Training Order" means the Industrial Training (Gas Industry Board) Order 1965(**c**),

(**a**) 1964 c. 16. (**b**) 1972 c. 60. (**c**) S.I. 1965/1257 (1965 II, p. 3552).

(g) "the remaining assets" means any amount by which the assets of the Board immediately before 1st April 1974 may exceed the amount which has been required to meet the liabilities of the Board and the expenses of the winding up.

(5) The Interpretation Act 1889(**a**) shall apply to the interpretation of this Order as it applies to the interpretation of an Act of Parliament and as if this Order and the Industrial Training Order were Acts of Parliament.

Winding up of the Board

2.—(1) The Board shall be wound up in accordance with the provisions of this Article.

(2) On the coming into operation of this Article the Board shall cease to exercise its functions except insofar as continued exercise of those functions may be necessary or expedient for the purpose of the winding up.

(3) Between the coming into operation of this Article and 1st April 1974 the Board shall discharge its liabilities.

(4) Immediately before 1st April 1974 the Board shall transfer to, or to the order of, the Secretary of State in such manner as he may direct the remaining assets of the Board and those assets shall be applied by the Secretary of State for the purpose specified in paragraph (5) of this Article.

(5) The specified purpose shall be the repayment (as the case may allow in whole or in part) to the Corporation of levies paid by the Corporation and by the former employers in the gas industry.

(6) The accounts of the Board up to 1st April 1974 shall be prepared and audited in accordance with section 8 and those accounts and the final report of the Board shall be laid before Parliament in accordance with that section.

Revocation of Industrial Training Order

3. The Industrial Training Order is hereby revoked.

Signed by order of the Secretary of State.
27th November 1973.

R. Chichester-Clark,
Minister of State,
Department of Employment.

(**a**) 1889 c. 63.

EXPLANATORY NOTE

(This Note is not part of the Order.)

This Order provides with effect from 1st January 1974 for the winding up of the Gas Industry Training Board, which was established by the Industrial Training (Gas Industry Board) Order 1965, and for the revocation of that Order with effect from 1st April 1974. Any assets remaining on the completion of the winding up are to be applied for the purpose of repaying levy to the British Gas Corporation, now the sole employer in the industry, which was formerly called the Gas Council and is the successor body to the Area Boards who until 1st January 1973 were, together with the Gas Council, the employers in the industry.

STATUTORY INSTRUMENTS

1973 No. 2009

COMPENSATION

The Courts (Compensation to Officers) (Amendment) Regulations 1973

Made - - -	*27th November* 1973
Laid before Parliament	*11th December* 1973
Coming into Operation	*1st January* 1974

The Lord Chancellor, in exercise of the powers conferred on him by section 44 of the Courts Act 1971(**a**) and with the concurrence of the Minister for the Civil Service, hereby makes the following Regulations:—

1.—(1) These Regulations may be cited as the Courts (Compensation to Officers) (Amendment) Regulations 1973 and shall come into operation on 1st January 1974.

(2) In these Regulations "the principal Regulations" means the Courts (Compensation to Officers) Regulations 1971(**b**) and a reference to a regulation by number means the regulation so numbered in those Regulations.

(3) The Interpretation Act 1889(**c**) shall apply to the interpretation of these Regulations as it applies to the interpretation of an Act of Parliament.

2.—(1) In the definition of "normal retiring age" in regulation 2(1) of the principal Regulations, there shall be inserted after paragraph (*a*) the following paragraph—

"(*aa*) in relation to a person claiming compensation in respect of the office of chairman or deputy chairman of county quarter sessions or of recorder or deputy, assistant or temporary recorder of a borough, seventy-two years; and".

(2) The compensating authority may review any decision made before the coming into operation of these Regulations in respect of a claim in relation to any of the offices mentioned in paragraph (1) above, provided that any compensation payable by virtue of that decision shall not be reduced by reason only of a review under this paragraph.

3. For the tables in the Schedule to the principal Regulations there shall be substituted the tables in the Schedule to these Regulations.

Dated 26th November 1973.

Hailsham of St. Marylebone, C.

Concurrence of the Minister for the Civil Service given under his Official Seal on 27th November 1973.

(L.S.)

K. H. McNeill,
Authorised by the
Minister for the Civil Service.

(**a**) 1971 c. 23. (**b**) S.I. 1971/2008 (1971 III, p. 5700). (**c**) 1889 c. 63.

SCHEDULE

Substitution of Tables in the Schedule to the Principal Regulations

Regulation 2(3)

Table 1(*a*)

The capital value of an amount of £1 per annum, payable for life, which attracts pensions increase from age 55, or retirement age if greater

Age last birthday	*Capital value*	
	Female	*Male*
	£·p	£·p
30	14·82	14·34
31	14·86	14·37
32	14·91	14·39
33	14·95	14·41
34	14·99	14·42
35	15·03	14·43
36	15·06	14·44
37	15·09	14·44
38	15·12	14·43
39	15·14	14·42
40	15·15	14·40
41	15·16	14·37
42	15·15	14·33
43	15·14	14·29
44	15·12	14·23
45	15·09	14·16
46	15·05	14·08
47	14·99	13·99
48	14·92	13·88
49	14·83	13·75
50	14·72	13·61
51	14·59	13·45
52	14·43	13·26
53	14·25	13·04
54	14·04	12·79
55	13·79	12·52
56	13·54	12·24
57	13·28	11·95
58	13·01	11·66
59	12·74	11·36
60	12·46	11·06
61	12·17	10·76
62	11·87	10·45
63	11·57	10·14
64	11·27	9·82

Table 1(*a*) (*continued*)

Age last birthday	*Capital value*	
	Female	*Male*
	£·p	£·p
65	10·96	9·51
66	10·64	9·19
67	10·32	8·87
68	10·00	8·56
69	9·68	8·25
70	9·36	7·94
71	9·03	7·63
72	8·70	7·32
73	8·38	7·02
74	8·05	6·72
75	7·73	6·43
76	7·41	6·14
77	7·09	5·86
78	6·78	5·59
79	6·47	5·32

NOTE:—This table is for use in connection with regulation 36(1) and (2) for the compounding of annual retirement compensation which a person is currently entitled to receive under regulation 20, 21, 22 or 23 and which attracts pensions increase when the person attains age 55, or retirement age if greater. Where the compensation is payable before age 60 (females), 65 (males), but will be reduced on the attainment of that age (in connection with National Insurance pension) the tables should be used in conjunction with Table 2(*a*), *i.e.*, Table 2(*a*) should be used for valuing that part of the compensation which ceases to be payable at 60 (65) and this table should be used for valuing the remainder.

TABLE 1(*b*)

The capital value of an amount of £1 per annum, payable for life, which attracts pensions increase from the outset

Age last birthday	*Capital value*	
	Female	*Male*
	£·p	£·p
23	18·59	18·24
24	18·52	18·15
25	18·44	18·05
26	18·36	17·95
27	18·28	17·85
28	18·19	17·74
29	18·10	17·63
30	18·00	17·51
31	17·90	17·38
32	17·79	17·25
33	17·68	17·12
34	17·57	16·98
35	17·45	16·83
36	17·32	16·68
37	17·19	16·52
38	17·05	16·35
39	16·91	16·18
40	16·76	16·00
41	16·61	15·81
42	16·45	15·62
43	16·29	15·42
44	16·12	15·21
45	15·94	15·00
46	15·76	14·78
47	15·57	14·56
48	15·37	14·33
49	15·17	14·09
50	14·96	13·84
51	14·74	13·59
52	14·51	13·33
53	14·28	13·07
54	14·04	12·80
55	13·79	12·52
56	13·54	12·24
57	13·28	11·95
58	13·01	11·66
59	12·74	11·36
60	12·46	11·06
61	12·17	10·76
62	11·87	10·45
63	11·57	10·14
64	11·27	9·82

Table 1(*b*) (*continued*)

Age last birthday	*Capital value*	
	Female	*Male*
	£·p	£·p
65	10·96	9·51
66	10·64	9·19
67	10·32	8·87
68	10·00	8·56
69	9·68	8·25
70	9·36	7·94
71	9·03	7·63
72	8·70	7·32
73	8·38	7·02
74	8·05	6·72
75	7·73	6·43
76	7·41	6·14
77	7·09	5·86
78	6·78	5·59
79	6·47	5·32

NOTE:—This table is for use in connection with regulation 36(1) and (2) for the compounding of annual retirement compensation which a person is currently entitled to receive under regulation 20, 21, 22 or 23 and which attracts pensions increase from the outset. Where the compensation is payable before age 60 (females), 65 (males) but will be reduced on the attainment of that age (in connection with National Insurance pension) the tables should be used in conjunction with Table 2(*b*), *i.e.*, Table 2(*b*) should be used for valuing that part of the compensation which ceases to be payable at 60 (65) and this table should be used for valuing the remainder.

TABLE 2(*a*)

The capital value of an amount of £1 per annum, ceasing at age 60 (females), 65 (males), which attracts pensions increase from age 55, or retirement age if greater

Age last birthday	*Capital value*	
	Female	*Male*
	£·p	£·p
30	12·11	12·92
31	12·01	12·87
32	11·91	12·81
33	11·80	12·75
34	11·68	12·68
35	11·55	12·60
36	11·40	12·51
37	11·24	12·41
38	11·07	12·30
39	10·88	12·18
40	10·67	12·04
41	10·44	11·89
42	10·19	11·72
43	9·92	11·53
44	9·63	11·33
45	9·31	11·11
46	8·96	10·86
47	8·58	10·59
48	8·16	10·30
49	7·71	9·98
50	7·22	9·62
51	6·68	9·23
52	6·09	8·80
53	5·45	8·33
54	4·75	7·81
55	3·99	7·24
56	3·18	6·64
57	2·33	6·01
58	1·43	5·35
59	·49	4·65
60	—	3·91
61	—	3·13
62	—	2·30
63	—	1·42
64	—	·48

NOTE:—This table is for use in connection with regulation 36(1) and (2) for the compounding of any part of annual retirement compensation which will cease to be payable on the attainment of age 60 (females), 65 (males), and which attracts pensions increase from age 55, or retirement age if greater. Table 1(*a*) should be used in relation to the remainder of such compensation, *i.e.*, the part which is payable for life—see note on that table.

TABLE 2(*b*)

The capital value of an amount of £1 per annum, ceasing at age 60 (females), 65 (males), which attracts pensions increase from the outset

Age last birthday	*Capital value*	
	Female	*Male*
	£·p	£·p
23	16·68	17·24
24	16·51	17·10
25	16·33	16·95
26	16·14	16·79
27	15·94	16·63
28	15·74	16·46
29	15·52	16·28
30	15·29	16·09
31	15·05	15·89
32	14·80	15·68
33	14·54	15·46
34	14·26	15·23
35	13·97	15·00
36	13·66	14·75
37	13·34	14·49
38	13·01	14·22
39	12·66	13·94
40	12·29	13·64
41	11·90	13·33
42	11·49	13·01
43	11·07	12·67
44	10·63	12·31
45	10·16	11·94
46	9·67	11·56
47	9·15	11·16
48	8·61	10·74
49	8·04	10·30
50	7·45	9·85
51	6·83	9·38
52	6·17	8·88
53	5·48	8·36
54	4·75	7·81
55	3·99	7·24
56	3·18	6·64
57	2·33	6·01
58	1·43	5·35
59	·49	4·65

Table 2(*b*) (*continued*)

Age last birthday	*Capital value*	
	Female	*Male*
	£·p	£·p
60	—	3·91
61	—	3·13
62	—	2·30
63	—	1·42
64	—	·48

NOTE:—This table is for use in connection with regulation 36(1) and (2) for the compounding of any part of annual retirement compensation which will cease to be payable on the attainment of age 60 (females), 65 (males), and which attracts pensions increase from the outset. Table 1(*b*) should be used in relation to the remainder of such compensation, *i.e.*, the part which is payable for life—see note on that table.

TABLE 3

The capital value of an amount of £1 per annum, payable to a widow until death or remarriage, which attracts pensions increase from the outset

Age of widow at date of widowhood	*Capital value*	*Age of widow at date of widowhood*	*Capital value*
	£·p		£·p
20	6·00	45	13·14
21	6·00	46	13·25
22	6·00	47	13·34
23	6·00	48	13·40
24	6·13	49	13·44
25	6·58	50	13·46
26	7·01	51	13·46
27	7·41	52	13·43
28	7·78	53	13·38
29	8·11	54	13·31
30	8·41	55	13·22
31	8·72	56	13·10
32	9·06	57	12·96
33	9·42	58	12·80
34	9·82	59	12·61
35	10·24	60	12·39
36	10·65	61	12·14
37	11·04	62	11·87
38	11·40	63	11·57
39	11·73	64	11·27
40	12·04	65	10·96
41	12·33	66	10·64
42	12·59	67	10·32
43	12·81	68	10·00
44	12·99	69	9·68
		70	9·35

NOTE:—This table is for use in connection with regulation 36(1) for compounding annual compensation to a widow which attracts pensions increase from the outset under regulation 26. It should also be used, where a reduction of compensation under regulation 26(6) falls to be apportioned between the compensation payable under that regulation and under regulation 27, for ascertaining the capital value of annual compensation to a widow.

TABLE 4(*a*)

The annual amount, payable for life, and attracting pensions increase from age 55, or retirement age if greater, equal in value to a lump sum of £100

Age	Annual amount	
	Female	*Male*
	£·p	£·p
30	6·75	6·97
31	6·73	6·96
32	6·71	6·95
33	6·69	6·94
34	6·67	6·93
35	6·65	6·93
36	6·64	6·93
37	6·63	6·93
38	6·61	6·93
39	6·61	6·93
40	6·60	6·94
41	6·60	6·96
42	6·60	6·98
43	6·61	7·00
44	6·61	7·03
45	6·63	7·06
46	6·64	7·10
47	6·67	7·15
48	6·70	7·20
49	6·74	7·27
50	6·79	7·35
51	6·85	7·43
52	6·93	7·54
53	7·02	7·67
54	7·12	7·82
55	7·25	7·99
56	7·39	8·17
57	7·53	8·37
58	7·69	8·58
59	7·85	8·80
60	8·03	9·04
61	8·22	9·29
62	8·42	9·57
63	8·64	9·86
64	8·87	10·18
65	9·12	10·52
66	9·40	10·88
67	9·69	11·27
68	10·00	11·68
69	10·33	12·12
70	10·68	12·59

Table 4(a) (continued)

Age	*Annual amount*	
	Female	*Male*
	£·p	£·p
71	11·07	13·11
72	11·49	13·66
73	11·93	14·25
74	12·42	14·88
75	12·94	15·55
76	13·50	16·29
77	14·10	17·06
78	14·75	17·89
79	15·46	18·80

NOTE:—This table is for use in connection with regulation 24(1) for ascertaining the annual amount (which attracts pensions increase from age 55, or retirement age if greater) by which retirement compensation under regulation 20, 21 or 22 is to be reduced where a claimant has not paid to the compensating authority an amount equal to any sum paid to him by way of superannuation contributions or that amount has been repaid to him by the compensating authority at his request. It should also be used in connection with regulation 36(2) for calculating for the purposes of that paragraph the annual value of retirement compensation awarded as a lump sum.

TABLE 4(*b*)

The annual amount, payable for life, and attracting pensions increase from the outset, equal in value to a lump sum of £100

Age last birthday	*Annual amount*	
	Female	*Male*
	£·p	£·p
23	5·38	5·48
24	5·40	5·51
25	5·42	5·54
26	5·45	5·57
27	5·47	5·60
28	5·50	5·64
29	5·52	5·67
30	5·56	5·71
31	5·59	5·75
32	5·62	5·80
33	5·66	5·84
34	5·69	5·89
35	5·73	5·94
36	5·77	6·00
37	5·82	6·05
38	5·87	6·12
39	5·91	6·18
40	5·97	6·25
41	6·02	6·33
42	6·08	6·40
43	6·14	6·49
44	6·20	6·57
45	6·27	6·67
46	6·35	6·77
47	6·42	6·87
48	6·51	6·98
49	6·59	7·10
50	6·68	7·23
51	6·78	7·36
52	6·89	7·50
53	7·00	7·65
54	7·12	7·81
55	7·25	7·99
56	7·39	8·17
57	7·53	8·37
58	7·69	8·58
59	7·85	8·80

Table 4(*b*) (*continued*)

Age last birthday	*Annual amount*	
	Female	*Male*
	£·p	£·p
60	8·03	9·04
61	8·22	9·29
62	8·42	9·57
63	8·61	9·86
64	8·87	10·18
65	9·12	10·52
66	9·40	10·88
67	9·69	11·27
68	10·00	11·68
69	10·33	12·12
70	10·68	12·59
71	11·07	13·11
72	11·49	13·66
73	11·93	14·25
74	12·42	14·88
75	12·94	15·55
76	13·50	16·29
77	14·10	17·06
78	14·75	17·89
79	15·46	18·80

NOTE:—This table is for use in connection with regulation 24(1) for ascertaining the annual amount (attracting pensions increase throughout life) by which retirement compensation under regulation 20, 21 or 22 is to be reduced where a claimant has not paid to the compensating authority an amount equal to any sum paid to him by way of superannuation contributions or that amount has been repaid to him by the compensating authority at his request. It should also be used in connection with regulation 36(2) for calculating for the purposes of that paragraph the annual value of retirement compensation awarded as a lump sum.

TABLE 5

The annual amount, attracting pensions increase from the outset, payable to a widow until death or remarriage, equal in value to a lump sum of £100

Age of widow at date of widowhood	*Annual amount*	*Age of widow at date of widowhood*	*Annual amount*
	£·p		£·p
20	16·67	45	7·61
21	16·67	46	7·55
22	16·67	47	7·50
23	16·67	48	7·46
24	16·31	49	7·44
25	15·20	50	7·43
26	14·27	51	7·43
27	13·50	52	7·45
28	12·85	53	7·47
29	12·33	54	7·51
30	11·89	55	7·56
31	11·47	56	7·63
32	11·04	57	7·72
33	10·62	58	7·81
34	10·18	59	7·93
35	9·77	60	8·07
36	9·39	61	8·24
37	9·06	62	8·42
38	8·77	63	8·64
39	8·53	64	8·87
40	8·31	65	9·12
41	8·11	66	9·40
42	7·94	67	9·69
43	7·81	68	10·00
44	7·70	69	10·33
		70	10·70

NOTE:—This table is for use in connection with regulation 26(6) for ascertaining the annual amount (which attracts pensions increase from the outset) by which compensation to a widow is to be reduced in the circumstances described in that paragraph. If a reduction is required to be apportioned between compensation payable under regulations 26 and 27, the capital value of annual compensation to a widow should be ascertained by reference to Table 3.

TABLE 6

The capital value of each £100 per annum of long-term compensation, attracting pensions increase from age 55, according to the outstanding period of long-term compensation

Outstanding number of complete years of long-term compensation	*Capital value*	
	Female	*Male*
	£·p	£·p
0	98·65	98·50
1	95·95	95·50
2	93·25	92·60
3	90·65	89·80
4	88·20	87·15
5	85·90	84·70
6	83·70	82·40
7	81·60	80·25
8	79·60	78·20
9	77·70	76·30
10	75·80	74·40
11	73·85	72·45
12	71·80	70·45
13	69·75	68·40
14	67·70	66·40
15	65·65	64·40
16	63·65	62·45
17	61·70	60·55
18	59·80	58·75
19	58·00	57·00
20	56·25	55·30
21	54·55	53·65
22	52·95	52·10
23	51·40	50·60
24	49·90	49·15
25	48·45	47·75
26	47·05	46·40
27	45·75	45·10
28	44·45	43·90
29	43·20	42·75
30	42·05	41·60

NOTE:—This table is for use in connection with regulation 36(1) and (2) for compounding awards of long-term compensation which attracts pensions increase from age 55 under Part IV of these Regulations. The total amount of the annual long-term compensation which is to be compounded must first be calculated, *i.e.*, the amount which the person would receive on account of that compensation or the part of it which is to be compounded, if it were paid until "normal retiring age" (as defined in these Regulations). The capital value of that annual long-term compensation will be the total calculated multiplied by the appropriate factor.

EXPLANATORY NOTE

(This Note is not part of the Regulations.)

These Regulations amend the Courts (Compensation to Officers) Regulations 1971 by applying a definition of "normal retiring age" of 72 years to persons claiming compensation in respect of certain quarter sessions offices which were abolished by the Courts Act 1971. The Regulations also substitute revised commutation tables in the Schedule to the 1971 Regulations which take account of pension increase legislation.

STATUTORY INSTRUMENTS

1973 No. 2010

FAIR TRADING

RESTRICTIVE TRADE PRACTICES

The Restrictive Practices Court (Protection of Consumers) Rules 1973

Made - - -	*28th November* 1973
Laid before Parliament	*7th December* 1973
Coming into Operation	*1st January* 1974

The Lord Chancellor, in exercise of the powers conferred on him by section 23 of the Restrictive Trade Practices Act 1956(**a**), as amended by section 16(1) of, and Schedule 2 to, the Restrictive Trade Practices Act 1968(**b**), and section 139(1)(*a*) of, and Schedule 12 to, the Fair Trading Act 1973(**c**), hereby makes the following Rules:—

Introductory

1. These Rules may be cited as the Restrictive Practices Court (Protection of Consumers) Rules 1973 and shall come into operation on 1st January 1974.

2.—(1) In these Rules, unless the context otherwise requires—

"the Act" means the Fair Trading Act 1973;

"the Director" means the Director General of Fair Trading;

"the principal rules" means the Restrictive Practices Court Rules 1957(**d**), as amended (**e**);

expressions defined by the principal rules (except the expression "the Act") have the same meanings in these Rules.

(2) The Interpretation Act 1889(**f**) shall apply to the interpretation of these Rules as it applies to the interpretation of an Act of Parliament.

(**a**) 1956 c. 68.
(**b**) 1968 c. 66.
(**c**) 1973 c. 41.
(**d**) S.I. 1957/603 (1957 II, p. 1955).
(**e**) S.I. 1962/2705, 1965/22, 1968/1802, 1973/1653 (1962 III, p. 3662; 1965 I, p. 14; 1968 III p. 4819; 1973 III, p. 5112).
(**f**) 1889 c. 63.

Notice of application under section 35 *or* 38 *of Fair Trading Act* 1973

3.—(1) Proceedings before the Court under section 35 and section 38 of the Act shall be instituted by a notice of application issued out of the central office of the Court, or the office of the Court in Scotland or Northern Ireland, as the case may be, specifying the part of the United Kingdom in which the hearing is to take place and the persons against whom an order is sought, and containing the particulars and other information required by this rule.

(2) Every notice of application shall contain particulars—

(*a*) of the person carrying on a business;

(*b*) of the course of conduct complained of;

(*c*) of the ground or grounds upon which it is alleged that the course of conduct is—

(i) detrimental to the interests of consumers in the United Kingdom, and

(ii) to be regarded as unfair to consumers;

(*d*) of the facts and matters on which the Director intends to rely in order to show that the person carrying on a business—

(i) has persisted in the course of conduct, and

(ii) has so persisted in the course of that business.

(3) A notice of application under section 35 of the Act shall further state—

(*a*) that the Director is unable, despite his best endeavours (of which particulars shall be given), to obtain a satisfactory written assurance from the person carrying on a business that he will refrain from continuing the course of conduct complained of and from carrying on any similar course of conduct in the course of that business; or

(*b*) the facts and matters from which it appears to the Director that the person who has given such an assurance has failed to observe it.

(4) A notice of application under section 38 of the Act shall further state—

(*a*) the name and address of each alleged accessory;

(*b*) except where the same notice of application relates to proceedings under section 35 as well as under section 38, whether or not proceedings have been commenced under section 35 against the body corporate, and if so where and when they were commenced and what stage they have reached;

(*c*) the facts and matters from which it appears to the Director that each alleged accessory—

(i) consented to or connived at the course of conduct,

(ii) fulfilled at a material time, which shall also be stated, the relevant conditions in relation to the body corporate;

(*d*) in relation to each alleged accessory, the particulars corresponding to those required by paragraph (3) of this rule in relation to a person carrying on a business.

(5) If the Director, in reliance on section 11 of the Civil Evidence Act 1968(**a**), section 10 of the Law Reform (Miscellaneous Provisions) (Scotland) Act 1968(**b**), section 7 of the Civil Evidence Act (Northern Ireland) 1971(**c**) or section 36(2) of the Act, intends to adduce evidence of a conviction or a finding of breach of contract or breach of duty in civil proceedings he must include in the notice of application under this rule a statement of his intention with particulars of—

(*a*) the conviction or finding and the date thereof;

(*b*) the court which made the conviction or finding and, in the case of a finding, the proceedings in which it was made;

(*c*) the person or persons convicted or, as the case may be, against whom the finding was made; and

(*d*) the issue in the proceedings to which the conviction or finding is relevant.

(6) A notice of application shall be accompanied by a list of all documents relevant to the application which are or have been in the Director's possession or power.

4. A notice of application shall be issued by being sealed with the Court's seal by the proper officer of the Court with whom a copy of the notice shall be left to be filed by him.

5. The Director shall serve a copy of the notice of application and of the list referred to in rule 3(6) on all persons or bodies against whom an order is sought, and those persons or bodies shall be respondents to the proceedings.

Entry of appearance

6. Every respondent who wishes to be heard in the proceedings shall within fourteen days of service upon him of a copy of the notice of application enter an appearance in accordance with rule 14 of the principal rules.

Delivery of answer

7. Every respondent who has entered an appearance shall, within four weeks of his entry of appearance, deliver to the Director and file with the proper officer of the Court an answer which shall be accompanied by a list of all the documents relevant to the proceedings which are or have been in his possession or power, indicating for which (if any) of those documents he claims privilege and the grounds of the claim.

8. Every allegation of fact in a notice of application shall be deemed to be admitted unless in the answer it is denied specifically or by necessary implication, or is stated not to be admitted, and any respondent who wishes to allege that a conviction or finding referred to in the notice was erroneous or irrelevant must do so in his answer.

(**a**) 1968 c. 64. (**b**) 1968 c. 70. (**c**) 1971 c. 36 (N.I.).

9. No reply or further pleading may be filed without leave.

Inspection of documents

10. Without prejudice to the provisions of these Rules relating to discovery, the Director and any respondent shall within seven days after receiving notice in that behalf from any opposite party, provide for his inspection the documents specified in the list referred to in rule 3(6) or rule 7 or such of them as may be specified in the notice, and shall permit that party to take copies thereof:

Provided that nothing in this rule shall affect the right of a respondent to claim privilege for any of the said documents.

Particulars

11.—(1) In proceedings in England and Wales or in Northern Ireland, any party may apply to any opposite party for further and better particulars of the notice of application, answer or reply and, if such particulars are not supplied within fourteen days or such further time as may be agreed, he may apply to the Court which may order the delivery of such further and better particulars as it considers necessary.

(2) In proceedings in Scotland—

(*a*) the Director shall, within seven days after the expiration of the time limited for filing an answer, make up an open record consisting of the notice of application and the answer and file two copies thereof with the proper officer of the Court, at the same time delivering a copy thereof to each of the respondents and thereafter the parties shall forthwith proceed to adjust their pleadings;

(*b*) upon expiration of twenty-eight days from the filing of the open record, or of such period of continuation as may be allowed by the Court on cause shown, the record shall be deemed to be closed, and thereafter no amendment of the pleadings shall be made except by leave of the Court; and

(*c*) within fourteen days after the closing of the record the Director shall file two copies of the closed record with the proper officer of the Court, and shall at the same time deliver fifteen copies thereof to each of the respondents.

Amendment of pleadings

12. In proceedings in England and Wales or in Northern Ireland a notice of application, answer or reply may be amended—

(*a*) at any time by leave of the Court;

(*b*) at any time before the hearing of the application for directions without leave, if—

(i) in the case of a notice of application or reply, the Director and all respondents who have entered an appearance or, as the case may be, to whose answer the reply is directed, agree; or

(ii) in the case of an answer, the Director and all respondents seeking to amend agree:

and a copy of the pleading as amended shall be delivered to all opposite parties and filed with the proper officer of the Court within such time as may be allowed by the Court or agreed between the parties concerned.

Application for directions

13.—(1) With a view to providing an occasion for the consideration of the preparations for the final hearing, so that—

(*a*) all matters which can be dealt with on interlocutory applications and have not already been dealt with (including, in Scotland, any preliminary question of relevance or sufficiency of specification arising on the pleadings) may, so far as possible, be dealt with; and

(*b*) such directions may be given as to the future course of the proceedings as appear best adapted to secure the just, expeditious and economical disposal thereof,

the Director shall, as soon as practicable after every respondent has delivered an answer or after the time for doing so has expired (or in Scotland as soon as practicable after the closing of the record), make an application to the Court for directions and shall serve notice of the application on every respondent who has entered an appearance.

(2) The proper officer of the Court shall fix a date for the hearing of the application for directions and serve notice of the time and place of the hearing on every respondent who has entered an appearance and rule 36 of the principal rules (except paragraph (*k*)) shall apply, with the necessary modifications, to the application for directions as if—

(*a*) references to the notice of reference or to any statement of case were references to the notice of application; and

(*b*) for the word "agreement" in paragraph (*i*) there were substituted the words "course of conduct".

Application of principal rules

14. Rule 17, rules 28 to 32, rules 37 to 58 (except rules 43 and 47) and rule 64 of the principal rules shall apply, with the necessary modifications, to proceedings instituted by a notice of application under these Rules as they apply to proceedings instituted by a notice of reference under the principal rules.

Final hearing

15. Subject to the provisions of paragraph 4 of the Schedule to the Restrictive Trade Practices Act 1956 the final hearing shall take place in open court before such members of the Court as the President thereof may nominate for the purpose.

Interconnected bodies corporate

16.—(1) Where in any proceedings under section 35 or section 38 of the Act the Director intends to apply for a direction under section 40 thereof that any order made against a body corporate which is a member of a group of interconnected bodies corporate shall be binding on all members of the group, he shall serve a notice to that effect on each of them and shall file a copy thereof with the proper officer of the Court.

(2) As soon as a date and place have been fixed for the final hearing of the proceedings or for any hearing under rule 20(4), the Director shall give notice thereof to each of the bodies corporate other than the respondent on which notice under paragraph (1) was served.

(3) Every body corporate on which notice is served under paragraph (1) may appear at the final hearing or at any hearing under rule 20(4) notwithstanding that it is not a respondent to the proceedings and may be heard on the question whether any order made under section 37 or section 39 of the Act should be directed to be binding on each member of the group.

(4) The respondent may at any time serve on the Director and file with the proper officer of the Court a notice containing particulars of any other interconnected body corporate not mentioned in a notice served under paragraph (1), and thereupon paragraph (3) shall apply to that other body as if it had been served with notice under paragraph (1).

(5) With a view to deciding whether or on whom to serve notice under paragraph (1) the Director may, at any time before applying for directions under rule 14 or rule 20(2), serve on the respondent a notice requiring it to give to the Director within fourteen days after service of the notice particulars of any interconnected bodies corporate which are members of a group of which the respondent is a member and shall file a copy of any such notice with the proper officer of the Court.

(6) The respondent shall comply with any notice served under paragraph (5) by delivering to the Director and filing with the proper officer of the Court the particulars required by the notice within the time thereby prescribed.

17. Any directions given by the Court under section 40(2) of the Act shall be contained in an order of the Court which shall be drawn up in accordance with rule 21.

Applications under section 40(3) *of the Act of* 1973

18.—(1) An application by the Director for a direction under section 40(3) of the Act may be made by notice in writing issued out of the central office of the Court, or the office of the Court in Scotland or Northern Ireland, as the case may be, specifying the bodies corporate against which the order was made and the bodies corporate in respect of which a direction is sought.

(2) The notice of application shall be issued by being sealed with the Court's seal by the proper officer of the Court with whom a copy of the notice shall be left to be filed by him.

(3) The Director shall serve a copy of the notice on every body corporate specified therein and those bodies shall be respondents to the notice.

(4) The provisions of these Rules shall apply, with the necessary modifications, to all further proceedings on an application under this rule as they apply to an application under rule 3.

Costs

19.—(1) In exercising its discretion as to costs the Court shall, subject to paragraph (2), have regard to the practice observed in civil proceedings in the High Court, the Court of Session or the High Court in Northern Ireland, as the case may be, and, without prejudice to the generality of the foregoing, may order the payment by any party of costs incurred by any person entitled under these Rules to be heard in the proceedings.

(2) Where the Court makes an order for the payment of costs by any party it may direct that the proper officer of the Court refer the costs to be taxed or assessed by a Master of the Supreme Court (Taxing Office) or by the Auditor of the Court of Session in Scotland or by the Taxing Master of the Supreme Court of Northern Ireland.

(3) Where the Court gives a direction under paragraph (2) in proceedings in England and Wales, the provisions of Order 62 of the Rules of the Supreme Court 1965(**a**) shall apply, with the necessary modifications, to the taxation of the costs as if the proceedings in the Court were a cause or matter in the Supreme Court.

(4) Where the Court gives a direction under paragraph (2) in proceedings in Northern Ireland, the provisions of Order 65 of the Rules of the Supreme Court (Northern Ireland) 1936(**b**) shall apply, with the necessary modifications, to the taxation of the costs as if those proceedings were a cause or matter in the High Court in Northern Ireland.

Discontinuance and summary application for final order

20.—(1) The Director may at any time discontinue the proceedings against any or all of the respondents without the leave of the Court, on giving notice to every respondent who has entered an appearance and on his undertaking to pay the costs incurred by any respondent against whom the proceedings are discontinued.

(2) If at any time before the final hearing any respondent informs the Director that he is willing to submit to an order under section 37 or section 39 of the Act or to give an undertaking under either of those sections, the Director shall apply to the Court for directions and shall serve notice on every other party that he has done so.

(3) On receipt of an application under paragraph (2) the proper officer of the Court shall fix a date for the hearing of the application and serve notice of the time and place of the hearing on all respondents who have entered an appearance.

(4) On the hearing of the application the Court may take such steps as it thinks fit for disposing of the proceedings against any respondent who is willing to submit to an order or to give such an undertaking as aforesaid and for continuing the proceedings against any other respondent, and, without prejudice to the generality of the foregoing, may—

(*a*) make and record any finding against any respondent if he consents;

(*b*) make an order that the proceedings against any respondent be stayed,

(**a**) S.I. 1965/1776 (1965 III, p. 4995). (**b**) S.R. & O. 1936/70 (1936 II, p. 2559) except for the purpose of carrying into effect the agreed terms on which the proceedings are stayed; and

(*c*) make such order as to costs as it thinks fit.

Drawing up and enforcement of orders

21.—(1) The proper officer of the Court shall deliver or send to the Director a copy, sealed with the seal of the Court, of every order made under section 37 or section 39 of the Act or containing directions given under section 40(2) thereof as well as of any order made under rule 20(4) as soon as may be after the order has been drawn up.

Supplementary

22. Rules 79 to 90 (except rule 81) of the principal rules shall apply, with the necessary modifications, to proceedings instituted by a notice of application under these Rules as they apply to proceedings instituted by a notice of reference under the principal rules.

Hailsham of St. Marylebone, C.

Dated 28th November 1973.

EXPLANATORY NOTE

(*This Note is not part of the Rules.*)

These Rules prescribe the procedure to be followed in proceedings before the Restrictive Practices Court under Part III of the Fair Trading Act 1973.

Proceedings will be begun by a notice of application issued by the Director General of Fair Trading and served by him on all the persons against whom an order is sought (Rules 3 to 5). Every respondent who wishes to be heard must within four weeks of entering an appearance deliver an answer (Rules 6 to 8). The Director must then apply for directions for the future conduct of the proceedings (Rule 13). The wide powers of direction conferred on the Court by the Restrictive Practices Court Rules 1957 will be available in these proceedings for the purposes of which many of those Rules are also attracted (Rules 14 and 22). When a case is ready for hearing it will be heard in open court (Rule 15).

Provision is made for notifying members of a group of interconnected bodies corporate in cases where an order made against a body corporate may be directed to be binding on all members of the group of which it is a member (Rules 16 and 18).

Rule 20 provides for discontinuance of proceedings by the Director and for a summary procedure for determining proceedings against any respondent who is willing to submit to an order or to give an undertaking under section 37 or 39 of the Act.

STATUTORY INSTRUMENTS

1973 No. 2012

NATIONAL HEALTH SERVICE, ENGLAND AND WALES

The National Health Service (Family Practitioner Committees: Membership and Procedure) Regulations 1973

Made - - - -	*29th November* 1973
Laid before Parliament	*7th December* 1973
Coming into Operation	*28th December* 1973

The Secretary of State for Social Services, as respects England, and the Secretary of State for Wales, as respects Wales, in exercise of powers conferred upon them by sections 6 and 7(4) of, and paragraphs 6(1) and 12 of Schedule 1 to, the National Health Service Reorganisation Act 1973**(a)** and of all other powers enabling them in that behalf, hereby make the following regulations:—

PART I

GENERAL

Citation and commencement

1. These regulations may be cited as the National Health Service (Family Practitioner Committees: Membership and Procedure) Regulations 1973 and shall come into operation on 28th December 1973.

Interpretation

2.—(1) In these regulations, unless the context otherwise requires:—

"The Act of 1946" means the National Health Service Act 1946**(b)**;

"The Act of 1973" means the National Health Service Reorganisation Act 1973;

"Administrator" means the officer appointed by an Area Health Authority by which a Family Practitioner Committee is established to act as Administrator to that Committee;

"appointing body" means, as appropriate, an Area Health Authority, a local authority, a Local Medical Committee, a Local Dental Committee, a Local Pharmaceutical Committee, such members of a Local Optical Committee as are ophthalmic opticians and such members of a Local Optical Committee as are dispensing opticians;

"Authority" means an Area Health Authority;

"Committee" means a Family Practitioner Committee;

(a) 1973 c. 32. **(b)** 1946 c. 81.

"health authority" means any one of the following authorities:—

A Regional Health Authority, an Area Health Authority, a special health authority, a Preserved Board, a Regional Hospital Board, a Hospital Management Committee, a Board of Governors of a Teaching Hospital, an Executive Council or a local health authority;

"local authority" in relation to any Committee means a local authority specified, in the Order constituting the Authority by which the Committee was established, as entitled to make appointments to that Authority;

"local representative body" in relation to any Committee means the Local Medical Committee, Local Dental Committee, Local Pharmaceutical Committee, ophthalmic opticians who are members of the Local Optical Committee and dispensing opticians who are members of the Local Optical Committees, in each case for the area of the Authority by which the Committee was established;

"member" means the chairman or other member of a Committee and

"members" shall be construed accordingly;

"the relevant Authority" means the Authority by which the Committee in question was established;

"securities" and "shares" have the same meanings respectively as in the Prevention of Fraud (Investments) Act 1958**(a)**;

and any other expression to which a meaning is assigned by the Act of 1946 has that meaning in these regulations.

(2) In regulation 13 of these regulations "public body" includes any body established for the purpose of carrying on under national ownership any industry or part of an industry or undertaking, the governing body of any university, university college or college, school or hall of a university and the National Trust for Places of Historic Interest or Natural Beauty incorporated by the National Trust Act 1907**(b)**.

(3) The rules for the construction of Acts of Parliament contained in the Interpretation Act 1889**(c)** shall apply for the purposes of the interpretation of these regulations as they apply for the purposes of the interpretation of an Act of Parliament.

PART II

MEMBERSHIP

Term of office of members appointed by an Authority or by a local representative body

3.—(1) Subject to the provisions of these regulations the term of office of members appointed by an Authority or by a local representative body shall be four years expiring on 31st March in any year.

(2) Where a Committee is established in England before 1st April 1977 the original members appointed by the relevant Authority or by any local representative body shall be appointed for a period ending on 31st March 1977, and one half of the members appointed by the relevant Authority or by each local representative body whose appointments take effect from 1st April 1977 shall be appointed for a period ending on 31st March 1979 and the remainder of such members shall be appointed for a period ending on 31st March 1981.

(a) 1958 c. 45. **(b)** 1907 c. cxxxvi. **(c)** 1889 c. 63.

(3) Where a Committee is established in Wales before 1st April 1974 one half of the original members appointed by the relevant Authority or by each local representative body shall be appointed for a period ending on 31st March 1976 and the remainder of such members shall be appointed for a period ending on 31st March 1978.

(4) Where a Committee is established in Wales after 31st March 1974 and in England after 31st March 1977 one half of the original members appointed by the relevant Authority or by each local representative body shall be appointed for such a period, not exceeding two years, expiring on 31st March in any year as the relevant Authority shall, in the case of such Committee, determine and the remainder of such members shall be appointed for a period two years greater than the period of office of the first half of such original members.

(5) For the purposes of this regulation where, in accordance with paragraph 6 of Schedule 1 to the Act of 1973 or with an Order made under paragraph 7 of that Schedule, an uneven number of members greater than one falls to be appointed by the relevant Authority or a local representative body, one half of such members shall be calculated by reference to the number of those members less one and where only one member is to be appointed by a local representative body the period of office of such member shall in all cases be that prescribed for the remainder of members appointed by local representative bodies.

(6) On making an appointment of any member in accordance with the provisions of this regulation, the appointing body shall give notice in writing to that member and to the Administrator of the period for which such member is appointed.

Term of office of members appointed by local authority

4. Subject to the provisions of these regulations the term of office of members appointed by a local authority or appointed jointly by two or more local authorities shall be for a period terminating on such date or in such event as the appointing body or appointing bodies acting jointly may determine on making the appointment.

Variation of membership of Committees

5.—(1) Where the Secretary of State has by Order provided that paragraph 6 of Schedule 1 to the Act of 1973 should apply with such modifications as are specified in the Order to a Committee established in accordance with that paragraph or where he makes an Order revoking or varying such Order as aforesaid, he may terminate the appointment of any member of the Committee as established before the date of coming into operation of the Order, and the term of office of any original member appointed in accordance with provisions taking effect upon that date shall be for such a period, not exceeding four years, expiring on 31st March in any year as the relevant Authority shall, in each case, determine.

(2) Where, for any reason, a person ceases to be a member before the expiration of the period for which he was appointed, the term of office of any member appointed in his place shall be the remainder of such period, and, if the person ceasing to be a member was appointed by virtue of paragraph 6(2) of Schedule 1 to the Act of 1973, the appointment of any member appointed in his place shall, subject to provisions of the said paragraph 6(2), be made by such local representative body as should have made the preceding appointment.

Eligibility of members for re-appointment

6. Subject to the provisions of regulation 7 of these regulations a member shall, on the expiration of his term of office, be eligible for re-appointment.

Disqualification for membership

7.—(1) A person shall be disqualified for appointment to, or being a member of, a Committee if he—

(*a*) is a person who in the preceding five years has been convicted in the United Kingdom, Channel Islands or the Isle of Man of any offence and has had passed on him a sentence of imprisonment (whether suspended or not) for a period of not less than three months without the option of a fine; or

(*b*) is a person who has been adjudged bankrupt or made a composition or arrangement with his creditors; or

(*c*) being a person who has held any paid appointment or office, other than as chairman thereof, with any health authority, has been dismissed from such appointment or office otherwise than by reason of redundancy; or

(*d*) being a person whose name has been included in any list prepared under Part IV of the Act of 1946, has had his name removed from the list under the provisions of section 42 of that Act and has not subsequently had his name restored to such list.

(2) For the purposes of paragraph (1)(*a*) of this regulation the ordinary date on which the period allowed for making an appeal or application with respect to the conviction expires, or if such an appeal or application is made, the date on which the appeal or application is finally disposed of, or abandoned or fails by reason of the non-prosecution thereof, shall be deemed to be the date of conviction.

(3) When a person is disqualified under paragraph (1)(*b*) of this regulation by reason of his having been adjudged bankrupt, then—

(*a*) if the bankruptcy is annulled on the grounds that he ought not to have been adjudged bankrupt or on the grounds that his debts have been paid in full, the disqualification shall cease on the date of the annulment;

(*b*) if he is discharged with a certificate that the bankruptcy was caused by misfortune without any misconduct on his part, the disqualification shall cease on the date of his discharge;

(*c*) if he was discharged without such a certificate his disqualification shall cease on the expiration of five years from the date of his discharge.

(4) Where a person is disqualified under the said paragraph (1)(*b*) by reason of his having made a composition or arrangement with his creditors and he pays his debts in full, the disqualification shall cease on the date on which the payment is completed and in any other case it shall cease on the expiration of five years from the date on which the terms of the deed of composition or arrangement are fulfilled.

Termination of membership

8.—(1) Any member may resign at any time during the period for which he was appointed on giving notice in writing to the Administrator and his resignation shall take effect upon the receipt of the notice by the Administrator who shall forthwith send a copy of such notice to the appointing body by which such member had been appointed.

(2) If a member has not attended a meeting of the Committee to which he belongs or of a sub-committee or joint committee thereof for a period of six months, the Administrator shall inform the Committee which, after consultation with any appointing body by which that member was appointed, shall, unless satisfied that the absence was due to illness or other reasonable cause, declare that his place on the Committee has become vacant and that person shall forthwith cease to be a member.

(3) A member being either—

(*a*) a person who, holding any paid appointment or office with any health authority, resigns from such appointment or office, or

(*b*) a person, whose name being included in any list prepared under Part IV of the Act of 1946, has his name withdrawn from such list on his own application,

shall, if the Secretary of State so directs, cease to be a member.

(4) If an appointing body is of the opinion that it is not in the interest of the national health service that a person whom it has appointed as a member should continue to be a member, such appointing body may terminate the appointment of that member who shall, on such termination, forthwith cease to be a member.

PART III

CONSTITUTION AND PROCEEDINGS

Election of chairman and vice-chairman

9.—(1) The members shall elect one of their number to be chairman for such period as the Committee may determine on making the election, not being a longer period than four years or, where the remainder of the period of his membership of the Committee during which he is elected has less than four years to run, not being longer than the remainder of such period, and such election shall take place at a meeting of the Committee specially summoned for such purpose at which those members present shall choose one of their number to preside.

(2) The members shall elect one of their number, other than the chairman, to be vice-chairman for such period as the Committee may determine on making the election, not being a longer period than four years or, where the remainder of the period of his membership of the Committee during which he is elected has less than four years to run, not being longer than the remainder of such period.

(3) Any member elected to be chairman or vice-chairman may at any time resign from such office by giving notice in writing to the Administrator, and the members shall thereupon elect another of their number as chairman or vice-chairman in accordance with the provisions of this regulation.

Appointment of committees and joint committees

10. Subject to any directions given by the Secretary of State, a Committee may and if directed as aforesaid shall, appoint committees of the Committee, which shall be known as, and are in these regulations referred to as, sub-committees or, together with one or more other health authorities, appoint joint committees, consisting in either case wholly or partly of persons who are members of the Committee or health authorities.

Arrangements for the exercise of functions

11. Subject to any directions by the Secretary of State, a Committee may make arrangements for the exercise, on their behalf, of any of their functions by a sub-committee or joint committee appointed by virtue of regulation 10 of these regulations or by an officer of the relevant Authority; in each case subject to such restrictions and conditions as the Committee may, with the agreement of the relevant Authority if they concern an officer of that Authority, think fit, or as the Secretary of State may direct.

Meetings and proceedings

12.—(1) The meetings and proceedings of a Committee shall be conducted in accordance with the rules set out in the Schedule to these regulations and with Standing Orders made under the next following paragraph of this regulation.

(2) Subject to the aforesaid rules, to regulation 13 of these regulations and to such directions as may be given by the Secretary of State, a Committee shall make and may vary or revoke, Standing Orders for the regulation of their proceedings and business, including provision for the time and place of each meeting of the Committee and for the suspension of all or part of such Standing Orders.

(3) Subject to such directions as may be given by the Secretary of State, a Committee may, on its own in the case of a sub-committee of the Committee or jointly with any other health authorities concerned in the case of a joint committee, make, vary and revoke Standing Orders respecting the quorum, proceedings and place of meeting of such sub-committee or joint committee, but subject to any such Standing Orders the quorum, proceedings and place of meeting shall, subject to such directions as aforesaid, be such as the sub-committee or joint comittee may determine.

Disability of members in proceedings on account of pecuniary interests

13.—(1) Subject to the provisions of this regulation, if a member has any pecuniary interest, direct or indirect, in any contract, proposed contract or other matter and is present at a meeting of the Committee at which the contract or other matter is the subject of consideration, he shall at the meeting and as soon as practicable after its commencement disclose the fact and shall not take part in the consideration or discussion of the contract or other matter, or vote on any question with respect to it.

(2) A Committee may by Standing Orders, made by virtue of regulation 12 of these regulations, provide for the exclusion of a member from a meeting of the Committee while any contract, proposed contact, or other matter in which he has a pecuniary interest, direct or indirect, is under consideration.

(3) For the purposes of this regulation any arrangement made in pursuance of Part IV of the Act of 1946 for the provision of general medical services, general dental services, general ophthalmic services or pharmaceutical services shall be deemed not to be a contract, proposed contract or other matter and any allowances payable to a member by virtue of paragraph 9 of Schedule 1 to the Act of 1973 shall not be treated as a pecuniary interest.

(4) For the purposes of this regulation a member shall be treated, subject to the next following paragraph, as having indirectly a pecuniary interest in a contract, proposed contract, or other matter, if—

(*a*) he or a nominee of his is a member of a company or other body, not being a public body, with which the contract was made or is proposed to be made or which has a pecuniary interest in the other matter under consideration; or

(*b*) he is a partner, or is in the employment of a person with whom the contract was made or is proposed to be made or who has a direct pecuniary interest in the other matter under consideration;

and in the case of married persons living together the interest of one spouse shall, if known to the other, be deemed for the purposes of this regulation to be also an interest of the other.

(5) A member shall not be treated as having a pecuniary interest in any contract, proposed contract or other matter by reason only—

(*a*) of his membership of a company or other body if he has no beneficial interest in any securities of that company or other body;

(*b*) of an interest of his, or any company, body or person with which he is connected as mentioned in paragraph (4) of this regulation, which is so remote or insignificant that it cannot be regarded as likely to influence a member in the consideration or discussion of, or in voting on, any question with respect to that contract or matter.

(6) Where a member has an indirect pecuniary interest in a contract, proposed contract or other matter by reason only of a beneficial interest in securities of a company or other body, and the total nominal value of those securities does not exceed £1,000 or one-hundredth of the total nominal value of the issued share capital of the company or body, whichever is the less, and, if the share capital is of more than one class, the total nominal value of shares of any one class in which he has a beneficial interest does not exceed one-hundredth of the total issued share capital of that class, this regulation shall not prohibit him from taking part in the consideration or discussion of the contract or other matter or from voting on any question with respect to it, without prejudice, however, to his duty to disclose his interest.

(7) The Secretary of State may, subject to such conditions as he may think fit to impose, remove any disability imposed by this regulation, or by Standing Orders made by virtue of regulation 12 of these regulations, in any case in which it appears to be in the interests of the national health service that the disability should be removed.

Provision as to committees or sub-committees authorised by other provisions

14. Nothing in this part of these regulations shall apply to any committee or sub-committee which a Committee is authorised or required to appoint by any enactment, Order or regulations other than these regulations except in so far as any provision hereof is specificially applied to such committee or sub-committee by such enactment, Order or regulations.

Keith Joseph,
Secretary of State for Social Services.

29th November 1973.

Peter Thomas,
Secretary of State for Wales.

29th November 1973.

Regulation 12(1)

SCHEDULE

Rules as to Meetings and Proceedings of Committees

1. The first meeting of a Committee shall be held on such day and at such place as may be fixed by the relevant Authority which shall be responsible for convening the meeting after such consultation with members as the Authority thinks fit.

2. A meeting of the Committee shall take place at least once in every three months.

3. Before each meeting of the Committee a notice of the meeting which, subject to any exceptions which may have been determined by the Committee, shall specify the business proposed to be transacted thereat, and which shall be signed by the Administrator or by an officer of the relevant Authority authorised by the Administrator to sign on his behalf, shall be delivered to every member, or sent by post to the usual place of residence of such member, so as to be available to such member at least three clear days before the meeting:

Provided that want of service of such notice on any member shall not affect the validity of a meeting.

4.—(1) At any meeting of a Committee the chairman, if present, shall preside.

(2) If the chairman is absent from the meeting the vice-chairman, if present, shall preside.

(3) If the chairman and vice-chairman are absent, such one of their number as the members present shall choose shall preside.

5. Every question at a meeting shall be determined by a majority of the votes of members present and voting on the question, and in the case of an equality of votes, the person presiding shall have a second and casting vote.

6. The names of members present at the meeting shall be recorded.

7. No business shall be transacted at a meeting unless at least one-third of the whole number of members is present.

8. The minutes of the proceedings of a meeting shall be drawn up and entered in a book kept for that purpose and shall be signed at the same or the next ensuing meeting by the person presiding thereat.

EXPLANATORY NOTE

(*This Note is not part of the Regulations.*)

These Regulations provide for the appointment and term of office of members of Family Practitioner Committees and for the procedure of such bodies.

STATUTORY INSTRUMENTS

1973 No. 2013

ROAD TRAFFIC

The Motor Cars (Driving Instruction) (Amendment) Regulations 1973

Made - - -	25*th November* 1973
Laid before Parliament	10*th December* 1973
Coming into Operation	31*st December* 1973

The Secretary of State for the Environment, in exercise of his powers under sections 128(1) and 142 of the Road Traffic Act 1972(**a**) and of all other enabling powers, hereby makes the following Regulations:—

1.—(1) These Regulations shall come into operation on 31st December 1973 and may be cited as the Motor Cars (Driving Instruction) (Amendment) Regulations 1973.

(2) The Interpretation Act 1889(**b**) shall apply for the interpretation of these Regulations as it applies for the interpretation of an Act of Parliament.

2. The Motor Cars (Driving Instruction) Regulations 1969(**c**), as amended(**d**), shall have effect as though in Regulation 11, at the end of paragraph (5), there were added the following words—

"or if he is exempt from the condition specified in section 128(1)(*a*) of the Road Traffic Act 1972 by virtue of subsection (4) of that section.".

Signed by authority of the Secretary of State.

John Peyton,
Minister for Transport Industries,
Department of the Environment.

25th November 1973.

(**a**) 1972 c. 20.
(**b**) 1889 c. 63.
(**c**) S.I. 1969/85 (1969 I, p. 248).
(**d**) The relevant amending instruments are S.I. 1970/966, 1971/351 (1970 II, p. 3071; 1971 I, p. 1096).

EXPLANATORY NOTE

(This Note is not part of the Regulations.)

These Regulations further amend the Motor Cars (Driving Instruction) Regulations 1969 by prescribing that the fee of £15 payable by a person who applies for his name to be entered in the Register and who is exempt from the requirement of passing an examination of his ability to give driving instruction shall be payable also by one who satisfies the Registrar that his name is in the Northern Ireland register of persons qualified to give driving instruction and that he is resident in Great Britain.

STATUTORY INSTRUMENTS

1973 No. 2014

WATER, ENGLAND AND WALES

The Northumbrian Water Authority (Regional Land Drainage Committee) Order 1973

Made - - -	*28th November* 1973
Coming into Operation	*17th December* 1973

Whereas—

(1) the Northumbrian Water Authority (hereafter in this Order referred to as "the Water Authority") are required by paragraph 1(1) of Schedule 5 to the Water Act 1973(**a**) to establish a committee to be known as a regional land drainage committee and, in accordance with paragraph 1(7) and (9) of the said Schedule, have submitted to the Minister of Agriculture, Fisheries and Food (hereafter in this Order referred to as "the Minister") a determination that the total number of members of their regional land drainage committee (hereafter in this Order referred to as "the committee") shall be seventeen;

(2) the constituent councils for the committee are the councils of the counties specified in the first column of the Schedule to this Order;

(3) the Minister, having had regard to the appropriate penny rate product and proportion mentioned in paragraph 3(1) of the said Schedule 5 relating to each of the said constituent councils, considers it to be inappropriate that the councils of the counties of Cumbria and North Yorkshire (being two of the said constituent councils) should appoint a member of the committee:

Now, therefore, the Minister, in exercise of the powers conferred on him by paragraphs 1(12) and 3(1) of Schedule 5 to the Water Act 1973, and of every other power enabling him in that behalf, and having had regard to the appropriate penny rate product and proportion mentioned in the said paragraph 3(1) relating to each of the said constituent councils, hereby orders as follows:—

Citation and commencement

1. This Order may be cited as the Northumbrian Water Authority (Regional Land Drainage Committee) Order 1973 and shall come into operation on 17th December 1973.

Interpretation

2.—(1) In this Order—

"the Act of 1972" means the Local Government Act 1972(**b**);

"constituent council" means the council of any county established by the Act of 1972 any part of which is in the Water Authority area;

"the Water Authority area" means the area of the Water Authority for the purposes of their functions relating to land drainage.

(**a**) 1973 c. 37. (**b**) 1972 c. 70.

(2) Any reference in this Order to a specified county or to the council thereof is a reference to the county of that name established by the Act of 1972 or to the council so established for that county, as the case may be.

(3) The Interpretation Act 1889(**a**) shall apply for the interpretation of this Order as it applies for the interpretation of an Act of Parliament.

Constituent councils appointments of committee members

3.—(1) The number of members to be appointed to the committee by or on behalf of constituent councils for the committee shall be nine.

(2) The number of members of the committee to be appointed by each of the councils of the counties specified in the first column of the Schedule to this Order shall be the number specified in relation to that county in the second column of that Schedule.

In witness whereof the Official Seal of the Minister of Agriculture, Fisheries and Food is hereunto affixed on 28th November 1973.

(L.S.)

Joseph Godber,
Minister of Agriculture,
Fisheries and Food.

Article 3

SCHEDULE

Counties	*Number of Members*
Cleveland	Two
Cumbria	None
Durham	Two
Northumberland	One
North Yorkshire	None
Tyne and Wear	Four

(**a**) 1889 c. 63.

EXPLANATORY NOTE

(This Note is not part of the Order.)

Paragraph 1 of Schedule 5 to the Water Act provides that each water authority shall establish a regional land drainage committee consisting of:—

(*a*) a Chairman and a number of other members appointed by the Minister of Agriculture, Fisheries and Food;

(*b*) two members appointed by the water authority; and

(*c*) a number of members appointed by constituent councils being, where no part of Greater London is in the water authority area, councils of counties any part of whose area is in the water authority area.

When the total number of members of a water authority's regional land drainage committee, being not less than eleven nor more than seventeen, has been fixed by them, the Minister is required by paragraph 1(12) of the Schedule by Order to specify the number of members to be appointed to the committee by the constituent councils, their number being required by paragraph 1(13) of the Schedule to exceed by one the number of the other members. In determining the number of such members to be appointed by each constituent council, the Minister is required by paragraph 3(1) of the Schedule to have regard to the appropriate penny rate product and proportion mentioned in that paragraph and where, having regard thereto, the Minister considers it inappropriate that a constituent council should appoint a member of the committee he may by the Order so provide.

The Northumbrian Water Authority, established on 26th July 1973, has determined that the total number of the members of their regional land drainage committee should be seventeen and this Order specifies the number of members of that committee which are to be appointed by constituent councils and by which of those councils such members are to be appointed.

1973 No. 2015

ROAD TRAFFIC

The Motor Vehicles (Driving Licences) (Amendment) Regulations 1973

Made - - - -	30*th November* 1973
Laid before Parliament	11*th December* 1973
Coming into Operation	1*st January* 1974

The Secretary of State for the Environment, in exercise of his powers under sections 87(1) and (3), 88(2) and (5), 107 and 190(11) of the Road Traffic Act 1972**(a)** and of all other enabling powers, and after consultation with representative organisations in accordance with section 199(2) of that Act, hereby makes the following Regulations:—

1. These Regulations shall come into operation on 1st January 1974 and may be cited as the Motor Vehicles (Driving Licences) (Amendment) Regulations 1973.

2. The Motor Vehicles (Driving Licences) Regulations 1971**(b)** shall be amended so as to have effect in accordance with the following provisions of these Regulations.

3. In Regulation 6 (conditions attached to provisional licences), for sub-paragraph (*b*) of paragraph (1) there shall be substituted the following sub-paragraph:—

"(*b*) unless a distinguishing mark in the form set out in Schedule 2 to these Regulations is displayed on the vehicle in such a manner as to be clearly visible to other persons using the road from within a reasonable distance from the front and from the back of the vehicle;".

4. In Regulation 8 (full licences not carrying provisional entitlement), in paragraph (*a*), after the word "design" there shall be inserted the words "whether pursuant to an application in that behalf made by the holder of the licence or".

5. In Regulation 20 (disabilities which operate as a bar to holding a licence)—

(a) 1972 c. 20.

(b) S.I. 1971/451 (1971 I, p. 1338).

(*a*) for sub-paragraph (*g*) of paragraph (1) there shall be substituted the following sub-paragraphs:—

"(*g*) liability to sudden attacks of disabling giddiness or fainting, other than such attacks falling within sub-paragraph (*gg*) below;

(*gg*) liability to sudden attacks of disabling giddiness or fainting which are caused by any disorder or defect of the heart as a result of which the applicant for the licence or, as the case may be, the holder of the licence has a device implanted in his body, being a device which, by operating on the heart so as to regulate its action, is designed to correct the disorder or defect; and";

(*b*) after paragraph (2) there shall be inserted the following paragraph:—

"(2A) The disability prescribed in paragraph (1)(*gg*) above is prescribed for the purpose of section 87(3)(*b*) of the Road Traffic Act 1972 and an applicant for a licence suffering from that disability shall satisfy the conditions that—

(*a*) the driving of a vehicle by him in pursuance of the licence is not likely to be a source of danger to the public; and

(*b*) he has made adequate arrangements to receive regular medical supervision by a cardiologist (being a supervision to be continued throughout the period of the licence) and is conforming to those arrangements.

In this paragraph, the expession "cardiologist" means a registered medical practitioner (as that expression is construed by section 52(2) of the Medical Act 1956**(a)**), being a practitioner who specialises in disorders or defects of the heart and who, in that connection, holds a hospital appointment.".

6. In Regulation 23 (increase of maximum weight of invalid carriages for certain purposes), for the words "eight hundredweight" there shall be substituted the words "ten hundredweight".

Signed by authority of the Secretary of State.

John Peyton,
Minister for Transport Industries,
Department of the Environment.

30th November 1973.

(a) 1956 c. 76.

EXPLANATORY NOTE

(*This Note is not part of the Regulations.*)

1. These Regulations amend the Motor Vehicles (Driving Licences) Regulations 1971 to provide as follows:—

(*a*) that the "L" plate required to be displayed on a vehicle when driven by a learner driver shall be clearly visible from within a reasonable distance from the front and the back of the vehicle (Regulation 3);

(*b*) that the restriction on a full driving licence carrying provisional entitlement, where it has effect by virtue of the licence being limited to vehicles of a particular construction or design in pursuance of a notice under section 87(4) of the Road Traffic Act 1972, shall also have effect where the limitation is one applied for by the licence holder himself (Regulation 4);

(*c*) that a liability to sudden attacks of disabling giddiness or fainting caused by a heart disorder, where the person concerned has implanted in his body a heart-regulating device which is designed to correct the disorder, shall be a disability which operates as a bar to holding a driving licence unless the person concerned satisfies certain conditions (Regulation 5); and

(*d*) that for the purposes of Part III of the 1972 Act (which relates to driving licences) and the Regulations thereunder the maximum weight specified in the definition of an invalid carriage shall be 10, instead of 8, hundredweight (Regulation 6).

STATUTORY INSTRUMENTS

1973 No. 2016 (L.29)

MATRIMONIAL CAUSES
SUPREME COURT OF JUDICATURE, ENGLAND
COUNTY COURTS

The Matrimonial Causes Rules 1973

Made - - - -	29*th November* 1973
Laid before Parliament	18*th December* 1973
Coming into Operation	11*th January* 1974

ARRANGEMENT OF RULES

PRELIMINARY

Rule

COMMENCEMENT ETC. OF PROCEEDINGS

SERVICE OF PETITION, ETC.

PLEADINGS AND AMENDMENT

PREPARATIONS FOR TRIAL

EVIDENCE

TRIAL, ETC.

Decrees and Orders

Ancillary Relief

Enforcement of Orders

Applications relating to Children

Other Applications

Disability

Procedure: General

Miscellaneous

We, the authority having power to make rules of court for the purposes mentioned in section 50 of the Matrimonial Causes Act 1973(**a**), hereby exercise that power and all other powers enabling us in that behalf as follows:—

PRELIMINARY

Citation and commencement

1. These Rules may be cited as the Matrimonial Causes Rules 1973 and shall come into operation on 11th January 1974.

Interpretation

2.—(1) The Interpretation Act 1889(**b**) shall apply to the interpretation of these Rules as it applies to the interpretation of an Act of Parliament.

(2) In these Rules, unless the context otherwise requires—

"the Act of 1882" means the Married Women's Property Act 1882(**c**);

"the Act of 1965" means the Matrimonial Causes Act 1965(**d**);

"the Act of 1967" means the Matrimonial Causes Act 1967(**e**);

"the Act of 1973" means the Matrimonial Causes Act 1973;

"ancillary relief" means—

(*a*) an avoidance of disposition order,

(*b*) a financial provision order,

(*c*) an order for maintenance pending suit,

(*d*) a property adjustment order, or

(*e*) a variation order;

"avoidance of disposition order" means an order under section 37(2)(*b*) or (*c*) of the Act of 1973;

"cause" means a matrimonial cause as defined by section 10(1) of the Act of 1967;

"court" means a judge or the registrar;

"court of trial" means a divorce county court designated by the Lord Chancellor as a court of trial pursuant to section 1(1) of the Act of 1967 and, in relation to matrimonial proceedings pending in a divorce county court, the divorce registry shall be treated as a court of trial having its place of sitting at the Royal Courts of Justice;

"defended cause" means a cause not being an undefended cause;

"directions for trial" means directions for trial given under rule 33;

"district registry" means any district registry having a divorce county court within its district;

"divorce county court" means a county court so designated by the Lord Chancellor pursuant to section 1(1) of the Act of 1967;

"divorce registry" means the principal registry of the Family Division;

(**a**) 1973 c. 18. (**b**) 1889 c. 63. (**c**) 1882 c. 75.
(**d**) 1965 c. 72. (**e**) 1967 c. 56.

"divorce town", in relation to any matrimonial proceedings, means a town at which sittings of the High Court are authorised to be held outside the Royal Courts of Justice for the hearing of those proceedings or proceedings of the class to which they belong;

"financial provision order" means any of the orders mentioned in section 21(1) of the Act of 1973 except an order under section 27(6) of that Act;

"financial relief" has the same meaning as in section 37 of the Act of 1973;

"judge", in relation to proceedings pending in a divorce county court, means one of the circuit judges assigned by the Lord Chancellor to exercise the jurisdiction conferred by the Act of 1967 on divorce county courts;

"matrimonial proceedings" means any proceedings with respect to which rules may be made under section 50 of the Act of 1973;

"notice of intention to defend" has the meaning assigned to it by rule 15;

"person named" includes a person described as "passing under the name of A.B.";

"the President" means the President of the Family Division or, in the case of his incapacity through illness or otherwise or of a vacancy in the office of President, the senior puisne judge of that Division;

"registrar", in relation to proceedings pending in a divorce county court, the divorce registry or a district registry, means the registrar or one of the registrars of that county court or registry, as the case may be;

"registry for the divorce town" shall be construed in accordance with rule 44(4);

"Royal Courts of Justice", in relation to matrimonial proceedings pending in a divorce county court, means such place, being the Royal Courts of Justice or elsewhere, as may be specified in directions given by the Lord Chancellor pursuant to section 4(2)(*a*) of the Act of 1967;

"senior registrar" means the senior registrar of the divorce registry or, in his absence, the senior of the registrars in attendance at the divorce registry;

"special procedure list" has the meaning assigned to it by rule 33(3);

"undefended cause" means—

(*a*) in the case of an application under section 3 of the Act of 1973, a cause in which the respondent has not given notice of intention to defend within the time limited;

(*b*) in any other case—

(i) a cause in which no answer has been filed or any answer filed has been struck out, or

(ii) a cause which is proceeding only on the respondent's answer and in which no reply or answer to the respondent's answer has been filed or any such reply or answer has been struck out, or

(iii) a cause to which rule 18(4) applies and in which no notice has been given under that rule or any notice so given has been withdrawn;

"variation order" means an order under section 31 of the Act of 1973;

"welfare" has the same meaning as in section 41 of the Act of 1973.

(3) Unless the context otherwise requires, a cause begun by petition shall be treated as pending for the purposes of these Rules notwithstanding that a final decree or order has been made on the petition.

(4) Unless the context otherwise requires, a rule referred to by number means the rule so numbered in these Rules.

(5) In these Rules a form referred to by number means the form so numbered in the Appendix to these Rules, or a form substantially to the like effect, with such variations as the circumstances of the particular case may require.

(6) In these Rules any reference to an Order and rule is—

(*a*) if prefixed by the letters "C.C.R.", a reference to that Order and rule in the County Court Rules 1936(**a**), and

(*b*) if prefixed by the letters "R.S.C.", a reference to that Order and rule in the Rules of the Supreme Court 1965(**b**).

(7) Unless the context otherwise requires, any reference in these Rules to any rule or enactment shall be construed as a reference to that rule or enactment as amended, extended or applied by any other rule or enactment.

Application of other rules

3.—(1) Subject to the provisions of these Rules and of any enactment, the County Court Rules 1936 and the Rules of the Supreme Court 1965 shall apply, with the necessary modifications, to the commencement of matrimonial proceedings in, and to the practice and procedure in matrimonial proceedings pending in, a divorce county court and the High Court respectively.

(2) For the purposes of paragraph (1) any provision of these Rules authorising or requiring anything to be done in matrimonial proceedings shall be treated as if it were, in the case of proceedings pending in a divorce county court, a provision of the County Court Rules 1936 and, in the case of proceedings pending in the High Court, a provision of the Rules of the Supreme Court 1965.

County court proceedings in divorce registry

4.—(1) Subject to the provisions of these Rules, matrimonial proceedings pending at any time in the divorce registry which, if they had been begun in a divorce county court, would be pending at that time in such a court shall be treated, for the purposes of these Rules and of any provision of the County Court Rules 1936 and the County Courts Act 1959(**c**), as pending in a divorce county court and not in the High Court.

In this paragraph "matrimonial proceedings" includes proceedings for the exercise of any power under Part II or III of the Act of 1973 if, but only if, the power is exercisable in connection with any petition, decree or order pending in or made by, or treated as pending in or made by, a divorce county court.

(2) Unless the context otherwise requires, any reference to a divorce county court in any provision of these Rules or of the County Court Rules 1936 as applied by these Rules, which relates to the commencement or prosecution of proceedings in a divorce county court, or the transfer of proceedings to or from such a court, includes a reference to the divorce registry.

(**a**) S.R. & O. 1936/626 (1936 I, p. 282). (**b**) S.I. 1965/1776 (1965 III, p. 4995).
(**c**) 1959 c. 22.

Commencement etc. of Proceedings

Application under section 3 *of Act of* 1973

5.—(1) An application under section 3 of the Act of 1973 for leave to present a petition for divorce before the expiration of three years from the date of the marriage shall be made by originating application.

(2) The application shall be filed in the divorce county court to which it is proposed to present the petition, together with—

(*a*) an affidavit by the applicant exhibiting a copy of the proposed petition and stating—

(i) the grounds of the application,

(ii) particulars of the hardship or depravity alleged,

(iii) whether there has been any previous application for leave,

(iv) whether any, and if so what, attempts at reconciliation have been made,

(v) particulars of any circumstances which may assist the court in determining whether there is a reasonable probability of reconciliation between the parties,

(vi) the date of birth of each of the parties or, if it be the case, that he or she has attained 18;

(*b*) a copy of the application and of the supporting affidavit for service on the respondent; and

(*c*) unless otherwise directed on an application made *ex parte*, a certificate of the marriage.

(3) C.C.R. Order 6, rule 4(2)(*c*)(ii) and (*d*) (which deal with the service of an originating application), shall not apply but the registrar shall annex to the copy of the application for service a copy of the supporting affidavit and a notice in Form 1 with Form 6 attached.

Proceedings after service of application under section 3 *of Act of* 1973

6.—(1) If, within the time limited, the respondent gives notice of intention to defend an application under section 3 of the Act of 1973, the registrar shall order that the application be transferred to the High Court.

(2) Where the application is filed in a divorce county court which is not a court of trial or has been transferred to the High Court and is proceeding in a district registry which is not in a divorce town, the hearing shall be fixed to take place at such court of trial or divorce town as in the opinion of the registrar is the nearest or most convenient.

For the purposes of this paragraph the Royal Courts of Justice shall be treated as a divorce town.

(3) The application shall be heard by a judge and shall, unless otherwise directed, be heard in chambers.

(4) Subject to the provisions of this rule, these Rules shall, so far as applicable, apply, with the necessary modifications, to the application as if the originating application were a petition and the applicant a petitioner.

Discontinuance of cause before service of petition

7. Before a petition is served on any person, the petitioner may file a notice of discontinuance and the cause shall thereupon stand dismissed.

Cause to be begun by petition

8.—(1) Every cause other than an application under section 3 of the Act of 1973 shall be begun by petition.

(2) Where a petition for divorce, nullity or judicial separation discloses that there is a minor child of the family who is under 16 or who is over that age and is receiving instruction at an educational establishment or undergoing training for a trade or profession, the petition shall be accompanied by a separate written statement containing the information required by Form 4, to which shall be attached a copy of any medical report mentioned therein.

(3) Where a petition for divorce alleging five years' separation contains a proposal by the petitioner (not being a proposal agreed between the petitioner and the respondent) to make financial provision for the respondent, the petition shall be accompanied by an affidavit by the petitioner giving brief particulars of his means and commitments.

Contents of petition

9.—(1) Unless otherwise directed, every petition, other than a petition for jactitation of marriage or under rule 109 or 110, shall contain the information required by Form 2 as near as may be in the order there set out and any further or other information required by such of the following paragraphs of this rule and by rule 108 as may be applicable.

(2) A petition for divorce, nullity or judicial separation—

(*a*) shall state whether or not there are to the knowledge of the petitioner any proceedings continuing in any country outside England and Wales which are in respect of the marriage to which the petition relates or are capable of affecting its validity or subsistence, and

(*b*) if there are any such proceedings, shall give particulars of them including—

(i) the court in or tribunal or authority before which they were begun,

(ii) the date when they were begun,

(iii) the names of the parties,

(iv) the date, or as the case may be, the expected date of any trial in the proceedings, and

(v) such other facts as may be relevant to the question whether the proceedings on the petition should be stayed under Schedule 1 to the Domicile and Matrimonial Proceedings Act 1973**(a)**.

In this paragraph "proceedings continuing in any country outside England and Wales" includes any proceedings which are not instituted in a court of

(a) 1973 c. 45.

law in that country, if those proceedings are instituted before a tribunal or other authority in that country having power under the law having effect there to determine questions of status, and proceedings shall be treated as continuing in a country outside England and Wales if they have been begun and have not been finally disposed of.

(3) A petition for a decree of nullity under section 12(*e*) or (*f*) of the Act of 1973 shall state whether the petitioner was at the time of the marriage ignorant of the facts alleged.

(4) A petition for a decree of presumption of death and dissolution of marriage shall state the last place at which the parties to the marriage cohabited, the circumstances in which the parties ceased to cohabit, the date when and the place where the respondent was last seen or heard of, and the steps which have been taken to trace the respondent.

(5) A petitioner who, in reliance on section 11 or 12 of the Civil Evidence Act 1968**(a)**, intends to adduce evidence that a person—

(*a*) was convicted of an offence by or before a court in the United Kingdom or by a court-martial there or elsewhere, or

(*b*) was found guilty of adultery in matrimonial proceedings or was adjudged to be the father of a child in affiliation proceedings before a court in the United Kingdom,

must include in his petition a statement of his intention with particulars of—

(i) the conviction, finding or adjudication and the date thereof,

(ii) the court or court-martial which made the conviction, finding or adjudication and, in the case of a finding or adjudication, the proceedings in which it was made, and

(iii) the issue in the proceedings to which the conviction, finding or adjudication is relevant.

Petition for jactitation of marriage

10. A petition for jactitation of marriage shall state—

(*a*) the residence and domicile of the petitioner and the respondent at the date of the institution of the cause;

(*b*) the dates, times and places of the alleged boastings and assertions;

(*c*) that the alleged boastings and assertions are false and that the petitioner has not acquiesced therein.

Signing of petition

11. Every petition shall be signed by counsel if settled by him and, if not, by the petitioner's solicitor in his own name or the name of his firm, or by the petitioner if he sues in person.

Presentation of petition

12.—(1) A petition, other than a petition under rule 109 or 110, may be presented to any divorce county court.

(a) 1968 c. 64.

(2) Unless otherwise directed on an application made *ex parte*, a certificate of the marriage to which the cause relates shall be filed with the petition.

(3) Where a solicitor is acting for a petitioner for divorce or judicial separation, a certificate in Form 3 shall be filed with the petition, unless otherwise directed on an application made *ex parte*.

(4) Where there is before a divorce county court or the High Court a petition which has not been dismissed or otherwise disposed of by a final order, another petition by the same petitioner in respect of the same marriage shall not be presented without leave granted on an application made in the pending proceedings:

Provided that no such leave shall be required where it is proposed, after the expiration of the period of three years from the date of the marriage, to present a petition for divorce alleging such of the facts mentioned in section 1(2) of the Act of 1973 as were alleged in a petition for judicial separation presented before the expiration of that period.

(5) The petition shall be presented by filing it, together with any statement, report and affidavit required by rule 8(2) and (3), in the court office, with as many copies of the petition as there are persons to be served and a copy of the statement, report and affidavit required by rule 8(2) and (3) for service on the respondent.

(6) C.C.R. Order 6, rule 4(2) (which, as applied by rule 5 of that Order, deals with the filing and service of petitions), shall not apply but on the filing of the petition the registrar shall—

(*a*) enter the cause in the books of the court, and

(*b*) annex to every copy of the petition for service a notice in Form 5 with Form 6 attached and shall also annex to the copy petition for service on a respondent the copy of any statement, report and affidavit filed pursuant to paragraph (5) of this rule.

Parties

13.—(1) Subject to paragraph (2), where a petition alleges that the respondent has committed adultery, the person with whom the adultery is alleged to have been committed shall be made a co-respondent in the cause unless—

(*a*) that person is not named in the petition and, if the adultery is relied on for the purpose of section 1(2)(*a*) of the Act of 1973, the petition contains a statement that his or her identity is not known to the petitioner, or

(*b*) the court otherwise directs.

(2) Where a petition alleges that the respondent has been guilty of rape upon a person named, then, notwithstanding anything in paragraph (1), that person shall not be made a co-respondent in the cause unless the court so directs.

(3) Where a petition alleges that the respondent has been guilty of an improper association (other than adultery) with a person named, the petitioner

shall, as soon as practicable after the time limited for the respondent to give notice of intention to defend has expired, apply to the court for directions as to whether the person named shall be made a co-respondent in the cause.

(4) An application for directions under paragraph (1) or (3) may be made *ex parte* if no notice of intention to defend has been given.

(5) Paragraphs (1) and (3) of this rule do not apply where the person named has died before the filing of the petition.

SERVICE OF PETITION, ETC.

Service of petition

14.—(1) Subject to the provisions of this rule and rules 113 and 117, a copy of every petition shall be served personally or by post on every respondent or co-respondent.

(2) Service may be effected—

(*a*) where the party to be served is a person under disability within the meaning of rule 112, through the petitioner, and

(*b*) in any other case, through the court or, if the petitioner so requests, through the petitioner.

(3) Personal service shall in no case be effected by the petitioner himself.

(4) A copy of any petition which is to be served through the court shall be served by post by an officer of the court.

(5) For the purposes of the foregoing paragraphs, a copy of a petition shall be deemed to be duly served if—

(*a*) an acknowledgment of service in Form 6 is signed by the party to be served or by a solicitor on his behalf and is returned to the court office, and

(*b*) where the form purports to be signed by the respondent, his signature is proved at the hearing.

(6) Where a copy of a petition has been sent to a party and no acknowledgment of service has been returned to the court office, the registrar, if satisfied by affidavit or otherwise that the party has nevertheless received the document, may direct that the document shall be deemed to have been duly served on him.

(7) Where a copy of a petition has been served on a party personally and no acknowledgment of service has been returned to the court office, service shall be proved by filing an affidavit of service showing, in the case of a respondent, the server's means of knowledge of the identity of the party served.

(8) Where an acknowledgment of service is returned to the court office, the registrar shall send a photographic copy thereof to the petitioner.

(9) An application for leave to substitute some other mode of service for the modes of service prescribed by paragraph (1), or to substitute notice of the proceedings by advertisement or otherwise, shall be made *ex parte* by lodging an affidavit setting out the grounds on which the application is made; and the form of any advertisement shall be settled by the registrar.

(10) Where it appears necessary or expedient to do so the registrar may by order dispense with service of a copy of a petition on the respondent or on any other person, and an application to a registrar for an order under this paragraph may, if no notice of intention to defend has been given, be made *ex parte* by lodging an affidavit setting out the grounds of the application.

Notice of intention to defend

15.—(1) In these Rules any reference to a notice of intention to defend is a reference to an acknowledgment of service in Form 6 containing a statement to the effect that the person by whom or on whose behalf it is signed intends to defend the proceedings to which the acknowledgment relates, and any reference to giving notice of intention to defend is a reference to returning such a notice to the court office.

(2) In relation to any person on whom there is served a document requiring or authorising an acknowledgment of service to be returned to the court office, references in these Rules to the time limited for giving notice of intention to defend are references to eight days after service of the document, inclusive of the day of service, or such other time as may be fixed.

(3) Notice of intention to defend a cause begun by petition may be given at any time before directions for trial are given, notwithstanding that the time limited for giving the notice has expired.

(4) Subject to paragraphs (2) and (3), a person may give notice of intention to defend notwithstanding that he has already returned to the court office an acknowledgment of service not constituting such a notice.

Consent to the grant of a decree

16.—(1) Where, before the hearing of a petition alleging two years' separation coupled with the respondent's consent to a decree being granted, the respondent wishes to indicate to the court that he consents to the grant of a decree, he must do so by giving the registrar a notice to that effect signed by the respondent personally.

For the purposes of this paragraph an acknowledgment of service containing a statement that the respondent consents to the grant of a decree shall be treated as such a notice if the acknowledgment is signed—

(*a*) in the case of a respondent acting in person, by the respondent, or

(*b*) in the case of a respondent represented by a solicitor, by the respondent as well as by the solicitor.

(2) A respondent to a petition which alleges any such fact as is mentioned in paragraph (1) may give notice to the court either that he does not consent to a decree being granted or that he withdraws any consent which he has already given.

Where any such notice is given and none of the other facts mentioned in section 1(2) of the Act of 1973 is alleged, the proceedings on the petition shall be stayed and the registrar shall thereupon give notice of the stay to all parties.

Pleadings and Amendment

Supplemental petition and amendment of petition

17.—(1) A supplemental petition may be filed only with leave.

(2) A petition may be amended without leave before it is served but only with leave after it has been served.

(3) Subject to paragraph (4), an application for leave under this rule—

(*a*) may, if every opposite party consents in writing to the supplemental petition being filed or the petition being amended, be made *ex parte* by lodging in the court office the supplemental petition or a copy of the petition as proposed to be amended, and

(*b*) shall, in any other case, be made on notice (or in the High Court by summons), to be served, unless otherwise directed, on every opposite party.

(4) The registrar may, if he thinks fit, require an application for leave to be supported by an affidavit.

(5) An order granting leave shall—

(*a*) where any party has given notice of intention to defend, fix the time within which his answer must be filed or amended;

(*b*) where the order is made after directions for trial have been given, provide for a stay of the hearing until after the directions have been renewed.

(6) An amendment authorised to be made under this rule shall be made by filing a copy of the amended petition.

(7) Rules 11 and 13 shall apply to a supplemental or amended petition as they apply to the original petition.

(8) Unless otherwise directed, a copy of a supplemental or amended petition, together with a copy of the order (if any) made under this rule shall be served on every respondent and co-respondent named in the original petition or in the supplemental or amended petition.

(9) The petitioner shall file the documents required by paragraph (8) to be served on any person and thereupon, unless otherwise directed, rules 12(6)

(except sub-paragraph (*a*)) and 14 shall apply in relation to that person as they apply in relation to a person required to be served with an original petition.

Filing of answer to petition

18.—(1) Subject to paragraph (2) and to rules 16, 20 and 49, a respondent or co-respondent who—

(*a*) wishes to defend the petition or to dispute any of the facts alleged in it,

(*b*) being the respondent wishes to make in the proceedings any charge against the petitioner in respect of which the respondent prays for relief, or

(*c*) being the respondent to a petition to which section 5(1) of the Act of 1973 applies, wishes to oppose the grant of a decree on the ground mentioned in that subsection,

shall, within 21 days after the expiration of the time limited for giving notice of intention to defend, file an answer to the petition.

(2) An answer may be filed at any time before directions have been given for the trial of the cause, notwithstanding that the time for filing the answer has expired or that the person filing the answer has not given notice of intention to defend.

(3) Any reference in these Rules to a person who has given notice of intention to defend shall be construed as including a reference to a person who has filed an answer without giving notice of intention to defend.

(4) Where in a cause in which relief is sought under section 12(*d*) of the Act of 1973 the respondent files an answer containing no more than a simple denial of the facts stated in the petition, he shall, if he intends to rebut the charges in the petition, give the registrar notice to that effect when filing his answer.

(5) On the filing of an answer the registrar shall order the cause to be transferred to the High Court, unless in a case to which paragraph (4) applies the respondent has not given such a notice as is mentioned in that paragraph.

Filing of reply and subsequent pleadings

19.—(1) A petitioner may file a reply to an answer within 14 days after he has received a copy of the answer pursuant to rule 23.

(2) If the petitioner does not file a reply to an answer, he shall, unless the answer prays for a decree, be deemed, on making a request for directions for trial, to have denied every material allegation of fact made in the answer.

(3) No pleading subsequent to a reply shall be filed without leave.

Filing of pleadings after directions for trial

20. No pleading shall be filed without leave after directions for trial have been given.

Contents of answer and subsequent pleadings

21.—(1) Where an answer, reply or subsequent pleading contains more than a simple denial of the facts stated in the petition, answer or reply, as the case may be, the pleading shall set out with sufficient particularity the facts relied on but not the evidence by which they are to be proved and, if the pleading is filed by the husband or wife, it shall, in relation to those facts, contain the information required in the case of a petition by paragraphs (11) and (12) of Form 2.

(2) Unless otherwise directed, an answer by a husband or wife who disputes any statement required by paragraphs (4), (5) and (6) of Form 2 to be included in the petition shall contain full particulars of the facts relied on.

(3) Paragraph (8) of Form 2 and so much of that form as requires the petition to conclude with a prayer giving details of the relief claimed shall, where appropriate, apply, with the necessary modifications, to a respondent's answer as they apply to a petition:

Provided that it shall not be necessary to include in the answer any claim for costs against the petitioner.

(4) Where an answer to any petition to which rule 9(2) applies contains a prayer for relief, it shall contain the information required by that paragraph in the case of the petition in so far as it has not been given by the petitioner.

(5) Rule 9(5) shall apply, with the necessary modifications, to a pleading other than a petition as it applies to a petition.

(6) Where a party's pleading includes such a statement as is mentioned in rule 9(5), then if the opposite party—

(*a*) denies the conviction, finding or adjudication to which the statement relates, or

(*b*) alleges that the conviction, finding or adjudication was erroneous, or

(*c*) denies that the conviction, finding or adjudication is relevant to any issue in the proceedings,

he must make the denial or allegation in his pleading.

(7) Rule 11 shall apply, with the necessary modifications, to a pleading other than a petition as it applies to a petition.

Allegation against third person in pleading

22.—(1) Rules 13 and 14 shall apply, with the necessary modifications, to a pleading other than a petition as they apply to a petition, so however that for the references in those rules to a co-respondent there shall be substituted references to a party cited.

(2) Rule 18 shall apply, with the necessary modifications, to a party cited as it applies to a co-respondent.

Service of pleadings

23. A party who files an answer, reply or subsequent pleading shall at the same time file a copy for service on every opposite party and thereupon the registrar shall annex to every copy for service on a party cited in the pleading a notice in Form 5 with Form 6 attached and shall send a copy to every other opposite party.

Supplemental answer and amendment of pleadings

24. Rule 17 shall apply, with the necessary modifications, to the filing of a supplemental answer, and the amendment of a pleading or other document not being a petition, as they apply to the filing of a supplemental petition and the amendment of a petition.

Service and amendment of pleadings in Long Vacation

25. R.S.C. Order 3, rule 3, R.S.C. Order 18, rule 5, and R.S.C. Order 20, rule 6 (which restrict the service and amendment of pleadings in the Long Vacation), shall not apply to any matrimonial proceedings pending in the High Court.

Particulars

26.—(1) A party on whom a pleading has been served may in writing request the party whose pleading it is to give particulars of any allegation or other matter pleaded and, if that party fails to give the particulars within a reasonable time, the party requiring them may apply for an order that the particulars be given.

(2) The request or order in pursuance of which particulars are given shall be incorporated with the particulars, each item of the particulars following immediately after the corresponding item of the request or order.

(3) A party giving particulars, whether in pursuance of an order or otherwise, shall at the same time file a copy of them.

Re-transfer of cause to divorce county court

27.—(1) Where a cause begun by petition has been transferred to the High Court under rule 18(5) and subsequently becomes undefended, the court shall order it to be re-transferred to a divorce county court, unless (because of the proximity of the probable date of trial or otherwise) the court thinks it desirable that the cause should be heard and determined in the High Court.

(2) Nothing in paragraph (1) shall require a cause to be re-transferred at the time when it becomes undefended if in the opinion of the court the question whether it is desirable to retain it in the High Court cannot conveniently be considered until later.

PREPARATIONS FOR TRIAL

Discovery of documents in defended cause

28.—(1) R.S.C. Order 24 (which deals with the discovery and inspection of documents) shall apply to a defended cause begun by petition as it applies to an action begun by writ, with the following modifications:—

(*a*) rule 1(2), the second paragraph of rule 2(1), rule 2(2) to (4), rules 4(2) and 6, and in rule 16(1) the words from "including" to the end, shall be omitted,

(*b*) in rule 2(7) for the words "the summons for directions is taken out" there shall be substituted the words "directions for trial are given".

(2) For the purposes of R.S.C. Order 24, rule 2(1), as applied by paragraph (1) of this rule, pleadings shall be deemed to be closed at the expiration of 14 days after the service of the reply or, if there is no reply, at the expiration of 14 days after service of the answer, and are deemed to be closed then notwithstanding that any request or order for particulars previously made has not been complied with.

(3) The petitioner and any party who has filed an answer shall be entitled to have a copy of any list of documents served on any other party under R.S.C. Order 24 as applied by paragraph (1) of this rule, and such copy shall, on request, be supplied to him free of charge by the party who served the list.

In this paragraph "list of documents" includes an affidavit verifying the list.

Discovery by interrogatories in defended cause

29.—(1) R.S.C. Order 26 (which deals with discovery by interrogatories) shall apply to a defended cause begun by petition as it applies to a cause within the meaning of that Order, but with the omission of—

(*a*) in rule 1(2), the words "or the notice under Order 25, rule 7",

(*b*) rule 2, and

(*c*) in rule 6(1), the words from "including" to the end.

(2) A copy of the proposed interrogatories shall be filed when the summons for an order under R.S.C. Order 26, rule 1, is issued.

Medical examination in proceedings for nullity

30.—(1) In proceedings for nullity on the ground of incapacity to consummate the marriage the petitioner shall, subject to paragraph (2), apply to the registrar to determine whether medical inspectors should be appointed to examine the parties.

(2) An application under paragraph (1) shall not be made in an undefended cause—

(*a*) if the husband is the petitioner, or

(*b*) if the wife is the petitioner and—

(i) it appears from the petition that she was either a widow or divorced at the time of marriage in question, or

(ii) it appears from the petition or otherwise that she has borne a child, or

(iii) a statement by the wife that she is not a virgin is filed, unless, in any such case, the petitioner is alleging his or her own incapacity.

(3) References in paragraphs (1) and (2) to the petitioner shall, where the cause is proceeding only on the respondent's answer or where the allegation of incapacity is made only in the respondent's answer, be construed as references to the respondent.

(4) An application under paragraph (1) by the petitioner shall be made—

(*a*) where the respondent has not given notice of intention to defend, after the time limited for giving the notice has expired;

(*b*) where the respondent has given notice of intention to defend, after the expiration of the time allowed for filing his answer or, if he has filed an answer, after it has been filed;

and an application under paragraph (1) by the respondent shall be made after he has filed an answer.

(5) Where the party required to make an application under paragraph (1) fails to do so within a reasonable time, the other party may, if he is prosecuting or defending the cause, make an application under that paragraph.

(6) In proceedings for nullity on the ground that the marriage has not been consummated owing to the wilful refusal of the respondent, either party may apply to the registrar for the appointment of medical inspectors to examine the parties.

(7) If the respondent has not given notice of intention to defend, an application by the petitioner under paragraph (1) or (6) may be made *ex parte.*

(8) If the registrar hearing an application under paragraph (1) or (6) considers it expedient to do so, he shall appoint a medical inspector or, if he thinks it necessary, two medical inspectors to examine the parties and report to the court the result of the examination.

(9) At the hearing of any such proceedings as are referred to in paragraph (1) the court may, if it thinks fit, appoint a medical inspector or two medical inspectors to examine any party who has not been examined or to examine further any party who has been examined.

(10) The party on whose application an order under paragraph (8) is made or who has the conduct of proceedings in which an order under paragraph (9) has been made for the examination of the other party, shall serve on the other party notice of the time and place appointed for his or her examination.

Conduct of medical examination

31.—(1) Every medical examination under rule 30 shall be held at the consulting room of the medical inspector or, as the case may be, of one of the medical inspectors appointed to conduct the examination:

Provided that the registrar may, on the application of a party, direct that the examination of that party shall be held at the court office or at such other place as the registrar thinks convenient.

(2) Every party presenting himself for examination shall sign, in the presence of the inspector or inspectors, a statement that he is the person referred to as the petitioner or respondent, as the case may be, in the order for the examination, and at the conclusion of the examination the inspector or inspectors shall certify on the statement that it was signed in his or their presence by the person who has been examined.

(3) Every report made in pursuance of rule 30 shall be filed and either party shall be entitled to be supplied with a copy on payment of the prescribed fee.

(4) In an undefended cause it shall not be necessary for the inspector or inspectors to attend and give evidence at the trial unless so directed.

(5) In a defended cause, if the report made in pursuance of rule 30 is accepted by both parties, notice to that effect shall be given by the parties to the registrar and to the inspector or inspectors not less than seven clear days before the date fixed for the trial; and where such notice is given, it shall not be necessary for the inspector or inspectors to attend and give evidence at the trial.

(6) Where pursuant to paragraph (4) or (5) the evidence of the inspector or inspectors is not given at the trial, his or their report shall be treated as information furnished to the court by a court expert and be given such weight as the court thinks fit.

Order for transfer of cause

32.—(1) The court may order that a cause pending in a divorce county court be transferred to the High Court, where, having regard to all the circumstances including the difficulty or importance of the cause or of any issue arising therein, the court thinks it desirable that the cause should be heard and determined in the High Court.

(2) The court may order that any cause pending in a divorce county court shall be transferred to another divorce county court.

(3) Where a cause has been transferred to the High Court, the registrar of the registry in which it is proceeding or a judge may order that the cause be transferred to another registry.

(4) An order under any of the foregoing paragraphs may be made by the judge or registrar, as the case may be, of his own motion or on the application of a party, but before making an order of his own motion the judge or registrar shall give the parties an opportunity of being heard on the question of transfer and for that purpose the registrar may give the parties notice of a date, time and place at which the question will be considered.

Directions for trial

33.—(1) On the written request of the petitioner or of any party who is defending a cause begun by petition, the registrar shall give directions for the trial of the cause if he is satisfied—

(*a*) that any application for directions required by rule 13(3), or by that rule as applied by rule 17(7) or 22(1), has been made;

(*b*) that a copy of the petition (including any supplemental or amended petition) and any subsequent pleading has been duly served on every party required to be served and, where that party is a person under disability, that any affidavit required by rule 113(2) has been filed;

(*c*) if no notice of intention to defend has been given by any party entitled to give it, that the time limited for giving such notice has expired;

(*d*) if notice of intention to defend has been given by any party, that the time allowed him for filing an answer has expired;

(*e*) if an answer has been filed, that the time allowed for filing any subsequent pleading has expired;

(*f*) in proceedings for nullity—

(i) that any application required by rule 30(1) has been made, and

(ii) where an order for the examination of the parties has been made on an application under rule 30, that the notice required by paragraph (10) of that rule has been served and that the report of the inspector or inspectors has been filed.

(2) Subject to paragraph (3), where the cause is pending in a divorce county court other than the divorce registry and is to be tried at that court, the registrar shall, if he considers it practicable to do so, give directions for trial by fixing the date, place and, as nearly as may be, the time of the trial and giving notice thereof to every party to the cause.

(3) Where in the case of a petition for divorce or judicial separation pending in a divorce county court—

(*a*) the only fact mentioned in section 1(2) of the Act of 1973 on which the petitioner relies in support of the petition is that specified in paragraph (*d*) of that subsection,

(*b*) there are no children of the family to whom section 41 of the Act of 1973 applies, and

(*c*) the respondent has returned to the court office an acknowledgement of service containing a statement to the effect that he consents to a decree being granted or a statement to that effect signed by the respondent has been lodged in the court office,

then, unless otherwise directed,—

(i) there shall be filed with the request for directions for trial an affidavit by the petitioner containing the information required by Form 7, as near as may be in the order there set out, together with any corroborative evidence on which the petitioner intends to rely; and

(ii) the registrar shall give directions for trial by entering the cause in a list to be known as the special procedure list.

(4) In any other case the registrar shall give directions for trial by setting the cause down for trial and giving notice that he has done so to every party to the cause.

Determination of place of trial

34.—(1) Directions for trial, except where given under rule 33(3), shall determine the place of trial.

(2) In the case of an undefended cause to which rule 33(3) does not apply, the request for directions shall state—

(*a*) the place of trial desired,

(*b*) the place where the witnesses whom it is proposed to call at the trial reside,

(*c*) an estimate of the probable length of trial, and

(*d*) any other fact which may be relevant for determing the place of trial.

(3) In the case of a defended cause, the party intending to make a request for directions shall, not less than eight days before making his request, give notice of the place of trial desired to every other party who has given notice of intention to defend and, if the party intending to make the request is the respondent, to the petitioner.

The notice shall state the number of witnesses to be called on behalf of the party giving the notice and the places where he and his witnesses reside.

(4) If any party to whom notice is given under paragraph (3) does not consent to the place of trial specified in the notice, he may, within eight days after receiving it, apply to the registrar to direct trial at some other place; and if he does consent to the place so specified, he shall within that period send to the party by whom the notice was given a statement signed by his solicitor (or by him, if he is acting in person) indicating that the notice has been received and specifying the number of witnesses to be called on his behalf and the places where he and his witnesses reside.

(5) Where no application for trial at some other place is made under paragraph (4) within the period specified in that paragraph, the party making the request for directions shall state in his request—

(*a*) the place of trial desired;

(*b*) the number of witnesses to be called on his behalf and the places where he and his witnesses reside;

(*c*) if it be the case, that no statement has been received from any party (naming him) to whom notice was given under paragraph (3); and

(*d*) an estimate of the probable length of the trial;

and shall file with the request any statement sent to him by any other party in accordance with paragraph (4).

(6) If circumstances arise tending to show that the estimate of the probable length of the trial given under paragraph (2)(*c*) or (5)(*d*) or made on an application under paragraph (4) is inaccurate, a further estimate shall be filed.

(7) In determining the place of trial the registrar shall have regard to all the circumstances of the case so far as it is possible for him to do so on the basis of the information available to him, including the convenience of the parties

and their witnesses, the costs likely to be incurred, the date on which the trial can take place, the estimated length of the trial and the respective facilities for trial at the Royal Courts of Justice and elsewhere.

(8) Directions determining the place of trial of any cause may be varied by the registrar of the court or registry in which the cause is proceeding on the application of any party to the cause.

Directions as to allegations under section 1(2)(*b*) *of Act of* 1973

35.—(1) Where in a defended cause the petitioner alleges that the respondent has behaved in such a way that the petitioner cannot reasonably be expected to live with the respondent, the registrar may, of his own motion on giving directions for trial or on the application of any party made at any time before the trial, order or authorise the party who has made the request for or obtained such directions to file a schedule of the allegations and counter-allegations made in the pleadings or particulars.

(2) Where such an order is made or authority given, the allegations and counter-allegations shall, unless otherwise directed, be listed concisely in chronological order, each counter-allegation being set out against the allegation to which it relates, and the party filing the schedule shall serve a copy of it on any other party to the cause who has filed a pleading.

Stay under Domicile and Matrimonial Proceedings Act 1973

36.—(1) An application to the court by the petitioner or respondent in proceedings for divorce for an order under paragraph 8 of Schedule 1 to the Domicile and Matrimonial Proceedings Act 1973 (in this rule referred to as "Schedule 1") shall be made to the registrar, who may determine the application or refer the application, or any question arising thereon, to a judge for his decision as if the application were an application for ancillary relief.

(2) An application for an order under paragraph 9 of Schedule 1 shall be made to a judge.

(3) Where, on giving directions for trial, it appears to the registrar from any information given pursuant to rule 9(2) or 21(4) or paragraph (4) of this rule that any proceedings which are in respect of the marriage in question or which are capable of affecting its validity or subsistence are continuing in any country outside England and Wales and he considers that the question whether the proceedings on the petition should be stayed under paragraph 9 of Schedule 1 ought to be determined by the court, he shall fix a date and time for the consideration of that question by a judge and give notice thereof to all parties.

In this paragraph "proceedings continuing in any country outside England and Wales" has the same meaning as in rule 9(2).

(4) Any party who makes a request for directions for trial in matrimonial proceedings within the meaning of paragraph 2 of Schedule 1 shall, if there has been a change in the information given pursuant to rules 9(2) and 21(4), file a statement giving particulars of the change.

(5) An application by a party to the proceedings for an order under paragraph 10 of Schedule 1 may be made to the registrar, and he may determine the application or may refer the application, or any question arising thereon, to a judge as if the application were an application for ancillary relief.

EVIDENCE

Evidence generally

37.—(1) Subject to the provisions of rules 39, 40 and 48 and of the Civil Evidence Act 1968 and any other enactment, any fact required to be proved by the evidence of witnesses at the trial of a cause begun by petition shall be proved by the examination of the witnesses orally and in open court.

(2) Nothing in rules 39 and 40 shall affect the power of the judge at the trial to refuse to admit any evidence if in the interest of justice he thinks fit to do so.

Taking of affidavit in county court proceedings

38. In relation to matrimonial proceedings pending or treated as pending in a divorce county court, section 87(1) of the County Courts Act 1959 shall have effect as if after paragraph (*c*) there were inserted the following words:—

"or

(*d*) a registrar of the divorce registry; or

(*e*) any officer of the divorce registry authorised by the President under section 2 of the Commissioners for Oaths Act 1889(**a**); or

(*f*) any clerk in the Central Office of the Royal Courts of Justice authorised to take affidavits for the purpose of proceedings in the Supreme Court.

Evidence by affidavit, etc.

39.—(1) The court may order—

(*a*) that the affidavit of any witness may be read at the trial on such conditions as the court thinks reasonable;

(*b*) that the evidence of any particular fact shall be given at the trial in such manner as may be specified in the order and in particular—

(i) by statement on oath of information or belief, or

(ii) by the production of documents or entries in books, or

(iii) by copies of documents or entries in books, or

(iv) in the case of a fact which is or was a matter of common knowledge either generally or in a particular district, by the production of a specified newspaper containing a statement of that fact; and

(*c*) that not more than a specified number of expert witnesses may be called.

(**a**) 1889 c. 10.

(2) An application to the registrar for an order under paragraph (1) shall—

(*a*) if no notice of intention to defend has been given, or

(*b*) if the petitioner and every party who has given notice of intention to defend consents to the order sought, or

(*c*) if the cause is undefended and directions for trial have been given,

be made *ex parte* by filing an affidavit stating the grounds on which the application is made.

(3) Where an application is made before the trial for an order that the affidavit of a witness may be read at the trial or that evidence of a particular fact may be given at the trial by affidavit, the proposed affidavit or a draft thereof shall be submitted with the application; and where the affidavit is sworn before the hearing of the application and sufficiently states the grounds on which the application is made, no other affidavit shall be required under paragraph (2).

(4) The court may, on the application of any party to a cause begun by petition, make an order under C.C.R. Order 20, rule 18, or (if the cause is pending in the High Court) under R.S.C. Order 39, rule 1, for the examination on oath of any person, and C.C.R. Order 20, rule 18, or (if the cause is pending in the High Court) R.S.C. Order 38, rule 9, and Order 39, rules 1 to 14, (which regulate the procedure where evidence is to be taken by deposition) shall have effect accordingly with the appropriate modifications.

(5) On any application made—

(*a*) in a divorce county court, by originating application or in accordance with C.C.R. Order 13, rule 1 (which deals with applications in the course of proceedings), or

(*b*) in the High Court, by originating summons, summons, notice or motion,

evidence may be given by affidavit unless these Rules otherwise provide or the court otherwise directs, but the court may, on the application of any party, order the attendance for cross-examination of the person making any such affidavit; and where, after such an order has been made, that person does not attend, his affidavit shall not be used as evidence without the leave of the court.

(6) C.C.R. Order 20, rule 19(6) (which enables the opposite party by notice to require the attendance of a deponent), shall not apply to an affidavit made in matrimonial proceedings.

Evidence of marriage outside England and Wales

40.—(1) The celebration of a marriage outside England and Wales and its validity under the law of the country where it was celebrated may, in any matrimonial proceedings in which the existence and validity of the marriage is not disputed, be proved by the evidence of one of the parties to the marriage and the production of a document purporting to be—

(*a*) a marriage certificate or similar document issued under the law in force in that country; or

(*b*) a certified copy of an entry in a register of marriages kept under the law in force in that country.

(2) Where a document produced by virtue of paragraph (1) is not in English it shall, unless otherwise directed, be accompanied by a translation certified by a notary public or authenticated by affidavit.

(3) This rule shall not be construed as precluding the proof of a marriage in accordance with the Evidence (Foreign, Dominion and Colonial Documents) Act 1933**(a)** or in any other manner authorised apart from this rule.

Issue of witness summons or subpoena

41.—(1) A witness summons in a cause pending in a divorce county court may be issued in that court or in the court of trial at which the cause is to be tried.

(2) A writ of subpoena in a cause pending in the High Court may issue out of—

(*a*) the registry in which the cause is proceeding, or

(*b*) if the cause is to be tried at the Royal Courts of Justice, the divorce registry, or

(*c*) if the cause is to be tried at a divorce town, the registry for that town.

Hearsay evidence

42.—(1) R.S.C. Order 38, rules 20 to 33 (which deal with hearsay evidence), shall apply in relation to a defended cause as if in rule 21—

(*a*) for the reference in paragraph (4) to Order 38, rule 3, there were substituted a reference to rule 39 of these Rules;

(*b*) paragraph (5) were omitted.

(2) Unless in any particular case the court otherwise directs—

(*a*) R.S.C. Order 38, rule 21(1) shall not apply in relation to an undefended cause pending in the High Court;

(*b*) C.C.R. Order 20, rule 21(1), shall not apply in relation to an undefended cause pending in a divorce county court,

(a) 1933 c. 4.

and where the court otherwise directs, then—

(i) if the cause is pending in the High Court, paragraph (1) shall apply as it applies in the case of a defended cause;

(ii) if the cause is pending in a divorce county court, C.C.R. Order 20, rules 20 to 30, shall apply as if paragraph (2) of rule 21 were omitted.

TRIAL, ETC.

Mode and place of trial

43.—(1) Unless otherwise directed and subject to rule 48, every cause and any issue arising therein shall be tried by a judge without a jury.

(2) Any cause begun by petition (except one entered in the special procedure list) which is pending in a divorce county court may be tried at any court of trial.

(2) Any cause begun by petition which is pending in the High Court may be tried at the Royal Courts of Justice or at any divorce town.

(3) A judge or the district registrar of the registry for the divorce town at which any cause has been set down for trial may, where it appears to him that the cause cannot conveniently be tried at that town, change the place of trial to some other divorce town.

The power conferred by this paragraph may be exercised by the judge or district registrar of his own motion or on the application of a party, but before acting of his own motion the judge or district registrar shall give the parties an opportunity of being heard on the question of change, and for that purpose the district registrar may give the parties notice of a date, time and place at which the question will be considered.

Transmission of file etc. on setting down cause

44.—(1) Where a cause pending in a divorce county court is set down for trial at another divorce county court, the registrar of the court in which the cause is pending shall send the file of the cause to the registrar of the court of trial.

(2) As soon as practicable after a cause pending in a divorce county court has been set down for trial, the registrar of the court of trial shall fix the date, place and, as nearly as may be, the time of the trial and give notice thereof to every party to the cause.

(3) On setting down for trial a cause pending in the High Court, the registrar of the registry in which the cause is proceeding shall—

(*a*) if the cause is to be tried at the Royal Courts of Justice and is not proceeding in the divorce registry, send the file of the cause to that registry, and (*b*) if the cause is to be tried at a divorce town and is not proceeding in the registry for that town, send the file of the cause to that registry.

(4) In these Rules any reference to the registry for the divorce town at which a cause is to be tried shall, in relation to a divorce town in which there is no district registry, be construed as a reference to such district registry as the Lord Chancellor may designate for the purpose.

Trial of issue

45. Where directions are given for the separate trial of any issue, the registrar shall, after those directions have been complied with, set down the issue for trial and thereupon rule 44 shall apply as if the issue were a cause.

Lists at divorce towns and exercise of registrar's jurisdiction

46.—(1) The registrar of the registry for each divorce town shall prepare and keep up to date a list of the causes which are for the time being set down for trial at that divorce town.

(2) Causes shall be entered in each of the lists in the order in which they were set down for trial and for the purpose of this paragraph—

(*a*) a cause proceeding in another registry shall, subject to sub-paragraph (*b*), be treated as having been set down for trial when the file of the cause is received in the registry for the divorce town at which it is to be tried;

(*b*) a cause remitted for trial from another divorce town shall be treated as having been set down for trial at the end of the day on which it was originally set down for trial.

(3) The district registrar of the registry for the divorce town at which a cause has been set down for trial or, in the case of a cause set down for trial at the Royal Courts of Justice, a registrar of the divorce registry may, if it appears to him to be desirable having regard to the proximity of the date of the trial or otherwise, exercise in the cause any jurisdiction of the registrar of the registry in which the cause is proceeding.

Further provisions as to date of trial

47. Except with the consent of the parties or by leave of a judge, no cause, whether defended or undefended, shall be tried until after the expiration of 10 days from the date on which directions for trial were given:

Provided that nothing in this rule shall apply to a cause entered in the special procedure list.

Disposal of causes in special procedure list

48.—(1) As soon as practicable after a cause has been entered in the special procedure list, the registrar shall consider the evidence filed by the petitioner and—

(*a*) if he is satisfied that the petitioner has sufficiently proved the contents of the petition and is entitled to a decree and any costs for which he prays and that there are no children of the family to whom section 41 of the Act of 1973 applies, the registrar shall make and file a certificate to that effect;

(*b*) if he is not so satisfied he may either give the petitioner an opportunity of filing further evidence or remove the cause from the special procedure list whereupon rule 33(3) shall cease to apply.

(2) On the filing of a certificate under paragraph (1) a day shall be fixed for the pronouncement of a decree by a judge in open court at a court of trial and the registrar shall send to each party notice of the day and place so fixed and a copy of the certificate but it shall not be necessary for either party to appear on that day.

(3) Within 14 days after the pronouncement of a decree in accordance with a certificate under paragraph (1), any person may inspect the certificate and the evidence filed under rule 33(3) and may bespeak copies on payment of the prescribed fee.

Right to be heard on ancillary questions

49.—(1) A respondent may, without filing an answer, be heard on—

(*a*) any question of custody of, or access to, any child of the family,

(*b*) any question whether any such child should be committed to the care of a local authority under section 43 of the Act of 1973,

(*c*) any question whether a supervision order should be made as respects any such child under section 44 of that Act, and

(*d*) any question of ancillary relief.

(2) A respondent, co-respondent or party cited may, without filing an answer, be heard on any question as to costs but no allegation shall be made against a party claiming costs unless the party making the allegation has filed an answer.

(3) A party shall be entitled to be heard on any question pursuant to paragraph (1) or (2) whether or not he has returned to the court office an acknowledgement of service stating his wish to be heard on that question.

(4) In proceedings after a decree nisi of divorce or a decree of judicial separation no order the effect of which would be to make a co-respondent or party cited liable for costs which are not directly referable to the decree shall be made unless the co-respondent or party cited is a party to such proceedings or has been given notice of the intention to apply for such an order.

Respondent's statement as to arrangements for children

50. A respondent on whom there is served a statement in accordance with rule 8(2) may, at any time before the judge makes an order under section 41 of the Act of 1973, file in the court office a written statement of his views on the present and proposed arrangements for the children, and on receipt of such a statement from the respondent the registrar shall send a copy to the petitioner.

Order as to arrangements for children to be drawn up

51. Any order made pursuant to section 41(1) or (4) of the Act of 1973 shall be drawn up.

Restoration of matters adjourned etc. at the hearing

52.—(1) Where at the trial of a cause any application is adjourned by the judge for hearing in chambers, it may be restored—

(*a*) in the High Court, by notice without a summons, or

(*b*) in a divorce county court, on notice under C.C.R. Order 13, rule 1 (which deals with applications in the course of proceedings),

(*c*) in the High Court or a divorce county court, by notice given by the registrar when in his opinion the matter ought to be further considered,

and the notice shall state the place and time for the hearing of the restored application and be served on every party concerned.

(2) Where in proceedings for divorce, nullity of marriage or judicial separation the judge has not made an order pursuant to section 41(1) of the Act of 1973, paragraph (1) shall, unless the judge otherwise directs, apply as if an application with respect to the arrangements for the care and upbringing of any such child had been adjourned for hearing in chambers.

Shorthand note etc. of proceedings at trial

53.—(1) Official shorthand writers shall be appointed by the Lord Chancellor for the purpose of trials of causes in the High Court:

Provided that if at any divorce town no shorthand writer has been appointed under this paragraph or the person so appointed is not available, a shorthand writer may be appointed by the judge hearing causes at that town.

(2) Unless the judge otherwise directs, a shorthand note shall be taken of the proceedings at the trial in open court of every cause pending in the High Court.

(3) A shorthand note may be taken of any other proceedings before a judge if directions for the taking of such a note are given by or on behalf of the Lord Chancellor.

(4) The shorthand writer shall sign the note and certify it to be a correct shorthand note of the proceedings and shall retain the note unless he is directed by the registrar to forward it to him.

(5) On being so directed the shorthand writer shall furnish the registrar with a transcript of the whole or such part as may be directed of the shorthand note.

(6) Any party, any person who has intervened in a cause or the Queen's Proctor shall be entitled to require from the shorthand writer a transcript of the shorthand note, and the shorthand writer shall, at the request of any person so entitled, supply that person with a transcript of the whole or any part of the note on payment of the shorthand writer's charges at such rate as may be fixed by the Minister for the Civil Service.

(7) Except as aforesaid, the shorthand writer shall not, without the permission of the court, furnish the shorthand note or a transcript of the whole or any part thereof to anyone.

(8) In these Rules references to a shorthand note include references to a record of the proceedings made by mechanical means and in relation to such a record references to the shorthand writer shall have effect as if they were references to the person responsible for transcribing the record.

Application for re-hearing

54.—(1) An application for re-hearing of a cause tried by a judge alone (whether in the High Court or a divorce county court), where no error of the court at the hearing is alleged, shall be made to a judge.

(2) Unless otherwise directed, the application shall be made to the judge by whom the cause was tried and shall be heard in open court.

(3) The application shall be made—

(*a*) in the High Court, by a notice to attend before the judge on a day specified in the notice, and

(*b*) in the county court, on notice in accordance with C.C.R. Order 13, rule 1 (which deals with applications in the course of proceedings),

and the notice shall state the grounds of the application.

(4) Unless otherwise directed, the notice must be issued within six weeks after the judgment and served on every other party to the cause not less than 14 days before the day fixed for the hearing of the application.

(5) The applicant shall file a certificate that the notice has been duly served on each person required to be served therewith.

(6) The application shall be supported by an affidavit setting out the allegations on which the applicant relies or exhibiting a copy of any pleading which he proposes to file if the application is granted, and a copy of the affidavit shall be served on every other party to the cause.

(7) Not less than seven days before the application is heard the applicant shall file a copy of a transcript of so much as is relevant of any official shorthand note of the proceedings at the trial.

(8) Any other application for re-hearing shall be made by way of appeal to the Court of Appeal.

(9) This rule shall apply, with the necessary modifications, to a cause disposed of under rule 48 as it applies to a cause tried by a judge alone.

DECREES AND ORDERS

Decrees and orders

55.—(1) Every decree, every order made in open court and every other order which is required to be drawn up shall be drawn up—

(*a*) in the case of a decree or order made at a divorce county court, by the registrar of that court;

(*b*) in the case of a decree or order made at the Royal Courts of Justice, by a registrar of the divorce registry;

(*c*) in the case of a decree or order made at a divorce town, by the registrar of the registry for that town.

(2) C.C.R. Order 24, rule 5 (which deals with the preparation of a decree) shall not apply to a decree made in a cause pending in a divorce county court.

(3) The registrar to whom the file of a cause has been sent under rule 44 shall, as soon as practicable after the cause has been tried, return the file to the registrar from whom he received it, together with any documentary evidence produced during the trial which has not been ordered to be returned to the party who produced it and the decree or order pronounced or made in the cause.

Application for rescission of decree

56.—(1) An application by a respondent under section 10(1) of the Act of 1973 for the rescission of a decree of divorce shall be made to a judge and shall be heard in open court.

(2) Paragraphs (3) and (5) of rule 54 shall apply to an application under this rule as they apply to an application under that rule.

(3) Unless otherwise directed, the notice of the application shall be served on the petitioner not less than 14 days before the day fixed for the hearing of the application.

(4) The application shall be supported by an affidavit setting out the allegations on which the applicant relies and a copy of the affidavit shall be served on the petitioner.

Application under section 10(2) *of Act of* 1973

57.—(1) An application by the respondent to a petition for divorce for the court to consider the financial position of the respondent after the divorce shall be made by notice in Form 12.

(2) Where a petitioner is served with a notice in Form 12, then, unless he has already filed an affidavit under rule 8(3) or rule 73(2), he shall, within 14

days after the service of the notice, file an affidavit in answer to the application containing full particulars of his property and income, and if he does not do so, the court may order him to file an affidavit containing such particulars.

(3) Within 14 days after service of any affidavit under paragraph (2) or within such other time as the court may fix, the respondent shall file an affidavit in reply containing full particulars of his property and income unless already given in an affidavit filed by him under rule 73(3).

(4) The powers of the court on the hearing of the application may be exercised by the registrar.

(5) If a decree nisi has been granted on the basis of a finding that the petitioner was entitled to rely in support of his petition on the fact of two years' or five years' separation and has made no such finding as to any other fact mentioned in section 1(2) of the Act of 1973, the registrar by whom an application under section 10(2) is to be heard shall fix an appointment for the hearing, and rules 77(3) to (7), 80 and 81 shall apply to the application as if it were an application for ancillary relief.

(6) At any time before the hearing of the application is concluded (and without prejudice to any right of appeal), the registrar may, and if so requested by either party shall, refer the application, or any question arising thereon, to a judge.

(7) A statement of any of the matters mentioned in subsection (3) of section 10 of the Act of 1973 with respect to which the court is satisfied, or, where the court has proceeded under subsection (4) of the said section, a statement that the conditions for which that subsection provides have been fulfilled, shall be entered in the court minutes.

Copies of decrees and orders

58.—(1) A copy of every decree shall be sent by the registrar to every party to the cause.

(2) A sealed or other copy of a decree or order made in open court shall be issued to any person requiring it on payment of the prescribed fee.

Service of order

59.—(1) Where an order made in matrimonial proceedings has been drawn up, the registrar shall, unless otherwise directed, send a copy of the order to every party affected by it.

(2) Where a party against whom the order is made is acting by a solicitor, a copy may, if the registrar thinks fit, be sent to that party as if he were acting in person, as well as to his solicitor.

(3) It shall not be necessary for the person in whose favour the order was made to prove that a copy of the order has reached any other party to whom it is required to be sent.

(4) This rule is without prejudice to R.S.C. Order 45, rule 7 (which deals with the service of an order to do or abstain from doing an act), C.C.R. Order 25, rule 68 (which deals with orders enforceable by attachment), and any other rule or enactment for the purposes of which an order is required to be served in a particular way.

Service of decree or order requiring act to be done

60. Where a decree or order requires a person to do or abstain from doing an act, the copy required by R.S.C. Order 45, rule 7, or C.C.R. Order 25, rule 68, to be served on the person mentioned in those rules may either be served on him personally or delivered to his solicitor.

Intervention to show cause by Queen's Proctor

61.—(1) If the Queen's Proctor wishes to show cause against a decree nisi being made absolute, he shall give notice to that effect to the registrar and to the party in whose favour it was pronounced, and, if the cause is pending in a divorce county court, the registrar shall thereupon order it to be transferred to the High Court.

(2) Within 21 days after giving notice under paragraph (1) the Queen's Proctor shall file his plea setting out the grounds on which he desires to show cause, together with a copy for service on the party in whose favour the decree was pronounced and every other party affected by the decree.

(3) The registrar shall serve a copy of the plea on each of the persons mentioned in paragraph (2).

(4) Subject to the following provisions of this rule, these Rules shall apply to all subsequent pleadings and proceedings in respect of the plea as if it were a petition by which a cause is begun.

(5) If no answer to the plea is filed within the time limited or, if an answer is filed and struck out or not proceeded with, the Queen's Proctor may apply forthwith by motion for an order rescinding the decree and dismissing the petition.

(6) Rule 33 shall apply to proceedings in respect of a plea by the Queen's Proctor as it applies to the trial of a cause, so however that if all the charges in the plea are denied in the answer the application for directions shall be made by the Queen's Proctor and in any other case it shall be made by the party in whose favour the decree nisi has been pronounced.

Intervention to show cause by person other than Queen's Proctor

62.—(1) If any person other than the Queen's Proctor wishes to show cause under section 9 of the Act of 1973 against a decree nisi being made absolute, he shall file an affidavit stating the facts on which he relies and a copy shall be served on the party in whose favour the decree was pronounced.

(2) A party on whom a copy of an affidavit has been served under paragraph (1) may, within 14 days after service, file an affidavit in answer and, if he does so, a copy thereof shall be served on the person showing cause.

(3) The person showing cause may file an affidavit in reply within 14 days

after service of the affidavit in answer and, if he does so, a copy shall be served on each party who was served with a copy of his original affidavit.

(4) No affidavit after an affidavit in reply shall be filed without leave.

(5) Any person who files an affidavit under paragraph (1), (2) or (3) shall at the same time file a copy for service on each person required to be served therewith and the registrar shall thereupon serve the copy on that person.

(6) A person showing cause shall apply to the judge for directions within 14 days after expiry of the time allowed for filing an affidavit in reply or, where no affidavit in answer has been filed, within 14 days after expiry of the time allowed for filing such an affidavit.

(7) If the person showing cause does not apply under paragraph (6) within the time limited, the person in whose favour the decree was pronounced may do so.

(8) If directions are given for the trial of an intervention in a cause pending in a divorce county court, the registrar shall thereupon order the cause to be transferred to the High Court.

Intervention to show cause to be tried in London

63. The trial of any intervention under rule 61 or 62, whether the cause is proceeding in the divorce registry or a district registry, shall take place at the Royal Courts of Justice, unless the President otherwise directs.

Rescission of decree nisi by consent

64.—(1) Where, after a decree nisi has been pronounced but before it has been made absolute, a reconciliation has been effected between the petitioner and the respondent, either party may apply for an order rescinding the decree by consent.

(2) Where the cause is pending in a divorce county court, the application shall be made on notice to the other spouse and to any other party against whom costs have been awarded or who is otherwise affected by the decree, and where the cause is pending in the High Court, a copy of the summons by which the application is made shall be served on every such person.

(3) The application shall be made to a judge and may be heard in chambers.

Decree absolute on lodging notice

65.—(1) Subject to rule 66(1), an application by a spouse to make absolute a decree nisi pronounced in his favour may be made by lodging with the registrar a notice in Form 8.

(2) On the lodging of such a notice, the registrar shall search the court minutes and if he is satisfied—

(*a*) that no appeal against the decree and no application for re-hearing of the cause or for rescission of the decree is pending;

(*b*) that no order has been made by the Court of Appeal extending the time for appealing against the decree or by a judge extending the time for making an application for re-hearing of the cause or, if any such order has been made, that the time so extended has expired;

(*c*) that no application for such an order as is mentioned in sub-paragraph (*b*) is pending;

(*d*) that no intervention under rule 61 or 62 is pending;

(*e*) that the judge has made an order under section 41(1) of the Act of 1973;

(*f*) where a certificate has been granted under section 12 of the Administration of Justice Act 1969**(a)** in respect of the decree—

(i) that no application for leave to appeal directly to the House of Lords is pending;

(ii) that no extension of the time to apply for leave to appeal directly to the House of Lords has been granted or, if any such extension has been granted, that the time so extended has expired; and

(iii) that the time for any appeal to the Court of Appeal has expired; and

(*g*) that the provisions of section 10(2) to (4) of the Act of 1973 do not apply or have been complied with,

the registrar shall make the decree absolute:

Provided that if the notice is lodged more than 12 months after the decree nisi, the registrar may require the applicant to file an affidavit accounting for the delay and may make such order on the application as he thinks fit or refer the application to a judge.

Decree absolute on application

66.—(1) In the following cases an application for a decree nisi to be made absolute shall be made to a judge, that is to say—

(*a*) where, within six weeks after a decree nisi has been pronounced, the Queen's Proctor gives to the registrar and to the party in whose favour the decree was pronounced a notice that he requires more time to decide whether to show cause against the decree being made absolute and the notice has not been withdrawn, or

(*b*) where there are other circumstances which ought to be brought to the attention of the court before a decree nisi is made absolute.

Unless otherwise directed, the summons by which the application is made (or, where the cause is pending in a divorce county court, notice of the application) shall be served on every party to the cause (other than the applicant) and, in a case to which sub-paragraph (*a*) applies, on the Queen's Proctor.

(2) An application by a spouse for a decree nisi pronounced against him to

(**a**) 1969 c. 58.

be made absolute may be made to a judge or the registrar, and the summons by which the application is made (or, where the cause is pending in a divorce county court, notice of the application) shall be served on the other spouse not less than four clear days before the day on which the application is heard.

(3) An order granting an application under this rule shall not take effect until the registrar has searched the court minutes and is satisfied as to the matters mentioned in rule 65(2).

Indorsement and certificate of decree absolute

67.—(1) Where a decree nisi is made absolute, the registrar shall make an indorsement to that effect on the decree, stating the precise time at which it was made absolute.

(2) On a decree nisi being made absolute, the registrar shall—

(*a*) send to the petitioner and the respondent a certificate in Form 9 or 10, whichever is appropriate, authenticated by the seal of the divorce county court or registry from which it is issued, and

(*b*) if the cause is proceeding in a district registry or a divorce county court other than the divorce registry, send to the divorce registry an index card relating to the cause.

(3) A central index of decrees absolute shall be kept at the divorce registry and any person shall be entitled to require a search to be made therein, and to be furnished with a certificate of the result of the search, on payment of the prescribed fee.

(4) A certificate in Form 9 or 10 that a decree nisi has been made absolute shall be issued to any person requiring it on payment of the prescribed fee.

Ancillary Relief

Application by petitioner or respondent for ancillary relief

68.—(1) Any application by a petitioner or by a respondent who files an answer claiming relief, for—

(*a*) an order for maintenance pending suit,

(*b*) a financial provision order,

(*c*) a property adjustment order,

shall be made in the petition or answer, as the case may be.

(2) Notwithstanding anything in paragraph (1), an application for ancillary relief which should have been made in the petition or answer may be made subsequently—

(*a*) by leave of the court, either by notice in Form 11 or at the trial, or (*b*) where the parties are agreed upon the terms of the proposed order, without leave by notice in Form 11.

(3) An application by a petitioner or respondent for ancillary relief, not being an application which is required to be made in the petition or answer, shall be made by notice in Form 11.

Application by guardian etc. for ancillary relief in respect of children

69. Any of the following persons, namely—

(*a*) the guardian of any child of the family,

(*b*) any person who has the custody or the care and control of a child of the family under an order of the High Court or a divorce county court,

(*c*) a local authority to whom the care of a child of the family has been committed by an order made under section 43 of the Act of 1973,

(*d*) any person who has obtained leave to intervene in the cause for the purpose of applying for the custody of a child of the family,

(*e*) the Official Solicitor if appointed the guardian *ad litem* of a child of the family under rule 115, and

(*f*) any other person in whose care a child of the family is and who has obtained leave to intervene in the cause for the purpose of applying for ancillary relief in respect of that child,

may apply for an order for ancillary relief as respects that child by notice in Form 11.

Application in Form 11 *or* 12

70. Where an application for ancillary relief is made by notice in Form 11 or an application under rule 57 is made by notice in Form 12, the notice shall be filed—

(*a*) if the cause is pending in a divorce county court, in that court, or

(*b*) if the cause is pending in the High Court, in the registry in which it is proceeding,

and within four days after filing the notice the applicant shall serve a copy on the respondent to the application.

Application for ancillary relief after order of magistrates' court

71. Where an application for ancillary relief is made while there is in force an order of a magistrates' court for maintenance of a spouse or child, the applicant shall file a copy of the order on or before the hearing of the application.

Children to be separately represented on certain applications

72.—(1) Where an application is made to the High Court or a divorce county court for an order for a variation of settlement, the court shall, unless it is satisfied that the proposed variation does not adversely affect the rights or interests of any children concerned, direct that the children be separately represented on the application, either by a solicitor or by a solicitor and counsel, and may appoint the Official Solicitor or other fit person to be guardian *ad litem* of the children for the purpose of the application.

(2) On any other application for ancillary relief the court may give such a direction or make such appointment as it is empowered to give or make by paragraph (1).

(3) Before a person other than the Official Solicitor is appointed guardian *ad litem* under this rule there shall be filed a certificate by the solicitor acting for the children that the person proposed as guardian has no interest in the matter adverse to that of the children and that he is a proper person to be such guardian.

General provisions as to evidence etc. on application for ancillary relief

73.—(1) A petitioner or respondent who has applied for ancillary relief in his petition or answer and who intends to proceed with the application before a registrar shall, subject to rule 83, file a notice in Form 13 and within four days after doing so serve a copy on the other spouse.

(2) Where a respondent or a petitioner is served with a notice in Form 11 or 13 in respect of an application for ancillary relief, not being an application to which rule 74 or 75 applies, then, unless the parties are agreed upon the terms of the proposed order, he shall, within 14 days after service of the notice, file an affidavit in answer to the application containing full particulars of his property and income, and if he does not do so, the court may order him to file an affidavit containing such particulars.

(3) Within 14 days after service of any affidavit under paragraph (2) or within such other time as the court may fix, the applicant shall file an affidavit in reply containing full particulars of his property and income.

Evidence on application for property adjustment or avoidance of disposition order

74.—(1) Where an application is made for a property adjustment order or an avoidance of disposition order, the application shall state briefly the nature of the adjustment proposed or the disposition to be set aside and the notice in Form 11 or 13, as the case may be, shall, unless otherwise directed, be supported by an affidavit by the applicant stating the facts relied on in support of the application.

(2) The affidavit in support shall contain, so far as known to the applicant, full particulars—

(*a*) in the case of an application for a transfer or settlement of property—

(i) of the property in respect of which the application is made,

(ii) of the property to which the party against whom the application is made is entitled either in possession or reversion;

(*b*) in the case of an application for an order for a variation of settlement—

(i) of all settlements, whether ante-nuptial or post-nuptial, made on the spouses, and

(ii) of the funds brought into settlement by each spouse;

(*c*) in the case of an application for an avoidance of disposition order—

(i) of the property to which the disposition relates,

(ii) of the persons in whose favour the disposition is alleged to have been made, and in the case of a disposition alleged to have been made by way of settlement, of the trustees and the beneficiaries of the settlement.

(3) Where an application for a property adjustment order or an avoidance of disposition order relates to land, the affidavit in support shall, in addition to containing any particulars required by paragraph (2)—

(*a*) state whether the title to the land is registered or unregistered and, if registered, the Land Registry title number,

(*b*) give particulars, so far as known to the applicant, of any mortgage of the land or any interest therein.

(4) A copy of Form 11 or 13, as the case may be, together with a copy of the supporting affidavit, shall be served on the following persons as well as on the respondent to the application, that is to say—

(*a*) in the case of an application for an order for a variation of settlement order, the trustees of the settlement and the settlor if living,

(*b*) in the case of an application for an avoidance of disposition order, the person in whose favour the disposition is alleged to have been made,

(*c*) in the case of an application to which paragraph (3) refers, any mortgagee of whom particulars are given pursuant to that paragraph,

and such other persons, if any, as the registrar may direct.

(5) Any person served with notice of an application to which this rule applies may, within 14 days after service, file an affidavit in answer.

Evidence on application for variation order

75.—(1) An application for a variation order shall be supported by an affidavit by the applicant setting out full particulars of his property and income and the grounds on which the application is made.

(2) The respondent to the application may, within 14 days after service of the affidavit, file an affidavit in answer.

Service of affidavit in answer or reply

76.—(1) A person who files an affidavit for use on an application under rule 73, 74 or 75 shall at the same time serve a copy on the opposite party and, where the affidavit contains an allegation of adultery or of an improper association with a named person, then, unless otherwise directed, it shall be indorsed with a notice in Form 14 and a copy of the affidavit or of such part thereof as the court may direct, indorsed as aforesaid, shall be served on that person by the person who files the affidavit, and the person against whom the allegation is made shall be entitled to intervene in the proceedings by applying for directions under rule 77(6) within eight days of service of the affidavit on him, inclusive of the day of service.

(2) Rule 49(4) shall apply to a person served with an affidavit under paragraph (1) of this rule as it applies to a co-respondent.

Investigation by registrar of application for ancillary relief

77.—(1) On or after the filing of a notice in Form 11 or 13 an appointment shall be fixed for the hearing of the application by the registrar.

(2) An application for an avoidance of disposition order shall, if practicable, be heard at the same time as any related application for financial relief.

(3) Notice of the appointment, unless given in Form 11 or 13 (as the case may be) shall be given by the registrar to every party to the application.

(4) Any party to an application for ancillary relief may by letter require any other party to give further information concerning any matter contained in any affidavit filed by or on behalf of that other party or any other relevant matter, or to furnish a list of relevant documents or to allow inspection of any such document, and may, in default of compliance by such other party, apply to the registrar for directions.

(5) At the hearing of an application for ancillary relief the registrar shall, subject to rules 78, 80 and 81, investigate the allegations made in support of and in answer to the application, and may take evidence orally and may order the attendance of any person for the purpose of being examined or cross-examined, and may at any stage of the proceedings order the discovery and production of any document or require further affidavits.

(6) The registrar may at any stage of the proceedings give directions as to the filing and service of pleadings and as to the further conduct of the proceedings.

(7) Where any party to such an application intends on the day appointed for the hearing to apply only for directions, he shall file and serve on every other party a notice to that effect.

Applications heard by registrar

78.—(1) Except in a case to which rule 79 applies and subject to paragraph (2), the registrar shall, after completing his investigation under rule 77, make such order as he thinks just.

(2) The registrar may at any time refer the application, or any question arising thereon, to a judge for his decision.

(3) Pending the final determination of the application, the registrar may make an interim order upon such terms as he thinks just.

Applications heard by judge

79.—(1) In the case of an application for an avoidance of disposition order and any related application for financial relief which is being heard at the same time, the registrar shall, after completing his investigation under rule 77, report the result thereof in writing to a judge to whom the application shall be adjourned.

(2) The registrar's report shall contain an estimate of the financial relief to which, in his opinion, the applicant is entitled (if he has not already obtained an order for financial relief), and of the relief to which, in the registrar's opinion, the applicant would be entitled if the application were granted.

(3) The registrar's report shall be filed and any party shall be entitled to inspect the report and to be supplied with a copy on payment of the prescribed fee.

(4) On the hearing of the application the judge may confirm or vary the registrar's report or make such other order as he thinks just.

(5) Where the parties come to an agreement as to the terms of the order to be made on the application, an order in those terms may be made by the registrar and the foregoing provisions of this rule shall not apply.

Transfer of application for ancillary relief: general provisions

80.—(1) If the court considers that an application for ancillary relief pending in a divorce county court gives rise to a contested issue of conduct of a nature which is likely materially to affect the question whether any, or what, order should be made therein and for that reason the application should be transferred to the High Court, the court shall, subject to paragraph (5) of this rule, make an order for transfer accordingly and, where an application is transferred to the High Court under this paragraph, it shall be heard by a judge of that Court.

(2) Where an application for ancillary relief is pending in a divorce county court and the parties to the proceedings consent to the making of an order for the transfer of the application to the High Court, an application for that purpose may be made to a judge or the registrar who shall, subject to paragraph (5) of this rule, order the transfer unless he is of opinion that it would not be justified.

(3) Without prejudice to paragraphs (1) and (2) of this rule, the court in which an application for ancillary relief is pending may, if it is a divorce county court, order the transfer of the application to the High Court or, if it is the High Court, order the transfer of the application to a divorce county court, where the transfer appears to the court to be desirable.

(4) The judge before hearing and the registrar before investigating under rule 77 an application for ancillary relief pending in a divorce county court shall consider whether the case is one in which the court should exercise its powers under paragraph (1) or (3) of this rule.

(5) In considering whether an application should be transferred from a divorce county court to the High Court or from the High Court to a divorce county court, the court shall have regard to all relevant considerations, including the nature and value of the property involved, the relief sought and the financial limits for the time being relating to the jurisdiction of county courts in other matters.

(6) Where a decree nisi has been pronounced in the cause, the court shall, before making an order for the transfer of the application to the High Court, consider whether it would be more convenient to transfer the cause to the High Court under rule 32.

(7) Where pursuant to the provisions of this rule an application for ancillary relief or the cause is transferred to the High Court, the court may, on making the order for transfer, give directions as to the further conduct of the proceedings.

(8) Where an application for ancillary relief is pending in a divorce county court, the court may order that the application be transferred to another divorce county court.

(9) Where an application for ancillary relief is pending in the High Court, the registrar of the registry in which the application is proceeding or a judge may order that the application be transferred to another registry.

(10) An order under paragraph (1), (3), (8) or (9) may be made by the court of its own motion or on the application of a party, but before making an order of its own motion the court shall give the parties an opportunity of being heard on the question of transfer and for that purpose the registrar may give the parties notice of a date, time and place at which the question will be considered.

Transfer to High Court for purpose of expedition

81. Without prejudice to the last foregoing rule, a judge or the registrar may, on the application of a party or of his own motion, order that an application for ancillary relief pending in a divorce county court shall be transferred to the High Court if he is of opinion that the transfer is desirable for the purpose of expediting the hearing of the application ; but where a transfer is ordered under this rule, the costs of the application for ancillary relief shall be on the county court scale unless the judge or registrar who hears the application considers that a transfer would have been justified otherwise than for expediting the hearing and for that reason directs that the costs incurred after the transfer of the application shall be on the High Court scale.

Arrangements for hearing of application etc. by judge

82.—(1) Where an application for ancillary relief or any question arising thereon has been referred or adjourned to a judge, the registrar shall fix a date and time for the hearing of the application or the consideration of the question and give notice thereof to all parties.

(2) The hearing or consideration shall, unless otherwise directed, take place in chambers.

(3) Where the application is proceeding in a divorce county court which is not a court of trial or is pending in the High Court and proceeding in a district registry which is not in a divorce town, the hearing or consideration shall take place at such court of trial or divorce town as in the opinion of the registrar is the nearest or most convenient.

For the purposes of this paragraph the Royal Courts of Justice shall be treated as a divorce town.

Request for periodical payments order at same rate as order for maintenance pending suit

83.—(1) Where at or after the date of a decree nisi of divorce or nullity of marriage an order for maintenance pending suit is in force, the party in whose favour the order was made may, if he has made an application for an order for periodical payments for himself in his petition or answer, as the case may be, request the registrar in writing to make such an order (in this rule referred to as a "corresponding order") providing for payments at the same rate as those provided for by the order for maintenance pending suit.

(2) Where such a request is made, the registrar shall serve on the other spouse a notice in Form 15 requiring him, if he objects to the making of a corresponding order, to give notice to that effect to the registrar and to the applicant within 14 days after service of the notice in Form 15.

(3) If the other spouse does not give notice of objection within the time aforesaid, the registrar may make a corresponding order without further notice to that spouse and without requiring the attendance of the applicant or his solicitor, and shall in that case serve a copy of the order on the applicant as well as on the other spouse.

Application for order under section 37(2)(*a*) *of Act of* 1973

84.—(1) An application under section 37(2)(*a*) of the Act of 1973 for an order restraining any person from attempting to defeat a claim for financial provision or otherwise for protecting the claim shall be made to a judge.

(2) Rule 82 (except paragraph (2)) shall apply, with the necessary modifications, to the application as if it were an application for ancillary relief.

Exclusion of sections 99 *and* 101 *of County Courts Act* 1959

85.—(1) Section 99 of the County Courts Act 1959 (satisfaction of money judgments) shall not apply to an order made on an application for ancillary relief in proceedings pending in a divorce county court.

(2) Section 101 of the County Courts Act 1959 (register of judgments and orders) shall not apply to any decree or order made in proceedings pending in a divorce county court.

Enforcement of Orders

Enforcement of order for payment of money, etc.

86.—(1) Before any process is issued for the enforcement of an order made in matrimonial proceedings for the payment of money to any person, an affidavit shall be filed verifying the amount due under the order and showing how that amount is arrived at.

In a case to which C.C.R. Order 25, rule 13A (which deals with the execution of a High Court judgment in the county court), applies, the information required to be given in an affidavit under this paragraph may be given in the affidavit filed pursuant to that rule.

(2) Except with the leave of the registrar, no writ of *fieri facias* or warrant of execution shall be issued to enforce payment of any sum due under an order for ancillary relief or an order made under the provisions of section 27 of the Act of 1973 where an application for a variation order is pending.

(3) For the purposes of R.S.C. Order 46, rule 6 (which deals with the issue of a writ of execution), the divorce registry shall be the appropriate office for the issue of a writ of execution to enforce an order made in matrimonial proceedings in the High Court which are proceeding in that registry.

(4) Where a warrant of execution has been issued to enforce an order made in matrimonial proceedings pending in the divorce registry which are treated as pending in a divorce county court, the goods and chattels against which the warrant has been issued shall, wherever they are situate, be treated for the purposes of section 138 of the County Courts Act 1959 as being out of the jurisdiction of the divorce registry.

(5) The Attachment of Earnings Act 1971(**a**) and Part VII of C.C.R. Order 25 (which deals with attachment of earnings) shall apply to the enforcement of an order made in matrimonial proceedings in the divorce registry which are treated as pending in a divorce county court as if the order were an order made by such a court.

(6) Where an application under C.C.R. Order 25, rule 2 (which deals with the oral examination of a judgment debtor), relates to an order made by a divorce county court—

(*a*) the application shall be made to such divorce county court as in the opinion of the applicant is nearest to the place where the debtor resides or carries on business, and

(*b*) there shall be filed with the application the affidavit required by paragraph (1) of this rule and, except where the application is made to the court in which the order sought to be enforced was made, a copy of the order shall be exhibited to the affidavit;

and accordingly paragraph (2) of the said rule 2 shall not apply.

Judgment summonses: general provisions

87.—(1) In this rule and in rules 88 and 89, unless the context otherwise requires—

"order" means an order made in matrimonial proceedings for the payment of money;

"judgment creditor" means a person entitled to enforce an order under section 5 of the Debtors Act 1869(**b**);

"debtor" means a person liable under an order;

"judgment summons" means a summons under the said section 5 requiring a debtor to appear and be examined on oath as to his means.

(2) An application for the issue of a judgment summons may be made—

(*a*) in the case of an order of the High Court, to the divorce registry, a district registry or a divorce county court, whichever in the opinion of the judgment creditor is most convenient,

(**a**) 1971 c. 32.

(**b**) 1869 c. 62.

(*b*) in the case of an order of a divorce county court, to whichever divorce county court is in the opinion of the judgment creditor most convenient,

having regard (in either case) to the place where the debtor resides or carries on business and irrespective of the court or registry in which the order was made.

(3) The application shall be made by filing a request in Form 16 together with the affidavit required by rule 86(1) and, except where the application is made to the registry or divorce county court in which the order was made, a copy of the order shall be exhibited to the affidavit.

(4) A judgment summons shall not be issued without the leave of a judge if the debtor is in default under an order of commitment made on a previous judgment summons in respect of the same order.

(5) Every judgment summons shall be in Form 17 and shall be served on the debtor personally not less than 10 clear days before the hearing and at the time of service there shall be paid or tendered to the debtor a sum reasonably sufficient to cover his expenses in travelling to and from the court at which he is summoned to appear.

(6) C.C.R. Order 25, rule 41 (which deals with the issue of successive judgment summonses), shall apply to a judgment summons, whether issued in the High Court or a divorce county court, as if for the words "within the district" in paragraph (2) of that rule there were substituted the words "at the address stated in Form 16".

(7) Where the order was made in a different registry or divorce county court from that in which the judgment summons is issued, the registrar of the first-mentioned registry or court shall, if so requested by the registrar of the registry or court in which the summons is issued, send him the file of the matrimonial proceedings for the purpose of the hearing of the summons.

(8) On the hearing of the judgment summons the judge may—

(*a*) where the order is for lump sum provision or costs, or

(*b*) where the order is for maintenance pending suit or other periodical payments and it appears to him that the order would have been varied or suspended if the debtor had made an application for that purpose,

make a new order for payment of the amount due under the original order, together with the costs of the judgment summons, either at a specified time or by instalments.

(9) If the judge makes an order of commitment, he may direct its execution to be suspended on terms that the debtor pays to the judgment creditor the amount due, together with the costs of the judgment summons, either at a specified time or by instalments, in addition to any sums accruing due under the original order.

(10) All payments under a new order or an order of commitment shall be made to the judgment creditor unless the judge otherwise directs.

(11) Where an order of commitment is suspended on such terms as are mentioned in paragraph (9)—

(*a*) all payments thereafter made under the said order shall be deemed to be made, first, in or towards the discharge of any sums from time to time accruing due under the original order and, secondly, in or towards the discharge of the debt in respect of which the judgment summons was issued and the costs of the summons ;

(*b*) C.C.R. Order 25, rule 54(4) and (5) (which deal with an application for a further suspension), shall apply to the said order, whether it was made in the High Court or a divorce county court ; and

(*c*) the said order shall not be issued until the judgment creditor has filed an affidavit of default on the part of the debtor.

Special provisions as to judgment summonses in the High Court

88.—(1) R.S.C. Order 38, rule 2(3) (which enables evidence to be given by affidavit in certain cases), shall apply to a judgment summons issued in the High Court as if it were an originating summons.

(2) Witnesses may be summoned to prove the means of the debtor in the same manner as witnesses are summoned to give evidence on the hearing of a cause, and writs of subpoena may for that purpose be issued out of the registry in which the judgment summons is issued.

(3) Where the debtor appears at the hearing, the travelling expenses paid to him may, if the judge so directs, be allowed as expenses of a witness, but if the debtor appears at the hearing and no order of commitment is made, the judge may allow to the debtor, by way of set-off or otherwise, his proper costs, including compensation for loss of time, as upon an attendance by a defendant at a trial in court.

(4) Where a new order or an order of commitment is made, the registrar of the registry in which the judgment summons was issued shall send notice of the order to the debtor and, if the original order was made in another registry, to the registrar of that registry.

(5) An order of commitment shall be directed to the tipstaff, for execution by him, or to the registrar of the county court within the district of which the debtor is to be found, for execution by a deputy tipstaff.

(6) Unless the judge otherwise directs, the judgment creditor's costs of and incidental to the judgment summons shall be fixed without taxation in accordance with the following provisions :—

(*a*) Subject to sub-paragraph (*c*), where the amount in respect of which the judgment summons is issued is paid before the hearing, there may be allowed—

(i) the court fees paid by the judgment creditor,

(ii) any travelling expenses paid to the judgment debtor,

(iii) the fee paid to the commissioner on the affidavit filed under rule 86(1), and

(iv) if the judgment creditor is represented by a solicitor, £3 in respect of the solicitor's charges.

(*b*) Where an order is made on the hearing and the judgment creditor is awarded costs, there may be allowed—

(i) the court fees paid by the judgment creditor,

(ii) subject to paragraph (3), any travelling expenses paid to the judgment debtor,

(iii) the fees paid to the commissioner on any necessary affidavit,

(iv) if the judgment creditor is represented by a solicitor without counsel, £8 in respect of the solicitor's charges, and

(v) if the judgment creditor is represented by solicitor and counsel, £6 in respect of the solicitor's charges and £9 in respect of counsel's fees.

(*c*) Where the amount in respect of which the judgment summons is issued is paid too late to prevent the attendance of the judgment creditor or, as the case may be, his solicitor or counsel, at the hearing, the sums specified in sub-paragraph (*b*) may, if the judge so orders, be allowed instead of the sums specified in sub-paragraph (*a*).

(*d*) Where the costs of and incidental to a judgment summons are directed to be taxed, R.S.C. Order 62 (which deals generally with the costs of proceedings in the High Court) shall have effect in relation to those costs with such modifications as may be necessary.

Special provisions as to judgment summonses in divorce county courts

89.—(1) C.C.R. Order 25, rules 33, 37, 38, 39, 40(4), 48, 49(2), 54(1) and (3) and 55 (which deal with the issue of a judgment summons in a county court and the subsequent procedure), shall not apply to a judgment summons issued in a divorce county court.

(2) C.C.R. Order 25, rule 49(1) (which relates to a judgment summons heard in a county court on the order of another court), shall apply to such a summons as if for the words "any court other than a county court" there were substituted the words "any other court".

(3) C.C.R. Order 25, rule 54(2) (which relates to the suspension of an order of commitment), shall apply to such a summons subject to rule 87(9) and (10) of these Rules.

Committal and injunction

90.—(1) Notwithstanding anything in R.S.C. Order 52, rule 4(1) (which requires an application for an order of committal to be made by motion), but subject to rule 6 of that Order (which, except in certain cases, requires such an application to be heard in open court), an application for an order of committal in matrimonial proceedings pending in the High Court shall be made by summons.

(2) Where no judge is conveniently available to hear the application, then, without prejudice to C.C.R. Order 25, rule 70(3) (which in certain circumstances gives jurisdiction to a county court registrar), an application for—

(*a*) the discharge of any person committed, or

(*b*) the discharge by consent of an injunction granted by a judge,

may be made to the registrar who may, if satisfied of the urgency of the matter and that it is expedient to do so, make any order on the application which a judge could have made.

(3) Where an order or warrant for the committal of any person to prison has been made or issued in matrimonial proceedings pending in the divorce registry which are treated as pending in a divorce county court, that person shall, wherever he may be, be treated for the purposes of section 161 of the

County Courts Act 1959 as being out of the jurisdiction of the divorce registry; but if the committal is for failure to comply with the terms of an injunction, the order or warrant may, if a judge so directs, be executed by the tipstaff within any county court district.

(4) For the purposes of section 157 of the County Courts Act 1959 in its application to the hearing of matrimonial proceedings at the Royal Courts of Justice, the tipstaff shall be deemed to be an officer of the court.

Removal of county court order into High Court

91.—(1) Any order made by a divorce county court in matrimonial proceedings may, on an application made *ex parte* by affidavit by the person entitled to enforce the order, be removed into the High Court by direction of a registrar of the divorce registry or the registrar of the nearest district registry, if he is satisfied that the order cannot conveniently be enforced in the county court.

(2) Where an order is so removed, it shall have the same force and effect and the same proceedings may be taken on it as if it were an order of the High Court.

Applications relating to Children

Custody, care and supervision of children

92.—(1) Subject to paragraph (2), an application for an order relating to the custody or education of a child, or for an order committing him to the care of a local authority under section 43 of the Act of 1973 or providing for his supervision under section 44 of that Act, shall be made to a judge.

(2) An application by the petitioner or the respondent for access to a child of the family, where the other party consents to give access and the only question for determination is the extent to which access is to be given, may be made to the registrar.

(3) Without prejudice to the right of any other person entitled to apply for an order as respects a child, the guardian of any child of the family and any other person who, by virtue of an order of a court, has the custody or control of such a child or his care or supervision in pursuance of section 43 or 44 of the Act of 1973 may, without obtaining leave to intervene in the cause, apply by summons or (where the cause is proceeding in a divorce county court) by notice under C.C.R. Order 13, rule 1 (which deals with applications in the course of proceedings), for such an order as is mentioned in paragraph (1).

(4) On any application to a judge relating to the custody, care and control of, or access to, a child—

(*a*) neither the applicant nor the respondent shall be entitled to be heard in support of or, as the case may be, in opposition to the application unless he is available at the hearing to give oral evidence or the judge otherwise directs;

(*b*) the judge may refuse to admit any affidavit by any person (other than the applicant or respondent) who is or is proposed to be responsible for the child's care and upbringing or with whom the child is living or is proposed to live unless that person is available at the hearing to give oral evidence;

(*c*) a witness summons or writ of subpoena to compel the attendance of any such person as is mentioned in sub-paragraph (*b*) may issue in accordance with rule 41 without (in the case of a writ of subpoena) the production of the note from a judge or registrar mentioned in R.S.C. Order 32, rule 7;

(*d*) no witness summons or writ of subpoena shall be issued to compel the attendance of any other witness except with the production of such a note and accordingly in any such case R.S.C. Order 32, rule 7, shall apply, with such modifications as may be appropriate, to a witness summons as it applies to a writ of subpoena.

(5) Where an affidavit filed for use in proceedings relating to a child contains an allegation of adultery or of an improper association with a named person, then, unless otherwise directed, it shall be indorsed with a notice in Form 14 and a copy of the affidavit, or of such part thereof as the court may direct, indorsed as aforesaid, shall be served on that person by the person who files the affidavit, and the person against whom the allegation is made shall be entitled to intervene in the proceedings by applying for directions under paragraph (7) within eight days of service of the affidavit on him, inclusive of the day of service.

(6) Rule 49(4) shall apply to a person served with an affidavit under paragraph (5) of this rule as it applies to a co-respondent.

(7) The court may at any stage of the proceedings give directions as to the filing and service of pleadings and as to the further conduct of the proceedings.

Further provisions as to orders under sections 43 *and* 44 *of Act of* 1973

93.—(1) Before an order is made committing a child to the care of a local authority under section 43 of the Act of 1973, the registrar shall fix a date, time and place for the hearing of any representations by the local authority and shall send notice in Form 18 to the authority not less than 14 days before the date so fixed.

(2) If the local authority wish to represent that, in the event of an order being made under section 43, the court should make a financial provision order in favour of the child, the authority shall, within seven days after receipt of the notice, file an affidavit setting out such facts relevant to the property and income of the person against whom the financial provision order is sought as are known to the authority and shall at the same time serve a copy of the affidavit on that person.

(3) A person on whom a copy of the local authority's affidavit is served under paragraph (2) may, within four days after service, file an affidavit in answer and, if he does so, he shall at the same time serve a copy of the affidavit on the local authority.

(4) An application by a local authority or by an officer appointed under section 44 of the Act of 1973 for the variation or discharge of an order made under section 43 or 44 of that Act or for directions as to the exercise of the powers of the authority or officer under the order may, in case of urgency or where the application is unlikely to be opposed, be made by letter addressed to the court and the authority or officer shall, if practicable, notify any interested party of the intention to make the application.

(5) In proceedings under section 43 or 44 a local authority may be represented by their director of social services or other officer employed by them for the

purposes of their social services functions under the Local Authority Social Services Act 1970(**a**).

Removal of child out of England and Wales

94.—(1) In any cause begun by petition the petitioner or the respondent may apply at any time for an order prohibiting the removal of any child of the family under 18 out of England and Wales without the leave of the court except on such terms as may be specified in the order.

Unless otherwise directed, an application under this paragraph may be made *ex parte*.

(2) Unless otherwise directed, any order relating to the custody or care and control of a child shall provide for the child not to be removed out of England and Wales without the leave of the court except on such terms as may be specified in the order.

(3) Subject to rule 97(2), an application for leave to remove a child out of England and Wales shall be made to a judge except in the following cases when it may be made to the registrar, namely—

(*a*) where the application is unopposed, or

(*b*) where the application is for the temporary removal of the child and is opposed on a ground which in the opinion of the registrar relates only to the arrangements for the care of the child during the removal or any other incidental matter.

Reference to court welfare officer

95.—(1) A judge or the registrar may at any time refer to a court welfare officer for investigation and report any matter arising in matrimonial proceedings which concerns the welfare of a child.

(2) Without prejudice to paragraph (1), any party to an application to which rule 92 applies may, before the application is heard, request the registrar to call for a report from a court welfare officer on any matter arising on the application, and if the registrar is satisfied that the other parties to the application consent and that sufficient information is available to enable the officer to carry out the investigation, the registrar may refer the matter to a court welfare officer for investigation and report before the hearing.

(3) Where a reference is made under this rule—

(*a*) the court welfare officer may inspect the court file;

(*b*) after completing his investigation, the officer shall file his report and the registrar shall thereupon notify the parties that they may inspect it and may bespeak copies on payment of the prescribed fee;

(*c*) the registrar shall give notice to the officer of the date of hearing of the application or other proceeding.

Notice of other proceedings relating to children

96. If, while a cause is pending, proceedings relating to any child of the family are begun in the High Court, a county court or a magistrates' court,

(**a**) 1970 c. 42.

a concise statement of the nature of the proceedings shall forthwith be filed by the person beginning the proceedings or, if he is not a party to the cause, by the petitioner.

Transfer of proceedings relating to children

97.—(1) Rules 80 and 81 shall, so far as applicable, apply to proceedings for the exercise of any power under Part III of the Act of 1973 as they apply to an application for ancillary relief with the following modifications:—

(*a*) for the words "The judge before hearing and the registrar before investigating under rule 77 an application for ancillary relief" in paragraph (4) of rule 80 there shall be substituted the words "The court before hearing an application";

(*b*) paragraph (5) of rule 80 shall be omitted.

(2) Where it appears to the court that an application pending in a divorce county court for leave to remove a child permanently out of England and Wales or for an order under section 43 of the Act of 1973 is contested, or that any such proceedings pending in a divorce county court as are mentioned in paragraph (1) of this rule relate to a child who is a ward of court, the court shall order that the proceedings be transferred to the High Court:

Provided that, if a decree nisi has been pronounced in the cause, the court shall, before ordering a transfer as aforesaid, consider whether it would be more convenient to transfer the cause to the High Court under rule 32.

(3) Where in any cause it appears to the court that an application pending in a divorce county court for a declaration under section 42(3) of the Act of 1973 is contested, the court shall make an order that the cause be transferred to the High Court.

OTHER APPLICATIONS

Application in case of wilful neglect to maintain

98.—(1) Every application under section 27 of the Act of 1973 shall be made by originating application, which must, unless otherwise directed, contain the information required by Form 19.

(2) The application may be made to any divorce county court and there shall be filed with the application an affidavit by the applicant verifying the statements in the application and also a copy of the application and of the affidavit for service on the respondent.

(3) C.C.R. Order 6, rule 4(2)(*c*)(ii) and (*d*) (which deal with the service of an originating application), shall not apply but there shall be annexed to the copy of the application for service a copy of the affidavit referred to in paragraph (2) and a notice in Form 20 with Form 6 attached.

(4) If the registrar does not consider it practicable to fix a day for the hearing of the application at the time when it is issued, he may do so subsequently and in that case he shall forthwith give notice of the day to all parties.

(5) Within 14 days after the time limited for giving notice of intention to defend, the respondent shall, if he intends to contest the application, file an answer setting out the grounds on which he relies (including any allegation which he wishes to make against the applicant), and shall in any case, unless

otherwise directed, file an affidavit containing full particulars of his property and income, and the registrar shall serve a copy of the answer, if any, and of the affidavit on the applicant.

(6) Where an answer is filed alleging adultery the alleged adulterer shall, unless otherwise directed, be made a party cited and be served with a copy of the answer, and rules 12(6) and 14 shall apply, with the necessary modifications, as if the answer were a petition and the party cited were a co-respondent.

(7) A party cited who wishes to defend all or any of the charges made against him shall, within 21 days after the time limited for giving notice of intention to defend, file an answer and the registrar shall serve a copy of the answer on the respondent.

(8) If the respondent does not file an affidavit in accordance with paragraph (5), the court may order him to file an affidavit containing full particulars of his property and income, and the registrar shall serve a copy of any such affidavit on the applicant.

(9) Within 14 days after being served with a copy of any answer filed by the respondent, the applicant may file a reply, and in that case the registrar shall serve a copy on the respondent and on any party cited.

(10) Within 14 days after being served with a copy of the respondent's affidavit, the applicant may file a further affidavit as to means and as to any fact stated in the respondent's affidavit which he wishes to dispute, and in that case the registrar shall serve a copy on the respondent.

No further affidavit shall be filed without leave.

(11) An applicant, respondent or party cited who files an answer, affidavit or reply under any of the preceding paragraphs of this rule shall at the same time file a copy for service on every party required to be served therewith.

Transfer and hearing of applications under rule 98

99.—(1) Where it appears to the court that the respondent intends to contest an application under the last foregoing rule on the ground that—

(*a*) by reason of the applicant's conduct or otherwise the respondent is not liable to maintain the applicant, or

(*b*) no court in England or Wales has jurisdiction to entertain the application,

the court shall order that the application be transferred to the High Court.

(2) Without prejudice to the provisions of paragraph (1) of this rule, rules 80 (except paragraphs (5) and (7) thereof) and 81 shall apply with the necessary modifications to an appplication for an order under section 27 of the Act of 1973 as if the application were an application for ancillary relief.

(3) The application shall be heard by a judge in court, and where the application is proceeding in a divorce county court which is not a court of trial or where it has been transferred to the High Court and is proceeding in a district registry which is not in a divorce town, the hearing shall be fixed to take place at such court of trial or divorce town as in the opinion of the registrar is the nearest or most convenient.

For the purpose of this paragraph the Royal Courts of Justice shall be treated as a divorce town.

(4) On the hearing of the application the judge may make such order as he thinks just or may refer the application (except any claim for custody), or

any application for an order under section 27(5) of the Act of 1973, to the registrar for him to investigate the means of the parties to the marriage.

(5) Where an application is referred to the registrar under paragraph (4) he shall fix an appointment for the hearing of the application and the provisions of these Rules relating to ancillary relief shall apply subject to the modification that in rule 79(1) for the words from "In the case of" to "the same time" there shall be substituted the words "Except where the application is for an order made under section 27(5) of the Act of 1973 or the judge has made a finding that there has been wilful neglect to maintain".

(6) Where a person has been made a party cited, the judge may, if after the close of the evidence on the part of the respondent he is of opinion that there is not sufficient evidence against the party cited, dismiss him from the proceedings.

(7) Subject to the provisions of this and the last foregoing rule, these Rules shall, so far as applicable, apply, with the necessary modifications, to an application under section 27 of the Act of 1973 as if—

(*a*) the application were a cause, and

(*b*) the originating application were a petition and the applicant the petitioner.

Application for alteration of maintenance agreement during lifetime of parties

100.—(1) An application under section 35 of the Act of 1973 for the alteration of a maintenance agreement shall be made by originating application containing, unless otherwise directed, the information required by Form 21.

(2) The application may be filed in any divorce county court and may be heard and determined by the registrar.

(3) There shall be filed with the application an affidavit by the applicant exhibiting a copy of the agreement and verifying the statements in the application and also a copy of the application and of the affidavit for service on the respondent.

(4) C.C.R. Order 6, rule 4(2)(*c*)(ii) and (*d*) (which deal with the service of an originating application), shall not apply but there shall be annexed to the copy of the application for service a copy of the affidavit referred to in paragraph (2) and a notice in Form 20 with Form 6 attached.

(5) The respondent shall, within 14 days after the time limited for giving notice of intention to defend, file an affidavit in answer to the application containing full particulars of his property and income and, if he does not do so, the court may order him to file an affidavit containing such particulars.

(6) A respondent who files an affidavit under paragraph (5) shall at the same time file a copy which the registrar shall serve on the applicant.

(7) Rules 76, 77(4) to (7), 78 and 80 to 82 shall apply, with the necessary modifications, to an application under section 35 of the Act of 1973 as if it were an application for ancillary relief.

(8) Subject to the provisions of this rule, these Rules shall, so far as applicable, apply, with the necessary modifications, to an application under section 35 of the Act of 1973 as if the application were a cause, the originating application a petition, and the applicant the petitioner.

Application for alteration of maintenance agreement after death of one party

101.—(1) An application to the High Court under section 36 of the Act of 1973 for the alteration of a maintenance agreement after the death of one of the parties shall be made by originating summons in Form 22.

(2) The summons may be issued out of the divorce registry or any district registry.

(3) There shall be filed in support of the summons an affidavit by the applicant exhibiting a copy of the agreement and an official copy of the grant of representation to the deceased's estate and of every testamentary document admitted to proof and stating—

(*a*) whether the deceased died domiciled in England and Wales;

(*b*) the place and date of the marriage between the parties to the agreement and the name and status of the wife before the marriage;

(*c*) the name of every child of the family and of any other child for whom the agreement makes financial arrangements, and—

(i) the date of birth of each such child who is still living (or, if it be the case, that he has attained 18), and the place where and the person with whom any such minor child is residing,

(ii) the date of death of any such child who has died since the agreement was made;

(*d*) whether there have been in any court any, and if so what, previous proceedings with reference to the agreement or to the marriage or to the children of the family or to any other children for whom the agreement makes financial arrangements, and the date and effect of any order or decree made in such proceedings;

(*e*) whether there have been in any court any proceedings by the applicant against the deceased's estate under the Inheritance (Family Provision) Act 1938(**a**) and the date and effect of any order made in such proceedings;

(*f*) in the case of an application by the surviving party, the applicant's means;

(*g*) in the case of an application by the personal representatives of the deceased, the surviving party's means, so far as they are known to the applicants, and the information mentioned in sub-paragraph (*a*), (*b*) and (*c*) of rule 102(3);

(*h*) the facts alleged by the applicant as justifying an alteration in the agreement and the nature of the alteration sought;

(*i*) if the application is made after the end of the period of six months from the date on which representation in regard to the deceased's estate was first taken out, the grounds on which the court's permission to entertain the application is sought.

(4) There shall be lodged in the court office a copy of the summons and of the affidavit for service on every respondent.

(5) The registrar shall annex to every copy of the summons for service a copy of the affidavit in support and an acknowledgment of service in Form 6.

(**a**) 1938 c. 45.

Further proceedings on application under rule 101

102.—(1) Without prejudice to his powers under R.S.C. Order 15 (which deals with parties and other matters), the registrar may at any stage of the proceedings direct that any person be added as a respondent to an application under the last foregoing rule.

(2) R.S.C. Order 15, rule 13 (which enables the court to make representation orders in certain cases), shall apply to the proceedings as if they were mentioned in paragraph (1) of the said rule 13.

(3) A respondent who is a personal representative of the deceased shall, within 14 days after the time limited for giving notice of intention to defend, file an affidavit in answer to the application stating—

(*a*) full particulars of the value of the deceased's estate for probate, after providing for the discharge of the funeral, testamentary and administration expenses, debts and liabilities payable thereout, including the amount of the estate duty and interest thereon;

(*b*) the person or classes of persons beneficially interested in the estate (giving the names and addresses of all living beneficiaries) and the value of their interests so far as ascertained, and

(*c*) if such be the case, that any living beneficiary (naming him) is a minor or a patient within the meaning of rule 112.

(4) If a respondent who is a personal representative of the deceased does not file an affidavit stating the matters mentioned in paragraph (3), the registrar may order him to do so.

(5) A respondent who is not a personal representative of the deceased may, within 14 days after the time limited for giving notice of intention to defend, file an affidavit in answer to the application.

(6) Every respondent who files an affidavit in answer to the application shall at the same time lodge a copy, which the registrar shall serve on the applicant.

(7) The registrar shall, after investigating the allegations in support of and in answer to the application, report the result of his investigation in writing to a judge and the application shall be determined by a judge at the Royal Courts of Justice:

Provided that where the parties come to an agreement as to the terms of the order to be made on the application, an order in those terms may be made by the registrar.

(8) Paragraph (7) shall not affect the power of the judge under R.S.C. Order 4, rule 3 (which deals with transfer from one Division to another), to order the application to be transferred to the Chancery Division.

(9) Rules 76, 77(4) to (7), 79(3) and (4), 80(9) and (10) and 82(1) and (2) shall apply, with the necessary modifications, to an application under section 36 of the Act of 1973 as if it were an application for ancillary relief.

(10) Subject to the provisions of this rule, these Rules shall, so far as applicable, apply, with the necessary modifications, to an application under section 36 of the Act of 1973 as if the application were a cause, the originating summons a petition, and the applicant the petitioner.

Application for maintenance from deceased's estate

103.—(1) An application under section 26 of the Act of 1965 by the former spouse of a deceased person for an order that reasonable provision for his or her maintenance be made out of the net estate of the deceased shall be made by originating summons in Form 23.

(2) If the decree dissolving or annulling the applicant's marriage with the deceased was made in a cause proceeding in the divorce registry, the summons shall be issued out of that registry, and in any other case it may be issued out of the divorce registry or out of any district registry.

(3) There shall be filed in support of the summons an affidavit by the applicant exhibiting an official copy of the grant of representation to the deceased's estate and of every testamentary document admitted to proof and stating—

(*a*) the residence of the applicant;

(*b*) the place and date of the marriage between the applicant and the deceased and the name and status of the wife before the marriage;

(*c*) the name of any child of the family and—

(i) the date of birth of each such child who is still living (or, if such be the case, that he has attained 18), and the place where and the person with whom any such minor child is residing,

(ii) the date of death of any such child who has died since the marriage was dissolved or annulled;

(*d*) particulars of all previous proceedings with reference to the marriage or the children of the family, and the date and effect of any order or decree made in those proceedings;

(*e*) whether any such application as is mentioned in section 26(4)(*c*) of the Act of 1965 was made or deemed to be made by the applicant during the lifetime of the deceased and, if so, the date and effect of the order (if any) made on the application, or (if no such application was made by the applicant or such an application was made by the applicant and no order was made on the application) the reasons why no such application or order was made, in so far as they are within the applicant's knowledge or belief;

(*f*) the date of the deceased's death and whether he died domiciled in England and Wales;

(*g*) the applicant's means;

(*h*) the nature of the provision which the applicant desires to be made for his or her maintenance out of the deceased's estate;

(*i*) that the applicant has not remarried;

(*j*) if the application is made after the end of the period of six months from the date on which representation in regard to the deceased's estate was first taken out, the grounds on which the court's permission to entertain the application is sought.

(4) The procedure on an application to which this rule applies shall be the same as on an application to which rule 101 applies and paragraphs (4) and (5) of that rule and rule 102 shall apply accordingly, with any necessary modifications.

(5) On the hearing of the application the personal representatives shall produce to the judge the grant of representation to the deceased's estate and, if an order is made, the grant shall remain in the custody of the court until a memorandum of the order has been indorsed thereon or permanently affixed thereto.

Proceedings in High Court under section 17 of Act of 1882

104.—(1) An application to the High Court under section 17 of the Act of 1882 shall be made by originating summons in Form 24, which may be issued out of the divorce registry or a district registry, and at the same time the applicant shall, unless otherwise directed, file an affidavit in support of the summons and shall lodge in the court office a copy of the summons and of the affidavit for service on the respondent and on any mortgagee mentioned therein pursuant to paragraph (3).

(2) The jurisdiction of a judge of the High Court under the said section 17 may be exercised by a registrar.

(3) Where the application concerns the title to or possession of land, the originating summons or the affidavit in support shall—

(*a*) state, whether the title to the land is registered or unregistered, and, if registered, the Land Registry title number; and

(*b*) give particulars, so far as known to the applicant, of any mortgage of the land or any interest therein.

(4) The registrar shall annex to the copy of the originating summons for service on the respondent a copy of the affidavit in support and an acknowledgment of service in Form 6.

(5) Where particulars of a mortgage are given pursuant to paragraph (3), the registrar shall serve on the mortgagee a copy of the originating summons with a copy of the affidavit in support and any person so served shall be entitled to be heard on the application.

(6) No appearance need be entered to the originating summons.

(7) If the respondent intends to contest the application, he shall within 14 days after the time limited for giving notice to defend file an affidavit in answer to the application setting out the grounds on which he relies and lodge in the court office a copy of the affidavit for service by the registrar on the applicant.

(8) If the respondent fails to file an affidavit under paragraph (7), the registrar may by order specify a time within which the respondent must, if he wishes to defend, file an affidavit, and may, on or after making such an order, direct that the respondent shall be debarred from defending the application unless an affidavit is filed within that time.

(9) The registrar may grant an injunction in proceedings under the said section 17 if, but only so far as, the injunction is ancillary or incidental to any relief sought in those proceedings.

(10) Without prejudice to paragraph (7) of this rule, R.S.C. Order 28, rule 7 (which enables a counterclaim to be made in an action begun by originating

summons), shall apply, with the necessary modifications, to a respondent to an originating summons under this rule as it applies to a defendant who has entered an appearance to an originating summons.

(11) Rules 77(4) to (7), 78 and 82 shall apply, with the necessary modifications, to an application under section 17 of the Act of 1882 as they apply to an application for ancillary relief.

(12) Subject to the provisions of this rule, these Rules shall, so far as applicable, apply, with the necessary modifications, to an application under section 17 of the Act of 1882 as if the application were a cause, the originating summons a petition, and the applicant the petitioner.

Transfer of proceedings under section 17 *of Act of* 1882, *etc.*

105.—(1) The court in which an application under section 17 of the Act of 1882, section 26 of the Act of 1965 or section 36 of the Act of 1973 is pending may, if it is a county court, order the transfer of the application to the High Court or, if it is the High Court, order the transfer of the application to a divorce county court, where the transfer appears to the court to be desirable.

(2) In considering whether an application should be transferred under paragraph (1) from a county court to the High Court or from the High Court to a divorce county court, the court shall have regard to all relevant considerations, including the nature and value of the property involved, and, in the case of an application under section 26 of the Act of 1965 or section 36 of the Act of 1973, the limits for the time being of the jurisdiction of county courts under section 7 of the Family Provision Act 1966**(a)**.

(3) Rule 80(10) shall apply to an order under paragraph (1) of this rule as it applies to an order under paragraph (3) of that rule.

Exercise in divorce registry of county court jurisdiction under section 17 *of Act of* 1882, *etc.*

106.—(1) Where any proceedings for divorce, nullity or judicial separation pending in the divorce registry are treated as pending in a divorce county court, an application under section 17 of the Act of 1882 by one of the parties to the marriage may be made to the divorce registry as if it were a county court.

(2) In relation to proceedings begun in the divorce registry under paragraph (1) of this rule or transferred from the High Court to the divorce registry under rule 105(1)—

(*a*) section 4 of the Act of 1967 and the rules made thereunder shall have effect, with the necessary modifications, as they have effect in relation to proceedings begun in or transferred to the divorce registry under that section;

(*b*) C.C.R. Order 2, rule 13 (which relates to venue), and C.C.R. Order 46, rule 11(2) (which deals with reference to the registrar), shall not apply, and a registrar may exercise the jurisdiction conferred on a circuit judge by the said section 17.

(a) 1966 c. 35.

Proceedings under sections 1 *and* 7 *of Matrimonial Homes Act* 1967

107.—(1) The jurisdiction of the High Court under section 1 of the Matrimonial Homes Act 1967**(a)** may be exercised in chambers and the provisions of rule 104 (except paragraph (2)) shall apply, with the necessary modifications, to proceedings under that section as they apply to an application under section 17 of the Act of 1882.

(2) Where the applicant asks for an order under the said section 1 terminating the respondent's rights of occupation and it appears to the court, on the *ex parte* application of the applicant, that the respondent is not in occupation of the dwelling house to which the application relates and his whereabouts cannot after reasonable inquiries be ascertained, the court may dispense with service of the originating summons on him.

(3) The jurisdiction of the court under section 7 of the said Act of 1967 may be exercised by the registrar.

(4) Where an application is made for an order under the said section 7, notice of the application (or, in the High Court, the summons by which the application is made) shall be served on—

(*a*) the spouse entitled as mentioned in subsection (1) of that section to occupy the dwelling house to which the application relates, and

(*b*) the landlord of the dwelling house,

and any person so served shall be entitled to be heard on the application.

Proceedings in respect of polygamous marriage

108.—(1) The provisions of this rule shall have effect where a petition, originating application or originating summons asks for matrimonial relief within the meaning of section 47(2) of the Act of 1973 in respect of a marriage entered into under a law which permits polygamy (in this rule referred to as a polygamous marriage).

(2) The petition, originating application or originating summons—

(*a*) shall state that the marriage in question is polygamous;

(*b*) shall state whether or not there is, to the knowledge of the petitioner or applicant, any living spouse of his or hers additional to the respondent or, as the case may be, any living spouse of the respondent additional to the petitioner or applicant (in this rule referred to as an additional spouse); and

(*c*) if there is any additional spouse, shall give his or her full name and address and the date and place of his or her marriage to the petitioner or applicant or, as the case may be, to the respondent, or state, so far as may be applicable, that such information is unknown to the petitioner or applicant.

(3) Without prejudice to its powers under R.S.C. Order 15 (which deals with parties) or C.C.R. Order 15 (which deals with amendment), the court may order that any additional spouse be added as a party to the proceedings or be given notice of the proceedings or of any application in the proceedings for any such order as is mentioned in section 47(2)(*d*) of the Act of 1973.

(a) 1967 c. 75.

(4) Any order under paragraph (3) may be made at any stage of the proceedings and either on the application of any party or by the court of its own motion and, where an additional spouse is mentioned in a petition or an acknowledgement of service of a petition, the petitioner shall, on making any application in the proceedings or, if no previous application has been made in the proceedings, on making a request for directions for trial, ask for directions as to whether an order should be made under paragraph (3).

(5) Any person to whom notice is given pursuant to an order under paragraph (3) shall be entitled, without filing an answer or affidavit, to be heard in the proceedings or on the application to which the notice relates.

Application for declaration affecting matrimonial status

109.—(1) Where, apart from costs, the only relief sought in any proceedings is a declaration with respect to a person's matrimonial status, the proceedings shall be begun by petition.

(2) The petition shall state—

(*a*) the names of the parties and the residential address of each of them at the date of presentation of the petition;

(*b*) the place and date of any ceremony of marriage to which the application relates;

(*c*) whether there have been any previous proceedings in any court in England and Wales or elsewhere between the parties with reference to the marriage or the ceremony of marriage to which the application relates or with respect to the matrimonial status of either of them, and, if so, the nature of the proceedings;

(*d*) all other material facts alleged by the petitioner to justify the making of the declaration and the grounds on which he alleges that the court has jurisdiction to make it;

and shall conclude with a prayer setting out the declaration sought and any claim for costs.

(3) Nothing in the foregoing provisions shall be construed—

(*a*) as conferring any jurisdiction to make a declaration in circumstances in which the court could not otherwise make it, or

(*b*) as affecting the power of the court to refuse to make a declaration notwithstanding that it has jurisdiction to make it.

(4) This rule does not apply to proceedings to which rule 110 applies.

Application under section 45 *of Act of* 1973

110.—(1) A petition by which proceedings in the High Court are begun under section 45 of the Act of 1973 shall, in addition to stating the grounds on which the petitioner relies, set out the date and place of birth of the petitioner and the maiden name of his mother, and, if the petitioner is known by a name other than that which appears in the certificate of his birth, that fact shall be stated in the petition and in any decree made thereon.

(2) The petition shall be supported by an affidavit by the petitioner verifying the petition and giving particulars of every person whose interest may be affected by the proceedings and his relationship to the petitioner:

Provided that if the petitioner is under 16, the affidavit shall, unless otherwise directed, be made by his next friend:

(3) An affidavit for the purposes of paragraph (2) may contain statements of information or belief with the sources and grounds thereof.

(4) On filing the petition the petitioner shall issue and serve on the Attorney-General a summons for directions as to the persons, other than the Attorney-General, who are to be made respondents to the petition.

(5) It shall not be necessary to serve the petition on the Attorney-General otherwise than by delivering a copy of it to him in accordance with subsection (6) of the said section 45.

(6) The Attorney-General may file an answer to the petition within 21 days after directions have been given under paragraph (4) and no directions for trial shall be given until that period has expired.

(7) A respondent who files an answer shall at the same time lodge in the divorce registry as many copies of the answer as there are other parties to the proceedings and the registrar shall send one of the copies to each of those parties.

General provisions as to proceedings under rule 109 *or* 110

111.—(1) Proceedings to which rule 109 or 110 relates shall be begun in the divorce registry.

(2) Where the proceedings are proceedings for a declaration as to the validity or subsistence of a marriage of the petitioner, rule 9(2) shall apply to the petition as if it were a petition for divorce.

(3) Unless a judge otherwise directs, the trial of the proceedings shall take place at the Royal Courts of Justice.

(4) Subject to rules 109 and 110 and paragraphs (2) and (3) of this rule, these Rules shall, so far as applicable, apply, with the necessary modifications, to the proceedings as if they were a cause.

DISABILITY

Person under disability must sue by next friend, etc.

112.—(1) In this rule—

"patient" means a person who, by reason of mental disorder within the meaning of the Mental Health Act 1959**(a)**, is incapable of managing and administering his property and affairs;

"person under disability" means a person who is a minor or a patient;

"Part VIII" means Part VIII of the Mental Health Act 1959.

(2) A person under disability may begin and prosecute any matrimonial proceedings by his next friend and may defend any such proceedings by his guardian *ad litem* and, except as otherwise provided by this rule, it shall not be necessary for a guardian *ad litem* to be appointed by the court.

(a) 1959 c. 72.

(3) No person's name shall be used in any proceedings as next friend of a person under disability unless he is the Official Solicitor or the documents mentioned in paragraph (8) have been filed.

(4) Where a person is authorised under Part VIII to conduct legal proceedings in the name of a patient or on his behalf, that person shall, subject to paragraph (3), be entitled to be next friend or guardian *ad litem* of the patient in any matrimonial proceedings to which his authority extends.

(5) Where a person entitled to defend any matrimonial proceedings is a patient and there is no person authorised under Part VIII to defend the proceedings in his name or on his behalf, then—

(*a*) the Official Solicitor shall, if he consents, be the patient's guardian *ad litem*, but at any stage of the proceedings an application may be made on not less than four days' notice to the Official Solicitor, for the appointment of some other person as guardian;

(*b*) in any other case, an application may be made on behalf of the patient for the appointment of a guardian *ad litem*;

and there shall be filed in support of any application under this paragraph the documents mentioned in paragraph (8).

(6) Where a petition, answer, originating application or originating summons has been served on a person whom there is reasonable ground for believing to be a person under disability and no notice of intention to defend has been given, or answer or affidavit in answer filed, on his behalf, the party at whose instance the document was served shall, before taking any further step in the proceedings, apply to a registrar for directions as to whether a guardian *ad litem* should be appointed to act for that person in the cause, and on any such application the registrar may, if he considers it necessary in order to protect the interests of the person served, order that some proper person be appointed his guardian *ad litem*.

(7) No notice of intention to defend shall be given, or answer or affidavit in answer filed, by or on behalf of a person under disability unless the person giving the notice or filing the answer or affidavit—

(*a*) is the Official Solicitor or, in a case to which paragraph (5) applies, is the Official Solicitor or has been appointed by the court to be guardian *ad litem*; or

(*b*) in any other case, has filed the documents mentioned in paragraph (8).

(8) The documents referred to in paragraphs (3), (5) and (7) are—

(*a*) a written consent to act by the proposed next friend or guardian *ad litem*;

(*b*) where the person under disability is a patient and the proposed next friend or guardian *ad litem* is authorised under Part VIII to conduct the proceedings in his name or on his behalf, an office copy, sealed with the seal of the Court of Protection, of the order or other authorisation made or given under Part VIII; and

(*c*) except where the proposed next friend or guardian *ad litem* is authorised as mentioned in sub-paragraph (*b*), a certificate by the solicitor acting for the person under disability—

(i) that he knows or believes that the person to whom the certificate relates is a minor or patient stating (in the case of a patient) the grounds of his knowledge or belief and, where the person under disability is a patient, that there is no person authorised as aforesaid, and

(ii) that the person named in the certificate as next friend or guardian *ad litem* has no interest in the cause or matter in question adverse to that of the person under disability and that he is a proper person to be next friend or guardian.

Service on person under disability

113.—(1) Where a document to which rule 14 applies is required to be served on a person under disability within the meaning of the last foregoing rule, it shall be served—

(*a*) in the case of a minor who is not also a patient, on his father or guardian or, if he has no father or guardian, on the person with whom he resides or in whose care he is;

(*b*) in the case of a patient—

(i) on the person (if any) who is authorised under Part VIII of the Mental Health Act 1959 to conduct in the name of the patient or on his behalf the proceedings in connection with which the document is to be served, or

(ii) if there is no person so authorised, on the Official Solicitor if he has consented under rule 112(5) to be the guardian *ad litem* of the patient, or

(iii) in any other case, on the person with whom the patient resides or in whose care he is:

Provided that the court may order that a document which has been, or is to be, served on the person under disability or on a person other than one mentioned in sub-paragraph (*a*) or (*b*) shall be deemed to be duly served on the person under disability.

(2) Where a document is served in accordance with paragraph (1), it shall be indorsed with a notice in Form 25; and after service has been effected the person at whose instance the document was served shall, unless the Official Solicitor is the guardian *ad litem* of the person under disability or the court otherwise directs, file an affidavit by the person on whom the document was served stating whether the contents of the document were, or its purport was, communicated to the person under disability and, if not, the reasons for not doing so.

Petition for nullity on ground of insanity, etc.

114.—(1) Where a petition for nullity has been presented on the ground that at the time of the marriage the respondent was suffering from mental disorder within the meaning of the Mental Health Act 1959 of such a kind or to such an extent as to be unfitted for marriage, then, whether or not the respondent gives notice of intention to defend, the petitioner shall not proceed with the cause without the leave of the registrar.

(2) The registrar by whom an application for leave is heard may make it a condition of granting leave that some proper person be appointed to act as guardian *ad litem* of the respondent.

Separate representation of children

115.—(1) Without prejudice to rule 72, if in any matrimonial proceedings it appears to the court that any child ought to be separately represented, the court may—

(*a*) of its own motion, appoint the Official Solicitor if he consents, or

(*b*) on the application of any other proper person, appoint that person to be guardian *ad litem* of the child with authority to take part in the proceedings on the child's behalf.

(2) The applicant for an order under paragraph (1)(*b*) shall, on making the application, file a certificate by a solicitor certifying that the person named in the certificate as the proposed guardian *ad litem* has no interest in the proceedings adverse to that of the child and that he is a proper person to be such guardian.

PROCEDURE: GENERAL

Security for costs

116. C.C.R. Order 3, rule 1 (which requires a person bringing proceedings to give security for costs if he is not resident in England or Wales), shall not apply to matrimonial proceedings in a county court.

Service out of England and Wales

117.—(1) Any document in matrimonial proceedings may be served out of England and Wales without leave either in the manner prescribed by these Rules or—

(*a*) where the proceedings are pending in the High Court, in accordance with R.S.C. Order 11, rules 5 and 6 (which relate to the service of a writ abroad); or

(*b*) where the proceedings are pending in a divorce county court, in accordance with C.C.R. Order 8, rules 46 to 48 (which relate to the service of process abroad).

(2) Where the document is served in accordance with R.S.C. Order 11, rules 5 and 6, those rules and rule 8 of the said Order 11 (which deals with the expenses incurred by the Secretary of State) shall have effect in relation to service of the document as they have effect in relation to service of notice of a writ, except that the official certificate of service referred to in paragraph (5) of the said rule 5 shall, if the document was served personally, show the server's means of knowledge of the identity of the person served.

(3) Where the document is served in accordance with C.C.R. Order 8, rules 46 to 48, those rules shall have effect subject to the following modifications:—

(*a*) paragraph (5) of the said rule 46 (which in certain circumstances requires the document to be annexed to a notice of process) shall not apply;

(*b*) the document need not be served personally on the person required to be served so long as it is served in accordance with the law of the country in which service is effected;

(*c*) the official certificate or declaration with regard to service referred to in paragraph (6) of the said rule 48 shall, if the document was served personally, show the server's means of knowledge of the identity of the person served; and

(*d*) in paragraph (7) of the said rule 48 (which deals with the method of service through the court) the words "or in the manner in which default summonses are required to be served" shall be omitted.

(4) Where a petition is to be served on a person out of England and Wales, then—

(*a*) the time within which that person must give notice of intention to defend shall be determined having regard to the practice adopted under R.S.C. Order 11, rule 4(4) (which requires an order for leave to serve a writ out of the jurisdiction to limit the time for appearance), and the notice in Form 5 shall be amended accordingly;

(*b*) if the petition is to be served otherwise than in accordance with R.S.C. Order 11, rules 5 and 6, or C.C.R. Order 8, rules 46 to 48, and there is reasonable ground for believing that the person to be served does not understand English, the petition shall be accompanied by a translation, approved by the registrar, of the notice in Form 5, in the official language of the country in which service is to be effected or, if there is more than one official language of that country, in any one of those languages which is appropriate to the place where service is to be effected:

Provided that this sub-paragraph shall not apply in relation to a document which is to be served in a country in which the official language, or one of the official languages, is English.

(5) Where a document specifying the date of hearing of any proceedings is to be served out of England and Wales, the date shall be fixed having regard to the time which would be limited under paragraph (4)(*a*) for giving notice of intention to defend if the document were a petition.

Service by post

118. Where a document is required by these rules to be sent to any person, it shall, unless otherwise directed, be sent by post—

(*a*) if a solicitor is acting for him, to the solicitor's address;

(*b*) if he is acting in person, to the address for service given by him or, if he has not given an address for service, his last known address, but if in the opinion of the registrar the document would be unlikely to reach him if sent to that address, the registrar may dispense with sending the document to him.

Service of documents where no special mode of service prescribed

119. Unless otherwise directed, service of any document in matrimonial proceedings shall, if no other mode of service is prescribed or ordered, be effected—

(*a*) if a solicitor is acting for the person to be served, by leaving the document at, or sending it by post to, the solicitor's address;

(*b*) if the person to be served is acting in person, by delivering the document to him or by leaving it at, or sending it by post to, the address for service given by him or, if he has not given an address for service, his last known address:

Provided that where, in a case to which sub-paragraph (*b*) applies, it appears to the registrar that it is impracticable to deliver the document to the person to be served and that, if the document were left at, or sent by post to, the address specified in that sub-paragraph, it would be unlikely to reach him, the registrar may dispense with service of the document.

Service by bailiff in proceedings in divorce registry

120. Where, in any proceedings pending in the divorce registry which are treated as pending in a divorce county court, a document is to be served by bailiff, it shall be sent for service to the registrar of the county court within the district of which the document is to be served.

Proof of service by officer of court, etc.

121.—(1) Where a petition is sent to any person by an officer of the court, he shall indorse on a copy of Form 5 the date of posting and the address written on the letter and shall sign the indorsement and add the name of the court or registry to which he is attached.

(2) Without prejudice to section 186 of the County Courts Act 1959, an indorsement made pursuant to paragraph (1) shall be evidence of the facts stated therein.

(3) Where the court has authorised notice by advertisement to be substituted for service and the advertisement has been inserted by some person other than the registrar, that person shall file copies of the newspapers containing the advertisement.

Mode of making applications

122.—(1) Except where these Rules, or any rules applied by these Rules, otherwise provide, every application in matrimonial proceedings—

(*a*) shall be made to a registrar;

(*b*) shall, if the proceedings are pending in the High Court, be made by summons or, if the proceedings are pending in a divorce county court, be made in accordance with C.C.R. Order 13, rule 1 (which deals with applications in the course of proceedings).

(2) For the purposes of paragraph (1), C.C.R. Order 13, rule 1, shall have effect as if for the period of one clear day mentioned in paragraph (1)(*b*)(i) of that rule (which prescribes the length of notice to be given) there were substituted a period of two clear days.

Place of hearing of application by judge

123.—(1) Any application in a cause which is to be heard by a judge otherwise than at the trial may, except where these Rules otherwise provide or the court otherwise directs, be heard—

(*a*) if the cause is pending in the High Court—

(i) at the Royal Courts of Justice, or

(ii) in the case of an application in a cause proceeding in a district registry, at the divorce town in which that registry is situated or, if it is not situated in a divorce town, then at the appropriate divorce town, or

(iii) in the case of an application in a cause which has been set down for trial at a divorce town, at that town;

(*b*) if the cause is pending in a divorce county court—

(i) at that court if it is a court of trial and otherwise at the appropriate court of trial, or

(ii) in the case of an application in a cause which has been set down for trial at a court of trial, at that court.

(2) In this rule "application" includes an appeal from an order or decision made or given by the registrar and "appropriate divorce town" and "appropriate court of trial" mean such divorce town or court of trial as in the opinion of the registrar is the nearest or most convenient.

Appeal from registrar in county court proceedings

124.—(1) C.C.R. Order 13, rule 1(1)(*h*) (which enables the judge to vary or rescind an order made by the registrar in the course of proceedings), and C.C.R. Order 37, rule 5 (which gives a right of appeal to the judge from a judgment or final decision of the registrar), shall not apply to an order or decision made or given by the registrar in matrimonial proceedings pending in a divorce county court, but any party may appeal from such an order or decision to a judge on notice filed within five days after the order or decision was made or given and served not less than two clear days before the day fixed for hearing of the appeal, which shall be heard in chambers unless the judge otherwise orders.

(2) Except so far as may be otherwise ordered, an appeal under paragraph (1) shall not operate as a stay of proceedings on the order or decision appealed against.

No notice of intention to proceed after year's delay

125. R.S.C. Order 3, rule 6 (which requires a party to give notice of intention to proceed after a year's delay), shall not apply to any matrimonial proceedings pending in the High Court.

Filing of documents at place of hearing, etc.

126. Where the file of any matrimonial proceedings has been sent from one divorce county court or registry to another for the purpose of a hearing or for some other purpose, any document needed for that purpose and required to be filed shall be filed in the other court or registry.

Mode of giving notice

127. Unless otherwise directed, any notice which is required by these Rules to be given to any person shall be in writing and, if it is to be given by the registrar, shall be given by post.

Removal of proceedings to High Court under section 115 *of County Courts Act* 1959

128.—(1) The power of the High Court or a judge thereof under section 115 of the County Courts Act 1959 to order the removal into the High Court, otherwise than by order of certiorari, of matrimonial proceedings pending in a divorce county court may be exercised by a registrar of the divorce registry or by the registrar of any district registry having that county court within its district, except where a judge of the county court has refused to order the transfer of the proceedings to the High Court.

(2) Proceedings for the exercise of the power shall be begun by originating summons.

No appearance need be entered to the summons.

(3) Rule 129(3) shall have effect in relation to an order for the removal of matrimonial proceedings into the High Court as if it were an order for the transfer of the proceedings to the High Court.

(4) Where by virtue of any provision of these Rules a county court has power to order that any proceedings pending in the court be transferred to the High Court, the High Court shall have power, exercisable in the like circumstances, to order the removal of the proceedings into the High Court, and the foregoing paragraphs of this rule shall apply as if the power conferred by this paragraph were conferred by the said section 115.

Procedure on transfer of cause or application

129.—(1) Where any cause or application is ordered to be transferred from one court or registry to another, the registrar of the first-mentioned court or registry shall, unless otherwise directed, give notice of the transfer to the parties and send a copy of the notice and the file of the proceedings to the registrar of the other court or registry.

(2) Any provision in these Rules, or in any order made or notice given pursuant to these Rules, for the transfer of proceedings between a divorce county court and the High Court shall, in relation to proceedings which, after the transfer, are to continue in the divorce registry, be construed—

(*a*) in the case of a transfer from the High Court to a divorce county court, as a provision for the proceedings to be treated as pending in a divorce county court, and

(*b*) in the case of a transfer from a divorce county court to the High Court, as a provision for the proceedings no longer to be treated as pending in a divorce county court.

(3) Proceedings transferred from a divorce county court to the High Court pursuant to any provision in these Rules shall, unless the order of transfer otherwise directs, proceed in the registry nearest to the divorce county court from which they are transferred, but nothing in this paragraph shall prejudice any power under these Rules to order the transfer of the proceedings to a different registry.

MISCELLANEOUS

Inspection etc. of documents retained in court

130.—(1) A party to any matrimonial proceedings or his solicitor or the Queen's Proctor may have a search made for, and may inspect and bespeak a copy of, any document filed or lodged in the court office in those proceedings.

(2) Except as provided by rules 48(3) and 95(3) and paragraph (1) of this rule, no document filed or lodged in the court office other than a decree or order made in open court, shall be open to inspection by any person without the leave of the registrar, and no copy of any such document, or of an extract from any such document, shall be taken by, or issued to, any person without such leave.

Practice to be observed in district registries and divorce county courts

131.—(1) The President and the senior registrar may, with the concurrence of the Lord Chancellor, issue directions for the purpose of securing in the district registries and the divorce county courts due observance of statutory requirements and uniformity of practice in matrimonial proceedings.

(2) R.S.C. Order 63, rule 11 (which requires the practice of the Central Office to be followed in the district registries), shall not apply to matrimonial proceedings.

Revocations

132. The rules specified in column 1 of the Schedule to these Rules are hereby revoked to the extent specified in column 2 of the Schedule, so, however, that the provisions of those rules in force immediately before 11th January 1974 shall continue to apply to such extent as may be necessary for giving effect to the transitional provisions and savings in the Act of 1973.

Dated 29th November 1973.

Hailsham of St. Marylebone, C.
George Baker, P.
John Latey, J.
Ifor Lloyd.
Irvon Sunderland.
W. D. S. Caird.
J. L. Williams.
F. B. Purchas.
Margaret Puxon.
J. D. Clarke.
D. E. Morris.

SCHEDULE

Rule 132

RULES REVOKED

Title and Reference	*Extent of Revocation*
The Rules of the Supreme Court 1965 (S.I. 1965/1776 (1965 III, p. 4995), as amended **(a)**)	Order 89, rules 1 and 3 Order 90, rules 13, 14 and 15
The Matrimonial Causes Rules 1971 (S.I. 1971/953 (1971 II, p. 2713))	The whole Instrument
The Matrimonial Causes (Amendment) Rules 1971 (S.I. 1971/1923 (1971 III, p. 5243))	The whole Instrument
The Matrimonial Causes (Amendment) Rules 1972 (S.I. 1972/1095 (1972 II, p. 3248))	The whole Instrument
The Matrimonial Causes (Amendment) Rules 1973 (S.I. 1973/777 (1973 I, p. 2459))	The whole Instrument
The Matrimonial Causes (Amendment No. 2) Rules 1973 (S.I. 1973/1413 (1973 II, p. 4340))	The whole Instrument
The Matrimonial Causes (Amendment No. 3) Rules 1973 (S.I. 1973/1973)	The whole Instrument

(a) The relevant amending instruments are S.I. 1967/1809, 1968/1244, 1971/1269, 1971/1955 (1967 III, p. 4832; 1968 II, p. 3360; 1971 II, p. 3634; III, p. 5274).

APPENDIX

FORMS

Rule 5(3)

Form 1

NOTICE OF APPLICATION UNDER RULE 5

In the County Court
[Divorce Registry]
No. of
Matter

(Seal)

In the Matter of a proposed petition for dissolution of marriage

Between Applicant

and Respondent

TAKE NOTICE THAT an application has been made by the above-named Applicant for leave to present a petition for dissolution of his [her] marriage with you before the expiration of the period of three years from the date of the said marriage. If the application is undefended, it will be heard at County Court [*insert address of court-house*] on the day of 19 , at o'clock, and if you do not attend at that time and place, such order will be made as the Court thinks just.

A sealed copy of the application and of the affidavit to be used in support of the application is delivered with this notice.

You must complete and detach the acknowledgment of service and send it so as to reach the Court within eight days after you receive this notice, inclusive of the day of receipt. Delay in returning the form may add to the costs. If the reply to Question 4 in the acknowledgment is Yes, the application will be transferred to the High Court and will not be heard at the place and time above-mentioned. If you intend to instruct a solicitor to act for you, you should at once give him all the documents which have been served on you, so that he may send the acknowledgment to the Court on your behalf.

Dated this day of 19 .

Registrar

To the Respondent

[*Here set out Form* 6]

Rule 9(1)

Form 2

GENERAL FORM OF PETITION

In the County Court
[Divorce Registry]
No. of
Matter

THE PETITION OF SHOWS THAT—

(1) On the day of 19 the petitioner was lawfully married to (hereinafter called the respondent) at

(2) The petitioner and the respondent have cohabited at [*state the last address at which they have cohabited in England or Wales*] [*or* The petitioner and the respondent have not cohabited in England or Wales].

(3) [*In the case of a petition for divorce, nullity, judicial separation or presumption of death and dissolution of marriage where it is alleged that the court has jurisdiction based on domicile*] The petitioner is domiciled in England and Wales [*or* The petitioner is domiciled in and the respondent is domiciled in England and Wales] [*or, where it is alleged that*

the court has jurisdiction based on habitual residence] The petitioner has [*or* The respondent has] [*or* The petitioner and the respondent have] been habitually resident in England and Wales throughout the period of one year ending with the date of the presentation of the petition [*or as the case may be*] [*give details of the habitual residence relied on including the addresses of places of residence during the one year period and the length of residence at each place*]; the petitioner is a [*state occupation*] [and resides at], and the respondent is a [*state occupation*] [and resides at].

(4) There is [are] [no [*or state number*] child[ren] of the family now living] [namely [*state the full names (including surname) of each child and his date of birth or, if it be the case, that he is over 18 and in the case of each minor child over the age of 16, whether he is receiving instruction at an educational establishment or undergoing training for a trade, profession or vocation*]].

(5) [*In the case of a husband's petition*] No other child now living has been born to the respondent during the marriage so far as is known to the petitioner [*or in the case of a wife's petition*] No other child now living has been born to the petitioner during the marriage [except [*state the name of any such child and his date of birth, or if it be the case, that he is over 18*]].

(6) [*Where there is a dispute whether a child is a child of the family*] The petitioner alleges that is [not] a child of the family because [*give full particulars of the facts relied on by the petitioner in support of his or her allegation that the child is or, as the case may be, is not, a child of the family*].

(7) [*Where appropriate in the case of a child who is under 18*] The said was, on the day of 19 , received into the care of [*or* is a child with respect to whom a resolution was, on the day of 19 , passed by] [*name of local authority*] under section 1 [*or* 2] of the Children Act 1948.

(8) [*Where an application is made in the petition for an order for the support of a child of whom the respondent is not a parent*] The respondent assumed responsibility for the maintenance of the said to the following extent and for the following time namely [*give details*]. There is no other person liable to maintain the said child [except].

(9) There have been no previous proceedings in any court in England and Wales or elsewhere with reference to the marriage [or to any children of the family] [or between the petitioner and the respondent with reference to any property of either or both of them] [except [*state the nature of the proceedings, the date and effect of any decree or order and, in the case of proceedings with reference to the marriage, whether there has been any resumption of cohabitation since the making of the decree or order*]].

(10) There are no proceedings continuing in any country outside England and Wales which are in respect of the marriage or are capable of affecting its validity or subsistence [except [*give particulars of the proceedings, including the court in or tribunal or authority before which they were begun, the date when they were begun, the names of the parties, the date or expected date of any trial in the proceedings and such other facts as may be relevant to the question whether the proceedings on the petition should be stayed under Schedule 1 to the Domicile and Matrimonial Proceedings Act* 1973]].

(11) The following [*or* No] agreement or arrangement has been made or is proposed to be made between the parties for the support of the respondent [*or* the petitioner] [and the said children] [namely [*state details*]].

(12) [*In the case of a petition for divorce alleging five years' separation*] The petitioner proposes, if a decree nisi is granted, to make the following financial provision for the respondent [*give details of any proposal not mentioned in paragraph* (11)] [*or* The petitioner makes no proposals for financial provision for the respondent in the event of a decree nisi being granted].

(13) [*In the case of a petition for divorce*] The said marriage has broken down irretrievably.

(14) The respondent has committed adultery with and the petitioner finds it intolerable to live with the respondent [*or* The respondent has behaved in such a way that the petitioner cannot reasonably be expected to live with the respondent] [*or* The respondent has deserted the petitioner for a continuous period of at least two years immediately preceding the presentation of this petition] [*or* The parties to the marriage have lived apart for a continuous period of at least two years immediately preceding the presentation of this petition and the respondent consents to a decree being granted] [*or* The parties to the marriage have lived apart for a continous period of at least five years immediately preceding the presentation of the petition] [*or, where the petition is not for divorce or judicial separation, set out the ground on which relief is sought, and in any case state with sufficient particularity the facts relied on but not the evidence by which they are to be proved*].

The petitioner therefore prays—

(1) That the said marriage may be dissolved [*or* declared void] [*or* annulled] [*or as the case may be*].

(2) That he [she] may be granted the custody of [*state name*[*s*] *of the child*[*ren*] *and add any application for a declaration under section* 42(3) *of the Matrimonial Causes Act* 1973].

(3) [*Where appropriate*] That may be ordered to pay the costs of this suit.

(4) That he [she] may be granted the following ancillary relief, namely [*state particulars of any application for ancillary relief which it is intended to claim*].

The names and addresses of the persons who are to be served with this petition are [*give particulars, stating if any of them is a person under disability*].

The petitioner's address for service is [*Where the petitioner sues by a solicitor, state the solicitor's name or firm and address, or, where the petitioner sues in person, state his place of residence as given in paragraph* 3 *of the petition or, if no place of residence in England or Wales is given, the address of a place in England or Wales at or to which documents for him may be delivered or sent*].

Dated this day of 19 .

Note: Under the Matrimonial Causes Rules 1973 *further information is required in certain cases.*

Rule 12(3)

Form 3

Certificate with Regard to Reconciliation

[*Heading as in Form* 5]

I, , the solicitor acting for the petitioner in the above cause do hereby certify that I have [*or* have not] discussed with the petitioner the possibility of a reconciliation and that I have [*or* have not] given to the petitioner the names and addresses of persons qualified to help effect a reconciliation.

Dated this day of 19 .

Signed

Solicitor for the Petitioner

Rule 8(2)

Form 4

STATEMENT AS TO ARRANGEMENTS FOR CHILDREN

[*Heading as in Form 5*]

The present arrangements for the minor children of the family under 16 and those over 16 who are receiving instruction at an educational establishment or undergoing training for a trade, profession or vocation are as follows:—[*State in respect of each child*]

(i) residence [*state where the child is living, particulars of the accommodation, what other persons (naming them) live there and who looks after the child*]

(ii) education etc. [*state the school or other educational establishment which the child is attending or, if he is working, his place of employment, the nature of his work and details of any training he is receiving*]

(iii) financial provision [*state who is supporting the child or contributing to his support and the extent thereof*]

(iv) access [*state any arrangements which have been agreed for access by either of the parties and the extent to which access is and has been afforded*].

The arrangements proposed for the children in the event of a decree being granted are as follows:—

(i) residence

(ii) education, etc.

(iii) financial provision

(iv) access.

[*In each of these paragraphs state whether the grant of a decree will affect the present arrangements set out above, whether it is proposed that those arrangements should continue, and if not, and to the extent that they are likely to alter, state what alteration is anticipated and what proposals in substitution are proposed. In the case of residence, where it is proposed that for any period a child should be in the immediate care of a person other than the petitioner, give details of that person's willingness and ability to care for the child. In the case of education state, if possible, any long-term proposals for further education or training. In the case of financial provision give details of any application which will be made for ancillary relief in respect of the children and, where applicable, state the object of any application which is other than for the day-to-day support of the child.*]

The said child[ren] is [are] [not] suffering from [any] serious disability or chronic illness or from the effects of [any] serious illness [namely [*state, in respect of each child so suffering, the nature of the disability or illness and attach a copy of any up-to-date medical report which is available*]].

The said child[ren] is [are] [not] under the care or supervision of a welfare officer or officer appointed by a local authority or other person or organisation [namely [*state the date of any order for care or supervision and the circumstances which gave rise to its being made*]].

Dated this day of 19 .

Signed

[Solicitor for the] Petitioner

Rule 12(6)

Form 5

NOTICE OF PROCEEDINGS

In the County Court(1) [Divorce Registry]

(1) Amend if the proceedings are pending in High Court.

No. of Matter

(Seal)

Between Petitioner

and Respondent

[and Co-Respondent]

TAKE NOTICE THAT a petition [for divorce] (2) has been presented to this Court. A sealed copy of it [and a copy of the petitioner's proposals regarding the children] [is] [are] delivered with this notice.

(2) Or as the case may be.

1. You must complete and detach the acknowledgment of service and send it so as to reach the Court within eight days after you receive this notice, inclusive of the day of receipt. Delay in returning the form may add to the costs.

2. (3) If you wish to do so, you may send to the Court a statement setting out your views on the proposals regarding the children. If you send a statement it will be placed before the Judge dealing with the arrangements for the child[ren] and a copy of your statement will be sent to the petitioner.

(3) Delete if inapplicable.

3. If the reply to Question 4 [or 6] (3) in the acknowledgment is Yes, you must, within 29 days after you receive this notice, inclusive of the day of receipt, file in the Court office an answer to the petition (2), together with a copy for every other party to the proceedings. The case will then be transferred to the High Court (4).

(4) Delete if case has already been transferred to High Court.

4. (3) If the reply to Question 5 in the acknowledgment is Yes, the consequences to you are that—

(*a*) provided the petitioner establishes the fact that the parties to the marriage have lived apart for two years immediately preceding the presentation of the petition and that you consent, a decree will be granted unless, in the case of a petition for divorce, the Court is satisfied that the marriage has not broken down irretrievably;

(*b*) your right to inherit from the petitioner if he or she dies without having made a will ceases on the grant of a decree of judicial separation or on a decree nisi of divorce being made absolute;

(*c*) in the case of divorce the making absolute of the decree will end the marriage thereby affecting any right to a pension which depends upon the marriage continuing or upon your being left a widow; the State widow's pension will not be payable to you when the petitioner dies, and any rights of occupation you may have in the matrimonial home under the Matrimonial Homes Act 1967 will cease unless the Court directs otherwise during the subsistence of the marriage;

(*d*) apart from the consequences listed above there may be others applicable to you depending on your particular circumstances. About these you should obtain legal advice from a solicitor.

5. (3) If after consenting you wish to withdraw your consent you must immediately inform the Court and give notice to the petitioner.

6. (3) The petitioner relies in support of the petition on the fact that the parties to the marriage have lived apart for at least five years. Section 10 of the Matrimonial Causes Act 1973 provides that if in such a case the respondent applies to the Court for it to consider the respondent's financial

position after the divorce, a decree nisi based on five years' separation only cannot be made absolute unless the Court is satisfied that the petitioner has made or will make proper financial provision for the respondent, or else that the petitioner should not be required to make any financial provision for the respondent. Paragraph (12) of the petition will tell you whether the petitioner proposes to make any financial provision for you. It is important that you should consider this information carefully before answering Question 7 in the acknowledgment.

7. (3) If the reply to Question 7 in the acknowledgment is Yes, you must, before the decree is made absolute, make application to the Court by filing and serving on the petitioner a notice in Form 12, which may be obtained from the Court.

8. If you intend to instruct a solicitor to act for you, you should at once give him all the documents which have been served on you, so that he may send the acknowledgment to the Court on your behalf. If you do not intend to instruct a solicitor, you should nevertheless give an address for service in the acknowledgment so that any documents affecting your interests which are sent to you will in fact reach you. Change of address should be notified to the Court.

Dated this day of 19 .

Registrar

To

[*Here set out Form* 6]

Rule 14(5)

Form 6

ACKNOWLEDGMENT OF SERVICE

If you intend to instruct a solicitor to act for you, give him this form immediately.

[*Heading as in Form* 5]

(2) Or as the case may be.

1. Have you received the originating application [*or* summons] [and copy of the supporting affidavit] [*or* the petition for [divorce](2)] delivered with this form?

2. On what date and at what address did you receive it?

3. Are you the person named as the Respondent in the application [or as in the petition](2)?

4. Do you intend to defend the case?

(3) Delete if inapplicable.

5. (3) [*In the case of a petition alleging two years' separation coupled with the respondent's consent to a decree being granted*] Do you consent to a decree being granted?

6. (3) [*In the case of a petition asking for divorce and alleging five years' separation*] Do you intend to oppose the grant of a decree on the ground that the divorce will result in grave financial or other hardship to you and that in all the circumstances it would be wrong to dissolve the marriage?

7. (3) In the event of a decree nisi being granted on the basis of two years' separation coupled with the respondent's consent, or five years' separation, do you intend to apply to the Court for it to consider your financial position as it will be after the divorce?

(4) Delete Question 8 except in the case of a petition.

(5) Insert whichever of the following items is applicable.

8. (4) Even if you do not intend to defend the case do you wish to be heard on the claim[s] in the petition for (5)—

(*a*) costs ....
(*b*) custody of the children..
(*c*) maintenance pending suit..
(*d*) periodical payments..
(*e*) secured periodical payments......................................

(*f*) lump sum provision..
(*g*) settlement or transfer of property.................................
(*h*) variation of a settlement...

9. (6) Do you wish to make any application on your own account for—
(*a*) access to the children..
(*b*) custody of the children...
(*c*) periodical payments or secured periodical payments for the children..
(*d*) maintenance pending suit..
(*e*) periodical payments or secured periodical payments for yourself ....
(*f*) lump sum provision..
(*g*) settlement or transfer of property.................................
(*h*) variation of a settlement...

(6) Delete Question 9 (except in the case of a respondent in proceedings begun by petition).

(If possible answer YES or NO against each item in Question[s] 8 [and 9]. If you are uncertain leave a blank).

10. (3) [*In the case of proceedings relating to a polygamous marriage*] If you have any wife [*or* husband] in addition to the petitioner [*or* applicant] who is not mentioned in the petition [*or* originating application [*or* summons]], what is the name and address of each such wife [*or* husband] and the date and place of your marriage to her [*or* him]?

Dated this day of 19 .

[*If a solicitor is instructed, he will sign below on your behalf* [*but if the answer to Question 5 is Yes, you must also sign here*]]

Signed

Address for service [*Unless you intend to instruct a solicitor, give your place of residence, or if you do not reside in England or Wales, the address of a place in England or Wales to which documents may be sent to you. If you subsequently wish to change your address for service, you must notify the Court.*]

[I am [We are] acting for the Respondent [*or* the above-named] in this matter.

Signed
Address for service:]

Rule 33(3)

Form 7

AFFIDAVIT BY PETITIONER IN SUPPORT OF PETITION UNDER SECTION 1(2)(*d*) OF MATRIMONIAL CAUSES ACT 1973

[*Heading as in Form 5*]

QUESTION	ANSWER
1. Have you read your petition dated ?	
2. Do you wish to alter or add to any statement in the petition?	
If so, state the alterations or additions.	
3. Subject to these alterations and additions (if any), is everything stated in your petition true? Indicate which statements are true to your own knowledge and which to the best of your information and belief.	
4. State the date on which you and the respondent separated.	
5. State briefly the reason or main reason for the separation.	
6. When and in what circumstances did you come to the conclusion that the marriage was in fact at an end?	

7. State as far as you know the various addresses at which you and the respondent have respectively lived since the date given in the answer to Question 4, and the periods of residence at each address:

	Petitioner's Address		*Respondent's Address*
From to		From to	

8. Since the date given in the answer to Question 6, have you ever lived with the respondent in the same household? If so, state for which period or periods, giving dates.	

I, (*full name*)

of (*full residential address*) (*occupation*)

make oath and say as follows:—

1. I am the petitioner in this cause.

2. The answers to Questions 1 to 8 above are true.

3. I identify the signature

appearing on the copy acknowledgment of service now produced to me and marked "A" as the signature of my husband [wife], the respondent in this cause.

4. [*Exhibit any other documents on which the petitioner wishes to rely.*]

5. I ask the Court to grant a decree dissolving my marriage with [*or* a decree that I be judicially separated from] the respondent on the grounds stated in my petition [and to order the respondent to pay the costs of this suit *or as the case may be*].

Sworn at

in the County of

this day of , 19 .

Before me,

A Commissioner for Oaths
[*or as the case may be*]

Rule 65(1)

Form 8

NOTICE OF APPLICATION FOR DECREE NISI TO BE MADE ABSOLUTE

[*Heading as in Form* 5]

TAKE NOTICE THAT the petitioner [*or* respondent] applies for the decree nisi pronounced in his [her] favour on the day of 19 , to be made absolute.

Dated this day of 19 .

Signed
[Solicitor for the] Petitioner
[*or* Respondent]

Rule 67(2)

Form 9

CERTIFICATE OF MAKING DECREE NISI ABSOLUTE (DIVORCE)

(Seal)

[*Heading as in Form* 5]

Referring to the decree made in this cause on the day of 19 , whereby it was decreed that the marriage solemnised on the day of 19 at between the petitioner and the respondent be dissolved unless sufficient cause be shown to the court within from the making thereof why the said decree should not be made absolute, and no such cause having been shown, it is hereby certified that the said decree was on the day of 19 , made final and absolute and that the said marriage was thereby dissolved.

Dated this day of 19 .

Rule 67(2)

Form 10

CERTIFICATE OF MAKING DECREE NISI ABSOLUTE (NULLITY)

(Seal)

[*Heading as in Form* 5]

Referring to the decree made in this cause on the day of 19 , whereby it was ordered that the marriage in fact solemnised on the day of 19 , at between the petitioner and the respondent [*in the case of a void marriage* be pronounced and declared to have been by law void and the said petitioner be pronounced to have been and to be free of all bond of marriage with the said respondent] [*in the case of a voidable marriage* be annulled] unless sufficient cause be shown to the court within from the making thereof why the said decree should not be made absolute, and no such cause having been shown, it is hereby certified that the said decree was on the day of 19 , made final and absolute [*in the case of a void marriage* and that the said marriage was by law void and that the said petitioner was and is free from all bond of marriage with the said respondent] [*in the case of a voidable marriage* and that the said petitioner was from that date and is free from all bond of marriage with the said respondent].

Dated this day of 19 .

Rule 68(2) and (3)

Form 11

NOTICE OF APPLICATION FOR ANCILLARY RELIEF

[*Heading as in Form* 5]

TAKE NOTICE THAT the petitioner [*or* respondent] intends to apply to the Court for [*here set out the ancillary relief claimed, stating the terms of any agreement as to the order which the court is to be asked to make and, in the case of an application for a property adjustment order or an avoidance of disposition order, stating briefly the nature of the adjustment proposed or the disposition to be set aside*].

Notice will be given to you of the place and time fixed for the hearing of the application [*or* The application will be heard by the registrar in chambers at on day, the day of 19 , at o'clock].

[*Unless the parties are agreed upon the terms of the proposed order, add in the case of an application for an order for maintenance pending suit or a financial provision order:*

TAKE NOTICE ALSO THAT you must send to the registrar, so as to reach him within 14 days after you receive this notice, an affidavit giving full particulars of your property and income. You must at the same time send a copy of your affidavit to the [solicitor for] the applicant.

If you wish to allege that the petitioner has property or income, you should say so in your affidavit].

Dated this day of 19 .

Signed

[Solicitor for the] Respondent
[*or* Petitioner]

Rule 57

Form 12

NOTICE OF APPLICATION UNDER RULE 57

[*Heading as in Form* 5]

TAKE NOTICE THAT the respondent applies to the Court under section 10(2) of the Matrimonial Causes Act 1973 for the Court to consider the financial position of the respondent after the divorce.

The application will be heard on a date to be fixed [*or if, in the case of an application made after a decree nisi, a date has been fixed* by the registrar in chambers at on day, the day of 19 , at o'clock].

[*Unless the petitioner has already filed an affidavit with his petition under rule* 8(3) *or in connection with an application for ancillary relief under rule 73(2):*

TAKE NOTICE ALSO THAT you must send to the registrar, so as to reach him within 14 days after you receive this notice, an affidavit giving full particulars of your property and income. You must at the same time send a copy of your affidavit to the [solicitor for the] respondent.

If you wish to allege that the respondent has property or income, you should say so in your affidavit].

Dated this day of 19 .

Signed

[Solicitor for the] Respondent

Rule 73(1)

Form 13

NOTICE OF INTENTION TO PROCEED WITH APPLICATION FOR ANCILLARY RELIEF MADE IN PETITION OR ANSWER

[*Heading as in Form* 5]

The petitioner [*or* respondent] having applied in his [her] petition [*or* answer] for [*here set out the ancillary relief claimed and intended to be proceeded with, stating the terms of any agreement as to the order which the court is to be asked to make*].

[*Add where applicable* TAKE NOTICE THAT the application will be heard by the registrar in chambers at on day, the day of 19 , at o'clock].

[TAKE NOTICE [ALSO] THAT [*continue as in third paragraph of Form* 11]]

Dated this day of 19 .

Signed

[Solicitor for the] Petitioner [*or* Respondent]

Rules 76 and 92(5)

Form 14

NOTICE OF ALLEGATION IN PROCEEDINGS FOR ANCILLARY RELIEF

[*Heading as in Form* 5]

TAKE NOTICE THAT this affidavit has been filed in proceedings for [*state nature of application*] and that if you wish to be heard on any matter affecting you in the proceedings you may intervene by applying to the Court, within eight days after you receive this notice, inclusive of the day of receipt, for directions as to the filing and service of pleadings and as to the further conduct of the proceedings.

Dated this day of 19 .

Issued by

[Solicitor for the] Petitioner [*or* Respondent]

Rule 83(2)

Form 15

NOTICE OF REQUEST FOR PERIODICAL PAYMENTS ORDER AT SAME RATE AS ORDER FOR MAINTENANCE PENDING SUIT

[*Heading as in Form* 5]

TO of

The petitioner [*or* respondent] having on the day of 19 , obtained an order for payment by you of maintenance pending suit at the rate of

AND the petitioner [*or* respondent] having applied in his [her] petition [*or* answer] for a periodical payments order for himself [*or* herself],

TAKE NOTICE THAT the petitioner [*or* respondent] has requested the Court to make a periodical payments order for himself [*or* herself] providing for payments by you at the same rate as those mentioned above.

AND TAKE NOTICE THAT if you object to the making of such a periodical payments order, you must give notice to that effect to the registrar and the petitioner [*or* respondent] within 14 days after service of this notice on you, and if you do not do so, the registrar may make such a periodical payments order without further notice to you.

Dated this day of 19 .

Registrar

Rule 87(3)

Form 16

REQUEST FOR ISSUE OF JUDGMENT SUMMONS

In the High Court of Justice [*or* In the County Court
Family Division [Divorce Registry]
(Divorce) .
[District Registry]

No. of {Matter / Judgment Summons}

Between Petitioner [*or* Applicant]
and Respondent
[and Co-Respondent]

Judgment creditor's full name and address..

Debtor's full name and address..

I apply for the issue of a judgment summons against the above-named debtor in respect of an order made in this Court [*or as the case may be*] on the day of 19 , for [*state nature of order*].

[*If it be the case* I intend to apply to the Court at the hearing of the proposed judgment summons for leave to enforce arrears which became due more than twelve months before the date of the proposed summons].

I am aware that, if I do not prove to the satisfaction of the Court at the hearing that the debtor has, or has had since the date of the said order, the means to pay the sum in respect of which he has made default and that he has refused or neglected, or refuses or neglects, to pay it I may have to pay the costs of the summons.

[*Add, except where judgment summons is to issue in divorce county court in which order was made:* I certify that the said order has not been modified or discharged and that there is no order of commitment in this matter which remains unsatisfied.

I further certify that no [writ or] warrant of execution has been issued to enforce the said order [*or, if a writ or warrant has been issued, give details and state what return to it has been made*].]

Dated this day of 19 .

[Solicitor for the] Judgment Creditor

	£
Amount due and unpaid in respect of the order and costs ...	
Costs of this summons	
Travelling expenses to be paid to debtor	

Rule 87(5)

Form 17

(Seal)

JUDGMENT SUMMONS

[*Heading as in Form* 16]

WHEREAS the above-named (hereinafter called "the judgment creditor") obtained an order in this Court [*or as the case may be*] on the day of 19 , against (hereinafter called "the debtor") for [*state nature of order*].

AND WHEREAS default has been made in payment of the sum of £ payable under the said order and the judgment creditor has required this judgment summons to be issued against you, the said debtor.

YOU ARE HEREBY SUMMONED to appear personally before one of the Judges sitting in this Division at the Royal Courts of Justice, Strand, London, WC2A 2LL [*or as the case may be*] on the day of 19 , at o'clock, to be examined on oath touching the means you have or have had since the date of the said order to pay the said sum in payment of which you have made default and also to show cause why you should not be committed to prison for such default.

[AND TAKE NOTICE THAT the judgment creditor intends to apply to the Court at the hearing of this judgment summons for leave to enforce arrears which became due more than twelve months before the date of this summons].

Dated this day of 19 .

	£
Amount due and unpaid in respect of order and costs ...	
Costs of this summons	
Travelling expenses to be paid to the debtor	
Sum on payment of which this summons will be discharged ...	

Note: If payment is made too late to prevent the judgment creditor's attendance on the day of hearing, you may be liable for further costs.

[The judgment creditor's solicitor is].

Rule 93(1)

Form 18

NOTICE OF APPOINTMENT TO HEAR REPRESENTATIONS BEFORE CHILD IS COMMITTED TO CARE OF LOCAL AUTHORITY

[*Heading as in Form* 5]

TO

TAKE NOTICE THAT if you wish to make representation before an order

is made committing to the care of the

council, you should attend before at

on the day of 19 , and that if you do

not attend at the time and place mentioned, such order will be made and proceedings taken as the judge thinks fit.

Note: Where a local authority to whose care a child is committed wish to ask for a financial provision order in favour of the child, they must, within seven days after receiving this notice, file an affidavit as to the property and income of the party against whom the order is sought and must at the same time send him a copy of the affidavit. Within four days after receiving the local authority's affidavit the party against whom the order is sought may file an affidavit in reply and, if he does so, he must send a copy of his affidavit to the local authority.

Dated this day of 19 .

Registrar

Rule 98(1)

Form 19

ORIGINATING APPLICATION ON GROUND OF WILFUL NEGLECT TO MAINTAIN

In the County Court
[Divorce Registry]
No. of
Matter
(Seal)

In the Matter of an Application under section 27 *of the Matrimonial Causes Act* 1973

Between Applicant

and Respondent

1. I, , of ,the wife [husband] of

of (hereinafter called the "respondent") say that the respondent [*in the case of a wife's application* has wilfully neglected to provide [reasonable maintenance for me] *or in the case of a husband's application* has wilfully neglected to provide [*or* make a proper contribution towards] reasonable maintenance [for me] [and] [the child[ren] of our family]].

2. On the day of 19 , I [*in the case of an application by a wife* being then [*state full name and status before the marriage*]] was lawfully married to the respondent [*in the case of an application by a husband* who was then [*state respondent's full name and status before marriage*]] at .

3. There is [are] [no [*or state number*] children of the family now living] [namely [*state the full name (including surname) of each child and his date of birth or, if it be the case, that he is over* 18 *and, in the case of each minor child over the age of* 16 *whether, he is, or will be, or if an order or provision were made would be, receiving instruction at an educational establishment or undergoing training for a trade, profession or vocation*] who is now residing at [*state the place*] with [*state the person*]].

4. There have been no previous proceedings in any court in England and Wales or elsewhere with reference to the marriage [or the children of the family] [or between the applicant and the respondent with reference to any property of either or both of them] [except *state the nature of the proceedings, the date and effect of any decree or order and, in the case of proceedings with reference to the marriage, whether there has been any resumption of cohabitation since the making of the decree or order*].

5. [*Where appropriate in the case of a child who is under* 18] The said was, on the day of 19 , received into the care of [*or* is a child with respect to whom a resolution was, on the day of 19 , passed by] [*name of local authority*] under section 1 [*or* 2] of the Children Act 1948.

6. The following are particulars of the wilful neglect [*give particulars adding the name*[*s*] *of the child*[*ren*] *concerned and in the case of a husband's application in respect of himself the matters set out in section* 27(1)(*b*)(i) *of the Act of* 1973 *on which he relies*].

7. The respondent has not made any payments to me by way of maintenance for myself [or the said child[ren] [except [*give particulars*]].

8. My means are as follows:—

9. To the best of my knowledge and belief the respondent's means are as follows:—

10. I apply for an order that the respondent do make provision by way of [periodical payments, secured periodical payments, a lump sum *delete as appropriate*] for me [and [*such of the said provisions as may be claimed*] for [*state name*[*s*] *of child*[*ren*] *in respect of whom such claim is made*]].

11. I ask that I may be granted the custody of the said [*state name*[*s*] *of the child*[*ren*]].

12. This Court has jurisdiction to entertain these proceedings by reason of the fact that [*in the case of an application based on domicile* I am [*or* the respondent is] [*or* the respondent and I are] domiciled in England and Wales] [*or in the case of an application based on residence* I have been habitually resident in England and Wales throughout the period of one year ending with the date of this application [*or* the respondent is now resident in England and Wales]].

My address for service is [*Where the applicant sues by a solicitor, state the solicitor's name or firm and address or, where the applicant sues in person, state her place of residence as given in paragraph* 1 *or, if no place of residence in England or Wales is given, the address of a place in England or Wales at or to which documents for her may be delivered or sent*].

Dated this day of 19 .

Rules 98(3) and 100(4)

Form 20

NOTICE OF APPLICATION UNDER RULE 98 OR 100

[*Heading as in Form* 19] *or* [21]

TAKE NOTICE THAT this application will be heard at County Court [*insert address of court-house*] on the day of 19 , at o'clock [*or* on a day to be fixed], and if you do not attend at that place and time, such order will be made as the Court thinks just.

A sealed copy of the application [and of the affidavit in verification] is delivered with this notice.

You must complete and detach the acknowledgment of service and send it so as to reach the Court within eight days after you receive this notice inclusive of the day of receipt. Delay in returning the form may add to the costs.

[*Where the application is under rule* 98] If you intend to contest the application, you must file an answer setting out the grounds on which you rely (including any allegation which you wish to make against the applicant), and in any case, unless otherwise directed, you must file an affidavit containing full particulars of your property and income. The affidavit and any answer you wish to file must be sent, together with a copy for the applicant, so as to reach the Court within 14 days after the time allowed for sending the acknowledgment of service. If you file an answer alleging adultery it must be accompanied by a copy for the alleged adulterer.

[*Where the application is under rule* 100] You must also swear an affidavit in answer to the application, setting out any grounds on which you intend to contest the application and containing full particulars of your property and income, and send the affidavit, together with a copy for the applicant, so as to reach the Court within 14 days after the time allowed for sending the acknowledgment of service.

If you intend to instruct a solicitor to act for you, you should at once give him all the documents which have been served on you, so that he may take the necessary steps on your behalf.

Dated this day of 19 .

Registrar

To the Respondent

[*Here set out Form* 6]

Rule 100(1)

Form 21

ORIGINATING APPLICATION FOR ALTERATION OF MAINTENANCE AGREEMENT DURING PARTIES' LIFETIME

In the County Court
[Divorce Registry]

No. of
Matter

(Seal)

In the Matter of an Application under section 35 *of the Matrimonial Causes Act* 1973

Between Applicant

and Respondent

1. I, ,the wife [*or* husband] of (hereinafter called "the respondent"), apply for an order altering the maintenance agreement made between me and the respondent on the day of 19 .

2. I reside at , and the respondent resides at

[*Add, unless both parties are resident in England or Wales* We are both domiciled in England and Wales [*or as the case may be*]].

3. On the day of 19 , I was lawfully married to the respondent at .
I [*or in the case of an application by the husband* The respondent] was then [*state full name and status of wife before marriage*].

4. There is [are] [no [*or state number*] child[ren] of the family [namely [*state the full name (including surname) of each child now living and his date of birth or, if it be the case, that he is over* 18 *and, in the case of each minor child over the age of* 16, *whether he is, or will be, or if an order or provision were made would be, receiving instruction at an educational establishment or undergoing training for a trade, profession or vocation*] who is now residing at [*state the place*] with [*state the person*] [and [*state name of any child who has died since the date of the agreement*] who died on the day of 19 .] [The agreement also makes financial arrangements for [*give similar particulars of any other child for whom the agreement makes such arrangements*]].

5. There have been no previous proceedings in any court with reference to the agreement or to the marriage [or to the child[ren] of the family] [or to the other child[ren] for whom the agreement makes financial arrangements] or between the applicant and the respondent with reference to any property of either or both of them [except *state the nature of the proceedings and the date and effect of any order or decree*].

6. My means are as follows:—

7. I ask for the following alteration[s] to be made in the agreement:—

8. The facts on which I rely to justify the alteration[s] are:—

My address for service is [*Where the applicant sues by a solicitor, state the solicitor's name or firm and address, or, where the applicant sues in person, state his or her place of residence as given in paragraph* 2 *or, if no place of residence in England or Wales is given, the address of a place in England or Wales at or to which documents for him or her may be delivered or sent*].

Dated this day of 19 .

Rule 101(1)

Form 22

ORIGINATING SUMMONS FOR ALTERATION OF MAINTENANCE AGREEMENT AFTER DEATH OF ONE OF THE PARTIES

In the High Court of Justice
Family Division

(Divorce)
[District Registry]

In the Matter of an Application by *under section* 36 *of the Matrimonial Causes Act* 1973

Between Applicant[s]
and Respondent[s]

Let of attend before Mr. Registrar in chambers at the Divorce Registry, Somerset House, London, WC2R 1LP, [*or as the case may be*] on day, the day of 19 , at o'clock, on the hearing of an application by that the agreement made on the day of 19 , between [the applicant and] who died on the day of 19 , [and the respondent] should be altered as shown in the affidavit accompanying this summons so as to make different [*or* contain] financial arrangements.

Dated this day of 19 .

This summons was taken out by [Solicitor for] the above-named applicant[s].

To the Respondent.

TAKE NOTICE THAT:—

1. A copy of the affidavit to be used in support of the application is delivered herewith.

2. You must complete the accompanying acknowledgment of service and send it so as to reach the Court within eight days after you receive this summons.

3. [*If the respondent is a personal representative of the deceased:* You must also file an affidavit in answer to the applicant's application containing full particulars of the value of the deceased's estate for probate, after providing for the discharge of the funeral, testamentary and administration expenses, debts and liabilities, including the amount of the estate duty and interest thereon, and the persons or classes of persons beneficially interested in the estate, with the names and addresses of all living beneficiaries and stating whether any beneficiary is a minor or incapable, by reason of mental disorder, of managing and administering his property and affairs.]

[*Or, if the respondent is not a personal representative of the deceased:* You may also file an affidavit in answer to the application.]

[*Add, in either case:* The affidavit must be filed by sending or delivering it, together with a copy for the applicant, so as to reach the Court within 14 days after the time allowed for sending the acknowledgment of service.]

4. If you intend to instruct a solicitor to act for you, you should at once give him all the documents which have been served on you, so that he may take the necessary steps on your behalf.

Rule 103(1)

Form 23

ORIGINATING SUMMONS FOR MAINTENANCE OUT OF ESTATE OF DECEASED FORMER SPOUSE

In the High Court of Justice
Family Division

(Divorce)
[District Registry]

In the Matter of an Application by *under section* 26 *of the Matrimonial Causes Act* 1965

Between Applicant
and Respondent

Let of
attend before Mr. Registrar in chambers at the Divorce Registry, Somerset House, London, WC2R 1LP, [*or as the case may be*] on day, the day of 19 , at o'clock, on the hearing of an application by that provision for her maintenance be made out of the estate of of , who died on the day of 19 , on the ground that he has not made reasonable provision for her maintenance after his death.

Dated this day of 19 .

This summons was taken out by
[Solicitor for] the above-named applicant.

To the Respondent.

TAKE NOTICE THAT:—

[*Continue as in Form* 22]

Rule 104(1)

Form 24

ORIGINATING SUMMONS UNDER SECTION 17 OF THE MARRIED WOMEN'S PROPERTY ACT 1882 [OR SECTION 1 OF THE MATRIMONIAL HOMES ACT 1967]

In the High Court of Justice
Family Division

[District Registry]

In the Matter of an Application by *under section* 17 *of the Married Women's Property Act* 1882 [or *section* 1 *of the Matrimonial Homes Act* 1967]

Between Applicant

and Respondent

Let of
attend before Mr. Registrar in chambers at the Divorce Registry, Somerset House, London WC2R 1LP, [*or as the case may be*] on day, the day of 19 , at o'clock, on the hearing of an application by for an order in the following terms:—
[here set out terms of order sought]

Dated this day of 19 .

This summons was taken out by
[Solicitor for] the above-named applicant

To the Respondent

TAKE NOTICE THAT:—

1. A copy of the affidavit to be used in support of the application is delivered herewith.

2. You must complete the accompanying acknowledgment of service and send it so as to reach the court within eight days after you receive this summons.

3. If you wish to dispute the claim made by the applicant you must file an affidavit in answer within 14 days after the time allowed for sending the acknowledgment of service.

4. If you intend to instruct a solicitor to act for you you should at once give him all the documents served on you, so that he may take the necessary steps on your behalf.

Rule 113(2)

Form 25

NOTICE TO BE INDORSED ON DOCUMENT SERVED IN ACCORDANCE WITH RULE 113(1)

To of .

TAKE NOTICE THAT the contents or purport of this document are to be communicated to the respondent [*or as the case may be*], the said , if he is over 16 [*add, if the person to be served is by reason of mental disorder within the meaning of the Mental Health Act* 1959 *incapable of managing and administering his property and affairs:* unless you are satisfied [after consultation with the responsible medical officer within the meaning of the Mental Health Act 1959 or, if the said is not liable to be detained or subject to guardianship under that Act, his medical attendant]* that communication will be detrimental to his mental condition].

*Delete these words if the document is served on the responsible medical officer or medical attendant.

EXPLANATORY NOTE

(This Note is not part of the Rules.)

These Rules consolidate with amendments the Matrimonial Causes Rules 1971 and subsequent amending instruments. Apart from drafting changes and minor changes rendered necessary by the Matrimonial Causes Act 1973, the main alterations are as follows:—

(1) The provisions relating to applications for the consideration of agreements or arrangements between the parties to a marriage are omitted.

(2) Fresh provision is made for the parties to proceedings in which adultery is alleged (Rule 13).

(3) An order to dispense with service of a copy of the petition on the respondent may be made by the registrar instead of only by a judge (Rule 14 (10)).

(4) Applications for evidence to be given on affidavit can be made in undefended cases, despite a notice of intention to defend, without the consent of all the parties concerned (Rule 39(2)).

(5) Time limits are set for service of notices in connection with all applications for ancillary relief (Rules 70 and 73(1)).

(6) It is made plain that any affidavit in reply by an applicant on an application for ancillary relief should contain full particulars of the applicant's property and income (Rule 73(3)).

(7) Details of mortgages have to be given in affidavits in support of certain applications for ancillary relief (Rule 74(3)) and in relation to matrimonial property (Rule 104(3)), and provision is made for service of notice of such applications on mortgagees.

(8) Those making or opposing applications relating to the custody etc. of children and deponents who are responsible for the child's care will now normally have to be available at the hearing to give oral evidence (Rule 92(4)).

(9) Rules for applications in the High Court—

(*a*) under section 17 of the Married Women's Property Act 1882,

(*b*) under section 1 of the Matrimonial Homes Act 1967,

(*c*) for declarations affecting matrimonial status, and

(*d*) for declarations of legitimacy,

are inserted in lieu of the corresponding provisions in the Rules of the Supreme Court which are revoked (Rules 104, 107(1) and (2), 109-111 and the Schedule).

As far as possible, rules and forms have been kept in the same order as in the Matrimonial Causes Rules 1971 as amended. Where there is a divergence in numbering the following tables show the correspondence between the two sets of Rules.

TABLE A

CORRESPONDENCE OF RULES

Matrimonial Causes Rules 1971	1973
5	5-6
6	—
36	116
36A	36
37	37(1)
37A	38
38	39
39	40
40	37(2)
42A	48
43	43(2), (3) and (4)
48	43(1)
65–66	65–67
67	—
104	107(3) and (4)
104A	105
104B	106
104C	108
105–108	112–115
109–123	117–131
124	
	104 } are new.
	107(1)–(2) } are new.
	109–111 } are new.
	132 } are new.

TABLE B

CORRESPONDENCE OF FORMS

Matrimonial Causes Rules 1971	1973
24	7
7–12	8–13
23	14
13–21	15–23
22	25
	24 is new.

STATUTORY INSTRUMENTS

1973 No. 2019

TRANSPORT

PENSIONS AND COMPENSATION

The British Railways Board (Alteration of Pension Schemes) Order 1973

Made - - -	*30th November* 1973
Laid before Parliament	*7th December* 1973
Coming into Operation	*2nd January* 1974

The Secretary of State for the Environment, in exercise of powers conferred by section 74 of the Transport Act 1962(**a**) and now vested in him(**b**) and of all other enabling powers, hereby makes the following Order:—

Commencement, citation and interpretation

1.—(1) This Order shall come into operation on 2nd January 1974 and may be cited as the British Railways Board (Alteration of Pension Schemes) Order 1973.

(2) In this Order, unless the context otherwise requires—

"the Board" means the British Railways Board;

"the persons administering", in relation to a pension fund, means the persons responsible for administering the fund under the terms applicable thereto, and includes the trustees (if any) of the fund;

"term", in relation to a pension fund to which this Order applies, includes any rule or provision of the fund, or of any statutory provision relating to the fund, or of any deed or other instrument made for the purposes of the fund.

(3) Where provision is made in this Order for any sum to be paid by the Board to the persons administering a pension fund and the persons administering a particular pension fund are the Board themselves, that provision shall be construed in relation to that fund as a provision for the sum in question to be credited by the Board to that fund.

(**a**) 1962 c.46. (**b**) S.I. 1970/1681(1970 III, p.5551).

(4) The Interpretation Act 1889(**a**) shall apply for the interpretation of this Order as it applies for the interpretation of an Act of Parliament.

Application of Order

2.—(1) This Order applies to the pension funds which are specified in Schedule 1 to this Order and to any other pension fund maintained by the Board for the provision of pensions or other benefits for, or for the dependants of, persons of any of the following categories, that is to say:—

(*a*) persons who are, or have been, employed by the Board or by any subsidiary of theirs,

(*b*) persons who are, or have been, employed by, or by a subsidiary of, a body whose undertaking immediately before 1st January 1963 formed part of the undertaking of the British Transport Commission,

(*c*) persons who were employed by the British Transport Commission,

(*d*) persons who were employed by a predecessor body as defined in Article 1 of the British Transport Reorganisation (Pensions of Employees) (No. 3) Order 1962(**b**), in connection with a transferred undertaking as defined in that Article,

and also to the pension fund which is specified in Schedule 2 to this Order.

(2) Every pension fund to which this Order applies shall be construed and have effect as if the relevant provisions of this Order were terms of, or applicable to, the fund, any other terms thereof, whether expressed or implied, to the contrary notwithstanding.

Termination of certain investment powers

3. (1) Subject to paragraph (2) below, the power of the Board or other persons administering a pension fund to which this Order applies to apply to the general purposes of the Board's undertaking or to invest by way of deposit with the Board moneys which belong to any such pension fund but which have not previously been so applied or invested shall cease on the date on which this Order comes into operation and no further moneys belonging to any such fund shall be so applied or invested by the Board or by such persons on or after that date.

(2) Nothing in paragraph (1) above shall affect the powers of the persons administering the pension fund which is specified in Schedule 2 to this Order to make or vary investments, or the powers of the persons administering any other pension fund to which this Order applies to make deposits in a railway savings bank mentioned in section 65 of the Transport Act 1962.

Provisions with respect to existing deposits

4. Where before the date of the coming into operation of this Order moneys belonging to a pension fund to which this Order applies have been applied or invested in exercise of a power referred to in Article 3(1) of this Order (whether by the Board or by any other body referred to in Article 2(1) above) and those moneys on that date remain so applied or invested and constitute assets of that fund, the provisions of Articles 5 and 6 of this Order shall have effect in relation to those moneys on and after that date.

(**a**) 1889 c.63. (**b**) S.I. 1962/2758 (1962 III, p. 3866)

Interest on deposits

5.—(1) The Board shall pay to the fund in question at intervals of not more than 6 months interest at a rate determined in accordance with the provisions of paragraph (2) of this Article on so much of the moneys referred to in Article 4 above as have for the time being not been repaid by the Board.

(2) Subject to paragraphs (3) and (4) below, the rate of interest to be paid as mentioned in paragraph (1) above on a particular date shall be the rate which has been determined by the Treasury under section 5 of the National Loans Act 1968(**a**) for loans from the National Loans Fund repayable at maturity for periods of more than one year and not more than 5 years and which is in operation for such loans on the 2nd January next preceding that date.

(3) The provisions of paragraph (2) above shall not apply to interest accruing before the date on which this Order comes into operation.

(4) The rate of interest to be paid under this Article shall not be less than 5% per annum.

(5) The provisions of this Article shall, in relation to the pension funds to which the provisions of Article 3(*c*) and (*d*) of the British Transport (Alteration of Pension Schemes) Order 1969(**b**) or Article 5(3) of the British Transport (Amalgamation of Railways' Pension Funds) (No. 1) Order 1970(**c**) apply, have effect in substitution for those provisions.

Redemption of capital of deposits

6.—(1) The capital of the moneys referred to in Article 4 above shall be repaid by the Board to the fund to which they belong by five annual instalments on 2nd January in each of the years 1974 to 1978 (inclusive).

(2) The instalments referred to in paragraph (1) above shall, so far as practicable, be of equal amounts, but if the total capital repayable to a particular fund has not been finally determined by 2nd January 1974, an appropriate adjustment shall be made in one or other of the succeeding instalments.

(3) Payment of the instalments referred to in paragraph (1) above shall be made at the same time to each of the funds concerned on the basis of that fund's entitlement on the date of the coming into operation of this Order to the capital of the moneys which have been applied or invested in exercise of a power referred to in Article 3(1) above and which on that date remain so applied or invested.

(4) Moneys of a pension fund repaid by the Board under the provisions of this Article shall be invested by the persons administering the fund in investments which they have power to make in relation to the fund, or shall otherwise be applied in accordance with the terms of the fund.

Widened investment powers for certain funds

7.—(1) Subject to paragraph (2) below, the persons administering each of the pension funds which are specified in Schedule 3 to this Order shall, in addition to their existing powers of investment in relation to those funds, have power to apply and invest moneys belonging to those funds in or upon any invest-

(**a**) 1968 c.13. (**b**) S.I. 1969/1858 (1969 III, p.5797).
(**c**) S.I. 1970/477 (1970 I, p.1582).

ments which any person could make if he were absolutely and beneficially entitled to those moneys.

(2) Nothing in this Article shall entitle the persons administering a pension fund referred to in paragraph (1) above to apply or invest moneys in the manner mentioned in Article 3(1) of this Order.

Saving for existing provisions with respect to transfer values

8. Nothing in this Order shall prevent the payment by any pension fund to which this Order applies of transfer values to another pension fund in the form of moneys which have been applied or invested in exercise of a power referred to in Article 3(1) of this Order in any case where payment in such form is provided for by any existing provision applicable to the funds in question, but where payment is made in such form after the coming into operation of this Order the payment shall have the benefit of the provisions of this Order.

Signed by authority of the Secretary of State.
30th November 1973.

John Peyton,
Minister for Transport Industries,
Department of the Environment.

SCHEDULE 1

Railway Pension Funds holding deposits with the Board

British Railways (North Eastern Region) Employees' Accident and Death Fund.

British Railways Southern Region Employees' Supplementary Pension Society.

British Railways Superannuation Fund:

LNER Section.

GWR Section.

SR Section.

LMSR Section.

New Section.

British Transport Police Force Superannuation Fund.

British Transport Police Force Retirement Benefit Fund.

1970 Section of the British Transport Police Force Superannuation Fund.

Great Eastern Railway Employees' Sick and Orphan Society.

Great Eastern Railway New Pension Fund and New Pension (Supplemental) Fund Trust Account.

Great Northern Railway Locomotive Friendly Society.

Great Northern Railway Superannuation Fund.

Great Western Railway Inspectors and Foremen's Special Pension Fund.

Great Western Railway Pension Society.

Great Western Railway Salaried Staff Supplemental Pension Fund.

Great Western Railway Salaried Staff Widows and Orphans' Pension Society.

Great Western Railway Supplemental Pensions Reserve Fund.

Great Western Railway Widows' and Orphans' Benevolent Fund.

London, Brighton and South Coast Railway Pension Fund.

London Midland and Scottish Railway (LNW) Insurance Society.

London Midland and Scottish Railway, Midland Friendly Society.

London and North Western Railway Provident Society for providing pensions for Widows and Orphans of Members of the Salaried Staff.

London and South Western Railway Company's Engine Drivers, Firemen, Locomotive and Electrical Engineering Departments Pension Society.

North Eastern Railway Servants' Pension Society.

North Eastern Railway Servants' Sickness and Assurance Society.

North Eastern and Great Eastern Superannuation Societies and Pension Funds Joint Trust Account.

Port Talbot Railway and Docks Company Augmentation Fund.

Southern Railway (South Eastern and Chatham Section), Enginemen and Motormen's Pension Fund Society.

Southern Railway (Western Section) Provident and Sick Benefit Society.

Thos. Bantock and Co. Benevolent and Pensions Fund.

Thos. Bantock and Co. Superannuation Fund.

SCHEDULE 2

Other Pension Fund of national transport authority holding deposits with the Board

British Transport Docks Board (Salaried Staff) Pension Scheme.

SCHEDULE 3

Railway Pension Funds to which widened investment powers are given

British Railways Superannuation Fund:

LNER Section.

GWR Section.

SR Section.

LMSR Section.

Great Eastern Railway New Pension Fund and New Pension (Supplemental) Fund Trust Account.

Great Western Railway Inspectors and Foremen's Special Pension Fund.

Great Western Railway Salaried Staff Supplemental Pension Fund.

Great Western Railway Salaried Staff Widows and Orphans' Pension Society.

Great Western Railway Supplemental Pensions Reserve Fund.

Great Western Railway Widows' and Orphans' Benevolent Fund.

London, Brighton and South Coast Railway Pension Fund.

London & North Western Railway Provident Society for providing pensions for Widows and Orphans of Members of the Salaried Staff.

North Eastern and Great Eastern Superannuation Societies and Pension Funds Joint Trust Account.

North Eastern Railway Servants' Pension Society.

Port Talbot Railway and Docks Company Augmentation Fund

EXPLANATORY NOTE

(This Note is not part of the Order.)

This Order relates to certain railway pension funds of the British Railways Board and to the British Transport Docks Board (Salaried Staff) Pension Scheme. It terminates (Article 3) the existing powers of the persons administering the railway pension funds to apply to the general purposes of the Board's undertaking, or to invest by way of deposit with the Board, moneys belonging to those funds. It also provides (Articles 4, 5 and 6) for the payment by the Board of interest at current rates on the existing deposits with the Board belonging to the railway pension funds and to the British Transport Docks Board (Salaried Staff) Pension Scheme, and for the redemption by the Board of the capital of those deposits in annual instalments spread over the years 1974 to 1978 (inclusive). Additional investment powers are given to certain pension funds (Article 7 and Schedule 3) and provision is made for certain transfer value payments to have the benefit of the effect of the Order (Article 8).

STATUTORY INSTRUMENTS

1973 No. 2020

SEA FISHERIES

BOATS AND METHODS OF FISHING

The Herring (Atlanto-Scandian) (Prohibition of Fishing) Order 1973

Made - - -	21*st November* 1973
Laid before Parliament	10*th December* 1973
Coming into Operation	1*st January* 1974

The Minister of Agriculture, Fisheries and Food and the Secretaries of State respectively concerned with the sea fishing industry in Scotland and Northern Ireland in exercise of the powers conferred on them by sections 5(1) and (2) and 15 of the Sea Fish (Conservation) Act 1967(**a**) as the latter section is amended by section 22(1) of, and paragraph 38 of Part II of Schedule I to, the Sea Fisheries Act 1968(**b**) and of all other powers enabling them in that behalf, hereby make the following order:—

Citation and commencement

1. This order may be cited as the Herring (Atlanto-Scandian) (Prohibition of Fishing) Order 1973 and shall come into operation on 1st January 1974.

Interpretation

2. The Interpretation Act 1889(**c**) shall apply to the interpretation of this order as it applies to the interpretation of an Act of Parliament.

Prohibition

3. During the period from 1st January 1974 to 31st December 1974, both dates inclusive, fishing for herring (Clupea harengus) within the areas of sea specified in the Schedule to this order (being parts of an area to which the North-East Atlantic Fisheries Convention (**d**) applies) is hereby prohibited.

Enforcement

4. For the purpose of the enforcement of this order, there are hereby conferred on every British sea-fishery officer the powers of a British sea-fishery officer under section 8(2) and (3) of the Sea Fisheries Act 1968.

(**a**) 1967 c. 84.
(**b**) 1968 c. 77.
(**c**) 1889 c. 63.
(**d**) Cmnd. 2190.

In Witness whereof the Official Seal of the Minister of Agriculture, Fisheries and Food is hereunto affixed on 18th November 1973.

Joseph Godber,
Minister of Agriculture, Fisheries and Food.

Gordon Campbell,
Secretary of State for Scotland.

18th November 1973.

W. S. I. Whitelaw,
Secretary of State for Northern Ireland.

21st November 1973.

SCHEDULE

Areas to which the Order relates

(1) The areas of sea lying between longitudes 11°W and 68° 30′E to the north of a line running from a position longitude 11°W and latitude 63°N in an easterly direction along the parallel of latitude 63°N to longitude 4°W thence due south to latitude 62°N thence due east to the coast of Norway; and

(2) The areas of sea bounded by a line drawn east from the meridian of 15°W longitude along the parallel of 60°N latitude to the meridian of 5°W longitude thence due north to the parallel of 60° 30′ thence due east to the meridian of 4°W longitude thence due north to the parallel of 63°N latitude thence due west to the meridian of 15°W longitude thence due south to the parallel of 60°N latitude.

EXPLANATORY NOTE

(This Note is not part of the Order.)

This Order which implements a recommendation of the North-East-Atlantic Fisheries Commission prohibits fishing for herring in specified northerly parts of the north-east Atlantic ocean during 1974.

By virtue of section 5(8) of the Sea Fish (Conservation) Act 1967 the Order applies to all British fishing boats registered in the United Kingdom.

STATUTORY INSTRUMENTS

1973 No. 2021

EDUCATION, ENGLAND AND WALES

The Schools (Qualified Teachers) Regulations 1973

Made - - - -	*3rd December* 1973
Laid before Parliament	*10th December* 1973
Coming into Operation	*1st January* 1974

The Secretary of State for Education and Science, in exercise of the powers conferred on her by section 4(2) of the Local Government Act 1966**(a)** and section 33(3) of the Education Act 1944**(b)**, hereby makes the following regulations:—

Citation, commencement and interpretation

1.—(1) These regulations may be cited as the Schools (Qualified Teachers) Regulations 1973 and shall come into operation on 1st January 1974.

(2) The Interpretation Act 1889**(c)** shall apply for the interpretation of these regulations as it applies for the interpretation of an Act of Parliament.

Amendment of regulations

2. Regulation 16 (employment of teachers) of the Schools Regulations 1959**(d)** as amended**(e)** shall have effect subject to—

(*a*) in paragraph (1), the omission of sub-paragraph (*a*);

(*b*) in paragraph (1)(*b*), the omission of the word "other";

(*c*) in paragraph (2)(*b*), the omission of "(acquired in the case of a teacher in a primary school before 1st January 1970)" and, at the end of paragraph (2), the addition of the following:

"provided that a person who is eligible for acceptance as a qualified teacher by virtue only of sub-paragraph (*b*) above—

(i) may not be accepted as a teacher in a primary school (but, subject to sub-paragraph (ii) below, may be accepted as a teacher in a secondary school) if his qualification was acquired after 31st December 1969;

(a) 1958 c. 55.

(b) 1944 c. 31.

(c) 1889 c. 63.

(d) S.I. 1959/364 (1959 I, p. 1584).

(e) The relevant amending instruments are S.I. 1969/1777, 1971/342 (1969 III, p. 5573; 1971 I, p. 1082).

(ii) may be accepted as a teacher in a secondary school if his qualification was acquired after 31st December 1973 only where it is one for the time being recognised by the Secretary of State as a qualification in a subject for teachers of which there is a special need";

(*d*) in paragraph 2(*e*), the substitution for the words "as may be" of the words "or such experience, as may on the recommendation of an authority be"; and

(*e*) in paragraph (3), the omission of sub-paragraph (*b*).

Consequential amendment

3.—(1) In regulation 15(2) (teachers in special schools) of the Handicapped Pupils and Special Schools Regulations 1959**(a)** as amended**(b)** the reference to regulation 16(2) of the Schools Regulations 1959 shall be construed as a reference to that regulation as amended, subject to the substitution for the proviso of the following proviso:—

"provided that a person who is eligible for acceptance as a qualified teacher by virtue only of sub-paragraph(*b*) above may not be accepted as a teacher in a special school if his qualification was acquired after 31st December 1969".

(2) Regulation 3 of the Schools (Qualified Teachers) Regulations 1969**(c)**, which is superseded by paragraph (1) above, is hereby revoked.

Given under the Official Seal of the Secretary of State for Education and Science on 3rd December 1973.

(L.S.)

Margaret H. Thatcher,
Secretary of State for
Education and Science.

EXPLANATORY NOTE

(This Note is not part of the Regulations.)

These Regulations provide that from 1st January 1974 a person shall be eligible for appointment as a qualified teacher in a maintained secondary school by virtue of a special qualification only if he acquired it before that date or it is in a subject for teachers of which there is a special need. They also make minor amendments to the provisions of the regulations which regulate the employment of teachers in maintained schools.

(a) S.I. 1959/365 (1959 I, p. 1024).
(b) The relevant amending instrument is S.I. 1971/342 (1971 I, p. 1082).
(c) S.I. 1969/1777 (1969 III, p. 5573).

STATUTORY INSTRUMENTS

1973 No. 2023

LOCAL GOVERNMENT, ENGLAND AND WALES

The Fire Services (Retirement of Senior Officers) (Amendment) Regulations 1973

Made - - -	*29th November* 1973
Laid before Parliament	*11th December* 1973
Coming into Operation	*24th December* 1973

In exercise of the powers conferred on me by section 260 of the Local Government Act 1972(**a**), I hereby make the following Regulations:—

1. These Regulations may be cited as the Fire Services (Retirement of Senior Officers) (Amendment) Regulations 1973 and shall come into operation on 24th December 1973.

2. In Regulation 3(1)(*a*) of the Fire Services (Retirement of Senior Officers) Regulations 1973(**b**) (application of section 260 of the Local Government Act 1972) for the date "1st January 1974" there shall be substituted the date "24th December 1973".

Robert Carr,
One of Her Majesty's Principal
Secretaries of State.

Home Office,
Whitehall.

29th November 1973.

EXPLANATORY NOTE

(*This Note is not part of the Regulations.*)

These Regulations amend the Fire Services (Retirement of Senior Officers) Regulations 1973 (which come into operation on 24th December 1973) under Regulation 3(1)(*a*) of which only senior fire service officers serving as such on 1st January 1974 can qualify for the benefit of the Regulations. The present Regulations change this qualiying date to 24th December 1973.

(**a**) 1972 c. 70. (**b**) S.I. 1973/1951 (1973 III, p. 6772).

STATUTORY INSTRUMENTS

1973 No. 2024

LOCAL GOVERNMENT, ENGLAND AND WALES

The Police (Retirement of Senior Officers) (Amendment) Regulations 1973

Made - - -	*29th November* 1973
Laid before Parliament	*11th December* 1973
Coming into Operation	*24th December* 1973

In exercise of the powers conferred on me by section 260 of the Local Government Act 1972(**a**), I hereby make the following Regulations:—

1. These Regulations may be cited as the Police (Retirement of Senior Officers) (Amendment) Regulations 1973 and shall come into operation on 24th December 1973.

2. In Regulation 3(1)(*a*) of the Police (Retirement of Senior Officers) Regulations 1973(**b**) (application of section 260 of the Local Government Act 1972) for the date "1st January 1974" there shall be substituted the date "24th December 1973".

Robert Carr,
One of Her Majesty's Principal
Secretaries of State.

Home Office,
Whitehall.

29th November 1973.

EXPLANATORY NOTE

(*This Note is not part of the Regulations.*)

These Regulations amend the Police (Retirement of Senior Officers) Regulations 1973 (which come into operation on 24th December 1973) under Regulation 3(1)(*a*) of which only senior police officers serving as such on 1st January 1974 can qualify for the benefit of the Regulations. The present Regulations change this qualifying date to 24th December 1973.

(**a**) 1972 c. 70.
(**b**) S.I. 1973/1944 (1973 III, p. 6693)

1973 No. 2025

LOCAL GOVERNMENT, ENGLAND AND WALES

The Local Government (Voluntary Schools and Educational Charities) Order 1973

Made - - -	29*th November* 1973
Laid before Parliament	12*th December* 1973
Coming into Operation	1*st April* 1974

The Secretary of State for Education and Science and the Secretary of State for Wales, in exercise of the powers conferred on them by section 254(1) and (2)(*b*) of the Local Government Act 1972(**a**), hereby make the following Order:—

Citation, commencement and interpretation

1.—(1) This Order may be cited as the Local Government (Voluntary Schools and Educational Charities) Order 1973 and shall come into operation on 1st April 1974.

(2) In this Order, except where the context otherwise requires—

"educational charity" means a charity, not being a charity incorporated under the Companies Acts or by charter, registered in the register established under section 4 of the Charities Act 1960(**b**) in a part of the register which immediately before 1st February 1974 is maintained by the Secretary of State by virtue of section 2 of the Charities Act 1960 or excepted from registration by virtue of the Charities (Exception of Voluntary Schools from Registration) Regulations 1960(**c**);

"instrument" means an instrument of government or of management made under section 17(2) of the Education Act 1944(**d**);

"representative", in references to a manager or governor, means a manager or governor who is not a foundation manager or governor;

"trust deed" includes any instrument regulating a charity, except an instrument of government or of management made under section 17(2) of the Education Act 1944;

"Wales" means the area comprising the counties named in Part I of schedule 4 to the Local Government Act 1972 and "England" does not include any part of that area;

other expressions have the meanings assigned to them by the Education Acts 1944 to 1973.

(3) The Interpretation Act 1889(**e**) shall apply for the interpretation of this Order as it applies for the interpretation of an Act of Parliament.

(**a**) 1972 c. 70. (**b**) 1960 c. 58. (**c**) S.I. 1960/2366 (1960 I, p. 522).
(**d**) 1944 c. 31. (**e**) 1889 c. 63.

Managers of primary schools

2.—(1) The instrument for any voluntary primary school maintained by the council of an existing county which as from 1st April 1974 will not serve the area of any minor authority shall have effect as if it provided for all the representative managers of the school to be appointed by the local education authority; and any manager of such a school who was appointed by an existing minor authority shall vacate his office on 1st April 1974.

(2) The instrument for any voluntary primary school maintained by the council of an existing county borough which as from 1st April 1974 will serve the area of a minor authority shall have effect as if it provided for the appointment by that minor authority of one third of the number of representative managers or, if the number of such managers is not divisible by three, of one half of that number; and the representative managers of all such schools shall vacate their offices on 1st April 1974.

Terms of office of managers and governors

3.—(1) There shall be substituted for any provision in an instrument relating to the term of office of the representative managers or governors of a voluntary school which—

(*a*) is maintained by the council of an existing county borough; and

(*b*) as from 1st April 1974 will be maintained by the council of a non-metropolitan county—

a provision that any such manager or governor shall hold office until the appointment of his successor, which may be made at any time after the ordinary day of election of county councillors next after his appointment; and the representative managers and governors of all such schools who are in office immediately before 1st April 1974 shall, unless article 2(2) above applies to them, hold their offices for the terms for which they were respectively appointed.

(2) There shall be substituted for any provision in an instrument relating to the term of office of the representative managers or governors of a voluntary school which—

(*a*) is maintained by the council of an existing county; and

(*b*) as from 1st April 1974 will be maintained by the council of a metropolitan district—

a provision that any such manager or governor shall hold office for a period of three years.

(3) There shall be substituted for any provision in an instrument relating to the term of office of the representative managers or governors of a voluntary school which—

(*a*) is maintained by the council of an existing county; and

(*b*) as from 1st April 1974 will be maintained by the council of a non-metropolitan county—

a provision that any such manager or governor shall hold office until the appointment of his successor, which may be made at any time after the ordinary day of election of county councillors next after his appointment.

Construction of references to officers

4. Any reference (in whatever terms) contained in an instrument, or in articles of government, for a voluntary school to the chief education officer of a divisional executive or the council of an excepted district shall, unless the context otherwise requires, be construed as a reference to the chief education officer of the local education authority by which the school is maintained.

Educational charities

5. Article 8 of the Local Government (New Councils, etc.) Order 1973(**a**) and article 3 above shall, with the necessary adaptations, apply to a provision contained in a trust deed of an educational charity which specifies the term of office of any trustee appointed by a local education authority as they apply to any provision in the instrument for a voluntary school which specifies the term of office of any manager or governor so appointed (references to the authority having the power of appointment being substituted for references to the authority maintaining the school).

Given under the Official Seal of the Secretary of State for Education and Science on 23rd November 1973.

(L.S.)

Margaret H. Thatcher,
Secretary of State for Education and Science.

Given under my hand on 29th November 1973.

Peter Thomas,
Secretary of State for Wales.

EXPLANATORY NOTE

(*This Note is not part of the Order.*)

This Order makes provision consequential upon the Local Government Act 1972 with regard to the composition of the managing bodies of voluntary primary schools; the terms of office of managers and governors of voluntary schools and of trustees of educational charities who are appointed by local education authorities; and the construction of references to the chief education officers of certain bodies which will cease to exist as a result of the repeal by the Act of Part III of schedule 1 to the Education Act 1944.

(**a**) S.I. 1973/444 (1973 I, p. 1535).

1973 No. 2030

ANIMALS

DISEASES OF ANIMALS

The Tuberculosis (Amendment) Order 1973

Made - - -	*3rd December* 1973
Laid before Parliament	*11th December* 1973
Coming into Operation	*1st January* 1974

The Minister of Agriculture, Fisheries and Food in exercise of the powers conferred on him by sections 1, 8(3), 20, 77(3) and 85(1) of the Diseases of Animals Act 1950(**a**) and of all his other enabling powers, hereby makes the following order:—

Citation and commencement

1. This order, which may be cited as the Tuberculosis (Amendment) Order 1973, shall come into operation on 1st January 1974.

Interpretation

2.—(1) This order shall be construed as one with the Tuberculosis Order 1964(**b**), hereinafter referred to as "the principal order".

(2) The Interpretation Act 1889(**c**) applies to the interpretation of this order as it applies to the interpretation of an Act of Parliament.

Amendments of principal order

3. There shall be inserted in Article 3(1) of the principal order (interpretation) the following definition:

"carcase" means the carcase of any bovine animal and includes any part of the carcase or any flesh, bone, hide, skin, hooves, offal or other part of a bovine animal, separately or otherwise or any part thereof.

4. The following Article shall be inserted in the principal order immediately following Article 5 thereof, namely:—

"*Notice of disease in a carcase*

5A.—(1) Every person having in his possession or under his charge on any premises any carcase which is affected with or is suspected of being affected with tuberculosis, and every veterinary surgeon or veterinary practitioner who in his private practice, and every person who in the course of his duties under the Meat Inspection Regulations 1963(**d**), or in the course of meat inspection carried out for the purposes of export certification of meat

(**a**) 1950 c. 36.
(**b**) S.I. 1964/1151 (1964 II, p. 2634).
(**c**) 1889 c. 63.
(**d**) S.I. 1963/1229 (1963 II, p. 2041).

examines any carcase, and is of opinion or suspects that such carcase is affected with tuberculosis, shall with all practicable speed give notice of the fact to a veterinary inspector.

(2) Any person having in his possession or under his charge a carcase which is affected with or suspected of being affected with tuberculosis shall detain it (or the part thereof affected with or suspected of being affected with tuberculosis) until it has been examined by a veterinary inspector."

5. Article 8 of the principal order (tuberculosis tests and vaccination) shall be amended by the addition after paragraph (3) thereof of the following paragraph:—

"(4) If any person fails to comply with any reasonable requirement of a veterinary inspector or other officer of the Ministry made in accordance with the provisions of paragraph (1) of this Article the Minister may, without prejudice to any proceedings for an offence arising out of such default, take or cause to be taken all such steps as may be necessary to facilitate the examination of such bovine animal, or the application thereto of any diagnostic test for tuberculosis, and the amount of any expenses reasonably incurred by the Minister for the purpose of making good the default shall be recoverable by him as a civil debt from the person in default."

6. There shall be inserted at the end of Article 11(1) of the principal order (precautions against the spread of infection) the words "and may, by such notice, require the isolation of any bovine animals specified in the notice in a specified part of the premises to which the notice relates."

In Witness whereof the Official Seal of the Minister of Agriculture, Fisheries and Food is hereunto affixed on 3rd December 1973.

(L.S.) *Joseph Godber,*
Minister of Agriculture, Fisheries and Food.

EXPLANATORY NOTE

(This Note is not part of the Order.)

This Order amends the Tuberculosis Order 1964 so as to include provisions requiring notification in respect of the carcase of a bovine animal which is suspected of being affected with tuberculosis, and detention of the whole or part of such a carcase pending inspection by a veterinary inspector.

The Order also enables the Minister, where the owner or person in charge of a bovine animal fails to take steps to facilitate the examination of such an animal or the application thereto of any diagnostic test for tuberculosis, to recover from him the expenses reasonably incurred in making good the default as a civil debt.

Provision is also made for the isolation of bovine animals in a certain part of any premises if this appears necessary for the prevention of the spread of disease.

STATUTORY INSTRUMENTS

1973 No. 2031

TRADE DESCRIPTIONS

The Trade Descriptions (Indication of Origin) (Exemptions No. 5) Directions 1973

Made - - -	*3rd December* 1973
Coming into Operation	*29th December* 1973

The Secretary of State, in exercise of the powers conferred on him by section 1(5) of the Trade Descriptions Act 1972(**a**) hereby gives the following Directions:—

1. These Directions may be cited as the Trade Descriptions (Indication of Origin) (Exemptions No. 5) Directions 1973, and shall come into operation on 29th December 1973.

2. Subsection (2) of section 1 of the Trade Descriptions Act 1972 shall be excluded in relation to goods described in Schedule 1 hereto.

3. The said subsection shall be excluded in relation to goods described in Schedule 2 hereto if any United Kingdom name or mark applied to such goods, which that subsection would, but for the provisions of this paragraph, have required to be accompanied by an indication of the country in which the goods were manufactured or produced, is accompanied by "imported", "foreign", or other words indicating that the goods were manufactured or produced outside the United Kingdom appearing conspicuously.

C. E. Coffin,
An Under Secretary of the
Department of Trade and Industry.

3rd December 1973.

SCHEDULE 1

1. Dyestuffs, colouring matter and luminophores falling within Chapters 32.05, 32.06 and 32.07 of the Customs Tariff 1959 as set out in Schedule 1 to the Import Duties (General) (No. 8) Order 1973(**b**).

2. Natural micaceous iron oxides falling within Chapter 25.09 of the said Customs Tariff.

3. Medicinal products as defined in section 130 of the Medicines Act 1968(**c**).

(**a**) 1972 c. 34. (**b**) S.I. 1973/1845(1973 III, p. 5601) (**c**) 1968. c. 67.

SCHEDULE 2

1. Plant growth regulators and anti-sprouting agents.
2. Weed killers, fungicides, insecticides, nematocides, molluscicides, rodenticides and other preparations used as pesticides.

EXPLANATORY NOTE

(This Note is not part of the Directions.)

These Directions exclude section 1(2) of the Trade Descriptions Act 1972 (which requires that a United Kingdom name or mark applied to imported goods be accompanied by an indication of the country of origin of those goods) in relation to goods of the descriptions mentioned in Schedule 1 to the Directions. They also permit alternative origin markings for goods of the descriptions mentioned in Schedule 2 to the Directions.

STATUTORY INSTRUMENTS

1973 No. 2035 (C.61)

LEGAL AID AND ADVICE, ENGLAND

The Legal Aid and Advice Act 1949 (Commencement No. 13) Order 1973

Made - - - *29th November* 1973

The Lord Chancellor, in exercise of the powers conferred on him by section 17(2) of the Legal Aid and Advice Act 1949(**a**), hereby makes the following Order:—

1.—(1) The Interpretation Act 1889(**b**) shall apply to the interpretation of this Order as it applies to the interpretation of an Act of Parliament.

(2) This Order may be cited as the Legal Aid and Advice Act 1949 (Commencement No. 13) Order 1973.

2. The provisions of Part I of the Legal Aid and Advice Act 1949 shall come into operation on 1st January 1974 for the purpose of making legal aid available in connection with proceedings in the Restrictive Practices Court under Part III of the Fair Trading Act 1973(**c**), and any proceedings in that Court in consequence of an order made, or undertaking given to the Court, under that Part of that Act.

Dated 29th November 1973.

Hailsham of St. Marylebone, C.

EXPLANATORY NOTE

(*This Note is not part of the Order.*)

This Order brings the provisions of Part I of the Legal Aid and Advice Act 1949 into operation on 1st January 1974 so as to make legal aid available in connection with proceedings in the Restrictive Practices Court under Part III of the Fair Trading Act 1973.

(**a**) 1949 c. 51. (**b**) 1889 c. 63. (**c**) 1973 c. 41.

1973 No. 2036

LEGAL AID AND ADVICE, ENGLAND

The Legal Aid (General) (Amendment) Regulations 1973

Made - - -	29*th November* 1973
Laid before Parliament	12*th December* 1973
Coming into Operation	1*st January* 1974

The Lord Chancellor, in exercise of the powers conferred on him by sections 2 and 12 of, and the Third Schedule to, the Legal Aid and Advice Act 1949(**a**), hereby makes the following Regulations:—

1.—(1) These Regulations may be cited as the Legal Aid (General) (Amendment) Regulations 1973 and shall come into operation on 1st January 1974.

(2) The Interpretation Act 1889(**b**) shall apply to the interpretation of these Regulations as it applies to the interpretation of an Act of Parliament.

(3) In these Regulations a regulation referred to by number means a regulation so numbered in the Legal Aid (General) Regulations 1971(**c**), as amended (**d**).

2. In the Arrangement of Regulations at the beginning of the Legal Aid (General) Regulations 1971 after "26(B). The Commons Commissioners." there shall be inserted "26(C). The Restrictive Practices Court.".

3. The following regulation shall be inserted after regulation 26(B):—

"*The Restrictive Practices Court*

26(C).—(1) In this regulation the expression "the Restrictive Practices Court" means the Court established by section 2 of the Restrictive Trade Practices Act 1956(**e**) and the expression "the proper officer of the Court" shall have the same meaning as in the Restrictive Practices Rules 1957(**f**).

(2) Except in so far as otherwise provided by this regulation, these Regulations shall apply to applications for legal aid for proceedings in the Restrictive Practices Court under Part III of the Fair Trading Act 1973(**g**) and for any proceedings in that Court in consequence of an order made, or undertaking given to the Court, under that Part of that Act, and to the conduct of all such proceedings for which a certificate is granted, in like manner as they apply to applications for legal aid for, and the conduct of, proceedings in any court.

(**a**) 1949 c. 51.
(**b**) 1889 c. 63.
(**c**) S.I. 1971/62 (1971 I, p. 75).
(**d**) There are no relevant amendments.
(**e**) 1956 c. 68.
(**f**) S.I. 1957/603 (1957 II, p. 1955).
(**g**) 1973 c. 41.

(3) Where any power to do any act or exercise any jurisdiction or discretion is conferred by these Regulations on a court it shall, in relation to proceedings in the Restrictive Practices Court, be exercised by that Court and may, unless it is exercisable only during the hearing of the proceedings by a judge or by the Court, be exercisable by the proper officer of the Court.

(4) (*a*) Where it appears to the appropriate committee that an application for a certificate relates to proceedings which are likely to be conducted in Scotland or Northern Ireland, they shall transmit the application forthwith to the Secretary of the Legal Aid Central Committee of the Law Society of Scotland or the Secretary of the Legal Aid Department of the Incorporated Law Society of Northern Ireland as the case may be and shall notify the applicant and his solicitor that they have done so.

(*b*) Where it appears to the appropriate committee doubtful whether the proceedings to which an application for a certificate relates will be conducted in the Restrictive Practices Court when sitting in England and Wales or in Scotland or Northern Ireland they shall request the proper officer of the Court to determine that question, and that determination shall be binding upon the committee.

(5) Where a certificate has been issued and there is a change of circumstances regarding the conduct of the proceedings in that, by order of the Restrictive Practices Court, they will be wholly or partly conducted in Scotland or Northern Ireland—

(*a*) the certificate shall remain in force;

(*b*) for any proceedings in Scotland—

(i) the assisted person shall continue to be represented in the proceedings by the solicitor who represented him in England and Wales and that solicitor may instruct a member of the bar of England and Wales or of Scotland from the panel maintained by The Law Society of barristers and advocates willing to act for assisted persons before the Restrictive Practices Court, and

(ii) no question as to the propriety of appearing in Scotland shall be raised on a taxation in accordance with the provisions of the Third Schedule to the Act or on an assessment by an area committee in accordance with regulation 22.

(*c*) for any proceedings in Northern Ireland, the assisted person shall continue to be represented in the proceedings by the solicitor who represented him in England and Wales and that solicitor shall instruct as his agent a solicitor on the panel maintained by the Incorporated Law Society of Northern Ireland of solicitors willing to act for assisted persons before the Restrictive Practices Court.

(6) (*a*) The provisions of the Third Schedule to the Act shall apply to proceedings in the Restrictive Practices Court as they apply to proceedings in the House of Lords, the Court of Appeal and the High Court, and the sums allowed in connection with those proceedings shall be, to a solicitor, the full amount allowed on taxation of the costs on account of disbursements and 90% of the amount so allowed on account of profit costs and, to counsel, 90% of the amount so allowed.

(*b*) The costs of an assisted person shall be assessed by an area committee in accordance with regulation 22 or taxed in accordance with the

Third Schedule to the Act by a Taxing Master of the Supreme Court, and the provisions of Order 62 of the Rules of the Supreme Court shall apply, with the necessary modifications, to the taxation of those costs as if the proceedings in the Restrictive Practices Court were a cause or matter in the Supreme Court."

Dated 29th November 1973.

Hailsham of St. Marylebone, C.

EXPLANATORY NOTE

(*This Note is not part of the Regulations.*)

These Regulations amend the Legal Aid (General) Regulations 1971, as amended, so as to extend them to applications for and the grant of legal aid for proceedings brought before the Restrictive Practices Court under Part III of the Fair Trading Act 1973, to make provision for applications in England where those proceedings are likely to be conducted in Scotland or Northern Ireland, or where those proceedings are transferred to Scotland or Northern Ireland after a certificate is issued, for the taxation of costs in those proceedings and for the remuneration of solicitors and counsel.

STATUTORY INSTRUMENTS

1973 No. 2037

CUSTOMS AND EXCISE

The Anti-Dumping and Countervailing Duties Order 1973

Made - - - -	*4th December* 1973
Laid before the House of Commons	*10th December* 1973
Coming into Operation	*1st January* 1974

The Secretary of State, in exercise of powers conferred by sections 1, 2, 7, 15 and 18(2) of the Customs Duties (Dumping and Subsidies) Act 1969(**a**) and now vested in him(**b**) and all other powers enabling him in that behalf, hereby makes the following Order:

1.—(1) This Order may be cited as the Anti-Dumping and Countervailing Duties Order 1973 and shall come into operation on 1st January 1974.

(2) The Interpretation Act 1889(**c**) shall apply to the interpretation of this Order as it applies to the interpretation of an Act of Parliament and as if this Order and the Orders hereby revoked were Acts of Parliament.

(3) The Orders specified in Schedule 2 hereto are hereby revoked.

2. The anti-dumping and countervailing duties chargeable immediately before the commencement of this Order by virtue of Orders mentioned in Schedule 2 hereto on the importation into the United Kingdom of goods of the descriptions mentioned in column 2 of Schedule 1 shall be chargeable on and after 1st January 1974 by virtue of this Order at the relevant rate set out in column 3.

3. There shall be charged on the importation into the United Kingdom of any goods of the description set out in column 2 of Schedule 1 hereto (being goods classified in the Customs Tariff 1959(**d**) under the heading mentioned in column 1 of that Schedule) a duty of customs at the rate mentioned in column 3.

4. Section 2 of the Customs Duties (Dumping and Subsidies) Act 1969 (which allows relief to be given where goods are shown not to have been dumped or where the margin of dumping is less than the amount of the duty) shall apply to the duties imposed by this Order.

Limerick,
Parliamentary Under-Secretary of State for Trade,
Department of Trade and Industry.

4th December 1973.

(**a**) 1969 c. 16. (**b**) S.I. 1970/1537 (1970 III, p. 5293). (**c**) 1889 c. 63.
(**d**) S.I. 1973/1845 (1973 III, p. 5601).

SCHEDULE 1

Anti-Dumping Duties

Relevant Tariff Heading	Description	Rate chargeable from 1st January 1974
11.02 C.III.	Pearled Barley (including blocked, pot and pearl barley) originating in the Federal Republic of Germany	£0·6000 per cwt
ex 28.21 B.	Chromic anhydride (CrO_3) originating in the Union of Soviet Socialist Republics	£49·2100 per tonne
ex 28.28 IJ.II.	Zirconium dioxide originating in the Union of Soviet Socialist Republics	£270·6565 per tonne
29.26 A.I.	Saccharin and its salts (*a*) originating in Japan (*b*) originating in the Republic of Korea	£0·0917 per kilogramme £0·5511 per kilogramme
ex 31.02 C.IV.	Calcium ammonium nitrate originating in the Republic of South Africa	£14·7630 per tonne
ex 73.01 B.III. ex 73.01 C.II. ex 73.01 D.I.b) ex 73.01 D.II.e)	Pig iron and cast iron originating in the German Democratic Republic and Berlin (East)	£5 per tonne
77.01 A.II.	Unwrought magnesium originating in the Union of Soviet Socialist Republics	£62 per tonne
91.04 B.I.b)	Mechanical alarm clocks of a value less than £0·6000 each originating in the People's Republic of China	£0·1000 each
	Countervailing Duties	
ex 84.15 B.	Domestic refrigerators electrically operated of a storage capacity not exceeding 12 cubic feet originating in Italy but excluding food freezers and refrigerators cum freezers	£0·0238 per kilogramme

SCHEDULE 2

Revocations

The Anti-Dumping (No. 1) Order 1959 S.I. 1959/917 (1959 I, p. 901).
The Anti-Dumping Duty Order 1966 S.I. 1966/319 (1966 I, p. 774).
The Anti-Dumping Duty (No. 1) Order 1969 S.I. 1969/895 (1969 II, p. 2563).
The Anti-Dumping and Countervailing Duties (Metric Rates) Order 1971 S.I. 1971/2001 (1971 III, p. 5691).
The Anti-Dumping Duty Order 1972 S.I. 1972/569 (1972 I, p. 1897).
The Anti-Dumping (Provisional Charge to Duty) Order 1972 S.I. 1972/1361 (1972 III, p. 4194).
The Anti-Dumping (Provisional Charge to Duty) (Extension) Order 1972 S.I. 1972/1907 (1972 III, p. 5548).
The Anti-Dumping and Countervailing Duties (Metric Rates) Order 1971 (Amendment) Order 1972 S.I. 1972/2024 (S.I. 1972 III, p. 6003).
The Anti-Dumping Duty Order 1973 S.I. 1973/419 (1973 I, p. 1384).

EXPLANATORY NOTE

(This Note is not part of the Order.)

This Order replaces certain current anti-dumping and countervailing duty Orders. The way in which most of the headings of the Customs Tariff are at present subdivided will be changed with effect from 1st January 1974. This Order takes account of these and other minor drafting changes. The duties are to be chargeable on and after 1st January 1974 on specified goods classified in the relevant tariff headings of the amended Tariff. There is no increase in duty as a result of these changes.

The Order applies section 2 of the Customs Duties (Dumping and Subsidies) Act 1969 to the duties. This section enables relief to be granted where particular goods have not been dumped or the margin of dumping is shown to be less than the amount of duty payable.

Some spent Orders are included among the Orders revoked.

1973 No. 2038

CUSTOMS AND EXCISE

The Composite Goods Order 1968 (Amendment) (No. 2) Order 1973

Made - - -	*4th December* 1973
Laid before the House of Commons	*10th December* 1973
Coming into Operation	*1st January* 1974

The Lords Commissioners of Her Majesty's Treasury by virtue of the powers conferred on them by Schedule 2 to the Finance Act 1957(**a**) and all other powers enabling them in that behalf, hereby make the following Order:—

1. This Order shall be cited as the Composite Goods Order 1968 (Amendment) (No. 2) Order 1973 and shall come into operation on 1st January 1974.

2. In this Order "the Principal Order" means The Composite Goods Order 1968(**b**).

3. The Interpretation Act 1889(**c**) applies for the interpretation of this Order as it applies for the interpretation of an Act of Parliament.

4. The Principal Order shall be amended by deleting from the column of the Schedule thereto bearing the heading "Tariff Subheading" the figures and letters in column 1 and by substituting therefor the figures and letters in column 2 hereunder—

Existing Tariff Subheading	*New Tariff Subheading*
34.03(B)(1)	34.03 A.II.*a*)
38.18(B)(1)(*a*))	38.18 B.I.*a*)
38.18(B)(2)(*a*))	B.II.*a*)
36.08(C)	36.08 C.

Hamish Gray,
Hugh Rossi,
Two of the Lords Commissioners of Her Majesty's Treasury.

4th December 1973.

(**a**) 1957 c. 49.
(**b**) S.I. 1968/1381 (1968 II, p. 3932).
(**c**) 1889 c. 63.

EXPLANATORY NOTE

(*This Note is not part of the Order.*)

Some subheadings of Chapters 34, 36 and 38 of the Customs Tariff are altered with effect from 1st January 1974. This Order amends the Schedule to the Composite Goods Order 1968 so that the same imported composite goods as heretofore continue to be charged with hydrocarbon oil duty at ad valorem rates.

The Order makes no change in the liability to duty of the goods concerned.

STATUTORY INSTRUMENTS

1973 No. 2044

IRON AND STEEL

The Iron and Steel Act 1969 (Continuance of Provisions) Order 1973

Laid before Parliament in draft

Made - - - *4th December* 1973

Coming into Operation 30*th March* 1974

The Secretary of State, in exercise of powers conferred by section 6(2) of the Iron and Steel Act 1969(**a**) and now vested in him(**b**) and of all other powers enabling him in that behalf, hereby makes the following Order, a draft of which has, in accordance with the said section 6(2), been approved by a resolution of each House of Parliament:—

1. This Order may be cited as the Iron and Steel Act 1969 (Continuance of Provisions) Order 1973 and shall come into operation on 30th March 1974.

2. Sections 2(1), 4 and 5 of the Iron and Steel Act 1969 shall continue in force permanently.

Tom Boardman,
Minister for Industry,
Department of Trade and Industry.

4th December 1973.

EXPLANATORY NOTE

(*This Note is not part of the Order.*)

This Order exercises the powers conferred by section 6 of the Iron and Steel Act 1969 to continue in force sections 2(1), 4 and 5 of that Act which would otherwise expire on 30th March 1974, which is the end of the financial year of the British Steel Corporation's that first ends after 1973.

The provisions which are continued in force permanently relate to investment in the British Steel Corporation by way of public dividend capital, the notional capitalisation of the Corporation's reserves and the financial duties of the Corporation.

(**a**) 1969 c. 45. (**b**) S.I. 1969/1498, 1970/1537 (1969 III, p, 4797; 1970 III, p. 5293).

STATUTORY INSTRUMENTS

1973 No. 2045 (L.30)

COUNTY COURTS

The County Court Districts (Miscellaneous) Order 1973

Made - - - -	*6th December* 1973
Coming into Operation	*1st January* 1974

The Lord Chancellor, in exercise of the powers conferred on him by section 2 of the County Courts Act 1959**(a)**, hereby makes the following Order:—

1.—(1) The County Court Districts Order 1970**(b)**, as amended**(c)**, (hereinafter called the principal Order) shall have effect as further amended by this Order.

(2) This Order may be cited as the County Court Districts (Miscellaneous) Order 1973 and shall come into operation on 1st January 1974.

(3) The Interpretation Act 1889**(d)** shall apply to the interpretation of this Order as it applies to the interpretation of an Act of Parliament.

2.—(1) The holding of the Thetford County Court shall be discontinued and the entry relating to that court in Schedule 1 to the principal Order shall be deleted.

(2) The amendments set out in columns 2 and 3 of Schedule 1 to this Order shall be made in their proper alphabetical position in the corresponding columns of Schedule 1 to the principal Order opposite the names of the courts mentioned in column 1.

(3) In Schedule 2 to the principal Order, there shall be inserted, after the entry relating to the Bridgend County Court, the following entry:—

Column 1	*Column* 2
"Bury St. Edmunds	Bury St. Edmunds and Thetford".

(4) The Bury St. Edmunds County Court shall have jurisdiction in proceedings in the Thetford County Court commenced before this Order comes into operation.

3. The amendments set out in columns 2 and 3 of Schedule 2 to this Order shall be made in the corresponding columns of Schedule 1 to the principal Order opposite the names of the courts mentioned in column 1:

(a) 1959 c. 22. **(b)** S.I. 1970/16 (1970 I, p. 17).
(c) The relevant amending instrument is S.I. 1970/904 (1970 II, p. 2833).
(d) 1889 c. 63.

Provided that nothing in this Order shall affect the jurisdiction of the Edmonton County Court to hear and determine any proceedings pending therein on the coming into operation of this Order.

Hailsham of St. Marylebone, C.

Dated 6th December 1973.

SCHEDULE 1

AMENDMENTS CONSEQUENT ON CLOSURE OF THETFORD COUNTY COURT

Column 1	*Column* 2	*Column* 3
BURY ST. EDMUNDS	In the entry relating to the Mildenhall Rural District:—	
	For "*Other parts* in Newmarket and Thetford County Court Districts" substitute "*Other part* in Newmarket County Court District."	Insert "Brandon, Elvedon, Santon, Downham and Wangford."
	After the entry relating to the Thedwastre Rural District insert the following entry:—	
	"Thetford Municipal Borough.	Thetford."
	In the entry relating to the Thingoe Rural District:—	
	Delete "(part)" and "*Other part* in Thetford County Court District."	Insert "Barnham, Barningham, Coney Weston, Euston, Fakenham Magna, Hepworth, Honington, Hopton, Knettishall, Market Weston, Sapiston and Thelnetham."
	Immediately after the entry relating to the Thingoe Rural District insert the following entry:—	
	"Wayland Rural District (part). *Other parts* in King's Lynn and Norwich County Court Districts.	Brettenham, Bridgham, Caston, Croxton, Harling, Hockham, Kenninghall, Kilverstone, Riddlesworth, Roudham, Stow Bedon, Thompson, Tottington, Wretham."
EAST DEREHAM	In the entry relating to the Swaffham Rural District:—	
	For "*Other parts* in King's Lynn and Thetford County Court Districts" substitute "*Other part* in King's Lynn County Court District."	

Column 1	*Column* 2	*Column* 3
KING'S LYNN	In the entry relating to the Downham Rural District:—	
	Delete "(part)" and "*Other part* in Thetford County Court District."	Insert "Feltwell, Hockwold cum Wilton, Methwold and Northwold".
	In the entry relating to the Swaffham Rural District:—	
	For "*Other parts* in East Dereham and Thetford County Court Districts" substitute "*Other part* in East Dereham County Court District."	Insert "Cranwich, Lynford, Mundford, Stanford, Sturston and Weeting with Broomhill".
	In the entry relating to the Wayland Rural District:—	
	For "Thetford" substitute "Bury St. Edmunds."	
NEWMARKET	In the entry relating to the Mildenhall Rural District:—	
	For "*Other parts* in Bury St. Edmunds and Thetford County Court Districts" substitute "*Other part* in Bury St. Edmunds County Court District."	
NORWICH	In the entry relating to the Wayland Rural District:—	
	For "Thetford" substitute "Bury St. Edmunds".	

SCHEDULE 2

BARNET AND EDMONTON COUNTY COURTS
BOUNDARY ALTERATION AND CONSEQUENT AMENDMENTS

Column 1	*Column* 2	*Column* 3
BARNET	In the entry relating to the London Borough of Enfield substitute the following:—	
		"That part of the Borough west of a line drawn from the point where the Borough boundary crosses Cattlegate Road, south-eastwards along the west side of Cattlegate Road to East Lodge Lane, southwards along the west side of East Lodge Lane to The Ridgway, then along the east side of The Ridgway to the junction with Windmill Hill, along the south side of Windmill Hill and Church Street to the New River and then southwards

Column 1	Column 2	Column 3
		along the centre of the New River to Bush Hill, then along the north side of Bush Hill to its junction with London Road, south-east across the junction and along the south side of Bush Hill to the New River and then along the middle of the New River to Bush Hill Road, along the east side of Bush Hill Road and the east side of Church Street to Gt. Cambridge Road thence southwards along the west side of Gt. Cambridge Road to its junction with Hedge Lane, westwards along the north side of Hedge Lane to its junction with Green Lanes and then southwards along the east side of Green Lanes to its junction with Bowes Road, westwards along the south side of Bowes Road to the middle of the Hertford North railway line and thence southwards along the middle of the railway line to the Borough boundary."

Immediately after the entry relating to the London Borough of Enfield insert the following entry:—

Column 1	Column 2	Column 3
	"London Borough of Haringey (part). *Other parts* in Clerkenwell and Edmonton County Court Districts.	That part of the Borough north of a line drawn from the point where the Borough boundary crosses Grosvenor Road, easterly along the east side of Grosvenor Road to Albert Road, thence along the south side of Albert Road and Durnsford Road to the point where it meets the Welwyn Garden City railway line and thence south-east along the middle of the railway line to the intersection of the Hertford North railway line and thence northward along the middle of the railway line to the point where it crosses the Borough boundary."

Column 1	*Column* 2	*Column* 3
CLERKENWELL	In the entry relating to the London Borough of Haringey:— For "*Other part* in Edmonton County Court District" substitute "*Other parts* in Barnet and Edmonton County Court Districts".	
EDMONTON	In the entry relating to the London Borough of Enfield substitute the following entry:—	"That part of the Borough east of a line drawn from the point where the Borough boundary crosses Cattlegate Road, south-eastwards along the west side of Cattlegate Road to East Lodge Lane, southwards along the west side of East Lodge Lane to The Ridgway, then along the east side of The Ridgway to the junction with Windmill Hill, along the south side of Windmill Hill and Church Street to the New River and then southwards along the centre of the New River to Bush Hill, then along the north side of Bush Hill to its junction with London Road, south-east across the junction and along the south side of Bush Hill to the New River and then along the middle of the New River to Bush Hill Road, along the east side of Bush Hill Road and the east side of Church Street to Gt. Cambridge Road thence southwards along the west side of Gt. Cambridge Road to its junction with Hedge Lane, westwards along the north side of Hedge Lane to its junction with Green Lanes and then southwards along the east side of Green Lanes to its junction with Bowes Road, westwards along the south side of Bowes Road to the middle of the Hertford North railway line and thence southwards along the middle of the railway line to the Borough boundary."

Column 1	*Column* 2	*Column* 3
	In the entry relating to the London Borough of Haringey:—	
	For "*Other part* in Clerkenwell County Court District" substitute "*Other parts* in Barnet and Clerkenwell County Court Districts."	Delete "and Grosvenor Road to the Borough boundary" and substitute "to Albert Road, and thence along the south side of Albert Road and Durnsford Road to the point where it meets the Welwyn Garden City railway and thence south-east along the middle of the railway line to the intersection of the Hertford North railway line and thence northward along the middle of the railway line to the point where it crosses the Borough boundary."

EXPLANATORY NOTE

(*This Note is not part of the Order.*)

This Order closes the Thetford County Court, divides its district among those of neighbouring courts, and provides for sittings of the Bury St. Edmunds County Court to be held at Bury St. Edmunds and Thetford. The Order also transfers certain parts of the London Boroughs of Enfield and Haringey from the district of the Edmonton County Court to the district of the Barnet County Court.

STATUTORY INSTRUMENTS

1973 No. 2046 (L.31)

SUPREME COURT OF JUDICATURE, ENGLAND

PROCEDURE

The Rules of the Supreme Court (Amendment No. 2) 1973

Made - - - *27th November* 1973

Laid before Parliament *13th December* 1973

Coming into Operation in accordance with Rule 1(1)

We, the Rule Committee of the Supreme Court, being the authority having for the time being power under section 99(4) of the Supreme Court of Judicature (Consolidation) Act 1925(**a**) to make, amend or revoke rules regulating the practice and procedure of the Supreme Court of Judicature, hereby exercise those powers and all other powers enabling us in that behalf as follows:—

1.—(1) These Rules may be cited as the Rules of the Supreme Court (Amendment No. 2) 1973 and shall come into operation on the day appointed for the coming into force of Part I of the Guardianship Act 1973(**b**).

(2) In these Rules an Order referred to by number means the Order so numbered in the Rules of the Supreme Court 1965(**c**), as amended(**d**).

(3) The Interpretation Act 1889(**e**) shall apply to the interpretation of these Rules as it applies to the interpretation of an Act of Parliament.

2. Order 90 shall be amended as follows:—

(1) In rule 3 after paragraph (3) there shall be inserted the following paragraph:—

"(3A) The date of the minor's birth shall, unless otherwise directed, be stated in the summons and the plaintiff shall—

(*a*) on issuing the summons or before or at the first hearing thereof lodge in the registry out of which the summons issued a certified copy of the entry in the Register of Births or, as the case may be, in the Adopted Children Register relating to the minor, or

(*b*) at the first hearing of the summons apply for directions as to proof of birth of the minor in some other manner."

(2) In rule 5, for the words "the Guardianship of Minors Act 1971(**f**)", wherever they appear, there shall be substituted the words "the Guardianship of Minors Acts 1971 and 1973" and for the words "(hereafter in this Part of this Order referred to as "the Act of 1971")" there shall be substituted the words "(in this Part of this Order referred to as "the Guardianship Acts")".

(**a**) 1925 c. 49. (**b**) 1973 c. 29. (**c**) S.I. 1965/1776 (1965 III, p. 4995).
(**d**) The relevant amending instruments are S.I. 1971/1269, 1972/813, 1898 (1971 II, p. 3634; 1972 II, p. 2618; III, p. 5523). (**e**) 1889 c. 63. (**f**) 1971 c. 3.

(3) The words "the Guardianship Acts" shall be substituted for the words "the Act of 1971" in the first place where they appear in rule 6(1) and in each place where they appear in rules 7 and 8(1).

(4) In rule 6(1), for the words "the Act of 1971" in the second place where they appear, there shall be substituted the words "the Guardianship of Minors Act 1971 (in this Part of this Order referred to as "the Act of 1971")".

(5) For rule 11, there shall be substituted the following rule:—

"*Application of matrimonial causes rules*

11.—(1) The provisions of the matrimonial causes rules relating to proceedings under section 43 or 44 of the Matrimonial Causes Act 1973(**a**) shall apply, with the necessary modifications, to proceedings under section 7 of the Family Law Reform Act 1969(**b**), or sections 2(2), 3 and 4 of the Guardianship Act 1973.

(2) The provisions of the matrimonial causes rules relating to the drawing up and service of orders shall apply to proceedings under this Part of this Order as if they were proceedings under those rules."

(6) In rule 12(2), after the words "without prejudice to" there shall be inserted the words "rule 11(1) and to".

Dated 27th November 1973.

Hailsham of St. Marylebone, C.
Widgery, C. J.
Denning, M. R.
George Baker, P.
John Pennycuick, V-C.
Eustace Roskill, L. J.
P. J. Millett.
Michael Wright.
William Carter.
H. Montgomery-Campbell.

EXPLANATORY NOTE

(*This Note is not part of the Rules.*)

These Rules make amendments to the Rules of the Supreme Court relating to wardship and guardianship of minors. Rule 2(1) requires the plaintiff in wardship proceedings to state the date of birth of the minor in the summons and to provide evidence of the birth by lodging a birth certificate or in accordance with directions of the Court. Paragraphs (2) to (6) of Rule 2 are mainly consequential on the coming into operation of the Guardianship Act 1973. The provisions of the matrimonial causes rules relating to applications for supervision orders and for orders committing a child to the care of a local authority are to govern applications for such orders under the Act of 1973 or under section 7 of the Family Law Reform Act 1969.

(**a**) 1973 c. 18. (**b**) 1969 c. 46.

STATUTORY INSTRUMENTS

1973 No. 2051

CONTROL OF FUEL AND ELECTRICITY

The Fuel Control (Modification of Enactments) (Speed Limits) Order 1973

Made - - -	*7th December* 1973
Laid before Parliament	*7th December* 1973
Coming into Operation	*7th December* 1973

At the Court at Buckingham Palace, the 7th day of December 1973

Present,

The Queen's Most Excellent Majesty in Council

Her Majesty, in exercise of the powers conferred on Her by section 4(3) of the Fuel and Electricity (Control) Act 1973(**a**), is pleased, by and with the advice of Her Privy Council, to order, and it is hereby ordered, as follows:—

1.—(1) This Order may be cited as the Fuel Control (Modification of Enactments) (Speed Limits) Order 1973 and shall come into operation on 7th December 1973.

(2) In this Order, "the Act of 1967" means the Road Traffic Regulation Act 1967(**b**) and "fuel" means a substance to which the Fuel and Electricity (Control) Act 1973 applies.

(3) The Interpretation Act 1889(**c**) shall apply for the interpretation of this Order as it applies for the interpretation of an Act of Parliament.

2. The power of the Secretary of State under section 77 of the Act of 1967 to impose temporary speed limits on roads where it appears to him desirable to do so in the interest of safety or for the purpose of facilitating the movement of traffic shall be exercisable also where it appears to him desirable in the interests of regulating the use of fuel.

3. The requirement under section 77(1) of the Act of 1967 for the giving of public notice by the Secretary of State of his intention to impose a temporary speed limit under that section shall not apply in any case where he exercises the power under that section in the interests of regulating the use of fuel.

4. The following provisions of the Act of 1967, that is to say—

(*a*) section 107(2) (which requires the Secretary of State to consult with representative organisations before making regulations under that Act), and

(*b*) section 107(4) (which provides that regulations under the said section 78 of that Act shall not have effect unless approved by resolution of each House of Parliament),

---

(**a**) 1973 c. 67.
(**b**) 1967 c. 76.
(**c**) 1889 c. 63.

shall not apply in relation to the power of the Secretary of State to make regulations under—

(i) section 13 of the Act of 1967 (regulation of traffic on special roads) or

(ii) section 78 of that Act (speed limits on vehicles of different classes),

in any case where he exercises any of those powers in the interests of regulating the use of fuel.

N. E. Leigh.

EXPLANATORY NOTE

(This Note is not part of the Order.)

This Order extends the power of the Secretary of State under the Road Traffic Regulation Act 1967 to impose temporary speed limits on roads so that the power is exercisable in the interests of regulating the use of motor fuel (Article 2). The Order also provides for the exclusion of certain procedural obligations and restrictions applicable to that power and to Regulations of the Secretary of State under the 1967 Act by which speed limits on motorways or on particular classes of vehicle may be imposed where the Regulations are made in the interests aforesaid. (Articles 3 and 4.)

STATUTORY INSTRUMENTS

1973 No. 2052

CONTROL OF FUEL AND ELECTRICITY

The Fuel Control (Modification of Enactments) (Speed Limits) (Northern Ireland) Order 1973

Made - - -	*7th December* 1973
Laid before Parliament	*7th December* 1973
Coming into Operation	*7th December* 1973

At the Court at Buckingham Palace, the 7th day of December 1973

Present,

The Queen's Most Excellent Majesty in Council

Her Majesty, in exercise of the powers conferred on Her by section 4(3) of the Fuel and Electricity (Control) Act 1973(**a**), is pleased, by and with the advice of Her Privy Council, to order, and it is hereby ordered, as follows:—

1.—(1) This Order may be cited as the Fuel Control (Modification of Enactments) (Speed Limits) (Northern Ireland) Order 1973 and shall come into operation on 7th December 1973.

(2) In this Order, "the Act of 1970" means the Road Traffic Act (Northern Ireland) 1970(**b**) and "fuel" means a substance to which the Fuel and Electricity (Control) Act 1973 applies.

(3) The Interpretation Act 1889(**c**) shall apply for the interpretation of this Order as it applies for the interpretation of an Act of Parliament.

2. The power of the Ministry of Home Affairs under section 44 of the Act of 1970 to impose temporary speed limits on roads where it is satisfied that it is desirable to do so in the interests of safety or for the purpose of facilitating the movement of traffic shall be exercisable also where it is satisfied that it is desirable to do so in the interests of regulating the use of fuel.

3. The requirement under section 44(1) of the Act of 1970 for the giving of public notice by the Ministry of Home Affairs of its intention to impose a temporary speed limit under that section shall not apply in any case where it exercises its power under section 44 in the interests of regulating the use of fuel.

N. E. Leigh.

(**a**) 1973 c. 67.
(**b**) 1970 c. 2 (N.I.).
(**c**) 1889 c. 63.

EXPLANATORY NOTE

(*This Note is not part of the Order.*)

This Order extends the power of the Ministry of Home Affairs for Northern Ireland, by Order under the Road Traffic Act (Northern Ireland) 1970, to impose temporary speed limits on roads so that the power is exercisable in the interests of regulating the use of motor fuel. It also relieves the Ministry of its obligation to give public notice of its intention to exercise this power.

STATUTORY INSTRUMENTS

1973 No. 2053

CONTROL OF FUEL AND ELECTRICITY

The Fuel and Electricity (Control) Act 1973 (Guernsey) Order 1973

Made - - - -	*7th December* 1973
Coming into Operation	*7th December* 1973

At the Court at Buckingham Palace, the 7th day of December 1973

Present,

The Queen's Most Excellent Majesty in Council

Her Majesty, in exercise of the powers conferred upon Her by section 9 of the Fuel and Electricity (Control) Act 1973(**a**), is pleased, by and with the advice of Her Privy Council, to order, and it is hereby ordered, as follows:—

1. This Order may be cited as the Fuel and Electricity (Control) Act 1973 (Guernsey) Order 1973 and shall come into operation forthwith.

2. The Interpretation Act 1889 (**b**) shall apply for the interpretation of this Order as it applies for the interpretation of an Act of Parliament.

3. The Fuel and Electricity (Control) Act 1973 shall extend to the Bailiwick of Guernsey subject to the exceptions, adaptations and modifications specified in the Schedule to this Order.

N. E. Leigh.

(**a**) 1973 c. 67. (**b**) 1889 c. 63.

SCHEDULE

EXCEPTIONS, ADAPTATIONS AND MODIFICATIONS TO THE FUEL AND ELECTRICITY (CONTROL) ACT 1973

1. Any reference to the Fuel and Electricity (Control) Act 1973 shall be construed as a reference to that Act as extended to the Bailiwick of Guernsey by this Order.

2. For the words " Secretary of State ", wherever they occur, there shall be substituted—

(*a*) in relation to any part of the Bailiwick of Guernsey other than the Island of Alderney, the words " States of Guernsey Emergency Council", and

(*b*) in relation to the Island of Alderney, the words " States of Alderney Finance Committee ".

3. Section 4(2) shall be omitted.

4. In section 4(3) for the words " Her Majesty may by Order in Council " there shall be substituted the words " The States of Guernsey may by Ordinance.".

5. Section 4(4) and (5) shall be omitted.

6. For section 4(6) there shall be substituted the following provision:—

" (6) Any Ordinance made under this section may be varied or repealed by a subsequent Ordinance of the States of Guernsey.".

7. For section 5 there shall be substituted the following sections:—

" *Application of provisions of Defence (General) (Guernsey) Regulations* 1945 *as continued in force*

5.—(1) The following Regulations set out in Part V of Schedule 2 to the Defence (General) (Guernsey) Regulations Continuance Order 1960(**a**), as continued in force by the Defence (General) (Guernsey) Regulations Continuance Order 1964(**b**), that is to say Regulations 82 (false documents and false statements), 84 (restrictions on disclosing information), 87(3) (permits, licences, etc.), 91 (offences by corporations), 97 (service of notices) and 98 (revocation and variation of orders, etc.), shall have effect for the purposes of this Act as if in those provisions any reference to a Regulation were a reference to this Act: and in the following provisions of this Act any reference to an offence under this Act shall be construed as including an offence under the provisions applied by this subsection.

(2) The supplementary provisions of paragraphs 2 and 4 of Schedule 3 to the said Order of 1960 shall have effect for the purposes of this Act as if in those provisions—

(*a*) any reference to such a Regulation as is mentioned in paragraph 1 of the said Schedule 3 were a reference to this Act (including the provisions applied by subsection (1) above), and

(*b*) any reference to British ships or aircraft not being excepted ships or aircraft or to persons on board such a ship or aircraft were omitted.

Production of documents

5A.—(1) For the purposes—

(*a*) of securing compliance with any order made or direction given under this Act by or on behalf of a competent authority or

(*b*) of verifying any estimates, returns or information furnished to a competent authority in connection with this Act or any order made or direction given thereunder,

an officer of a competent authority duly authorised in that behalf shall have power, on producing (if required to do so) evidence of his authority, to require any person carrying on an undertaking or employed in connection with an undertaking to produce to the officer forthwith any documents relating to the undertaking which the officer may reasonably require for the purposes set out above in this section.

(**a**) S.I. 1960/208 (1960 I, p. 1323). (**b**) S.I. 1964/2035 (1964 III, p. 5118).

(2) The power conferred by this section to require any person to produce documents shall include power—

(*a*) if the documents are produced—

(i) to take copies of them or extracts from them, and

(ii) to require that person, or, where that person is a body corporate, any other person who is a present or past officer of, or is employed by, the body corporate, to provide an explanation of any of them,

(*b*) if the documents are not produced, to require the person who was required to produce them to state, to the best of his knowledge and belief, where they are.

(3) If the Bailiff is satisfied, on information on oath given on behalf of a competent authority that there are any reasonable grounds for suspecting that there are on any premises any documents of which production has been required by virtue of the foregoing provisions of this section and which have not been produced in compliance with that requirement, the Bailiff may issue a warrant authorising any officer of police, together with any other persons named in the warrant and any other officers of police, to enter the premises specified in the information (using such force as is reasonably necessary for the purpose) and to search the premises and take possession of any documents appearing to be such documents as aforesaid, or to take in relation to any documents so appearing any other steps which may appear necessary for preserving them and preventing interference with them.

(4) Every warrant issued under the last preceding subsection shall continue in force until the end of the period of one month after the date on which it is issued.

(5) Any documents of which possession is taken under subsection (3) of this section may be retained for a period of three months or, if within that period there are commenced any proceedings for an offence under this Act to which they are relevant, until the conclusion of those proceedings.

(6) Any person who obstructs the exercise of any right of entry or search conferred by virtue of a warrant under subsection (3) of this section, or who obstructs the exercise of any rights so conferred to take possession of any documents shall be guilty of an offence under this Act.

(7) In this section—

" Bailiff " means—

(*a*) in relation to the Islands of Guernsey, Herm and Jethou, the Bailiff, the Deputy Bailiff, a Lieutenant Bailiff or the Juge Délégué;

(*b*) in relation to the Island of Alderney, the Chairman of the Court of Alderney; and

(*c*) in relation to the Island of Sark, the Seneschal;

" competent authority " means—

(*a*) in relation to any part of the Bailiwick of Guernsey other than the Island of Alderney, the States of Guernsey Emergency Council;

(*b*) in relation to the Island of Alderney, the States of Alderney Finance Committee;

" officer of police " means—

(*a*) in relation to the Islands of Guernsey, Herm and Jethou, a member of the salaried police force of the Island of Guernsey and, within the limit of his jurisdiction, a member of the special constabulary of the Island of Guernsey;

(*b*) in relation to the Island of Alderney, a member of the said police force and a member of any police force which may be established by the States of Alderney and, within the limit of his jurisdiction, a special constable appointed by the Court of Alderney under section 65 of the Government of Alderney Law 1948; and

(*c*) in relation to the Island of Sark, the Constable, the Vingtenier and a member of the said police force of Guernsey.".

8. In section 6(1) for the words " subject, however " to the end there shall be substituted the following words:—

" Provided that where a person is charged with an offence by reason of a failure to comply with a requirement to produce documents imposed under subsection (1) of section 5A of this Act, it shall be a defence to prove that the documents were not in his possession or under his control and that it was not reasonably practicable for him to comply with the requirement.".

9. In section 6(3) for the words " United Kingdom " there shall be substituted the words " Bailiwick of Guernsey ".

10. Section 7 shall be omitted.

11. For section 8 there shall be substituted the following section:—

" *Interpretation*

8.—(1) In this Act " enactment " means any provision contained in a Law or in an Ordinance in force in the Bailiwick of Guernsey or in any part thereof.

(2) In this Act " petroleum " includes any mineral oil or relative hydro-carbon and natural gas existing in its natural condition in strata, but does not include coal or bituminous shales or other stratified deposits from which oil can be extracted by destructive distillation.".

12. Section 9 shall be omitted.

13. Section 10(5) shall be omitted.

14. Section 11(2) shall be omitted.

EXPLANATORY NOTE

(*This Note is not part of the Order.*)

This Order extends the Fuel and Electricity (Control) Act 1973 to the Bailiwick of Guernsey subject to specified exceptions, adaptations and modifications.

STATUTORY INSTRUMENTS

1973 No. 2054

CONTROL OF FUEL AND ELECTRICITY

The Fuel and Electricity (Control) Act 1973 (Isle of Man) Order 1973

Made - - - -	*7th December* 1973
Coming into Operation	*7th December* 1973

At the Court at Buckingham Palace, the 7th day of December 1973

Present,

The Queen's Most Excellent Majesty in Council

Her Majesty, in exercise of the powers conferred upon Her by section 9 of the Fuel and Electricity (Control) Act 1973(**a**), is pleased, by and with the advice of Her Privy Council, to order, and it is hereby ordered, as follows:—

1. This Order may be cited as the Fuel and Electricity (Control) Act 1973 (Isle of Man) Order 1973 and shall come into operation forthwith.

2. The Interpretation Act 1889 (**b**) shall apply for the interpretation of this Order as it applies for the interpretation of an Act of Parliament.

3. The Fuel and Electricity (Control) Act 1973 shall extend to the Isle of Man subject to the exceptions, adaptations and modifications specified in the Schedule to this Order.

N. E. Leigh.

(**a**) 1973 c. 67. (**b**) 1889 c. 63.

SCHEDULE

EXCEPTIONS, ADAPTATIONS AND MODIFICATIONS TO THE FUEL AND ELECTRICITY (CONTROL) ACT 1973

1. Any reference to the Fuel and Electricity (Control) Act 1973 shall be construed as a reference to that Act as extended to the Bailiwick of Guernsey by this Order.

2. For the words " Secretary of State ", wherever they occur, there shall be substituted—

(*a*) in relation to any part of the Bailiwick of Guernsey other than the Island of Alderney, the words " States of Guernsey Emergency Council", and

(*b*) in relation to the Island of Alderney, the words " States of Alderney Finance Committee ".

3. Section 4(2) shall be omitted.

4. In section 4(3) for the words " Her Majesty may by Order in Council " there shall be substituted the words " The States of Guernsey may by Ordinance.".

5. Section 4(4) and (5) shall be omitted.

6. For section 4(6) there shall be substituted the following provision:—

" (6) Any Ordinance made under this section may be varied or repealed by a subsequent Ordinance of the States of Guernsey.".

7. For section 5 there shall be substituted the following sections:—

" *Application of provisions of Defence (General) (Guernsey) Regulations* 1945 *as continued in force*

5.—(1) The following Regulations set out in Part V of Schedule 2 to the Defence (General) (Guernsey) Regulations Continuance Order 1960(**a**), as continued in force by the Defence (General) (Guernsey) Regulations Continuance Order 1964(**b**), that is to say Regulations 82 (false documents and false statements), 84 (restrictions on disclosing information), 87(3) (permits, licences, etc.), 91 (offences by corporations), 97 (service of notices) and 98 (revocation and variation of orders, etc.), shall have effect for the purposes of this Act as if in those provisions any reference to a Regulation were a reference to this Act: and in the following provisions of this Act any reference to an offence under this Act shall be construed as including an offence under the provisions applied by this subsection.

(2) The supplementary provisions of paragraphs 2 and 4 of Schedule 3 to the said Order of 1960 shall have effect for the purposes of this Act as if in those provisions—

(*a*) any reference to such a Regulation as is mentioned in paragraph 1 of the said Schedule 3 were a reference to this Act (including the provisions applied by subsection (1) above), and

(*b*) any reference to British ships or aircraft not being excepted ships or aircraft or to persons on board such a ship or aircraft were omitted.

Production of documents

5A.—(1) For the purposes—

(*a*) of securing compliance with any order made or direction given under this Act by or on behalf of a competent authority or

(*b*) of verifying any estimates, returns or information furnished to a competent authority in connection with this Act or any order made or direction given thereunder,

an officer of a competent authority duly authorised in that behalf shall have power, on producing (if required to do so) evidence of his authority, to require any person carrying on an undertaking or employed in connection with an undertaking to produce to the officer forthwith any documents relating to the undertaking which the officer may reasonably require for the purposes set out above in this section.

(**a**) S.I. 1960/208 (1960 I, p. 1323). (**b**) S.I. 1964/2035 (1964 III, p. 5118).

(5) An order under this Act shall take effect on such day or days as may be specified in the order, not being earlier than that on which the order is made, and different days may be specified for different purposes and different provisions of the order.

(6) An order under this Act shall be laid before Tynwald as soon as may be after it is made and unless it is approved by Tynwald at the sitting of Tynwald before which it is laid, or at the next sitting of Tynwald after the sitting before which it is laid, the order shall become void without prejudice, however, to the validity of anything previously done thereunder or to the making of a new order.

(7) In this section any reference to an order or directions is a reference to an order made, or directions given, by the Governor.

Notices, authorisations and proof of documents

5A.—(1) A notice to be served on any person for the purposes of this Act, or of any order or direction made or given under this Act, shall be deemed to have been duly served on the person to whom it is directed if—

(*a*) it is delivered to him personally, or

(*b*) it is sent by registered post or the recorded delivery service addressed to him at his last or usual place of abode or place of business.

(2) Any permit, licence, permission or authorisation granted for the purposes of this Act may be revoked at any time by the authority or person empowered to grant it.

(3) Every document purporting to be an instrument made or issued by any person or body in pursuance of this Act, or of any provision having effect under this Act, and to be signed by or on behalf of that person or body shall be received in evidence and shall, until the contrary is proved, be deemed to be an instrument made or issued by that person or body; and prima facie evidence of any such instrument as aforesaid may, in any legal proceedings (including arbitrations), be given by the production of a document purporting to be certified to be a true copy of the instrument by or on behalf of the person or body having power to make or issue the instrument.

Territorial extent

5B. Unless the contrary intention appears therefrom, any provisions contained in, or having effect under, this Act shall, in so far as they impose prohibitions, restrictions or obligations on persons, apply to all persons in the Isle of Man, and to all other persons, wherever they may be, who are ordinarily resident in the Isle of Man and who are citizens of the United Kingdom and Colonies or British protected persons (within the meaning of the British Nationality Act 1948 (**a**)).

False documents and false statements

5C.—(1) If, with intent to deceive, any person—

(*a*) uses any document issued for the purposes of this Act or of any order made under this Act; or

(*b*) has in his possession any document so closely resembling such a document as aforesaid as to be calculated to deceive; or

(*c*) produces, furnishes, sends or otherwise makes use of, for purposes connected with this Act or any order or direction made or given under this Act, any book, account, estimate, return, declaration or other document which is false in a material particular,

he shall be guilty of an offence under this Act.

(2) If, in furnishing any information for the purposes of this Act or of any order made under this Act, any person makes any statement which he knows to be false in a material particular, or recklessly makes any statement which is false in a material particular, he shall be guilty of an offence under this Act.

Restrictions on disclosing information

5D. No person who obtains any information by virtue of this Act shall, otherwise than in connection with the execution of this Act or of an order made under this

(**a**) 1948 c. 56.

Act, disclose that information except for the purposes of any criminal proceedings, or of a report of any criminal proceedings, or with permission granted by or on behalf of the Governor.

Offences by corporations

5E.—(1) Where an offence under this Act committed by a body corporate is proved to have been committed with the consent or connivance of, or to be attributable to any neglect on the part of, any director, manager, secretary or other similar officer of the body corporate or any person who was purporting to act in any such capacity, he, as well as the body corporate, shall be guilty of that offence and shall be liable to be proceeded against and punished accordingly.

(2) In this section, the expression " director ", in relation to a body corporate established by or under any enactment for the purpose of carrying on under national ownership any industry or part of an industry or undertaking, being a body corporate whose affairs are managed by its members, means a member of that body corporate.

Production of documents

5F.—(1) For the purposes—

(*a*) of securing compliance with any order made or direction given under this Act by or on behalf of the Governor, or

(*b*) of verifying any estimates, returns or information furnished to the Governor in connection with this Act or any order made or direction given thereunder,

an officer appointed by the Governor and duly authorised in that behalf shall have power, on producing (if required to do so) evidence of his authority, to require any person carrying on an undertaking or employed in connection with an undertaking to produce to the officer forthwith any documents relating to the undertaking which the officer may reasonably require for the purposes set out above in this section.

(2) The power conferred by this section to require any person to produce documents shall include power—

(*a*) if the documents are produced—

(i) to take copies of them or extracts from them, and

(ii) to require that person, or, where that person is a body corporate, any other person who is a present or past officer of, or is employed by, the body corporate, to provide an explanation of any of them,

(*b*) if the documents are not produced, to require the person who was required to produce them to state, to the best of his knowledge and belief, where they are.

(3) If a justice of the peace is satisfied, on information on oath given on behalf of the Governor that there are any reasonable grounds for suspecting that there are on any premises any documents of which production has been required by virtue of the foregoing provisions of this section and which have not been produced in compliance with that requirement, the justice of the peace may issue a warrant authorising any officer of police, together with any other persons named in the warrant and any other officers of police, to enter the premises specified in the information (using such force as is reasonably necessary for the purpose) and to search the premises and take possession of any documents appearing to be such documents as aforesaid, or to take in relation to any documents so appearing any other steps which may appear necessary for preserving them and preventing interference with them.

(4) Every warrant issued under the last preceding subsection shall continue in force until the end of the period of one month after the date on which it is issued.

(5) Any documents of which possession is taken under subsection (3) of this section may be retained for a period of three months or, if within that period there are commenced any proceedings for an offence under this Act to which they are relevant, until the conclusion of those proceedings.

(6) Any person who obstructs the exercise of any right of entry or search conferred by virtue of a warrant under subsection (3) of this section, or who obstructs the exercise of any rights so conferred to take possession of any documents shall be guilty of an offence under this Act.

(7) In this section the expression " officer of police " means a member of the Isle of Man constabulary.".

9. In section 6(1) for the words " subject, however " to the end there shall be substituted the following words:—

" Provided that where a person is charged with an offence by reason of a failure to comply with a requirement to produce documents imposed under subsection (1) of section 5F of this Act, it shall be a defence to prove that the documents were not in his possession or under his control and that it was not reasonably practicable for him to comply with the requirement.".

10. In section 6(3) for the words " United Kingdom " there shall be substituted the words " Isle of Man ".

11. Section 7 shall be omitted.

12. For section 8 there shall be substituted the following section:—

" *Interpretation*

8.—(1) In this Act " enactment " means an Act of Tynwald.

(2) In this Act " petroleum " includes any mineral oil or relative hydro-carbon and natural gas existing in its natural condition in strata, but does not include coal or bituminous shales or other stratified deposits from which oil can be extracted by destructive distillation.

(3) In this Act " Governor " means the Lieutenant Governor of the Isle of Man and includes a Deputy or Acting Lieutenant Governor.".

13. Section 9 shall be omitted.

14. Section 10(5) shall be omitted.

15. Section 11(2) shall be omitted.

EXPLANATORY NOTE

(*This Note is not part of the Order.*)

This Order extends the Fuel and Electricity (Control) Act 1973 to the Isle of Man subject to specified exceptions, adaptations and modifications.

1973 No. 2058

ROAD TRAFFIC

The Motor Vehicles (Speed Limits on Motorways) (Amendment) Regulations 1973

Made - - - - *7th December* 1973

Coming into Operation *8th December* 1973

The Secretary of State for the Environment, in exercise of his powers under section 78(2) and (4) of the Road Traffic Regulation Act 1967(**a**) and of all other enabling powers, hereby makes the following Regulations:—

1. These Regulations may be cited as the Motor Vehicles (Speed Limits on Motorways) (Amendment) Regulations 1973 and shall come into operation on 8th December 1973.

2. The Motor Vehicles (Speed Limits on Motorways) Regulations 1973(**b**) (which, in relation to certain classes of vehicle, vary the speed limit for those classes imposed under Schedule 5 to the Road Traffic Regulation Act 1967) shall have effect as though in paragraph 1 of Schedule 1—

(*a*) the words "except when falling within paragraph 2 below" were omitted, and

(*b*) for the figure "60" there were substituted the figure "50".

John Peyton,
Minister for Transport Industries,
Department of the Environment.

Signed by authority of
the Secretary of State.
7th December 1973.

EXPLANATORY NOTE

(*This Note is not part of the Regulations.*)

Schedule 5 to the Road Traffic Regulation Act 1967, as varied by the Motor Vehicles (Speed Limits on Motorways) Regulations 1973, specifies speed limits for certain classes of vehicles when being driven on a motorway. These Regulations amend the Regulations of 1973 so as to provide that the maximum speed for goods vehicles having an unladen weight exceeding 3 tons shall be 50 (instead of 60) miles per hour.

(**a**) 1967 c. 76.

(**b**) S.I. 1973/748 (1973 I, p. 2389).

STATUTORY INSTRUMENTS

1973 No. 2059

ROAD TRAFFIC

The Motorways Traffic (Speed Limit) Regulations 1973

Made - - - -	*7th December* 1973
Laid before Parliament	*7th December* 1973
Coming into Operation	*8th December* 1973

The Secretary of State for the Environment (so far as relating to motorways in England), the Secretary of State for Scotland (so far as relating to motorways in Scotland) and the Secretary of State for Wales (so far as relating to motorways in Wales), in exercise respectively of their powers under section 13 of the Road Traffic Regulation Act 1967(**a**) and of all other enabling powers, hereby make the following Regulations:—

1. These Regulations shall come into operation on 8th December 1973 and may be cited as the Motorways Traffic (Speed Limit) Regulations 1973.

2.—(1) In these Regulations the expression "motorway" has the meaning assigned to it in the Motorways Traffic Regulations 1959(**b**).

(2) The Interpretation Act 1889(**c**) shall apply for the interpretation of these Regulations as it applies for the interpretation of an Act of Parliament, and as if for the purposes of section 38 of that Act these Regulations were an Act of Parliament and the Regulations revoked by Regulation 4 below were Acts of Parliament thereby repealed.

3. No person shall drive a motor vehicle on a motorway at a speed greater than 50 miles per hour:

Provided that this Regulation shall not apply to the driving of a motor vehicle on any length of motorway on which there is for the time being a restriction imposed under section 13 of the said Act of 1967 on the driving of a motor vehicle in excess of a maximum speed which is less than 50 miles per hour.

4. The Motorways Traffic (Speed Limit) (England) Regulations 1967(**d**), the Motorways Traffic (Speed Limit) (Scotland) Regulations 1967(**e**) and the Motorways Traffic (Speed Limit) (Wales) Regulations 1967(**f**), and any other regulations made or having effect as if made under section 13 of the said Act of 1967 which are in force on the date of coming into operation of these Regulations and which impose a restriction on the driving of motor vehicles

(**a**) 1967 c. 76.
(**b**) S.I. 1959/1147 (1959 II, p. 2507).
(**c**) 1889 c. 63.
(**d**) S.I. 1967/1041 (1967 II, p. 3125).
(**e**) S.I. 1967/1044 (1967 II, p. 3133).
(**f**) S.I. 1967/1039 (1967 II, p. 3122).

on specified lengths of motorway at a speed greater than 50 miles per hour or in excess of a maximum speed which is greater than 50 miles per hour, are hereby revoked.

Signed by authority of
the Secretary of State.

John Peyton,
Minister for Transport Industries,
Department of the Environment.

7th December 1973.

Gordon Campbell,
Secretary of State for Scotland.

7th December 1973.

Peter Thomas,
Secretary of State for Wales.

7th December 1973.

EXPLANATORY NOTE

(*This Note is not part of the Regulations.*)

These Regulations impose indefinitely a maximum speed limit of 50 miles per hour on the driving of motor vehicles on motorways (other than lengths of motorway which are subject to lower maximum speed limits) after midnight at the end of Friday 7th December 1973.

On roads other than motorways the same speed limit is imposed by virtue of the 50 miles per hour Speed Limit Order 1973.

STATUTORY INSTRUMENTS

1973 No. 2060

COMPANIES

The Companies (Fees) Regulations 1973

Laid before Parliament in draft

Made - - - -	*6th December* 1973
Coming into Operation	*8th December* 1973

Whereas a draft of these regulations has been laid before Parliament and approved by resolution of each House pursuant to section 48(3) of the Companies Act 1967(**a**) (hereinafter referred to as " the Act "):

Now, therefore, the Secretary of State in exercise of his powers under section 48(2) of the Act hereby makes the following regulations:

1. These regulations may be cited as the Companies (Fees) Regulations 1973 and shall come into operation two days after they have been approved by resolution of each House of Parliament.

2. The Interpretation Act 1889(**b**) shall apply to the interpretation of these regulations as it applies to the interpretation of an Act of Parliament.

3. For Schedule 3 to the Act there shall be substituted the Schedule to these regulations.

Geoffrey Howe,
Minister for Trade and Consumer Affairs,
Department of Trade and Industry.

6th December 1973.

(**a**) 1967 c. 81. (**b**) 1889 c 63.

SCHEDULE

Fees to be Paid to the Registrar of Companies

Matter in respect of which Fee is payable	Amount of Fee
	£
For registration of a company on its formation under the Companies Act 1948(a), re-registration of a company under that Act in pursuance of section 44 of the Companies Act 1967 or registration of a company under the Companies Act 1948 in pursuance of Part VIII thereof as a limited company (not being a company in whose case the liability of the members thereof was, before registration in pursuance of that Part, limited by some other Act or by letters patent)	50
For re-registration of a company under the Companies Act 1948 in pursuance of section 43 of the Companies Act 1967	5
For registration of a copy of an annual return or copies of documents delivered to the registrar of companies in compliance with section 410 of the Companies Act 1948	3
For entering on the register the name of a company assumed by virtue of the passing of a special resolution by virtue of section 18(1) of the Companies Act 1948	40

EXPLANATORY NOTE

(This Note is not part of the Regulations.)

These Regulations come into operation on 8th December 1973 and alter the fees payable to the registrar of companies in the following respects:—

1. The fee for registration of a company is to be a fixed fee of £50 instead of a fee varying from £20 to £68 according to the amount of the nominal capital with which the company is registered or varying from £20 to £38, in the case of a company without a share capital, according to the number of members.

2. The fees payable for registration of an increase in the share capital or the membership of a company are abolished.

3. The fee for registration of a change in a company's name is increased from £10 to £40.

(a) 1948 c. 38.

STATUTORY INSTRUMENTS

1973 No. 2062

WAGES COUNCILS

The Flax and Hemp Wages Council (Great Britain) (Variation) Order 1973

Made - - - -	6*th December* 1973
Laid before Parliament	17*th December* 1973
Coming into Operation	14*th January* 1974

Whereas the Secretary of State has published in accordance with section 4(6) of, and Schedule 1 to, the Wages Councils Act 1959(**a**), notice of his intention to make an Order varying the field of operation of the Flax and Hemp Wages Council (Great Britain):

And whereas no objections have been made to the draft of the said Order referred to in the said notice:

Now, therefore, the Secretary of State in exercise of powers conferred by section 4(2) of the Wages Councils Act 1959 and now vested in him (**b**), and of all other powers enabling him in that behalf hereby makes the following Order:—

1. The field of operation of the Flax and Hemp Wages Council (Great Britain) is hereby varied by the inclusion therein of workers employed in the activity of calendering which variation is set out as item (2) of the activities included in the trade specified in the Schedule to this Order and accordingly the said Wages Council shall operate in relation to workers employed in Great Britain in the trade so specified and their employers.

2.—(1) This Order may be cited as the Flax and Hemp Wages Council (Great Britain) (Variation) Order 1973 and shall come into operation on 14th January 1974.

(2) The Schedule to the Trade Boards (Flax and Hemp Trade, Great Britain) (Constitution and Proceedings) Regulations 1940(**c**) shall cease to have effect.

(3) The Interpretation Act 1889(**d**) shall apply to the interpretation of this Order as it applies to the interpretation of an Act of Parliament.

(**a**) 1959 c. 69.

(**b**) S.I. 1959/1769, 1968/729 (1959 I, p. 1795; 1968 II, p. 2108).

(**c**) S.R. & O 1940/1886 (1940 I, p. 1031). (**d**) 1889 c. 63.

Signed by order of the Secretary of State.

6th December 1973.

R. Chichester-Clark,

Minister of State,
Department of Employment.

Article 1

SCHEDULE

The Flax and Hemp Trade

The preparing, spinning and weaving (*a*) of scutched flax, (*b*) of hemp, (*c*) of a mixture of scutched flax and any other fibre, or (*d*) of a mixture of hemp and any other fibre;
including:—

(1) preparing and spinning of waste reclaimed at any stage;

(2) calendering when carried on at an establishment engaged in any of the above-mentioned activities;

(3) all packing, despatching, warehousing, storing or other operations incidental to or appertaining to any of the above-mentioned activities;

but excluding:—

(1) bleaching, dyeing or finishing;

(2) preparing or spinning of materials required for the making or re-making of (*a*) rope (including driving rope and banding), (*b*) cord (including blind and window cord, but excluding silk, worsted and other fancy cords), (*c*) core for wire ropes, (*d*) lines, (*e*) twine (including binder and trawl twine), (*f*) lanyards, (*g*) net and similar articles when such spinning or preparing is carried on in the same factory or workshop as the said making or re-making;

(3) making or repair of sacks or bags;

(4) weaving of carpets, rugs and mats.

EXPLANATORY NOTE

(*This Note is not part of the Order.*)

The Flax and Hemp Wages Council (Great Britain) which was established as a Trade Board under the Trade Boards Act 1909 (c.22) became a Wages Council by virtue of the Wages Councils Act 1945 (c.17).

This Order, which comes into operation on 14th January 1974, varies the field of operation of the Wages Council by the inclusion therein of workers employed in the activity of calendering.

1973 No. 2063 (C. 62)

TERMS AND CONDITIONS OF EMPLOYMENT

INDUSTRIAL TRAINING

The Employment and Training Act 1973 (Commencement No. 1) Order 1973

Made - - - - *6th December* 1973

The Secretary of State, in exercise of the powers conferred on him by section 15(2) of the Employment and Training Act 1973(a) and of all other powers enabling him in that behalf, hereby makes the following Order:—

Citation and interpretation

1.—(1) This Order may be cited as the Employment and Training Act 1973 (Commencement No. 1) Order 1973.

(2) In this Order—

"the 1973 Act" means the Employment and Training Act 1973; and
"the 1964 Act" means the Industrial Training Act 1964(b).

Appointed days for certain provisions other than section 6 *and Schedule* 2

2.—The provisions mentioned in the first column of Schedule 1 to this Order (which relate to the matters specified in the second column of that Schedule) shall come into operation—

(*a*) in the case of the provisions mentioned in Part I of that Schedule, on 1st January 1974;

(*b*) in the case of the provision mentioned in Part II of that Schedule, on 1st April 1974; and

(*c*) in the case of the provision mentioned in Part III of that Schedule, on 16th May 1975.

Appointed days for section 6(1) *and* (2) *and Parts I and II of Schedule* 2

3.—(1) This Article shall have effect subject to Article 4.

(2) The provisions of Part I of Schedule 2 to the 1973 Act mentioned in the first column of Schedule 2 to this Order (which relate to the matters specified in the second column of that Schedule) shall come into operation—

(*a*) in the case of the provisions mentioned in Part I of that Schedule, on 1st January 1974;

(*b*) in the case of the provisions mentioned in Part II of that Schedule, on 1st April 1974;

(*c*) in the case of the provisions mentioned in Part III of that Schedule, on 1st April 1975; and

(*d*) in the case of the provision mentioned in Part IV of that Schedule, on 16th May 1975.

(3) Section 6(1) of the 1973 Act shall come into operation in relation to each of the provisions of Part I of Schedule 2 to the 1973 Act referred to in paragraph (2) of this Article, on the date specified in the said paragraph for the coming into operation of the said provision.

(a) 1973 c. 50. (b) 1964 c. 16.

(4) Section 6(1) of the 1973 Act, in relation to the provisions of paragraph 5 of Part I of Schedule 2 to the 1973 Act, and that paragraph (amendments to section 4 of the 1964 Act which relate to the making of levy orders) shall, in relation to the industrial training boards specified in the first column of Schedule 3 to this Order, come into operation on the corresponding date specified in respect of each board in the second column of that Schedule.

(5) Section 6(2) of and Part II of Schedule 2 to the 1973 Act shall come into operation on 16th May 1975.

Transitional provisions

4.—(1) The coming into operation of the following provisions of Part I of Schedule 2 to the 1973 Act—

(*a*) so much of paragraph 1 as relates to the substitution of a reference to the Commission for a reference to the Secretary of State in section 4(2) and section 7(2) of the 1964 Act ;

(*b*) paragraph 6 ; and

(*c*) so much of paragraph 10 as relates to the submission to the Commission of proposals for the raising and collection of a levy ;

shall, as respects an industrial training board specified in the first column of Schedule 3 to this Order, have effect only as respects levy which is to be raised and collected under a levy order coming into operation on or after the date specified in relation to that board in the second column of that Schedule.

(2) The coming into operation of the following provisions of Part I of Schedule 2 to the 1973 Act—

(*a*) so much of paragraph 1 as relates to the substitution of a reference to the Commission for a reference to the Secretary of State in section 2(5) of the 1964 Act ; and

(*b*) so much of paragraph 10 as relates to the submission to the Commission of proposals for the exercise of an industrial training board's functions ;

shall, as respects an industrial training board specified in the first column of Schedule 3 to this Order, have effect only in relation to functions which are to be exercised on or after the date specified in relation to that board in the third column of that Schedule: Provided that in respect of proposals relating to functions of the Engineering Industry Training Board which at the date of this Order have been delegated to a committee under section 3(1) of the 1964 Act the provisions of (*a*) and (*b*) of this paragraph shall have effect only in relation to functions which are to be exercised on or after 1st September 1975.

(3) The coming into operation on 1st April 1974 of the following provisions of Part I of Schedule 2 to the 1973 Act (amendments to the 1964 Act which relate to accounts and reports of industrial training boards)—

(*a*) so much of paragraph 1 as relates to the substitution of a reference to the Commission for a reference to the Secretary of State in section 8(3) of the 1964 Act ; and

(*b*) paragraph 11

shall have effect only in relation to accounts and reports which relate to a period commencing on or after 1st April 1974.

Appointed days for section 6(3) *and* (4) *and Parts III and IV of Schedule* 2

5.—(1) The provisions of Part III of Schedule 2 to the 1973 Act mentioned in the first column of Schedule 4 to this Order (which relate to the matters specified in the second column of that Schedule) shall come into operation—

(*a*) in the case of the provisions mentioned in Part I of that Schedule, on 1st January 1974 ;

(*b*) in the case of the provisions mentioned in Part II of that Schedule, on 1st April 1974 ; and

(*c*) in the case of the provisions mentioned in Part III of that Schedule, on 1st April 1975.

(2) Section 6(3) (except for section 6(3)(*b*)) of the 1973 Act shall come into operation in relation to each of the provisions of Part III of Schedule 2 to the 1973 Act referred to in paragraph (1) of this Article, on the date specified in the said paragraph for the coming into operation of the said provision and section 6(3)(*b*) of the said Act shall come into operation on 1st April 1974.

(3) Section 6(4) of and Part IV of Schedule 2 to the 1973 Act shall come into operation on 1st April 1975.

Appointed day for section 6(5)

6. Section 6(5) of the 1973 Act shall come into operation on 1st January 1974.

Signed by order of the Secretary of State.

R. Chichester-Clark,
Minister of State,
Department of Employment.

6th December 1973.

Article 2.

SCHEDULE 1

PART I

PROVISIONS, OTHER THAN SECTION 6 OF AND SCHEDULE 2 TO THE 1973 ACT, COMING INTO OPERATION ON 1ST JANUARY 1974

Provisions	Subject matter of provisions
Section 1(1) (so far as it relates to the Commission).	Establishment of Commission.
Section 1(2) and (3) and (except so far as it relates to paragraph 21 of Schedule 1) section 1(5).	Constitution of Commission.
Section 1(6) (so far as it relates to the Commission).	Power to transfer property to Commission.
Section 1(7) (so far as it relates to the Commission).	Status of Commission.
Section 2 (1) to (3)	Functions of Commission.
Section 2(5) (so far as it relates to the Commission).	Incidental powers of Commission.
Section 3	Control of Commission by Secretary of State.
Section 4	Obtaining and disclosure of information.

Provisions	Subject matter of provisions
Section 5	Powers of the Secretary of State relating to the provision of temporary employment, the appointment of advisers and research.
Section 7(1) to (4) (so far as it relates to the Commission).	Modification and exclusion of enactments relating to redundancy payments, employers' liability insurance and contracts of employment.
Section 7(5)	Secretary of State's power to exclude or modify enactments relating to the carrying on of employment agencies.
Section 11(1) (so far as it relates to payments to the Commission).	Finance.
Section 11(2)	Expenses and receipts under the Act.
Section 11(3)	Power to make payments analogous to industrial injury benefit.
Section 12(1)	Preference for disabled ex-service men and women in relation to training and other courses and submissions for engagements.
Section 12(2) (so far as it relates to the Commission).	Duty to furnish information relating to social security questions.
Section 12(4)	Payments to persons attending for examinations connected with a claim under section 11(3).
Section 12(6)	Extension of terms of office of members of Youth Employment Committees.
Section 13	Interpretation.
Section 14(1) (so far as it relates to paragraphs 3 to 5, 7(3), 9, 10, 11(2) and 13 of Schedule 3).	Minor amendments of other enactments.
Section 14(2) (so far as it relates to sections 4 and 20(2) of the Employment and Training Act 1948(**a**), sections 3(1), 6, 11 and 13 and paragraph 6(2) of the Schedule to the 1964 Act and to section 13(2) of the Chronically Sick and Disable Persons Act 1970(**b**)).	Repeals.
Section 15	Short title, commencement and extent.
Schedule 1 (except paragraph 21) ...	Constitution of Commission.
Schedule 3, paragraphs 3 to 5, 7(3), 9, 10, 11(2) and 13.	Minor amendments of other enactments.
Schedule 4 (to the extent mentioned above in relation to section 14(2)).	Repeals.

(**a**) 1948 c. 46. (**b**) 1970 c. 44.

Part II

Provision, other than section 6 of and Schedule 2 to the 1973 Act, coming into operation on 1st April 1974

Provision	Subject matter of provision
Section 14(2) (so far as it relates to sections 2(1)(*f*) (so far as it relates to arrangements made by local education authorities in England and Wales), 5 and 17 of the 1964 Act).	Repeals.

Part III

Provision, other than section 6 of and Schedule 2 to the 1973 Act, coming into operation on 16th May 1975

Provision	Subject matter of provision
Section 14(2) (so far as it relates to section 2(1)(*f*) of the 1964 Act (so far as that provision is not already in force)).	Repeal.

Article 3.

SCHEDULE 2

Part I

Provisions of Part I of Schedule 2 to the 1973 Act coming into operation on 1st January 1974

Provisions	Subject matter of provisions
Paragraph 1 (except so far as it amends section 5(1), (2) and (5) and section 8(3) of the 1964 Act).	Substitution of Commission for Secretary of State in section 1(4), section 2(5), section 2(6), section 4(2) and section 7(2) of the 1964 Act.
Paragraph 2	(i) Proposal by Commission for establishment of an industrial training board ; (ii) Definitions.
Paragraph 3	Functions of industrial training boards.
Paragraph 4(1)	Establishment of committees by industrial training boards and delegation of functions.
Paragraph 4(2) (except so far as it relates to the determination by Ministers of travelling, subsistence and other allowances (other than allowances for loss of remunerative time)).	Determination by Ministers of allowances for committee members and remuneration of committee chairmen.

Provisions	Subject matter of provisions
Paragraph 4(3)	Arrangements for pensions etc. for committee chairmen.
Paragraph 6	(i) Proposals for exemption by certificate from certain levies ; (ii) Certificates of exemption from levy.
Paragraphs 8 and 9	Power of industrial training boards to obtain information from employers.
Paragraph 10	Proposals to the Commission for the exercise of industrial training boards' functions and for levies.
Paragraph 12	Commission's recommendations for amendment or revocation by Minister of industrial training order.
Paragraph 13	Transfer of establishments' activities from industry of one board to that of another.
Paragraph 14	Accidents happening in connection with training provided or approved by the Commission or the Minister.
Paragraph 15	Remuneration of Presidents and full-time chairmen of industrial tribunals established under the 1964 Act.
Paragraph 16	Consent of Commission with approval of Minister to exercise by industrial training board of functions with respect to training for employment overseas and power of board to enter into agreements for payment to board in respect of the exercise of such functions.
Paragraph 17(*a*) and (*b*)	Pensions etc. for chairmen of industrial training boards.
Paragraph 17(*c*) and (*d*)	Power of Commission to appoint persons to attend meetings of boards and committees.
Paragraph 17(*f*) (except so far as it relates to the determination by Ministers of travelling, subsistence and other allowances (other than allowances for loss of remunerative time)).	Determination by Ministers of allowances for loss of remunerative time for board members.
Paragraph 18(*b*), (*d*), (*e*) and (*f*) (except so far as sub-paragraph (*e*) repeals section 17).	Consequential repeals and repeals of provisions of 1964 Act relating to the Central Training Council (section 11) and the Cotton Board (section 13).

PART II

PROVISIONS OF PART I OF SCHEDULE 2 TO THE 1973 ACT COMING INTO OPERATION ON 1ST APRIL 1974

Provisions	Subject matter of provisions
Paragraph 1 (so far as it is not already in operation).	Substitution of Commission for Secretary of State in section 5(1), (2) and (5) and section 8(3) of the 1964 Act.
Paragraph 7(1)	Making of grants and loans by the Commission.
Paragraph 11	Reports and accounts of industrial training boards.
Paragraph 18(*a*) (so far as it relates to arrangements made by local education authorities in England and Wales).	Consequential repeal.
Paragraph 18(*c*) and (*e*) (so far as it is not already in operation).	Consequential repeal and repeal of provision relating to contributions out of National Insurance Fund towards Minister's expenses.

PART III

PROVISIONS OF PART I OF SCHEDULE 2 TO THE 1973 ACT COMING INTO OPERATION ON 1ST APRIL 1975

Provisions	Subject matter of provisions
Paragraph 4(2) (so far as it is not already in operation).	Determination by Ministers of travelling, subsistence and other allowances for committee members.
Paragraph 7(2)	Commission's power of direction in relation to boards' expenditure.
Paragraph 17(*e*)	Ministerial approval of conditions of appointment of board officers and servants.
Paragraph 17(*f*) (so far as it is not already in operation).	Determination by Ministers of travelling, subsistence and other allowances for board members.

PART IV

PROVISION OF PART I OF SCHEDULE 2 TO THE 1973 ACT COMING INTO OPERATION ON 16TH MAY 1975

Provision	Subject matter of provision
Paragraph 18(*a*) (so far as it is not already in operation).	Consequential repeal.

Article 3.

SCHEDULE 3

SPECIFIED DATES FOR THE PURPOSES OF ARTICLE 3(4) AND ARTICLE 4(1) AND (2)

Column 1 (Industrial Training Board)	Column 2 (Article 3(4) and Article 4(1))	Column 3 (Article 4(2))
Air Transport and Travel	1st April 1975	1st April 1975
Carpet	1st April 1975	1st August 1974
Ceramics, Glass and Mineral Products	1st April 1975	1st August 1974
Chemical and Allied Products ...	1st August 1976	1st August 1975
Clothing and Allied Products ...	1st April 1975	1st August 1974
Construction	1st March 1975	1st August 1974
Cotton and Allied Textiles	1st April 1976	1st April 1975
Distributive	1st July 1976	1st August 1975
Engineering	15th October 1974	1st August 1974, subject to the proviso to Article 4(2) of this Order.
Food, Drink and Tobacco	1st August 1974	1st August 1974
Footwear, Leather and Fur Skin ...	1st April 1976	1st August 1974
Furniture and Timber	6th April 1975	1st August 1974
Hotel and Catering	1st April 1975	1st April 1975
Iron and Steel	1st April 1975	1st August 1974
Knitting, Lace and Net	1st April 1975	1st August 1974
Man-made Fibres Producing ...	1st April 1975	1st April 1975
Paper and Paper Products	6th April 1975	1st September 1974
Petroleum	1st April 1975	1st September 1974
Printing and Publishing	1st April 1975	1st April 1975
Road Transport	6th April 1975	1st August 1974
Rubber and Plastics Processing ...	1st April 1975	1st April 1975
Shipbuilding	1st April 1975	1st April 1975
Wool, Jute and Flax	1st April 1975	1st April 1975

Article 5.

SCHEDULE 4

PART I

PROVISIONS OF PART III OF SCHEDULE 2 TO THE 1973 ACT COMING INTO OPERATION ON 1ST JANUARY 1974

Provisions	Subject matter of provisions
Paragraph 1(*f*) (so far as it refers to section 11 of the 1964 Act).	Repeal of provision of 1964 Act relating to the Central Training Council (section 11).
Paragraph 2 (except so far as it relates to the definition of "the Minister").	Definitions.
Paragraph 3 (except so far as it relates to section 2(1)(*f*) of the 1964 Act).	Functions of industrial training boards.

Provisions	Subject matter of provisions
Paragraph 5(2) (except so far as it relates to the determination by Ministers of travelling, subsistence and other allowances (other than allowances for loss of remunerative time)).	Determination by Ministers of allowances for committee members and remuneration of committee chairmen.
Paragraph 5(3)	Arrangements for pensions etc. for committee chairmen.
Paragraph 8	Power of industrial training board with consent of Minister to exercise functions with respect to training for employment overseas.
Paragraph 9(*a*) and (*b*)	Pensions etc. for chairmen of industrial training boards.
Paragraph 9(*c*)	Power of Commission to appoint persons to attend meetings of boards.
Paragraph 9(*e*) (except so far as it relates to the determination by Ministers of travelling, subsistence and other allowances (other than allowances for loss of remunerative time)).	Determination by Ministers of allowances for loss of remunerative time for board members.

PART II

PROVISIONS OF PART III OF SCHEDULE 2 TO THE 1973 ACT COMING INTO OPERATION ON 1ST APRIL 1974

Provisions	Subject matter of provisions
Paragraph 1 (so far as it is not already in operation).	Consequential repeals and repeals of provisions of 1964 Act relating to the Cotton Board (section 13) and contributions out of National Insurance Fund towards Minister's expenses (section 17).
Paragraph 2 (so far as it is not already in operation).	Definitions.
Paragraph 3 (so far as it is not already in operation).	Further functions of industrial training boards.
Paragraph 4	(i) Control of Agricultural Training Board by the Minister ; (ii) Disclosure of information to Agricultural Training Board.
Paragraph 5 (1)	Delegation of functions to committees.
Paragraph 6	Substitution of reference to Minister of Agriculture, Fisheries and Food for reference to the Minister in section 5(1) of 1964 Act.
Paragraph 7	Amendment or revocation of industrial training order.

PART III

PROVISIONS OF PART III OF SCHEDULE 2 TO THE 1973 ACT COMING INTO OPERATION ON 1ST APRIL 1975

Provisions	Subject matter of provisions
Paragraph 5(2) (so far as it is not already in operation).	Determination by Ministers of travelling, subsistence and other allowances for committee members.
Paragraph 9(*d*)	Ministerial approval of conditions of appointment of board officers and servants.
Paragraph 9(*e*) (so far as it is not already in operation).	Determination by Ministers of travelling, subsistence and other allowances for board members.

EXPLANATORY NOTE

(*This Note is not part of the Order.*)

This Order brings into operation—

(*a*) the provisions of the Employment and Training Act 1973 which relate to the establishment and the functions of the Manpower Services Commission ;

(*b*) the provisions which relate to the powers of the Secretary of State to make arrangements for the purpose of providing temporary employment for persons who are without employment and to appoint advisers and conduct research in connection with his functions relating to employment, unemployment and training for employment ;

(*c*) the provisions relating to industrial training (including transitional provisions) which modify the Industrial Training Act 1964 so as to establish the relationships between the Secretary of State, the Manpower Services Commission and industrial training boards ; provide for an upper limit for levy of 1 per cent. of an employer's payroll, unless there is an affirmative resolution of each House of Parliament ; for exemption from levy of small firms and of firms in respect of establishments where training is adequate ; and for such matters as the payment, subject to Ministerial approval, of pensions to chairmen of industrial training boards and of certain committees and of allowances for loss of remunerative time to board and committee members ;

(*d*) the special modifications to the Industrial Training Act 1964 which relate to the Agricultural Training Board only, and provide for the control of that Board by the Agricultural Ministers.

1973 No. 2064

INSURANCE

The Insurance Companies (Identification of Long Term Assets and Liabilities) Regulations 1973

Made - - -	*7th December* 1973
Laid before Parliament	10*th December* 1973
Coming into Operation	1*st January* 1974

The Secretary of State in exercise of the powers conferred upon him by sections 7(3) and (4) and 53(1) of the Insurance Companies Amendment Act 1973(**a**) hereby makes the following Regulations:—

Citation and Commencement

1. These Regulations may be cited as the Insurance Companies (Identification of Long Term Assets and Liabilities) Regulations 1973 and shall come into operation on 1st January 1974.

Interpretation

2.—(1) In these Regulations—

"asset" includes any part of an asset;

"liability" includes any part of a liability;

"current financial year", in relation to a company, means the financial year of the company which ends next after the date on which these Regulations are made;

"next financial year", in relation to a company, means the financial year of the company which begins next after the date on which these Regulations are made;

"base date", in relation to a company, means the last day of its current financial year;

"relevant date", in relation to a company, means the last day of its next financial year;

"other business", in relation to a company, means such of that company's business as is not long term business; and

"the apportionment fraction" has the meaning assigned to it by the Schedule to these Regulations.

(2) The Interpretation Act 1889(**b**) shall apply to the interpretation of these Regulations as it applies to the interpretation of an Act of Parliament.

Application

3.—(1) These Regulations apply to every insurance company to which the Insurance Companies Act 1958(**c**) applies which was carrying on long term business at 25th July 1973 and are made for the purposes of paragraph (*a*) of section 7(3) of the Insurance Companies Amendment Act 1973.

(**a**) 1973 c. 58.
(**b**) 1889 c. 63.
(**c**) 1958 c. 72.

(2) The arrangements to be made during the next financial year by companies to which these Regulations apply for identifying their assets and liabilities as on the relevant date which are attributable to their long term business shall be made in accordance with the provisions of Regulations 4, 5 and 6 of these Regulations.

Assets and liabilities unidentified at the base date

4.—(1) This Regulation applies for the purposes of identifying as attributable to the long term business assets and liabilities on the base date which were then neither identified as attributable to the long term business nor identified as attributable to the other business.

(2) The assets and liabilities to which this Regulation applies may be identified either—

(*a*) by the identification of a proportion equal to the apportionment fraction of any such asset or liability as attributable to the long term business as on the base date; or

(*b*) by the identification and apportionment of such assets and liabilities having regard to their value as on the base date, which in the case of assets shall be a fair market value.

(3) In the case of identification in accordance with paragraph 2(*b*) above the apportionment shall be such that—

(*a*) in the case of assets, the aggregate of the values of the assets so identified when divided by the aggregate of the values of all the assets valued, and

(*b*) in the case of liabilities, the aggregate of the values of the liabilities so identified when divided by the aggregate of the values of all the liabilities valued,

is in each case a fraction equal to the apportionment fraction.

Further identification during next financial year

5.—(1) Assets and liabilities which were already identified as attributable to the long term business on the base date or which are to be so identified as on the base date shall, if they are still assets and liabilities on the relevant date, be identified as attributable to the long term business as on the relevant date.

(2) Assets acquired during the next financial year, to the extent that they are acquired out of receipts of the company during that financial year in respect of its long term business, shall, if they are still assets on the relevant date, be identified to that extent as assets attributable to the company's long term business as on the relevant date.

(3) Where any such assets as are referred to in paragraphs (1) and (2) have been disposed of before the relevant date, the proceeds of that disposal or the relevant part thereof or any assets acquired therewith shall be identified as assets attributable to the company's long term business as on the relevant date.

(4) Any income accruing during the next financial year from any asset of the company which falls to be identified as an asset attributable to the company's long term business shall also be so identified as on the relevant date.

(5) Liabilities of the company assumed during the next financial year, to the extent that they are assumed in the course or for the purposes of the company's long term business, shall, if they are still liabilities on the relevant date, be identified to that extent as liabilities attributable to the company's long term business as on the relevant date.

Records during next financial year

6. The company shall during its next financial year make arrangements for the establishment and maintenance of such books of account and other records as are necessary for identifying as attributable to the long term business as on the relevant date those assets and liabilities which are to be so identified in accordance with the provisions of Regulation 5.

Certificates

7.—(1) Every company to which these Regulations apply shall, not later than two months after the relevant date, deposit with the Secretary of State a certificate that the company has in accordance with these Regulations—

(*a*) apportioned in accordance with the provisions of Regulation 4 any assets and liabilities which were not already identified on the base date as attributable to the long term business or as attributable to the other business of the company;

(*b*) identified as assets attributable to the long term business all those assets which are required to be so identified in accordance with Regulation 5; and

(*c*) established and maintained those books of account and other records which are required to be established and maintained by Regulation 6,

and that certificate shall be signed by at least two directors of the company and the chief executive thereof or, in the case of a company which has no chief executive, by at least two directors and the secretary thereof.

(2) There shall be annexed to every such certificate a report signed by the auditor of the company and stating whether or not in his opinion that certificate was properly given.

Limerick,
Parliamentary Under-Secretary of State for Trade,
Department of Trade and Industry.

7th December 1973.

SCHEDULE

THE APPORTIONMENT FRACTION

1. "The Apportionment Fraction" in relation to a company is the amount of that company's Long Term Business Index divided by the aggregate of that amount and the amount of its Other Business Index.

2. "The Long Term Business Index" in relation to a company is the amount by which the amount determined in accordance with paragraph 3 of this Schedule exceeds the amount determined in accordance with paragraph 4 of this Schedule.

3. The amount to be determined in accordance with this paragraph in relation to a company is the aggregate of the following:—

(i) the amount of the long term business fund or funds carried forward in the company's revenue account;

(ii) the amount of any accounting liabilities, reserves or provisions, other than those mentioned in sub-paragraph (i) of this paragraph, shown in the company's balance sheet as attributable only to the company's long term business;

(iii) the amounts of any accounting liabilities, reserves or provisions, other than those mentioned in sub-paragraphs (i) and (ii) of this paragraph, shown or included in the company's balance sheet in relation to which there are records which identify them as attributable only to the company's long term business.

4. The amount to be determined in accordance with this paragraph is the aggregate of the amounts at which assets already identified at the base date as attributable to the company's long term business are shown or included in the company's balance sheet.

5. "The Other Business Index" in relation to a company is the amount by which the amount determined in accordance with paragraph 6 below exceeds the amount determined in accordance with paragraph 7 below.

6. The amount to be determined in accordance with this paragraph is the aggregate of all the amounts shown or included as accounting liabilities, reserves or provisions in the company's balance sheet excluding:—

(i) any amount referred to in paragraph 3 of this Schedule;

(ii) any amount which constituted a reserve, provision or other allowance in respect of depreciation, renewals or diminution in value (whether actual or potential) of assets which were not already identified either as attributable to the long term business or as attributable to the other business on the base date;

(iii) any other amount which corresponded to a legal liability which was not already identified either as attributable to the long term business or as attributable to the other business on the base date.

7. The amount to be determined in accordance with this paragraph is the aggregate of the amounts at which assets already identified at the base date as attributable to the company's other business are shown or included in the company's balance sheet.

8. In this Schedule references to a company's balance sheet or revenue account are references to the balance sheet and revenue account prepared by the company in relation to its current financial year for the purposes of section 4 of the Insurance Companies Act 1958.

EXPLANATORY NOTE

(This Note is not part of the Regulations.)

These Regulations describe the arrangements which, according to section 7(3)(*a*) of the Insurance Companies Amendment Act 1973, are required to be made by insurance companies carrying on long term business for identifying assets and liabilities as attributable to their long term business. The Regulations apply to all insurance companies to which the Insurance Companies Act 1958 applies which were carrying on long term business at 25th July 1973.

The Regulations also require such companies to furnish to the Secretary of State certificates that such arrangements have been made.

STATUTORY INSTRUMENTS

1973 No. 2065

CUSTOMS AND EXCISE

The Import Duties (Quota Relief) (Paper, Paperboard and Printed Products) Order 1973

Made - - -	7*th December* 1973
Laid before the House of Commons	10*th December* 1973
Coming into Operation	1*st January* 1974

The Secretary of State, in exercise of the powers conferred on him by section 5(1) and (4) of the Import Duties Act 1958**(a)**, as amended by paragraph 1 of Schedule 4 to the European Communities Act 1972**(b)**, and of all other powers enabling him in that behalf, hereby makes the following Order:

1.—(1) This Order may be cited as the Import Duties (Quota Relief) (Paper, Paperboard and Printed Products) Order 1973 and shall operate from the beginning of 1st January 1974 up to and including 31st December 1974.

(2) The Interpretation Act 1889**(c)** shall apply for the interpretation of this Order as it applies for the interpretation of an Act of Parliament.

(3) In this Order—

"the Agreements" means the Agreements, signed on 22nd July 1972, between the European Economic Community and, respectively, Austria, Iceland, Portugal, Sweden and Switzerland, the Agreement, signed on 14th May 1973, between the Community and Norway and the Agreement, signed on 5th October 1973, between the Community and Finland**(d)** and references to an Agreement shall be construed accordingly;

references to goods originating in any of the above-mentioned countries are references to products which, under the provisions of the Agreements, are to be regarded as originating there.

2.—(1) No import duty shall be charged on the relevant quota of goods which—

(*a*) fall within a heading or subheading of the Customs Tariff 1959 specified in column 3 of any of the Schedules hereto,

(*b*) are of a description specified in column 1 of such a Schedule in relation to the heading or subheading and

---

(a) 1958 c. 6. **(b)** 1972 c. 68.
(c) 1889 c. 63.
(d) The Agreements with Austria, Iceland, Portugal, Sweden, Switzerland and Norway are annexed respectively to Regulations (EEC) Nos. 2836/72 (O.J. No. L 300, p. 1), 2842/72 (O.J. No. L 301, p. 1), 2844/72 (O.J. No. L 301, p.166), 2838/72, (O.J. No. L 300, p. 96), 2840/72 (O.J. No. L 300, p. 188) and 1691/73 (O.J. No. L 171, p. 1); the Agreement with Finland has yet to be published in the Official Journal.

(*c*) originate in the country to which the Schedule relates and satisfy the provisions of Article 25(1) of Protocol No. 3 (relating to origin of goods) to the Agreement between the Community and that country.

(2) For the purposes of this Article, the "relevant quota" of goods of a description specified in column 1 of any Schedule hereto is the quantity of goods specified in column 2 of such a Schedule in relation to the description (such quantities being expressed as a number of tonnes or a value in pounds), and any entry in column 2 of a Schedule prescribing a limit to a subclass of goods within a quota shall have effect.

(3) The Schedules to this Order relate to the countries named in Article 1(3) above as follows:

Schedule 1 to Austria,
Schedule 2 to Iceland,
Schedule 3 to Portugal,
Schedule 4 to Sweden,
Schedule 5 to Switzerland,
Schedule 6 to Norway and
Schedule 7 to Finland.

(4) Goods shall be treated as forming part of a quota in the order in which they are entered for home use (within the meaning of the Customs and Excise Act 1952(**a**)) in the United Kingdom on or after 1st January 1974.

3. A description of goods in column 1 or 2 of any of the Schedules hereto, other than one covering a whole heading or subheading, shall be taken to comprise all goods which would be classified under a description in the same terms constituting a subheading (other than the final subheading) in the relevant heading of the Customs Tariff 1959.

Limerick,
Parliamentary Under-Secretary
of State for Trade,
Department of Trade and Industry.

7th December 1973.

SCHEDULE 1

AUSTRIA

1 *Description of Goods*	2 *Quota*	3 *Tariff Heading or Subheading*
All goods of these subheadings excluding kraft liner and sack kraft	3,300 tonnes	Ex 48.01.C.II.a) Ex 48.01.C.II.b)1 48.01.C.II.b)2 48.01.C.II.b)3
Bible paper (India paper), copying tissue, other printing paper and other writing paper, not containing mechanical wood pulp or in which mechanical wood pulp does not represent more than 5%	2,200 tonnes	Ex 48.01.E.II.b)1 Ex 48.01.E.II.b)2.bb) Ex 48.01.E.II.b)3 Ex 48.01.E.II.b)5

(**a**) 1952 c. 44.

1 *Description of Goods*	2 *Quota*	3 *Tariff Heading or Subheading*
Printing paper and writing paper, containing mechanical wood pulp, excluding copying tissue.	750 tonnes	48.01.E.II.b)2.aa) Ex 48.01.E.II.b)2.bb) Ex 48.01.E.II.b)3 Ex 48.01.E.II.b)5
All goods of these subheadings other than sulphite paper for wrapping purposes, semi-chemical fluting paper, cellulose wadding and than paper covered by the two entries in this column immediately preceding this one.	560 tonnes	Ex 48.01.E.II.a) Ex 48.01.E.II.b)1 48.01.E.II.b)4 Ex 48.01.E.II.b)5
All goods of this subheading	750 tonnes	48.01.E.I
Coated printing paper	15,000 tonnes	Ex 48.07.B.I.c)1
All goods of these sub-headings other than coated printing paper	2,700 tonnes	48.07.B.I.a) 48.07.B.I.b) Ex 48.07.B.I.c)1 48.07.B.I.c)2 48.07.B.I.c)3 48.07.B.I.c)4 48.07.B.II
All goods of this subheading	3,000 tonnes	48.15.B
All goods of these subheadings other than those covered by any of the preceding entries in this column relating to subheadings 48.01.C.II.a), 48.01.C.II.b)1, 48.01.E.II.a), 48.01.E.II.b)1 and 48.01.E.II.b)5	3,000 tonnes	48.01.B 48.01.C.I Ex 48.01.C.II.a) Ex 48.01.C.II.b)1 48.01.D Ex 48.01.E.II.a) Ex 48.01.E.II.b)1 Ex 48.01.E.II.b)5 48.02 48.03 48.04 48.05 48.06 48.07.A 48.08 48.10 48.11 48.12 48.13 48.14 48.15.A 48.16 48.17 48.18 48.19 48.20 48.21

1 *Description of Goods*	2 *Quota*	3 *Tariff Heading or Subheading*
All goods of these headings and subheadings	£178,249	49.03 49.05.A 49.07.A 49.07.C.II 49.08 49.09 49.10 49.11.B

SCHEDULE 2

ICELAND

1 *Description of Goods*	2 *Quota*	3 *Tariff Heading or Subheading*
All goods of these headings and subheadings	10 tonnes	All subheadings of 48.01 other than 48.01.A, and all headings from 48.02 to 48.21 (inclusive) other than 48.09.
All goods of these headings and subheadings	£1,804	49.03 49.05.A 49.07.A 49.07.C.II 49.08 49.09 49.10 49.11.B

SCHEDULE 3

PORTUGAL

1 *Description of Goods*	2 *Quota*	3 *Tariff Heading or Subheading*
All goods of these headings and subheadings	569 tonnes	All subheadings of 48.01 other than 48.01.A, and all headings from 48.02 to 48.21 (inclusive) other than 48.09

1 *Description of Goods*	2 *Quota*	3 *Tariff Heading or Subheading*
All goods of these headings and subheadings	£10,713	49.03 49.05.A 49.07.A 49.07.C.II 49.08 49.09 49.10 49.11.B

SCHEDULE 4

SWEDEN

1 *Description of Goods*	2 *Quota*	3 *Tariff Heading or Subheading*
Kraft liner	111,500 tonnes (of which not more than 95,500 tonnes weighing less than 220 g/m^2, and not more than 16,000 tonnes weighing more than 220 g/m^2)	Ex 48.01.C.II.a) Ex 48.01.C.II.b)1
Sack kraft	115,700 tonnes	Ex 48.01.C.II.b)1
All goods of these subheadings other than kraft liner and sack kraft	66,500 tonnes (of which not more than 11,500 tonnes bleached and semi-bleached and not more than 55,000 tonnes unbleached)	Ex 48.01.C.II.a) Ex 48.01.C.II.b)1 48.01.C.II.b)2 48.01.C.II.b)3
Bible paper (India paper), copying tissue, other printing paper and other writing paper, not containing mechanical woodpulp or in which mechanical woodpulp does not represent more than 5%	12,000 tonnes	Ex 48.01.E.II.b)1 Ex 48.01.E.II.b)2.bb) Ex 48.01.E.II.b)3 Ex 48.01.E.II.b)5
Printing paper and writing paper, containing mechanical wood pulp, excluding copying tissue	55,000 tonnes	48.01.E.II.b)2.aa) Ex 48.01.E.II.b)2.bb) Ex 48.01.E.II.b)3 Ex 48.01.E.II.b)5
Fluting paper for corrugated paperboard	38,700 tonnes	Ex 48.01.E.II.b)5
Sulphite paper for wrapping purposes	17,800 tonnes	Ex 48.01.E.II.a)

1 *Description of Goods*	2 *Quota*	3 *Tariff Heading or Subheading*
All goods of these subheadings other than cellulose wadding and than paper covered by the four entries in this column immediately preceding this one	25,000 tonnes (of which not more than 8,000 tonnes test liner (including jute liner), not more than 3,000 tonnes tissue paper (hard) not more than 1,000 tonnes base paper for sensitising with solutions other than silver salts, not more than 5,000 tonnes wallpaper base and not more than 8,000 tonnes other papers not mentioned in the four entries in this column immediately preceding this one)	Ex 48.01.E.II.a) Ex 48.01.E.II.b)1 48.01.E.II.b)4 Ex 48.01.E.II.b)5
Paperboard other than kraft board	30,750 tonnes (of which not more than 7,500 tonnes test linerboard (including jute linerboard), not more than 16,000 tonnes folding box board, not more than 250 tonnes electrical insulating pressboard and not more than 7,000 tonnes other paperboard not mentioned in the three entries in this column immediately preceding this one)	48.01.E.I
All goods of this heading	8,500 tonnes	48.03
All goods of this heading	530 tonnes	48.04
All goods of these subheadings	9,000 tonnes	48.05.B.I.b) 48.05.B.I.c)1 48.05.B.I.c)2 48.05.B.I.c)3 48.05.B.I.c)4 48.05.B.II
Coated printing paper	6,750 tonnes (of which not more than 3,500 tonnes mechanical and not more than 3,250 tonnes other than mechanical)	Ex 48.07.B.I.c)1

1 *Description of Goods*	2 *Quota*	3 *Tariff Heading or Subheading*
All goods of these subheadings other than coated printing paper	30,000 tonnes (of which not more than 6,000 tonnes folding box board and not more than 24,000 tonnes other than folding box board)	48.07.B.I.a) 48.07.B.I.b) Ex 48.07.B.I.c)1 48.07.B.I.c)2 48.07.B.I.c)3 48.07.B.I.c)4 48.07.B.II
All goods of this subheading	2,250 tonnes	48.15.B
All goods of this heading	425 tonnes	48.16
All goods of this subheading	850 tonnes (of which not more than 525 tonnes sanitary products and not more than 325 tonnes other than sanitary products)	48.21.B
All goods of these subheadings other than those covered by any of the preceding entries in this column relating to subheadings 48.01.E.II.b)1 and 48.01.E.II.b)5	4,600 tonnes (of which not more than 2,100 tonnes paper manufactured wholly of bleached or unbleached sulphate cellulose fibre excluding that for spinning into yarn and corrugated and not more than 2,500 tonnes other than paper manufactured wholly of bleached or unbleached sulphate cellulose fibre but including paper for spinning into yarn and corrugated)	48.01.B 48.01.C.I 48.01.D Ex 48.01.E.II.b)1 Ex 48.01.E.II.b)5 48.02 48.05.A 48.05.B.I.a) 48.06 48.07.A 48.08 48.10 48.11 48.12 48.13 48.14 48.15.A 48.17 48.18 48.19 48.20 48.21.A
All goods of these headings and subheadings	£674,473	49.03 49.05.A 49.07.A 49.07.C.II 49.08 49.09 49.10 49.11.B

SCHEDULE 5

Switzerland

1 *Description of Goods*	2 *Quota*	3 *Tariff Heading or Subheading*
All goods of these subheadings except kraft liner and sack kraft	145 tonnes	Ex 48.01.C.II.a) Ex 48.01.C.II.b)1 48.01.C.II.b)2 48.01.C.II.b)3
Bible paper (India paper), copying tissue, other printing paper and other writing paper, not containing mechanical wood pulp or in which mechanical wood pulp does not represent more than 5%	202 tonnes	Ex 48.01.E.II.b)1 Ex 48.01.E.II.b)2.bb) Ex 48.01.E.II.b)3 Ex 48.01.E.II.b)5
Wallpaper base	244 tonnes	Ex 48.01.E.II.b)5
All goods of this heading	126 tonnes	48.03
Coated printing paper	152 tonnes	Ex 48.07.B.I.c)1
All goods of these subheadings other than coated printing paper	586 tonnes	48.07.B.I.a) 48.07.B.I.b) Ex 48.07.B.I.c)1 48.07.B.I.c)2 48.07.B.I.c)3 48.07.B.I.c)4 48.07.B.II
All goods of this heading	207 tonnes	48.16
All goods of this subheading	147 tonnes	48.21.B
All goods of these subheadings other than those covered by any of the preceding entries in this column	522 tonnes	48.01.B 48.01.C.I Ex 48.01.C.II.a) Ex 48.01.C.II.b)1 48.01.D 48.01.E.I 48.01.E.II.a) Ex 48.01.E.II.b)1 48.01.E.II.b)2.aa) Ex 48.01.E.II.b)2.bb) Ex 48.01.E.II.b)3 48.01.E.II.b)4 Ex 48.01.E.II.b)5 48.02 48.04 48.05 48.06 48.07.A 48.08 48.10 48.11

1 *Description of Goods*	2 *Quota*	3 *Tariff Heading or Subheading*
All goods of these headings and subheadings	£756,918	48.12 48.13 48.14 48.15 48.17 48.18 48.19 48.20 48.21.A 49.03 49.05.A 49.07.A 49.07.C.II 49.08 49.09 49.10 49.11.B

SCHEDULE 6

NORWAY

1 *Description of Goods*	2 *Quota*	3 *Tariff Heading or Subheading*
Kraft liner	7,650 tonnes	Ex 48.01.C.II.a) Ex 48.01.C.II.b)1
Sack kraft	15,400 tonnes	Ex 48.01.C.II.b)1
All goods of these subheadings other than kraft liner and sack kraft	11,500 tonnes (of which not more than 3,000 tonnes bleached and semi-bleached and not more than 8,500 tonnes unbleached)	Ex 48.01.C.II.a) Ex 48.01.C.II.b)1 48.01.C.II.b)2 48.01.C.II.b)3
Bible paper (India paper), copying tissue, other printing paper and other writing paper, not containing mechanical woodpulp or in which mechanical woodpulp does not represent more than 5%	12,000 tonnes	Ex 48.01.E.II.b)1 Ex 48.01.E.II.b)2.bb) Ex 48.01.E.II.b)3 Ex 48.01.E.II.b)5
Printing paper and writing paper, containing mechanical wood pulp, excluding copying tissue	27,000 tonnes	48.01.E.II.b)2.aa) Ex 48.01.E.II.b)2.bb) Ex 48.01.E.II.b)3 Ex 48.01.E.II.b)5
Fluting paper for corrugated paperboard	16,000 tonnes	Ex 48.01.E.II.b)5
Sulphite paper for wrapping purposes	10,350 tonnes	Ex 48.01.E.II.a)

1 *Description of Goods*	2 *Quota*	3 *Tariff Heading or Subheading*
All goods of these subheadings other than cellulose wadding and than paper covered by the four entries in this column immediately preceding this one	9,500 tonnes (of which not more than 4,000 tonnes tissue paper (hard) and not more than 5,500 tonnes other papers)	Ex 48.01.E.II.a) Ex 48.01.E.II.b)1 48.01.E.II.b)4 Ex 48.01.E.II.b)5
Paperboard other than kraft board	8,950 tonnes (of which not more than 5,000 tonnes folding box board made from 100% woodpulp, not more than 2,250 tonnes folding box board made from furnishes including waste paper and not more than 1,700 tonnes other paperboard not mentioned in the two entries in this column immediately preceeding this one)	48.01.E.I
All goods of this heading	16,000 tonnes	48.03
All goods of this subheading	5,400 tonnes (of which not more than 3,000 tonnes folding box board made from 100% woodpulp, not more than 700 tonnes folding box board made from other furnishes and not more than 1,700 tonnes other paper and paperboard not mentioned in the two entries in this column immediately preceeding this one)	48.07.B
All goods of these subheadings other than those covered by the preceding entries in this column relating to subheadings 48.01.E.II.b)1 and 48.01.E.II.b)5	5,600 tonnes (of which not more than 2,000 tonnes crêped tissue paper and not more than 3,600 tonnes other than crêped tissue)	48.01.B 48.01.C.I 48.01.D Ex 48.01.E.II.b)1 Ex 48.01.E.II.b)5 48.02 48.04 48.05 48.06 48.07.A 48.08 48.10 48.11 48.12 48.13 48.14

1 *Description of Goods*	2 *Quota*	3 *Tariff Heading or Subheading*
All goods of these headings and subheadings	£45,396	48.15 48.16 48.17 48.18 48.19 48.20 48.21 49.03 49.05.A 49.07.A 49.07.C.II 49.08 49.09 49.10 49.11.B

SCHEDULE 7

FINLAND

1 *Description of Goods*	2 *Quota*	3 *Tariff Heading or Subheading*
Kraft liner	51,100 tonnes (of which not more than 44,000 tonnes weighing less than 220 g/m^2 and not more than 7,100 tonnes weighing more than 220 g/m^2)	Ex 48.01.C.II.a) Ex 48.01.C.II.b)1
Sack kraft	25,100 tonnes	Ex 48.01.C.II.b)1
All goods of these subheadings other than kraft liner and sack kraft	26,000 tonnes (of which not more than 1,000 tonnes bleached and semi-bleached and not more than 25,000 tonnes unbleached)	Ex 48.01.C.II.a) Ex 48.01.C.II.b)1 48.01.C.II.b)2 48.01.C.II.b)3
Bible paper (India paper), copying tissue, other printing paper and other writing paper, not containing mechanical woodpulp or in which mechanical woodpulp does not represent more than 5%	14,500 tonnes	Ex 48.01.E.II.b)1 Ex 48.01.E.II.b)2.bb) Ex 48.01.E.II.b)3 Ex 48.01.E.II.b)5
Printing paper and writing paper containing mechanical wood pulp, excluding copying tissue	103,000 tonnes	48.01.E.II.b)2.aa) Ex 48.01.E.II.b)2.bb) Ex 48.01.E.II.b)3 Ex 48.01.E.II.b)5

1 *Description of Goods*	2 *Quota*	3 *Tariff Heading or Subheading*
Fluting paper for corrugated paperboard	42,000 tonnes	Ex 48.01.E.II.b)5
Sulphite paper for wrapping purposes	5,400 tonnes	Ex 48.01.E.II.a)
All goods of these subheadings other than cellulose wadding and than paper covered by the four entries in this column immediately preceding this one	28,000 tonnes (of which not more than 22,500 tonnes wallpaper base and not more than 5,500 tonnes other than wallpaper base)	Ex 48.01.E.II.a) Ex 48.01.E.II.b)1 48.01.E.II.b)4 Ex 48.01.E.II.b)5
Paper board other than kraft board	36,700 tonnes (of which not more than 20,000 tonnes folding box-board made from 100% woodpulp, not more than 3,700 tonnes folding box-board made from furnishes including waste paper and not more than 13,000 tonnes other paper-board not mentioned in the two entries in this column immediately preceding this one)	48.01.E.I
All goods of this heading	4,500 tonnes	48.03
All goods of these subheadings	21,000 tonnes	48.05.B.I.b) 48.05.B.I.c)1 48.05.B.I.c)2 48.05.B.I.c)3 48.05.B.I.c)4 48.05.B.II
Coated printing paper	13,150 tonnes (of which not more than 11,000 tonnes mechanical and not more than 2,150 tonnes other than mechanical)	Ex 48.07.B.I.c)1
All goods of these subheadings other than coated printing paper	39,100 tonnes (of which not more than 19,500 tonnes folding box board made from 100% wood pulp, not more than 1,600 tonnes folding box board made from furnishes including waste paper and not more than 18,000 tonnes other paper and paperboard not mentioned in the two entries in this column immediately preceding this one)	48.07.B.I.a) 48.07.B.I.b) Ex 48.07.B.I.c)1 48.07.B.I.c)2 48.07.B.I.c)3 48.07.B.I.c)4 48.07.B.II

1 *Description of Goods*	2 *Quota*	3 *Tariff Heading or Subheading*
All goods of this subheading	5,000 tonnes (of which not more than 4,000 tonnes toilet paper and not more than 1,000 tonnes other than toilet paper)	48.15.B
All goods of these subheadings other than those covered by any of the preceding entries in this column relating to Subheadings 48.01.E.II.b)1 and 48.01.E.II.b)5	4,000 tonnes	48.01.B 48.01.C.I 48.01.D Ex 48.01.E.II.b)1 Ex 48.01.E.II.b)5 48.02 48.05 48.05.A 48.05.B.I.a) 48.06. 48.07.A 48.08 48.10 48.11 48.12 48.13 48.14 48.15.A 48.16 48.17 48.18 48.19 48.20 48.21
All goods of these headings and subheadings	£192,477	49.03 49.05.A 49.07.A 49.07.C.II 49.08 49.09 49.10 49.11.B

EXPLANATORY NOTE

(*This Note is not part of the Order.*)

This Order, which comes into operation on 1st January 1974, provides for the opening and administration during 1974 of duty-free tariff quotas for paper, paperboard, and printed products originating in Austria, Iceland, Portugal, Sweden, Switzerland, Norway and Finland. In order to qualify for duty-free treatment within the quotas goods must satisfy the conditions relating to origin in Article 25(1) of Protocol 3 to the Agreements between the European Economic Community and these countries. Goods which form part of these tariff quotas do so in the order in which they are entered for home use.

STATUTORY INSTRUMENTS

1973 No. 2066

CUSTOMS AND EXCISE

The Import Duties (Quota Relief) (Phosphorus and Wood Pulp) Order 1973

Made - - - -	*7th December* 1973
Laid before the House of Commons	10*th December* 1973
Coming into Operation	1*st January* 1974

The Secretary of State, in exercise of the powers conferred on him by section 5(1) and (4) of the Import Duties Act 1958**(a)**, as amended by paragraph 1 of Schedule 4 to the European Communities Act 1972**(b)**, and of all other powers enabling him in that behalf, hereby makes the following Order:

1.—(1) This Order may be cited as the Import Duties (Quota Relief) (Phosphorus and Wood Pulp) Order 1973 and shall operate from the beginning of 1st January 1974 up to and including 31st December 1974.

(2) The Interpretation Act 1889**(c)** shall apply for the interpretation of this Order as it applies for the interpretation of an Act of Parliament.

2.—(1) No import duty shall be charged on the following quantities (hereinafter referred to as "quotas") of goods of subheadings 28.04 C IV (phosphorus) and 47.01 A II (certain wood pulp) of the Customs Tariff 1959, namely:

(*a*) in the case of subheading 28.04 C IV, 36,000 tonnes;

(*b*) in the case of subheading 47.01 A II, 3,000,000 tonnes.

(2) The following classes of goods shall not be treated as forming part of a quota, namely goods on which, even if this Order had not been made, no import duty would be chargeable (whether because they originate in a particular country or area or in a developing country or otherwise).

(3) Goods shall be treated as forming part of a quota in the order in which they are entered for home use (within the meaning of the Customs and Excise Act 1952**(d)**) in the United Kingdom on or after 1st January 1974.

Limerick,
Parliamentary Under-Secretary
of State for Trade,
Department of Trade and Industry.

7th December 1973.

(a) 1958 c.6. **(b)** 1972 c.68. **(c)** 1889 c.63. **(d)** 1952 c.44.

EXPLANATORY NOTE

(This Note is not part of the Order.)

This Order, which comes into operation on 1st January 1974, provides for the opening and administration during 1974 of duty free tariff quotas to the amounts specified in Article 2(1) for phosphorus and wood pulp. The United Kingdom is authorised to establish such quotas under the Act annexed to the Treaty of Accession to the European Economic Community.

The Order provides that goods which would not in any case be subject to duty do not form part of these tariff quotas and that any goods which do form part of these tariff quotas do so as soon as they are entered for home use.

STATUTORY INSTRUMENTS

1973 No. 2067

CUSTOMS AND EXCISE

The Origin of Goods (Republic of Ireland) (Amendment) Regulations 1973

Made - - - -	*7th December* 1973
Laid before House of Commons	*10th December* 1973
Coming into Operation -	*1st January* 1974

The Secretary of State, in exercise of powers conferred by section 12(2) of the Import Duties Act 1958(**a**) and extended by section 7 of the Finance Act 1966(**b**) and now vested in him(**c**) and of all other powers enabling him in that behalf, hereby makes the following Regulations.

1.—(1) These Regulations may be cited as the Origin of Goods (Republic of Ireland) (Amendment) Regulations 1973 and shall come into operation on 1st January 1974.

(2) In these Regulations "the Regulations of 1966" means the Origin of Goods (Republic of Ireland) Regulations 1966(**d**), as amended (**e**).

(3) The Interpretation Act 1889(**f**) shall apply to the interpretation of these Regulations as it applies to the interpretation of an Act of Parliament.

2. The Regulations of 1966 shall have effect subject to the further amendments provided for in regulations 3, 4, 5 and 6 below.

3. For Regulations 1 and 2 of the Regulations of 1966 there shall be substituted the following:—

"1.—(1) For the purposes of the Import Duties Act 1958 goods shall not be treated as grown, produced or manufactured in the Republic of Ireland unless they are consigned to the United Kingdom from a place in that country and, unless they are in free circulation in that country.

(2) For the purposes of paragraph (1) above goods shall not be treated as being in free circulation unless—

(*a*) any customs duty or charge of equivalent effect payable on the import of the goods, or on the import of materials and parts used in the production or manufacture of the goods, into the Republic of Ireland, has been paid and has not subsequently been refunded or,

(**a**) 1958 c. 6.
(**b**) 1966 c. 18.
(**c**) S.I. 1970/1537 (1970 III, p. 5293).
(**d**) S.I. 1966/667 (1966 II, p. 1463).
(**e**) S.I. 1966/1098, 1968/988, 1223, 1972/388 (1966 III, p. 2699; 1968 II, pp. 2612, 2380; 1972 I, p. 1392).
(**f**) 1889 c. 63.

(*b*) if any such customs duty or charge of equivalent effect has been refunded, compensatory levy has been paid in respect of the goods on export to the United Kingdom by virtue of an instrument of the European Economic Community made under article 45(2) of the Act annexed to the Treaty concerning United Kingdom Accession to the Community.

2.—(1) Subject to Regulation 1 above, for the purposes of the Import Duties Act 1958 and of section 1 of the Finance Act 1973(**a**) and any Order made thereunder, goods of a description specified in Schedule 1, 2 or 3 hereto shall be treated as manufactured in the Republic of Ireland if, but only if—

(*a*) in the case of goods of a description specified in column 2 of Part I or II of Schedule 1 to these Regulations, they were manufactured in the Republic of Ireland and the appropriate proportion of the costs of their manufacture is attributable to expenditure within the area defined in regulation 6(1) (hereinafter referred to as "the area");

(*b*) in the case of goods of a description specified in column 2 of Schedule 2 to these Regulations, the last stage of their manufacture took place in the Republic of Ireland and they have undergone in the area the relevant qualifying process specified in column 3 of that Schedule;

(*c*) in the case of goods of a description specified in Part II of Schedule 3 not being goods of a description specified in Schedule 2, the relevant conditions set out in Part I of Schedule 3 have been fulfilled.

(2) The appropriate proportion referred to in regulation 2(1)(*a*) of these Regulations shall be—

(*a*) in the case of goods of a description specified in Part I of Schedule 1, 25%;

(*b*) in the case of goods of a description specified in Part II of Schedule 1, 50%.

4. In the first line of Regulation 3(1) of the Regulations of 1966, for "regulation 1(*a*)" there shall be substituted "regulation 2(1)(*a*)".

5. Regulations 5 and 6 of the Regulations of 1966 shall be renumbered as 6 and 7 respectively and there shall be inserted as regulation 5 the following:—

"5. Subject to regulation 1 above, for the purposes of the Import Duties Act 1958 and of section 1 of the Finance Act 1973 and any Order made thereunder, goods of a description other than one specified in Schedule 1, 2 or 3 hereto shall be treated as grown, produced or manufactured in Ireland if they qualify for Commonwealth preference".

6. Schedules 2 and 3 to the Regulations of 1966 shall be amended as specified in the Schedule to these Regulations.

7. The Origin of Goods (Republic of Ireland) (Amendment) Regulations 1966 are hereby revoked.

Limerick,
Parliamentary Under-Secretary of State for Trade,
Department of Trade and Industry.

7th December 1973.

(**a**) 1973 c. 51.
(**b**) S.I. 1966/1098 (1966 III, p. 2699).

SCHEDULE

AMENDMENTS TO SCHEDULES 2 AND 3 TO THE REGULATIONS OF 1966.

1. In Schedule 2 to the Regulations of 1966—

(*a*) in Introductory Note (1), for "regulation 1(*b*)" there shall be substituted "regulation 2(1)(*b*)";

(*b*) in Introductory Note 8, after "E.F.T.A." in the first three places where it occurs, there shall be substituted "or Danish";

(*c*) for the last paragraph of the said Introductory Note 8 there shall be substituted the following:

"References in this note to goods of E.F.T.A. or Danish origin are references to goods—

(*a*) which, under the Agreements, signed on 22nd July 1972, between the European Economic Community and respectively Austria, Iceland, Portugal, Sweden and Switzerland, the Agreement, signed on 14th May 1973, between the Community and Norway and the Agreement, signed on 5th October 1973, between the Community and Finland, are to be regarded as products originating in those countries and satisfy the provisions of Article 25(1) of Protocol 3 to these Agreements(**a**), and

(*b*) which, for the purposes of duties under the Import Duties Act 1958, are to be treated as goods of Denmark:

Provided (in all cases) that the goods have not benefitted from drawback or other relief from import duty in whichever of the abovementioned countries they underwent their last process of production.".

2. In Schedule 3 to the Regulations of 1966—

(*a*) in Introductory Note 1, for "Regulation 5" (in line 2) and "Regulation 1(*c*)" (in line 11) there shall be substituted respectively "Regulation 6" and "Regulation 2(1)(*c*)";

(*b*) in Introductory Note 3, for "Regulation 1(*c*)" (in line 2) and "Regulation 1(*a*)" (in line 4) there shall be substituted respectively "Regulation 2(1)(*c*)" and "Regulation 2(1)(*a*)".

(a) The Agreements are annexed respectively to Regulations (E.E.C.) Nos. 2836/72 (O. J. No. L.300, p. 1), 2842/72 (O. J. No. L.301, p. 1), 2844/72 (O. J. No. L.301, p. 167), 2838/72 (O. J. No. L.300 p. 96), 2840/72 (O. J. No. L.300 p. 188), 1691(73 (O. J. No. L.171 p. 1), the Agreement with Finland has yet to be published in the Official Journal.

EXPLANATORY NOTE

(This Note is not part of the Regulations.)

These Regulations further amend the Origin of Goods (Republic of Ireland) Regulations 1966.

They provide that in order to qualify as goods of the Republic of Ireland for the purposes of exemption from import duties or from any protective elements in revenue duties, goods must, in addition to being consigned to the United Kingdom from the Republic of Ireland, have been in free circulation in the Republic. This condition is met if any duty chargeable on import into the Republic of Ireland of the goods or materials and parts used in their production or manufacture has been paid and not drawn back or, where duty has been drawn back, if a compensatory levy is paid in accordance with E.E.C. Regulations in respect of the goods on export to the United Kingdom.

The Regulations also provide that, subject to those conditions, goods for which specific content and processing requirements are not laid down in the Regulations of 1966 (as amended) are to be treated as originating in the Republic of Ireland if they qualify for commonwealth preference.

The Schedule to these Regulations provides for consequential amendments to the Regulations of 1966 and amendments resulting from the alteration of the arrangements applying to E.F.T.A. goods.

The Origin of Goods (Republic of Ireland) (Amendment) Regulations 1966, which become otiose as a result of these Regulations, are revoked.

1973 No. 2068

CONTROL OF FUEL AND ELECTRICITY

The Fuel and Electricity (Heating) (Control) Order 1973

Made - - -	8*th December* 1973
Laid before Parliament	10*th December* 1973
Coming into Operation	11*th December* 1973

The Secretary of State, in exercise of his powers under section 2(1) of the Fuel and Electricity (Control) Act 1973(a) and section 7 of the Emergency Laws (Re-enactments and Repeals) Act 1964(b) as having effect by virtue of section 5(1) of the Fuel and Electricity (Control) Act 1973, and of all other powers in that behalf enabling him, hereby orders as follows:

1. This Order may be cited as the Fuel and Electricity (Heating) (Control) Order 1973 and shall come into operation on 11th December 1973.

2. (1) In this Order:

"electricity" means electricity whether or not supplied by an Electricity Board within the meaning of section 1 of the Electricity Act 1947(c);

"fuel" means any substance, whether solid, liquid or gaseous, used as a fuel; and

"school" means any institution providing primary or secondary education or both within the meaning of the Education Acts 1944 to 1971 or the Education (Scotland) Acts 1939 to 1971.

(2) In this Order "premises to which this Order applies" means—

(*a*) any premises used wholly or mainly—

(i) as an office or showroom;

(ii) as a retail shop, bank or petrol station;

(iii) as a restaurant or catering establishment (whether or not licensed for the sale of intoxicating liquor) or for the sale or consumption of intoxicating liquor;

(iv) as a warehouse or store;

(v) as a film, television or photographic studio;

(vi) as a library, museum, art gallery, exhibition hall or other public hall;

(vii) as a place of education;

(viii) as a church, chapel or other place of public worship; or

(ix) for recreation, entertainment or sport; or

(*b*) any part so used of any premises, not otherwise so used, if the heating for that part is effected separately from the heating for the other part of the premises.

(a) 1973 c. 67. (b) 1964 c. 60. (c) 1947 c. 54.

(3) Any reference in this Order to any enactment shall be construed as a reference thereto as amended or extended and as a reference to any regulation or Order made under any enactment.

3. (1) Subject to the Electricity (Heating) (Restriction) Order 1973(a)and to paragraph (2) of this Article, no person shall use or permit the use of electricity or fuel for the purpose of heating any premises to which this Order applies so as to cause the temperature of those premises to exceed 63 degrees Fahrenheit (which is equivalent to 17.25 degrees Centigrade):

Provided that if any enactment requires the heating of any premises to which this Order applies or any part thereof to be maintained in certain circumstances at a specific temperature or at not less than a specific temperature, nothing in this Article shall require the heating of such premises or part thereof (as the case may be) in those circumstances to fall below the minimum temperature so specified even if in consequence thereof the temperature of any other part of such premises is thereby caused to exceed that specified in the last foregoing paragraph.

(2) Nothing in paragraph (1) of this Article shall apply to the use of electricity or fuel for the purpose of heating any part of any premises to which this Order applies—

(*a*) which is used for living accommodation;

(*b*) to the extent that such use is necessary for the maintenance of the health of any person on those premises who is ill, disabled, infirm, pregnant, under the age of 5 years or over the age of 60 years;

(*c*) which is used as a school during such times as it is so used;

(*d*) to the extent necessary to prevent damage or deterioration to food, goods or material or to prevent damage to or impairment of the functioning of any apparatus or equipment on the premises which is sensitive to changes of temperature or humidity;

(*e*) for preserving the health of any livestock on any such premises; or

(*f*) in respect of which a licence has been granted by the Secretary of State under this Order.

4. Any licence granted under this Order may be subject to conditions and may be revoked without prior notice.

5. It shall be a defence for a person who contravenes or fails to comply with a provision of this Order to prove that he used all due diligence to secure compliance with that provision.

6. This Order shall not extend to Northern Ireland.

Tom Boardman,
Minister for Industry,
Department of Trade and Industry.

8th December 1973.

(a)S.I. 1973/1900 (1973 III, p. 6587)

EXPLANATORY NOTE

(This Note is not part of the Order.)

This Order prohibits the heating above a temperature of 63°F (17.25°C) by electricity or any fuel of premises specified in Article 2(2) of the Order. These premises include offices, showrooms, shops, banks, petrol stations, restaurants, bars, studios, public halls, places of education (except schools), churches and places of recreation, entertainment or sport. This temperature may however be exceeded for certain purposes including the maintenance of health, the prevention of damage to food, goods and material or so as to conform with certain minimum temperature requirements imposed by other legislation.

1973 No. 2069

CUSTOMS AND EXCISE

The Commonwealth Preference (Standstill Area) Regulations 1973

Made - - - -	7*th December* 1973
Laid before the Houses of Commons	10*th December* 1973
Coming into Operation	1*st January* 1974

The Secretary of State, by virtue of powers conferred by section 12(2) of the Import Duties Act 1958**(a)** and now vested in him**(b)** and of the powers conferred on him by section 2(1) of the Finance Act 1973**(c)** and of all other powers enabling him in that behalf, hereby makes the following Regulations:—

Citation, Commencement and Interpretation

1.—(1) These Regulations may be cited as the Commonwealth Preference (Standstill Area) Regulations 1973 and shall come into operation on 1st January 1974.

(2) The Interpretation Act 1889**(d)** shall apply for the interpretation of these Regulations as it applies for the interpretation of an Act of Parliament.

(3) In these Regulations—

(*a*) "factory", in relation to any goods, means the place where the goods were manufactured and

(*b*) references to goods include references to any containers or other forms of interior packing in which the goods are packed, being containers or packing of a type ordinarily sold with similar goods when they are sold retail.

2. For the purposes of any Order made under the Import Duties Act 1958 or under the Finance Act 1973, the question whether goods are of the part of the Commonwealth Preference area formed by the countries named in Schedule 1 hereto (hereinafter referred to as "the standstill area") shall be determined in accordance with the following Regulations.

Consignment of Goods

3. Goods grown, produced or manufactured in a country of the standstill area shall not be treated as goods of that area unless they are consigned to the United Kingdom from such a country:

Provided that nothing in this Regulation shall affect the operation of section 2(9) of the Import Duties Act 1958 (under which goods of Swaziland, Botswana,

(a) 1958 c. 6.
(b) *See* S.I. 1970/1537 (1970 III, p. 5293).
(c) 1973 c. 51.
(d) 1889 c. 63.

Malawi or Zambia are deemed to be consigned from those countries if consigned from Lourenço Marques or, in the case of the three last-mentioned countries, from Beira).

Goods manufactured in the Commonwealth Preference standstill Area

4.—(1) Goods manufactured in the standstill area shall nonetheless not be treated as manufactured there unless at least the appropriate proportion of the costs of their manufacture is attributable to area expenditure, as defined in Regulation 6.

(2) Subject to the provisions of Regulation 7 (which relates to manufactured sugar and tobacco), the appropriate proportion, for the purposes of duties chargeable on any goods either as such or in respect of any article contained in them as a part or ingredient, shall be—

(*a*) in the case of goods falling within a description of goods specified in Part I of Schedule 2 hereto ... ... 75 per cent;

(*b*) in the case of goods not falling within any such description but falling within a description of goods specified in Part II of Schedule 2 hereto ... ... 50 per cent;

(*c*) in the case of any other goods ... ... 25 per cent.

Costs of manufacture

5.—(1) For the purposes of these Regulations, the costs of manufacture of any goods shall be the costs incurred by the manufacturer in relation to those goods before they are dispatched in their finished state and shall include the following items:—

(*a*) the costs to the manufacturer as received into the factory of any materials (including components and unfinished goods) used in the manufacture of the goods, less the amount of any customs or excise duty or any other duty or tax incurred in respect of such materials which is subsequently refunded on the exportation of the goods;

(*b*) the cost of labour directly employed in the manufacture of the goods;

(*c*) the factory overhead costs incurred in relation to the manufacture of the goods in respect of—

(i) rent, rates and taxes, motive power, electricity, gas, fuel, water, lighting and heating;

(ii) factory supervision, including the costs of employing managers, foremen, timekeepers, watchmen and other similar officers and servants of the manufacturer;

(iii) maintenance, repairs and renewals of plant, machinery, tools and factory buildings;

(iv) depreciation of plant, machinery and tools;

(v) interest on capital outlay on the factory buildings and land;

(vi) interest on depreciated value of plant, machinery and tools;

(*d*) the cost of any process carried out in the course of the manufacture of the goods by any independent contractor in performance of a contract with the manufacturer.

(2) In computing the costs of manufacture as aforesaid the following items shall not be included:—

(*a*) the cost of exterior packing;

(*b*) the manufacturer's profit or the profit or remuneration of any trader, broker, exporter or other person dealing with the goods in their finished manufactured state;

(*c*) royalties;

(*d*) the cost of carriage and freight or insurance or any other charges incurred in respect of the goods after their manufacture.

Area expenditure

6.—(1) Without prejudice to the provisions of paragraph (2) of this Regulation area expenditure shall include any costs mentioned in head (*a*), (*b*), or (*c*) of paragraph (1) of Regulation 5 which are incurred in respect of materials grown or produced in the standstill area, or in respect of work done or factories situated in that area.

(2) Where any costs mentioned in head (*a*) of paragraph (1) of Regulation 5 are incurred in respect of materials which have been manufactured or processed in the standstill area, area expenditure means a proportion of those costs equal to the proportion of area expenditure which is shown to the satisfaction of the Commissioners of Customs and Excise to be included in the costs incurred by the manufacturer or processor of those materials in that area.

(3) In relation to any cost mentioned in head(*d*) of paragraph (1) of Regulation 5 area expenditure means a proportion of that cost equal to the proportion of area expenditure which is shown to the satisfaction of the Commissioners of Customs and Excise to be included in the costs of the person who carried out the process.

Sugar and Tobacco

7. In the case of refined sugar, extracts from sugar, molasses, and manufactured tobacco, while there is in force in respect of such goods a direction given by the Board of Trade or Secretary of State under subsection (2) of section 8 of the Finance Act, 1919**(a)** providing that a preferential rate of duty shall be charged only upon such proportion of the goods as corresponds to the proportion of dutiable material used in their manufacture shown to the satisfaction of the Commissioners of Customs and Excise to have been grown or produced in the Commonwealth preference area, the appropriate proportion under paragraph (1) of Regulation 4 shall be 5 per cent.

Miscellaneous

8.—(1) Any goods falling within a description of goods set out in Schedule 2 hereto shall for the purpose of these Regulations be treated as within that description, notwithstanding that for the purpose of any duty of customs chargeable on the importation thereof such goods are treated as falling within some other description of goods.

(2) Where a number of separate articles are included in one parcel or shipment, each and every article shall be treated separately for the purpose of calculating the proportion of the costs of manufacture thereof attributable to area expenditure.

Limerick,
Parliamentary Under-Secretary of State for Trade,
Department of Trade and Industry.

7th December 1973.

(a) 1919 c. 32.

SCHEDULE 1

Regulation 2

Associated States in the Carribbean:
Antigua, Dominica, Grenada, St Lucia, St Vincent, St Kitts-Nevis-Anguilla

The Bahamas

Barbados

Bermuda

Botswana

British Antarctic Territory

Belize

British Indian Ocean Territory

British Solomon Islands

British Virgin Islands

Brunei

Cayman Islands

Central and Southern Line Islands

Cyprus

Falkland Islands and Dependencies

Fiji

The Gambia

Ghana

Gilbert and Ellice Islands

Guyana

Jamaica

Kenya

Lesotho

Malawi

Malta

Mauritius

Montserrat

Nigeria

Papua-New Guinea

Pitcairn

The Seychelles

Sierra Leone

St Helena and Dependencies

Swaziland

Tanzania

Tonga

Trinidad and Tobago

Turks and Caicos Islands

Uganda

Western Samoa

Zambia

SCHEDULE 2

Regulation 4(2)

PART I

Optical glass and optical elements, whether finished or not, microscopes, field and opera glasses, theodolites, sextants, spectroscopes and other optical instruments and component parts thereof.

PART II

Pottery and all other clay products.

Glass and glassware:—

Plate and sheet glass, whether bevelled, silvered, or otherwise finished or not.

Illuminating glassware.

Domestic glassware, including cooking utensils, table glassware, toilet glassware and ornamental glassware.

Glass bottles and glass jars, including glass stoppers.

Furniture made wholly or mainly of metal, of the following descriptions:—

(i) Tables, bedsteads, wire mattresses, stands, desks and counters.

(ii) Chairs, stools and seats.

(iii) Bookcases and bookshelves.

(iv) Cabinets, safes, cash and deed boxes, drawers and cupboards.

(v) Shelving, storage bins and storage racks.

(vi) Office letter racks and letter trays.

(vii) Lockers.

(viii) Parts of any of the above-mentioned articles.

Hollow-ware of iron or steel (including tinned plate).

Baths of iron or steel.

Metal door and window frames and casements.

Stoves, grates and ranges for domestic cooking or heating and parts and fittings therefor.

Iron and steel products of the following descriptions:—

(i) Tubes, pipes and pipe and tube fittings of all kinds.

(ii) Railway and tramway construction material of all kinds.

(iii) Springs.

(iv) Wire, wire netting, wire nails and cable and rope (except insulated telephone and telegraph cables).

(v) Screws (except screws for wood, other than screw hooks, screw rings and screw knobs), nails, tacks, studs and spikes.

(vi) Rivets and washers.

(vii) Bolts and nuts.

(viii) Anchors and grapnels and parts thereof, chains and ships' cables.

(ix) Screws for wood (other than screw hooks, screw rings and screw knobs) whether wholly of iron or steel, or of iron or steel coated or plated with some other metal or substance.

(x) Wagons for use on railways and parts of such wagons.

The following articles manufactured wholly or partly of the metals aluminium, copper, lead, nickel, tin, zinc and alloys containing any of those metals:—

Sheets and strip, rods, plates, angles, shapes and sections, wire, tubes, foil and hollow-ware.

Screws for wood of brass, copper or any alloy containing copper, whether coated with any other metal or other substance or not.

Cutlery:—

(i) Knives with one or more blades made wholly or partly of steel or iron.

(ii) Scissors, including tailor's shears and secateurs, made wholly or partly of steel or iron.

(iii) Razors, including safety-razors and blades therefor.

(iv) Hair clippers.

(v) Carving forks.

(vi) Knife sharpeners, wholly or partly of steel.

(vii) Component parts of or blanks for any of the above-mentioned articles.

Locks, padlocks, keys, bolts, latches, hasps and hinges of metal.

Needles and pins.

Implements and tools and parts thereof, other than handles of hickory.

Unexposed sensitised photographic paper, cloth, plates and film and spools therefor.

Electrical goods including:—

Electric wires and cables, insulated.

Telegraph and telephone apparatus.

Wireless apparatus.

Electric carbons other than graphitized carbon electrodes.

Electric lighting appliances and fittings.

Batteries and accumulators.

Electric bell apparatus.

Electric cooking and heating apparatus.

Electric meters.

Parts of, and accessories to, the above.

Machinery and parts thereof (including ball bearings, roller bearings and parts thereof).

Twine of the following description:—

Hard fibre singles.

Boots, booties, shoes, overshoes, slippers and sandals of all descriptions and of whatever material, finished or unfinished, and shaped parts and laces therefor.

Paints, painters, enamels, lacquers, varnishes and printers' inks.

Distempers, whether dry or not.

Pigments and extenders (whether dry or with oil or other medium) other than the following:—Natural dyes; synthetic organic dyestuffs, colours and colouring matters; dry earth colours, barytes, silica, graphite and carbon black from natural gas.

Saddlery and harness (including horse boots) wholly or partly of leather.

Trunks, bags, wallets, pouches and other receptacles made wholly or partly of leather or material resembling leather, whether fitted or not.

Transparent cellulose wrapping.

Locomotives and parts thereof.

Aircraft and parts thereof.

Cycles (other than motor cycles) and parts and accessories thereof.

Perambulators and mailcarts and parts thereof.

Manufactures wholly or partly of rubber, balata or gutta percha (including vulcanite and ebonite).

Arms and ammunition:—

(i) Sporting guns, sporting rifles and sporting carbines and parts thereof.

(ii) Military rifles and military carbines and parts thereof.

(iii) Miniature rifles and carbines and cadet rifles and carbines and parts thereof.

(iv) Air guns and air rifles and air pistols and parts thereof.

(v) Revolvers and pistols and parts thereof.

(vi) Loaded cartridges and empty cartridge cases.

Toilet preparations (excluding essential oils) of the following descriptions:—

Toilet soap.

Tooth paste or powder and liquid preparations for dental purposes and mouth washes.

Toilet paste or powder.

Toilet cream.

Hair dyes.

Scented sachets.

Lipstick, rouge and grease paint.

Preparations for use in manicure or chiropody.

Preparations for use on the hair, face or body.

Bath salts and essences.

Smelling salts.

Prepared fuller's earth.

Toilet requisites of the following descriptions:—

Powder bowls or boxes and powder puffs.

Nail polishers.

Nail clippers, nail cleaners and nail files.

Denture bowls.

Manicure sets.

Parts of the above articles.

Brooms and brushes of all descriptions and parts thereof (other than prepared bristles and other prepared animal hair).

Buttons, snap and slide fasteners, push buttons, studs, hooks and eyes.

Machinery belting (including conveyor and elevator bands).

Appliances, apparatus, accessories and requisites for sports, games, gymnastics and athletics (other than apparel and boots and shoes) and parts thereof.

Toys of all kinds and parts thereof of whatever material composed.

Pen nibs, fountain pens, stylographic and other pens, propelling pencils, paper clips and fasteners, stationery glassware and parts of any such articles.

Hair combs.

Iron or steel guides, T section, of a description commonly used for lifts or elevators.

Manufactures wholly or partly of cotton, wool (including alpaca, mohair, cashmere, llama, vicuna and camel's hair), hemp of all kinds, flax or jute, of the following descriptions (but excluding coir, rush, grass, raffia, straw or reed mats and matting):—

Carpets, carpeting, floor rugs, floor mats and matting.

Motor cars, including motor bicycles and motor tricycles; accessories and component parts of motor cars, motor bicyles and motor tricycles.

Musical instruments (including gramophones, pianolas, and other similar instruments; accessories and component parts of musical instruments, and records and other means of ıeproducing music).

Clocks and clock cases.

Beakers, flasks, burettes, measuring cylinders, thermometers, tubing and other scientific glassware and lamp-blown ware.

Evaporating dishes, crucibles, combustion boats and other laboratory porcelain.

Galvanometers, pyrometers, electroscopes, barometers, analytical and other precision balances, and other scientific instruments and component parts thereof, gauges and measuring instruments of precision of the types used in engineering machine shops and viewing rooms, whether for use in such shops or rooms or not (but not including microscopes, field and opera glasses, theodolites, sextants, spectroscopes and other optical instruments and component parts thereof).

Hosiery latch needles.

Unexposed sensitised cinematograph film.

Arc lamp carbons and amorphous carbon electrodes.

Wireless valves and similar rectifiers and vacuum tubes.

Ignition magnetos and permanent magnets.

EXPLANATORY NOTE

(*This Note is not part of the Regulations.*)

These Regulations prescribe the circumstances in which goods are to be treated as originating in the part of the Commonwealth preference area formed by the countries named in Schedule 1 to the Regulations (the "Commonwealth preference standstill area") for the purposes of import duties under the Import Duties Act 1958 or the protective elements of other customs duties. The countries in question are the Commonwealth preference area countries which are entitled under the Treaty concerning United Kingdom Accession to the European Economic Community to benefit from the continuance of the Commonwealth preference treatment which applied on 1st January 1972 where that is more favourable than the treatment which will apply to goods qualifying for Commonwealth preference generally.

The conditions prescribed by these Regulations are generally speaking those which would result if the origin rules for Commonwealth preference qualification (The Commonwealth Preference Regulations 1958) applied to the Common wealth preference standstill area alone.

In order to qualify under these Regulations, goods must be consigned from a country in the standstill area (subject to an exception relating to the ports of Beira and Lourenço Marques) (Regulation 3).

In the case of goods manufactured in the Commonwealth preference standstill area, the appropriate proportion of the costs of their manufacture must be attributable to work done or materials grown or produced in the area (Regulation 4). The appropriate proportion varies in the case of goods in Part I and II of Schedule 2 to the Regulations and other goods.

1973 No. 2070

CIVIL AVIATION

The Civil Aviation (Route Charges for Navigation Services) (Amendment) Regulations 1973

Made - - -	*7th December* 1973
Laid before Parliament	*10th December* 1973
Coming into Operation	*1st January* 1974

Whereas in pursuance of tariffs approved under the Eurocontrol Convention(**a**) and under the Multilateral Agreement relating to the Collection of Route Charges concluded at Brussels on 8th September 1970(**b**) (being an international agreement to which the United Kingdom is a party) the Secretary of State has determined that the rates of charges, payable to the Eurocontrol Organisation under the Civil Aviation (Route Charges for Navigation Services) Regulations 1973(**c**), in respect of the navigation services specified in the said Regulations, shall be amended as provided in the following Regulations:

Now, therefore, the Secretary of State, in exercise of his powers under sections 4 and 7(1) of the Civil Aviation (Eurocontrol) Act 1962(**d**), section 15(3) of the Civil Aviation Act 1968(**e**), and paragraph 6 of Schedule 10 to the Civil Aviation Act 1971(**f**) and of all other powers enabling him in that behalf, hereby makes the following Regulations:—

1. These Regulations may be cited as the Civil Aviation (Route Charges for Navigation Services) (Amendment) Regulations 1973 and shall come into operation on 1st January 1974.

2. The Interpretation Act 1889(**g**) applies for the purpose of the interpretation of these Regulations as it applies for the purpose of the interpretation of an Act of Parliament.

3. The Civil Aviation (Route Charges for Navigation Services) Regulations 1973 shall be amended by substituting for Schedule 1 the Schedule to these Regulations.

Michael Heseltine,
Minister for Aerospace and Shipping,
Department of Trade and Industry.

7th December 1973.

(**a**) Cmnd. 2114.
(**b**) Cmnd. 4916.
(**c**) S.I. 1973/1678 (1973 II, p. 5154).
(**d**) 1962 c. 8.
(**e**) 1968 c. 61.
(**f**) 1971 c. 75.
(**g**) 1889 c. 63.

SCHEDULE

(1) Aerodromes of departure (or of first destination) situated	(2) Aerodromes of first destination (or of departure)	(3) Amount of the charge in US dollars
between 14°W and 110°W and North of 55°N. (ZONE I)	Amsterdam	91.24
	Belfast	24.45
	Berlin	126.82
	Brussels	95.78
	Coventry	71.95
	Dusseldorf	108.78
	Edinburgh	42.42
	Frankfurt/Main	122.41
	Glasgow	34.46
	Gutersloh	113.60
	Hamburg	110.35
	Hanover	118.15
	Lahr	111.90
	London	74.45
	Luton	74.45
	Luxembourg	109.38
	Lyneham	77.17
	Manchester	56.55
	Mildenhall	76.95
	Ostend	90.38
	Paris	98.96
	Prestwick	42.27
	Ramstein	110.55
	Rotterdam	92.46
	Shannon	5.25
	Valkenburg	90.92
	Wiesbaden	121.60
	Woodbridge	75.77
	Zurich	144.63
West of 110°W and North of 55°N. (ZONE II)	Amsterdam	24.41
	Hamburg	8.98
	London	83.21
	Ramstein	48.01
between 30°W and 110°W and between 28°N and 55°N. (ZONE III)	Albenga	65.53
	Amsterdam	72.66
	Ankara	77.90
	Athens	77.90
	Barcelona	38.57
	Basle-Mulhouse	66.40
	Beirut	77.90
	Belfast	21.70
	Bergen/Flesland	44.85
	Bordeaux	40.45
	Brize Norton	35.25
	Brussels	70.00
	Budapest	145.82
	Casablanca	13.02
	Cologne-Bonn	81.47
	Copenhagen	58.25
	Dublin	14.81

(1) Aerodromes of departure (or of first destination) situated	(2) Aerodromes of first destination (or of departure)	(3) Amount of the charge in US dollars
(ZONE III) *continued*	Dusseldorf	79.71
	East Midlands	40.84
	Frankfurt/Main	89.10
	Geneva	66.38
	Glasgow	25.99
	Hamburg	100.19
	Hanover	104.00
	Helsinki	47.72
	Lahr	78.46
	Las Palmas (Canary Islands)	11.81
	Lisbon	14.23
	London	46.12
	Luton	46.12
	Luxembourg	71.48
	Lyneham	34.05
	Lyon	66.73
	Madrid	29.53
	Malaga	31.24
	Manchester	36.80
	Marham	53.49
	Milan	65.53
	Mildenhall	50.22
	Moscow	58.25
	Munich	114.03
	Naples...	65.08
	Nice	46.23
	Northolt	46.12
	Ostend	64.36
	Oslo	44.85
	Palma (Majorca)	44.90
	Paris	52.94
	Pisa	65.53
	Prague...	105.15
	Prestwick	25.99
	Rabat	13.02
	Rome	82.70
	Rota	26.31
	Seville	26.31
	Shannon	8.22
	Sollingen	74.84
	Stavanger	44.85
	St. Mawgan	28.04
	Stockholm	44.85
	Stuttgart	96.24
	Tel Aviv/Lod	77.90
	Thorney Island	40.85
	Turin	65.53
	Upper Heyford	43.21
	Venice	65.53
	Vienna	143.69
	Waddington	43.21
	Warsaw	69.66
	Zagreb	131.65
	Zurich	72.03

(1) Aerodromes of departure (or of first destination) situated	(2) Aerodromes of first destination (or of departure)	(3) Amount of the charge in US dollars
West of 110°W and between 28°N and 55°N. (ZONE IV)	Amsterdam	87.04
	Berlin	126.89
	Brussels	81.29
	Dusseldorf	103.99
	Frankfurt/Main	117.25
	London	72.36
	Luton	72.36
	Manchester	36.80
	Paris	74.12
	Prestwick	34.02
	Shannon	6.54
West of 30°W and between the equator and 28°N. (ZONE V)	Amsterdam	62.67
	Brussels	54.71
	Casablanca	8.57
	Charleroi	53.61
	Cologne-Bonn	65.53
	Copenhagen	101.73
	Dusseldorf	65.93
	Frankfurt/Main	71.39
	Las Palmas (Canary Islands)	25.37
	Lisbon	15.35
	London	41.17
	Luxembourg	58.74
	Madrid	31.93
	Manchester	41.17
	Milan	47.53
	Munich	65.98
	Paris	49.24
	Rabat	8.57
	Rome	43.79
	Shannon	9.55
	Zurich	56.91

EXPLANATORY NOTE

(This Note is not part of the Regulations.)

These Regulations amend the Civil Aviation (Route Charges for Navigation Services) Regulations 1973 so as to give effect to new tariffs relating to transatlantic flights which enter the airspace, specified in the 1973 Regulations, where the United Kingdom provides air navigation services. The tariffs have been agreed internationally under the Eurocontrol Convention and the Multilateral Agreement relating to the Collection of Route Charges. They reflect recent changes in the effective parity relationships of currencies.

1973 No. 2071

CUSTOMS AND EXCISE

The Origin of Goods (Petroleum Products) Regulations 1973

Made - - - -	*7th December* 1973
Laid before the House of Commons -	*10th December* 1973
Coming into Operation	*1st January* 1974

The Secretary of State, in exercise of powers conferred by section 12(2) of the Import Duties Act 1958**(a)** and now vested in him **(b)** and of the powers conferred on him by section 2(1) of the Finance Act 1973**(c)**, hereby makes the following Regulations:

1.—(1) These Regulations may be cited as the Origin of Goods (Petroleum Products) Regulations 1973 and shall come into operation on 1st January 1974.

(2) The Interpretation Act 1889**(d)** shall apply for the interpretation of these Regulations as it applies for the interpretation of an Act of Parliament.

2.—(1) For the purposes of any Order under section 1, 3 or 13 of the Import Duties Act 1958, the question whether goods of a description specified in Schedule 1 hereto are to be treated as produced or manufactured in a country shall, except in the cases specified in paragraph (3) of this Regulation, be determined in accordance with these Regulations.

(2) For the purposes of any relief from customs duties available by virtue of any instrument of the European Communities in the case of goods of a description specified in Schedule 1 hereto which originate in a developing country and for the purposes of any preferential rate of customs duty, other than a duty under the Import Duties Act 1958, imposed on goods of such a description, goods shall, except in the cases specified in paragraph (3) of this Regulation, be regarded as originating in a country if they are to be regarded as produced or manufactured in a country in accordance with the following provisions of these Regulations.

(3) The preceding paragraphs of this Regulation shall not, however, apply to determine the question of production, manufacture or origin of goods for the purposes therein specified where such question falls to be determined under any regulation of the European Communities or any Act or other instrument having the force of law, and in particular under any such instrument relating to goods qualifying for commonwealth preference or goods of or originating in any of the following countries, namely, Denmark, the Republic of Ireland, the Channel Islands, Austria, Finland, Iceland, Norway, Portugal, Sweden or Switzerland.

3.—(1) For the purposes of these Regulations—

(*a*) a description of goods in the second column of Schedule 1 or 2 hereto,

(i) if in the same terms as the heading or subheading of the Customs Tariff 1959 specified in column 1 of the said Schedules in relation to the description, covers all goods of that heading or subheading and,

(a) 1958 c. 6.
(b) *See* S.I. 1970/1537 (1970 III, p. 5293).
(c) 1973 c. 51.
(d) 1889 c. 63.

(ii) in other cases, covers all goods of that description which would fall within a subheading in the same terms in the heading of the Customs Tariff 1959 specified in the said column 1 in relation to the description (the said heading being prefixed by "ex");

(*b*) materials shall be treated as having been imported into a country unless they are shown to the satisfaction of the Commissioners of Customs and Excise not to have been so imported.

(2) Notwithstanding the provisions of the following Regulations, goods specified in Schedule 1 hereto shall not be treated as produced or manufactured in a country unless—

(*a*) they were consigned to the United Kingdom from that country or from another member State of the European Economic Community or,

(*b*) if not so consigned, they remained under customs control in any country (other than one described in paragraph (*a*) above) through which they were moved, were not entered for home use there and were not subject to any operation there other than unloading, reloading or any operation intended to keep them in good condition.

4.—(1) Goods which have been wholly produced or manufactured in a country without the use of any imported materials shall be treated as produced or manufactured in that country.

(2) For the purpose of paragraph (1) above, waste products shall be treated as wholly produced in a country from materials produced there if they result from the carrying on of any process of manufacture in that country.

5. Goods produced or manufactured in a country from imported materials not falling within the same heading of the Customs Tariff 1959 as those goods shall be treated as produced or manufactured in that country except in the following cases—

(*a*) being goods mentioned in column 2 of Part I of Schedule 2 hereto, if they fall to be classified in a different tariff heading by reason only of the performance of the process mentioned in relation to them in column 3 of Part I of that Schedule or a combination of such a process and a process or processes mentioned in head (*b*) of this paragraph, or

(*b*) if they fall to be classified in a different tariff heading by reason only of the performance of one or more of the following minor processes, namely:

(i) operations intended solely to ensure that the goods remain in good condition during transit or storage, (including freezing);

(ii) packing, repacking, bottling or splitting up into, or assembling into, consignments;

(iii) marking or labelling;

(iv) mixing—where any of the components mixed is a product imported into the country in question.

6. Goods mentioned in column 2 of Part II of Schedule 2 hereto which have undergone in a country the process mentioned in column 3 of that Part of that Schedule shall be treated as produced or manufactured in that country.

Limerick,
Parliamentary Under-Secretary of State for Trade,
Department of Trade and Industry.

7th December 1973.

SCHEDULE 1

1. *Tariff heading*	2. *Description of goods*
ex 27.07	Assimilated aromatic oils as defined in Note 2 to Chapter 27, of which more than 65 per cent. by volume distils at a temperature of up to 250°C (including mixtures of petroleum spirit and benzole), intended for use as power or heating fuels.
27.09	Petroleum oils and oils obtained from bituminous minerals, crude.
27.10	Petroleum oils and oils obtained from bituminous minerals, other than crude; preparations not elsewhere specified or included, containing not less than 70 per cent. by weight of petroleum oils or of oils obtained from bituminous minerals, these oils being the basic constituents of the preparations.
27.11	Petroleum gases and other gaseous hydrocarbons.
27.12	Petroleum jelly.
27.13	Paraffin wax, micro-crystalline wax, slack wax, ozokerite, lignite wax, peat wax and other mineral waxes, whether or not coloured.
27.14	Petroleum bitumen, petroleum coke and other residues of petroleum oils obtained from bituminous materials.
27.15	Bitumen and asphalt, natural; bituminous shale, asphaltic rock and tar sands.
27.16	Bituminous mixtures based on natural asphalt, on natural bitumen, on petroleum bitumen, on mineral tar or on mineral tar pitch (for example, bituminous mastics, cut-backs).
29.01 A.I	Hydrocarbons, acyclic, for use as power or heating fuels.
29.01 B.II	Cyclanes and Cyclenes (excluding azulenes) for use as power or heating fuels.
ex 34.03	Lubricating preparations containing petroleum oils or oils obtained from bituminous minerals, but not including preparations containing 70 per cent. or more by weight of petroleum oils or of oils obtained from bituminous minerals.
ex 34.04	Waxes with a basis of paraffin wax, of petroleum wax, of waxes obtained from bituminous minerals, of slack wax or of scale wax.
ex 38.14	Prepared additives for lubricants.
ex 38.19	Mixed alkylenes.

SCHEDULE 2

PART I

1. *Tariff Heading*	2. *Description of goods*	3. *Processing that does not confer the status of originating product*
ex 34.04	Waxes with a basis of paraffin wax, of petroleum wax, of waxes obtained from bituminous minerals, of slack wax or scale wax	Manufacture from organic chemicals of Chapter 29.

PART II

Tariff Heading	*Description of goods*	*Processing which, even if not resulting in a change of tariff heading of the materials, confers originating status*
ex 27.07	Assimilated aromatic oils as defined in Note 2 to Chapter 27, of which more than 65 per cent. by volume distils at a temperature of up to 250°C (including mixtures of petroleum spirit and benzole) for use as power or heating fuels	Manufacture by processes not consisting solely of mixing or blending or packing or any combination of these processes
ex 27.10	Petroleum oils and oils obtained from bituminous minerals, other than crude; preparations not elsewhere specified or included containing not less than 70 per cent. by weight of petroleum oils or of oils obtained from bituminous minerals, these oils being the basic constituents of the preparations	Manufacture by processes not consisting solely of mixing or blending or packing or any combination of these processes
ex 27.12	Refined petroleum jelly	Manufacture from unrefined petroleum jelly
ex 27.13	Paraffin wax	Manufacture from slack wax or scale wax
ex 27.13	Micro-crystalline wax, slack wax, purified ozokerite, lignite wax, peat wax and other mineral waxes (other than crude ozokerite), whether or not coloured	Manufacture from crude ozokerite
ex 38.14	Prepared additives for lubricants	Manufacture in which the value of non-originating products used does not exceed 50 per cent. of the value of the finished product

EXPLANATORY NOTE

(This Note is not part of the Regulations.)

These Regulations lay down the conditions under which certain petroleum products, specified in Schedule 1 to the Regulations, are to be treated as originating in a country for the purposes of preferential rates of duty under the Import Duties Act 1958 or of other customs duties or for the purposes of reliefs from such duties under the European Economic Community's Scheme of Preferences for developing countries.

Preferential rates of import duty on products specified in Schedule 1 apply in the case of Egypt and Cyprus and are to apply in the case of other Mediterranean countries having Agreements with the Community when those Agreements take effect in the United Kingdom. The Regulations do not apply to determine the question of origin to the extent that there are other legal provisions which do so (for example, Regulations relating to commonwealth preference or the E.F.T.A. countries).

Goods to which the Regulations apply which are wholly produced or manufactured in a country are treated as originating there (Regulation 4). The use of imported materials of a different Customs Tariff heading from that of the goods does not disqualify the goods from originating in the country of production unless the materials undergo only minor processes there (Regulation 5(*b*)) or, in the case of goods listed in Part I of Schedule 2, unless they undergo the process specified in that Part (Regulation 5 *(a)*). The goods listed in Part II of Schedule 2 may be processed as described there with the use of imported materials of a different tariff heading without losing their originating status (Regulation 6).

1973 No. 2072

ACQUISITION OF LAND

COMPENSATION

The Acquisition of Land (Rate of Interest after Entry) (No. 5) Regulations 1973

Made - - -	*6th December* 1973
Laid before Parliament	17th *December* 1973
Coming into Operation	18*th December* 1973

The Treasury, in exercise of the powers conferred upon them by section 32(1) of the Land Compensation Act 1961(**a**), and of all other powers enabling them in that behalf, hereby make the following Regulations:—

1. These Regulations may be cited as the Acquisition of Land (Rate of Interest after Entry) (No. 5) Regulations 1973, and shall come into operation on 18th December 1973.

2. The Interpretation Act 1889(**b**) shall apply for the interpretation of these Regulations as it applies for the interpretation of an Act of Parliament.

3. The rate of interest on any compensation in respect of the compulsory acquisition of an interest in any land on which entry has been made before the payment of the compensation shall be $13\frac{1}{2}$ per cent. per annum.

4. The Acquisition of Land (Rate of Interest after Entry) (No. 4) Regulations 1973(**c**) are hereby revoked.

Michael Jopling,
Hamish Gray,
Two of the Lords Commissioners
of Her Majesty's Treasury.

6th December 1973.

EXPLANATORY NOTE

(*This Note is not part of the Regulations.*)

These Regulations increase from 12 per cent. to $13\frac{1}{2}$ per cent. per annum, in respect of any period after the coming into operation of these Regulations, the rate of interest payable where entry is made, before payment of compensation, on land in England and Wales which is being purchased compulsorily, and revoke the Acquisition of Land (Rate of Interest after Entry) (No. 4) Regulations 1973.

(**a**) 1961 c. 33. (**b**) 1889 c. 63. (**c**) S.I. 1973/1542 (1973 III, p. 4830).

1973 No. 2073

ACQUISITION OF LAND

COMPENSATION

The Acquisition of Land (Rate of Interest after Entry) (Scotland) (No. 5) Regulations 1973

Made - - -	*6th December* 1973
Laid before Parliament	*17th December* 1973
Coming into Operation	*18th December* 1973

The Treasury, in exercise of the powers conferred upon them by section 40(1) of the Land Compensation (Scotland) Act 1963(**a**), and of all other powers enabling them in that behalf, hereby make the following Regulations:—

1.—(1) These Regulations may be cited as the Acquisition of Land (Rate of Interest after Entry) (Scotland) (No. 5) Regulations 1973, and shall come into operation on 18th December 1973.

(2) These Regulations shall extend to Scotland only.

2. The Interpretation Act 1889(**b**) shall apply for the interpretation of these Regulations as it applies for the interpretation of an Act of Parliament.

3. The rate of interest on any compensation in respect of the compulsory acquisition of an interest in any land on which entry has been made before the payment of the compensation shall be 13½ per cent. per annum.

4. The Acquisition of Land (Rate of Interest after Entry) (Scotland) (No. 4) Regulations 1973(**c**) are hereby revoked.

Michael Jopling,
Hamish Gray,
Two of the Lords Commissioners
of Her Majesty's Treasury.

6th December 1973.

(**a**) 1963 c. 51. (**b**) 1889 c. 63.
(**c**) S.I. 1973/1543 (1973 III, p. 4831).

EXPLANATORY NOTE

(This Note is not part of the Regulations.)

These Regulations increase from 12 per cent. to 13½ per cent. per annum, in respect of any period after the coming into operation of these Regulations, the rate of interest payable where entry is made, before payment of compensation, on land in Scotland which is being purchased compulsorily, and revoke the Acquisition of Land (Rate of Interest after Entry) (Scotland) (No. 4) Regulations 1973.

1973 No. 2074

COAL INDUSTRY

The Opencast Coal (Rate of Interest on Compensation) (No. 5) Order 1973

Made - - -	*6th December* 1973
Laid before Parliament	*17th December* 1973
Coming into Operation	*18th December* 1973

The Treasury, in exercise of the powers conferred upon them by sections 35(8) and 49(4) of the Opencast Coal Act 1958(**a**) and of all other powers enabling them in that behalf, hereby make the following Order:—

1. This Order may be cited as the Opencast Coal (Rate of Interest on Compensation) (No. 5) Order 1973, and shall come into operation on 18th December 1973.

2. The Interpretation Act 1889(**b**) shall apply for the interpretation of this Order as it applies for the interpretation of an Act of Parliament.

3. The rate of interest for the purposes of section 35 of the Opencast Coal Act 1958 shall be 14 per cent. per annum.

4. The Opencast Coal (Rate of Interest on Compensation) (No. 4) Order 1973(**c**) is hereby revoked.

Michael Jopling,
Hamish Gray,
Two of the Lords Commissioners
of Her Majesty's Treasury.

6th December 1973.

EXPLANATORY NOTE

(*This Note is not part of the Order.*)

Section 35 of the Opencast Coal Act 1958 provides that interest shall be payable in addition to compensation in certain circumstances. This Order increases the rate of interest from 12 per cent. to 14 per cent. per annum and revokes the Opencast Coal (Rate of Interest on Compensation) (No. 4) Order 1973.

(**a**) 1958 c. 69. (**b**) 1889 c. 63. (**c**) S.I. 1973/1544 (1973 III, p. 4833).

STATUTORY INSTRUMENTS

1973 No. 2075

WAGES COUNCILS

The Wages Regulation (Linen and Cotton Handkerchief etc.) Order 1973

Made - - - -	*7th December* 1973
Coming into Operation	14*th January* 1974

Whereas the Secretary of State has received from the Linen and Cotton Handkerchief and Household Goods and Linen Piece Goods Wages Council (Great Britain) the wages regulation proposals set out in the Schedule hereto;

Now, therefore, the Secretary of State in exercise of powers conferred by section 11 of the Wages Councils Act 1959(**a**), as modified by Article 2 of the Counter-Inflation (Modification of Wages Councils Act 1959) Order 1973(**b**), and now vested in him(**c**), and of all other powers enabling him in that behalf, hereby makes the following Order:—

1. This Order may be cited as the Wages Regulation (Linen and Cotton Handkerchief etc.) Order 1973.

2.—(1) In this Order, the expression "the specified date" means the 14th January 1974, provided that where, as respects any worker who is paid wages at intervals not exceeding seven days, that date does not correspond with the beginning of the period for which the wages are paid, the expression "the specified date" means, as respects that worker, the beginning of the next such period following that date.

(2) The Interpretation Act 1889(**d**) shall apply to the interpretation of this Order as it applies to the interpretation of an Act of Parliament and as if this Order and the Order hereby revoked were Acts of Parliament.

3. The wages regulation proposals set out in the Schedule hereto shall have effect as from the specified date and as from that date the Wages Regulation (Linen and Cotton Handkerchief etc.) Order 1972(**e**) shall cease to have effect.

Signed by order of the Secretary of State.

7th December 1973.

W. H. Marsh,
Assistant Secretary,
Department of Employment.

(**a**) 1959 c. 69.
(**b**) S.I. 1973/661 (1973 I, p. 2141).
(**c**) S.I. 1959/1769, 1968/729 (1959 I, p. 1795; 1968 II, p. 2108).
(**d**) 1889 c. 63.
(**e**) S.I. 1972/1312 (1972 II, p. 3974).

Article 3

SCHEDULE

The following minimum remuneration shall be substituted for the statutory minimum remuneration fixed by the Wages Regulation (Linen and Cotton Handkerchief etc.) Order 1972 (Order H.L. (79)).

STATUTORY MINIMUM REMUNERATION

PART I

GENERAL

1. The minimum remuneration payable to a worker to whom this Schedule applies for all work except work to which a minimum overtime rate applies under Part IV of this Schedule is:—

(1) in the case of a time worker, the hourly general minimum time rate payable to the worker under Part II of this Schedule;

(2) in the case of a male worker employed on piece work, piece rates each of which would yield, in the circumstances of the case, to an ordinary worker at least the same amount of money as the hourly general minimum time rate which would be payable to the worker under Part II of this Schedule if he were a time worker;

(3) in the case of a female worker employed on piece work, piece rates each of which would yield, in the circumstances of the case, to an ordinary worker at least the same amount of money as the hourly piece work basis time rate applicable to the worker under Part III of this Schedule.

PART II

GENERAL MINIMUM TIME RATES

2. The general minimum time rates are as follows:

	Per hour p
(1) Male workers aged 18 years or over	
(*a*) up to and including 31st August 1974	
aged 19 years or over	*41·50*
„ 18 and under 19 years	*37·35*
(*b*) from 1st September 1974 up to and including 31st August 1975	
aged 19 years or over	*41·50*
„ 18 and under 19 years	*39·43*
(*c*) on and after 1st September 1975	
aged 18 years or over	*41·50*
(2) Female workers aged 18 years or over	
(*a*) up to and including 31st August 1974	*37·35*
(*b*) from 1st September 1974 up to and including 31st August 1975	*39·43*
(*c*) on and after 1st September 1975	*41·50*

Provided that the general minimum time rates payable, during the first year's employment in the trade, to a female worker who enters, or has entered, the trade for the first time at or over the age of 18 years shall be:—

(*a*) up to and including 31st August 1974

during the first 3 months of such employment	*27·46*
during the second 3 months of such employment	*28·50*
during the third 3 months of such employment	*31·62*
during the fourth 3 months of such employment	*33·70*

(*b*) from 1st September 1974 up to and including 31st August 1975

during the first 3 months of such employment	*28·50*
during the second 3 months of such employment	*29·54*
during the third 3 months of such employment	*32·66*
during the fourth 3 months of such employment	*35·26*

(*c*) on and after 1st September 1975

during the first 3 months of such employment	*30·06*
during the second 3 months of such employment	*31·10*
during the third 3 months of such employment	*34·22*
during the fourth 3 months of such employment	*37·34*

(3) All workers aged:—

17 and under 18 years	*27·46*
16 and under 17 years	*22·78*

PART III

PIECE WORK BASIS TIME RATES APPLICABLE TO FEMALE WORKERS

3. The piece work basis time rates applicable to female workers of any age employed on piece work are as follows:—

	Per hour p
(i) up to and including 31st August 1974	*38·35*
(ii) from 1st September 1974 up to and including 31st August 1975	*40·43*
(iii) from 1st September 1975	*42·50*

PART IV

OVERTIME AND WAITING TIME
MINIMUM OVERTIME RATES

4. (1) Minimum overtime rates are payable to any worker to whom this Schedule applies as follows:—

(*a*) on any day other than a Saturday or Sunday—

(i) for the first two hours worked in excess of 8 hours	time-and-a-quarter
(ii) thereafter	time-and-a-half

Provided that where the employer and the worker by agreement in writing fix in respect of each weekday the number of hours after which a minimum overtime rate shall be payable and the total number of such hours amounts to 40 weekly, the following minimum overtime rates shall be payable in substitution for those set out above—

(i) for the first two hours worked in excess of the agreed number of hours .. .. .. time-and-a-quarter

(ii) thereafter .. .. time-and-a-half

(*b*) on a Saturday—

(i) for the first two hours worked .. .. .. time-and-a-quarter

(ii) thereafter .. .. time-and-a-half

(*c*) on a Sunday—

for all time worked .. .. double time

(2) In this Part of this Schedule the expressions "time-and-a-quarter", "time-and-a-half" and "double time" mean, respectively, one and a quarter times, one and a half times and twice the minimum remuneration otherwise payable to the worker.

WAITING TIME

5.—(1) A worker is entitled to payment of the minimum remuneration specified in this Schedule for all time during which he is present on the premises of his employer, unless he is present thereon in any of the following circumstances:—

(*a*) without the employer's consent, express or implied;

(*b*) for some purpose unconnected with his work and other than that of waiting for work to be given to him to perform;

(*c*) by reason only of the fact that he is resident thereon;

(*d*) during the normal meal times in a room or place in which no work is being done, and he is not waiting for work to be given to him to perform.

(2) The minimum remuneration payable under sub-paragraph (1) of this paragraph to a piece worker when not engaged on piece work is that which would be payable if he were a time worker.

PART V

APPLICABILITY OF STATUTORY MINIMUM REMUNERATION

6. Subject to paragraph 7, this Schedule applies to workers in relation to whom the Linen and Cotton Handkerchief and Household Goods and Linen Piece Goods Wages Council (Great Britain) operates, that is to say, workers employed in Great Britain in the trade specified in the Regulations made by the Minister and dated 28th May 1920(**a**), with respect to the Constitution and Proceedings of the Trade Board for the Linen and Cotton Handkerchief and Household Goods and Linen Piece Goods Trade (Great Britain) namely:—

(1) The making of such articles as are specified in (*a*) and (*b*) below, from linen or cotton or mixed linen and cotton fabrics (excepting knitted fabrics), or from other textile fabrics when the work is carried on in establishments mainly engaged in the making of such articles from the before-mentioned fabrics, viz.:—

(*a*) Handkerchiefs (including mufflers or flags when made in association or conjunction with handkerchiefs);

(**a**) S.R. & O. 1920/854 (1920 II, p. 854).

(*b*) Bed-linen, towels, dusters, table-napery, bed-spreads, tea-cloths, table-centres, sideboard-covers, cushion-covers, or similar household articles; including all or any of the following operations:—

(i) Hooking, cutting or tearing the material;

(ii) Vice-folding;

(iii) Machine hemming, hem-stitching, spoking, over-locking, tambouring, button-holing, and other plain or fancy machine stitching;

(iv) All processes of embroidery or decorative needlework done by machine, whether before or after the making of the articles of the description specified above;

(v) The following processes if done by machine—thread-drawing, thread-clipping, top-sewing, scalloping, nickelling and paring;

(vi) All processes of laundering, smoothing, folding, ornamenting, boxing, finishing, warehousing, packing and other similar operations incidental to or appertaining to the making of the articles of the description specified above.

(2) The making up in linen warehouses or in establishments mainly engaged in linen lapping, of linen or mixed linen and cotton or other textile fabrics in the piece, or of linen or mixed linen and cotton or other textile articles cut from the piece, including—

Measuring, cutting, lapping, ornamenting, boxing, warehousing, packing and similar operations.

7. Notwithstanding paragraph 6, this schedule does not apply to workers who are persons registered as handicapped by disablement in pursuance of the Disabled Persons (Employment) Acts 1944 and 1958(**a**), in respect of their employment by Remploy Limited.

EXPLANATORY NOTE

(*This Note is not part of the Order.*)

This Order, which has effect from 14th January 1974, sets out the increased statutory minimum remuneration payable to workers in relation to whom the Linen and Cotton Handkerchief and Household Goods and Linen Piece Goods Wages Council (Great Britain) operates, in substitution for that fixed by the Wages Regulation (Linen and Cotton Handkerchief etc.) Order, 1972 (H.L.(79)). The Order sets out the stages by which equal pay for men and women workers in the trade is to be achieved. Order H.L.(79) is revoked.

New provisions are printed in italics.

(**a**) 1949 c. 10; 1958 c. 33.

1973 No. 2076

WAGES COUNCILS

The Wages Regulation (Linen and Cotton Handkerchief etc.) (Holidays) Order 1973

Made - - -	*7th December* 1973
Coming into Operation	14*th January* 1974

Whereas the Secretary of State has received from the Linen and Cotton Handkerchief and Household Goods and Linen Piece Goods Wages Council (Great Britain) the wages regulation proposals set out in the Schedule hereto;

Now, therefore, the Secretary of State in exercise of powers conferred by section 11 of the Wages Councils Act 1959(**a**), as modified by Article 2 of the Counter-Inflation (Modification of Wages Councils Act 1959) Order 1973(**b**), and now vested in him(**c**), and of all other powers enabling him in that behalf, hereby makes the following Order:—

1. This Order may be cited as the Wages Regulation (Linen and Cotton Handkerchief etc.) (Holidays) Order 1973.

2.—(1) In this Order the expression "the specified date" means the 14th January 1974, provided that where, as respects any worker who is paid wages at intervals not exceeding seven days, that date does not correspond with the beginning of the period for which the wages are paid, the expression "the specified date" means, as respects that worker, the beginning of the next such period following that date.

(2) The Interpretation Act 1889(**d**) shall apply to the interpretation of this Order as it applies to the interpretation of an Act of Parliament and as if this Order and the Order hereby revoked were Acts of Parliament.

3. The wages regulation proposals set out in the Schedule hereto shall have effect as from the specified date and as from that date the Wages Regulation (Linen and Cotton Handkerchief etc.) (Holidays) Order 1969(**e**) shall cease to have effect.

Signed by order of the Secretary of State.
7th December 1973.

W. H. Marsh,
Assistant Secretary,
Department of Employment.

(**a**) 1959 c. 69.
(**b**) S.I. 1973/661 (1973 I, p. 2141).
(**c**) S.I. 1959/1769, 1968/729 (1959 I, p. 1795; 1968 II, p. 2108).
(**d**) 1889 c. 63.
(**e**) S.I. 1969/869 (1969 II, p. 2470).

Article 3

SCHEDULE

The following provisions as to holidays and holiday remuneration shall be substituted for the provisions as to holidays and holiday remuneration set out in the Wages Regulation (Linen and Cotton Handkerchief etc.) (Holidays) Order 1969 (hereinafter referred to as "Order H.L.(73)").

PART I

APPLICATION

1. This Schedule applies to every worker (other than an outworker) for whom statutory minimum remuneration has been fixed.

PART II

CUSTOMARY HOLIDAYS

2.—(1) Subject to the provisions of sub-paragraph (3) of this paragraph an employer shall allow a day of holiday (hereinafter referred to as a "customary holiday") in each year on each of the days specified in the next following sub-paragraph to every worker in his employment to whom this Schedule applies who:—

(*a*) has been in his employment throughout the 8 weeks immediately preceding the said day; and

(*b*) has worked for the employer during the whole or part of that period; and

(*c*) is in his employment on the day of customary holiday.

(2) The said customary holidays are:—

(*a*) (i) in England and Wales—

Christmas Day;
26th December if it be not a Sunday;
27th December in a year when 25th or 26th December is a Sunday;
New Year's Day;
Good Friday;
Easter Monday; and
the last Monday in May; (*or, where a day is substituted for any of the above days by national proclamation, that day*);

(ii) in Scotland—

New Year's Day and the day following or, if New Year's Day falls on a Sunday, the following Monday and Tuesday, or, if New Year's Day falls on a Saturday, New Year's Day and the following Monday, the local Spring holiday, the local Autumn holiday, and two other days (being days on which the worker normally works for the employer) in the course of each calendar year, to be fixed by the employer in consultation with the worker or his representative and notified to the worker not less than three weeks in advance;

or (*b*) in the case of each of the said days (other than a day fixed by the employer in Scotland and notified to the worker as aforesaid) a day substituted therefor by agreement between the employer and the worker to be allowed within the period of six weeks next ensuing.

(3) Notwithstanding the preceding provisions of this paragraph an employer may (except where in the case of a woman or young person such requirement would be unlawful) require a worker who is otherwise entitled to any customary holiday under the foregoing provisions of this Schedule to work thereon and, in lieu of any customary holiday on which he so works, the employer shall allow the worker a day's holiday (hereinafter referred to as "a holiday in lieu of a customary holiday") on a weekday on which he would normally work for the employer within the period of six weeks next ensuing.

PART III

ANNUAL HOLIDAY

3.—(1) Subject to the provisions of paragraph 4, in addition to the holidays specified in Part II of this Schedule an employer shall, between the date on which the provisions of this Schedule become effective and 5th April 1974 and in each succeeding period of 12 months commencing on 6th April allow a holiday (hereinafter referred to as an "annual holiday") to every worker in his employment to whom this Schedule applies who has been employed by him during the 12 months ending on 5th April immediately preceding the commencement of the holiday season (hereinafter referred to as the "qualifying period") for any of the periods of employment (calculated in accordance with the provisions of paragraph 10) specified below and the duration of the annual holiday shall, in the case of each such worker, be related to his period of employment during that 12 months as follows:—

Period of employment	Duration of annual holiday in 12 months commencing 6th April
At least 48 weeks	15 days
" " 43 "	9 "
" " 38 "	8 "
" " 33 "	7 "
" " 28 "	6 "
" " 24 "	5 "
" " 19 "	4 "
" " 14 "	3 "
" " 9 "	2 "
" " 4 "	1 day

(2) Notwithstanding the provisions of the foregoing sub-paragraph the number of days of annual holiday which an employer is required to allow to a worker in the holiday season commencing 6th April 1974 and in each succeeding holiday season commencing on 6th April, shall not exceed in the aggregate three times the number of days constituting the worker's normal working week.

(3) In this Schedule the expression "holiday season" means in relation to the year 1974 the period commencing on 6th April 1974 and ending on 5th April 1975 and each succeeding year, the period commencing on 6th April and ending on the next following 5th April.

(4) The duration of the worker's annual holiday in the holiday season ending on 5th April 1974 shall be reduced by any days of annual holiday duly allowed to him by the employer under the provisions of Order H.L. (73) between 6th April 1973 and the date on which the provisions of this Schedule become effective.

4.—(1) Subject to the provisions of this paragraph an annual holiday under this Schedule shall be allowed in accordance with an agreement between the employer and the worker or his representative on consecutive working days being days on which the worker normally works for the employer, and days of annual holiday shall be treated as consecutive notwithstanding that a holiday under the provisions of Part II of this Schedule intervenes.

(2)(*a*) Where the number of days of annual holiday for which a worker has qualified exceeds the number of days constituting his normal working week, but does not exceed twice that number, the holiday may be allowed in two periods of consecutive working days; so, however, that when a holiday is so allowed, one of the periods shall consist of a number of such days not less than the number of days constituting the worker's normal working week.

(*b*) Where the number of days of annual holiday for which a worker has qualified exceeds twice the number of days constituting his normal working week the holiday may be allowed in the holiday season as follows:—

(i) as to two periods of consecutive working days, each such period not being less than the period constituting the worker's normal working week; and

(ii) as to any additional days, on working days being days on which the worker normally works for the employer.

(3) Subject to the provisions of sub-paragraph (1) of this paragraph, any day of annual holiday under this Schedule may be allowed on a day on which the worker is entitled to a day of holiday or to a half-holiday under any enactment other than the Wages Councils Act 1959.

5. The employer shall give to the worker notice of the commencing date and duration of his annual holiday either individually or by a notice which the worker has reasonable opportunities of reading in the course of his employment or which is reasonably accessible to him in some other way. Such notice shall be given not later than the 31st December immediately preceding the annual holiday or when the worker commences employment with the employer, whichever is the later.

PART IV

HOLIDAY REMUNERATION

A.—CUSTOMARY HOLIDAYS AND HOLIDAYS IN LIEU OF CUSTOMARY HOLIDAYS

6.—(1) Subject to the provisions of this paragraph, for each day allowed as a holiday under Part II of this Schedule the worker shall be paid by his employer the following remuneration:—

(*a*) in respect of days allowed in the holiday season commencing on 6th April 1973 and each succeeding holiday season, in the case of a worker who has been in the employment of the employer for the whole of the 12 months ending on 5th April immediately preceding, an amount equal to one-fifteenth of 5·8 per cent of his total remuneration (determined in accordance with paragraph 11) during that period;

(*b*) in the case of a worker who has been in the employment of the employer for any lesser period, one-fifth of his average weekly earnings, such average weekly earnings to be determined by dividing the worker's total remuneration (determined in accordance with paragraph 11) by the number of weeks of employment (calculated in accordance with paragraph 10).

(2) Subject to the provisions of sub-paragraphs (3) and (4) of this paragraph, the holiday remuneration in respect of any holiday allowed under Part II of this Schedule shall be paid by the employer to the worker on the pay day on which wages are paid for the week including the holiday.

(3) Where a worker ceases to be employed before being allowed a holiday in lieu of a customary holiday to which he has become entitled he shall be paid the holiday remuneration for that day immediately on the termination of his employment and in such a case sub-paragraph (4) of this paragraph shall not apply.

(4) Payment of remuneration in respect of the said holiday is subject to the condition that the worker (unless excused by the employer or absent by reason of proved incapacity due to sickness or injury) works for the employer the number of hours ordinarily worked by him or such lesser number of hours as may be required by the employer, on the first working day on which work is available to him following the holiday.

B.—ANNUAL HOLIDAY

7.—(1) Subject to the provisions of this paragraph and of paragraph 8, a worker qualified to be allowed an annual holiday under Part III of this Schedule shall be paid as holiday remuneration by his employer in respect thereof, on the last pay day preceding such annual holiday in relation to the holiday season commencing

6th April 1973, and to each succeeding holiday season, an amount equal to 5·8 per cent of his total remuneration (determined in accordance with paragraph 11) during the qualifying period.

(2) Where under the provisions of paragraph 4 an annual holiday is allowed in more than one period, the holiday remuneration shall be apportioned accordingly.

8. Where any accrued holiday remuneration has been paid by the employer to the worker (in accordance with paragraph 9 of this Schedule or with Order H.L. (73)) in respect of employment during any of the periods referred to in that paragraph or that Order, the amount of holiday remuneration payable by the employer in respect of any annual holiday for which the worker has qualified by reason of employment during the said period shall be reduced by the amount of the said accrued holiday remuneration unless that remuneration has been deducted from a previous payment of holiday remuneration made under the provisions of this Schedule or of Order H.L. (73).

ACCRUED HOLIDAY REMUNERATION PAYABLE ON TERMINATION OF EMPLOYMENT

9. Where a worker ceases to be employed by an employer after the provisions of this Schedule become effective, the employer shall, immediately on the termination of the employment (hereinafter called "the termination date"), pay to the worker as accrued holiday remuneration:—

(1) in respect of employment in the 12 months up to and including the 5th April immediately preceding the termination date, a sum equal to the holiday remuneration for any days of annual holiday for which he has qualified except days of annual holiday which he has been allowed or has become entitled to be allowed before leaving the employment; and

(2) in respect of any employment of at least four weeks duration since the said 5th April, a sum equal to the holiday remuneration which would have been payable to him if he could have been allowed an annual holiday in respect of that employment at the time of leaving it.

PART V

GENERAL

10. For the purposes of calculating any period of employment qualifying a worker for a holiday under this Schedule, the worker shall be treated:—

(1) as if he were employed for a week in respect of any week during the qualifying period in which—

(*a*) he has worked for the employer on at least three days and has performed some work for which statutory minimum remuneration is payable and any absence from work on the other days of the week is with the consent of the employer;

(*b*) he has been absent throughout the week or worked less than three days by reason of proved incapacity due to sickness or injury and has returned to the employment of the employer on the termination of the period of absence:

Provided that the number of weeks which may be so treated as weeks of employment shall not exceed:—

(i) 26 weeks in the case of proved incapacity in respect of which the worker is entitled to injury benefit under the National Insurance (Industrial Injuries) Act 1965(**a**);

and (ii) 8 weeks in the case of any other proved incapacity;

(2) as if he were employed on any day of holiday allowed under the provisions of this Schedule.

(**a**) 1965 c. 52.

11. A worker's total remuneration shall include:—

(1) all payments paid or payable to the worker by the employer in respect of his employment except:—

(*a*) payments by way of annual holiday remuneration;

(*b*) payments by way of accrued holiday remuneration; and

(*c*) payments in respect of any period of absence from work by reason of incapacity due to sickness or injury; and

(2) in respect of any period of absence which under the provisions of sub-paragraph (1)(*b*) of paragraph 10 is to be treated as a period of employment, the amount to which he would have been entitled if he had worked during that period as a time worker for the number of daily hours normally worked by him.

12. In this Schedule, unless the context otherwise requires, the following expressions have the meanings hereby respectively assigned to them, that is to say:—

"NORMAL WORKING WEEK" means the number of days on which it has been usual for the worker to work in a week in the employment of the employer during the qualifying period or, where under paragraph 9 accrued holiday remuneration is payable on the termination of the employment, in the 12 months immediately preceding the termination date:

Provided that—

(1) part of a day shall count as a day;

(2) no account shall be taken of any week in which the worker did not perform any work for which statutory minimum remuneration has been fixed.

"OUTWORKER" means a worker who works in his own home or in any other place not under the control or management of the employer.

"STATUTORY MINIMUM REMUNERATION" means minimum remuneration (other than holiday remuneration) fixed by a wages regulation order made by the Secretary of State to give effect to proposals submitted to him by the Linen and Cotton Handkerchief and Household Goods and Linen Piece Goods Wages Council (Great Britain).

"WEEK" means "pay week".

13. The provisions of this Schedule are without prejudice to any agreement for the allowance of any further holidays with pay or for the payment of additional holiday remuneration.

EXPLANATORY NOTE

(*This Note is not part of the Order.*)

This Order, which has effect from 14th January 1974, sets out the holidays to be allowed to workers in relation to whom the Linen and Cotton Handkerchief and Household Goods and Linen Piece Goods Wages Council (Great Britain) operates and the remuneration payable for those holidays. It also amends the provisions relating to customary holidays contained in Order H.L.(73) so as to take account of recent changes in the law and practice relating to public holidays. Order H.L.(73) is revoked.

New provisions are printed in italics.

1973 No. 2077

NATIONAL HEALTH SERVICE, ENGLAND AND WALES

The National Health Service (Constitution of Area Health Authorities) (Amendment) Order 1973

Made - - -	*7th December* 1973
Laid before Parliament	17th *December* 1973
Coming into Operation	*7th January* 1974

The Secretary of State for Social Services, in exercise of powers conferred upon him by section 5(1) of the National Health Service Reorganisation Act 1973(**a**) and of all other powers enabling him in that behalf, hereby makes the following Order:—

Citation, interpretation and commencement

1. This Order, which may be cited as the National Health Service (Constitution of Area Health Authorities) (Amendment) Order 1973, shall be read as one with the National Health Service (Constitution of Area Health Authorities) Order 1973(**b**) (hereinafter referred to as the "principal Order") and shall come into operation on 7th January 1974.

Amendment of Schedule 1 *to the principal Order*

2.—(1) In Schedule 1 to the principal Order, column (2) (total number of members other than chairman appointed to Authority) and column (5) (number of members appointed to Authority by the relevant Regional Authority in accordance with paragraph (2)(1)(*b*) of Schedule 1 to the Act of 1973) shall be amended in accordance with the following paragraphs of this Article.

(2) In Part 2 of the said Schedule against the title of the Humberside Area Health Authority in column (1) there shall be substituted for the number "14" in column (2) the number "16" and for the number "9" in column (5) the number "11".

(3) In Part 5 of the said Schedule against the title of the Ealing, Hammersmith and Hounslow Area Health Authority (Teaching) in column (1) there shall be substituted for the number "22" in column (2) the number "24" and for the number "10" in column (5) the number "12".

(4) In Part 7 of the said Schedule against the title of the Lambeth, Southwark and Lewisham Area Health Authority (Teaching) in column (1) there shall be substituted for the number "25" in column (2) the number "27" and for the number "11" in column (5) the number "13".

(**a**) 1973 c. 32.

(**b**) S.I. 1973/1305 (1973 II, p. 3931).

(5) In Part 12 of the said Schedule against the title of the Birmingham Area Health Authority (Teaching) in column (1) there shall be substituted for the number "20" in column (2) the number "22" and for the number "11" in column (5) the number "13".

Keith Joseph,
Secretary of State for Social Services.

7th December 1973.

EXPLANATORY NOTE

(*This Note is not part of the Order.*)

This Order increases the specified number of members to be appointed by the relevant Regional Health Authorities to certain Area Health Authorities established in England for the purposes of local administration of the National Health Service as reorganised under the National Health Service Reorganisation Act 1973.

1973 No. 2078 (S.153)

EDUCATION, SCOTLAND

The Teachers Superannuation (Family Benefits) (Scotland) Amendment Regulations 1973

Made - - -	6*th December* 1973
Laid before Parliament	18*th December* 1973
Coming into Operation	8*th January* 1974

ARRANGEMENT OF REGULATIONS

Miscellaneous and Supplementary

Schedules

In exercise of the powers conferred upon me by section 9 of the Superannuation Act 1972(**a**) and of all other powers enabling me in that behalf, with the consent of the Minister for the Civil Service and after consultation with representatives of education authorities and of teachers and with such representatives of other persons likely to be affected as appear to me to be appropriate, I hereby make the following regulations:—

Introductory

Citation and Commencement

1.—(1) These regulations may be cited as the Teachers Superannuation (Family Benefits) (Scotland) Amendment Regulations 1973.

(2) The Teachers Superannuation (Family Benefits) (Scotland) Regulations 1971 to 1973(**b**) and these regulations may be cited together as the Teachers Superannuation (Family Benefits) (Scotland) Regulations 1971 to 1973.

(3) These regulations shall come into operation on 8th January 1974.

Interpretation

2.—(1) In these regulations, except where the context otherwise requires—

"The Actuary" means the Government Actuary;

"child" means, in reference to the child of a person, a child (including an illegitimate child or adopted child) of that person, or a child accepted by that person as a member of the family, and wholly or mainly dependent on him, who has not attained the age of 17 or, having attained the age of 17, is receiving full-time education or attending a course of not less than 2 years full-time training for a trade, profession or calling but does not include a married woman nor a person who is for the time being in receipt of a disqualifying income;

"deemed additional service" has the meaning assigned to it by regulation 3(1)(*b*);

"deemed normal service" has the meaning assigned to it by regulation 3(1)(*a*);

"disqualifying income" means remuneration payable to a person attending a course of full-time training at a rate not less than the annual rate for the time being payable of an official pension (within the meaning of the Pensions (Increase) Act 1971(**c**)) which began on 1st April 1972 at the annual rate of £250;

(**a**) 1972 c. 11.
(**b**) S.I. 1971/1775, 1972/442, 1239, 1973/547 (1971 III, p.4813; 1972 I, p. 1644; II, p. 3738; 1973 I, p. 1738).
(**c**) 1971 c. 56.

"member" means a teacher employed in reckonable service on or after 1st April 1972 who, immediately before that date, had service counting for benefit within the meaning of regulation 37 of the Family Benefits Regulations;

"non-member" means a teacher employed in reckonable service on or after 1st April 1972 who, immediately before that date, had no such service counting for benefit as is referred to above;

"notional service" has the meaning assigned to it by regulation 3(1)(*c*);

"the Family Benefits Regulations" means the Teachers Superannuation (Family Benefits) (Scotland) Regulations 1971(**a**) as amended(**b**);

"the Teachers Regulations" means the Teachers Superannuation (Scotland) Regulations 1969(**c**) as amended (**d**);

"the Teachers and Teachers Families Regulations" means the Superannuation (Teachers and Teachers' Families) (Scotland) Regulations 1973(**e**);

other expressions have the meanings assigned to them by the Family Benefits Regulations.

(2) References to a teacher's widow do not include a woman who married him after the day on which he was last employed in reckonable service.

(3) In these regulations, unless the context otherwise requires any reference to a regulation or schedule, shall be construed as a reference to a regulation or schedule contained therein, any reference in a regulation or schedule to a paragraph shall be construed as a reference to a paragraph of that regulation or schedule, and any reference in a paragraph to a sub-paragraph shall be construed as a reference to a sub-paragraph of that paragraph.

(4) The Interpretation Act 1889(**f**) shall apply for the interpretation of these regulations as it applies for the interpretation of an Act of Parliament.

Service before 1st April 1972

3.—(1) Subject to paragraph (2) the service before 1st April 1972 counting for benefit for the purposes of these regulations of a member shall, unless he retires without making an election for those purposes within the time prescribed by regulation 7(1), be the aggregate of—

(*a*) two-thirds of any such service in respect of which the full amount of normal contributions is held in the Fund ("deemed normal service");

(*b*) the number of years determined in accordance with Schedule 1 as the actuarial value of any additional contributions held in the Fund on 31st March 1972 in respect of such service ("deemed additional service"); and

(*c*) the number of years determined by the Actuary as the actuarial value of his interest in the balance (so determined) of the Fund as at 31st March 1972 ("notional service").

(2) For the purposes of these regulations the service before 1st April 1972 counting for benefit of a member who retired on pension after 31st March 1972 and before 8th January 1974, or after that date but without making

(**a**) S.I. 1971/1775 (1971 III, p. 4813).
(**b**) The relevant amending instrument is S.I. 1973/547 (1973 I, p. 1738).
(**c**) S.I. 1969/77 (1969 I, p. 133).
(**d**) The relevant amending instruments are S.I. 1972/551, 1973/547 (1972 I, p. 1855; 1973 I, p. 1738).
(**e**) S.I. 1973/547 (1973 I, p. 1738). (**f**) 1889 c. 63.

an election for those purposes within the time prescribed by regulation 7(1), shall be the aggregate of—

(*a*) two-thirds of any such service in respect of which contributions were paid to the Fund; and

(*b*) twice his notional service.

Non-member's Contributions

4.—(1) Subject to paragraph (2), a non-member shall, if he so elects, pay contributions in accordance with these regulations, in respect of his reckonable service before 1st April 1972.

(2) Any election for the purposes of this regulation shall relate to the whole of the reckonable service of the teacher before 1st April 1972 or, if that service amounts to 5 years or more, 5 or more complete years of that service, as he may elect.

Member's Contributions

5.—(1) As from 1st May 1974 contributions payable by teachers for the purposes of family benefits in respect of service before 1st April 1972 may, and as from 1st November 1974 shall, be paid in accordance with this regulation and not in accordance with regulations 29, 30, 31 and 36 of the Family Benefits Regulations.

(2) A member shall pay contributions in accordance with these regulations in respect of so much (if any) as he elects of his reckonable service before 1st April 1972 as exceeds the aggregate of his deemed normal service, his notional service, his deemed additional service (if any) and one-sixth of the period of previous service in respect of which prior to that date he paid or elected to pay family benefits contributions.

(3) A member who elected to pay additional contributions in respect of his previous service by Method III may, if he is employed in reckonable service on 1st May 1974, by notice in writing delivered to the Secretary of State before 1st November 1974, revoke his election to pay such contributions; and any such member who is not so employed or does not so revoke that election shall pay contributions in accordance with paragraph (2).

Retired Member's Contributions

6. A member who, having been employed in reckonable service on or after 1st April 1972 retires from such service before 8th January 1974, or after that date but without making an election for the purposes of these regulations within the time prescribed by regulation 7(1), shall, if he so elects, pay contributions in the form of a lump sum equal to the actuarial equivalent of the contributions payable in respect of so much of his service before 1st April 1972 as does not exceed one-half of the amount by which one-third of the service in respect of which normal and additional contributions are held in the Fund on 31st March 1972 exceeds twice his notional service.

ELECTIONS

Time for Making Elections

7.—(1) Subject to paragraph (3), the first election for the purposes of regulation 4, 5 or 6 shall be made so as to be received by the Secretary of State—

(*a*) for the purposes of regulation 4, if the teacher is employed in reckonable service on 8th January 1974, before 8th July 1974;

(*b*) for the purposes of regulation 5, if the teacher is employed in reckonable service on 1st May 1974, before 1st November 1974;

(*c*) for the purposes of regulation 6, before 1st November 1974; and

(*d*) for the purposes of regulation 4 and 5 in any case not falling within sub-paragraph (*a*) or (*b*), not later than 6 months from the date of the teacher becoming employed or as the case may be again employed in reckonable service or of the award to him of superannuation allowances under the Teachers Regulations.

(2) For the purposes of regulation 6, the election may, if the member dies before 1st November 1974, be made by his widow and the provisions of these regulations relating to the payment of contributions for the purposes of that regulation shall be construed accordingly.

(3) A man teacher who does not make an election within the time specified by paragraph (1) may, notwithstanding that paragraph, make a first election for the purposes of regulation 4 or 5 within the 6 months next following the first to occur of any of the following events—

(i) his marriage if he is then employed in reckonable service;

(ii) his becoming again employed in reckonable service after his marriage while not so employed;

(iii) the nomination by him of an adult dependant under regulation 18;

and a woman teacher who does not make an election within the time specified by paragraph (1) may, notwithstanding that paragraph, make a first election for the purposes of regulation 4 or 5 within the 6 months next following the nomination by her of an adult dependant under regulation 18.

Form of Elections

8.—(1) The first election by any teacher for the purposes of these regulations shall specify—

(*a*) the number of years in respect of which the teacher elects to pay contributions; and

(*b*) the rate at which the teacher elects to pay contributions expressed as a percentage, being a whole number not exceeding 8, of the rate of his salary from time to time.

(2) An election shall be made in writing and delivered to the Secretary of State and shall be effective from the date of its receipt by him.

(3) In so far as it specifies the number of years in respect of which contributions are to be paid an election shall be irrevocable; but in so far as it specifies the rate at which contributions are to be paid it may from time to time be varied by a subsequent election to pay contributions at a higher rate (expressed as is specified in paragraph (1)(*b*)) taking effect from 1st April in the year following the end of the year in which that subsequent election is received by the Secretary of State.

(4) The Secretary of State may treat as an election made for the purposes of this regulation any notification in writing received from a teacher before 8th January 1974 which

(*a*) states the teacher's intention to pay contributions in respect of any such benefits as are payable under these regulations; and (*b*) specifies the matters required by this regulation to be specified by an election—

and any notification so treated shall be effective as such an election from 8th January 1974.

Effect of Elections

9.—(1) Subject to paragraph (2), regulations 23, 24 and 26 of the Teachers and Teachers' Families Regulations shall, as regards any teacher, cease to have effect as from the date upon which any election by him under regulation 8 is effective or the time specified by regulation 7(1) for the making of election expires without his having made an election.

(2) The Secretary of State may, having regard to the special circumstances of a particular teacher, direct that paragraph (1) shall not apply to him; and in any such case regulations 23, 24 and 26 of the Teachers and Teachers' Families Regulations shall continue to apply in relation to that teacher until such time as is specified in the direction.

CONTRIBUTIONS

Payment of Contributions

10. Subject to regulation 14 contributions shall be paid, at the rate for the time being specified by the teacher in an election under these regulations, for so long as he continues to be employed, or is for purposes of the Teachers Regulations treated as if he were employed in reckonable service.

Restriction on Amount of Contributions

11. Regulation 72 of the Family Benefits Regulations shall be construed as if the contributions specified in paragraph (1) included contributions payable under these regulations and for the references in paragraph (2)(*a*)(ii) to 6 per cent and 13 per cent there were substituted references to $6\frac{1}{2}$ per cent and $14\frac{1}{2}$ per cent respectively.

Determination of Contributions, etc.

12.—(1) The Secretary of State shall as soon as may be after the receipt of any election made by a teacher for the purposes of these regulations determine—

(*a*) in accordance with table 1 of Schedule 2 the period for which contributions are required to be paid by the teacher; and

(*b*) the amount (if any) of any deduction that will fall to be made from the terminal sum payable to or in respect of the teacher under regulation 15 by reason of the fact that the teacher will attain the age of sixty before the end of the period determined under sub-paragraph (*a*).

(2) A determination under paragraph (1) may be varied by a subsequent determination, and shall be so varied if—

(*a*) payment of contributions is interrupted by a break in service; or

(*b*) the amount of his contributions is reduced by reason of the teacher being for the time being employed in part-time reckonable service or (in the case of a teacher so employed) being so employed for a smaller proportion of his time; or

(*c*) a contribution payable in accordance with regulation 10 is not paid.

Notices

13. The Secretary of State shall as soon as may be after making a determination under regulation 12 serve a notice in writing on the teacher specifying as may be appropriate—

(*a*) the day on which, in accordance with regulation 14, the payment of contributions is to begin;

(*b*) the period determined under regulation 12 for which contributions are required to be paid;

(*c*) any liability of the teacher to a deduction from the terminal sum payable to or in respect of him by virtue of regulation 15.

Duration of Contributions

14. Contributions shall begin to be paid by a teacher on the first day of the month next following the date of the notice served on him by the Secretary of State under regulation 13 and shall cease to be paid on whichever is the earlier of the day he retires from reckonable service and the day specified in that notice as the last day on which contributions are required to be paid by him.

Deduction from Terminal Sum

15.—(1) If a member who elected to pay contributions under Method III and did not revoke his election to pay such contributions either—

(*a*) does not elect to pay contributions under regulation 5(2); or

(*b*) elects to pay such contributions in respect of a period which is less than two-thirds of the period in respect of which he elected to pay contributions under Method III—

there shall be deducted from the terminal sum payable to or in respect of him the amount determined by the Actuary as the sum necessary to defray the cost of the benefits payable under these regulations in so far as they relate to his reckonable service before 1st April 1972.

(2) If, as regards any teacher, the period determined under regulation 12 ends after whichever is the later of his 60th birthday and the award to him of allowances under regulation 40(1)(*a*) or (*b*) of the Teachers Regulations there shall be deducted from the terminal sum payable to or in respect of him the amount determined in accordance with table 2 of Schedule 2 as outstanding for payment.

(3) There shall be deducted from any terminal sum payable to or in respect of a teacher before his 60th birthday the amount determined by the Actuary as the actuarial equivalent of the amount which would have been outstanding for payment on that birthday if he had continued to pay contributions at the last rate specified by him until he attained the age of 60; and if any such teacher becomes again employed in reckonable service he shall be treated as having paid those contributions.

Benefits

Service Counting for Pension

16.—(1) A pension shall be paid in accordance with regulations 17 to 21 upon the death of any person who was employed in reckonable service on or after 1st April 1972 and whose service to which this regulation applies amounts to not less than five years.

(2) This regulation applies to—

(*a*) any reckonable service on or after 1st April 1972;

(*b*) any such service before 1st April 1972 in respect of which the person elected to pay contributions under regulation 4 or 5 or paid or elected to pay contributions under the Family Benefits Regulations.

Entitlement to Pension

17. A pension shall be paid under these regulations—

(*a*) in respect of a man teacher—

(i) if he is survived by his wife, to her in accordance with regulation 19;

(ii) if he is survived by a child or children, subject to regulation 21(6) to or for the benefit of that child or those children in accordance with regulation 20 below;

(iii) if he is not survived by his wife or a child of his but is survived by a person nominated by him in pursuance of regulation 18 ("the nominated beneficiary"), to the nominated beneficiary in accordance with regulation 19 (if the beneficiary is an adult) or in accordance with regulation 20 (if the beneficiary is a child).

(*b*) in respect of a woman teacher—

(i) if she is survived by her husband and he is the nominated beneficiary, to him in accordance with regulation 19;

(ii) if she is survived by a child or children, subject to regulation 21(6) to or for the benefit of that child or those children in accordance with regulation 20;

(iii) if she is not survived by her husband or a child, but is survived by the nominated beneficiary, to the nominated beneficiary in accordance with regulation 19 (if the beneficiary is an adult) or in accordance with regulation 20 (if the beneficiary is a child).

Nomination of Beneficiaries

18.—(1) A teacher to whom this regulation applies may at any time when—

(*a*) he is employed in reckonable service; and

(*b*) there is not in force a nomination made by him for the purposes of Part V of the Family Benefits Regulations;

nominate to receive a pension under these regulations a person who at the time of the nomination is wholly or mainly dependent on the teacher and is—

(i) the teacher's parent; or

(ii) an unmarried descendant of either of the teacher's parents; or

(iii) the teacher's widowed stepmother or stepfather; or

(iv) any unmarried descendant of the deceased wife of a man teacher; or

(v) the husband of a woman teacher.

(2) This regulation applies to a man teacher who is unmarried and to any woman teacher.

(3) The nomination of a beneficiary under this regulation shall become void—

(*a*) on the receipt by the Secretary of State of a written notice of revocation by the teacher;

(*b*) on the death or marriage of the nominated beneficiary;

(*c*) if the teacher is a man, on his marriage;

(*d*) if the beneficiary was a child, on his ceasing to be a child.

Amount of Pension for Widow or Adult Beneficiary

19.—(1) The annual amount of a pension payable to a widow or an adult nominated beneficiary shall be equal to one one-hundred and sixtieth of the teacher's average salary in respect of every year of his reckonable service counting for benefit for the purposes of this regulation.

(2) The reckonable service of a teacher counting for benefit for the purposes of this regulation is—

(*a*) his reckonable service on or after 1st April 1972;

(*b*) any reckonable service before 1st April 1972 in respect of which the teacher elects to pay contributions under regulation 4;

(*c*) his deemed normal service, or its equivalent in a case to which regulation 3(2) applies;

(*d*) his deemed additional service, or its equivalent in a case to which regulation 3(2) applies;

(*e*) twice his notional service;

(*f*) any period of service as is specified in an election by him to pay contributions under regulation 5 or regulation 6;

(*g*) (i) Where the teacher has elected to pay contributions under regulation 5, one-fifth of the period of service in respect of which the teacher has so elected but not exceeding one-fifth of the maximum period for which the teacher could have elected to pay under regulation 5 if his reckonable service prior to 1st April 1972 had not exceeded the period of the previous service in respect of which prior to that date he paid, or elected to pay, family benefits contributions, or

(ii) Where the teacher has elected to pay contributions under regulation 6, a period equal to the period of service in respect of which the teacher has elected to pay such contributions.

(*h*) if the teacher died while employed in reckonable service or while in receipt of an annual allowance to which he became entitled by virtue of regulation 40(1)(*c*) of the Teachers Regulations, such number of years as bears to any period which was or could have been added to his reckonable service by virtue of regulation 41 of the Teachers Regulations the same proportion as the aggregate number of years of his reckonable service under sub-paragraphs (*a*), (*b*), (*c*), (*d*), (*e*), (*f*) and (*g*) of paragraph (2) bears to his total reckonable service.

Amount of Child's Pension

20.—(1) The annual amount of a pension payable to or for the benefit of a child or children shall be—

(*a*) if the teacher is survived by a widow or dependent husband—

(i) for so long as there are two or more children, an amount equal to one one-hundred and sixtieth of the teacher's average salary for every year of the teacher's service counting for benefit for the purposes of regulation 19;

(ii) for so long as there is one child, an amount equal to one three-hundred and twentieth of the teacher's average salary for each such year;

(*b*) if (in the case of a man teacher) he is not survived by his wife or (in the case of a woman teacher) immediately before her death she was not married—

(i) for so long as there are two or more children, an amount equal to one one-hundred and twentieth of the teacher's average salary for every year of his reckonable service counting for benefit for the purposes of this regulation;

(ii) for so long as there is one child, an amount equal to one two-hundred and fortieth of the teacher's average salary for each such year.

(2) The reckonable service of a teacher counting for benefit for the purposes of this regulation is—

(*a*) his reckonable service; and

(*b*) if the teacher died while employed in reckonable service or while in receipt of an annual allowance to which he became entitled by virtue of regulation 40(1)(*c*) of the Teachers Regulations such number of years as bears to any period which was or could have been added to his reckonable service by virtue of regulation 41 of the Teachers Regulations the same proportion as the aggregate number of years of his reckonable service under sub-paragraphs (*a*), (*b*), (*c*), (*d*), (*e*), (*f*) and (*g*) of paragraph (2) of regulation 19 bears to his total reckonable service.

Duration of Pensions

21.—(1) A pension payable to a teacher's widow or widower, or to a nominated beneficiary, shall subject to paragraph (2), if a short term pension is payable under regulation 19 or 20 of the Teachers and Teachers' Families Regulations, begin to accrue on the termination of that pension and, if no such pension is payable under those regulations, on the day following the death of the teacher.

(2) If the annual rate of the pension payable to a widow or widower under these regulations exceeds the annual rate of the pension payable under regulation 19 or 20 of the Teachers and Teachers' Families Regulations the pension provided for by these regulations shall be paid in substitution for the pension payable under those regulations.

(3) The amount payable to or for the benefit of a child by virtue of regulation 20(1)(*a*) shall, if a short term pension is payable under regulation 19 or 20 of the Teachers and Teachers' Families Regulations to the child's parent, begin to accrue on the termination of the short term pension and, if no such short term pension is payable, on the day following the death of the teacher.

(4) A pension payable to or for the benefit of a child of a teacher shall, if the teacher is survived by a widow or widower, begin to accrue on the day following the death of that widow or widower and otherwise on the day following the death of the teacher.

(5) Subject to paragraph (6) a pension payable under these regulations or under regulation 23 or 24 of the Teachers and Teachers' Families Regulations shall cease to be paid upon the death of the person to whom it is payable or, unless the Secretary of State otherwise directs, upon that person marrying or

commencing to cohabit with a person to whom he or she is not married; but any pension which has ceased to be payable under the above provisions by reason of marriage or cohabitation may, if the Secretary of State so decides, be paid upon the person again becoming a widow or widower or as the case may be ceasing to cohabit.

(6) A pension payable to or for the benefit of a child shall cease on the death of the child or when the child ceases to be a child within the meaning of these regulations, whichever first occurs.

MISCELLANEOUS AND SUPPLEMENTARY

Special Provision for Widows of Certain Non-members

22.—(1) A pension of an amount specified in paragraph (2) may be paid to the widow of any non-member who dies without having made an election for the purposes of regulation 4 if a death gratuity is payable to his personal representatives under regulation 46(2A) of the Teachers Regulations.

(2) The amount of a pension under paragraph (1) shall be equal to one one-hundred and sixtieth of the teacher's average salary for every year of the service by reference to which the gratuity under regulation 46(2A) of the Teachers Regulations falls to be calculated.

(3) There shall be deducted from the terminal sum payable to or in respect of the teacher, or paid to the Secretary of State in such manner as may be agreed, the actuarial equivalent of the pension paid under this regulation.

(4) Paragraphs (1) and (5) of regulation 21 shall apply to a pension paid under this regulation.

Application of Family Benefits Regulations

23. Except in so far as other provision is made by these regulations Part VI (Miscellaneous and Supplementary) of the Family Benefits Regulations shall, with the necessary modifications, apply for the purposes of these regulations as it applies for the purposes of those regulations.

Repayment of Contributions

24.—(1) There shall, as soon as may be, be repaid the amount, together with compound interest thereon calculated at three per cent per annum with yearly rests, certified by the Actuary as the amount by which the contributions paid under regulation 36A(1) of the Family Benefits Regulations before the commencement of these regulations exceeds the amount payable under that provision as affected by these regulations.

(2) If a teacher to whom regulation 5 applies does not elect to pay contributions under that regulation, such sums as are prescribed by regulations 39 to 41 of the Family Benefits Regulations, reduced in any case by a sum equal to the tax chargeable on that repayment under paragraph 2 of Part II of Schedule 5 to the Finance Act 1970(**a**) (charge to tax on repayment of employee's contributions) shall be paid to him by way of repayment of contributions paid by him—

(*a*) on his being repaid his superannuation contributions after ceasing to be employed in reckonable service;

(*b*) on his transfer to other employment if interchange rules apply to him on that transfer;

(*c*) on his becoming eligible for allowances if on his death no pension will

(**a**) 1970 c. 24.

be payable to his widow, or other adult beneficiary nominated by him, under any provision relating to the superannuation of teachers except a provision contained in Part VI of the Teachers Regulations.

Special Provision for Teachers with Certain External Service

25.—(1) On the death of a teacher or former teacher who is a former external contributor to an external scheme relating to such service as is mentioned in paragraph 1 (England and Wales) or 2 (Northern Ireland) of Schedule 2 to the Teachers Regulations the Secretary of State may in accordance with this regulation pay a pension to or for the benefit of any widow, widower, child or other nominated beneficiary of that teacher to or for whose benefit a pension is payable under the preceding provisions of these regulations.

(2) The annual amount of a pension payable under this regulation shall be equal to the amount that would have been payable under those provisions of the external scheme which correspond to these regulations if that part of the election under regulation 8(1)(*a*) as is made in pursuance of paragraph 2(1) of Schedule 3 had formed part of an election to the like effect for the purposes of the external scheme.

(3) There shall be deducted from the terminal sum payable to or in respect of the teacher, or paid to the Secretary of State in such manner as may be agreed, an amount equal to the sum of any contributions outstanding for payment in respect of the service to which the part of the election referred to in paragraph (2) relates.

(4) In connection with the provisions of the preceding paragraphs of this regulation, Schedule 3 shall have effect for the modification—

(*a*) in accordance with paragraph 1 of that Schedule, of the Teachers and Teachers' Families Regulations in their application to a former external contributor to such a scheme as is mentioned in paragraph (1) who dies within the time prescribed for making an election under regulation 8(1)(*a*) above without making such an election; and

(*b*) in accordance with paragraph 2 of that Schedule, of these regulations in their application to a teacher or former teacher to whom paragraph (1) applies.

Short Term Pensions for Dependants of Women Teachers

26. Regulations 19 (Widow's Short Term Pension) and 20 (Retired Teacher's Widow's Short Term Pension) of the Teachers and Teachers' Families Regulations shall with the necessary modifications apply on the death after 31st March 1972 of a woman teacher whose husband is her nominated beneficiary as they apply on the death of a man teacher; and regulation 21 (Children's Short Term Pension) of those regulations shall so apply on the death after 31st March 1972, survived by a child or children, of a woman teacher who immediately before her death was not married as it applies on the death of a man teacher survived by a child or children.

Minor and Consequential Amendments and Revocations

27. The minor and consequential amendments and revocations specified in Schedule 4 shall have effect.

Gordon Campbell,
One of Her Majesty's Principal
Secretaries of State.

St. Andrew's House,
Edinburgh.
3rd December 1973.

Consent of the Minister for the Civil Service given under his Official Seal on 6th December 1973.

(L.S.)

K. H. McNeill,
Authorised by the Minister
for the Civil Service.

SCHEDULE 1

Regulation 3(1)(b)

Deemed Additional Service

The deemed additional service of any teacher shall be determined in accordance with the formula $\frac{ab}{c}$ where—

a is the factor shown in the appropriate entry of column **B** of the table below

b is the amount (in pounds) of his additional contributions held in the Fund at 31st March 1972; and

c is the amount (in pounds) of his annual salary at that date.

A *Age of teacher at last birthday before 1st April 1972*	B *Factor*	A *Age of teacher at last birthday before 1st April 1972*	B *Factor*
18	21·4	45	49·4
19	23·9	46	49·3
20	26·2	47	49·2
21	28·4	48	49·1
22	30·6	49	49·0
23	32·6		
24	34·5	50	49·0
		51	49·0
25	36·3	52	49·0
26	38·0	53	48·9
27	39·6	54	48·9
28	41·1		
29	42·6	55	48·8
		56	48·8
30	43·9	57	48·7
31	45·2	58	48·7
32	46·4	59	48·6
33	47·4		
34	48·4	60 and over	48·6
35	49·2		
36	49·8		
37	50·0		
38	50·2		
39	50·3		
40	50·3		
41	50·2		
42	50·0		
43	49·8		
44	49·6		

Regulations 12 and 15

SCHEDULE 2

CONTRIBUTIONS AND DEDUCTIONS

TABLE 1

CONTRIBUTIONS

Age on the date from which additional contributions begin to be paid	Period in years for which contributions are required to be paid in respect of each year of service (regulation 8(1)(*a*))								
	Rate of contributions elected (regulaation 8(1)(*b*))	1%	2%	3%	4%	5%	6%	7%	8%
32 and under		3·15	1·58	1·05	·79	·63	·525	·45	·395
33—37		3·20	1·60	1·07	·80	·64	·535	·46	·40
38—42		3·30	1·65	1·10	·82	·66	·55	·47	·41
43—47		3·35	1·68	1·12	·84	·67	·56	·48	·42
48 and over		3·40	1·70	1·13	·85	·68	·565	·485	·425

NOTES:

1. A teacher who before the day specified in relation to him under regulation 13*(a)* pays in accordance with the Family Benefits Regulations additional contributions so payable after 31st March 1972 shall be taken to have paid contributions in accordance with regulation 5 at the rate specified by him in accordance with regulation 8(1)(*b*) for the number of years equal to the fraction of which the denominator is that rate and the numerator is the amount of those contributions expressed as a percentage of his annual salary on the day specified; and, as regards any such teacher, that number shall accordingly be deducted from the period determined in accordance with the table above.

2. The necessary interpolations are to be made where the period elected under regulation 8(1)(*a*) is not an exact number of years.

Regulations 12 and 15

TABLE 2

DEDUCTIONS

As regards any teacher the deduction to be made is the annual amount of his contributions at the last rate payable multiplied by the factor shown in column B against the entry in column A which specifies the number of further years during which contributions would have been payable.

A *Number of further years during which contributions would have been payable*	B *Rate of deduction per £ of contribution at last rate payable*
1	·990
2	1·961
3	2·913
4	3·846
5	4·760
6	5·657
7	6·536
8	7·398
9	8·244
10	9·072
11	9·884
12	10·681
13	11·461
14	12·227
15	12·977
16	13·713
17	14·434
18	15·141
19	15·835
20	16·514

Note: The necessary interpolations are to be made where the further period for which contributions would have been payable is not an exact number of years.

SCHEDULE 3

Regulation 25

MODIFICATIONS RELATING TO TEACHERS WITH SERVICE IN ENGLAND, WALES OR NORTHERN IRELAND

Modifications of the Teachers and Teachers' Families Regulations

1.—(1) In computing the period of service of a non-contributor for the purposes of regulation 23(1)(*a*) (Non-contributor's Widow's Pension) any period of external service in England, Wales or Northern Ireland shall be treated as a period of reckonable service.

(2) The reference in regulations 23(1) (Non-contributor's Widow's Pension) and 24(1) (Retired Non-contributor's Widow's Pension) to the annual allowance payable to the teacher shall, if his widow so elects, be construed as including references to the allowance that would have been payable to the teacher if in computing it any external service in England, Wales or Northern Ireland had been treated as reckonable service.

(3) The reference in regulation 25(1) (Adjustment of Terminal Sum) to the teacher's reckonable service before 1st April 1972 shall, if his widow has so elected as is mentioned in sub-paragraph (2) be construed as including a reference to his external service in England, Wales or Northern Ireland.

Modifications of the Regulations

2.—(1) Any election under regulation 8(1) shall in addition specify the period of external service in England, Wales or Northern Ireland which the teacher elects to be treated as reckonable service for the purposes of regulation 19 in the event of his death in, or after retirement from, reckonable service.

(2) There shall be added at the end of regulation 15 as a new paragraph—

"(4) There shall be deducted from the terminal sum payable to or in respect of the teacher, or paid to the Secretary of State in such manner as may be agreed, the actuarial equivalent of the cost of defraying any pension payable in pursuance of regulation 25."

(3) The references in sub-paragraph (*a*) of each of regulations 16(2) and 19(2) to reckonable service on or after 1st April 1972 shall be construed as including references to external service on or after that date in England, Wales or Northern Ireland; and the references in sub-paragraph (*b*) of each of those provisions to reckonable service before 1st April 1972 shall be construed as including references to such external service as is specified in that part of an election under regulation 8(1) of these regulations as is made in pursuance of paragraph 2(1).

Regulation 27

SCHEDULE 4

Minor and Consequential Amendments and Revocations

Amount of Pensions under the Teachers' Widows' and Children's Scheme

1. The words "and before 24th April 1973" shall be inserted immediately after the words "after 24th March 1972" in regulation 44(2)(*d*) (Amount of Widow's Pension), 47(*d*) (Amount of Short Service Widow's Pension) and 50(1)(*d*) (Amount of Children's Pension) of the Family Benefits Regulations.

Additional Contributions

2. No contributions shall be payable by a teacher under regulations 29, 30, 31 and 36 of the Family Benefits Regulations as from any date before 1st November 1974 upon which he commences to pay contributions in accordance with regulation 5 above or, as the case may be, revokes his election to pay contributions under regulation 31 of the Family Benefits Regulations; and regulations 29, 30, 31 and 36 of those regulations shall cease to have effect on 1st November 1974.

Nomination of Dependants

3. Regulation 57 (Nomination of Dependants) of the Family Benefits Regulations shall cease to have effect, but without prejudice to the validity of any nomination made under that regulation which had not become void before the commencement of these regulations.

Teacher's Contribution

4. Regulation 5(2) (Teacher's Contribution towards Financing of Benefits) of the Teachers Superannuation (Financial Provisions) (Scotland) Regulations 1972**(a)** as amended by regulation 3 of the Teachers Superannuation (Financial Provisions and Family Benefits) (Scotland) Regulations 1972**(b)** shall have effect subject to the substitution for the words "6½ per cent of his salary for the time being" of the words—

"the aggregate of—

(*a*) 6½ per cent of his salary for the time being; and

(*b*) any contributions which he has elected to pay under Part V of the Family Benefits Regulations or under the Teachers Superannuation (Family Benefits) (Scotland) Amendment Regulations 1973."

Short Term Pensions

5.—(1) In regulation 19 (Widow's Short-term Pension) and 20 (Retired Teacher's Widow's Short-term Pension) of the Teachers and Teachers' Families Regulations references to the annual rate of a teacher's salary are to be construed as references to his salary as calculated under regulation 3(1) of the Teachers Superannuation (Financial Provisions) (Scotland) Regulations 1972.

(a) S.I. 1972/551 (1972 I, p. 1855). **(b)** S.I. 1972/1239 (1972 II, p. 3738).

(2) In regulation 19 of the Teachers and Teachers' Families Regulations paragraph 2(*b*) shall be deleted and there shall be substituted the following:—

"(*b*) to a widow to whom a pension would have been payable under regulation 23 if she had not elected that that paragraph should not apply—

in either case if the teacher leaves a widow and one child, for one and a half months and if he leaves a widow and more than one child, for three months."

EXPLANATORY NOTE

(*This Note is not part of the Regulations.*)

These Regulations amend the provisions contained in the Teachers Superannuation (Family Benefits) (Scotland) Regulations 1971 to 1973 relating to the payment of pensions to the widows or widowers of teachers and their families and other dependants.

The Regulations enable all teachers employed in reckonable service on or after 1st April 1972 to elect to pay contributions or, as the case may be, further contributions in respect of their reckonable service before that date and make new provision with respect to the amount of pensions payable.

Special provision is made with regard to teachers with external service in England, Wales or Northern Ireland (Regulation 25). The Regulations also make a number of minor amendments to the existing Regulations.

Regulation 26 has retrospective effect by virtue of section 12(1) of the Superannuation Act 1972.

1973 No. 2079

MEDICINES

The Medicines (Exemption from Licences) (Foods and Cosmetics) Amendment Order 1973

Made - - -	10*th December* 1973
Laid before Parliament	18*th December* 1973
Coming into Operation	8*th January* 1974

The Secretaries of State respectively concerned with health in England, in Wales and in Scotland, and the Secretary of State for Northern Ireland, acting jointly, in exercise of powers conferred by section 15(1) of the Medicines Act 1968(**a**) and now vested in them(**b**) and of all other powers enabling them in that behalf, after consulting such organisations as appear to them to be representative of interests likely to be substantially affected by the following order, hereby make the following order:—

Citation, interpretation and commencement

1. This order, which may be cited as the Medicines (Exemption from Licences) (Foods and Cosmetics) Amendment Order 1973, shall be read as one with the Medicines (Exemption from Licences) (Foods and Cosmetics) Order 1971(**c**) (hereinafter referred to as "the principal order"), and shall come into operation on 8th January 1974.

Amendment of Article 2 of the principal order

2.—(1) Article 2 of the principal order (exemption from licences for certain foods and cosmetics) shall be amended in accordance with the following paragraphs of this Article and shall accordingly have effect as set out in the Schedule to this order.

(2) In Article 2(1) for the words "provisions of paragraph (2)" there shall be substituted the words "other provisions".

(3) In Article 2(2) for sub-paragraph (*c*) there shall be substituted the following sub-paragraph—

"(*c*) being a product for external use as a cosmetic as aforesaid contains—

(i) any antibiotic, or

(ii) hexachlorophane, except where the product is exempted from the prohibition imposed by the Medicines (Hexachlorophane Prohibi-

(**a**) 1968 c. 67.

(**b**) In the case of the Secretaries of State concerned with health in England and in Wales by virtue of Article 2(2) of, and Schedule 1 to, the Transfer of Functions (Wales) Order 1969 (S.I. 1969/388 (1969 I, p. 1070)), and in the case of the Secretary of State for Northern Ireland by virtue of the provisions of Section 1(1)(*a*) of the Northern Ireland (Temporary Provisions) Act 1972 (c. 22).

(**c**) S.I. 1971/1410 (1971 III, p. 3945).

tion) Order 1973(**a**) under paragraphs (2)(i)(*a*) or (2)(ii) of Article 2 of that order, or

(iii) any hormone in a proportion (calculated on the weight of the medicinal product) in excess of 0.004 per cent, or

(iv) resorcinol in a proportion (calculated as aforesaid) in excess of 1 per cent, or".

(4) After Article 2(2) there shall be added the following paragraph—

"(3) Without prejudice to paragraph (2) of this Article, the exemption from section 7 of the Act (product licences) conferred by paragraph (1) of this Article does not apply to a medicinal product as aforesaid in respect of which there are, or are to be directed to practitioners advertisements or representations of the nature and in the manner described in section 96(1) and (2) of the Act.".

Temporary provisions

3.—(1) Notwithstanding the provisions of paragraphs (2)(*c*)(ii) and (3) of Article 2 of the principal order, as amended by this order, during the periods set out in paragraph (2) below, the exemption conferred by Article 2(1) of the principal order shall apply to a medicinal product to which the said paragraphs (2)(*c*)(ii) or (3) apply, if—

(*a*) that product was effectively on the market in the United Kingdom immediately before the date of the coming into operation of this order, and

(*b*) dealings in or manufacture of that product would have been subject to the restrictions imposed by sections 7 or 8 of the Act as from that date but for the provisions of this Article.

(2) The periods referred to in the preceding paragraph are as follows:—

(*a*) the period of 28 days, or such extended period as the licensing authority may in a particular case allow, from the date of the coming into operation of this order;

(*b*) the period of 3 months or such extended period as aforesaid from that date, if during the period under (*a*) above the licensing authority have been notified of the intention to apply for a product licence in respect of the medicinal product to which paragraph (1) above relates;

(*c*) the period until the application for such product licence has been finally disposed of, if the licensing authority have been notified in accordance with (*b*) above and the application for such product licence is made during the period under the said sub-paragraph.

(3) For the purposes of this Article an application shall be taken as finally disposed of on (but not before) the occurrence of whichever of the events specified in paragraphs (*a*) to (*e*) of section 27(7) of the Act last occurs.

6th December 1973.

Keith Joseph,
Secretary of State for Social Services.

6th December 1973.

Peter Thomas,
Secretary of State for Wales.

7th December 1973.

Gordon Campbell,
Secretary of State for Scotland.

10th December 1973.

Francis Pym.
Secretary of State for Northern Ireland.

(a) S.I. 1973/1120 (1973 II, p.3453).

SCHEDULE

Article 2(1)

Containing Article 2 of the Principal Order
as amended by this Order*

2.—(1) Subject to the *other provisions* of this Article, the restrictions imposed by sections 7 and 8 of the Act (licences for dealings in and manufacture of medicinal products) shall not apply to anything done in relation to a medicinal product which is wholly or mainly for use by being administered to one or more human beings and which is or is to be for sale either for oral administration as a food or for external use as a cosmetic.

(2) The exemption conferred by the preceding paragraph of this Article does not apply to a medicinal product as aforesaid which—

(*a*) is or is to be sold with, accompanied by or having in relation to it, any particulars in writing specifying that product's curative or remedial function in relation to a disease specified or the use of that product for such curative or remedial purposes, or

(*b*) being a product for oral administration as a food as aforesaid, comes within any of the descriptions contained in the Schedule to this order, or

(*c*) *being a product for external use as a cosmetic as aforesaid contains*—

(i) *any antibiotic, or*

(ii) *hexachlorophane, except where the product is exempted from the prohibition imposed by the Medicines (Hexachlorophane Prohibition) Order* 1973(*a*) *under paragraphs* (2)(*i*)(*a*) *or* (2)(*ii*) *of Article* 2 *of that order, or*

(iii) *any hormone in a proportion (calculated on the weight of the medicinal product) in excess of* 0.004 *per cent. or*

(iv) *resorcinol in a proportion (calculated as aforesaid) in excess of* 1 *per cent, or*

(*d*) being neither a vitamin preparation nor a substance coming within the description in paragraph 3 of the said Schedule, is or is to be sold with, accompanied by or having in relation to it any particulars in writing specifying the dosage relevant to that product's medicinal purpose.

(3) *Without prejudice to paragraph* (2) *of this Article, the exemption from section* 7 *of the Act (product licences) conferred by paragraph* (1) *of this Article does not apply to a medicinal product in respect of which there are, or are to be, directed to practitioners advertisements or representations of the nature and in the manner described in section* 96(1) *and* (2) *of the Act.*

---

*The words substituted or added by this order are shown in italics.

EXPLANATORY NOTE

(This Note is not part of the Order.)

This Order amends the Medicines (Exemption from Licences) (Foods and Cosmetics) Order 1971 by adding to the cases to which the exemptions from licensing conferred by the Order of 1971 do not apply, the cases where the medicinal product is being advertised in a certain way to practitioners and cases where the medicinal product, being a cosmetic within the meaning of the Order of 1971, contains hexachlorophane. The Order provides for certain periods during which the exemptions from licensing will continue to apply after the coming into operation of the Order.

The Order also amends the proportion of hormone specified in Article 2(2)(*c*) of the Order of 1971 from 0·4 per cent to 0·004 per cent.

1973 No. 2080

CONTROL OF FUEL AND ELECTRICITY

The Electricity (Lighting) (Control) Order 1973

Made - - - 10*th December* 1973

Laid before Parliament 11*th December* 1973

Coming into Operation 12*th December* 1973

The Secretary of State, in exercise of his powers under section 2(1) of the Fuel and Electricity (Control) Act 1973(**a**) and section 7 of the Emergency Laws (Re-enactments and Repeals) Act 1964(**b**) as having effect by virtue of section 5(1) of the Fuel and Electricity (Control) Act 1973 hereby makes the following Order:—

1. This Order shall come into operation on the 12th December 1973 and may be cited as the Electricity (Lighting) (Control) Order 1973.

2. (1) In this Order—

"electricity" means electricity whether or not supplied by an Electricity Board within the meaning of section 1 of the Electricity Act (1947)(**c**);

"school" means any institution providing primary or secondary education or both within the meaning of the Education Acts 1944 to 1971 or the Education (Scotland) Acts 1939 to 1971.

(2) Any reference in this Order to any enactment shall be construed as a reference thereto as amended or extended.

3. This Order shall apply in relation to—

(*a*) any premises used wholly or mainly—

(i) as an office or showroom;

(ii) as a retail shop, bank or petrol station;

(iii) as a restaurant or catering establishment (whether or not licensed for the sale of intoxicating liquor) or for the sale or consumption of intoxicating liquor;

(iv) as a warehouse or store;

(v) as a library, museum, art gallery, exhibition hall or other public hall;

(vi) as a place of education;

(vii) as a church, chapel or other place of public worship;

(*b*) any part so used of any premises not otherwise so used, if the lighting of that part is controlled separately from the lighting for the other part of the premises;

(**a**) 1973 c. 67. (**b**) 1964 c. 60. (**c**) 1947 c. 54.

(*c*) any part of any premises licensed under the Cinematograph Act 1909(a) or the Theatres Act 1968(b) to which the public is admitted on payment or otherwise and any place other than premises so licensed used wholly or mainly for recreation, entertainment or sport;

(*d*) any part of any hotel, residential club or hostel to which the public is admitted or which is provided for the communal use of persons resident therein.

4. Except under a licence granted by the Secretary of State under this Order, no person shall use or permit the use of electricity for the purpose of lighting any room comprised in any premises in relation to which this Order applies at any time while that room is unoccupied, except to such extent as may be necessary for the safety of persons on those premises or the security of those premises.

5. Except under a licence granted by the Secretary of State under this Order, no person shall use or permit the use of electricity for the purpose of lighting any room or part of any premises in relation to which this Order applies in such a manner that the electrical load imposed by such lighting in relation to that part exceeds—

(*a*) two watts per square foot of floor area where that room or part is lighted by tungsten lamps;

(*b*) one watt per square foot of floor area where that room or part is lighted by fluorescent lamps or by both tungsten and fluorescent lamps:

Provided that nothing in this Article:

(i) shall apply in relation to any such room or part lighted solely by a single tungsten lamp not exceeding 40 watts, by a single fluorescent lamp or by any high intensity discharge lamp; or

(ii) shall have effect so as to require a reduction in the standard of lighting at any place in such premises below that necessary for the safety of persons on those premises or the security of those premises; or

(iii) shall apply in relation to any part of any premises used as a school during such times as the premises are so used.

6. Any licence granted under this Order may be subject to conditions and may be revoked without prior notice.

7. It shall be a defence for a person who contravenes or fails to comply with a provision of this Order to prove that he used all due diligence to secure compliance with that provision.

8. This Order shall not extend to Northern Ireland.

Tom Boardman,
Minister for Industry,
Department of Trade and Industry.

10th December 1973.

(a) 1909 c. 30. (b) 1968 c. 54.

EXPLANATORY NOTE

(This Note is not part of the Order.)

This Order relates to the electric lighting of the premises specified in Article 3 of the Order. These include offices, shops, catering establishments, warehouses, libraries, places of education, churches, places of recreation, entertainment or sport and the public parts of hotels. It prohibits the lighting by electricity of any room in such premises while it is unoccupied (Article 4). It also restricts (with certain exceptions) the electric lighting of any part of such premises to two watts per square foot for tungsten lamps and one watt per square foot for fluorescent tubes. This restriction does not apply to schools (Article 5). Lighting necessary for the safety of persons on the premises or the security of the premises is permitted.

1973 No. 2081

CHILDREN AND YOUNG PERSONS

The Cessation of Approved Institutions (Herts Training School) Order 1973

Made - - - - 10*th December* 1973

Coming into Operation 1*st January* 1974

The Secretary of State for Social Services in exercise of his power under section 46 of the Children and Young Persons Act 1969**(a)** and of all other powers enabling him in that behalf, hereby makes the following order:—

Citation and commencement

1. This order may be cited as the Cessation of Approved Institutions (Herts Training School) Order 1973, and shall come into operation on 1st January 1974.

Interpretation

2.—(1) In this order unless the context otherwise requires—

"the specified date" means 1st January 1974;

"the school" means the school approved by the Secretary of State in pursuance of section 79(1) of the Children and Young Persons Act 1933**(b)** and known as Herts Training School;

"the managers" means the managers of the school for the purpose of section 79(1) of the Children and Young Persons Act 1933;

"the tribunal" means a tribunal established under section 12 of the Industrial Training Act 1964**(c)** and referred to in section 100 of the Industrial Relations Act 1971**(d)**;

"terms and conditions of employment" includes any restriction arising under any Act or any instrument made under any Act on the termination of the employment of any officer;

(a) 1969 c. 54. **(b)** 1933 c. 12.
(c) 1964 c. 16. **(d)** 1971 c. 72.

"the Council" means the county council of Hertfordshire;

"approved institution" has the meaning assigned to it under section 46 of the Children and Young Persons Act 1969;

"Planning Area No. 7" is the area so designated in the Schedule to the Children and Young Persons (Planning Areas) Order 1970**(a)**.

(2) Any reference in this order to the Local Government Superannuation Acts 1937 to 1953**(b)**, to any provisions thereof or to the provisions of any instrument made under those Acts shall be construed as references to the said provisions as they have effect as regulations made under section 7 of the Superannuation Act 1972**(c)**.

(3) In this order, unless the context otherwise requires, references to any enactment shall be construed as references to that enactment as amended, extended or applied by or under any other enactment or by this order.

(4) Any reference in this order to a numbered article shall, unless the reference is to an article of a specified order, be construed as a reference to the article bearing that number in this order.

(5) Any reference in any article of this order to a numbered paragraph shall, unless the reference is to a paragraph of a specified article, be construed as a reference to the paragraph bearing that number in the first-mentioned article.

(6) The Interpretation Act 1889**(d)** shall apply to the interpretation of this order as it applies to the interpretation of an Act of Parliament.

Cessation as an approved institution

3. It having appeared to the Secretary of State that in consequence of the establishment of community homes in Planning Area No. 7, the school is no longer required he hereby orders that it shall cease to be an approved institution as from the specified date.

Transfer of staff and the safeguarding of their interests

4.—(1) Any person who immediately before the specified date is employed by the managers of the school wholly or substantially in respect of the school shall be transferred to the employment of the Council on the specified date.

(2) Any question whether a person is employed as described in paragraph (1) shall where necessary be determined by the tribunal and references to the tribunal may be made as soon as may be and in any case not later than 15th February 1974 and if any question that a person is not, or is, so employed is undecided on the specified date the person shall not be transferred as mentioned in paragraph (1) until the expiration of the second week following that in which the decision of the tribunal is notified.

(a) S.I. 1970/335 (1970 I, p. 1220).
(b) 1937 c. 68; 1939 c. 18; 1953 c. 25.
(c) 1972 c. 11.
(d) 1889 c. 63.

(3) (*a*) Every person transferred by paragraph (1) to the employment of the Council shall, so long as he continues in that employment by virtue of the transfer, and until he is served with a statement in writing of new terms and conditions of employment, enjoy terms and conditions of employment not less favourable than those he enjoyed immediately before the specified date and the said new terms and conditions shall be such that—

(i) so long as the person is engaged in duties reasonably comparable to those in which he was engaged immediately before the specified date, the scale of his salary or remuneration, and

(ii) the other terms and conditions of his employment, are not less favourable than those he enjoyed immediately before the specified date, and any question whether duties are reasonably comparable or whether terms and conditions of employment are less favourable shall where necessary be determined by the tribunal.

(*b*) A statement of new terms and conditions of employment shall not be served in respect of any person in relation to whom a question has been referred under paragraph (2) until the decision of the tribunal has been notified.

(*c*) Subject to sub-paragraph (*b*), a statement of new terms and conditions of employment may be served before the specified date.

(*d*) If after service upon a person of a statement of new terms and conditions of employment a question is referred to the tribunal in respect of such person under paragraph (2), the statement shall cease to have effect, sub-paragraph (*a*) of this paragraph shall have effect as if the statement had not been served, and no new statement shall be served until the decision on the question has been notified.

(4) A written statement given in accordance with section 4(1) of the Contracts of Employment Act 1972**(a)** shall not be regarded as a statement of new terms and conditions of employment for the purposes of paragraph (3) unless the statement so indicates.

(5) Any extension of service under section 7(1) of the Local Government Superannuation Act 1937 effective on the specified date in relation to a person transferred by paragraph (1) shall continue to have effect as if it had been made by the Council to whose employment he is transferred as aforesaid.

(6) (*a*) Any determination made by the tribunal as provided under paragraph (2) or (3)(*a*)(ii) shall be made in accordance with the Industrial Tribunals (Industrial Relations, etc.) Regulations 1972**(b)**, and this order, and in respect of any hearing of the tribunal for purposes of any such determination a person or persons may be appointed to sit with the tribunal as assessor or assessors.

(*b*) Any determination of the tribunal as mentioned in sub-paragraph (*a*) above shall, subject to any modification that may be required in consequence of any appeal from that determination on a point of law, be given effect to by the Council or the managers as the case may be.

(a) 1972 c. 53.
(b) S.I. 1972/38 (1972 I, p. 91).

(*c*) The Council shall inform everyone who is employed by the managers on 31st December 1973 of his right to make reference to the tribunal under paragraph (2) and shall inform every employee transferred by this order of his right to make reference to the tribunal under paragraph (3)(*a*)(ii) and shall at the same time give them the address to which the reference may be made, and with respect to a reference under paragraph (2) the Council shall inform the employee not later than 15th January 1974 that he must make reference to the tribunal not later than 15th February 1974, and with respect to a reference under paragraph (3)(*a*)(ii) the Council may inform the employee of his said right by means of an insertion in the statement in writing to be served under paragraph (3)(*a*).

Superannuation

5.—(1) For the purposes of this article unless the context otherwise requires—

"the Act" means the Local Government Superannuation Act 1937**(a)**;

"transferred employee" means a person transferred by article 4;

"existing employment" means employment by the managers of the school;

"new employment" means employment by the Council;

"servant" shall have the meaning assigned to it under section 40 of the Act.

(2) The admission agreement made by or on behalf of the managers and the Council on 27th August 1956 and approved by the Minister of Housing and Local Government on 28th August 1956 shall cease to have effect on the specified date but without prejudice to accrued rights or any liabilities thereunder.

(3) Any liabilities of the managers arising out of the agreement referred to in the last preceding paragraph shall become the liability of the Council with effect from the specified date.

(4) Any transferred employee who immediately before he is transferred is a contributory employee by virtue of the admission agreement mentioned in paragraph (2) shall continue to be a contributory employee in his new employment and for that purpose the Council shall be deemed to have passed any necessary statutory resolution.

(5) Subject to the provisions of this article, any enactment, instrument or other document contained in or made or issued under the Local Government Superannuation Acts 1937 to 1953, the Superannuation (Miscellaneous Provisions) Act 1948**(b)** or Part III of the National Insurance Act 1965**(c)** shall have effect in relation to any transferred employee to whom it applies as if his new employment and his existing employment were one continuous employment.

(6) Paragraph (5) shall not affect the operation of the Local Government Superannuation (Administration) Regulations 1954**(d)** (as amended **(e)**) in relation to any transferred employee.

(a) 1937 c. 68.
(b) 1948 c. 33.
(c) 1965 c. 51.
(d) S.I. 1954/1192 (1954 II, p. 1570).
(e) The amending Regulations are not relevant to the subject matter of this Order.

(7) Any transferred employee who is paying superannuation contributions immediately before the specified date at a rate appropriate to a servant shall continue to contribute at the like rate so long as he is employed without a break of 12 months or more by the Council on duties reasonably comparable to those on which he is engaged immediately before that day.

(8) Where immediately before a transferred employee is transferred it is the prevailing practice of the managers to exercise beneficially (that is to say, to secure the payment of gratuities, allowances or pensions, or of increased pensions or lump sum benefits) any discretionary power exercisable by them by virtue of any statutory provision relating to pensions it shall be the duty of the Council in relation to that transferred employee, if he has continued in their employment without a break of 12 months or more, to exercise that power (or any corresponding power under the statutory provisions relating to pensions for the time being in force) in a way which is not less beneficial than under the aforesaid practice prevailing; and section 35 of the Act shall apply to any question arising under this paragraph as if any statutory provision mentioned above were a provision under Part I of the Act.

(9) Where at any time before the specified date a gratuity or allowance by way of periodical payments or an annuity—

(*a*) has been granted to any person by the managers on or after his ceasing to be employed by them at or in connection with the school, or

(*b*) has been granted to the widow or other dependant of a person who died while in the employment of the managers at or in connection with the school or during the currency of a gratuity or allowance granted to him as mentioned in sub-paragraph (*a*) above,

and, if payment in respect of the gratuity or allowance or annuity had continued in accordance with the terms of the grant and of any subsequent increase, one or more payments would have been made on or after the specified date (whether under legal obligation or otherwise), such payments shall be made by the Council in place of the managers.

(10) Without prejudice to the last preceding paragraph, where, if this order had not been made, the managers would for the purpose of any statutory provision relating to pensions have been the employing authority or former employing authority in relation to a person who died before the specified date while in the employment of the managers at or in connection with the school or otherwise ceased to be employed by them at or in connection with the school or the widow or other dependant of such a person, the Council shall be treated as being at that time the employing authority or former employing authority for those purposes in relation to that person, his widow or other dependant.

(11) If any gratuity or allowance or annuity as is mentioned in paragraph (9) is paid as a supplement to a pension payable under the Home Office Superannuation Scheme the Council shall increase the said gratuity or allowance or annuity by such amounts as may from time to time be calculated in accordance with and by reference to increases under the Pensions (Increase) Act 1971**(a)** or any enactment repealed by it.

(a) 1971 c. 56.

Financial provisions

6. The Council shall repay to the Secretary of State before the expiry of 3 months from the specified date such sum as he may determine in accordance with paragraph 9(4) of Schedule 3 to the Children and Young Persons Act 1969, such sum being notified to the Council before the expiry of one month from the specified date.

Transfer of rights, liabilities and obligations

7. Except as specified in paragraphs (*b*) and (*c*) of the proviso to this article all liabilities attaching to the managers in relation to the carrying on of the school, including responsibility for the repayment of principal and payment of interest charges on loans, which subsist at the specified date shall as from such date become the liability of the Council; and all contracts, deeds, bonds, agreements and other instruments subsisting in favour of, or against, and all notices in force which were given by, or to, the managers in relation to the carrying on of the school subsisting at the specified date shall be in full force and effect in favour of, or against the Council as from the specified date, provided that:

(*a*) nothing in this article shall affect any trust under the terms of which the premises or any part of the premises of the school, or any property connected with the school is held,

(*b*) the obligation of the managers to prepare annual final accounts for the school and to deal with any questions arising on such accounts shall remain with the managers,

(*c*) (i) where an instrument of management ceases to have effect by virtue of an order under section 43(5) or 47(2) or (4)(*a*) of the Children and Young Persons Act 1969 and relates to a controlled community home which is conducted on premises formerly used as the school, but which was designated as a community home in a regional plan approved by the Secretary of State, the voluntary organisation by which the home was provided, or as the case may be, the trustees of the home shall pay to the Council a sum equal to that part of the value of the premises used for the purposes of the home and belonging to the voluntary organisation, or as the case may be, trustees which is attributable to the expenditure of that sum of money which on the specified date was an outstanding debt incurred in respect of the erection, extension or improvement of the premises and transferred to the Council by this article,

(ii) the amount of any sum payable under the foregoing sub-paragraph of this proviso shall be determined in accordance with arrangements as may be agreed between the voluntary organisation or, as the case may be, trustees and the Council, and in default of agreement as may be determined by the Secretary of State,

(iii) in this proviso "voluntary organisation" has the same meaning as in the Children Act 1948(**a**).

Signed by authority of the Secretary of State for Social Services.

M. G. Russell,
Assistant Secretary,
Department of Health and Social Security.

10th December 1973.

(**a**) 1948 c. 43.

EXPLANATORY NOTE

(*This Note is not part of the Order.*)

This Order makes provision for the cessation as an approved institution of Herts Training School and for the transfer of the staff of the school and of most of the rights, liabilities and obligations of the managers of the school to Hertfordshire County Council which is to assume responsibility after the school becomes a controlled community home (as provided in section 36 of the Children and Young Persons Act 1969). The Order also makes provision for the protection of the interests of the staff and pensioners of the school and for the repayment to the Secretary of State by Hertfordshire County Council of grants which had been made to the managers of the school.

1973 No. 2084

SEA FISHERIES

BOATS AND METHODS OF FISHING

The Sea Fishing (North-West Atlantic) Licensing Order 1973

Made - - -	*7th December* 1973
Laid before Parliament	*19th December* 1973
Coming into Operation	*10th January* 1974

The Minister of Agriculture, Fisheries and Food and the Secretaries of State respectively concerned with the sea fishing industry in Scotland and Northern Ireland, in exercise of the powers conferred on them by sections 4 and 15 of the Sea Fish (Conservation) Act 1967(**a**) as the latter section is amended by section 22(1) of, and paragraph 38 of Part II of Schedule 1 to, the Sea Fisheries Act 1968(**b**) and of all other powers enabling them in that behalf, being satisfied that substantially equivalent measures are being taken by governments of other countries concerned, hereby make the following Order:—

Citation and commencement

1. This Order may be cited as the Sea Fishing (North-West Atlantic) Licensing Order 1973 and shall come into operation on 10th January 1974.

Interpretation

2.—(1) In this Order "the Act" means the Sea Fish (Conservation) Act 1967.

(2) The Interpretation Act 1889(**c**) shall apply to the interpretation of this Order as it applies to the interpretation of an Act of Parliament.

Appointed day

3. The appointed day for the purposes of section 4 of the Act (which prohibits the use of British fishing boats for fishing by way of trade or business in any area specified in an order made under that section as from a day appointed by the order except under the authority of a licence) in conjunction with this Order, is 10th January 1974.

(**a**) 1967 c. 84. (**b**) 1968 c. 77.
(**c**) 1889 c. 63.

Area

4. This Order applies to fishing for all sea fish in the areas of sea specified in the Schedule to this Order.

Enforcement

5. For the purpose of the enforcement of section 4 of the Act in conjunction with this Order, there are hereby conferred on every British sea-fishery officer the powers of a British sea-fishery officer under section 8(2) and (3) of the Sea Fisheries Act 1968.

In Witness whereof the Official Seal of the Minister of Agriculture, Fisheries and Food is hereunto affixed on 6th December 1973.

(L.S.)

Joseph Godber,
Minister of Agriculture, Fisheries and Food.

Gordon Campbell,
Secretary of State for Scotland.

7th December 1973.

Francis Pym,
Secretary of State for Northern Ireland.

7th December 1973.

SCHEDULE

Specified areas to which the Order applies:—

(*a*) All waters, except territorial waters, bounded by a line beginning at a point on the coast of Rhode Island in 71° 40′ west longitude; thence due south to 39° north latitude; thence due east to 42° west longitude; thence due north to 59° north latitude; thence due west to 44° west longitude; thence due north to the coast of Greenland; thence along the west coast of Greenland to 78° 10′ north latitude; thence southwards to a point in 75° north latitude and 73° 30′ west longitude; thence along a rhumb line to a point in 69° north latitude and 59° west longitude; thence due south to 61° north latitude; thence due west to 64° 30′ west longitude; thence due south to the coast of Labrador; thence in a southerly direction along the coast of Labrador to the southern terminus of its boundary with Quebec; thence in a westerly direction along the coast of Quebec; and in an easterly and southerly direction along the coasts of New Brunswick, Nova Scotia, and Cape Breton Island to Cabot Strait, thence along the coasts of Cape Breton Island, Nova Scotia, New Brunswick, Maine, New Hampshire, Massachusetts, and Rhode Island to the point of beginning; and

(*b*) All waters, except territorial waters, bounded by a line beginning at a point on the coast of Rhode Island in 71° 40′ west longitude; thence due south to 39° north latitude; thence due east to 65° 40′ west longitude; thence due south to 35° north latitude; thence due west to the coast of North Carolina; thence in a northerly direction along the coasts of North Carolina, Virginia, Maryland, Delaware, New Jersey, New York, Connecticut, and Rhode Island to the point of beginning.

EXPLANATORY NOTE

(This Note is not part of the Order.)

Section 4 of the Sea Fish (Conservation) Act 1967 provides that from a day appointed by an Order no British fishing boat registered in the United Kingdom shall be used by way of trade or business for fishing in any area specified in the Order except under the authority of a licence granted by one of the fisheries Ministers.

This Order, which implements the recommendations of the International Commission for the North-West Atlantic Fisheries, appoints 10th January 1974 as the date from which no such fishing boat shall so fish for sea fish in specified areas of the North-West Atlantic except under the authority of such a licence. Waters referred to in paragraph (*a*) of the Schedule to the Order are the waters to which the International Convention for the North-West Atlantic Fisheries applies; and the waters referred to in paragraph (*b*) form part of the area known as the Statistical Area 6.

1973 No. 2085

CUSTOMS AND EXCISE

The Customs Duties and Drawbacks (Revenue, including Hydrocarbon Oil, Duties) (Miscellaneous Amendments) Order 1973

Made - - -	10*th December* 1973
Laid before the House of Commons	11*th December* 1973
Coming into Operation	1*st January* 1974

The Treasury, by virtue of the powers conferred upon them by section 1(4), (5) and (6) of the Finance Act 1973(**a**), and of all other powers enabling them in that behalf, hereby make the following Order:—

1.—(1) This Order may be cited as the Customs Duties and Drawbacks (Revenue, including Hydrocarbon Oil, Duties) (Miscellaneous Amendments) Order 1973 and shall come into operation on 1st January 1974.

(2) The Interpretation Act 1889(**b**) shall apply for the interpretation of this Order as it applies for the interpretation of an Act of Parliament.

2. The Customs Duties and Drawbacks (Revenue Duties) Order 1973(**c**) shall be amended—

(*a*) in Article 4 by inserting after the figure 13 in the eighth line the word and figure "to 15";

(*b*) in Article 6(1) by inserting after the words "Article 25(1)" in the first and second lines of the column headed "Goods" opposite "FTA" the words "of Protocol No. 3";

(*c*) after Article 13 by adding the following:—

"14.—(1) The rates of customs duty chargeable and of drawback, if any, allowable on goods originating in Algeria, Greece, Israel, Lebanon, Morocco, Spain and Tunisia, other than goods to which Articles 10 or 11 of the Customs Duties and Drawbacks (Revenue Duties) (Algeria, Cyprus, Egypt, Morocco, Tunisia and Turkey) Order 1973(**d**) apply, shall be the lower of the rates applicable on 31st December 1973 and those provided by this Order.

(2) For the purpose of Article 6, Malta shall be deemed to be part of the Commonwealth preference area formed by the countries named in Part 1 of Schedule 8.

(3) In the case of goods originating in Malta, other than goods which qualify for rates under the column headings "Commonwealth

---

(**a**) 1973 c. 51. (**b**) 1889 c. 63.
(**c**) S.I. 1973/1946 (1973 III, p. 6707). (**d**) S.I. 1973/1947 (1973 III, p. 6742).

2" in the new schedules, the rates of customs duty chargeable and of drawback, if any, allowable shall be the lowest of those applicable on 31st December 1973, at the full rate and the rates provided under this Order.

15.—(1) For the purpose of Article 6, the Channel Islands shall be deemed to be a state which is a member of the Community.

(2) Where goods originating in the Channel Islands qualify for rates of customs duty or drawback under the column headings "Commonwealth 1" or "FTA" in the new schedules the rates applicable shall be the respective rates expressed in pounds ignoring any additional amount expressed in "UA" or as a percentage."; and

(*d*) in Schedule 5 thereto by substituting for the figure "0.5255", shown under the column heading "Commonwealth 2", the figure "0.5225".

3. The Customs Duties and Drawbacks (Revenue Duties) (Algeria, Cyprus, Egypt, Morocco, Tunisia and Turkey) Order 1973 shall be amended—

(*a*) in Schedule 1 thereto by substituting for the figures and word "4 Table 2", wherever they occur opposite goods of heading 33.06, the figures and word "1 Table 2";

(*b*) in Schedule 2, Table 1, thereto by deleting the letters "UA" after the figure 0.1440 in the last line of the second column; and

(*c*) in Schedule 2, Table 2, thereto by inserting immediately after the words "Total dry extract not in excess of", in the column heading to the second column, the figure and words "330 but exceeding".

4. The Hydrocarbon Oil (Customs Duties) Order 1973(**a**) shall be amended—

(*a*) by the deletion of the comma in Article 3(1)(*a*) and by the addition thereto of the words "in the Channel Islands, or"

(*b*) by the addition to Schedule 2 thereto of the following countries:—

"Algeria
Greece
Israel
Lebanon
Malta
Morocco
Spain
Tunisia".

10th December 1973.

John Stradling Thomas,
Michael Jopling,
Two of the Lords Commissioners
of Her Majesty's Treasury.

(**a**) S.I. 1973/1948 (1973 III, p. 6753).

EXPLANATORY NOTE

(This Note is not part of the Order)

(1) This Order comes into force on 1st January 1974 and modifies three Orders which establish rates of Customs revenue duties and drawbacks for 1974. Those Orders implement certain EEC obligations of the United Kingdom in relation to revenue duties and are—

(*a*) The Customs Duties and Drawbacks (Revenue Duties) Order 1973 (S.I. 1973/1946);

(*b*) The Customs and Drawbacks (Revenue Duties) (Algeria, Cyprus, Egypt, Morocco, Tunisia and Turkey) Order 1973 (S.I. 1973/1947); and

(*c*) The Hydrocarbon Oil (Customs Duties) Order 1973 (S.I. 1973/1948).

(2) The modifications have the following effect:

(*a*) pending the conclusion, or entry into force, of agreements between the EEC and Algeria, Greece, Israel, Lebanon, Malta, Morocco, Spain and Tunisia, to prevent the charging of protective elements in the duties on goods of those countries (other than certain wines covered by S.I. 1973/1947) at rates higher than those prevailing in 1973 (Articles 2(*c*) and 4);

(*b*) for goods of the Channel Islands, to reduce any protective element in the revenue duties by 2/5 (Article 2(*c*)) and to prevent the charging of any protective element in respect of hydrocarbon oil duty (Article 4); and

(*c*) to correct certain typographical errors in the first two of the Orders listed above (Articles 2(*a*), (*b*) and (*d*) and 3).

1973 No. 2086

CUSTOMS AND EXCISE

The Customs Duties and Drawbacks (Revenue, including Hydrocarbon Oil, Duties) (Turkey) Order 1973

Made - - -	10*th December* 1973
Laid before the House of Commons	11*th December* 1973
Coming into Operation	1*st January* 1974

The Treasury, by virtue of the powers conferred upon them by section 1(4), (5) and (6) of the Finance Act 1973(**a**), and of all other powers enabling them in that behalf, hereby make the following Order:—

1.—(1) This Order may be cited as the Customs Duties and Drawbacks (Revenue, including Hydrocarbon Oil, Duties) (Turkey) Order 1973.

(2) The Interpretation Act 1889(**b**) shall apply for the interpretation of this Order as it applies for the interpretation of an Act of Parliament.

(3) This Order shall come into operation on 1st January 1974 and shall cease to have effect on the 1st January 1975 in relation to Article 4(2).

2. In this Order references to a heading or subheading other than a column heading are references to a heading or subheading of the Customs Tariff 1959; and the description of goods in Schedule 1 hereto shall be interpreted and applied in accordance with the Interpretative Rules of the said Tariff.

3.—(1) The substitution by or under this Order of a rate of drawback for a rate previously in force shall apply only in relation to goods in respect of which duty at the corresponding rate has been paid.

(2) Notwithstanding that Article 4(2) of this Order shall cease to have effect on 1st January 1975, it shall be without prejudice to any claim to drawback on goods imported before that time.

4.—(1) This Article shall apply only to goods of Turkey which are entitled to the benefit of reduced rates of customs duty under the Interim Agreement signed on 30th June 1973 between the European Economic Community and Turkey (**c**).

(2) Notwithstanding the provisions of Article 4 of the Customs Duties and Drawbacks (Revenue Duties) Order 1973(**d**), in the case of goods to which this

(**a**) 1973 c. 51. (**b**) 1889 c. 63.
(**c**) Annexed to Regulation (EEC) No. 2682/73 OJ No. L.277, 3.10.73, p. 1.
(**d**) S.I. 1973/1946 (1973 III, p. 6707).

Article applies of the headings and subheadings described in the following Schedules to the said Order the rates of customs duty chargeable and of drawback, if any, allowable shall be in—

(*a*) Schedule 1 (Table 1),	Spirits of 22.08 and 22.09,
Schedule 1 (Table 2),	Perfumed spirits of 33.06. B.I.,
Schedule 2,	Beer of 22.03A.,
Schedule 3 (Table 1),	Residues and Waste from the Food Industries of 23.05 A.,
Schedule 4 (Table 1),	Manufactured tobacco of 24.02,
Schedule 5,	Matches 36.05 B.I. and 36.06, and
Schedule 6,	Mechanical lighters of 98.10 A.I.a)2. and 98.10 B.I.b)

the rates shown under the column headings "Republic of Ireland" in the said schedules;

(*b*) Schedule 2 and Schedule 3 (Table 1),	Fermented Beverages of 22.07,
Schedule 4 (Tables 1 and 2),	Unmanufactured tobacco of 24.01

the rates shown under the column headings "EEC" in the said schedules; and

(*c*) Schedule 3, wine of 22.06, the rates shown in Schedule 1 to this Order.

(3) Notwithstanding the provisions of Article 3(2) of the Hydrocarbon Oil (Customs Duties) Order 1973(**a**), the additional duty chargeable thereunder shall not be charged in the case of hydrocarbon oil of the subheadings set out in Schedule 2 to this Order.

10th December 1973.

John Stradling Thomas,
Michael Jopling,
Two of the Lords Commissioners
of Her Majesty's Treasury.

(**a**) S.I. 1973/1948 (1973 III, p. 6753).

SCHEDULE 1

WINE OF 22.06 (RATES OF CUSTOMS DUTIES FOR TURKEY)

Description of wine by heading and subheading	Rate of duty (per gallon)
	£
A.I.a) 1.	0.7500
A.I.a) 2.	1.4000
A.I.c) 1.	1.4750
A.I.c) 2.	2.1000
A.II.a) 1. aa) and bb)	0.7500
A.II.a) 2.	1.4000
A.II.c) 1. aa) and bb)	1.4750
A.II.c) 2.	2.1000
B.I.b) 1.	1.4750
B.I.b) 2.	2.1000
B.II.b) 1. aa) and bb)	1.4750
B.II.b) 2.	2.1000
C.I.a) 1.	1.4750
C.I.a) 2.	2.1000
C.I.b) 1.	1.4750*
C.I.b) 2.	2.1000*
C.II.a) 1. aa) and bb)	1.4750
C.II.a) 2.	2.1000
C.II.b) 1. aa) and bb)	1.4750*
C.II.b) 2.	2.1000*
*Together in the case of wine exceeding 42 degrees of proof spirit, with an addition for each additional degree or fraction of degree of	0.1200

SCHEDULE 2

TARIFF SUBHEADING

27.07 A.I.a)
27.07 A.II.a)
27.07 B.I.
27.07 G.II.a)
27.16 A.I.
27.16 B.I.
29.01 A.I.b)
29.01 C.I.a)
29.01 C.II.a)
29.01 D.I.a) 1.
29.01 D.VI.a)
32.09 A.II.a)
36.08 A.
38.07 A.
38.07 B.
38.07 C.I.
38.08 B.I.
38.14 B.I.a) 1.
38.14 B.III.a)
38.18 A.
38.19 E.I.
38.19 T.I.
39.02 C.V.a)
39.02 C.VI.a) 1.
39.02 C.XIII.a)
39.02 C.XIV.a) 1.

EXPLANATORY NOTE

(This Note is not part of the Order.)

(1) This Order, which comes into effect on 1st January 1974 implements the obligations of the United Kingdom under the Interim Agreement of 30th June 1973 between the EEC and Turkey. It provides for the abolition of the protective element in the customs duties on most revenue duty goods, namely, spirits and perfumed spirits, beer, wine lees, vermouth, manufactured tobacco, matches and mechanical lighters. It also provides for the customs duties on fermented beverages other than wine of fresh grapes and on unmanufactured tobacco to be reduced to the rates applicable to imports from EEC countries. It provides for relief from the additional duties on certain hydrocarbon oils introduced by the Hydrocarbon Oil (Customs Duties) Order 1973.

(2) The Order provides for like reductions in drawback rates where applicable.

1973 No. 2087

CONTROL OF FUEL AND ELECTRICITY

The Motor Fuel (Restriction of Acquisition) Order 1973

Made - - -	11*th December* 1973
Laid before Parliament	12*th December* 1973
Coming into Operation	13*th December* 1973

The Secretary of State, in exercise of his powers under section 2(1) of the Fuel and Electricity (Control) Act 1973(**a**) and section 7 of the Emergency Laws (Re-enactments and Repeals) Act 1964(**b**) as having effect by virtue of section 5 of the Fuel and Electricity (Control) Act 1973, and all other powers in that behalf enabling him, hereby orders as follows:

Citation and commencement

1. This Order may be cited as the Motor Fuel (Restriction of Acquisition) Order 1973 and shall come into operation on 13th December 1973.

Interpretation

2. In this Order—

"business" includes a trade, profession or employment and includes any activity carried on by a body of persons whether corporate or unincorporate and the performance by a local or public authority of its functions;

"dealer" means a person carrying on an undertaking for the supply of motor fuel by retail;

"motor fuel" means—

(*a*) light oil (within the meaning of the Hydrocarbon Oil (Customs & Excise) Act 1971(**c**) of a kind intended for use as fuel for propelling a motor vehicle; or

(*b*) heavy oil (within the meaning of that Act) of a kind intended for use as fuel for propelling a motor vehicle other than heavy oil in respect of which rebate of duty has been allowed under section 9 of that Act;

"motor vehicle" means a mechanically propelled vehicle intended or adapted for use on roads;

(**a**) 1973 c. 67. (**b**) 1964 c. 60.
(**c**) 1971 c. 12.

"normal quantity", in relation to the acquisition of motor fuel, means a quantity not exceeding the greatest quantity acquired by the acquirer from his normal supplier on any single occasion after 20th May 1973 and before the date of the coming into operation of this Order;

"normal supplier", in relation to the acquisition of motor fuel by a person, means the dealer or other supplier from whom that person has acquired motor fuel on at least 3 occasions after 20th May 1973 and before the date of the coming into operation of this Order;

"two-stroke mixture" means a mixture of motor fuel being light oil within the meaning of the Hydrocarbon Oil (Customs & Excise) Act 1971 and other oil consisting of not less than 16 nor more than 100 parts of motor fuel of that description to one part of other oil.

Restriction of Acquisition

3.—(1) Subject to this Article, no person shall acquire motor fuel unless—

(*a*) it is supplied by a dealer directly into the ordinary fuel tank of a motor vehicle; or

(*b*) it is acquired in a normal quantity from the acquirer's normal supplier for use within a reasonable time—

(i) in a motor vehicle which is an agricultural machine within the meaning of Schedule 3 to the Vehicles (Excise) Act 1971(**a**) or in respect of which no duty is chargeable under that Act;

(ii) otherwise than in a motor vehicle; or

(iii) in the course of the acquirer's business.

(2) Nothing in paragraph (1) of this Article shall prevent—

(*a*) the acquisition of two-stroke mixture in a normal quantity from the acquirer's normal supplier or the acquisition of motor fuel in a normal quantity from the acquirer's normal supplier for making two-stroke mixture within a reasonable time; or

(*b*) where motor fuel is supplied to an acquirer under sub-paragraph (*b*) of that paragraph—

(i) the subsequent issue or distribution of that fuel by the acquirer for use by any officer, servant or agent of the acquirer in the course of the acquirer's business;

(ii) the acquisition by any such officer, servant or agent of any such fuel for such use when it has been so issued or distributed.

Records

4.—(1) Every person shall keep a record of any motor fuel supplied by him under Article 3(1)(*b*) of this Order showing—

(*a*) the quantity supplied;

(*b*) the date of the supply; and

(*c*) the identity of the acquirer.

(**a**) 1971 c. 10.

(2) Notwithstanding the expiry of the Motor Fuel (Restriction of Supplies) Order 1973(**a**) any person required to keep a record by Article 4 of that Order shall preserve that record for the period of 6 months beginning with the date of the coming into operation of this Order.

Directions

5. Nothing in this Order shall prevent the acquisition by a person of such motor fuel as is required to be supplied to that person by a direction given by the Secretary of State under section 2(2)(*b*) of the Fuel and Electricity (Control) Act 1973.

Licences

6.—(1) Nothing in this Order shall prevent the acquisition of motor fuel under the authority of a licence granted by the Secretary of State under this Order.

(2) Any licence granted under this Order may be subject to conditions and may be revoked without prior notice.

(3) Every licence granted under this Order shall be the property of the Secretary of State and any person being in possession of any such licence shall, if requested to do so by the Secretary of State, produce or deliver it to such a person or to a person of such class or description, and within such time, as may be specified in or at the time of the request.

Application to Northern Ireland

7. This Order shall not extend to Northern Ireland.

Tom Boardman,
Minister for Industry,
Department of Trade and Industry.

11th December, 1973.

(a) S.I. 1973/1943 (1973 III, p. 6690).

EXPLANATORY NOTE

(*This Note is not part of the Order.*)

This Order restricts the acquisition of motor fuel by requiring it to be supplied directly into the fuel tank of a motor vehicle or, if it is for use in an agricultural motor vehicle or in a motor vehicle not chargeable with vehicle excise duty or for use otherwise than in a motor vehicle or for business use, by requiring it to be supplied in normal quantities from the acquirer's normal supplier. This Order does not extend to Northern Ireland.

STATUTORY INSTRUMENTS

1973 No. 2088

TRANSPORT

The Carriage by Railway (Parties to Convention) (Amendment) Order 1973

Made - - - *12th December* 1973

At the Court at Buckingham Palace, the 12th day of December 1973

Present,

The Queen's Most Excellent Majesty in Council

Her Majesty, in exercise of the powers conferred upon Her by sections 2(1) and (2) and 11 of the Carriage by Railway Act 1972(**a**), and of all other powers enabling Her in that behalf, is pleased, by and with the advice of Her Privy Council, to order, and it is hereby ordered, as follows:—

1. This Order may be cited as the Carriage by Railway (Parties to Convention) (Amendment) Order 1973.

2. The Carriage by Railway (Parties to Convention) Order 1972(**b**) is hereby amended by substituting the Schedule to this Order for Schedule 1 to that Order, and by adding in Schedule 2 to that Order, after the entry "The Republic of Finland" the words "The German Democratic Republic" and after the entry "The German Democratic Republic" the words "The People's Republic of Hungary".

W. G. Agnew.

(**a**) 1972 c.33.

(**b**) S.I. 1972/1580 (1972 III, p.4580).

SCHEDULE

The Contracting States for the purposes of the Convention and the date of entry into force of the Convention with respect to such States are as follows:

Contracting States	Date of entry into force
The United Kingdom of Great Britain and Northern Ireland	1st January 1973
The Democratic and Popular Republic of Algeria	1st January 1973
The Republic of Austria	7th September 1973
The Kingdom of Belgium	1st January 1973
The People's Republic of Bulgaria	1st January 1973
The Czechoslovak Socialist Republic	1st January 1973
The Kingdom of Denmark	1st January 1973
The Republic of Finland	1st January 1973
The French Republic	1st January 1973
The German Democratic Republic	1st May 1973
The People's Republic of Hungary	7th October 1973
The Republic of Iraq	1st January 1973
The Principality of Liechtenstein	1st January 1973
The Grand Duchy of Luxembourg	1st January 1973
The Kingdom of Morocco	1st September 1973
The Kingdom of the Netherlands	1st January 1973
The Kingdom of Norway	1st January 1973
The Polish People's Republic	1st January 1973
The Republic of Portugal	1st January 1973
The Spanish State	1st January 1973
The Swiss Confederation	1st January 1973
The Syrian Arab Republic	1st January 1973
The Republic of Turkey	1st January 1973
The Socialist Federal Republic of Yugoslavia	1st January 1973

EXPLANATORY NOTE

(This Note is not part of the Order.)

The Carriage by Railway (Parties to Convention) Order 1972 certifies that various States, listed in Schedule 1 to that Order, are Contracting States for the purposes of the Additional Convention to the International Convention concerning the Carriage of Passengers and Luggage by Rail signed at Berne, 1966 (Cmnd. 4969), and that certain of those States, listed in Schedule 2 to the Order, have made a declaration in accordance with Article 1(2) of the Convention. Since that Order was made the German Democratic Republic, the People's Republic of Hungary and the Kingdom of Morocco have become Contracting States to the Convention, and the German Democratic Republic and the People's Republic of Hungary have made a declaration in accordance with Article 1(2). The revised entry into force date for the Republic of Austria is made necessary by a correction issued by the depositary Government. The present Order amends the principal Order accordingly.

1973 No. 2089

EMERGENCY POWERS

The Emergency (No. 2) Regulations 1973

Made - - - -	12*th December* 1973
Laid before Parliament	12*th December* 1973
Coming into Operation	13*th December* 1973

ARRANGEMENT OF REGULATIONS

REQUISITIONING OF CHATTELS AND TAKING POSSESSION OF LAND

OFFENCES

SUPPLEMENTAL

At the Court at Buckingham Palace, the 12th day of December 1973

Present,

The Queen's Most Excellent Majesty in Council

Whereas on the 13th day of November 1973 a proclamation of emergency was made under section 1 of the Emergency Powers Act 1920(**a**), as amended by the Emergency Powers Act 1964(**b**) :

And whereas, by virtue of that section, such a proclamation does not remain in force for more than one month :

And whereas the Emergency Regulations 1973(**c**) were, in pursuance of section 2 of the said Act of 1920, made on the day aforesaid :

And whereas those Regulations will expire when the said proclamation ceases to be in force :

And whereas a further proclamation of emergency has been made as aforesaid and is now in force:

Now, therefore, Her Majesty, in pursuance of section 2 of the said Act of 1920, is pleased, by and with the advice of Her Privy Council, to order, and it is hereby ordered, as follows :—

PRELIMINARY

Title and commencement

1.—(1) These Regulations may be cited as the Emergency (No. 2) Regulations 1973.

(2) These Regulations shall come into operation on 13th December 1973.

(a) 1920 c. 55. (b) 1964 c. 38 (c) S.I. 1973/1881 (1973 III, p. 6516).

Interpretation

2.—(1) In these Regulations, except so far as the context otherwise requires, the following expressions have the meanings hereby respectively assigned to them, that is to say:—

"air transport licence" and "air transport service" have the same meanings as in the Civil Aviation Act 1971(**a**);

"animal feeding stuffs" includes any substance used in the composition or preparation of animal feeding stuffs;

"chattel", in relation to Scotland, means corporeal moveable;

"district", in relation to a sewerage authority, includes any area in which the authority exercise functions with respect to the reception of foul or surface water into their sewers;

"Electricity Board" has the same meaning as in the Electricity Act 1947(**b**);

"essential goods" means food, water, fuel, animal feeding stuffs and other necessities;

"essential services" means services essential to the life of the community;

"food" includes any substance used in the composition or preparation of food;

"hovercraft" has the same meaning as in the Hovercraft Act 1968(**c**);

"land" includes (without prejudice to any of the provisions of section 3 of the Interpretation Act 1889(**d**)) parts of houses or buildings;

"liquid fuel" means any liquid used as fuel, whether for the propulsion of vehicles or for industrial, domestic or any other purposes;

"port" includes any dock, harbour, pier, quay, wharf, mooring, anchorage or other similar place;

"port authority" means the authority or person having the control or management of a port;

"regional water board" has the same meaning as in the Water (Scotland) Act 1967(**e**);

"requisition" means, in relation to any chattel, take possession of the chattel or require the chattel to be placed at the disposal of the requisitioning authority;

"river authority" includes—

(*a*) the Conservators of the River Thames,

(*b*) the Lee Conservancy Catchment Board, and

(*c*) the Isle of Wight River and Water Authority;

"sewerage authority" means an authority which is a sewerage authority for the purposes of Part II of the Public Health Act 1936(**f**), the Common Council of the City of London, the council of a county in Scotland, the town council of a burgh, any combination of such county or town councils constituted for the purposes of the provision of sewerage works or sewage disposal services, a development corporation

(**a**) 1971 c. 75. (**b**) 1947 c. 54. (**c**) 1968 c. 59.
(**d**) 1889 c. 63. (**e**) 1967 c. 78. (**f**) 1936 c. 49.

established under the New Towns Act 1946(**a**), the New Towns Act 1965(**b**), or the New Towns (Scotland) Act 1968(**c**), and the Commission for the New Towns ;

"solid fuel" means coal, anthracite and coke and other manufactured fuel of which coal or anthracite is the principal constituent ;

"statutory water undertakers" has the same meaning as in the provisions of the Water Act 1945(**d**) other than Part II of that Act ;

"water development board" has the same meaning as in the Water (Scotland) Act 1967.

(2) The Interpretation Act 1889 shall apply to the interpretation of these Regulations as it applies to the interpretation of an Act of Parliament.

(3) Any reference in these Regulations to the doing of any act shall, unless the context otherwise requires, be construed as including a reference to the making of any statement.

(4) Any reference in these regulations to any enactment shall, without prejudice to any specific provision in that behalf, be construed as a reference thereto as amended or extended, and as including a reference thereto as applied, by or under any other enactment.

(5) Any reference in any document to these Regulations or to any of them shall, unless the contrary intention appears, be construed as a reference to these Regulations or to that Regulation as amended by any subsequent Regulations made under the Emergency Powers Act 1920.

REGULATION OF PORTS

Control of port traffic

3.—(1) The Secretary of State may, in the case of any port, give such directions to the port authority or any other person as appear to him to be necessary or expedient for securing that the most advantageous use is made in the public interest of the facilities provided at the port, and such directions may, in particular, make provision for excluding or removing from the port ships of any class or a specified ship and for all or any of the following matters, that is to say:—

(*a*) the berthing and movement of ships ;

(*b*) the movement and use of tugs, lighters, barges, floating cranes and elevators and other floating apparatus ;

(*c*) the loading and unloading of ships and the use of appliances therefor ;

(*d*) the movement and use of vehicles ;

(*e*) the prevention of entry by unauthorised persons ; and

(*f*) in connection with the loading and unloading of ships or the storage and warehousing of goods, the priority that should be given to particular cargoes or to particular operations ;

and such directions shall have effect notwithstanding any lease or appropriation of berths and storage or warehouse accommodation.

(2) The Secretary of State may give directions under the foregoing paragraph requiring goods lying at the port to be removed within such period as may be specified in the directions, and, in default of compliance with those directions and without prejudice to the taking of proceedings in

(**a**) 1946 c. 68. (**b**) 1965 c. 59. (**c**) 1968 c. 16. (**d**) 1945 c. 42.

respect of the default, the Secretary of State may remove, or authorise the removal of, the goods to such place, and by such means, as he thinks fit, and the owner or consignee of the goods shall pay to the Secretary of State such reasonable charges in respect of the removal and storage thereof by or on the authority of the Secretary of State as may be agreed or as may, in default of agreement, be determined by arbitration.

(3) All occupiers of public warehouses at or in the neighbourhood of the port shall, if so required by directions given by the Secretary of State, furnish to the Secretary of State from time to time information of vacant accommodation at their warehouses, and shall, to the extent of the accommodation available, accept for storage any goods removed by or on the authority of the Secretary of State under the last foregoing paragraph:

Provided that the Secretary of State shall, in exercising his power to require the storage of goods removed as aforesaid, have regard to the suitability of the accommodation for storing those goods.

(4) The Secretary of State may appoint for any port or group of ports a body of persons, to be known as the Port Emergency Committee for the port or, as the case may be, the group, and may authorise that Committee and persons designated by them for the purpose to exercise on his behalf in relation to the port or, as the case may be, each port comprised in the group all or any of his functions under this Regulation.

(5) Where the Secretary of State appoints a Port Emergency Committee under paragraph (4) of this Regulation, he—

(*a*) may appoint a member of the Committee to be chairman of the Committee, and

(*b*) may give (whether in the instrument of appointment of the Committee or otherwise) any general or special instructions as to the proceedings of the Committee and as to the exercise by the Committee of such of his functions under this Regulation as the Committee are authorised to exercise ; and any such Committee, and any person designated by them under that paragraph, shall comply with any instructions of the Secretary of State given under this paragraph.

(6) Paragraphs (1) to (5) of this Regulation shall have effect in relation to hovercraft as they have effect in relation to ships, and any reference in those paragraphs to ships shall be construed accordingly.

Default powers relating to port traffic

4.—(1) Where any directions have been given under paragraph (1) of the foregoing Regulation, other than any such directions as are mentioned in paragraph (2) of that Regulation, and those directions are not complied with within the time specified in the directions or, if no time is so specified, are not complied with within a reasonable time, the Secretary of State may take, or may authorise any other person to take, such steps as the Secretary of State may consider appropriate in the circumstances for effecting anything which would have been effected if the directions had been complied with.

(2) Without prejudice to the generality of the foregoing paragraph, the steps which may be taken by virtue of this Regulation in respect of any directions shall include entering upon, taking possession of, moving or using any ship, hovercraft or other vessel, apparatus, vehicle, premises or other property to which the directions related by such means as the Secretary of State or other person taking those steps may determine to be appropriate.

(3) Where any steps are taken by virtue of this Regulation in respect of any directions, the person to whom the directions were given shall pay to the Secretary of State or other person taking those steps such reasonable charges in respect of expenses incurred by the Secretary of State or person in taking those steps, or in consequence of having taken them, as may be agreed or as may, in default of agreement, be determined by arbitration.

(4) In Part VIII of the Merchant Shipping Act 1894(**a**) (liability of shipowners) " owner ", in relation to any ship, shall be construed as including the Secretary of State or other person by whom any steps are taken in relation to the ship by virtue of this Regulation.

In this paragraph " ship " has the same meaning as in Part VIII of that Act.

(5) The provisions of this Regulation shall have effect without prejudice to any power exercisable by virtue of paragraph (2) or paragraph (3) of the foregoing Regulation ; and the exercise of any power by virtue of this Regulation in respect of any directions shall be without prejudice to the taking of proceedings in respect of any contravention of, or failure to comply with, the directions.

(6) Paragraphs (4) and (5) of the foregoing Regulation shall have effect in relation to functions under this Regulation as they have effect in relation to functions under that Regulation.

Employment in ports

5.—(1) This Regulation shall apply to any port, or part of a port, specified in a direction given by the Secretary of State for Employment and for the time being in force, but not otherwise.

(2) Notwithstanding anything in any dock labour scheme or in section 1 of the Docks and Harbours Act 1966(**b**) (additional control of employment of dock workers), any employer, whether registered under such a scheme or not, and whether he holds a licence under that Act or not, may at any port—

(*a*) employ on dock work any person whom he has been requested by the Secretary of State to employ on such work ;

(*b*) employ any person on any such dock work, or dock work of any such class, as may be approved by the Secretary of State for the purposes of this Regulation ;

and such employment shall not constitute a contravention, either on the part of the employer or of the person employed, of any provision of any dock labour scheme or section 1 of that Act.

(3) Where the Secretary of State gives to an employer notice in writing that this paragraph is to apply to him, all earnings properly due to any person employed by that employer in the circumstances mentioned in sub-paragraph (*a*) of the last foregoing paragraph shall be paid to him by the Secretary of State as agent of the employer, and the employer shall, in such manner and at such time and place as may be directed by the Secretary of State,—

(*a*) furnish a statement of the gross wages (including overtime and allowances and without deductions of any kind) due to that person from the employer and of the period in respect of which they are due ; and

(**a**) 1894 c. 60. (**b**) 1966 c. 28.

(*b*) pay to the Secretary of State the total amount of the gross wages so due, and such further amount, calculated either by way of percentage of the gross wages or otherwise, as the Secretary of State may by notice require as a contribution towards the administrative expenses of the Secretary of State under this Regulation.

(4) If under Regulation 3 of these Regulations the Secretary of State appoints a Port Emergency Committee for a port to which this Regulation applies in whole or in part or for a group of ports of which that port is one, he may authorise that Committee to exercise on his behalf in relation to that port all or any of his functions under this Regulation ; and paragraph (5) of that Regulation shall have effect in relation to functions under this Regulation as it has effect in relation to functions under that Regulation.

(5) Where any person employed by the National Dock Labour Board for the purpose of the administration of a dock labour scheme performs services for the Secretary of State or a Port Emergency Committee under this Regulation, the performance of those services shall be deemed to have been authorised by the Board as part of his employment, and the Secretary of State shall pay to the Board such sums as may, in default of agreement, be determined by arbitration in respect of—

(*a*) the remuneration and allowances payable to that person by the Board for the period during which that person performs such services for the Secretary of State or Committee ; and

(*b*) the amount of the employer's contribution in respect of that person for that period and in respect of payments of his remuneration for that period.

(6) The Secretary of State, and, if any of his functions under this Regulation are delegated to a Port Emergency Committee for a port or for a group of ports, that Committee, shall be furnished by the National Dock Labour Board with such office accommodation and equipment as appears to the Secretary of State to be requisite for the proper exercise and performance of his functions under this Regulation, and the Secretary of State shall pay to the Board in respect of the use of that accommodation and equipment such sums as may, in default of agreement, be determined by arbitration.

(7) A direction given by the Secretary of State for Employment with respect to any port under paragraph (1) of this Regulation may be revoked by a subsequent direction given by him, and thereupon this Regulation shall cease to apply to that port, without prejudice to the giving of a new direction in relation thereto:

Provided that the revocation of such a direction with respect to any port or part thereof shall not affect the previous operation of this Regulation in relation to that port or part thereof, or the validity of any action taken thereunder, or any penalty or punishment incurred in respect of any contravention or failure to comply therewith, or any proceeding or remedy in respect of any such punishment or penalty.

(8) In this Regulation "dock labour scheme" means a scheme for the time being in force under the Dock Workers (Regulation of Employment)

Act 1946(**a**), "dock work", in relation to a port, means work which is treated for the purposes of a dock labour scheme as dock work at that port, and "the employer's contribution" means the employer's contribution (including any graduated contribution) under the National Insurance Act 1965(**b**), the National Insurance (Industrial Injuries) Act 1965(**c**), the National Health Service Contributions Act 1965(**d**) and section 27 of the Redundancy Payments Act 1965(**e**).

RELAXATION OF RESTRICTIONS AS TO USE OF ROAD VEHICLES

Goods vehicle licences

6. A goods vehicle with respect to which an operator's licence under Part V of the Transport Act 1968(**f**) is required, but no such licence is in force, may, notwithstanding anything in that Act, be used on a road for the carriage of goods for hire or reward, or for or in connection with any trade of business carried on by any person, so long as the use of the vehicle is under, and in accordance with, any general or special authority granted for the purposes of this paragraph by or on behalf of the Secretary of State.

Public service vehicle licences, road service licences, &c.

7.—(1) Notwithstanding anything in section 127 of the Road Traffic Act 1960(**g**), no public service vehicle licence shall be necessary for the use of a motor vehicle on a road as a stage carriage, an express carriage or a contract carriage so long as the use of the vehicle is under, and in accordance with, any general or special authority granted for the purposes of this paragraph by or on behalf of the Secretary of State.

(2) Notwithstanding anything in section 134 of the Road Traffic Act 1960, a vehicle may be used as a stage carriage or an express carriage otherwise than under a road service licence or a permit granted under section 30 of the Transport Act 1968, so long as the use of the vehicle is under, and in accordance with, any general or special authority granted for the purposes of this paragraph by or on behalf of the Secretary of State.

(3) So much of section 101 of the Road Traffic Act 1930(**h**) as requires the consent of a dock authority or a harbour authority to the running by a local authority of a public service vehicle on a road vested in a dock authority or harbour authority shall not apply so long as the running of the vehicle is under, and in accordance with, any general or special authority granted for the purposes of this paragraph by or on behalf of the Secretary of State.

(4) Notwithstanding anything in section 23 of the Transport (London) Act 1969(**i**), a vehicle may be used to provide a London bus service (as defined by subsection (7) of that section) otherwise than in pursuance of an agreement with, or consent granted by, the London Transport Executive, so long as the use of the vehicle is under, and in accordance with, any general or special authority granted for the purposes of this paragraph by or on behalf of the Secretary of State.

(**a**) 1946 c. 22 (**b**) 1965 c. 51. (**c**) 1965 c. 52. (**d**) 1965 c. 54. (**e**) 1965 c. 62.
(**f**) 1968 c. 73. (**g**) 1960 c. 16. (**h**) 1930 c. 43. (**i**) 1969 c. 35.

Other provisions as to road passenger vehicles

8.—(1) Nothing in section 144 of the Road Traffic Act 1960, in section 10 of the London Hackney Carriages Act 1843(**a**), in section 8 of the Metropolitan Public Carriage Act 1869(**b**), in section 48 of the Tramways Act 1870(**c**) or any rules or regulations thereunder, in Schedule 5 to the Burgh Police (Scotland) Act 1892(**d**) or in any local Act or any regulations or other instrument made or issued under any local Act shall apply so as to prevent any person from driving or acting as conductor of a vehicle although he is not licensed for the purpose so long as he is doing so under, and in accordance with, any general or special authority granted for the purposes of this paragraph by or on behalf of the Secretary of State.

(2) Notwithstanding anything in any enactment (whether public general or local) or in any regulations or other instrument made or issued under any enactment (whether public general or local) or in any condition of any road service licence—

(*a*) passengers may be carried (whether standing or otherwise) on any public service vehicle, tramcar or trolley vehicle without limit of number, and

(*b*) any public service vehicle, tramcar or trolley vehicle may be operated without a conductor's being carried thereon,

so long as the carriage of the passengers or, as the case may be, the operation of the vehicle is under, and in accordance with, any general or special authority granted for the purposes of this paragraph by or on behalf of the Secretary of State.

Construction and use regulations

9. Notwithstanding anything in section 40 of the Road Traffic Act 1972(**e**), a person may use on a road, or cause or permit to be so used, a motor vehicle or trailer which does not comply with regulations made or having effect as if made under the said section 40 so long as the use of the vehicle is under, and in accordance with, a special authority granted for the purposes of this Regulation by or on behalf of the Secretary of State.

Test and plating certificates

10.—(1) Notwithstanding anything in section 44 of the Road Traffic Act 1972, a person may use on a road, or cause or permit to be so used, a motor vehicle to which that section applies, and in respect of which no test certificate has been issued as therein mentioned, so long as the use of the vehicle is under, and in accordance with, any general or special authority granted for the purposes of this paragraph by or on behalf of the Secretary of State.

(2) Nothing in regulations made or having effect as if made under section 52(1) of the Road Traffic Act 1972 (which require the production of an effective test certificate or the making of a prescribed declaration on application for a vehicle excise licence for a vehicle) shall apply where the Secretary of State is satisfied that the vehicle is being used, or is to be used, under and in accordance with any general or special authority granted for the purposes of paragraph (1) of this Regulation.

(3) Notwithstanding anything in section 46 of the Road Traffic Act 1972, a person may use on a road, or cause or permit to be so used,—

(*a*) a goods vehicle which is of a class required by regulations under section 45 of that Act to have been submitted for examination for plating, and in respect of which no plating certificate is for the time being in force, or

(**a**) 1843 c. 86. (**b**) 1869 c. 115 (**c**) 1870 c. 78. (**d**) 1892 c. 55. (**e**) 1972 c. 20.

(*b*) a goods vehicle which is of a class required by such regulations to have been submitted for a goods vehicle test, and in respect of which no goods vehicle test certificate is for the time being in force,

so long as (in either case) the use of that vehicle is under, and in accordance with, any general or special authority granted for the purposes of this paragraph by or on behalf of the Secretary of State.

(4) Notwithstanding anything in section 51 of the Road Traffic Act 1972, a person may use a goods vehicle on a road for drawing a trailer, or cause or permit a goods vehicle to be so used, where the plating certificate issued for the goods vehicle does not specify a maximum laden weight for the vehicle together with any trailer which may be drawn by it, so long as the use of the vehicle for drawing the trailer is under, and in accordance with, any general or special authority granted for the purposes of this paragraph by or on behalf of the Secretary of State.

(5) Nothing in regulations made or having effect as if made under section 52(2) of the Road Traffic Act 1972 (which require the production of an effective goods vehicle test certificate, or a certificate of temporary exemption, or the making of a prescribed declaration, on application for a vehicle excise licence for a vehicle) shall apply where the Secretary of State is satisfied that the vehicle is being used, or is to be used, under and in accordance with any general or special authority granted for the purposes of paragraph (3) of this Regulation.

(6) Section 162(1) of the Road Traffic Act 1972 (which imposes requirements with respect to the production of certain documents) shall not, so far as it relates to the production of a test certificate, a plating certificate or a goods vehicle test certificate, apply in the case of a motor vehicle used under, and in accordance with, any general or special authority granted under this Regulation.

(7) In this Regulation " test certificate " has the meaning assigned to it by section 43(2) of the Road Traffic Act 1972, and " plating certificate " and " goods vehicle test certificate " have the meanings assigned to them by section 45(1) of that Act.

Drivers' hours

11.—(1) Nothing in subsections (1) to (6) of section 96 of the Transport Act 1968 (which relate to a driver's permitted hours and periods of duty and rest) shall apply to a driver so long as he is acting under, and in accordance with, any general or special authority granted for the purposes of this paragraph by or on behalf of the Secretary of State.

(2) Nothing in regulations under section 98 of the said Act—

(*a*) which concerns the entering of a current record in a driver's record book, or

(*b*) which requires a driver to have such a book in his possession,

shall apply to a driver so long as he is acting under, and in accordance with, any general or special authority granted for the purposes of this paragraph by or on behalf of the Secretary of State.

(3) An authority under paragraph (1) or paragraph (2) above may, instead of conferring all of the exemptions specified in the paragraph, confer only such exemptions as are specified in the authority.

Driver's licences

12.—(1) Notwithstanding anything in section 4 of the Road Traffic Act 1972 or in Part III or Part IV of that Act, a person who holds a valid licence granted under Part III of that Act authorising him to drive a motor car may drive on a road, and may be employed by another person so to drive, a vehicle to which this Regulation applies, so long as he drives it under, and in accordance with, a general or special authority granted for the purposes of this Regulation by or on behalf of the Secretary of State.

(2) The vehicles to which this Regulation applies are—

(*a*) heavy locomotives ;

(*b*) light locomotives ;

(*c*) motor tractors ;

(*d*) heavy motor cars ; and

(*e*) motor cars so constructed that a trailer may by partial superimposition be attached thereto in such a manner as to cause a substantial part of the weight of the trailer to be borne thereby.

(3) So much of any regulations for the time being in force and having effect as if made under section 119 of the Road Traffic Act 1972 as requires any person, or enables any person to be required, to produce a heavy goods vehicle driver's licence shall not apply in the case of a vehicle driven under, and in accordance with, any general or special authority granted under this Regulation.

(4) In this Regulation " heavy goods vehicle driver's licence " means a licence under Part IV of the Road Traffic Act 1972, and any expression which is defined in section 190 of that Act has the meaning assigned to it by that section.

Excise licences

13.—(1) Notwithstanding anything in the Vehicles (Excise) Act 1971(**a**), a person may use or keep on a public road a mechanically propelled vehicle without there being in force and fixed to and exhibited on that vehicle a licence issued under that Act for or in respect of the use of that vehicle, so long as the use or keeping of the vehicle is under, and in accordance with, any general or special authority granted for the purposes of this paragraph by or on behalf of the Secretary of State.

(2) Where an excise licence issued or having effect under the Vehicles (Excise) Act 1971 is in force with respect to any mechanically propelled vehicle, the uses of that vehicle which are authorised by the licence shall be deemed to extend to any use made of the vehicle under, and in accordance with, any general or special authority granted for the purposes of this paragraph by or on behalf of the Secretary of State, and the provisions of section 18 of that Act shall not apply to any use of any vehicle in respect of which such a licence is in force so long as that use of that vehicle is under, and in accordance with, any such general or special authority.

Third-party insurance

14.—(1) Notwithstanding anything in section 143(1) of the Road Traffic Act 1972, a person may use, or cause or permit another person to use, a motor vehicle on a road without there being in force in relation to the use thereof by that person or that other person, as the case may be, a policy of insurance or security in respect of third-party risks issued or given for the purposes of Part VI of that Act so long as—

(*a*) there is in force in relation to some other use of the vehicle a policy of insurance or security issued or given for those purposes and the use of the vehicle by that person or that other person, as the case may be,—

(**a**) 1971 c. 10.

(i) is one to which, as respects the period of the emergency, the policy or security is, by arrangement between the Secretary of State and the issuer or giver of the policy or security or some person acting on his behalf, treated as also relating, and

(ii) is under, and in accordance with, any general or special authority granted for the purposes of this paragraph by or on behalf of the Secretary of State ; or

(*b*) the use of the vehicle by that person or that other person, as the case may be, is under, and in accordance with, any such general or special authority and there is in force in relation to the use of the vehicle such an agreement to insure or make good failures to discharge liability in respect of third-party risks as may be specified in the authority ;

and sections 162(1) and 166(1) of the said Act of 1972 (which impose requirements with respect to the furnishing of the names and addresses of the driver and the owner of a motor vehicle and to the production of certificates of insurance or security) shall not, so far as they relate to the production of such certificates, apply in the case of a motor vehicle driven under, and in accordance with, any such general or special authority.

(2) So much of any regulations made or having effect as if made by virtue of section 153 of the Road Traffic Act 1972 as, on an application for a vehicle excise licence requires the production of a certificate of insurance, or evidence that the necessary security has been given or that the vehicle is exempt from the provisions of section 143 of the said Act, shall not apply where the Secretary of State is satisfied that the vehicle is being used, or is to be used, under, and in accordance with, any general or special authority granted for the purposes of paragraph (1) of this Regulation.

Transport of petroleum-spirit and other substances

15.—(1) Regulations made under section 6 of the Petroleum (Consolidation) Act 1928(**a**) (regulations as to the conveyance of petroleum-spirit by road) shall not have effect in relation to any vehicle, so long as the use of the vehicle is under, and in accordance with, any general or special authority granted for the purposes of this paragraph by or on behalf of the Secretary of State.

(2) Without prejudice to the foregoing paragraph, regulations made under that section, in so far as they are made for any of the purposes specified in subsection (1)(*d*) of that section, shall not have effect in relation to the loading or unloading of vehicles at any place, so long as that place is used under, and in accordance with, any general or special authority granted for the purposes of this paragraph by or on behalf of the Secretary of State.

(3) In this Regulation any reference to section 6 of the Petroleum (Consolidation) Act 1928 shall be construed as including a reference to that section as read with section 19 of that Act (which confers power to apply the Act to substances other than petroleum-spirit) and any Order in Council made thereunder which is for the time being in force, and any reference in this Regulation to regulations under section 6 of that Act shall be construed accordingly.

PUBLIC SERVICES AND FACILITIES

Transport services and facilities

16. The British Railways Board and the London Transport Executive may respectively, to such extent as appears to them to be necessary or expedient for providing or maintaining railway services and facilities in a manner

(**a**) 1928 c. 32.

best calculated to promote the public interest, disregard any obligation imposed by or under any enactment—

(*a*) to carry goods or passengers or to provide transport services or facilities ;

(*b*) to employ or provide a person for any particular purpose or to perform any particular duty ; or

(*c*) to keep gates on a level crossing over a public road closed across the road ;

so long as, in so doing, they are acting under, and in accordance with, any general or special authority granted for the purposes of this Regulation by or on behalf of the Secretary of State.

Electricity supply

17.—(1) Any Electricity Board may, to such extent as appears to them to be necessary or expedient for maintaining or making the best use of supplies of electricity available for distribution or for conserving and making the best use of supplies of fuel or power available for the generation of electricity, disregard or fall short in discharging any obligation imposed by or under any enactment, or any contractual obligation—

(*a*) to give or continue to give supplies of electricity ; or

(*b*) to supply electricity in accordance with standards prescribed by or under the enactment or contract in question ;

so long as, in so doing, they are acting under, and in accordance with, any general or special authority granted for the purposes of this Regulation by or on behalf of the Secretary of State.

(2) If and so far as it appears to the Secretary of State necessary or expedient for maintaining or making the best use of supplies of electricity available for distribution—

(*a*) he may give to the person carrying on business at, or appearing to be in charge of, or occupying, any premises, directions for regulating or prohibiting consumption of electricity on the premises ; and

(*b*) he may take, or authorise any person acting on his behalf to take, such steps as appear appropriate to cut off any supply of electricity.

(3) Without prejudice to the generality of the provisions of Regulation 40(2) below, the power of giving directions conferred by paragraph (2)(*a*) above may be exercised by means of an order—

(*a*) applicable to premises of any class or description specified in the order, or premises used for purposes of any class or description specified in the order, or

(*b*) where previous directions have been given otherwise than by order, applicable to the persons or premises as respects which the previous directions had effect, or such of them as may be specified in the order.

(4) If any person, without authority duly given by or on behalf of the Secretary of State, reconnects a supply cut off in pursuance of this Regulation, he shall be guilty of an offence against this Regulation.

(5) The Secretary of State may authorise any person acting on his behalf to enter any premises, if necessary by force, for the purpose—

(*a*) of ascertaining whether there has been any contravention of a direction under this Regulation, or

(*b*) of cutting off any supply of electricity in pursuance of this Regulation, or of ascertaining whether it remains duly cut off.

(6) The provisions of this Regulation are without prejudice to the generality of Regulation 21 below (regulation of consumption and supply of electricity and other products).

(7) The powers of the Secretary of State under paragraph (2) of this Regulation shall also be exercisable by such persons, being either servants of the Crown or persons acting on behalf of Her Majesty, as may be designated for the purposes of that paragraph by the Secretary of State, and references in that paragraph to the Secretary of State shall be construed accordingly.

Gas supply

18.—(1) The British Gas Corporation may, to such extent as appears to them to be necessary or expedient—

(*a*) for maintaining or making the best use of supplies of gas available for distribution ; or

(*b*) for conserving and making the best use of supplies of fuel or other material available for the manufacture of gas ; or

(*c*) for preserving public safety ;

disregard or fall short in discharging any obligation imposed by or under any enactment, or any contractual obligation—

(i) to give or continue to give supplies of gas ; or

(ii) to supply, transmit or distribute gas in accordance with standards prescribed by or under the enactment or contract in question ;

so long as, in so doing, they are acting under, and in accordance with, any general or special authority granted for the purposes of this paragraph by or on behalf of the Secretary of State.

(2) If and so far as it appears to the Secretary of State necessary or expedient for any of the purposes set out in sub-paragraphs (*a*), (*b*) and (*c*) of paragraph (1) above—

(*a*) he may give to the person carrying on business at, or appearing to be in charge of, or occupying, any premises, directions for regulating or prohibiting the consumption of gas on the premises ; and

(*b*) he may take, or authorise any person acting on his behalf to take, such steps as appear appropriate to cut off any supply, or means of supply, of gas by disconnecting any service pipe or by any other means.

(3) If any person, without authority duly given by or on behalf of the Secretary of State, reconnects a supply, or means of supply, cut off in pursuance of this Regulation, he shall be guilty of an offence against this Regulation.

(4) The Secretary of State may authorise any person acting on his behalf to enter any premises, if necessary by force, for the purpose—

(*a*) of ascertaining whether there has been any contravention of a direction under this Regulation,

(*b*) of cutting off any supply, or means of supply, of gas in pursuance of this Regulation, or of ascertaining whether it remains duly cut off, or

(*c*) of inspecting, examining or testing any plant or equipment for the supply or consumption of gas with a view to ensuring the preservation of public safety.

(5) The provisions of this Regulation are without prejudice to the generality of Regulation 21 below (regulation of consumption and supply of gas and other products).

(6) The powers of the Secretary of State under paragraphs (2) to (4) above shall also be exercisable by such persons, being either servants of the Crown or persons acting on behalf of Her Majesty, as may be designated for the purposes of those paragraphs by the Secretary of State, and references in those paragraphs to the Secretary of State shall be construed accordingly.

Water supply and resources

19.—(1) Any statutory water undertakers, regional water board or water development board may, for the purpose of maintaining supplies of water in any locality, disregard any restriction imposed by or under any enactment or rule of law with respect to the taking of water from any source or any obligation so imposed with respect to the discharge of compensation water, and may for that purpose take water from any source, so long as, in either case, in so doing, they are acting under, and in accordance with, any general or special authority granted for the purposes of this paragraph by or on behalf of the Secretary of State.

(2) Any statutory water undertakers, regional water board or water development board may, to such extent as appears to them to be necessary or expedient for conserving and making the best use of supplies of water in any locality, disregard or fall short in discharging any obligation imposed by or under any enactment or rule of law with respect to the provision by them of supplies of water (including, in particular, but without prejudice to the generality of the foregoing words, any obligation with respect to the filtration or other treatment of water or the pressure at which water is to be supplied) so long as, in so doing, they are acting under, and in accordance with, any general or special authority granted for the purposes of this paragraph by or on behalf of the Secretary of State.

(3) In the exercise of their new functions under the Water Resources Act 1963(a), any river authority may, for the purpose of maintaining supplies of water in any locality, disregard any restriction or obligation imposed by or under any enactment or rule of law with respect to—

(*a*) the taking or impounding of water from any source,

(*b*) the discharge of water into any inland water or underground strata, or

(*c*) in connection with their functions, the construction or alteration of any works,

and may for that purpose take or impound water from any source, or discharge water into any inland water or underground strata ; but the powers conferred by this paragraph shall only be exercisable so long as in exercising them the authority are acting under, and in accordance with, any general or special authority granted for the purposes of this paragraph by or on behalf of the Secretary of State.

(4) The Secretary of State may give any river authority, statutory water undertakers, regional water board or water development board or any other person managing an undertaking or business which is directly or indirectly concerned with the supply, abstraction or impounding of water such directions as appear to him to be necessary or expedient for maintaining and making the best use in the public interest of supplies of water, and, without prejudice to the generality of the foregoing, directions under this paragraph may—

(*a*) require the provision or continued provision, or regulate or prohibit the provision, of supplies of water by any such person to any person or class of persons specified in the directions ;

(*b*) require, regulate or prohibit the carrying out of any works or class of works so specified, either generally or during or within a time so specified.

(5) Where any directions have been given under paragraph (4) above and those directions are not complied with within the time specified in the directions or, if no time is so specified, are not complied with within a reasonable

(a) 1963 c. 38.

time, the Secretary of State may take such steps as he considers appropriate in the circumstances for effecting anything which would have been effected if the directions had been complied with.

(6) Without prejudice to the generality of paragraph (5) above, the steps which may be taken by virtue of that paragraph in respect of any directions shall include entering upon, taking possession of, moving or using any apparatus, vehicle, premises or other property to which the directions related by such means as the Secretary of State determines to be appropriate.

(7) Where any steps are taken by virtue of paragraph (5) or (6) above in respect of any directions, the Secretary of State may recover from the person to whom the directions were given such reasonable charges in respect of expenses incurred by him in taking those steps, or in consequence of having taken them, as may be agreed or as may, in default of agreement, be determined by arbitration.

(8) The powers of the Secretary of State under paragraphs (4) to (7) above shall also be exercisable by such persons, being either servants of the Crown or persons acting on behalf of Her Majesty, as may be designated for the purposes of those paragraphs by the Secretary of State, and references in these paragraphs to the Secretary of State shall be construed accordingly.

Sewerage and sewage disposal

20.—(1) Any sewerage authority may, for the purpose of effectively draining their district and dealing with the contents of their sewers, disregard any prohibition or restriction imposed by or under any enactment or rule of law with respect to the discharge of foul or surface water into any natural or artificial stream, watercourse, canal, pond or lake, so long as, in so doing, they are acting under, and in accordance with, any general or special authority granted for the purposes of this Regulation by or on behalf of the Secretary of State.

(2) The Secretary of State may give any sewerage authority or any other person managing an undertaking or business which is directly or indirectly concerned in sewerage or sewage disposal in a sewerage authority's district such directions as appear to him to be necessary or expedient for securing the most effective draining of the sewerage authority's district or of dealing with the contents of the sewers there and, without prejudice to the generality of the foregoing, directions under this paragraph may require, regulate or prohibit the carrying out of any works or class of works specified in the directions, either generally or during or within a time so specified.

(3) Where any directions have been given under paragraph (2) above and those directions are not complied with within the time specified in the directions or, if no time is so specified, are not complied with within a reasonable time, the Secretary of State may take such steps as he considers appropriate in the circumstances for effecting anything which would have been effected if the directions had been complied with.

(4) Without prejudice to the generality of paragraph (3) above, the steps which may be taken by virtue of that paragraph in respect of any directions shall include entering upon, taking possession of, moving or using any ship or other vessel, apparatus, vehicle, premises or other property to which the directions related by such means as the Secretary of State determines to be appropriate.

(5) Where any steps are taken by virtue of paragraph (3) or (4) above in respect of any directions, the Secretary of State may recover from the person to whom the directions were given such reasonable charges in respect of

expenses incurred by him in taking those steps, or in consequence of having taken them, as may be agreed or as may, in default of agreement, be determined by arbitration.

(6) The powers of the Secretary of State under paragraphs (2) to (5) above shall also be exercisable by such persons, being either servants of the Crown or persons acting on behalf of Her Majesty, as may be designated for the purposes of those paragraphs by the Secretary of State, and references in those paragraphs to the Secretary of State shall be construed accordingly.

(7) In Part VIII of the Merchant Shipping Act 1894 (liability of ship-owners) " owner ", in relation to any ship, shall be construed as including the Secretary of State or other person by whom any steps are taken in relation to the ship by virtue of paragraphs (3) to (6) above.

In this paragraph " ship " has the same meaning as in Part VIII of that Act.

CONSUMPTION AND SUPPLY

Supply, &c., of fuel, refinery products, electricity, gas and water

21.—(1) The Secretary of State may by order provide for regulating or prohibiting—

(*a*) the supply, acquisition or consumption of solid or liquid fuel or refinery products ;

(*b*) the supply or consumption of electricity or gas ; or

(*c*) the supply, acquisition, abstraction, impounding or consumption of water.

(2) References in this Regulation to consumption are references to consumption for any purposes whatsoever, whether domestic, industrial or other.

Directions as to solid or liquid fuel or refinery products

22.—(1) The Secretary of State—

(*a*) may give to any person carrying on business as a supplier of liquid fuel or as a supplier of solid fuel directions as to the supply by him of any such solid or liquid fuel as may be specified in the directions, and

(*b*) may give to any person carrying on business as a refiner of liquid fuel directions as to the production of any liquid fuel, or other refinery products, or as to the use, disposal or supply of any refinery products, including those forming part of any stock held by him for the purposes of his business.

(2) Directions under paragraph (1) of this Regulation may in particular—

(*a*) require any fuel or refinery product to be supplied, in accordance with such requirements as may be specified in the directions, to such persons as may be so specified, or

(*b*) prohibit or restrict the supply of any fuel or refinery product to persons so specified, or to persons other than those to be supplied in accordance with the directions,

and directions may be given under paragraph (1)(*b*) of this Regulation for securing that the liquid fuel produced is, or is to any extent, of a description specified in the direction.

(3) Where any fuel or refinery product is supplied to any person in pursuance of a direction under this Regulation, that person shall pay such price in respect thereof as may be reasonable.

(4) The foregoing provisions of this Regulation shall apply in relation to any person carrying on a trade or business (otherwise than as a supplier of fuel) for the purposes of which he is in possession of a stock of solid fuel, as if, in respect of that fuel, he were carrying on business as such a supplier; and any directions to such a person under this Regulation may include directions prohibiting the consumption of such fuel by him:

Provided that in relation to any such person any reference in this Regulation to supply shall be construed as a reference to delivery at the place where the fuel is kept.

Maximum prices for food and animal feeding stuffs

23. The Minister of Agriculture, Fisheries and Food may by order provide for regulating, to such extent and in such manner as may be specified in the order, the maximum prices which may be charged for such foods or animal feeding stuffs as may be so specified.

Distribution of food and animal feeding stuffs

24.—(1) The Minister of Agriculture, Fisheries and Food may give to any person carrying on business as a supplier of food or animal feeding stuffs directions as to the persons to whom he is to supply any such food or animal feeding stuffs as may be specified in the directions; and any such directions may in particular require any food or animal feeding stuffs to be supplied to such persons as may be specified in the directions in accordance with such requirements as may be so specified or may, to such extent as may be specified in the directions, prohibit the supply of food or animal feeding stuffs to persons so specified.

(2) Where anything is supplied to any person in pursuance of directions under this Regulation, that person shall pay such price in respect thereof as may be reasonable.

Supply of medicines

25.—(1) The restrictions and prohibitions imposed by or under the following provisions of the Medicines Act 1968(**a**), that is to say—

(*a*) Part II (licences and certificates relating to medicinal products),

(*b*) Part III (dealings with medicinal products), and

(*c*) Part V (containers, packages and identification of medicinal products),

shall not apply to a person so long as he is acting under, and in accordance with, any general or special authority granted for the purposes of this paragraph by or on behalf of the Secretary of State, or the Minister of Agriculture, Fisheries and Food.

(2) Nothing in any regulations made, or having effect, under the Medicines Act 1971(**b**) shall require the payment of a fee on an application made under and in accordance with, any general of special authority granted for the purposes of this paragraph by or on behalf of the Secretary of State, or the Minister of Agriculture, Fisheries and Food.

(3) An authority under paragraph (1) above may, instead of conferring exemptions from all the restrictions and prohibitions specified in the paragraph, confer only such exemptions as are specified in the authority.

(**a**) 1968 c. 67. (**b**) 1971 c. 69.

REGULATION OF TRANSPORT SERVICES

Transport of goods by road or rail

26.—(1) The Secretary of State may give to any person carrying on business as a carrier of goods by road or by rail for hire or reward directions as to the goods which are to be carried by him ; and any such directions may in particular require any essential goods to be carried for such persons, from and to such places, and in accordance with such requirements, as may be specified in the directions or may, to such extent as may be so specified, prohibit the carriage of goods for persons, or from or to places, so specified.

(2) Where in pursuance of directions given under this Regulation any goods are carried for the benefit of any person, that person shall pay such charge in respect of the carriage as may be reasonable.

(3) The powers of the Secretary of State under this Regulation shall also be exercisable by such persons, being either servants of the Crown or persons acting on behalf of Her Majesty, as may be designated for the purposes of this Regulation by the Secretary of State.

(4) The foregoing provisions of this Regulation shall apply in relation to any person carrying on a trade or business (otherwise than as a carrier of goods by road for hire or reward) for or in connection with which he uses any goods vehicles, as if, in respect of those vehicles, he were carrying on business as such a carrier of goods ; and any directions to such a person under this Regulation may include directions prohibiting the carriage of goods in the course of his own trade or business.

Transport of passengers by road or rail

27.—(1) The Secretary of State may give to any person carrying on the business of operating public service vehicles directions as to the passengers who are to be carried, or the road services which are to be provided, by him ; and any such directions may in particular require persons to be carried from and to places specified in the directions or may, to such extent as may be so specified, prohibit the carriage of persons from or to places so specified and may also specify requirements in accordance with which passengers are to be carried or, as the case may be, road services are to be provided.

(2) The Secretary of State may give to any person carrying on business as a carrier of passengers by rail directions as to the passengers who are to be carried by him, and any such directions may in particular require persons to be carried from and to places specified in the directions or may, to such extent as may be so specified, prohibit the carriage of persons from or to places so specified.

(3) Where in pursuance of directions given under this Regulation any passengers are carried for the benefit of any other person otherwise than at separate fares, that person shall pay such charge in respect of the carriage as may be reasonable.

(4) The powers of the Secretary of State under this Regulation shall also be exercisable by such persons, being either servants of the Crown or persons acting on behalf of Her Majesty, as may be designated for the purposes of this Regulation by the Secretary of State.

(5) The reference in this Regulation to public service vehicles shall be construed in accordance with sections 117 and 118 of the Road Traffic Act 1960.

Air transport

28.—(1) The Secretary of State may give to any person providing air transport services (being a person whose sole or principal place of business is in Great Britain) directions as to the passengers or cargo which are to be carried by him ; and any such directions in particular—

(*a*) may require any persons engaged in the performance of essential services to be carried from and to such places, and in accordance with such requirements, as may be specified in the directions or may, to such extent as may be so specified, prohibit the carriage of passengers from or to places so specified ;

(*b*) may require any essential goods to be carried for such persons, from and to such places, and in accordance with such requirements, as may be so specified or may, to such extent as may be so specified, prohibit the carriage of goods for persons, or from or to places, so specified.

(2) No air transport licence shall be required for a flight undertaken for the purpose of complying with directions given under this Regulation.

(3) Where in pursuance of directions given under this Regulation any passenger is carried, he (or, if he is carried for the benefit of any other person, that person) shall pay such charge in respect of the carriage as may be reasonable ; and where in pursuance of any such directions any goods are carried for the benefit of any person, that person shall pay such charge in respect of the carriage as may be reasonable.

(4) The powers of the Secretary of State under this Regulation shall also be exercisable by such persons, being either servants of the Crown or persons acting on behalf of Her Majesty, as may be designated for the purposes of this Regulation by the Secretary of State.

Transport by sea

29.—(1) The Secretary of State may give to any person having the management of a ship to which this Regulation applies (being a person in Great Britain or a person whose sole or principal place of business is in Great Britain) directions prohibiting that ship from proceeding to sea from any port in Great Britain except upon such voyages, or subject to such conditions as to the cargoes or classes of cargoes which may be carried in the ship, or as to the passengers who may be so carried, as may be specified in the directions.

(2) This Regulation applies to any ship registered in the United Kingdom, the Channel Islands or the Isle of Man.

(3) The powers of the Secretary of State under this Regulation shall also be exercisable by such persons, being either servants of the Crown or persons acting on behalf of Her Majesty, as may be designated for the purposes of this Regulation by the Secretary of State.

REQUISITIONING OF CHATTELS AND TAKING POSSESSION OF LAND

Requisitioning of chattels

30.—(1) A competent authority, if it appears to that authority to be necessary or expedient so to do for any of the purposes specified in section 2(1) of the Emergency Powers Act 1920, may requisition any chattel in Great Britain (including any vehicle, vessel or aircraft or anything on board a vehicle, vessel or aircraft and including also any detachable part of any vehicle or aircraft) and may give such directions as appear to the competent authority to be necessary or expedient in connection with the requisition.

(2) Where a competent authority requisitions any chattel under this Regulation, the competent authority may use or deal with, or authorise the use of, or dealing with, the chattel for such purpose and in such manner as the competent authority thinks expedient for any of the purposes specified in the said section 2(1) and may hold, or sell or otherwise dispose of, the chattel as if the competent authority were the owner thereof and as if the chattel were free from any mortgage, pledge, lien or other similar obligation.

(3) The powers conferred by the foregoing provisions of this Regulation on a competent authority shall also be exercisable by such persons, being either servants of the Crown or persons acting on behalf of Her Majesty, as may be designated for the purposes of those provisions by the competent authority, and references in those provisions to the competent authority shall be construed accordingly.

(4) Where a chattel is requisitioned under this Regulation, the competent authority shall pay to the owner of the chattel and to any other person interested in the chattel who suffers damage owing to the requisition such compensation as may be agreed or as may, in default of agreement, be determined by arbitration to be just having regard to all the circumstances of the particular case, so, however, that in assessing the compensation no account shall be taken of any appreciation of the value of the chattel due to the emergency.

(5) For the purposes of this Regulation, any of the following Ministers and authorities shall be a competent authority, that is to say, the Secretary of State, the Minister of Agriculture, Fisheries and Food and the Minister of Posts and Telecommunications.

Taking possession of land

31.—(1) The Secretary of State, if it appears to him to be necessary or expedient so to do for any of the purposes specified in section 2(1) of the Emergency Powers Act 1920, may take possession of any land in Great Britain, and may give such directions as appear to him to be necessary or expedient in connection with the taking of possession of that land.

(2) While any land is in the possession of the Secretary of State by virtue of this Regulation, the land may, notwithstanding any restriction imposed on the use thereof (whether by any Act or other instrument or otherwise), be used by, or under the authority of, the Secretary of State for such purpose, and in such manner, as he thinks expedient for any of the purposes specified in the said section 2(1).

(3) Without prejudice to the last foregoing paragraph, the Secretary of State may, so far as appears to him to be necessary or expedient in connection with the taking of possession of any land in pursuance of this Regulation, or with the use of any land in the possession of the Secretary of State by virtue of this Regulation, do, or authorise persons using the land under the authority of the Secretary of State to do, in relation to the land anything which any person having an interest in the land would be entitled to do by virtue of that interest.

(4) In respect of land of which possession is taken under this Regulation, the Secretary of State shall pay to the person who would otherwise be entitled to possession of the land, and to any other person having an estate or interest in the land who suffers damage by reason of the taking of possession or of anything done in relation to the land while in the possession of the Secretary of State, such compensation as may be agreed or as may, in default of agreement, be determined by arbitration to be just having regard to all the circumstances of the particular case.

OFFENCES

Sabotage

32.—(1) No person shall do any act with intent to impair the efficiency or impede the working or movement of any vessel, aircraft, hovercraft, vehicle, machinery, apparatus or other thing used or intended to be used in the performance of essential services, or to impair the usefulness of any works, structure or premises used or intended to be used as aforesaid.

(2) The foregoing provisions of this Regulation shall apply in relation to any omission on the part of a person to do anything which he is under a duty, either to the public or to any person, to do, as they apply in relation to the doing of any act by a person.

Trespassing and loitering

33.—(1) No person shall trespass on, or on premises in the vicinity of, any premises used or appropriated for the purposes of essential services; and if any person is found trespassing on any premises in contravention of this paragraph, then, without prejudice to any proceedings which may be taken against him, he may be removed by the appropriate person from the premises.

(2) No person shall, for any purpose prejudicial to the public safety, be in, or in the vicinity of, any premises used or appropriated for the purposes of essential services; and where, in any proceedings taken against a person by virtue of this paragraph, it is proved that at the material time he was present in, or in the vicinity of, the premises concerned, the prosecution may thereupon adduce such evidence of the character of that person (including evidence of his having been previously convicted of any offence) as tends to show that he was so present for a purpose prejudicial to the public safety.

(3) No person loitering in the vicinity of any premises used or appropriated for the purposes of essential services shall continue to loiter in that vicinity after being requested by the appropriate person to leave it.

(4) In this Regulation the expression " the appropriate person " means—

(*a*) any person acting on behalf of Her Majesty,

(*b*) any constable,

(*c*) the occupier of the premises or any person authorised by the occupier.

Interference with Her Majesty's forces, constables and other persons performing essential services

34.—(1) No person shall do any act having reasonable cause to believe that it would be likely to endanger the safety of any member of Her Majesty's forces or of any constable or of any person who is charged with the exercise or performance of any power or duty under any of these Regulations or is performing essential services.

(2) No person shall—

(*a*) wilfully obstruct any person acting in the course of his duty as a constable, or exercising or performing any power or duty under any of these Regulations, or performing essential services; or

(*b*) do any act having reasonable cause to believe that it would be likely to prevent any person from, or mislead or interfere with any person in, performing his duty as a constable, or exercising or performing any power or duty under any of these Regulations, or performing essential services.

Inducing persons to withhold services

35. No person shall—

(*a*) do any act calculated to induce any member of Her Majesty's forces or constable to withhold his services or commit breaches of discipline; or

(*b*) with intent to contravene, or to aid, abet, counsel or procure a contravention of, paragraph (*a*) of this Regulation, have in his possession or under his control any document of such a nature that the dissemination of copies thereof among members of Her Majesty's forces or constables would constitute such a contravention.

SUPPLEMENTAL

Power to arrest without warrant

36. Where a constable, with reasonable cause, suspects that an offence against any of these Regulations has been committed, he may arrest without warrant anyone whom he, with reasonable cause, suspects to be guilty of the offence.

Attempts to commit offences and assisting offenders

37.—(1) Without prejudice to the operation of section 8 of the Accessories and Abettors Act 1861(**a**) and section 35 of the Magistrates' Courts Act 1952(**b**), any person who attempts to commit, conspires with any other person to commit, or does any act preparatory to the commission of, an offence against any of these Regulations shall be guilty of an offence against that Regulation.

(2) Any person who, knowing or having reasonable cause to believe that another person is guilty of an offence against any of these Regulations, gives that other person any assistance with intent thereby to prevent, hinder or interfere with the apprehension, trial or punishment of that person for the said offence shall be guilty of an offence against that Regulation.

(3) This Regulation shall, in its application to Scotland, have effect as if, for the references to section 8 of the Accessories and Abettors Act 1861 and section 35 of the Magistrates' Courts Act 1952, there were substituted a reference to any rule of law relating to art and part guilt.

Penalties and place of trial

38.—(1) If any person contravenes or fails to comply with any of these Regulations or any order made, direction given or requirement imposed under any of these Regulations, he shall be guilty of an offence against that Regulation; and a person guilty of an offence against any of these Regulations shall, on summary conviction, be liable to imprisonment for a term not exceeding three months or to a fine not exceeding £100, or to both:

Provided that a person shall not be guilty of an offence against any of these Regulations by reason only of his taking part in, or peacefully persuading any other person or persons to take part in, a strike.

(2) Proceedings in respect of an offence alleged to have been committed by a person against any of these Regulations may be taken before the appropriate court in Great Britain having jurisdiction in the place where that person is for the time being.

(**a**) 1861 c. 94. (**b**) 1952 c. 55.

Arbitrations

39. An arbitration under these Regulations shall, unless otherwise agreed, be the arbitration, in England and Wales, of a single arbitrator to be appointed by the Lord Chancellor and, in Scotland, of a single arbiter to be appointed by the Lord President of the Court of Session.

Provisions as to orders and directions

40.—(1) Any power conferred by these Regulations to make an order includes power to revoke or vary the order by a subsequent order.

(2) Any power of giving directions conferred by any provision of these Regulations may be exercised by means of an order applicable to all persons to whom directions may be given under that provision, or to such of them as fall within any class or description specified in the order.

Transitional provisions

41.—(1) In so far as any direction, authority, instruction or notice given, order or appointment made or other thing done under the Emergency Regulations 1973 could have been given, made or done under a corresponding provision of these Regulations, it shall not be invalidated by the expiry of those Regulations, but shall have effect as if it had been given, made or done under that corresponding provision.

(2) Any document referring to a provision of the Emergency Regulations 1973 shall, so far as is necessary for preserving the effect thereof, be construed as referring or as including a reference to the corresponding provision of these Regulations.

W. G. Agnew.

EXPLANATORY NOTE

(This Note is not part of the Regulations.)

These Regulations replace the Emergency Regulations 1973, which expire on the proclamation of the state of emergency, made on 13th November 1973, ceasing to have effect. Under the Emergency Powers Act 1920 such a proclamation does not remain in force for more than a month.

The present Regulations reproduce the provisions of the expiring Regulations. The only additions are the transitional provisions contained in Regulation 41.

1973 No. 2090

CONTROL OF FUEL AND ELECTRICITY

The Fuel and Electricity (Control) (Northern Ireland) Order 1973

Made - - -	12*th* *December* 1973
Laid before Parliament	12*th* *December* 1973
Coming into Operation	13*th* *December* 1973

At the Court at Buckingham Palace, the 12th day of December 1973

Present,

The Queen's Most Excellent Majesty in Council

Her Majesty, in exercise of the powers conferred by section 4(3) and (5) of the Fuel and Electricity (Control) Act 1973(**a**), and of all other powers enabling Her in that behalf, is pleased, by and with the advice of Her Privy Council, to order, and it is hereby ordered, as follows:—

1.–(1) This Order may be cited as the Fuel and Electricity (Control) (Northern Ireland) Order 1973 and shall come into operation on 13th December 1973.

(2) The Interpretation Act 1889(**b**) shall apply to the interpretation of this Order as it applies to the interpretation of an Act of Parliament.

(3) This Order extends to Northern Ireland only.

2. Section 4 of the Fuel and Electricity (Control) Act 1973 shall, in its application to Northern Ireland, apply with the following modifications—

(*a*) subsection (1) shall, in relation to a transferred enactment (as defined in subsection (3A) as inserted by sub-paragraph (*d*) below) or any contractual obligation, have effect with the substitution for the reference to the Secretary of State of a reference to a Ministry of Northern Ireland·

(**a**) 1973 c. 67. (**b**) 1889 c. 63.

(*b*) in subsection (2)—

(i) for the reference to the Secretary of State substitute a reference to the Minister or Ministry of Northern Ireland exercising functions under the enactments specified in paragraphs (*a*) to (*c*) of that subsection, as modified by this Article;

(ii) for any reference to a stage carriage, an express carriage or a contract carriage substitute a reference to a public service vehicle;

(iii) for a reference to section 144 or 160 of the Road Traffic Act 1960(**a**) substitute a reference to section 65 or 61 of the Road Traffic Act (Northern Ireland) 1970(**b**), respectively;

(iv) for the reference to section 40 of the Road Traffic Act 1972(**c**) substitute a reference to section 26 of the Road Traffic Act (Northern Ireland) 1970;

(v) for the reference to subsections (1) to (6) of section 96 of the Transport Act 1968(**d**) substitute a reference to subsections (1) to (5) of section 49 of the Road Traffic Act (Northern Ireland) 1970, as applied by section 57 of that Act and as amended by Article 5 of the Road Traffic (Amendment) (Northern Ireland) Order 1973(**e**).

(*c*) in subsection (3), after "enactment" insert "(other than a transferred enactment within the meaning of subsection (3A) below)";

(*d*) after subsection (3), insert—

"(3A) A Ministry of Northern Ireland may by order make provision for modifying or excluding any obligation imposed, or extending any power conferred, by or under any transferred enactment which directly or indirectly affects the supply or use of a substance to which this Act applies.

In this subsection "transferred enactment" means an enactment which, if it is, or had been, in force before the expiration of section 1 of the Northern Ireland (Temporary Provisions) Act 1972(**f**) may be, or might have been, amended by an Order in Council under subsection (3) of that section.

(3B) Any order made under subsection (3A) above may be varied or revoked by a subsequent order and shall be subject to negative resolution within the meaning of section 41(6) of the Interpretation Act (Northern Ireland) 1954(**g**) as if it were a statutory instrument within the meaning of that Act.".

3. The Fuel Control (Modification of Enactments) (Speed Limits) (Northern Ireland) Order 1973(**h**) is, with effect from 8th April 1974, hereby revoked.

W. G. Agnew.

(**a**) 1960 c. 16. (**b**) 1970 c. 2 (N.I.). (**c**) 1972 c. 20.
(**d**) 1968 c. 73. (**e**) S.I. 1973/1229. (**f**) 1972 c. 22.
(**g**) 1954 c. 33 (N.I.). (**h**) S.I. 1973/2052 (1973 III, p. 7075)

EXPLANATORY NOTE

(This Note is not part of the Order.)

This Order modifies section 4 of the Fuel and Electricity (Control) Act 1973 (relaxation of statutory and contractual obligations) in its application to Northern Ireland and prospectively revokes the Fuel Control (Modification of Enactments) (Speed Limits) (Northern Ireland) Order 1973.

STATUTORY INSTRUMENTS

1973 No. 2091

CONTROL OF FUEL AND ELECTRICITY

The Electricity (Advertising, Display, etc.) (Control) Order 1973

Made - - - -	11*th December* 1973
Laid before Parliament	12*th December* 1973
Coming into Operation	13*th December* 1973

The Secretary of State, in exercise of his powers under section 2(1) of the Fuel and Electricity (Control) Act 1973(**a**) and section 7 of the Emergency Laws (Re-enactments and Repeals) Act 1964(**b**) as having effect by virtue of section 5(1) of the Fuel and Electricity (Control) Act 1973, hereby makes the following Order:—

1. This Order shall come into operation on the 13th December 1973 and may be cited as the Electricity (Advertising, Display, etc.) (Control) Order 1973.

2.—(1) In this Order " electricity " means electricity whether or not supplied by an Electricity Board within the meaning of section 1 of the Electricity Act 1947(**c**).

(2) Any reference in this Order to any enactment shall be construed as a reference thereto as amended or extended.

3.—(1) Subject to paragraphs (2) and (3) of this Article, and except under a licence granted by the Secretary of State under this Order, no person shall use or permit the use of electricity for the purpose of:—

(*a*) advertising any article, product or service;

(*b*) the display of any article, building or structure or any part thereof; or

(*c*) lighting (whether by means of floodlights or any other form of illumination) any area in the open air for the purpose of recreation, entertainment or sport.

(2) Nothing in paragraph (1) of this Article shall apply to the use of electricity for the purpose of:—

(*a*) broadcasting any advertisement from an authorised broadcasting station; or

(*b*) projecting any advertisement by means of any film or slide on to a screen in any premises licensed under the Cinematograph Act 1909(**d**) or the Theatres Act 1968(**e**); or

(*c*) displaying any article or structure which is a traffic sign within the meaning of section 54(1) of the Road Traffic Regulation Act 1967(**f**); or

(**a**) 1973 c. 67. (**b**) 1964 c. 60. (**c**) 1947 c. 54.
(**d**) 1909 c. 30. (**e**) 1968 c. 54. (**f**) 1967 c. 76.

(*d*) displaying any sign indicating the nature of the premises at any of the following:—

(i) ambulance stations;

(ii) fire stations;

(iii) first aid stations;

(iv) police stations;

(v) hospitals;

(vi) the premises of registered dentist;

(vii) the premises of a fully registered medical practitioner;

(viii) a registered pharmacy or the premises of a registered pharmacist;

(ix) the premises of a registered optician;

(x) the premises of a registered veterinary surgeon or registered veterinary practitioner;

(xi) the premises of a registered dispenser of hearing aids;

(xii) the premises of any person registered as a chiropodist or physiotherapist under the Professions Supplementary to Medicine Act 1960(**a**); or

(*e*) illuminating any telephone which is intended for public use.

(3) Nothing in paragraph (1) of this Article shall apply to the use of electricity at any premises used for the purpose of any railway undertaking.

4. Any licence granted under this Order may be subject to conditions and may be revoked without prior notice.

5. This Order shall not extend to Northern Ireland.

Tom Boardman,
Minister for Industry,
Department of Trade and Industry.

11th December 1973.

EXPLANATORY NOTE

(*This Note is not part of the Order.*)

This Order prohibits the use of electricity whether or not supplied by an Electricity Board for purposes of advertising or display, or lighting any area in the open air for the purpose of recreation, entertainment or sport, except under a licence granted by the Secretary of State or for certain purposes specified in the Order, including advertising on television or by radio, or in cinemas or theatres, and the illumination of traffic signs, public telephones and signs indicating hospitals, police and fire stations and other specified premises. The prohibition does not apply to railway premises.

(**a**) 1960 c. 66.

1973 No. 2092

CONTROL OF FUEL AND ELECTRICITY

The Electricity (Heating) (Control) Order 1973

Made - - - -	11*th December* 1973
Laid before Parliament	12*th December* 1973
Coming into Operation	13*th December* 1973

The Secretary of State, in exercise of his powers under section 2(1) of the Fuel and Electricity (Control) Act 1973(**a**) and section 7 of the Emergency Laws (Re-enactments and Repeals) Act 1964(**b**) as having effect by virtue of section 5(1) of the Fuel and Electricity (Control) Act 1973, hereby makes the following Order:—

1. This Order shall come into operation on the 13th December 1973 and may be cited as the Electricity (Heating) (Control) Order 1973.

2.—(1) In this Order " electricity " means electricity supplied by an Electricity Board within the meaning of section 1 of the Electricity Act 1947(**c**).

(2) Any reference in this Order to any enactment shall be construed as a reference thereto as amended or extended.

3.—(1) Subject to paragraph (2) of this Article, and except under a licence granted by the Secretary of State under this Order, no person shall use or permit the use of electricity for the purpose of heating—

(*a*) any premises used wholly or mainly—

(i) as an office or showroom;

(ii) as a retail shop, bank or petrol station;

(iii) as a restaurant or catering establishment (whether or not licensed for the sale of intoxicating liquor) or for the sale or consumption of intoxicating liquor;

(iv) as a warehouse or store;

(v) as a film, television or photographic studio;

(vi) as a library, museum, art gallery, exhibition hall or other public hall;

(vii) as a church, chapel or other place of public worship; or

(viii) for recreation, entertainment or sport; or

(*b*) any part so used of any premises not otherwise so used, if the heating for that part is controlled separately from the heating for the other part of the premises.

(2) Nothing in paragraph (1) of this Article shall apply to the use of electricity—

(*a*) during any period not exceeding eight hours falling between 2230 hours and 0730 hours on the following day;

(*b*) on any part of any such premises which is used for living accommodation;

(*c*) on any part of any such premises to the extent that such use is necessary for the maintenance of the health of any person on those premises who is ill, disabled, infirm, pregnant, under the age of 5 years or over the age of 60 years;

(**a**) 1973 c. 67. (**b**) 1964 c. 60. (**c**) 1947 c. 54.

(*d*) for the purpose of operating any fan, circulating pump or controlling mechanism installed in any central plant used for heating any such premises by means of solid fuel, gas or oil;

(*e*) for the purpose of preventing damage to any central heating plant on any such premises;

(*f*) for the purpose of operating apparatus for heating, cooling or air-conditioning on any such premises to the extent necessary to prevent damage or deterioration to food, goods or material or to prevent damage to or impairment of the functioning of any apparatus or equipment on the premises which is sensitive to changes in temperature or humidity;

(*g*) for preserving the health of any livestock on any such premises;

(*h*) on any part of such premises used as a registered pharmacy or used for the purpose of his practice or business by a registered medical practitioner, a registered dentist, a registered pharmacist, a registered optician, a registered veterinary surgeon, a registered veterinary practitioner or any person registered as a chiropodist or physiotherapist under the Professions Supplementary to Medicine Act 1960(**a**);

(*i*) on any part of such premises used for the purpose of dispensing hearing aids by any person registered as a dispenser of hearing aids under the Hearing Aid Council Act 1968(**b**);

(*j*) for the purpose of heating any premises for use as a church, chapel or other place of public worship or religious education, if such use does not exceed six hours in a period of seven days.

4. Any licence granted under this Order may be subject to conditions and may be revoked without prior notice.

5. This Order shall not extend to Northern Ireland.

Tom Boardman,
Minister for Industry,
Department of Trade and Industry.

11th December 1973.

EXPLANATORY NOTE

(*This Note is not part of the Order.*)

This Order prohibits the use of electricity for space heating, except under a licence granted by the Secretary of State, in premises used for certain purposes specified in Article 3(1) of the Order. These include offices, showrooms, shops, banks, petrol stations, restaurants, bars, warehouses, studios, public halls, churches and places of recreation, entertainment or sport. Such use is however permitted for a period of eight hours overnight, falling between 2230 hours and 0730 hours on the following day, and for certain purposes specified in Article 3(2). These include the maintenance of health, the prevention of damage to sensitive apparatus, goods and material (including food), and heating premises used for the purpose of their practice by doctors and other persons specified in the Article or (for a restricted period) for use as a church or other place of public worship or religious education.

(a) 1960 c. 66. (b) 1968 c. 50.

STATUTORY INSTRUMENTS

1973 No. 2093

RIVER, ENGLAND AND WALES
RIVER, SCOTLAND

SALMON AND FRESHWATER FISHERIES

The Diseases of Fish Order 1973

Laid before Parliament in draft

Made - - - 12*th December* 1973
Coming into Operation 1*st January* 1974

At the Court at Buckingham Palace, the 12th day of December 1973

Present,

The Queen's Most Excellent Majesty in Council

Whereas a draft of this Order has, in accordance with section 13 of the Diseases of Fish Act 1937(**a**) (as applied by section 6(2) of the Statutory Instruments Act 1946(**b**)), been laid before Parliament:

Now, therefore, Her Majesty, in exercise of the powers conferred on Her by the said section 13, and of all other powers enabling Her in that behalf, is pleased, by and with the advice of Her Privy Council, to order, and it is hereby ordered, as follows:—

Citation and commencement

1. This Order may be cited as the Diseases of Fish Order 1973 and shall come into operation on 1st January 1974.

Interpretation

2.—(1) In this Order "the Act" means the Diseases of Fish Act 1937.

(2) The Interpretation Act 1889(**c**) shall apply to the interpretation of this Order as it applies to the interpretation of an Act of Parliament.

Extension of Act to other diseases affecting fish

3. The provisions of the Act shall apply with respect to the diseases named in the Schedule to this Order (being diseases affecting fish of the salmon family or freshwater fish) as those provisions apply with respect to furunculosis and columnaris.

Modifications of certain definitions in Act

4. For the definitions of the expressions "infected" and "infected waters" contained in section 10(1) of the Act (as substituted by the Diseases of Fish

(**a**) 1937 c. 33. (**b**) 1946 c. 36. (**c**) 1889 c. 63.

Order 1966(**a**)) there shall be substituted the following definitions, that is to say—

" 'infected' means, in relation to fish, infected with any of the diseases respectively known as furunculosis, columnaris, infectious pancreatic necrosis (IPN), viral haemorrhagic septicaemia (VHS or Egtved disease), Myxosoma (Lentospora) cerebralis (whirling disease), infectious haematopoietic necrosis (IHN), ulcerative dermal necrosis (UDN) and infectious dropsy of cyprinids (IDC or IAD) in any of its forms including spring viraemia and erythrodermatitis;

'infected waters' means waters in which any of the diseases mentioned in the definition of the expression "infected" exists among fish, or in which the causative organisms of any of those diseases are present;"

W. G. Agnew.

SCHEDULE

Article 3

Diseases to which the Act is extended:—

Infectious pancreatic necrosis (IPN);

Viral haemorrhagic septicaemia (VHS or Egtved disease);

Myxosoma (Lentospora) cerebralis (whirling disease);

Infectious haematopoietic necrosis (IHN);

Ulcerative dermal necrosis (UDN); and

Infectious dropsy of cyprinids (IDC or IAD) in any of its forms including spring viraemia and erythrodermatitis.

EXPLANATORY NOTE

(This Note is not part of the Order.)

This Order extends the provisions of the Diseases of Fish Act 1937 to the diseases referred to in the Schedule to the Order and accordingly substitutes for the definitions in the Act of the expressions "infected" and "infected waters" the definitions provided in Article 4 of the Order. The diseases mentioned in the Schedule affect fish of the salmon family (i.e. salmon and trout) or freshwater fish.

(a) S.I. 1966/944 (1966 II, p. 2284).

STATUTORY INSTRUMENTS

1973 No. 2095

NORTHERN IRELAND

The Local Government Reorganisation (Consequential Provisions) (Northern Ireland) Order 1973

Laid before Parliament in draft

Made - - - -	12*th December* 1973
Coming into Operation	19*th December* 1973

At the Court at Buckingham Palace, the 12th day of December 1973

Present,

The Queen's Most Excellent Majesty in Council

Whereas a draft of this Order has been approved by a resolution of each House of Parliament:

Now, therefore, Her Majesty, in exercise of the powers conferred by section 38 of the Northern Ireland Constitution Act 1973**(a)**, and of all other powers enabling Her in that behalf, is pleased, by and with the advice of Her Privy Council, to order, and it is hereby ordered as follows:—

Citation, commencement, interpretation and extent

1.—(1) This Order may be cited as the Local Government Reorganisation (Consequential Provisions) (Northern Ireland) Order 1973.

(2) This Order shall come into operation on the seventh day after the day on which it is made.

(3) Any reference in this Order to any enactment is a reference to that enactment as amended by, and includes a reference to that enactment as extended or applied by, any other enactment.

(4) In this Order, any reference to an enactment is a reference to that enactment as it has effect in Northern Ireland.

(5) In this Order "enactment" includes an enactment of the Parliament of Northern Ireland.

(a) 1973 c. 36.

(6) The Interpretation Act 1889**(a)** shall apply to the interpretation of this Order as it applies to the interpretation of an Act of Parliament.

(7) This Order extends to Northern Ireland only.

Parliamentary elections: amendments consequential on reorganisation of local government in Northern Ireland

2.—(1) For the purposes of the Representation of the People Acts, the Chief Electoral Officer for Northern Ireland shall be—

(*a*) the electoral registration officer for each constituency in Northern Ireland; and

(*b*) the returning officer for a parliamentary election in the case of each such constituency.

(2) The Secretary of State shall pay to the Ministry of Home Affairs for Northern Ireland such sum as he considers appropriate in respect of the functions exercised under the Representation of the People Acts by the Chief Electoral Officer for Northern Ireland.

(3) Sections 14(5) and 14A(2) and (3) of the Electoral Law Act (Northern Ireland) 1962**(b)** (which were respectively substituted and inserted by Article 6 of the Electoral Law (Northern Ireland) Order 1972**(c)** and concern a temporary deputy for the Chief Electoral Officer and the appointment of persons to assist that Officer) and the definition of "Chief Electorial Officer" in section 130(1) of that Act (which was inserted by Schedule 2 to that Order) shall have effect in relation to the Chief Electoral Officer in his capacity as electoral registration officer and returning officer by virtue of this Article.

(4) For the purposes of section 12(4) of the Representation of the People Act 1949**(d)** (postal voting) and section 15 of that Act (voting by proxy) an address in Northern Ireland shall not be treated as in the same area as a qualifying address unless both addresses are within the same ward in Northern Ireland.

(5) In the proviso to section 136(3) of the said Act of 1949 (costs of election petition) for the words "the council of any county or county borough" there shall be substituted the words "the district council for the district".

(6) In the following provisions (which prescribe the persons before whom certain declarations are to be made), that is to say—

(*a*) proviso (*c*) to rule 32(3) of the parliamentary elections rules set out in Schedule 2 to the said Act of 1949;

(*b*) section 8(4)(*c*) of the Representation of the People Act 1969**(e)**;

(*c*) paragraph 8(3) of Part II of Schedule 1 to the said Act of 1969,

for the words "the secretary of a county council or a town clerk" there shall be substituted the words "the clerk of a district council".

(7) In paragraph 4(1)(*c*) of Schedule 2 to the House of Commons (Redistribution of Seats) Act 1949**(f)** (county district in Northern Ireland not to be included partly in one constituency and partly in another) for the words "county district" there shall be substituted the word "ward"; and in section 4(2) of the House of Commons (Redistribution of Seats) Act 1958**(g)** (objections to recommendation of Boundary Commission), "interested authority" in relation to any recommendation means the district council for a district which is wholly or partly comprised in the constituencies affected by the recommendation.

(a) 1889 c. 63. **(b)** 1962 c. 14 (N.I.). **(c)** S.I. 1972/1264 (N.I. 13).
(d) 1949 c. 68. **(e)** 1969 c. 15. **(f)** 1949 c. 66. **(g)** 1958 c. 26.

Appointment etc. of certain sheriffs

3.—(1) Notwithstanding any enactment, each person who is the holder of, or is executing, the office of sheriff of a county borough on 22nd June 1974 shall continue to hold, or, as the case may be, to execute, that office until 31st December 1974.

(2) The sheriff of a county borough shall be nominated and appointed for the year ending on 31st December 1975 and each subsequent year in the same manner as the sheriff of a county, and subject to the same terms and conditions; and the enactments which apply to the sheriff of a county shall apply to the sheriff of a county borough.

Extension of ss. 19(1) *and* 21 *of Northern Ireland Constitution Act* 1973

4. Subsection (1) of section 19 of the Northern Ireland Constitution Act 1973 shall have effect in relation to Enterprise Ulster, a Health and Social Services Board, the Northern Ireland Central Services Agency for the Health and Social Services and the Northern Ireland Staffs Council for the Health and Social Services as it has effect in relation to the persons referred to in that subsection and section 21 of that Act shall have effect in relation to those bodies as it has effect in relation to the bodies to which that section applies.

Amendments and repeals

5.—(1) The enactments set out in Schedule 1 shall have effect subject to the amendments specified in that Schedule (being amendments arising out of the reorganisation of local government in Northern Ireland and the establishment of certain bodies there).

(2) The enactments set out in Schedule 2 are hereby repealed to the extent specified in column 3 of that Schedule.

W. G. Agnew.

SCHEDULE 1

Article 5(1).

AMENDMENTS OF ACTS

The Telegraph Act 1863 (*c.* 112)

1. In section 21, in the first proviso, after "subject nevertheless" insert "to the provisions of sections 23 to 29 of this Act and".

The Telegraph Act 1892 (*c.* 59)

2. In section 3 for the words from the beginning to "those Acts" substitute "For the purposes of the Telegraph Acts 1863 and 1878"**(a)**.

3. In section 11 for the paragraph beginning "A reference to the Public Health Act 1875" substitute the following:—

"(1) For section 5(2) there shall be substituted the following subsection:—

'(2) Provided that, notwithstanding anything in the Telegraph Act 1878, a licensee shall not exercise any powers under the said enactments in any district without the consent of the district council and shall be subject to any terms and conditions which the district council may attach to any such consent and shall comply with any regulations of the district council from time to time in force in relation to telegraphic lines.'; and

(2) In section 6(1) for the words 'the Electric Lighting Act 1882', where they first occur, there shall be substituted the words 'the Electricity Supply (Northern Ireland) Order 1972'**(b)**; and for the words 'the local authority as defined by the Electric Lighting Act 1882' there shall be substituted the words 'the district council'. ".

(a) 1863 c. 112; 1878 c. 76.

(b) S.I. 1972/1072 (N.I.9).

The Northern Ireland Land Act 1929 (*c.* 14)

4. In section 7(1)(*c*) for the words from "the annual rateable value thereof as shown in the revised valuation lists" to "the amount certified by the Commissioner of Valuation to be the annual rateable value" substitute "the amount which the Commissioner of Valuation certifies would have been entered, at the time when the notice was given, in the valuation list in force under the Rates (Northern Ireland) Order 1972(**a**) as the net annual value of the holding or part of a holding, if the holding or part of a holding had been a hereditament within the meaning of that Order and if it had been valued under the provisions repealed by that Order".

The Food and Drugs Act 1955 (4 & 5 Eliz. 2 *c.* 16)

5. In Schedule 10—

(*a*) in paragraph 2(*c*) for "health authority or a port sanitary authority" substitute "district council";

(*b*) in the Table at the end of paragraph 2, in the paragraph substituted for paragraph (*a*) of section 87(3), for "health authorities, port sanitary authorities" substitute "district councils".

The Post Office Act 1969 (*c.* 48)

6. In section 12(4) and (6) for "(2) or (3)" substitute (in each case) "or (2)".

7. In section 54—

(*a*) in subsection (1)—

(i) for "valuation lists coming into force for the year beginning" substitute "valuation list coming into force on, or, as the case may be, in force on and after,",

(ii) for "rating authorities" (twice) substitute "district councils";

(*b*) in subsection (2)—

(i) for "lists" substitute "list", and

(ii) for "areas of local authorities" substitute "districts of district councils";

(*c*) in subsection (3) for "areas of the local authorities" substitute "districts of the district councils";

(*d*) in subsection (4) for "valuation lists" substitute "the valuation list";

(*e*) in subsection (9)for the definition of "relevant year" substitute—

" 'relevant year' means—

(*a*) the year 1973;

(*b*) the calendar year in which the third, and any subsequent, general revaluation first comes into force;

(*c*) each successive fifth year after 1973 unless a year such as is mentioned in paragraph (*b*) has occurred within the preceding five years.".

8. In section 86(1), in the definition of "local authority", for paragraph (*c*) substitute—

"(*c*) in relation to Northern Ireland, means a district council, the Northern Ireland Housing Executive, the Northern Ireland Electricity Service or an Education and Library Board;".

The National Savings Bank Act 1971 (*c.* 29)

9. In section 22(4) for "and (*e*)" substitute ",(*e*) and (*g*)".

10. In Schedule 1—

(*a*) in paragraph 1(*a*) for "section 7 of the Public Health and Local Government (Miscellaneous Provisions) Act (Northern Ireland) 1949" substitute "section 63 of the Local Government Act (Northern Ireland) 1972"(**b**);

(**a**) S.I. 1972/1633 (N.I. 16).

(**b**) 1972 c. 9 (N.I.).

(*b*) for paragraph 4(1) substitute—

"(1) For the purposes of section 70(2)(*b*) of the Local Government Act (Northern Ireland) 1972, so far as it relates to regulations with respect to registers of securities, 'security' shall include a charge arising by virtue of this Schedule, and such a charge shall be deemed to have been created on the date of the agreement giving rise to the charge.".

The Civil Aviation Act 1971 (*c.* 75)

11. In section 17(6), after "in Northern Ireland" insert "or under the Planning (Northern Ireland) Order 1972**(a)** by the Ministry of Development for Northern Ireland or the Planning Appeals Commission".

SCHEDULE 2

Article 5(2).

REPEALS

Chapter	Short Title	Extent of Repeal
3 & 4 Vict. c. 108.	The Municipal Corporations (Ireland) Act 1840.	Section 152.
26 & 27 Vict. c. 112.	The Telegraph Act 1863.	In section 9, the words from "within the limits" to "latest census)" and "within such respective limits". In section 21, in the first proviso, the words from "with respect" to "as a city or large town)", the words "in a city or large town" and paragraph (1). In section 23, the words from "(not being a street" to "large town)" and the words "(not being such a street as aforesaid)".
39 & 40 Vict. c. 76.	The Municipal Privilege Act, Ireland, 1876.	The whole Act so far as it relates to sheriffs.
55 & 56 Vict. c. 59.	The Telegraph Act 1892.	In section 9, the definitions of "urban sanitary authority" and "urban sanitary district".
61 & 62 Vict. c. 37.	The Local Government (Ireland) Act 1898.	In section 69(1) the words "sheriff and" where they twice occur and the words from "and as respects" to "Act provided". Section 94(12).
8 Edw. 7 c. 33.	The Telegraph (Construction) Act 1908.	In section 2, the words "which (as amended by section three of the Telegraph Act 1892) are not of general application", "be of general application, and", "to rural districts and" and the words from "; but, in the case" onwards.
24 & 25 Geo. 5 c. 22 (N.I.).	The Local Government Act (Northern Ireland) 1934.	Section 1(5).
12, 13 & 14 Geo. 6 c.66.	The House of Commons (Redistribution of Seats) Act 1949.	In Schedule 2, in paragraph 4(2), in the definition of "county district" the words "in sub-paragraph (*c*), the same meaning as in the Local Government (Ireland) Act 1898".

(a) S.I. **1972/1634** (N.I. 17).

Chapter	Short Title	Extent of Repeal
12, 13 & 14 Geo. 6 c.68.	The Representation of the People Act 1949.	Section 6(4). In section 9, in subsection (1)(*c*) the words "except in Northern Ireland " and subsection (2). Section 12(7). Section 15(3). Section 17(3). Section 19. Section 21. In section 41, subsection (4)(*b*), in subsection (5) the words from "and in Northern Ireland" onwards, and subsection (6). Section 43(4). Section 44. In section 136(3), in the proviso, the words from "and the said costs" onwards. In Schedule 4, paragraph 1.
4 & 5 Eliz. 2 c. 16.	The Food and Drugs Act 1955.	In Schedule 10, paragraphs 2(*d*) and 4.
1969 c.15.	The Representation of the People Act 1969.	Section 6(1).
1969 c. 48.	The Post Office Act 1969.	In section 12, subsection (3), in subsection (5), the words "or (3)" and subsection (9). In section 54, subsections (5) to (7) and in subsection (9), the definitions of "annual revision", "interim revision" and "local authorities".
1971 c. 75.	The Civil Aviation Act 1971.	In Schedule 9, paragraph 7(3) and (4).

EXPLANATORY NOTE

(*This Note is not part of the Order.*)

This Order makes consequential amendments in Acts of the United Kingdom Parliament to take account of local government reorganisation in Northern Ireland and extends sections 19 and 21 of the Northern Ireland Constitution Act 1973 to four named bodies. In particular, Article 2 makes the chief electoral officer for Northern Ireland the electoral registration officer and the returning officer for constituencies in Northern Ireland which return members to the Parliament of the United Kingdom.

STATUTORY INSTRUMENTS

1973 No. 2096

INCOME TAX

The Double Taxation Relief (Taxes on Income) (Barbados) Order 1973

Laid before the House of Commons in draft

Made - - - *12th December* 1973

At the Court at Buckingham Palace, the 12th day of December 1973

Present,

The Queen's Most Excellent Majesty in Council

Whereas a draft of this Order was laid before the Commons House of Parliament in accordance with the provisions of section 497(8) of the Income and Corporation Taxes Act 1970(**a**), and an Address has been presented to Her Majesty by that House praying that an Order may be made in the terms of this Order:

Now, therefore, Her Majesty, in exercise of the powers conferred upon Her by section 497 of the said Income and Corporation Taxes Act 1970, as amended by section 98 of the Finance Act 1972(**b**), and of all other powers enabling Her in that behalf, is pleased, by and with the advice of Her Privy Council, to order, and it is hereby ordered, as follows:—

1. This Order may be cited as the Double Taxation Relief (Taxes on Income) (Barbados) Order 1973.

2. It is hereby declared—

(*a*) that the arrangements specified in the Protocol set out in the Schedule to this Order, which vary the arrangements set out in the Schedule to the Double Taxation Relief (Taxes on Income) (Barbados) Order 1970(**c**), have been made with the Government of Barbados with a view to affording relief from double taxation in relation to income tax, or corporation tax and taxes of a similar character imposed by the laws of Barbados; and

(*b*) that it is expedient that those arrangements should have effect.

W. G. Agnew.

(**a**) 1970 c.10. (**b**) 1972 c.41. (**c**) S.I. 1970/952 (1970 II s.1, p.2944).

SCHEDULE

PROTOCOL AMENDING THE AGREEMENT BETWEEN THE GOVERNMENT OF THE UNITED KINGDOM OF GREAT BRITAIN AND NORTHERN IRELAND AND THE GOVERNMENT OF BARBADOS FOR THE AVOIDANCE OF DOUBLE TAXATION AND THE PREVENTION OF FISCAL EVASION WITH RESPECT TO TAXES ON INCOME AND CAPITAL GAINS, SIGNED AT BRIDGETOWN ON 26 MARCH 1970.

The Government of the United Kingdom of Great Britain and Northern Ireland and the Government of Barbados;

Desiring to conclude a protocol to amend the Agreement between the Contracting Governments for the avoidance of double taxation and the prevention of fiscal evasion with respect on taxes on income and capital gains, signed at Bridgetown on 26 March 1970 (hereinafter referred to as "the Agreement");

Have agreed as follows:

ARTICLE 1

Article 9 of the Agreement shall be deleted and replaced by the following:

"ARTICLE 9

Dividends

(1)(*a*) Dividends paid by a company which is a resident of the United Kingdom to a resident of Barbados may be taxed in Barbados.

(*b*) Where a resident of Barbados is entitled to a tax credit in respect of such a dividend under paragraph (2) of this Article tax may also be charged in the United Kingdom, and according to the laws of the United Kingdom, on the aggregate of the amount or value of that dividend and the amount of that tax credit at a rate not exceeding 15 per cent.

(*c*) Except as aforesaid, dividends paid by a company which is a resident of the United Kingdom to a resident of Barbados who is subject to tax in Barbados on them shall be exempt from any tax in the United Kingdom which is chargeable on dividends.

(2) A resident of Barbados who receives dividends from a company which is a resident of the United Kingdom shall, subject to the provisions of paragraph (3) of this Article and provided he is subject to tax in Barbados on those dividends, be entitled to the tax credit in respect thereof to which an individual resident in the United Kingdom would have been entitled had he received those dividends, and to the payment of any excess of such credit over his liability to United Kingdom tax.

(3) Paragraph (2) of this Article shall not apply where the recipient of the dividend is a company which, either alone or together with one or more associated companies, controls directly or indirectly at least 10 per cent of the voting power in the company paying the dividends. For the purposes of this paragraph two companies shall be deemed to be associated if one is controlled directly or indirectly by the other, or both are controlled directly or indirectly by a third company.

(4) Dividends paid by a company which is a resident of Barbados to a resident of the United Kingdom who is subject to tax in the United Kingdom in respect thereof shall be exempt from any tax in Barbados which is chargeable on dividends in addition to the tax chargeable in respect of the profits or income of the company.

(5) Subject to the provisions of paragraph (5) of Article 10 and paragraph (5) of Article 11 the term "dividends" includes any item which, under the law of the Contracting State of which the company paying the dividend is a resident, is treated as a distribution of a company.

(6) If the recipient of a dividend is a company which owns 10 per cent or more of the class of shares in respect of which the dividend is paid, then paragraphs (1) and (2) or, as the case may be, paragraph (4) of this Article shall not apply to the dividend to the extent that it can have been paid only out of profits which the company paying the dividend earned or other income which it received in a period ending twelve months or more before the relevant date. For the purposes of this paragraph the term "relevant date" means the date on which the beneficial owner of the dividend became the owner of 10 per cent or more of the class of shares in question.

Provided that this paragraph shall not apply if the beneficial owner of the dividend shows that the shares were acquired for bona fide commercial reasons and not primarily for the purpose of securing the benefit of this Article.

(7) The provisions of paragraphs (1) and (2) or, as the case may be, paragraph (4) of this Article shall not apply where a resident of a Contracting State has a permanent establishment in the other Contracting State and the holding by virtue of which the dividends are paid is effectively connected with a business carried on through that permanent establishment. In such a case the dividends shall be treated as if they were industrial or commercial profits to which the provisions of Article 6 are applicable.

(8) Where a company which is a resident of a Contracting State derives profits or income from sources within the other Contracting State, that other State shall not impose any form of taxation on dividends paid by the company to persons not resident in that other State, or any tax in the nature of an undistributed profits tax on undistributed profits of the company by reason of the fact that those dividends or undistributed profits represent, in whole or in part, profits or income so derived."

Article 2

This Protocol, which shall form an integral part of the Agreement, shall come into force when the last of all such things shall have been done in the United Kingdom and Barbados as are necessary to give the Protocol the force of law in the United Kingdom and Barbados respectively, and shall thereupon have effect in relation to dividends paid on or after 6 April 1973.

In witness whereof, the undersigned, duly authorised by their respective Governments, have signed this Protocol.

Done in duplicate at Bridgetown this eighteenth day of September, one thousand nine hundred and seventy-three.

For the Government of the United Kingdom of Great Britain and Northern Ireland:
J. R. Johnson,
Acting High Commissioner.

For the Government of Barbados:
Errol W. Barrow,
Prime Minister and Minister of Finance.

EXPLANATORY NOTE

(This Note is not part of the Order.)

The Protocol scheduled to this Order makes certain alterations to the Agreement with Barbados signed on 26th March 1970. These alterations follow from the introduction of the new United Kingdom corporation tax system which, so far as it relates to the tax treatment of dividends paid by a United Kingdom company to an overseas shareholder, came into operation on 6th April 1973. The Protocol provides that where a United Kingdom company pays a dividend to a resident of Barbados other than a company which controls 10 per cent or more of the voting power in the paying company, the recipient is, subject to certain conditions, to receive the tax credit to which an individual resident in the United Kingdom and in receipt of such a dividend would be entitled less income tax at a rate not exceeding 15 per cent on the aggregate of the dividend and the tax credit.

The Protocol is expressed to take effect in relation to dividends paid on or after 6th April 1973.

1973 No. 2097

INCOME TAX

The Double Taxation Relief (Taxes on Income) (Belize) Order 1973

Laid before the House of Commons in draft

Made - - - *12th December* 1973

At the Court at Buckingham Palace, the 12th day of December 1973

Present,

The Queen's Most Excellent Majesty in Council

Whereas a draft of this Order was laid before the Commons House of Parliament in accordance with the provisions of section 497(8) of the Income and Corporation Taxes Act 1970**(a)**, and an Address has been presented to Her Majesty by that House praying that an Order may be made in the terms of this Order:

Now, therefore, Her Majesty, in exercise of the powers conferred upon Her by section 497 of the said Income and Corporation Taxes Act 1970, as amended by section 98 of the Finance Act 1972**(b)** and of all other powers enabling Her in that behalf, is pleased, by and with the the advice of Her Privy Council, to order, and it is hereby ordered, as follows:—

1. This Order may be cited as the Double Taxation Relief (Taxes on Income) (Belize) Order 1973.

2. It is hereby declared—

(*a*) that the arrangements specified in the Supplementary Arrangement set out in the Schedule to this Order, which vary the arrangements set out in the Schedule to the Double Taxation Relief (Taxes on Income) (British Honduras) Order 1947**(c)** as amended by the arrangements set out in the Schedule to the Double Taxation Relief (Taxes on Income) (British Honduras) Order 1968**(d)** have been made with the Government of Belize with a view to affording relief from double taxation in relation to income tax or corporation tax and taxes of a similar character imposed by the laws of Belize; and

(*b*) that it is expedient that those arrangements should have effect.

W. G. Agnew.

(a) 1970 c. 10. **(b)** 1972 c. 41.
(c) S.R. & O. 1947/2866 (Rev. X, p. 363: 1947 I, p. 1084).
(d) S.I. 1968/573 (1968 I, p. 1312).

SCHEDULE

SUPPLEMENTARY ARRANGEMENT BETWEEN HER MAJESTY'S GOVERNMENT AND THE GOVERNMENT OF BELIZE TO AMEND THE EXISTING ARRANGEMENT MADE IN 1947 FOR THE AVOIDANCE OF DOUBLE TAXATION AND THE PREVENTION OF FISCAL EVASION WITH RESPECT TO TAXES ON INCOME, AS MODIFIED BY THE ARRANGEMENT MADE IN 1968.

1. The Arrangement made in 1947 between His Majesty's Government and the Government of British Honduras for the avoidance of double taxation and the prevention of fiscal evasion with respect to taxes on income as modified by the Arrangement made in 1968 (hereinafter referred to as "the existing Arrangement") shall be amended—

(*a*) by the deletion of paragraph 2(1)(*b*);

(*b*) by the substitution for the references therein to "the Colony", "Colonial enterprise" and "Colonial tax" of references to "Belize", "Belize enterprise" and "Belize tax" respectively;

(*c*) by the substitution for Paragraph 6 of the following new Paragraph—

"6.—(1) (*a*) Dividends paid by a company which is a resident of the United Kingdom to a resident of Belize may be taxed in Belize.

(*b*) Where a resident of Belize is entitled to a tax credit in respect of such a dividend under sub-paragraph (2) of this Paragraph tax may also be charged in the United Kingdom, and according to the laws of the United Kingdom, on the aggregate of the amount or value of that dividend and the amount of that tax credit at a rate not exceeding 15 per cent.

(*c*) Except as aforesaid, dividends paid by a company which is a resident of the United Kingdom to a resident of Belize who is subject to tax in Belize on them shall be exempt from any tax in the United Kingdom which is chargeable on dividends.

(2) A resident of Belize who receives dividends from a company which is a resident of the United Kingdom shall, subject to the provisions of sub-paragraph (3) of this Paragraph and provided he is subject to tax in Belize on those dividends, be entitled to the tax credit in respect thereof to which an individual resident in the United Kingdom would have been entitled had he received those dividends, and to the payment of any excess of that tax credit over his liability to United Kingdom tax.

(3) Sub-paragraph (2) of this Paragraph shall not apply where the recipient of the dividend is a company which, either alone or together with one or more associated companies, controls directly or indirectly at least 10 per cent of the voting power in the company paying the dividend. For the purposes of this sub-paragraph two companies shall be deemed to be associated if one is controlled directly or indirectly by the other, or both are controlled directly or indirectly by a third company.

(4) Dividends paid by a company which is a resident of Belize to a resident of the United Kingdom who is subject to tax in the United Kingdom in respect thereof shall be exempt from any tax in Belize which is chargeable on dividends in addition to the tax chargeable in respect of the profits or income of the company.

(5) The term "dividends" as used in this Paragraph means income from shares or any other item which, under the law of the territory of which the company paying the dividend is a resident, is treated as a dividend or distribution of the company.

(6) If the recipient of a dividend is a company which owns 10 per cent or more of the class of shares in respect of which the dividend is paid then sub-paragraphs (1) and (2) or, as the case may be, sub-paragraph (4) of this Paragraph shall not apply to the dividend to the extent that it can have been paid only out of profits which the company paying the dividend earned or other income which it received in a period ending twelve months or more before the relevant date. For the purposes of this sub-paragraph the term

"relevant date" means the date on which the beneficial owner of the dividend became the owner of 10 per cent or more of the class of shares in question. Provided that this sub-paragraph shall not apply if the beneficial owner of the dividend shows that the shares were acquired for bona fide commercial reasons and not primarily for the purpose of securing the benefit of this Paragraph.

(7) The provisions of sub-paragraphs (1) and (2) or, as the case may be, sub-paragraph (4) of this Paragraph shall not apply where a resident of one of the territories has in the other territory a permanent establishment and the holding by virtue of which the dividends are paid is effectively connected with a business carried on through that permanent establishment. In such a case the provisions of Paragraph 3 shall apply.

(8) Where a company which is a resident of one of the territories derives profits or income from sources within the other territory, the Government of that other territory shall not impose any form of taxation on dividends paid by the company to persons not resident in that other territory, or any tax in the nature of an undistributed profits tax on undistributed profits of the company, by reason of the fact that those dividends or undistributed profits represent, in whole or in part, profits or income so derived."

(*d*) by the addition immediately after sub-paragraph (1) of Paragraph 13 of the following new sub-paragraph—

"(1A) For the purposes of sub-paragraph (1) of this Paragraph, the term "Belize tax payable" shall be deemed to include any amount which would have been payable as Belize tax for any year but for an exemption or reduction of tax granted for that year or any part thereof under:

(*a*) the provisions of the Development Incentives Ordinance, 1960, so far as it was in force on, and has not been modified since, the date when this Supplementary Arrangement came into force, or has been modified only in minor respects so as not to affect its general character; or

(*b*) any other provision which may subsequently be made granting exemption or reduction of tax which is agreed by the taxation authorities of the United Kingdom and Belize to be of a substantially similar character, if it has not been modified thereafter or has been modified only in minor respects so as not to affect its general character."

2. This Supplementary Arrangement, which shall form an integral part of the existing Arrangement, shall enter into force when the last of all such things shall have been done in the United Kingdom and Belize as are necessary to give the Supplementary Arrangement the force of law in the United Kingdom and Belize respectively and shall thereupon have effect—

(*a*) as respects Paragraph 1(*c*), in relation to dividends paid on or after 6 April 1973; and

(*b*) as respects Paragraph 1(*d*)

(i) in relation to United Kingdom income tax, for any year of assessment beginning on or after 6 April 1973; and

(ii) in relation to United Kingdom corporation tax, for any financial year beginning or on after 1 April 1973.

EXPLANATORY NOTE

(*This Note is not part of the Order.*)

This Supplementary Arrangement makes two amendments to the Arrangement which was made in 1947 and amended in 1968 between the United Kingdom and British Honduras (renamed Belize as from 1st June 1973).

The first follows the introduction of the new system of corporation tax in the United Kingdom, which, so far as it relates to dividends paid by a United Kingdom company to an overseas shareholder, came into operation on 6th April 1973. The Supplementary Arrangement provides that where a United Kingdom company pays a dividend to an individual resident in Belize or to a Belize company which controls less than 10 per cent of the voting power in the paying company, the recipient is, subject to certain conditions, to receive the tax credit to which an individual resident in the United Kingdom and in receipt of such a dividend would be entitled, less income tax at a rate not exceeding 15 per cent on the aggregate of the dividend and the tax credit.

The second amendment provides for double taxation relief to be given by the United Kingdom for tax which would have been payable in Belize but for relief granted under certain provisions of Belize law in order to encourage development.

The Supplementary Arrangement is to take effect in the United Kingdom for 1973/74 and subsequent years.

STATUTORY INSTRUMENTS

1973 No. 2098

INCOME TAX

The Double Taxation Relief (Taxes on Income) (Brunei) Order 1973

Laid before the House of Commons in draft

Made - - - - - *12th December* 1973

At the Court at Buckingham Palace, the 12th day of December 1973

Present,

The Queen's Most Excellent Majesty in Council

Whereas a draft of this Order was laid before the Commons House of Parliament in accordance with the provisions of section 497(8) of the Income and Corporation Taxes Act 1970**(a)**, and an Address has been presented to Her Majesty by that House praying that an Order may be made in the terms of this Order:

Now, therefore, Her Majesty, in exercise of the powers conferred upon Her by section 497 of the said Income and Corporation Taxes Act 1970, as amended by section 98(2) of the Finance Act 1972**(b)**, and of all other powers enabling Her in that behalf, is pleased, by and with the advice of Her Privy Council, to order, and it is hereby ordered, as follows:—

1. This Order may be cited as the Double Taxation Relief (Taxes on Income) (Brunei) Order 1973.

2. It is hereby declared—

(*a*) that the arrangements specified in the Supplementary Arrangement set out in the Schedule to this Order, which vary the arrangements set out in the Schedule to the Double Taxation Relief (Taxes on Income) (Brunei) Order 1950**(c)**, as amended by the arrangements set out in the Schedule to the Double Taxation Relief (Taxes on Income) (Brunei) Order 1968**(d)**, have been made with the Government of Brunei with a view to affording relief from double taxation in relation to income tax or corporation tax and taxes of a similar character imposed by the laws of Brunei; and

(*b*) it is expedient that these arrangements should have effect.

W. G. Agnew.

(a) 1970 c. 10.
(b) 1972 c. 41.
(c) S.I. 1950/1977 (1950 I, p. 1004).
(d) S.I. 1968/306 (1968 I, p. 929).

SCHEDULE

SUPPLEMENTARY ARRANGEMENT BETWEEN HER MAJESTY'S GOVERNMENT AND THE GOVERNMENT OF BRUNEI TO AMEND THE EXISTING ARRANGEMENT FOR THE AVOIDANCE OF DOUBLE TAXATION AND THE PREVENTION OF FISCAL EVASION WITH RESPECT TO TAXES ON INCOME

1. The Arrangement made in 1950 between His Majesty's Government and the Government of Brunei as amended by the Arrangement made in 1968 between Her Majesty's Government and the Government of Brunei for the avoidance of double taxation and the prevention of fiscal evasion with respect to taxes on income (hereinafter referred to as "the existing Arrangement") shall be amended by the deletion of paragraph 6 and the substitution of the following—

"6.—(1) (*a*) Dividends paid by a company which is a resident of the United Kingdom to a resident of Brunei may be taxed in Brunei.

(*b*) Where a resident of Brunei is entitled to a tax credit in respect of such a dividend under sub-paragraph (2) of this paragraph tax may also be charged in the United Kingdom and according to the laws of the United Kingdom, on the aggregate of the amount or value of that dividend and the amount of that tax credit at a rate not exceeding 15 per cent.

(*c*) Except as aforesaid dividends paid by a company which is a resident of the United Kingdom to a resident of Brunei who is subject to tax in Brunei on them shall be exempt from any tax in the United Kingdom which is chargeable on dividends.

(2) A resident of Brunei who receives dividends from a company which is a resident of the United Kingdom shall, subject to the provisions of subparagraph (3) of this paragraph and provided he is subject to tax in Brunei on the dividends, be entitled to the tax credit in respect thereof to which an individual resident in the United Kingdom would have been entitled had he received those dividends, and to the payment of any excess of that tax credit over his liability to United Kingdom tax.

(3) Sub-paragraph (2) of this paragraph shall not apply where the recipient of the dividend is a company which either alone or together with one or more associated companies controls directly or indirectly at least 10 per cent of the voting power in the company paying the dividend. For the purpose of this sub-paragraph two companies shall be deemed to be associated if one is controlled directly or indirectly by the other, or both are controlled directly or indirectly by a third company.

(4) Dividends paid by a company resident in Brunei to a resident of the United Kingdom may be taxed in the United Kingdom. If the recipient of the dividends is subject to tax in the United Kingdom in respect thereof they shall be exempt from any tax in Brunei which is chargeable on dividends in addition to the tax chargeable in respect of the profits or income of the company.

(5) The term "dividends" as used in this paragraph means income from shares or other rights, not being debt-claims, participating in profits, as well as income from other corporate rights assimilated to income from shares by the taxation law of the territory of which the company making the distribution is a resident and also includes any other item (other than royalties exempt from tax under the provisions of paragraph 7 of this Arrangement) which, under the law of the territory of which the company paying the dividend is a resident, is treated as a dividend or distribution of a company.

(6) If the recipient of a dividend is a company which owns 10 per cent or more of the class of shares in respect of which the dividend is paid then sub-paragraphs (1) and (2) or as the case may be sub-paragraph (4) of this paragraph shall not apply to the dividend to the extent that it can have been paid only out of profits which the company paying the dividend earned or other income which it received in a period ending twelve months or more before the relevant date. For the purposes of this sub-paragraph the term "relevant date" means the date on which the beneficial owner of the dividend became the owner of 10 per cent or more of the class of

shares in question. Provided that this sub-paragraph shall not apply if the beneficial owner of the dividend shows that the shares were acquired for bona fide commercial reasons and not primarily for the purpose of securing the benefit of this paragraph.

(7) The provisions of sub-paragraphs (1) and (2) or as the case may be sub-paragraph (4) of this paragraph shall not apply where a resident of one of the territories has in the other territory a permanent establishment and the holding by virtue of which the dividends are paid is effectively connected with the business carried on through such permanent establishment.

(8) Where a company which is a resident of one of the territories derives profits or income from sources within the other territory, the Government of that other territory shall not impose any form of taxation on dividends paid by the company to persons not resident in that other territory, or any tax in the nature of an undistributed profits tax on undistributed profits of the company, by reason of the fact that those dividends or undistributed profits represent, in whole or in part, profits or income so derived."

2. This Supplementary Arrangement shall enter into force when the last of all such things shall have been done in the United Kingdom and Brunei as are necessary to give the Supplementary Arrangement the force of law in the United Kingdom and Brunei respectively, and the new paragraph 6 of the Arrangement shall thereupon have effect in relation to dividends paid on or after 6th April 1973.

EXPLANATORY NOTE

(*This Note is not part of the Order.*)

The Supplementary Arrangement scheduled to this Order makes certain alterations to the Arrangement made in 1950 with Brunei, as amended by the Arrangement made on 4th March 1968. These alterations follow from the introduction of the new United Kingdom corporation tax system which, so far as it relates to the tax treatment of dividends paid by a United Kingdom company to an overseas shareholder, came into operation on 6th April 1973. The Supplementary Arrangement provides that where a United Kingdom company pays a dividend to a resident of Brunei other than a company which controls 10 per cent or more of the voting power in the paying company, the recipient is, subject to certain conditions, to receive the tax credit to which an individual resident in the United Kingdom and in receipt of such a dividend would be entitled, less income tax at a rate not exceeding 15 per cent on the aggregate of the dividend and the tax credit. Dividends paid by a Brunei company to a resident of the United Kingdom will continue to be exempt from any tax in Brunei which is chargeable on dividends in addition to the tax chargeable in respect of the profits or income of the company.

The Supplementary Arrangement is expressed to take effect in relation to dividends paid on or after 6th April 1973.

1973 No. 2099

CLERK OF THE CROWN IN CHANCERY

The Crown Office (Commissions of the Peace) Rules 1973

Made - - -	12*th December* 1973
Laid before Parliament	18*th December* 1973
Coming into Operation	1*st February* 1974

At the Court at Buckingham Palace, the 12th day of December 1973

Present,

The Queen's Most Excellent Majesty in Council

Her Majesty, in exercise of the powers conferred on Her by section 3 of the Crown Office Act 1877(**a**) and of all other powers enabling Her in that behalf, is pleased, by and with the advice of Her Privy Council, to order, and it is hereby ordered, as follows:—

1. These Rules may be cited as the Crown Office (Commissions of the Peace) Rules 1973 and shall come into operation on 1st February 1974.

2. The forms set forth in the Schedule to these Rules shall be used for commissions of the peace under the Great Seal for counties in England and Wales, for the areas of Greater London and for the City of London respectively, being commissions issued after the coming into operation of these Rules and to take effect on or after 1st April 1974.

3. Rule 1 in the Schedule to the Order in Council made on the 22nd day of February 1878(**b**), so far as it applies to England and Wales, rule 4 in the said Schedule and the Crown Office (Commissions of the Peace) Rules 1969(**c**) are hereby revoked but without prejudice to the validity or effect of any commission of the peace issued in accordance with the provisions thereof.

W. G. Agnew.

SCHEDULE — Article 2

Form of Commission of the Peace

1. Counties of England and Wales.

ELIZABETH THE SECOND by the Grace of God of the United Kingdom of Great Britain and Northern Ireland and of Our other Realms and Territories Queen Head of the Commonwealth Defender of the Faith To all such persons as

(**a**) 1877 c.41. (**b**) Rev. III, p. 1009. (**c**) S.I. 1969/1070 (1969 II, p.3138).

may from time to time hold office as justices of the peace for Our County of
GREETING Know ye that you are and each of you is by these Presents assigned to keep Our peace in Our said county and to keep and cause to be kept in all points in Our said county the rules of law and enactments from time to time obtaining for the good of Our peace and for the preservation of the same and for the quiet rule and government of Our people And to deal according to law with all persons that offend against any of those rules of law or enactments And also to cause to come before you and to deal according to law with all persons against whom anything is alleged giving just cause under any rule of law or enactment for the time being in force why they should find security to keep the peace or be of good behaviour towards Us and Our people And to exercise all such other jurisdiction and powers as by any rule of law or enactment may from time to time belong to justices of the peace And therefore We command you and each of you that you diligently apply yourselves in Our said county to the keeping of Our peace and of the rules of law and enactments aforesaid and to the other matters hereinbefore mentioned doing therein what to justice appertains according to law

In Witness whereof We have caused these Our Letters to be made Patent

WITNESS Ourself at Westminster the day of in the year of Our Reign

2. The areas of Greater London.

The same form of commission of the peace as set forth in paragraph 1 shall be used for the areas of Greater London except that for any reference to the county there shall be substituted a reference to the area.

3. The City of London.

The same form of commission of the peace as set forth in paragraph 1 shall be used for the City of London except that

(*a*) the commission shall be addressed "To the Lord Mayor and Aldermen of the City of London now and for the time being who are by virtue of the Charter granted by his late Majesty King George the Second dated the twenty-fifth day of August 1741 a justice and justices of the peace within the City and to all such other persons as may from time to time hold office as justices of the peace for the City of London"; and

(*b*) for any reference to the county there shall be substituted a reference to the City.

EXPLANATORY NOTE

(This Note is not part of the Rules.)

These Rules prescribe a new form of Commission of the Peace for the counties of England and Wales, for the areas of Greater London and for the City of London, worded so as to take advantage of the power conferred by the Administration of Justice Act 1973 (c.15) to issue commissions generally, and not by name, to all persons who may from time to time hold office as justices by virtue of an appointment made by the Lord Chancellor or by the Chancellor of the Duchy of Lancaster in the name of Her Majesty and on Her behalf.

1973 No. 2100

ROAD TRAFFIC

The Goods Vehicles (Authorisation of International Journeys) (Fees) Regulations 1973

Made - - - -	10*th December* 1973
Laid before Parliament	12*th December* 1973
Coming into Operation	13*th December* 1973

The Secretary of State for the Environment, with the consent of the Treasury, in exercise of the powers conferred by section 56(1) and (2) of the Finance Act 1973**(a)**, and of all other enabling powers, hereby makes the following Regulations:—

1. These Regulations may be cited as the Goods Vehicles (Authorisation of International Journeys) (Fees) Regulations 1973 and shall come into operation on 13th December 1973.

2.—(1) In these Regulations—

"community authorisation" means an authorisation granted pursuant to Regulation No. 2829/72 dated 28th December 1972 of the Council of the European Communities **(b)**;

"E.C.M.T. licence" means a licence issued pursuant to the scheme adopted by Resolution of the Council of Ministers of the European Conference of Ministers of Transport on 14th June 1973;

"journey permit" means a permit issued pursuant to an agreement or arrangement mentioned in column 1 of the Schedule to these Regulations under the provision or one of the provisions of the agreement or arrangement mentioned opposite thereto in column 2 of the Schedule and providing for a number of outward and return journeys stated in the permit;

"period permit" means a permit issued pursuant to an agreement or arrangement mentioned in column 1 of the Schedule to these Regulations under the provision or one of the provisions of the agreement or arrangement mentioned opposite thereto in column 2 of the Schedule and providing for an unlimited number of journeys during a period stated in the permit.

(2) The Interpretation Act 1889**(c)** shall apply for the interpretation of these Regulations as it applies for the interpretation of an Act of Parliament.

3. The fee payable on the issue of a community authorisation shall be—

(*a*) if it is valid for a period of one year, £60, or

(*b*) if it is valid for a period of less than one year, for each such period of three months or part thereof, £15.

4. The fee payable on the issue of a E.C.M.T. licence shall be—

(*a*) if it is valid for a period of one year, £60, or

(*b*) if it is valid for a period of less than one year, for each such period of three months or part thereof, £15.

(a) 1973 c. 51.
(b) OJ No. L298, 31.12.1972, p. 16 (OJ/SE 1972 (30-31 Dec.) p. 43).
(c) 1889 c. 63.

5. The fee payable on the issue of a journey permit shall be £1·25 and the fee payable on the issue of a period permit shall be £25.

6. All fees received under these Regulations shall be paid into the Consolidated Fund.

Signed by authority of the Secretary of State.

John Peyton,
Minister for Transport Industries,
Department of the Environment.

4th December 1973.

We consent to the making of these Regulations.

Hugh Rossi,
John Stradling Thomas,

Two of the Lords Commissioners of Her Majesty's Treasury on 10th December 1973.

SCHEDULE

1 Agreement or Arrangement	2 Provision
Arrangement dated 29th May 1969 between the Minister of Transport in the Government of the United Kingdom of Great Britain and Northern Ireland and the Minister of Trade, Commerce and Industry of the Republic of Austria.	Clause 4
Agreement dated 10th November 1970 between the Government of the United Kingdom of Great Britain and Northern Ireland and the Czechoslovak Socialist Republic on International Road Transport **(a)**.	Article 7
Agreement dated 28th March 1969 between the Government of the United Kingdom of Great Britain and Northern Ireland and the Government of the French Republic on the International Carriage of Goods by Road **(b)**.	Articles 4, 6 & 7
Arrangement dated 2nd June 1967 between the Minister of Transport of the Federal Republic of Germany and the Minister of Transport in the Government of the United Kingdom of Great Britain and Northern Ireland.	Clauses 1, 3, 4, 5, 6 & 7
Agreement dated 23rd February 1970 between the Government of the United Kingdom of Great Britain and Northern Ireland and the Government of the Hungarian People's Republic on the International Carriage of Goods by Road **(c)**.	Article 4

(a) Cmnd. 4747. **(b)** Cmnd. 4324. **(c)** Cmnd. 4919

2 Agreement or Arrangement	1 Provision
Arrangement dated 17th July 1969 between the Minister of Transport in the Government of the United Kingdom of Great Britain and Northern Ireland and the Minister of Transport and Civil Aviation of the Italian Republic.	Clauses 2, 4 & 5
Agreement dated 26th April 1972 between the Government of the United Kingdom of Great Britain and Northern Ireland and the Government of the Spanish State on the International Carriage of Goods by Road **(a)**.	Article 3
Agreement dated 3rd February 1969 between the Government of the United Kingdom of Great Britain and Northern Ireland and the Government of the Socialist Federal Republic of Yugoslavia on the International Carriage of Goods by Road **(b)**.	Article 3

EXPLANATORY NOTE

(*This Note is not part of the Regulations.*)

These Regulations prescribe the fees to be paid on the issue of various documents authorising the operation of goods vehicles on journeys between the United Kingdom and—

(*a*) other member states of the European Community,

(*b*) other member countries of the European Conference of Ministers of Transport, and

(*c*) certain states with whom bilateral arrangements or agreements have been concluded.

(a) Cmnd. 5197. **(b)** Cmnd. 4284.

STATUTORY INSTRUMENTS

1973 No. 2101 (S.154)

ANIMALS

DISEASES OF ANIMALS

The Tuberculosis (Scotland) Amendment Order 1973

Made - - -	*7th December* 1973
Laid before Parliament	*20th December* 1973
Coming into Operation	*1st January* 1974

In exercise of the powers conferred by sections 1, 8(3), 20, 77(3) and 85(1) of the Diseases of Animals Act 1950(**a**) and now vested in me(**b**), and of all other powers enabling me in that behalf, I hereby make the following order:—

Citation and commencement

1. This order, which may be cited as the Tuberculosis (Scotland) Amendment Order 1973, shall come into operation on 1st January 1974.

Interpretation

2.—(1) This order shall be construed as one with the Tuberculosis (Scotland) Order 1964(**c**), hereinafter referred to as "the principal order".

(2) The Interpretation Act 1889(**d**) shall apply for the interpretation of this order as it applies for the interpretation of an Act of Parliament.

Amendment of Principal Order

3. There shall be inserted in Article 3(1) of the principal order (interpretation) the following definitions:—

"carcase" means the carcase of any bovine animal and includes any part of the carcase or any flesh, bone, hide, skin, hooves, offal or other part of a bovine animal, separately or otherwise or any part thereof;

"veterinary meat inspector" and "veterinary surgeon" have the meaning assigned to them by Article 2(1) of the Food (Meat Inspection) (Scotland) Regulations 1961(**e**).

4. The following Article shall be inserted in the principal order immediately following Article 5 thereof, namely:—

"*Notice of disease in a carcase*

5A.—(1) Every person having in his possession or under his charge on any premises any carcase which is affected with or suspected of being affected with tuberculosis, and every veterinary surgeon, veterinary prac-

(**a**) 1950 c.36.
(**b**) By the Transfer of Functions (Animal Health) Order 1955 (S.I. 1955/958 (1955 I, p.1184)).
(**c**) S.I. 1964/1109 (1964 II, p.2463).
(**d**) 1889 c.63.
(**e**) S.I. 1961/243 (1961, p.395).

titioner or veterinary meat inspector who examines any carcase and is of the opinion or suspects that such carcase is affected with tuberculosis shall give with all practical speed notice of the fact to a veterinary inspector.

(2) Any person having in his possession or under his charge a carcase which is affected with or suspected of being affected with tuberculosis shall detain it (or the part thereof affected with or suspected of being affected with tuberculosis) until it has been examined by a veterinary inspector."

5. Article 8 of the principal order (tuberculin tests and vaccination) shall be amended by the addition after paragraph (3) thereof of the following paragraph:—

"(4) If any person fails to comply with any reasonable requirement of a veterinary inspector or other officer of the Ministry or of the Secretary of State made in accordance with the provisions of paragraph (1) of this Article, the Secretary of State may, without prejudice to any proceedings for an offence arising out of such default, take or cause to be taken all such steps as may be necessary to facilitate the examination of such bovine animal, or the application thereto of any diagnostic test for tuberculosis, and the amount of any expenses reasonably incurred by the Secretary of State for the purpose of making good the default shall be recoverable by him as a civil debt from the person in default.

6. There shall be inserted at the end of Article 11(1) of the principal order (precautions against the spread of infection) the words "and may, by such notice, require the isolation of any bovine animals specified in the notice in a specified part of the premises to which the notice relates."

Gordon Campbell,
One of Her Majesty's
Principal Secretaries of State.

St. Andrew's House,
Edinburgh.
7th December 1973.

EXPLANATORY NOTE

(This Note is not part of the Order.)

This Order amends the Tuberculosis (Scotland) Order 1964 so as to include provisions requiring notification in respect of the carcase of a bovine animal which is suspected of being affected with tuberculosis, and detention of whole or part of such carcase pending inspection by a veterinary inspector.

The Order also enables the Secretary of State, where the owner or person in charge of a bovine animal fails to take steps to facilitate the examination of such an animal or the application thereto of any diagnostic test for tuberculosis, to recover from him the expenses reasonably incurred in making good the default as a civil debt.

Provision is also made for the isolation of bovine animals in a certain part of any premises if this appears necessary for the prevention of the spread of disease.

1973 No. 2102

AGRICULTURE

AGRICULTURAL GRANTS, GOODS AND SERVICES

Grants for Guarantees of Bank Loans (Extension of Period) Order 1973

Made - - -	13*th November* 1973
Laid before the House of Commons	22*nd November* 1973
Coming into Operation	1*st April* 1974

The Minister of Agriculture, Fisheries and Food in exercise of the powers conferred upon him by section 64(7) of the Agriculture Act 1967(**a**), with the approval of the Treasury, hereby makes the following order:—

1. This order may be cited as the Grants for Guarantees of Bank Loans (Extension of Period) Order 1973, and shall come into operation on 1st April 1974.

2. The period mentioned in subsection (2)(*a*) of section 64 of the Agriculture Act 1967 (being the period within which a guarantee must be given if expenditure incurred in fulfilling a guarantee given on or after 1st April 1966 is to attract grant under that section), having been extended for an additional period of five years beginning 1st April 1969 by virtue of the Grants for Guarantees of Bank Loans (Extension of Period) Order 1968(**b**), is hereby extended for a further additional period of five years beginning on 1st April 1974.

In Witness whereof the Official Seal of the Minister of Agriculture, Fisheries and Food is hereunto affixed on 12th November 1973.

(L.S.)

Joseph Godber,
Minister of Agriculture, Fisheries and Food.

Approved.
13th November 1973.

Michael Jopling,
P. L. Hawkins.
Two of the Lords Commissioners of Her Majesty's Treasury.

(**a**) 1967 c. 22.
(**b**) S.I. 1968/1146 (1968 II, p. 3131).

EXPLANATORY NOTE

(This Note is not part of the Order.)

Section 64 of the Agriculture Act 1967 empowers the Minister of Agriculture, Fisheries and Food, with the approval of the Treasury, to make a grant in respect of expenditure incurred in fulfilling a guarantee given as security for a loan made in the course of a banking business to a person requiring the loan for the purposes of an agriculture or horticulture business carried on by him where the guarantee was given during the period of three years beginning on 1st April 1966.

The Grants for Guarantees of Bank Loans (Extension of Period) Order 1968 extended that period, within which the guarantee must have been given, by an additional period of five years beginning on 1st April 1969 and this order extends that period by a further additional period of five years beginning on 1st April 1974.

In accordance with section 64(7), this order was approved by a resolution of the House of Commons on 12th December 1973.

1973 No. 2104

FAIR TRADING

The Restriction of Merger (Revocation) (No. 5) Order 1973

Made - - -	12*th December* 1973
Laid before Parliament	13*th December* 1973
Coming into Operation	14*th December* 1973

The Secretary of State in exercise of his powers under section 74(1)(*d*) and 134(2) of, and paragraph 12 of Schedule 8 to, the Fair Trading Act 1973(**a**) hereby orders as follows:—

1. This Order may be cited as the Restriction of Merger (Revocation) (No. 5) Order 1973, and shall come into operation on 14th December 1973.

2. The Restriction of Merger (No. 4) Order 1973(**b**) is hereby revoked.

Geoffrey Howe,
Minister for Trade and Consumer Affairs,
Department of Trade and Industry.

12th December 1973.

EXPLANATORY NOTE

(*This Note is not part of the Order.*)

This Order revokes the Restriction of Merger (No. 4) Order 1973.

The Order which is revoked imposed a temporary standstill on the proposed takeover of the Inveresk Group Limited by London and County Securities Group Limited while the Monopolies and Mergers Commission inquired into the matter.

The Secretary of State has, under section 75(5) of the Fair Trading Act 1973, consented to the Commission laying aside the reference on the grounds that the proposed merger has been abandoned.

(**a**) 1973 c. 41.

(**b**) S.I. 1973/1879. (1973 III, p. 6513)

STATUTORY INSTRUMENTS

1973 No. 2106

CONSUMER PROTECTION

The Heating Appliances (Fireguards) Regulations 1973

Made - - - -	8*th December* 1973
Laid before Parliament	20*th December* 1973
Coming into Operation	1*st April* 1974

In pursuance of sections 1, 2(4) and (6) and 6(2) of the Consumer Protection Act 1961**(a)** and, as respects Scotland, of paragraph 7 of the Schedule to that Act, and after consulting with such persons and bodies of persons as appear to me to be requisite, I hereby make the following Regulations:—

1. These Regulations may be cited as the Heating Appliances (Fireguards) Regulations 1973 and shall come into operation on 1st April 1974.

2.—(1) In these Regulations, unless the context otherwise requires—

"the Act" means the Consumer Protection Act 1961;

"excepted appliance" means—

(*a*) a gas or electric fire or oil heater—

(i) which is so constructed that when the appliance is burning, or, if it is an electric fire, consuming electricity, at the maximum rate for which it is designed, the heating element and, if it is a gas fire or oil heater, any flame is so enclosed within the body of the appliance that there is no likelihood of personal injury from burning, or of ignition of any fabric by reason of, in either case, contact with or proximity to, the heating element or any flame; or

(ii) which is not suitable for heating rooms in dwelling houses or other residential premises; or

(*b*) an electric fire which is so constructed as to require attachment to a ceiling;

"gas fire" includes a gas burning heating appliance in which the source of the gas is in liquid form or the gas is contained in a portable container;

"heating appliance" means—

(*a*) a gas or electric fire; or

(*b*) an oil heater;

(a) 1961 c. 40.

other than an excepted appliance:

"heating element" means—

(*a*) in relation to a gas fire or oil heater, that part of it which is designed to be directly heated by the impingement thereon of burning fuel:

(*b*) in relation to an electric fire, a heating resistor and element former including, where a resistor and former (if any) are a detachable unit, so much of the fire as makes them such a unit.

(2) Any reference in these Regulations to an enactment shall be construed as a reference to that enactment as amended or extended by or under any other enactment.

(3) The Interpretation Act 1889**(a)** applies for the interpretation of these Regulations as it applies for the interpretation of an Act of Parliament.

3.—(1) Subject to paragraph (2) below, a heating appliance shall be fitted with a guard such that the appliance is capable of satisfying the tests and requirements specified in Clause 1.3 (which contains design and performance requirements in relation to all types of heating appliances) and, as may be appropriate to the type of appliance, the tests and requirements specified in Clause 2 (which relates to gas fires), Clause 3 (which relates to electric fires) or Clause 4 (which relates to oil heaters) of the British Standard Specification for Fireguards for Heating Appliances (Gas, Electric and Oil-Burning) BS 1945: 1971, published on 30th July 1971, as amended by Amendment No. 1, published on 12th April 1972.

(2) This Regulation shall not have effect until 1st October 1974 except in the case of goods and component parts sold, or in the possession of any person for the purposes of being sold, by the manufacturer or importer into Great Britain of those goods or parts.

4. As respects the requirements of these Regulations, subsections (1) and (2) of section 2 of the Act (which prohibits sales and possession for sale of goods and component parts not complying with regulations) shall apply in relation to goods and component parts manufactured before the imposition of the requirements notwithstanding anything in subsection (4) of that section (which exempts such goods and parts unless regulations otherwise provide).

5. Section 2(1) to (3) of the Act (except subsection (3)(*d*) and (*e*)) (sale and possession for sale of goods and component parts not complying with regulations) shall, except as provided by the proviso to section 2(6), apply in relation to goods to which these Regulations apply as if references to selling or to a sale included references to letting under a hire-purchase agreement or on hire, and the reference to a sale under a credit-sale agreement were a reference to a letting under a hire-purchase agreement.

6.—(1) The Schedule to the Act (which relates to enforcement by local authorities) shall have effect in relation to goods to which these Regulations apply.

(a) 1889 c. 63.

(2) As respects Scotland, "local authority" in the Schedule to the Act shall mean, in relation to goods to which these Regulations apply, the council of any county or any town.

(3) Paragraph (2) above will cease to have effect on the coming into operation of paragraph 150 of Schedule 27 to the Local Government (Scotland) Act 1973**(a)** (which relates to the meaning of "local authority" in the Schedule to the Act).

7.—(1) In Schedule 2 to the Oil Heaters Regulations 1962**(b)**, as inserted by the Schedule to the Oil Heaters Regulations 1966**(c)**, in the last paragraph for the words from "by the Heating" onwards there shall be substituted the words "by the Heating Appliances (Fireguards) Regulations 1973".

(2) The Heating Appliances (Fireguards) Regulations 1953**(d)** and the Heating Appliances (Fireguards) (Scotland) Regulations 1953**(e)** shall, on 1st April 1974, cease to have effect in relation to the goods and component parts mentioned in Regulation 3(2) of these Regulations and are hereby revoked with effect from 1st October 1974.

Robert Carr,
One of Her Majesty's Principal Secretaries of State.

Home Office,
Whitehall.
8th December 1973.

(a) 1973 c. 65.
(b) S.I. 1962/884 (1962 I, p. 1017).
(c) S.I. 1966/588 (1966 II, p. 1348).
(d) S.I. 1953/526 (1953 I, p. 845).
(e) S.I. 1953/524 (1953 I, p. 848).

EXPLANATORY NOTE

(This Note is not part of the Regulations.)

The Consumer Protection Act 1961 gives the Secretary of State power to make Regulations imposing requirements, in respect of any class of goods, to prevent or reduce risk of death or personal injury. These Regulations impose such requirements in relation to gas and electric fires and oil heaters for heating rooms, and accordingly under the Act, subject to certain exceptions, no person may sell or have in his possession for sale such an appliance not complying with the Regulations. By virtue of Regulation 5, letting on hire or hire-purchase is similarly prohibited.

The substance of the Regulations is contained in Regulation 3, which requires heating appliances (as defined in Regulation 2) to have a fireguard which satisfies requirements of the British Standard BS 1945:1971 as amended in 1972. The requirements do not apply until 1st October 1974 except in the case of manufacturers and importers (Regulation 3(2)).

The Regulations supersede the Heating Appliances (Fireguards) Regulations 1953 and the Heating Appliances (Fireguards) (Scotland) Regulations 1953.

STATUTORY INSTRUMENTS

1973 No. 2110

EMERGENCY POWERS

The Electricity (Restrictions) (Revocation) Order 1973

Made - - - - -	*12th December* 1973
Coming into Operation	*13th December* 1973

The Secretary of State, in exercise of his powers under Regulations 21 and 40(1) of the Emergency Regulations 1973(**a**), hereby orders as follows:—

1. This Order shall come into operation on 13th December 1973 and may be cited as the Electricity (Restrictions) (Revocation) Order 1973.

2. The Electricity (Advertising, Display, etc.) (Restriction) Order 1973(**b**), the Electricity (Heating) (Restriction) Order 1973(**c**) and the Electricity (Heating) (Restriction) Variation Order 1973(**d**) are hereby revoked.

Tom Boardman,
Minister for Industry,
Department of Trade and Industry.

12th December 1973.

EXPLANATORY NOTE

(*This Note is not part of the Order.*)

This Order revokes the two Orders restricting the consumption of electricity made under the Emergency Regulations 1973 namely the Electricity (Advertising, Display, etc.) (Restriction) Order 1973 and the Electricity (Heating) (Restriction) Order 1973—together with the Order varying the latter Order.

(**a**) S.I. 1973/1881 (1973 III, p. 6516).
(**b**) S.I. 1973/1901 (1973 III, p. 6589).
(**c**) S.I. 1973/1900 (1973 III, p. 6587).
(**d**) S.I. 1973/1913 (1973 III, p. 6645).

1973 No. 2111

EMERGENCY POWERS

PETROLEUM

The Motor Fuel (Restriction of Supplies) (Revocation) Order 1973

Made - - - -	*12th December* 1973
Coming into Operation	*13th December* 1973

The Secretary of State, in exercise of his powers under Regulations 21 and 40(1) of the Emergency Regulations 1973(**a**), hereby orders as follows:—

1. This Order shall come into operation on 13th December 1973 and may be cited as the Motor Fuel (Restriction of Supplies) (Revocation) Order 1973.

2. The Interpretation Act 1889(**b**) shall apply for the interpretation of this Order as it applies for the interpretation of an Act of Parliament and as if this Order and the Order hereby revoked were Acts of Parliament.

3. The Motor Fuel (Restriction of Supplies) Order 1973(**c**) is hereby revoked.

12th December 1973.

Tom Boardman,
Minister for Industry,
Department of Trade and Industry.

EXPLANATORY NOTE

(*This Note is not part of the Order.*)

This Order revokes the Motor Fuel (Restriction of Supplies) Order 1973, restricting the acquisition of motor fuel, made under the Emergency Regulations 1973.

(a) S.I. 1973/1881 (1973 III, p. 6516). (b) 1889 c. 63. (c) S.I. 1973/1943 (1973 III, p. 6690).

1973 No. 2117 (S.155)

SHERIFF COURT, SCOTLAND

Act of Sederunt (Domicile and Matrimonial Proceedings Act 1973) 1973

Made - - -	12*th December* 1973
Coming into Operation	1*st January* 1974

The Lords of Council and Session, under and by virtue of the powers conferred upon them by section 32 of the Sheriff Courts (Scotland) Act 1971(**a**) and of all other powers competent to them in that behalf do hereby enact and declare as follows:—

1.—(1) This Act of Sederunt may be cited as the Act of Sederunt (Domicile and Matrimonial Proceedings Act 1973) 1973 and shall come into operation on 1st January 1974.

(2) The Interpretation Act 1889(**b**) shall apply for the interpretation of this Act of Sederunt as it applies for the interpretation of an Act of Parliament.

2.—(1) The condescendence of the initial writ (either in its original form or as amended at any time prior to the commencement of Proof) in every action of separation in the Sheriff Court shall contain a short statement of whether to the knowledge of the pursuer any proceedings are continuing in any country outside Scotland which are in respect of the marriage to which the initial writ relates or are capable of affecting its validity or subsistence.

(2) If there are any such proceedings said statement shall give particulars thereof including—

(*a*) The Court or Tribunal or authority before which they have been commenced;

(*b*) The date of commencement;

(*c*) The names of the parties;

(*d*) The date or expected date of any proof in the proceedings; and

(*e*) Such other facts as may be relevant to the question of whether the Sheriff Court action should be sisted under Schedule 3 of the Domicile and Matrimonial Proceedings Act 1973(**c**).

(3) For the purposes of this Act of Sederunt and said Schedule 3, proceedings shall be treated as "continuing" where proceedings in respect of that marriage or capable of affecting its validity have been instituted before a Court, Tribunal or other authority in any country outside Scotland and such proceedings have not been finally disposed of.

(**a**) 1971 c. 58. (**b**) 1889 c. 63.
(**c**) 1973 c. 45.

(4) A short statement such as is referred to in sub-section (1) hereof shall in all such actions be inserted in any defences or minutes lodged by any party in such action, containing the particulars referred to in sub-section (2) hereof insofar as these particulars are additional to or contradictory of any such particulars provided by the pursuer in the action, or in any case in which the pursuer has provided no such statement.

(5) Any application made by any party in an action of separation for an order in terms of Part I or Part II of Schedule 2 of the Domicile and Matrimonial Proceedings Act 1973 or for a sist of such an action or the recall of a sist in such an action in terms of said Schedule 3 shall be made by written motion.

And the Lords appoint this Act of Sederunt to be inserted in the Books of Sederunt.

G. C. Emslie,
I. P. D.

Edinburgh.
12th December 1973.

EXPLANATORY NOTE

(This Note is not part of the Act of Sederunt.)

This Act of Sederunt provides that a short statement shall be inserted in all initial writs in every action of separation and in defences and minutes lodged in such actions *inter alia* averring what other proceedings are continuing in any country other than Scotland in respect of that marriage or which may affect the validity of the marriage. It further provides that applications to the Court under Parts I and II of Schedule 2 and Schedule 3 of the Domicile and Matrimonial Proceedings Act 1973 shall be made by way of written motion.

STATUTORY INSTRUMENTS

1973 No. 2118

COUNTER-INFLATION

The Counter-Inflation (Notification of Increases in Prices and Charges) (No. 4) Order 1973

Made - - - 13*th December* 1973

Laid before Parliament 14*th December* 1973

Coming into operation 15*th December* 1973

The Secretary of State, in exercise of powers conferred on him by section 5 of, and paragraph 1(1), (4) and (6) of Schedule 3 to, the Counter-Inflation Act 1973(**a**) and of all other powers enabling him in that behalf, hereby makes the following Order: —

Citation, commencement and interpretation

1.–(1) This Order may be cited as the Counter-Inflation (Notification of Increases in Prices and Charges)(No. 4) Order 1973 and shall come into operation on 15th December 1973.

(2) The Interpretation Act 1889(**b**) shall apply for the interpretation of this Order as it applies for the interpretation of an Act of Parliament and as if this Order and the order hereby amended were Acts of Parliament.

Special provisions relating to petroleum and substances derived from petroleum

2.–(1) Where—

(*a*) a person specified in paragraph (2)(*a*)(*i*) or 2(*b*)(*i*) of article 5 of the Counter-Inflation (Notification of Increases in Prices and Charges)(No. 3) Order 1973(**c**) has before the date when this Order is made given notice to the Price Commission in accordance with that article of an increased price for the sale of petroleum oil or of petroleum oil and other related products derived from petroleum; and

(*b*) the period of 28 days or of 14 days (as may be appropriate) referred to in paragraph (5) of that article has not expired before the date when this Order comes into operation;

that period shall, in relation to any increase specified in the notice, be taken to expire immediately before that date.

(2) In this article, "petroleum oil" means petroleum oil of a kind intended for use as fuel for propelling a vehicle intended or adapted for use on roads.

13th December 1973.

Geoffrey Howe,
Minister for Trade and
Consumer Affairs,
Department of Trade and Industry.

(**a**) 1973 c. 9. (**b**) 1889 c. 63. (**c**) S.I. 1973/1786 (1973 III, p 5488)

EXPLANATORY NOTE

(This Note is not part of the Order.)

This Order amends the Counter-Inflation (Notification of Increases in Prices and Charges) (No 3) Order 1973.

Manufacturers who notified the Price Commission before 13th December 1973 of increases in the price of petroleum oil (or petroleum oil together with other related products) are released on 15th December 1973 from the restriction on implementation of the increase for 28 or 14 days beginning with the service of the notice on the Price Commission. Notifications served on or after 13th December remain subject to the 28 or 14 day restriction.

STATUTORY INSTRUMENTS

1973 No. 2119

CONTROL OF FUEL AND ELECTRICITY

The Motor Fuel (Maximum Retail Prices) Order 1973

Made - - -	14*th December* 1973
Laid before Parliament	14*th December* 1973
Coming into operation	15*th December* 1973

The Secretary of State, in exercise of his powers under Section 2(1)(b) of The Fuel and Electricity (Control) Act 1973(a)and Section 7 of the Emergency Laws (Re-enactments and Repeals) Act 1964(b) as having effect by virtue of Section 5 of the Fuel and Electricity (Control) Act 1973 hereby orders as follows:—

Citation and commencement

1. This Order may be cited as the Motor Fuel (Maximum Retail Prices) Order 1973 and shall come into operation on 15th December 1973.

Interpretation

2. (1) In this Order—

"by retail" means, in relation to the supply of any controlled motor fuel, supply to any person acquiring that fuel otherwise than for the purpose of resale;

"diesel fuel" means oil being heavy oil within the meaning of Section 1 of the Hydrocarbon Oil (Customs & Excise) Act 1971(c) derived from petroleum of a kind intended for use as fuel for propelling a motor vehicle, other than heavy oil in respect of which rebate of duty has been allowed under Section 9 of that Act;

"controlled motor fuel" means motor spirit of 5 star grade, 4 star grade, 3 star grade or 2 star grade or diesel fuel of Class A1 or Class A2;

"motor spirit" means oil being light oil within the meaning of Section 1 of the Hydrocarbon Oil (Customs & Excise) Act 1971 derived from petroleum of a kind intended for use as fuel for propelling a motor vehicle;

"motor vehicle" means a mechanically propelled vehicle intended or adapted for use on roads.

(2) In this Order—

(*a*) any reference to motor spirit of 5 star grade, 4 star grade, 3 star grade or 2 star grade shall be deemed to be a reference to motor spirit which complies with the requirements of British Standard Specification for Petrol (Gasoline) for Motor Vehicles (BS 4040 : 1971) published by the British Standards Institution on 31st March 1971 (as amended by Amendment Slip No. 1 published on 13th October 1972) for 5 star grade

(a) 1973 c. 67. (b) 1964 c. 60. (c) 1971 c. 12.

petrol, 4 star grade petrol, 3 star grade petrol or 2 star grade petrol respectively;

(*b*) any reference to diesel fuel of Class A1 or Class A2 shall be deemed to be a reference to diesel fuel which complies with the requirements of British Standard Specification for Petroleum Fuels for Oil Engines and Burners (BS 2869 : 1970) published by the British Standards Institution on 30th September 1970 (as amended by Amendment Slip No. 1 published on 9th June 1972) for Class A1 engine fuel and Class A2 engine fuel respectively;

(*c*) in relation to subdivisions of a grade of motor spirit, any reference to a minimum RON value shall be deemed to be a reference to the minimum value of the Research Octane Number of the motor spirit determined by the method referred to in Clause 4.2 of the British Standard Specification mentioned in subparagraph (a) of this paragraph.

Maximum retail prices

3. No person shall supply by retail motor spirit of a grade or subdivision of a grade or diesel fuel of a class specified in Column 1 of Schedule 1 to this Order at a price which exceeds:—

(*a*) the amount per gallon specified in Column 2 of that Schedule with respect to that grade, subdivision of a grade, or class; and

(*b*) where that motor spirit or diesel fuel is supplied by retail at or from premises situated in a zone or place specified in Column 1 of Schedule 2 to this Order the amount per gallon specified in Column 2 of that Schedule with respect to that zone or place in respect of the grade or subdivision of a grade of that motor spirit or the class of that diesel fuel mentioned in Column 3 of that Schedule.

Zones

4. For the purposes of this Order—

(*a*) premises shall be deemed to be situated in a zone named in Column 1 of Schedule 2 to this Order if those premises have, before the date of the making of this Order, been treated by a person supplying controlled motor fuel to those premises in the ordinary course of the wholesale business of that person as being situated in the zone so named; and

(*b*) where premises (not being premises situated in a place mentioned in Column 1 of Schedule 2 to this Order)—

(i) have not, before the date of the making of this Order, been treated by any person supplying controlled motor fuel to those premises in the ordinary course of the wholesale business of that person as being situated in a zone named in that Column; or

(ii) have, before the date of the making of this Order, been treated by different persons supplying controlled motor fuel to those premises in the ordinary course of the wholesale business of those persons as being situated in different zones so named.

the premises shall be deemed to be situated in the same zone as that in which the nearest to those premises of any premises to which paragraph (a) of this Article applies are deemed to be situated by virtue of that paragraph.

Notices

5. Every person who supplies by retail controlled motor fuel at or from premises at which controlled motor fuel is supplied by retail for use in motor vehicles shall keep displayed on those premises in a conspicuous position and so as to be clearly legible by all customers throughout the whole time during which any controlled motor fuel is offered for sale at those premises a notice stating:—

(*a*) the zone or place specified in Column 1 of Schedule 2 to this Order in which those premises are situated; and

(*b*) the grades or subdivisions of a grade of motor spirit and classes of diesel fuel specified in Column 1 of Schedule 1 to this Order; and

(*c*) with respect to those grades, subdivisions or classes, the maximum prices at which they may be sold at those premises in accordance with this Order.

Artificial transactions and unreasonable charges

6. No person shall, in connection with the supply by retail of any controlled motor fuel, enter or offer to enter into any artificial transaction or make or demand any unreasonable charge.

Directions

7. Nothing in this Order shall prevent the supply by retail of any controlled motor fuel required to be supplied by a direction under Section 2(2)(*b*) of the Fuel and Electricity (Control) Act 1973 at a price specified in the direction with respect to that fuel.

Licences

8.—(1) Nothing in this Order shall prevent the supply by retail of controlled motor fuel under the authority of a licence granted by the Secretary of State under this Order.

(2) Any licence granted under this Order may be subject to conditions and may be revoked without prior notice.

(3) Every licence granted under this Order shall be the property of the Secretary of State and any person being in possession of any such licence, shall, if requested to do so by the Secretary of State, produce or deliver it to such person or to a person of such class or description, and within such time, as may be specified in or at the time of the request.

Application to Northern Ireland

9. This Order shall not extend to Northern Ireland.

Geoffrey Howe,
Minister for Trade and Consumer Affairs,
Department of Trade and Industry.

14th December 1973.

Article 3

SCHEDULE 1

Column 1 Grades, subdivisions of a grade of motor spirit and classes of diesel fuel	Column 2 Amount in pence
Motor Spirit	
5 star grade	43.00
4 star grade	42.00
3 star grade of not less than 96 minimum RON value	41.50
Other 3 star grade	41.00
2 star grade of not less than 92 minimum RON value	40.50
Other 2 star grade	40.00
Diesel Fuel	
Class A1	41.50
Class A2	41.50

SCHEDULE 2

Article 3

Column 1 Zone or place	Column 2 Amount in pence	Column 3 Grades, subdivisions of a grade of motor spirit and classes of diesel fuel
Zones		
Inner zone	Nil	—
Outer zone	0.50	4 star grade
General zone	0.50	All grades, subdivisions of a grade of motor spirit and classes of diesel fuel
North Scotland (mainland only) zone	1.00	All grades, subdivisions of a grade of motor spirit
	2.50	Both classes of diesel fuel
Places		
Orkney Islands and West Cowal	1.00	All grades, subdivisions of a grade of motor spirit
	2.50	Both classes of diesel fuel
Lewis and Harris	0.50	Both classes of diesel fuel
Shetland Isles (mainland)	1.00	4 star grade and 2 star grade
	3.50	Both classes of diesel fuel
Other Shetland Isles	2.00	4 star grade and 2 star grade
Islay	3.00	4 star grade
	1.50	Both classes of diesel fuel
Mull	2.00	4 star grade
	0.50	Both classes of diesel fuel

EXPLANATORY NOTE

(This Note is not part of the Order.)

This Order imposes maximum retail prices in respect of the supply of 5 star, 4 star, 3 star and 2 star grades of motor spirit and Classes A1 and A2 of diesel fuel according to the zone or place at which it is supplied by retail.

It requires notices stating the maximum retail prices to be displayed at retail premises and prohibits artificial transactions and unreasonable charges. The Order does not extend to Northern Ireland.

Copies of the British Standard Specifications and Amendments referred to in this Order may be obtained from British Standards Institution, British Standards House, 2 Park Street, London W1A 2BS.